Microsoft Azure

Planning, Deploying, and Managing the Cloud

Second Edition

Julian Soh
Marshall Copeland
Anthony Puca
Micheleen Harris

Apress®

Microsoft Azure: Planning, Deploying, and Managing the Cloud

Julian Soh
Washington, WA, USA

Marshall Copeland
Texas, TX, USA

Anthony Puca
Colorado, CO, USA

Micheleen Harris
Washington, WA, USA

ISBN-13 (pbk): 978-1-4842-5957-3
ISBN-13 (electronic): 978-1-4842-5958-0
https://doi.org/10.1007/978-1-4842-5958-0

Managing Director, Apress Media LLC: Welmoed Spahr
Acquisitions Editor: Smriti Srivastava
Development Editor: Matthew Moodie
Coordinating Editor: Shrikant Vishwakarma

Cover designed by eStudioCalamar

Cover image designed by Pexels

Distributed to the book trade worldwide by Springer Science+Business Media New York, 233 Spring Street, 6th Floor, New York, NY 10013. Phone 1-800-SPRINGER, fax (201) 348-4505, e-mail orders-ny@springer-sbm.com, or visit www.springeronline.com. Apress Media, LLC is a California LLC and the sole member (owner) is Springer Science + Business Media Finance Inc (SSBM Finance Inc). SSBM Finance Inc is a **Delaware** corporation.

For information on translations, please e-mail rights@apress.com, or visit http://www.apress.com/rights-permissions.

Apress titles may be purchased in bulk for academic, corporate, or promotional use. eBook versions and licenses are also available for most titles. For more information, reference our Print and eBook Bulk Sales web page at http://www.apress.com/bulk-sales.

Any source code or other supplementary material referenced by the author in this book is available to readers on GitHub via the book's product page, located at www.apress.com/978-1-4842-5957-3. For more detailed information, please visit http://www.apress.com/source-code.

Printed on acid-free paper

Thank you to my family—Priscilla, Jasmine, and Makayla—for their continued support and all the great people I have had the honor to learn from, especially my co-authors and friends—Marshall Copeland, Anthony Puca, and Micheleen Harris. I also dedicate this book to those using technology to make the world a better place.

—Julian

Thank you to Angela Copeland, my wife, and I'm so happy every day. Thank you to Tara Larson for your friendship and continued support and guidance. Thanks to Keith Olinger and Mark Ghazai for their insight. Thank you to my fellow authors and friends—Julian Soh, Anthony Puca, and Micheleen Harris.

—Marshall

Writing a book requires a lot more time and effort than one would imagine. What made this effort unique was the life challenges that were underway while I did this. I would like to thank my lovely wife, Laura, for her patience, starting many dinners alone through, "I'm almost at a stopping point." The compounding of life, work, and loved ones makes the little free time one has all that much more valuable.

Special thanks go out to the other authors: Julian Soh, Marshall Copeland, and Micheleen Harris. Without them, this book would not have been completed. Each one of them stepped up at various times to make sure we stayed on track and kept moving forward. Their unique insights into the various aspects of Microsoft's Azure solutions provides an eloquent summary of some very complex technologies. Special thanks to our conductor, Julian, who kept this train on track!

Working at Microsoft for almost ten years has exposed me to a slew of clients, their challenges, and some of the brightest and most passionate IT professionals I have ever met. Thank you to Pete Luongo and Javier Vasquez for the Specialist teams they've built. A talented pool of individuals who continuously keep me and each other on their toes. Thank you to my Account Teams: PJ Kemp, Matt Chong, Chris Peacock, Matt Holzmann, Wole Moses, Jay Bhalodia, David Axinn, Gunnar Pribadi, Kent Cunningham, Susie Adams, and Angela Altimont. This group keeps the customers' business needs and challenges in the foreground and reminds me of the value these things provide to the customers and public.

—Anthony

Thank you to Rob Callaway, my fiancé, for always providing support and encouragement to keep me going—looking forward to our life together. Thank you to Marie and Steve Harris, my parents, for setting me down the road of science. Thank you to Rachelle Moore, Jessica Faulkner, Jennifer Flannery, and Jeremy Reynolds for your friendship and support. A big thanks to the reviewers, especially Priyanshi Singh, for their excellent work. Thank you to Apress and especially, Shrikant Vishwakarma, for all the tireless guidance and getting us to the finish line. Last, but not least, thank you to my co-authors—Julian Soh, Marshall Copeland, and Anthony Puca—for the partnership and amazing support.

—Micheleen

Table of Contents

About the Authors

Julian Soh is a solutions engineer and works at Microsoft, where he helps customers incorporate AI into software solutions, adopt modern data strategies, and use advanced analytics. A mechanical engineer by training with a background in information science, his career has primarily been in IT working with public, private, and nonprofit organizations in the United States and Asia. Find him at `https://juliansoh.github.io/` and on LinkedIn at `www.linkedin.com/in/juliansoh`.

Marshall Copeland is a Microsoft Alumni cloud security architect focused on cyber defenses in public cloud architecture using both cloud-native services and third-party risk management solutions. His work focuses on application and network security in hybrid deployments, secure Kubernetes design, and cloud security blueprints for training teams to enhance "blue team hunting" in the cloud. Find him on LinkedIn at `www.linkedin.com/in/marshallcopeland/`.

Anthony Puca is a director of Azure apps and infrastructure in Microsoft's US Federal Government division. Anthony has been consulting with US federal government departments and agencies on private, public, and hybrid cloud technologies for the last three years.

Micheleen Harris is a data scientist and technical program manager at Microsoft, where she focuses on AI and machine learning. She has been a developer for over ten years and was a bioinformatician before that. With a passion for learning, she has designed and delivered many courses and given workshops and talks at large conferences, such as Microsoft /build and ODSC West. She is the co-founder of the Seattle Artificial Intelligence Workshops meetup. Her personal website is `https://michhar.github.io`, and she can be followed on Twitter at @rheartpython.

About the Technical Reviewers

Kurtis Carlson is an independent consultant helping businesses migrate their mission-critical applications to Azure and apply governance across the organization's portfolio of applications. He also helps developers and operations teams modernize applications and practices using Azure DevOps and infrastructure as code. His IT career includes working for San Francisco–based companies like Visa International and First Republic Bank, as well as local government agencies.

Kurtis is on LinkedIn at `www.linkedin.com/in/kurtis-carlson/` and his website is at `http://KurtisCarlson.com/`.

Priyanshi Singh is a data scientist by training and a data enthusiast by nature. She specializes in machine learning techniques applied to predictive analytics, computer vision, and natural language processing. She has a master's degree in data science from New York University. Priyanshi is a cloud solution architect at Microsoft, where she helps the public sector transform citizen services with artificial intelligence. She also leads a meetup community based out of New York to help educate public sector employees via hands-on labs and discussions. Apart from her passion for learning new technologies and innovating with AI, she is a sports enthusiast, a great badminton player, and enjoys playing billiards.

Daren Child is a lifelong data professional with experience as a data architect in Fortune 100 companies, world financial organizations, and research organizations. Daren joined Microsoft as a government data architect in 2016. Since then, he has been involved in data transformation and aiding government organizations with developing a data culture. Daren is a fan of storage-based data access patterns and has taken on a personal initiative to revive enterprise data warehouses across US government organizations.

Acknowledgments

Special acknowledgment to Kurtis Carlson, a true professional and a great technical resource. Thank you to Priyanshi Singh and Daren Child for being such great colleagues and your willingness to help make this book a reality. Thank you to Shrikant Vishwakarma and the Apress team; we are so thankful for your dedication to this publication.

Introduction

Since the launch of the first edition of this book in 2015, Microsoft Azure, and cloud computing in general, has come a long way. This second edition is completely rewritten and updated, with more than 70% of the book containing brand-new topics and trends. In the first edition, we focused on managing a data center in the cloud, as reflected by the subtitle we chose at that time. Since then, Microsoft Azure is more than just your data center in the cloud. It is where you adopt advanced technologies like artificial intelligence (AI), Internet of Things (IoT), and machine learning, and handle vast amounts of data to help make data-driven decisions. With the focus on these new capabilities in Microsoft Azure, this second edition is all about adopting the intelligent cloud.

There are many resources online and by other authors that focus on all the topics covered in this book. But we found that there is a lack of updated material that goes into more than just an introduction of all the main technologies in Microsoft Azure. Thus, we wanted a book that ambitiously strives to give readers a strong foundation in all the important aspects of Microsoft Azure. If you are new to Microsoft Azure and cloud computing in general, Parts I and II of this book should give you a solid overview of Azure's capabilities and the business and environmental trends, including planning and adopting strategies. For the more seasoned readers, Parts III through VII cover the different categories of Azure services (IaaS, PaaS, data, cloud-based software development, and AI/ML). Although we tried to build the hands-on exercises in such a way that they are interrelated throughout the book, you can read any part in any order and still gain the benefits of the content without getting lost.

Due to the rapidly changing nature of technology, we have also incorporated a GitHub repository that is dedicated to updating the hands-on exercises and provide more content than we were able to fit within the physical constraints of these pages. We hope that you benefit greatly from this book as much as we enjoyed working on it. We wish you all the best in your quest for knowledge and making a difference in technology.

PART I

Introducing Microsoft Azure

CHAPTER 1

Microsoft Azure and Cloud Computing

Cloud computing as a platform does not require a review; however, the hundreds of new services and updated changes to the Microsoft Azure public cloud can be a great investment for your business. Updated Azure core services and new business services are explained in this book to further your knowledge. This book was written for both technical and business readers to gain greater skills through our guidance.

This book is updated in its second edition. We know that reader commitment goes beyond the cover price; it is spent in the value of your time learning. You cannot afford to waste one hour, so we are dedicated to earning your commitment on every page and in every chapter by providing you the most timely and updated guidance on Microsoft Azure services. We provide guidance and information to help you understand the details and completed code in the book as well as additional examples on the public GitHub location.

Note All the code for the software-defined infrastructure (both Microsoft Azure ARM templates and HashiCorp Terraform) can be downloaded at `https://github.com/harris-soh-copeland-puca`.

In this chapter, you learn about many new features and best-in-cloud improvements that are integrated and deployed through various methods in the Azure platform. This chapter is written as a high-level introduction to updated features that have been greatly enhanced or are new to the platform. The other chapters provide in-depth information on topics, to provide guidance and configuration.

J. Soh et al., *Microsoft Azure*, https://doi.org/10.1007/978-1-4842-5958-0_1

Where Is Microsoft Azure Today?

One of the challenges for technical readers may be having expertise in other cloud solutions and relating to Microsoft Azure terminology. You are first guided through Azure services and cloud products to identify a cloud service, and then in later chapters, we provide a deeper look at how to create, deploy, and manage that service. Azure services are continuously updated, and you need to understand the details to enable technologies to support your business and leverage updated Azure platform services. The market drives features that benefit business revenue, and cloud computing customers are requesting continuous innovation from Microsoft.

The Microsoft Azure additions have grown out of teams that expand beyond the Redmond campus to include global collaboration with businesses, customers, universities, and governments to expand Microsoft Azure services. The incorporated feedback provides a road map that, like software development, leverages a CI/CD (continuous integration/continuous deployment) pipeline. Azure services and resources change and adapt much more rapidly than traditional on-premises software deployment cycles.

The information provided is written with the intent to eliminate unnecessary acronyms. Some are unavoidable, and many are overused in online documentation. Depending on your business role, some acronyms are indispensable and are used in more than one workflow, and if you are skimming information, it can be confusing. For example, SDLC (software development life cycle) is used in Agile delivery conversations. If the topic also includes cybersecurity, then SDLC means *security development life cycle*.

Agile is a term used in software development conversations; it is not an acronym but a process for delivering software in a short schedule. Another example is continuous integration/continuous deployment (CICD or CI/CD). It is a term that is used in more than software delivery; for example, Azure documentation is updated on GitHub and delivered directly to websites.

Note This chapter provides an overview of many of the fundamental Azure features with additional chapters providing deep dives and guidance.

Azure Availability

Azure has an infrastructure that is geographically identified globally, regionally, and by zone. Azure regions are based on countries and broken into geographies. This is important because specific regions have failover availability and services that are available in a region. Not all services are available in all regions across the globe.

Azure regions are several datacenters deployed within a perimeter. They provide low network latency for communication within those regions and inside those datacenters. Many of the datacenters' physical buildings are aligned together as one location; they are described as a *datacenter campus* in some documentation. An entire datacenter can failover for another datacenter in the Azure region. Some of the Azure regions (in the United States, for example) are identified as Central US or East US in the Azure public cloud.

A Microsoft Azure region supports at least two physically separate locations that preserve data within a specific compliance boundary. *Geographies* allow customers to maintain data inside known locations by geographic boundaries. Geographic boundaries are connected using dedicated low-latency networks and include regions in the United States and around the globe, but it is more apparent when you look at geographic regions in Europe. For example, Azure regions in Europe include North Europe and West Europe, which support each other to provide high availability; likewise, North Germany and West Germany specifically maintain data inside Germany's borders.

Azure availability zones include at least two Azure regions, which are physically separated by hundreds of miles to support more than one location for high availability. The datacenter equipment includes redundant power, redundant cooling, and redundant network connectivity. High availability requires an architecture that considers both *infrastructure as a service* (IaaS) and *platform as a service* (PaaS). High availability does not include backup and recovery, which is included in the architecture for disaster recovery processes.

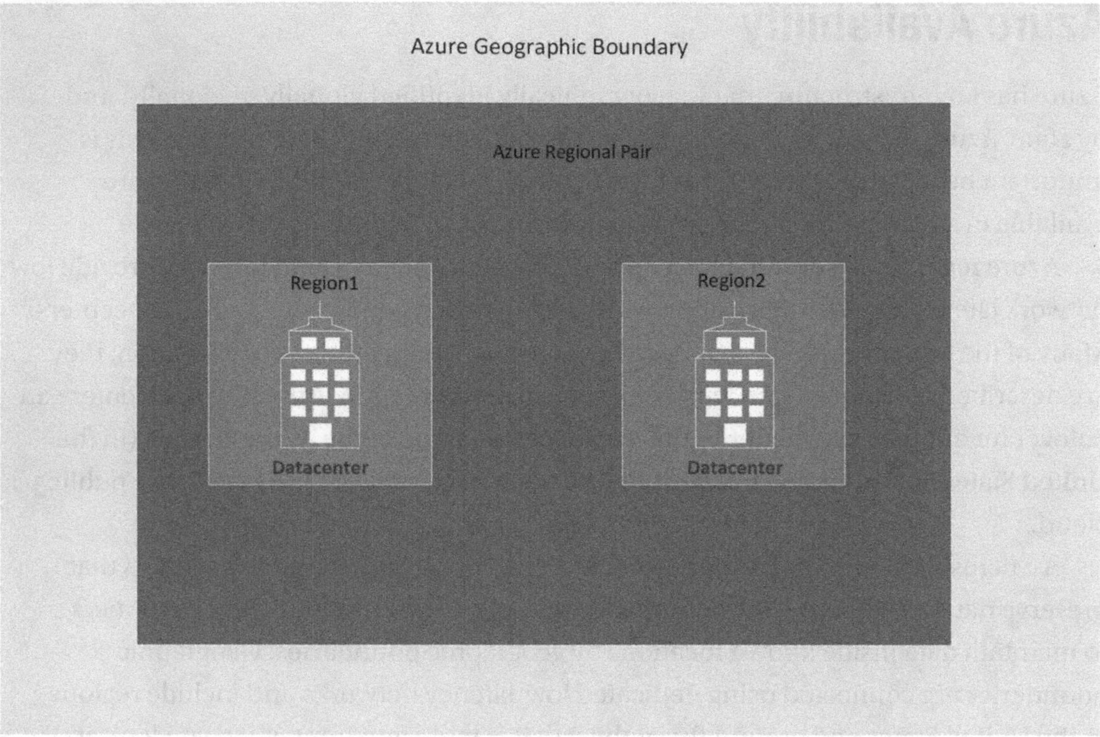

***Figure 1-1.** Azure geographic boundary with regional pairs*

For the Azure Government cloud, we use USDOD central or USDODE. Other regions support both the US public cloud and the US Azure Government clouds. To learn more about the Azure regions across the United States, Europe, and Asia, go to `https://azure.microsoft.com/is-is/global-infrastructure/geographies/`.

Azure Government is significantly different from other cloud services providers because it specifically addresses technical and mandatory regulatory requirements, such as

- FedRAMP
- FISMA
- FBI Criminal Justice Information Systems (CJIS)

Often, these government-specific requirements make it difficult for cloud services providers to scale up. Also, special SLAs (service-level agreements) and compliance requirements can cause providers to be penalized for noncompliance. For example, the FBI CJIS requires that a cloud service provider's personnel be background-checked and fingerprinted.

The Azure Government cloud was the first cloud to be consistent with the 13 areas defined in the CJIS security policy.

Note Standards apply to all customers using Azure cloud, Public or Government. Microsoft datacenter personnel are background-checked and fingerprinted, the same personnel are responsible for the service. Standards such as CJIS apply to all customers using Azure Government. Use the contact email cjis@microsoft.com for information on which services are currently available in specific states across the United States.

The Azure SLA for availability Each Microsoft Azure service has an SLA based on the region the service is available in. The most up-to-date SLA information is available at `https://azure.microsoft.com/en-us/support/legal/sla/`. The Azure SLA for availability zones offers 99.99% virtual machine (VM) uptime.

Azure Compliance

Azure maintains more than 90 compliance certifications, which include ones that specifically support regions and countries. These certifications are built to meet industry standards for IT and cloud-computing services. Azure's industry-recognized certifications are at `https://docs.microsoft.com/en-us/microsoft-365/compliance/offering-home?view=o365-worldwide`.

Figure 1-2. *Azure compliance offerings*

Certifications govern Azure's suitability for specific industry use, and they form the basis of customer trust. Third-party auditors, who are recognized by certification bodies, independently verify each certification. There is also a requirement for recertification and periodic audits to ensure compliance with all certifications.

Microsoft is a member of the advisory committee for many certification bodies, and it provides feedback and recommendations on proposed changes. Microsoft has visibility in many upcoming changes, which allows them to incorporate changes in the Azure platform in a timely manner.

Microsoft Azure Subscriptions

An Azure subscription is a large collection of services in your Azure account for identifying, controlling, and providing governance of those resources. Azure Active Directory is used in the provisioning of resources through ARM being able to use the role-based access control applied to specific resources. There are several ways to purchase an Azure subscription.

- Free trial
- Pay as you go
- Visual Studio MSDN (testing only)
- Microsoft resellers
- open license platform plus
- Microsoft enterprise account agreements

Azure role-based administration allows user and machine accounts access to resources in your Azure subscription; however, at a high level, there are administrative roles that are limited to the number of roles per subscription. Before we take a deeper dive into administration accounts, a few definitions need to be reviewed.

The term *Azure resource* designates an entity or an intelligent object that is managed by Azure. Simple examples are a virtual network (VNet), a storage account, or a virtual machine (VM). All three are Azure resources; they are not Azure services.

An *Azure service* is an automated deployment of a VM, VNet, or storage account.

An *Azure resource group* allows the grouping of resources that have the same life cycle and security requirements. Like individual services, a resource group can assign privileged access to multiple Azure roles.

Note One Azure account can have multiple Azure subscriptions associated with it.

An Azure subscription name is limited to a maximum of 64 characters, and the name cannot be changed. It is an important planning decision for administrative roles support for your Azure subscription.

Note Be aware the person who completes the Azure subscription sign up wizard is assigned the Global Administrator role.

It is important to realize that a Global Administrator and a Privileged Role Administrator can delegate administrator roles to other users in Azure AD. Table 1-1 provides key roles for Azure subscription users to consider for management and to support security needs, such as separation of duties.

Table 1-1. *Azure Account Roles, Limits, and Descriptions*

Admin Role	Limit	Description
Account Administrator	1/Azure account	Access to the Account Center
Service Administrator	1/Azure subscription	Access all subscriptions through the Azure management portal
Co-Administrator	Unlimited/Azure subscription	Cannot change permissions of Azure subscriptions
Global Administrator	1/Azure account	Read and modify every administrative setting in Azure AD

There is one Account Administrator per Azure subscription; this role authorizes and creates additional accounts for access to a subscription. This account allows you to change billing information and services administration. There is one Service Administrator account per Azure subscription, and it authorizes management access to the management portal for subscriptions. In a subscription, the Co-Administrator account is unlimited.

Note It is important to be aware of the current limits of a subscription. Review this at `https://docs.microsoft.com/en-us/azure/azure-resource-manager/management/azure-subscription-service-limits`.

Some of the Azure subscription resources include the default and maximum limit per subscription. If the Maximum Limit column reads *contact support*, it is known as a *soft limit*, which can be increased based on business needs.

Azure Cost Management

Investment in the Azure cloud should begin at the planning stage with an agreed approach to maximize the deployment investment and understand the total cost by breaking down the individual services and resources costs. The management of active work services with network flow and customer data storage costs are some of the information needed to budget Azure cloud utilization.

An *Azure subscription* is the primary purchasing vehicle for Azure services, your are charged based on utilization. Azure is billed monthly, with the billing data that is collected, processed, and displayed in the Azure portal.

Azure resources emit data for process billing usage differently, and active services maintain different reporting cycles. Cost factors include usage, Azure Marketplace third-party purchases, and service rates assessed based on subscription type (Government, Enterprise Agreement, pay-as-you-go, etc.).

Azure subscription pricing is found on the portal. Log in to the Azure portal, select Services ➤ Subscription to display the current costs, as shown in Figure 1-3.

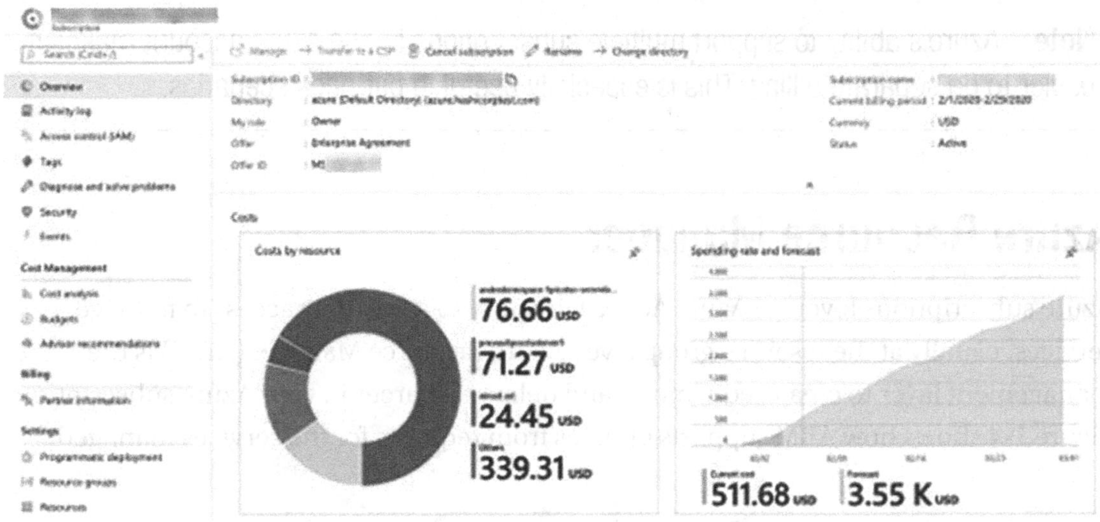

***Figure 1-3.** Azure cost by resource in the Azure portal*

Azure EA is a monetary commitment designed for large enterprises to pre-pay for Azure services on an annual basis based on estimated usage. An organization pays the estimated amount as part of the EA (enterprise agreement) renewal. It may be eligible for a discounted rate. Azure EA scopes and individual agreement scopes offer a finite view of resources; most often, Azure resources are grouped together.

The individual resources generally have the same life cycle and belong to a specific billing project in each resource group to better manage costs. The scopes are aligned to business groups to manage Azure resource costs. In addition to scopes, Microsoft supports two hierarchy roles above the Azure subscription level: one to manage billing data, payments, and invoices and one for cloud cost with cloud governance.

The methodology to support costs includes tools, processes, and resources. Microsoft Azure provides a pricing calculator, and closely estimate spending costs. You can create a plan to use the correctly sized resources based on estimated business needs. Azure services scale up (north and south) and out (east and west) on demand, so utilization costs can support the services used for optimal Azure services for better return of investment (ROI).

Note Azure's ability to support multiple subscriptions in one Azure account makes it easier to do separate billing. This is especially useful in bill-back scenarios.

Azure Resource Manager

Azure subscriptions leverage Azure Active Directory to apply user access to manage services, usually at the resource group level. Azure Resource Manager (ARM) is the management layer to create, edit, move, and delete resources in your Azure subscription. Figure 1-4 shows how ARM supports updates from requests for the services managed.

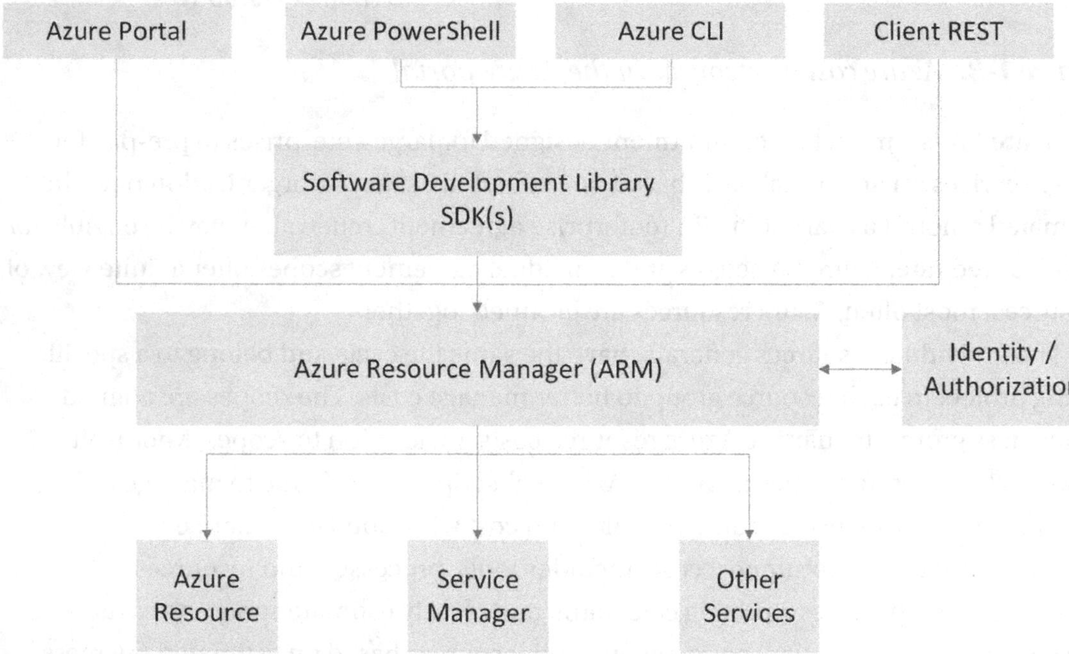

Figure 1-4. *Logical view of ARM processing*

In the first edition of this book, resources were deployed using both ARM and Azure Service Manager (ASM). ASM was the classic deployment model retired in June 2018. This edition supports Azure Resource Manager (ARM). Azure ARM supports Role Based Access Control (RBAC) It allows you to assign permissions at a more granular level.

You can configure Azure policies that directly support your overall governance security model. You can also use this information to analyze the cost of Azure with reports from log analytics.

Microsoft Azure Identity

Active Directory (AD) is the built-in identity and access management service available with your Microsoft Azure subscription. Azure AD authenticates users, machines, and services. Only after authentication is a request authorized to access Azure data or to perform work. AD also supports multifactor authentication (MFA) by using a second identification method, such as a mobile phone, a security token (or authentication token) device, or a certificate-based smart card. Strong, secure authentication is critical for businesses to support access to data or services. If Azure business policies follow the least privileged model, then users, applications, and services are granted appropriate access.

Identity services provided by the Azure platform are used in unison to provide *identity and access management* (IAM). The security access model includes tools and processes that support users, services, and systems by managing the workflow of access to data. Identity is the best security boundary for the validation of users, services, or services in the Azure cloud platform. In the cloud security architectures design with layers of security with management of identity being the most important security layer.

The security triad used to describe goals of security, CIA, confidentiality, integrity, and availability triad (see Figure 1-5).

Figure 1-5. *CIA security triad*

The triad is a visual representation of the Security triangle, one leg supports the other two legs. If they don't work together or security is compromised.

Confidentiality means that data cannot be viewed or used by anyone that has not been authorized. This pillar of information security immediately protects data from unauthorized use.

Integrity refers to data being changed or altered without the data owners' consent or knowledge. Microsoft Azure supports specific RBAC roles to prevent unauthorized changes and uses auditing to validate integrity.

Availability references the requirements to access data. It uses security availability and should not be included with Azure services that support high availability or virtual servers.

There is one other security consideration related to both identity and integrity: nonrepudiation. This security implication supports the legal claim that the authenticity of the author can be validated. Again, access control and authentication methods play a big part in Microsoft identity.

Our recommendation for businesses is to choose one of the two fully-featured Active Directory editions: Premium (P1) or Premium (P2). There are many features enabled with P1 or P2; however, some businesses benefit most from Premium 2.

Table 1-2 is a subset of features. It should be reviewed with your Chief Information Security Officer (CISO).

Table 1-2. *Subset of Azure Active Directory Premium Editions*

Advanced Feature	Premium 1	Premium 2
Conditional Access based on group, location, or device status	X	X
Third-party identity and MFA integration	X	X
Vulnerabilities and risky accounts detection		X
Risk-based conditional access policies		X
Identity Governance Supported		X

Note Please review the list of Azure Active Directory features at `https://azure.microsoft.com/en-us/pricing/details/active-directory/`.

Microsoft Azure Active Directory and Azure Resource Manager are used in multiple discussions throughout this book. The intent is to introduce them now and provide a foundation on the importance of identity, authorization, and least privileged.

Azure Security

Microsoft Azure cloud security services are designed with layers of cloud security and support a zero-trust security model. Cloud identity should be your network parameter, and not the TCP/IP security associated with an on-premises datacenter. During the process of moving workloads from on-premises to the cloud, commonly called a *lift and shift workflow*, we must leverage cloud identity to protect data. A DevOps team writes and tests code for the cloud differently from on-premises architecture applications.

As you learn about Azure infrastructure as a service (IaaS) and include platform as a service (PaaS) those responsibilities of access to data, services, and servers is critical in Azure. Public cloud providers have mastered physical security, which prevents access to the datacenter, and gaining access to physical servers. Now we must architect a network security model in the cloud with the software-defined network (SDN) and use the best security features available, including cloud-native, third-party, and software-defined security services.

The goal of Azure security is to reduce the attack surface area from bad actors or hackers. It reduces but does not eliminate all security threats; no cloud provider claims to eliminate all threats. They reduce threat risks. Some of this is from a layered approach that lowers the chance of a potential breach in your cloud infrastructure.

Security architecture follows the security baseline framework. Most companies that are new to the cloud start with a traditional model from a traditional IT security framework. Security for Microsoft Azure is designed to scale with the elasticity of the cloud model that supports high availability and scalability of both IaaS and PaaS when Azure services are created and deleted.

The Azure security framework supports a security life cycle that allows you to design threat mitigation, which includes testing with your security processes. The remediation and reduction of threats is a life cycle management goal, especially for security artifacts. Some of the individual components in security life cycle management are threat modeling, identification, and inventory. Security testing is an interactive process to support overall security. Microsoft Azure monitoring provides security alerts and security controls that identify threats and vulnerabilities in your Azure infrastructure. The cloud layered security model is shown in Figure 1-6.

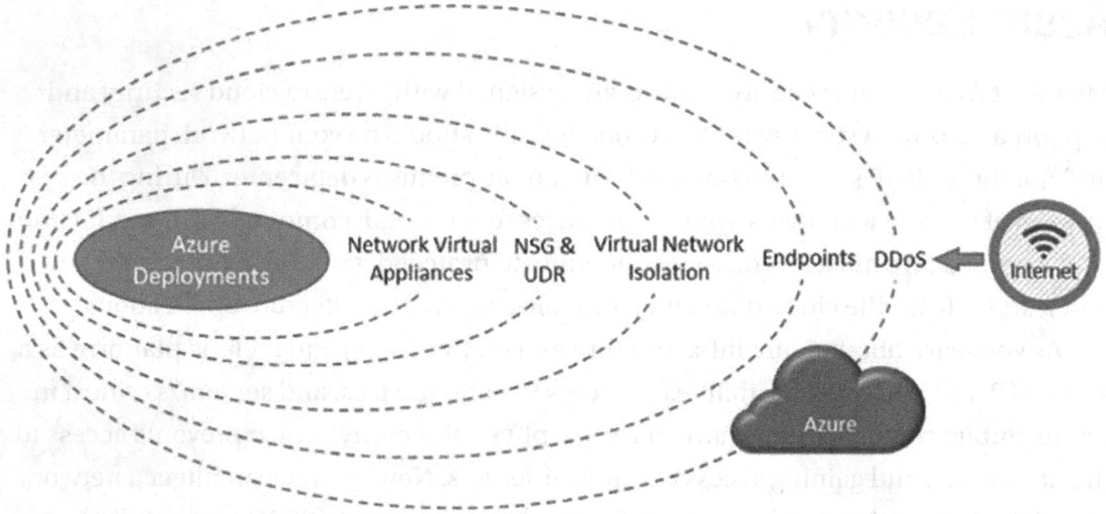

Figure 1-6. *Azure cloud-layered security*

Microsoft Azure security provides a layered security approach in the cloud from a virtual perspective and a physical perspective. The physical Azure datacenters are protected from intrusion. The way that Microsoft personnel and operations teams provide security is covered at `https://docs.microsoft.com/en-us/azure/security/fundamentals/physical-security`.

Microsoft Azure security layering includes, DDoS protection, Distributed Denial of Service. The prevention includes monitoring of public IP addresses, support for software-defined networks (VNet), and their isolation network security groups (NSG). The supporting those features all work together in a layered security model.

Azure network security groups are cloud-native implementations that allow or deny based on TCP/IP protocols, ports, origin IP addresses, and the destination IP address. The cloud-native network security group (NSG) applies inbound and outbound rules to TCP/IP data flow.

Firewalls can be used as cloud-native or third-party virtual systems in addition to the network security groups provided in Microsoft Azure. Firewalls are available through the Azure marketplace; you can use industry standards, including Palo Alto, Checkpoint, Barracuda, and F5. You can enable firewalls at the operating system level for both Windows machines and Linux servers, which increases your layered security in the Azure cloud.

Security is a broad topic. Cloud security teams and cloud administrators are familiar with the terms *jump server* and *bastion server* (see Chapter 13). It is a specific security implementation that has pros and cons. A jump server or a bastion host is normally deployed in a perimeter zone network and allows connectivity to support remote administration. You could limit a bastion host's network connectivity to allow access to only a few Azure security services.

A bastion server maintains access to support configuration and administration of the cloud services. Multiple jump servers compartmentalize connectivity from administrators into specific Azure servers and services, which reduces the vulnerability compromise.

Azure monitoring provides integration from the Azure portal, PowerShell, or the REST API to review, collect activity logs, and monitor logs specifically in an Azure subscription. Security metrics diagnostic settings and log searchers can be used inside Azure or exported into other SIEM solutions, such as Splunk or Sonra.

The Azure Security Center provides integration into both IaaS and PaaS. It provides recommendations based on compute workloads, network configurations, network security groups, data storage models, and applications, and it can configure security alerts.

Penetration testing is a standard part of any robust security program. Microsoft conducts regular penetration tests against the Azure platform. The program goes a step further by incorporating a *white hat* feature that allows customers to conduct their own penetration testing. Customers are required to agree to the terms of penetration testing, submit a request form, and receive approval before conducting such tests. The terms and the request form are at the Microsoft Azure Trust Center (see `https://security-forms.azure.com/penetration-testing/terms`).

Azure Sentinel

Changes are greatly anticipated, and the reduced development life cycle is one of the key benefits of Azure cloud computing. Microsoft Azure Sentinel is a cloud-native *security information and event management* (SIEM) solution. Sentinel can be enabled in your subscription to collect data from both Azure and on-premises log files. It was designed as artificial intelligence (AI) to investigate, detect, and respond to incidents using automation and orchestration.

Azure Sentinel supports cloud or on-premises data and supports connection to third-party security data sources, including network equipment and traditional security appliances, like firewalls. Once the data is flowing, the aggregated data provides insight from Azure cloud scaling to consume the data. This solution supports the Blue Team hunting techniques of using the IntelliSense query language, creating notebooks for automated investigation, and sharing the queries to Security Operations Centers (SOC).

Previewing New Security Features

Azure services are released once the preview period's goals have been achieved. They are often new services that are considered "opt-in" features. It is fair to use the milestone of achievement instead of a specific timeline, because preview features, some with partner co-engineering teams, may begin later than expected. They may also require more engineering time to validate the features on a global deployment scale with support in specific Azure regions.

You need to stay ahead of new features that help your business. You must opt into some preview features for specific resource testing. An example of this is the deployment of Field Programmable Gate Array (FPGA); The chip has specialized circuits used on the host hardware (Azure Hyper-V server) to increase virtual network efficiencies. Without FPGA circuits, there is network latency between software-based hosts that process the network IP packets through software layers. Using FPGA circuits allow the virtual network to interface directly with the hardware. The difference in latency (without FPGA) mid - 200 millisecond and (with FPGA) less than 10 millisecond latency. This single example illustrates the value of reviewing Azure preview features.

IaaS and PaaS Security

If you are new to Azure as a cloud provider, you need to identify the types of cloud services that are classified as *infrastructure as a service* (IaaS) or *platform as a service* (PaaS). In this book, we chose to remove conversations on *software as a service* (SaaS). If you want to learn about SaaS, please refer to the first edition of this book, *Microsoft Azure: Planning, Deploying and Managing Your Data Center in the Cloud* (Apress, 2015).

Azure provides foundational computing services; in fact, Azure is most recognized for its IaaS offerings. Examples of Azure IaaS offerings include Azure virtual machines and virtual networks, Azure storage solutions, and Azure recovery services. However, Azure is often mistaken as only an IaaS, when in fact, it has a large portfolio of PaaS offerings. Examples of its PaaS offerings include Azure SQL Database, Azure websites, Azure Content Delivery Network (CDN), and Azure Mobile Services.

Table 1-3 provides insight into Azure's PaaS security.

Table 1-3. *Microsoft Azure PaaS Security Considerations*

Attack Target	Control Plane	Responsibility
Data	Governance and rights management	100% Customer
Endpoints	Client and Network endpoints	100% Customer
Accounts, High-Value Target	Access and control management	100% Customer
Identity	AAD/ARM	50% Customer/ Azure
Applications, High-Value Target	Azure App Service	50% Customer/ Azure
Network	Software-Defined Network	50% Customer/ Azure
Operating System, High-Value Target	Hardening VM	100% Azure
Physical Host, Low ROI attack vector	Hyper-V Host	100% Azure
Physical Network, Low ROI attack vector	Network Providers	100% Azure
Physical Datacenter, Low ROI attack vector	Datacenter Buildings	100% Azure

Note The National Institute of Standards and Technology (NIST) provides definitions of the cloud models in their SP-800-145 publication at `https://csrc.nist.gov/publications/detail/sp/800-145/final`.

Summary

This chapter provided an overview of things to consider when evaluating Azure's geographically supported regions and availability zones. You learned about Azure accounts and subscriptions and how Azure is licensed. You learned how the Azure Resource Manager model leverages role-based access control and how RBAC supports Azure Active Directory. You also learned about Azure's layers of security.

The remaining chapters provide deep dives and exercise examples of Azure core features with IaaS and PaaS. The complete code for all chapters are available on GitHub.

CHAPTER 2

Overview of Azure Infrastructure as a Service (IaaS) Services

The National Institute of Standards and Technology (NIST), a division of the US Department of Commerce, defines *cloud computing* as "a model for enabling ubiquitous, convenient, on-demand network access to a shared pool of configurable computing resources (e.g., networks, servers, storage, applications, and services) that are rapidly provisioned and released with minimal management effort or service provider interaction." Within the NIST definition of cloud computing, three service models exist: software as a service (SaaS), platform as a service (PaaS), and infrastructure as a service (IaaS).

IaaS is defined as the consumer's ability to provision processing, storage, networks, and other fundamental computing resources, where the consumer can deploy and run arbitrary software, which includes operating systems and applications. The consumer does not manage or control the underlying cloud infrastructure but has control over operating systems, storage, and deployed applications; and possibly limited control of select networking components.

When this chapter was written, Microsoft Azure had 170 services, of which 55 were IaaS. In this chapter, we review the newest and most popular IaaS services and the major changes made to the existing ones. IaaS services run across all of Microsoft's various Azure clouds and regions. There are 15 compute, 19 networking, and 16 storage services. A full list of services by category is at `https://docs.microsoft.com/en-us/azure/index#pivot=products`.

J. Soh et al., *Microsoft Azure*, https://doi.org/10.1007/978-1-4842-5958-0_2

Azure Compute includes the following services.

- Linux virtual machines
- Windows virtual machines
- Virtual machine availability sets
- Virtual machine scale sets
- Dedicated hosts
- Proximity placement groups
- Azure Batch
- Azure Service Fabric
- Azure Kubernetes Service (AKS)
- CycleCloud
- Azure VMware Solutions by CloudSimple

Azure Virtual Machines

Each of the Azure compute services offer various scalability and service-level agreements (SLAs), ranging from 99% to 99.99%. We'll address this for each service reviewed in this chapter.

Each Azure virtual machine (VM) provides anywhere from 1 to 480 CPU cores or 960 CPU threads, which is the most compute power in the world. Memory-intensive workloads range from 1 GB to 24 TB for a single system, and local compute storage ranges from 4 GB to 64 TB and up to 160,000 IOPS, which is the *input/output operations per second*. This does not include the cloud storage options discussed later in this chapter.

Azure compute services offer networking speeds up to 100 Gbps InfiniBand interconnect.

One of the most overlooked aspects of virtual machines in Azure is the series. Too often, administrators provision virtual machines based on the number of cores and RAM, without understanding the underlying hardware architecture that the virtual machines reside on. Microsoft provides 12 hardware platforms for hosting virtual machines, and each one has a very specific purpose. The costs drastically differ.

Not all virtual machines are available in each Azure region. As discussed in Chapter 1, your workload may need to be in a specific Azure region due to hardware availability. For a detailed breakdown of the virtual machine series, refer to `https://azure.microsoft.com/en-us/pricing/details/virtual-machines/series/`. This page outlines not only the different underlying hardware architectures but also what each series is optimized for. The following list describes the virtual machine series.

- *A-series: Entry-level economical VMs for dev/test.* Development and test servers, low traffic web servers, small to medium databases, servers for proofs-of-concept, and code repositories
- *Bs-series: Economical burstable VMs.* Development and test servers, low-traffic web servers, small databases, microservices, servers for proofs-of-concept, build servers.
- *D-series: General-purpose compute*: Enterprise-grade applications, relational databases, in-memory caching, and analytics. The latest generations are ideal for applications that demand faster CPUs, better local disk performance, or higher memories.
- *DC-series: Protect data in use.* Confidential querying in databases, creation of scalable, confidential consortium networks, and secure multiparty machine learning algorithms. The DC-series VMs are ideal for building secure enclave-based applications to protect customers' code and data while it's in use.
- *E-series: Optimized for in-memory hyper-threaded applications.* SAP HANA, SAP S/4 HANA, SQL Hekaton, and other large in-memory business-critical workloads.
- *F-series: Compute optimized virtual machines.* Batch processing, web servers, analytics, and gaming.
- *G-series: Memory and storage optimized virtual machines.* Large SQL and NoSQL databases, ERP, SAP, and data warehousing solutions.
- *H-series: High-performance computing virtual machines.* Fluid dynamics, finite element analysis, seismic processing, reservoir simulation, risk analysis, electronic design automation, rendering, Spark, weather modeling, quantum simulation, computational chemistry, and heat-transfer simulation.

- *Ls-series: Storage-optimized virtual machines.* NoSQL databases such as Cassandra, MongoDB, Cloudera, and Redis. Data warehousing applications and large transactional databases are great use cases as well.
- *M-series: Memory-optimized virtual machines.* SAP HANA, SAP S/4 HANA, SQL Hekaton, and other large in-memory business-critical workloads requiring massive parallel compute power.
- *Mv2-series: Largest memory-optimized virtual machines.* SAP HANA, SAP S/4 HANA, SQL Hekaton, and other large in-memory business-critical workloads requiring massive parallel compute power.
- *N-series: GPU-enabled virtual machines.* Simulation, deep learning, graphics rendering, video editing, gaming, and remote visualization.

Note Azure services that support a single solution can span multiple Azure regions.

Don't worry about having all your cloud resources or services in the same Azure region. While some workloads may need this, traversing the Azure global network to get the service you need is not an issue thanks to high throughput and extremely low latency. For example, in the United States, a connection from the West Coast to the East Coast can be made in less than 60 ms (milliseconds). From Colorado, a user can connect to the East Coast in less than 45 ms. Your throughput may vary depending upon your location, the Internet service provider you're using to connect to Azure, the connection type, and so forth. The point is to be aware that your cloud services may be in multiple regions, not just the closest one to you. This is discussed later in this chapter.

Azure virtual machines provide on-demand compute resources at the scale, size, and price that meets a customer's budget. You can choose from a large variety of hardware architectures, while also designing for whatever availability needs you to have. SLAs range from 99% for a single virtual machine to 99.95% when you deploy two or more virtual machines in an availability set, this is covered in more detail in Chapter 10.

When building out Azure virtual machines, there are a few items that the administrator should consider.

- Naming conventions
- The Azure region
- The storage container configuration hosting the virtual machine
- The virtual machine series
- The size of the virtual machine
- The operating system
- The configuration of the virtual machine
- The ongoing monitoring and management of the virtual machine

Half of the Azure compute virtual machines run a flavor of Linux. Microsoft has the following distributions available in the virtual machines gallery, which is where Microsoft publishes images.

- Linux on Azure - Endorsed Distributions
- SUSE - Azure Marketplace - SUSE Linux Enterprise Server
- Red Hat - Azure Marketplace - Red Hat Enterprise Linux 7.2
- Canonical - Azure Marketplace - Ubuntu Server 16.04 LTS
- Debian - Azure Marketplace - Debian 8 "Jessie"
- FreeBSD - Azure Marketplace - FreeBSD 10.4
- CoreOS - Azure Marketplace - CoreOS (Stable)
- RancherOS - Azure Marketplace - RancherOS
- Bitnami - Bitnami Library for Azure
- Mesosphere - Azure Marketplace - Mesosphere DC/OS on Azure
- Docker - Azure Marketplace - Azure Container Service with Docker Swarm
- Jenkins - Azure Marketplace - CloudBees Jenkins Platform

Azure Batch

Azure Batch is a form of *high-performance computing* (HPC), optimized for parallel workloads that allow customers to deploy their software across pools of compute nodes (or virtual machines) and schedule the jobs to run when they want. Azure Batch allows large-scale execution when workloads are time-consuming, and the processing can be scaled out across multiple systems. Azure Batch only charges you for the compute, storage, and networking resources when you are using the service. The compute cost is included in the Batch execution. Batch supports two modes of execution.

- *Intrinsically parallel workloads* are processed in several independent parts, and access shared data, but don't communicate with each other.
- *Tightly coupled workloads* require communication with each other and use the Message Passing Interface (MPI) API to communicate with each other. HPC and GPU VM Series drastically improve this style of workload performance.

Azure Batch supports additional workloads, including, but not limited to, financial risk modeling using Monte Carlo simulations, VFX and 3D image rendering, image analysis and processing, media transcoding, genetic sequence analysis, optical character recognition (OCR), data ingestion, processing, ETL operations, software test execution, finite element analysis, fluid dynamics, multinode AI training, and execution of R algorithms.

Azure Service Fabric

To understand what Azure Service Fabric does, you must first understand the difference between monolithic and microservice applications. Briefly, monolithic applications are massive; they have numerous components that require updating the entire application at once, which incurs high risk due to potential issues and downtime. Microservice applications are made of several small services that communicate with each other. Since these scenario-focused services are separate, they can be updated and scaled independently, which reduces risk, increases flexibility, and provides a better long-term approach.

Azure Service Fabric is a service that provides packaging, deployment, and management of scalable and reliable microservices. While most of Service Fabric is viewed as a PaaS service because it is a platform on which to build highly scalable and resilient applications, it includes Service Fabric clusters, which leverage Azure compute and provide the ability to scale out to thousands of machines.

Azure CycleCloud

Azure CycleCloud is a new service that allows administrators to manage high-performance computing (HPC) clusters, also referred to as *big data*. CycleCloud supports deployment orchestration of all the necessary services, such as compute, networking, and storage. Deployment optimization, automation of operations like autoscaling, and delegation of administrators to clusters based on various constraints (including cost) are just a few of CycleCloud's capabilities.

CycleCloud's key advantage is that it is an open architecture, which allows any job-scheduler to be used with it. There are also advanced policy and governance features, such as cost reporting and controls, usage reporting, AD/LDAP integration, monitoring and alerting, and audit/event logging.

Azure VMware Solutions

Azure VMware Solutions (AVS) by CloudSimple is a fully managed service that allows customers to run their VMware-based virtual machines in Azure at any scale, without the lengthy and costly process of providing various vendors' hyper-converged solutions. AVS is an Azure service that enables you to bring your VMware-based environments to Azure without major modifications. This provides the customer with the ability to use the same operating framework, such as processes, training, code, scripts, and so forth, which they have been using in their on-premises or hosted VMware environments, now in Azure.

Common use cases for this solution include datacenter expansion needs that have an urgency where customers don't want to or don't have time to train their personnel on the Azure Resource Manager tooling. Another frequent use-case for Azure VMware Solutions is datacenter retirement. As the need to shut down datacenters increases due to high operating costs and low optimization scenarios, customers can quickly move their VMware assets to Azure without retooling or retraining. A VMware-focused hybrid architecture between on-premises and Azure is another popular reason for using AVS. The hybrid model of on-premises VMware with AVS facilitates backups, disaster recovery models, operations, and compliance due to the same platform in both locations.

Azure VMware Solutions include VMware vSphere, vCenter, vSAN, NSX-T, and their corresponding tools. Azure VMware Solutions runs natively on Azure bare metal, not Microsoft Hyper-V hosts, so customers pay the same for a host regardless of the number of virtual machines running on it. VMware workloads on Azure are easily modernized through integration with Azure services such as Azure Active Directory, Azure AI, and Analytics.

Customers deploy Azure VMware Solutions through the Azure portal. Microsoft provides and supports the management systems, networking services, operating platform, and back-end infrastructure required to run native VMware environments at scale in Azure. This service is built on a deep partnership with VMware and is part of the VMware cloud verified program.

Azure Storage Services

Azure Storage is a group of various Microsoft-managed services. These services include Azure Blobs, Azure Data Lake Storage, Azure Files, Azure Disks, Azure Archive, Azure Queues, and Azure Tables. Azure Storage services can be connected to public IPs, creating the debate on whether they're PaaS or IaaS services. For the sake of this book, and NIST's definition, we're going to treat Azure Storage as an IaaS service since you cannot run virtual machines without it!

All Azure Storage services replicate the data blocks stored to a minimum of three locations in one datacenter. Administrators can choose between the Azure Storage redundancy tiers shown in Table 2-1.

Table 2-1. *Azure Storage Redundancy Tiers*

Storage Redundancy Name	SLA on Storage Objects over a Year
Locally Redundant Storage (LRS)	99.999999999 % (11 9s)
Zone Redundant Storage (ZRS)	99.9999999999 % (12 9s)
Geographically Redundant Storage (GRS)	99.99999999999999 % (16 9s)
Geographically Zone Redundant Storage (GZRS)	99.99999999999999 % (16 9s)
Read-Access Geographically Redundant Storage (RA-GRS)	99.99999999999999 % (16 9s)

Locally redundant storage (LRS) places three copies of your data in one datacenter, providing resiliency from a drive failure or other unplanned outages within the datacenter. Zone Redundant Storage (ZRS) provides three copies of your data in both a primary and a secondary datacenter or Azure region, providing a total of six copies, three in each location. Geo-redundant storage (GRS) provides three copies to two datacenters as ZRS does, but only from one Azure region being replicated asynchronously to another Azure region 600 miles or more apart.

The replicas made in GRS are not accessible to the customer; they are designed for business continuity or disaster recovery (BC/DR) purposes. Geo-zone-redundant storage (GZRS) combines the high availability provided by redundancy across availability zones with protection from regional outages provided by geo-replication. Data in a GZRS storage account is copied across three Azure availability zones in the primary region and is also replicated to a second geographic region for protection from regional disasters.

Read-access geo-redundant storage (RA-GRS) provides three copies to two datacenters as GRS does, but the replica is accessible to be read from the second Azure region.

All Azure Storage is encrypted at rest using 256-bit AES encryption, which is one of the strongest encryptions and is FIPS 140-2 compliant. Azure Storage encryption is enabled by default, regardless of storage tier, for all Azure Storage accounts. Azure Storage Redundancy options utilize Azure Storage Encryption. No coding or configuration is necessary to leverage it. Azure Storage encryption is free and does not impact storage performance. It can use Microsoft-managed keys, or customers can use their own keys via Azure Key Vault.

Azure Storage services are billed differently than many other services in Azure because they are always in use. While you can turn off a virtual machine and not pay for the compute, you cannot turn off storage. Storage is only billed for the blocks used. If you have reserved a 1 TB Azure disk, you only pay for the part of the 1 TB that is used. This gets even more complicated when you're using workloads that are deduped or compressed, and the target amount of storage is hard to estimate. Certain Azure Storage services have tiers, also creating a tiered price model. For example, solid-state disks (SSDs) are more expensive than spinning disk drives. Another example is Azure Blob tiers, where moving from "hot" to "cool" to "archive" changes the price accordingly.

A detailed list of Azure Storage services is at `https://azure.microsoft.com/en-us/services/storage/`. For a more holistic view of all Azure Storage services, consider that they are available for any workload you run in Azure.

Blob Storage

Azure Blob storage is Microsoft's object storage solution for the cloud; it is optimized for storing massive amounts of unstructured data, such as images, video, writing to log files, backups, and streaming content. Azure Blob storage supports three tiers: hot, cold, and archive. Blob-level tiering allows block blobs to be configured programmatically as usage patterns change.

Hot Access Tier

The hot access tier is optimized for storing data that is accessed frequently. It has the highest cost and the lowest access costs. Data can be migrated from the hot tier to the cool or archive tiers.

Cool Access Tier

The cool access tier is optimized for storing data that is infrequently accessed and stored for at least 30 days. This tier has lower storage costs than the hot access tier, but has higher access costs, making backups a good use case since they are not frequently accessed. Unlike many other cloud service providers, Microsoft Azure hot and cool tiers have the same performance. The difference between these tiers is their respective SLAs; the hot access tier has a 99.99% RA-GRS SLA, while the cold access tier has a 99.9% RA-GRS SLA.

Archive Access Tier

The archive access tier is unique in several ways. It is the only tier that cannot be configured as the deployment of the storage container. It is the only tier that is required to be configured at the Blob level. It has the lowest storage costs, yet the highest cost for access. Storing data that is rarely accessed, such as legal hold, evidence, other compliance data types, and long-term backups are the ideal use cases.

Data stored in the archive access tier should be stored for at least 180 days; otherwise, there may be an early deletion charge. Finally, flexible retrieval requirements should be acceptable for the data type due to the retrieval taking hours instead of seconds.

The Azure Blob Storage archive access tier is supported by many third-party hardware manufacturers and software manufacturers, such as those who make backup solutions. At the time of writing, there were 69 partner solutions in the Azure marketplace. These partner solutions are found both on the Azure portal and the Microsoft Azure Marketplace website under the Storage section at `https://azuremarketplace.microsoft.com/en-us/marketplace/apps/category/storage?search=storage&page=1`.

Storage Explorer

Storage Explorer is a stand-alone application supported on all major Microsoft and non-Microsoft operating systems, including Mac and Linux. Storage Explorer enables users to upload, download, and copy managed disks, and create snapshots. Because of these additional capabilities, you can use Storage Explorer to migrate data from on-premises to Azure and migrate data across Azure regions.

Data Lake Storage Gen2

Azure Data Lake (ADL) Storage Gen2 is the successor to Azure Data Lake Storage Gen1. It is highly scalable and cost-effective due to being built on top of Azure Blob Storage. It supports fine-grained access control lists (ACLs), including Azure Active Directory integration, Azure Storage Encryption, automated life cycle policy management, atomic file operations, no limits on datastore size, optimizations for Spark and Hadoop integration, and tiered pricing.

The addition of a hierarchical namespace to Blob storage allows Azure Data Lake Storage Gen2 to treat operations the same way you do on a file system. You can delete a directory, which deletes all child objects. The need to enumerate all child objects is gone in Azure Data Lake Storage Gen2, making operations exponentially faster.

Azure Data Lake Storage Gen2 allows POSIX security ACLs to be applied to the folder or file level, which allows more granular permissions and security on the overall solution. These permissions are configurable through Azure Storage Explorer or frameworks like Hive and Spark.

Other key features include Hadoop integration emulating the Hadoop Distributed File System (HDFS) and big data analytics optimized ABFS driver.

Managed Disks

Azure Disk Storage offers persistent, high-performance disk solutions managed by Microsoft. It provides scalability to 50,000 disks in a single subscription within a single Azure region. Azure managed disks have a 99.999% availability SLA. Azure disks integrate with availability sets and zones, are supported by Azure backup, provide administrators with fine-grained, role-based access control (RBAC), and support two different types of disk encryption: server-side encryption and Azure Disk Encryption. Azure Disk Encryption uses Bitlocker for Microsoft volumes and DM-Crypt for Linux disk volumes.

When a virtual machine is built, there are three kinds of disks present to the administrator: OS disks, data disks, and temporary disks. Every VM that is created gets an OS disk; this is where the OS is installed and has a max size of 2 TB. Administrators have the option of adding a data disk at virtual machine deployment or after the fact. Data disks are managed disks attached to the virtual machine to store data and appear as local drives. Data disks are SCSI disks that have a maximum capacity of 35 TB. Temporary disks provide short-term storage for workloads. Temporary disks are deleted during a maintenance event, such as a reboot for patching. The temporary disk is re-created at each OS boot. Microsoft Windows virtual machines default the temporary disks to D: and Linux to /dev/sdb. This is ideal for applications that expect to have locations they can swap to. Many graphics-intensive apps have this requirement, and leveraging the temporary disk yields faster I/O than the OS disk. The size of the virtual machine determines the number of data disks that you can attach to it and the type of storage you can use to host the disks.

Queue Storage

Azure Queue Storage is designed to support standard queuing scenarios, such as decoupling application components to increase scalability and tolerance for failures, load leveling, and building process workflows. It provides asynchronous message queueing for communication between application components and a consistent programming model across other Azure Storage services.

Queue Storage messages are not always delivered in a *first in, first out* (FIFO) fashion. It is one of the two queue services offered by Microsoft Azure; the other is Azure Service Bus. Queue Storage is part of the Azure Storage service fabric. Storage queues should be used when many gigabytes of messages must be stored in a queue when tracking the progress of messages in a queue is desired or when there is a server-side log for all transactions requirement.

Azure Files

Azure Files is a new Azure Storage service that allows users to expose shares from Azure via SMB (Server Message Block). These shares are available to all major operations systems, both Microsoft and non-Microsoft. The Azure Files service allows customers to cache local copies of the data using Azure File Sync to minimize latency between on-premises and the cloud. This provides a pseudo local file server experience. The data shared via Azure Files is encrypted at rest, but also in transit via SMB 3.0 and HTTPS.

Azure Files has two tiers: Standard and Premium. The primary difference is the underlying storage architecture. Standard Azure Files reside on Microsoft's lowest-cost storage, whereas Premium Azure Files resides on SSD-based storage designed to support I/O-intensive workloads that require file share semantics with significantly high throughput and low latency.

Azure Files has multiple parts to its pricing structure, including the cost of storage, and the cost of ingress, egress, reads, writes, and so forth. For a detailed breakdown, refer to `https://azure.microsoft.com/en-us/pricing/details/storage/files/`. To model your own scenario, use the Azure Calculator at `https://azure.microsoft.com/en-us/pricing/calculator/`.

Data Box

Azure Data Box is a physical device-based storage solution that allows customers to copy and ship large amounts of data to Microsoft. Customers that have low-bandwidth challenges, large amounts of data, or time constraints on their data uploads to Azure are candidates for Azure Data Box. Customers order a Data Box solution that fits their storage needs; upon receiving it, they fill it with their data, and then ship it to Microsoft. Once Microsoft receives the Data Box solution, it inspects and uploads your data, and then wipes the device. Azure Data Box has three solutions.

- It provides customers up to five 8 TB SSDs, totaling 40 TB; 35 TB usable per order. These 2.5-inch drives come with an interface that uses 128-bit encryption. Data is copied over USB/SATA II, III interface using Robocopy or similar tools.

- It provides customers a 50 lb. 100 TB/80 TB usable enclosure per order that is AES 256-bit encrypted to copy and safely ship to Azure. Data is copied over 1×1/10 Gbps RJ45, 2×10 Gbps SFP+ interface using SMB or NFS protocols.
- Data Box Heavy is a self-contained, 500-lb. device capable of storing 1 PB/800 TB usable of data secured with AES 256-bit encryption. Data is copied over 4×1 Gbps RJ45, 4×40 Gbps QSFP+ interface.

All Azure Data Box solutions support Azure Block Blob, Page Blob, Azure Files, and managed disks. Data can only be accessed with a secure key provided via the Azure portal. Once your data is uploaded to Azure, the Data Box solutions are wiped clean and sanitized in accordance with NIST 800-88 R1 standards.

Ephemeral OS Disks

Ephemeral OS disks, which are only available to virtual machine series that support Premium Storage, are a new Azure Storage service that allows the disks that the OS is installed on to be deleted. Ephemeral OS Disks are free. They can be used with customer images or Azure Gallery images. They provide lower latency than an OS or data disk, and the ability to reimage or scale-out your virtual machine deployment or scale-set more quickly. Ephemeral OS disks are like the temporary disks, but for use where the OS resides. There are specific use cases for these disks in which the OS is always expected to run from a specific state, such as a "non-persistent" virtual desktop or server.

Azure Networking Services

Azure has 19 networking services, including applications, virtual machine–specific services like Azure Virtual Network or Azure Load Balancer, and unrestricted scalability-based services like Azure's Virtual WAN. Azure networking services allow you to configure any type of connectivity, security, or availability model. It used to take hundreds of hours, the coordination of numerous vendors, and lengthy procurement and deployment times. Today, Azure networking services can be deployed in minutes, and reconfigured, redeployed, and removed with the same elasticity and billing model as other Azure services.

Since the first edition of this book, several new Azure networking services have emerged. Each of them satisfies regulatory compliance and are audited to standards regularly. For more information on the regulatory compliance of any Azure service, please refer to `www.microsoft.com/en-us/TrustCenter/CloudServices/Azure/default.aspx`.

The rest of this chapter discusses new or enhanced services in Azure. There is more information on some of these services in Chapter 9.

Azure Virtual Network

Azure Virtual Network is the core component of all Azure IaaS services, and increasing PaaS usage as Azure Private Link and Azure service endpoints become broader offerings. Azure Virtual Network allows virtual machines to communicate with each other, the Internet, on-premises, and so forth. The key benefits of Azure Virtual Network are the scale, availability, being cloud native, and isolation offered by Azure. Azure Virtual Network has address spaces, subnets, and resides in regions, subscriptions, and management groups. It is also free of charge.

Compute, network, data, analytics, identity, containers, Web, and hosted Azure services can be deployed to an Azure virtual network. More than 20 Azure services support Azure Virtual Network deployments. Communication between these services is enabled via Point-to-Site (P2S), Site-to-Site (S2S), or ExpressRoute connectivity models. Traffic is filtered on an Azure virtual network by network security groups (NSG) or by network virtual appliances (NVA), which are virtual machines performing the functions of a firewall but running code usually provided by mainstream firewall manufacturers (Cisco, Palo Alto Networks, Riverbed, FortiGate, Barracuda, or Checkpoint to name just a few).

Finally, Azure virtual networks allow routing of traffic between subnets, in Azure or on-premises, by using routing tables or Border Gateway Protocol (BGP) routes.

For more information on Azure networking, please refer to Chapter 3 and Chapter 7.

Azure Application Gateway and Web Application Firewall

When we talk about load balancers, we're going to reference layer 4, the transport layer, and layer 7, the application layer, from the Open Systems Interconnection (OSI) model. Azure Application Gateway is a layer 7 load balancer. This is frequently confused with layer 4 load balancers, which are the most common; they route based on IP address or port data. Azure Load Balancer is layer 4. Azure Application Gateway can use URL or

HTTP headers to make routing determinations. Azure Application Gateway provides load balancing and routing based on layer 7 the same way Microsoft Forefront Unified Access Gateway (UAG) Server and Microsoft Intelligent Application Gateway (IAG) provided these services as a licensed product.

Azure Application Gateway and Azure Web Application Firewall have a second edition, known as v2. It was released in 2019, and it provides many features in addition to the ones in the v1 edition. Autoscaling and zone redundancy are key benefits of v2, while User Defined Routing (UDR) was a key difference between the first Azure Application Gateway and the Azure Application Gateway v2 version. UDR support on Azure AppGW v2 is available via PowerShell, and the v2 version should provide all of v1's functionality.

Azure DDoS Protection

DDoS (distributed denial-of-service) attacks are commonplace. They are in the news regularly, and companies can incur major financial losses from being the target of one. It is imperative for a cloud service provider (CSP) to protect itself and its customers from any kind of bad actors that try to cause their digital infrastructure harm. Almost anyone can fall victim to a DDoS attack, especially when they are hosted in countries that ignore them, can be launched for as little as $5, and can easily be purchased via a web service from a browser.

DDoS attacks cost lost revenue, sales, downtime, brand damage, lower brand value, operational expenses, and countless hours in personnel trying to mitigate or recover from them. In 2019, TechHQ reported that DDoS attacks cost US businesses $10 billion per year, and the average business lost $218,339. Go to `https://techhq.com/2019/03/ddos-attacks-cost-us-businesses-10bn-per-year/` for the article on the significance and growing landscape of DDoS attacks.

Azure DDoS protection comes in two tiers: Basic and Standard. Every Azure customer gets Basic for free and automatically, and it's always on. Azure's global network is a key element used in the Standard tier to mitigate workloads from DDoS attacks. Azure's Standard DDoS protection provides benefits specifically for customers using Azure Virtual Network resources. Azure network resources that expose workloads via public IP addresses are tuned by insights uncovered through machine learning of network traffic. DDoS Standard surfaces traffic insights through the Azure Monitor service. Several additional services are available with Standard DDoS Protection, including access to DDoS subject-matter experts (SME) during an attack, logs for SIEM integration, and post-attack mitigation reports.

ExpressRoute

Azure ExpressRoute is a private, dedicated, high bandwidth, low latency, SLA connection into the Microsoft Azure global network. ExpressRoute allows connectivity not only to Azure resources but Office 365 and Dynamics 365 as well. ExpressRoute uses private peering for connectivity to Azure virtual networks, and Microsoft peering for connectivity to PaaS and SaaS workloads, such as Cosmos DB, Azure SQL, Office 365, and Dynamics 365.

Azure Firewall

Azure Firewall is a stateful packet inspection (SPI) firewall managed by Microsoft. Firewall has unrestricted scalability and is highly available by default. It provides all the services you would expect from an enterprise-class firewall, but as a managed service. It includes a new service, Firewall Manager, where administrators can manage firewalls at scale, across Azure regions and subscriptions, with the ability to centrally manage the firewalls' configurations and routing via global and local policies.

Azure Firewall supports the following capabilities.

- Built-in high availability
- Availability zones
- Unrestricted cloud scalability
- Application FQDN filtering rules
- Network traffic filtering rules
- FQDN tags
- Service tags
- Threat intelligence
- Outbound SNAT support
- Inbound DNAT support
- Multiple public IP addresses
- Azure monitor logging

Azure Front Door

Azure Front Door allows the global management and routing of customers' web traffic. Front Door provides several ways to route traffic in the most efficient manner possible to the client. Front Door analyzes latency, priority, weight, and session affinity to determine the best routing for the traffic to be optimized. Front Door is highly available and can withstand an entire Azure region failure.

Azure Internet Analyzer

Azure Internet Analyzer provides customers the means to "benchmark" or measure the performance of network changes made within the environment. Internet Analyzer takes customers' data and mashes it with Microsoft's analytics to optimize network routing and topology. Internet Analyzer embeds a JavaScript client in a web application for customers to use for various measurements, such as latency. This new service allows customers to experiment with the "what if" scenarios before making major changes to their network, with the goal of understanding if the changes provide any performance gains.

Azure CDN

Azure Content Delivery Network (CDN) is a global caching service that allows high bandwidth and low latency to end users. It uses the closest point of presence (POP) to allow users to download data while minimizing the impact on their experience in a transparent fashion.

Microsoft Update is a great example of its usage. It's a predictable payload that can easily be pre-staged. This allows consumers to download their update data not from Redmond, WA, or their nearest Azure region, but instead from a local point of presence that minimized latency to the data/service.

Azure Content Delivery Network should be evaluated whenever dynamic content needs to be served, and the audience is geographically distributed, even within a single country.

Azure Load Balancer

Azure Load Balancer is a layer 4 load balancer in the OSI model. Azure Load Balancer acts as a public load balancer and translates private IPs for virtual machines to public IPs on Azure Edge. This service is called a network address translation (NAT); it allows virtual machines to have Internet access. Load Balancer also has a private mode, where it uses private IP addresses on both the outside and inside, such as when you need to use a load balancer inside a virtual network or between on-premises and a virtual network. The following are some of the use cases for Azure Load Balancer.

- Load balancing internal and external traffic to Azure virtual machines
- Increasing availability by distributing resources within and across zones
- Configuring outbound connectivity for Azure virtual machines
- Using health probes to monitor load-balanced resources
- Employing port forwarding to access virtual machines in a virtual network by public IP address and port
- Enabling support for load-balancing of IPv6

Standard Load Balancer provides multidimensional metrics through Azure Monitor. These metrics can be filtered, grouped, and broken out for a given dimension. They provide current and historical insights into the performance and health of your service. Azure Load Balancer allows customers to:

- Load balance services on multiple ports, multiple IP addresses, or both.
- Move internal and external load balancer resources across Azure regions.
- Load balance TCP and UDP flow on all ports simultaneously using HA ports.

Azure Load Balancer is priced on two tiers: Basic and Standard. Basic is free, while Standard is priced by a combination of the number of load balancing rules and the amount of data processed. For more pricing information, see `https://azure.microsoft.com/en-us/pricing/details/load-balancer/`.

Traffic Manager

Azure Traffic Manager is a DNS-based load balancer that allows the optimization of traffic to the most appropriate resources, determined by priority, weight, performance, geography, or subnets. Traffic Manager is the Microsoft version of Global Traffic Management (GTM) as an IaaS service. It is fully managed, highly available, and hosted in Azure. Common use cases for Traffic Manager include the ability to load balance between on-premise and Azure for mission-critical applications. Traffic Manager supports both Microsoft and non-Microsoft endpoints, as well as hybrid scenarios such as bursting into Azure for increased scale of a given workload.

VPN Gateway

A VPN gateway allows encrypted communication to flow between two Azure virtual networks or an Azure virtual network and an on-premises network. VPN gateways are made up of virtual machines deployed to a special subnet designed for routing. Because of this deployment model, the virtual machines are not configurable. Instead, all VPN gateway configuration is done through the Azure portal or as infrastructure as code.

A VPN gateway takes approximately 45 minutes to deploy due to the nature of its architecture and the VPN gateway subnet creation. Finally, VPN gateways support P2S, S2S, or ExpressRoute connectivity models. Bandwidth on VPN gateways can vary from 100 Mbps to 10 Gbps, depending upon the VPN gateway deployed. For a detailed breakdown of VPN gateway throughput, encryption used, and limitations, please refer to `https://docs.microsoft.com/en-us/azure/vpn-gateway/vpn-gateway-about-vpngateways`.

Summary

Azure has grown substantially, both in capability and customer adoption, since we wrote the first book in 2015. Azure IaaS has seen an explosion in networking, storage, and security-related solutions. Several non-Microsoft vendors are now offering their products or services on the Azure platform. Everything in Azure is built from the ground up with security as the top priority. Zero trust, which is outside the scope of this book, is largely based on the principles of securing applications through several mechanisms, including identity and multifactor authentication, but not relying solely on network segmentation. That architecture doesn't work in today's cybersecurity landscape. Hence, the intense investment in securing networks from the world's largest software provider is evident. This chapter provides an overview of some of the more popular services released over the past five years. Information on many of these cloud services is covered later in this book.

CHAPTER 3

Overview of Azure Platform as a Service

In this chapter, we provide a high-level view of the major services that are globally available, as well as elements of the Microsoft Azure platform as a service (PaaS). First, we discuss Azure Web Apps, support for developer frameworks, and apps that can run in containers. Next, you gain insight into database services and individual options for support. Then, we dive into Azure DNS as a powerful global service to support name resolution by customizing business service access. A companion service is Azure Traffic Manager, which supports DNS routing client requests based on profiles needed for business criteria.

We discuss Azure Content Delivery Network (CDN) and how to configure it to cache data on edge servers to speed content to end users and improve customer experience. We give insight into the Azure Batch service for scheduling and managing a compute platform and automatically scaling job size. Finally, you learn how Azure Private Link service supports a private connection from a virtual network to Azure PaaS services using a private endpoint.

This overview chapter skims topics that are key to support projects that your business wants to leverage. You learn about the PaaS service and then dive deeper into this topic with hands-on exercises in other chapters in this book.

Azure Web Apps

You may have many developers in your company—each with their own opinion on which software platform is best; however, the Azure App Service platform supports a wide variety of software choices. Azure Web Apps describes a managed application that is running in the Azure App Service. Earlier support options that used web and worker

J. Soh et al., *Microsoft Azure*, https://doi.org/10.1007/978-1-4842-5958-0_3

roles were a good start, but limited instance size changes with other management complexities. Today, Azure App Service and Web Apps provide services that remove management complexity, deploy quickly, and offer a service plan to match any project budget.

The application framework support includes

- .NET/.NET Core
- Node.js
- Java
- PHP
- Ruby
- Python

Azure App Service's advantages include global scaling to support security, compliance, and performance, which translates to easier maintenance. Azure App Service provides PaaS to support mobile back ends, RESTful APIs, and the ability to build and host web applications (a.k.a Web Apps). The Azure portal supports creating a web app easily; however, you should be familiar with the service plans and their features to best support your application's requirements.

Azure App Service is a traditional multitenant server deployment model. Your app service shares Hyper-V hosts with other Azure subscriptions. This is cost-effective, but Microsoft introduced several restrictions around scalability and security. This is a consideration for all the current service plans except the High-Performance, Security, and Isolation service plan. There is a free service plan that includes a limit of ten web mobile instances or APIs; however, it is the only plan that doesn't support a custom domain name.

There are a few other service plan attributes to be aware of as you plan and design a web application deployment model. The Auto Scale feature is only available in the Standard, Premium, and Isolated pricing models.

The last feature is VPN Hybrid connectivity. In the App Service platform, hybrid connections can be used in a hybrid connection manager (HCM) and bus relay configuration to access application resources in other networks. This feature does not allow a "side channel" to access your application.

Azure Database Services

Microsoft Azure has a database-as-a-service offering that is more than Microsoft SQL Server. Popular business database-hosted services include MySQL, MariaDB, and PostgreSQL. There are also other Azure services to help with access and migration. Microsoft SQL (services) include two offerings: one service is "SQL managed," and the other is Azure SQL Database.

The hardware, OS upgrades, and system configuration are included in the cloud services, so those requirements are removed from the traditional work of an IT Operations team or database administrators (DB Admin). The methods to maintain or gain high availability, disaster recovery, backup, and query performance insight are additional services that need to be configured and enabled.

Azure SQL Database is a multitenant database service. Microsoft services include supporting the network, storage, Hypervisor, and the hardware that a cloud provides with managed services. Upgrades are also included with SQL Database.

Azure SQL Database supports business applications and can be deployed using any of the following three configurations.

- Elastic pool
- Single
- Managed instance

You have the option to choose either a virtual core (vCore) or a database transaction unit (DTU). These options are important because they apply to specific Azure SQL database deployment models. The vCore purchasing model allows a choice between a compute tier and a serverless compute tier. You should spend time learning the differences between deployment models as they relate to vCore and DTU.

- Single, elastic pool deployment options in Azure SQL Database offer both DTU and vCore
- Managed instance options in Azure SQL Database only offer vCore
- The Hyperscale service tier is available for vCore

Before you review the database table limits of the Basic, Standard, and Premium tiers, you should first understand the formula used as part of the DTU cost model. The DTU and elastic DTU (eDTU) have benchmarks that include virtual computer characteristics, such as CPU, memory, and IO (input/output). The vCore purchasing model for a SQL Server managed instance supports Azure virtual machines (refer to Chapter 10) Gen4 and Gen 5 Hyper-V hosts. Additional processor chip sets include the Haswell and Broadwell CPU. Performance and security are always common areas of concern. You should understand the Azure SQL tier models to gain understanding of the total cost.

You should also become familuar with options available with the Microsoft migration tools. You can test a migration tools. You can test a migration process with the included guidance to select a database to see the recommendation of the migration to Azure (i.e., SAP migration to Azure SQL Database or SQL server). In addition to guidance, there are six services that help with migration:

- Data access toolkit: A Virtual Studio Code extension for Java and .NET source code
- Experimentation Assistant: Evaluates a specific version of SQL
- Migration Assistant: A tool to assess the source SQL database for potential compatibility issues
- Server Migration Assistant: Other than SQL database
- Azure Database Migration: Migrates multiple sources to the cloud platform (end to end)
- Azure Migrate: A hub for tracking all stages of a migration

Azure DNS

Azure DNS provides global name resolution using the Microsoft Azure cloud-native infrastructure. DNS (Domain Name System) has been an essential function of the Internet since the mid-1980s. This network service is responsible for assigning domain names (easy-to-remember names) to Internet resources. The resource is mostly used to provide principle namespace to an Internet Protocol (IP) subnet.

DNS uses a database back end to store relevant records and support lookup of most record types, including

- Start of Authority (SOA)
- IP address (A, AAAA-IPv6)

- Mail exchange (MX)
- Reverse DNS lookups (PTR)
- Domain aliases (CNAME)

Microsoft supports customized domain name integration, which includes features that support purchasing a domain name using the Azure App Service Domains page. Azure DNS supports controlled access to manage DNS services through role-based access control (RBAC). DNS writes to activity logs to troubleshoot and support Azure resources locking. Azure locks prevent subscriptions, resource groups, or individual resources (i.e., VM) from being accidentally modified. Locks support two settings: *cannot delete* and *read-only*.

Azure DNS services support internal Azure Private DNS services and external resources outside of your Azure subscription. Pricing information is based on two metrics: the number of DNS zones and the number of queries.

Azure Traffic Manager

Azure Traffic Manager is a component to support high availability. Relative to DNS, it supports IP traffic and distributes that traffic based on your Azure regional workloads. Traffic Manager uses DNS to direct end-user or client requests based on your preferred routing policy. No TCP/IP traffic flows through Azure Traffic Manager; it only routes the request to the appropriate endpoint based on the profile. It is not a proxy or gateway, so the traffic is only redirected between the endpoints.

Supported traffic can be routed based on profiles, which support the requirements of the business or application, such as

- Subnet
- Priority
- Geographic
- Performance
- Weighted
- Multivalue

Azure endpoints are publicly accessible URLs. An endpoint has a unique DNS CNAME to identify mapping for Traffic Manager. An example of a provision Traffic Manager extension resembles the following.

```
ACloudBiz.trafficmanger.net
```

Traffic Manager identifies regions to respond to the DNS server request. The DNS resolvers provide the correct endpoint. The two main benefits are traffic distribution support and failover. Both benefits support the high availability of client services.

Before you deploy Traffic Manager, you need to have a public IP address (URL) in DNS for the probes used for redirecting traffic and a profile of the routing method. From the Azure portal, search the Traffic Manager profile, as shown in Figure 3-1.

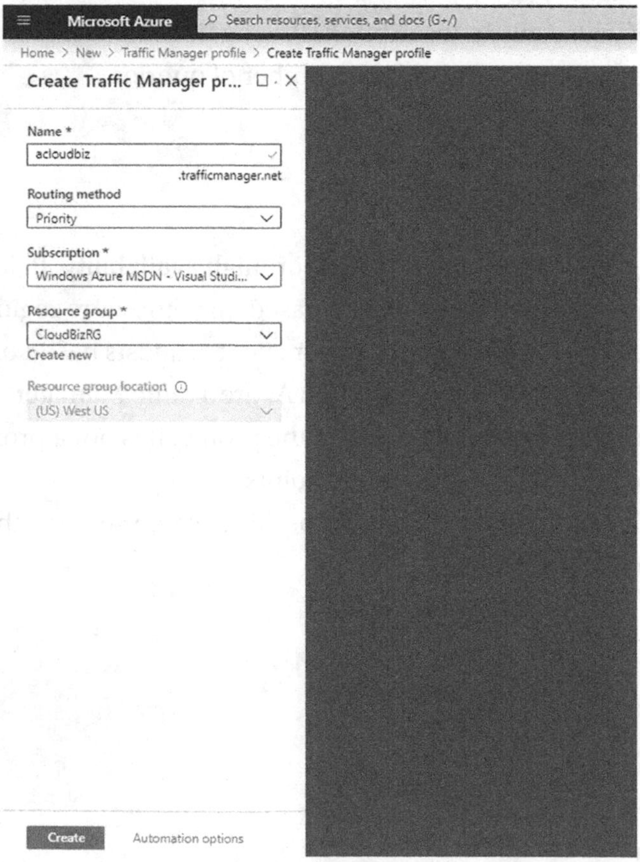

***Figure 3-1.** The Azure portal to create a Traffic Manager profile*

Once the profile is created, use the Azure portal to review the Traffic Manager settings, as shown in Figure 3-2. It shows the current profile status and settings, which can be changed using the Configuration icon on the left.

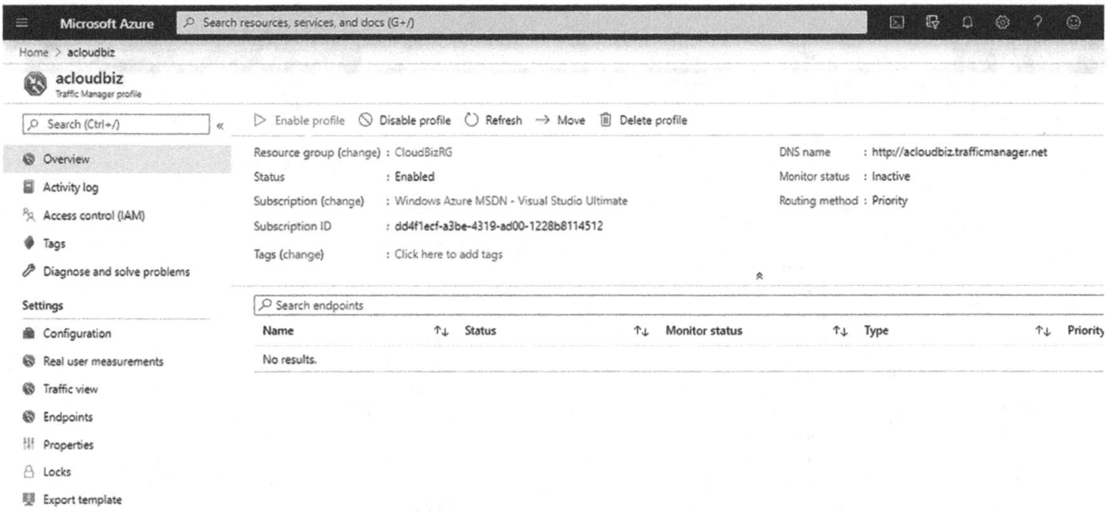

Figure 3-2. *Configuration settings for Azure Traffic Manager*

The endpoints are updated in the portal view to then efficiently route DNS traffic based on the "priority" selected in this example. It directs traffic to IP addresses that are associated with cloud services or on-premises networks. The DNS name is returned to the requesting client; however, if the endpoint is offline or degraded, the DNS name is not returned to the requesting client.

The most effective use of Azure Traffic Manager supports Azure georedundant Active Directory Federated Services (ADFS). Azure supports Transport Layer Security (TLS) and the management of SSL certificates for custom domains with DNS.

Content Delivery Network

You want to deliver web services and content (i.e., video files) efficiently and with the best user experience and fastest response times. The Azure Content Delivery Network (CDN) uses point-of-presence (POP) edge server repositories to store content and minimize network latency.

CDN servers enable content delivery and are globally available across Azure regions. Before you can create a CDN profile, you must register the Microsoft CDN service and a registered resource provider in your Azure subscription. Register the CDN service in the Azure portal, select your subscription, and locate `Microsoft.Cdn`, as shown in Figure 3-3.

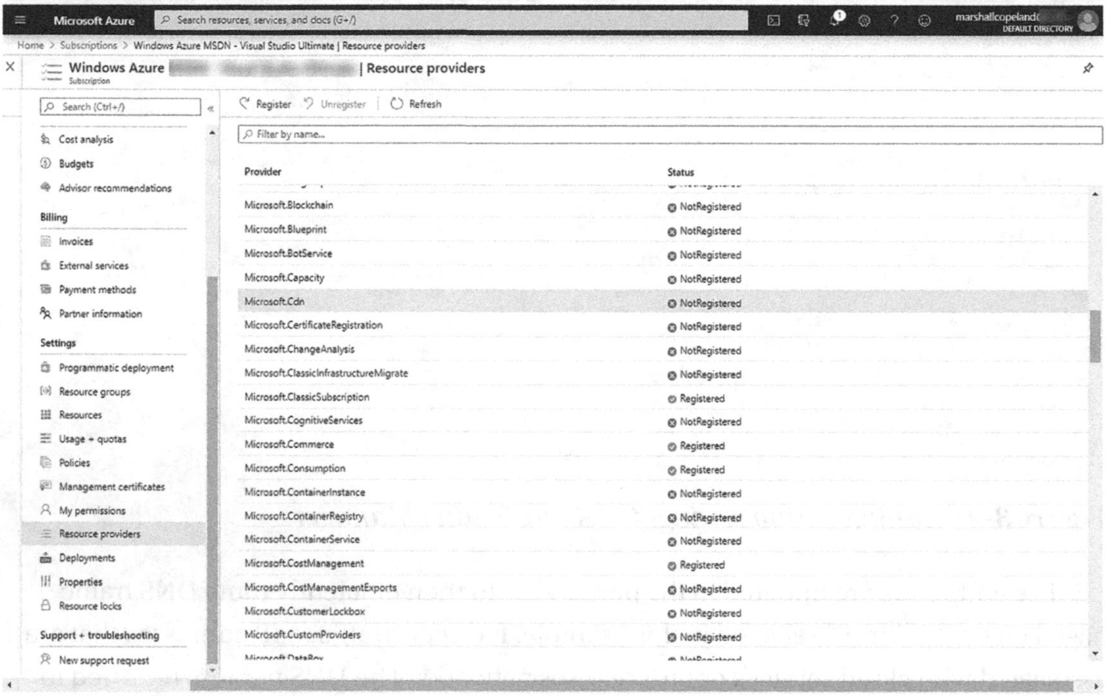

***Figure 3-3.** Azure portal registers Azure CDN services in an Azure subscription*

Once the service is registered, you can create a CDN profile to choose the specific collection of endpoints for that specific profile service, as shown in Figure 3-4.

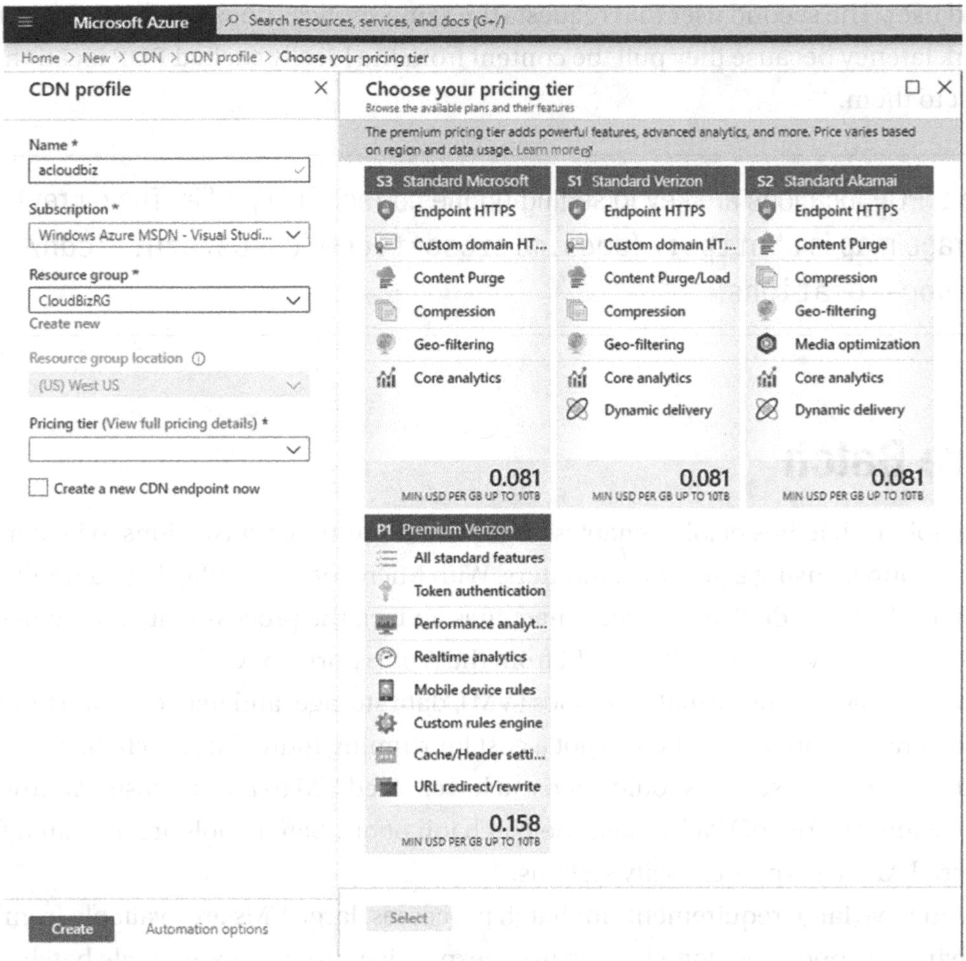

***Figure 3-4.** Azure portal view to create a CDN profile*

Note Pricing information for CDN standard updates based on region is at `https://azure.microsoft.com/en-us/pricing/details/cdn/`.

A CDN profile enables a better customer experience, which fosters a recurring customer. The Azure CDN can deliver better performance through high-bandwidth network caching. The first user that requests a service sends a request to review the content (i.e., video). The content originates from a server; it can have latency due to network distance. The content is cached to the edge servers in a POP location near the end user. The second user that requests the same services does not incur the same network latency because they pull the content from the locally cached POP location nearest to them.

Note POP locations are key to setting up the correct CDN profile. The current coverage map is at `https://docs.microsoft.com/en-us/azure/cdn/cdn-pop-locations`.

Azure Batch

A batch job (or batches of jobs) enables large jobs or multiple transactions to be part of a single group by using a pool of computers. With Microsoft Azure Batch, you don't need special hardware or dedicated virtual machines. In fact, the processes are automated to pool computers by using the Batch API from the Azure portal or CLI.

You only pay for the virtual machines (VM), data storage, and network traffic that run the parallel workloads. There is not a cost for running individual batch jobs. Virtual machine prices vary so you should choose a lower-sized VM to reduce costs. Another tip is using a low priority of VM because the Batch job pools. Batch pools are allocated from the overall Azure surplus capacity systems.

If you have large requirements for batch processes, large VMs are available from the underlying VM pool; you don't have to use inexpensive systems. Large-scale batch jobs run in parallel and use high-performance computing (HPC). The batch command-line tools include PowerShell cmdlets and the Azure CLI. For more functionality, you can use the Azure portal to review job stats and performance data.

You can also use new tools for reviewing batch processes from GitHub, such as Azure Batch Explorer (see `https://azure.github.io/BatchExplorer/`).

Azure Private Link

Azure Private Link is a newer service that allows connectivity to PaaS services by using an IaaS virtual network (vNET) as the endpoint. This provides the workload a private IP address instead of a public IP address, and hence, connectivity to the workload over

Azure VPN tunnels or ExpressRoute private peering. The service ties a PaaS service over its public IP address to the customer's virtual network over the Microsoft Azure backbone network. This means no "hair-pinning" of traffic over VPN or ExpressRoute to get the public IP address to talk to the private virtual network.

Services evolve on an almost daily schedule; however, Azure Private Link is only available for Azure Storage, Azure Cosmos DB, and Azure SQL Database. These are likely the three most used PaaS services in Azure. Azure Private Link can protect against data leakage because only an instance of a PaaS service is made available, not the entire service.

Network connectivity in Azure utilizes Microsoft virtual networks, and traffic is not routed over other network provider resources. To maintain a private connection between your applications deployed in different Microsoft Azure regions, you can deploy Private Link. You may think the network access is only to and from Microsoft Azure resources, but that is not the case.

Private Link is a service used with the Azure Standard load balancer; it also supports the Azure private endpoint. Azure deployments have leveraged the Private Link service to connect to Azure PaaS services like Azure Storage. Azure subscriptions can securely connect to on-premise networks and Azure partner services by using a private endpoint.

You do not need to expose a public IP address to the Internet to connect; with an Azure private endpoint, the IP address uses Azure Private Link services. Private Link is generally available in Azure regions and can be easily created from the portal, as shown in Figure 3-5.

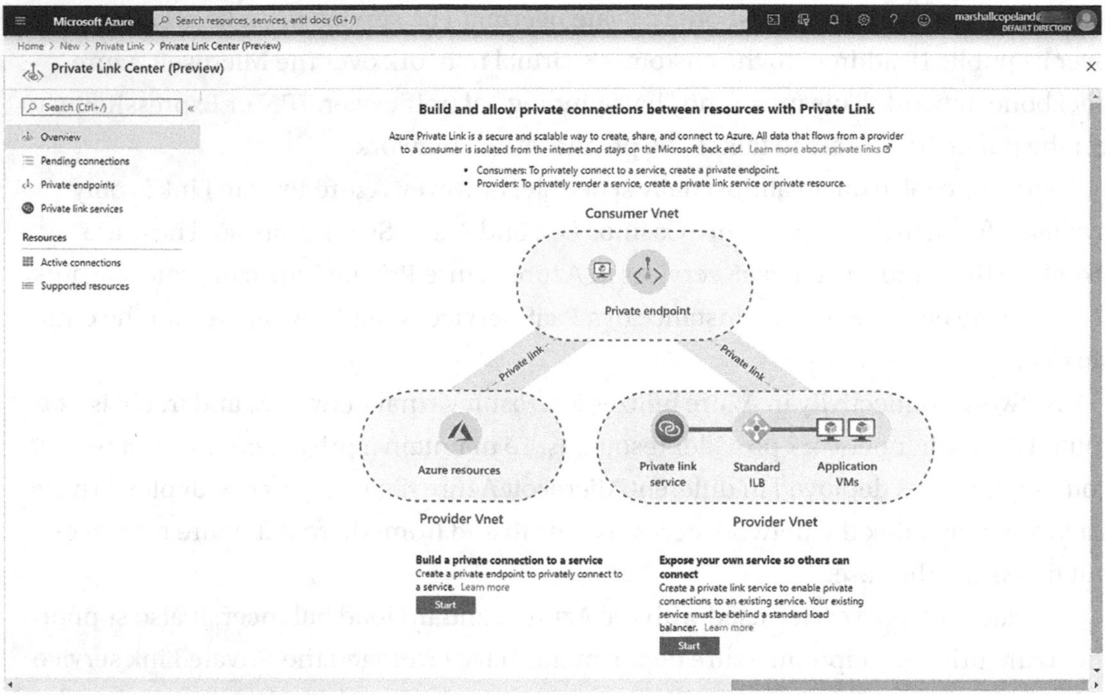

Figure 3-5. *Use the Azure portal to create an Azure Private Link*

Private Link provides connectivity using the Azure network to connect securely to Azure partner network services. You also have the choice to connect to your company's own service across a VPN or ExpressRoute (see Chapter 9). The Private Link platform supports the connection between a service provider and an Azure consumer.

Private endpoints supported by a VPN or ExpressRoute can connect directly using private links running over the VPN or ER. Another security feature is the risk reduction of data leakage. Mapping of PaaS services to specific user access can be blocked. Private Link features continue to be enhanced.

Summary

In this chapter, you learned about the Azure App Service for mobile back ends, APIs, and web app services with a global platform as a service (PaaS) solution. There are service tiers to support your application requirements, as well as the ability to leverage other PaaS Azure services. You were introduced to Azure database services and the many tools to help migrate databases to an Azure-hosted DB platform.

You gained insight into Azure DNS as a global service for client and server connectivity. You learned that Azure Traffic Manager redirects DNS requests to a localhost to reduce latency, or it can be used in failover mode. You learned that the Azure Content Delivery Network (CDN) is a global service that supports caching on Azure edge systems to speed up content delivery to clients. You gained insight into Azure Batch services, and, you learned about Azure Private Link services, including private endpoints.

CHAPTER 4

Azure AppDev Services Overview

The audience for this chapter includes business executives and technology decision-makers who want a quick overview of developer topics. This chapter connects the Azure developer services that span across the geographic regions of Azure datacenters. It overviews application development services in Microsoft Azure, making decisions for creating cloud applications, and how Azure supports code using popular programming languages.

This chapter is foundational and offers high-level explanations with later chapters providing deeper dives, configurations, and coding exercises. The support for developers or *Application development* (AppDev) includes application development with C#, .NET, Python, and others.

The goal of this chapter is to present high-level connections in the development triangle of people, processes, and technologies to leverage Azure AppDev. Applications run in the cloud, and every business wants to be competitive and create applications quickly in the nimble, software-defined network of cloud computing, but they may not know what is available in Azure. The cloud is disruptive for traditional IT operations and requires a refocus for the engineering team. Let's start with some of the languages supported by Azure services for developers.

- .NET
- Python
- JavaScript
- Java
- PHP
- Go Language

J. Soh et al., *Microsoft Azure*, https://doi.org/10.1007/978-1-4842-5958-0_4

The use of open source or non-Microsoft languages on a Microsoft platform may be surprising to some engineers; however, it is a key investment from Microsoft to support developers' languages of choice. Development language support is one leg of the development triangle.

Application development has evolved from longer, software development life cycles to embrace Agile deployment methods. Agile connects the second leg of the deployment triangle: people with processes. Azure DevOps (see Chapter 21) guides the Agile method of software creation and connectivity. In this chapter, you simply need to comprehend that code development using Agile deployment methods is achieved in an incremental process and requires team members, managers, and executives to support the method.

The third leg of the application development triangle is the technologies, Azure development services. Traditional development services depended on the hardware architecture to create a highly available service. Traditionally, budgets invested in servers, multiple processors, memory, and multiple networks with fiber to storage area networks (SAN). The cost of purpose-built datacenters goes further with the need to create highly available datacenter, including dual power feeds for buildings, dual power to the server racks, power backup systems, cooling, and humidity control. Developers need to understand which Azure services best support their application requirements for high availability (HA).

Note Learn more about business continuity and the high availability of the Azure global network at `https://azure.microsoft.com/en-us/features/resiliency/`.

Azure Development and GitHub

GitHub is a web-based management platform used as a collaboration and source control service to manage software development projects and files; it uses a distributed version control system called Git. Microsoft acquired GitHub in October 2018, and the announcement said that GitHub would operate independently. Although viewed skeptically by some people in the industry because of Microsoft's history with open source, the often-used "New Microsoft" moniker and the general change in the culture within Microsoft is still one that points to a 180-degree shift in support for open source.

GitHub adds unique features beyond the standard implementation of Git. The GitHub platform is designed to support developers' life cycle management of their applications from inception to delivery and beyond (e.g., maintenance, feature and fix releases, etc.). Updates, or versioning, include things like new coding features, vulnerabilities being patched, and different team members contributing. Git was created to support tracking changes to the Linux kernel in support of Linus Torvalds and other global contributing developers.

The information in GitHub is stored in a data structure called a *repository*, and data is changed using push-and-pull Git functions. You can download a copy of the repository, which is known as a *working copy*. As the development project files, or *objects*, change (called *commit objects*), the changes are tracked using a mandatory posting data attribute that includes who, what, why, and when. Role-based access identifies who made the change, and Git logs show what changed and when. Git commits are typically required to provide a tagging process for why a change was submitted. The life cycle of the development project supports the revisioning of software because the Git log shows the master branch, current branch (working on before commit back to the master), and committed code to create a new "merged" version.

GitHub offers developers and their teams many subscription access models, including free, professional, team, and enterprise. Many open source projects are hosted using the free plan, whereas businesses use professional and enterprise subscription models to have private repositories. Features for the plans vary, including unlimited repositories, limited collaborators, and storage size.

Note Learn more about GitHub's plans for developers at `https://github.com/pricing`.

Microsoft Azure continues to integrate directly with GitHub web services using Azure's current DevOps platform. GitHub's integration with Azure supports cloud security, like SAML (Secure Access Markup Language), visual and digital metrics for tracking and critical-issue support programs.

When the term *Azure DevOps* is used, clarification is often required because there are two distinctly different versions, and neither is a repository on GitHub. Azure DevOps Server has an on-premises version (a server running on a VM) and an online service (no VM). Both versions (server or service) implement the Git service through the formerly branded Microsoft Team Foundation Server.

Azure DevOps Services is Software as a Service (SaaS), offering that is directly supported using Microsoft Visual Studio. Visual Studio is an integrated development environment (IDE) running on Azure. Azure DevOps Services do not use GitHub as the back end for code repository. GitHub is a different hosting platform for repository management. Azure DevOps offers native cloud-based team collaboration for writing, editing, and sharing code. Azure DevOps services support connection into your GitHub account. GitHub can be used to update Azure app service directly or integrated with accounts to Azure DevOps "Boards" feature to link team text commits and DevOps pull requests (PR).

Chapter 21 provides configuration guidance and hands-on exercises. Azure App Service supports continuous deployment from GitHub, Bitbucket, and Azure repositories (part of Azure DevOps Services).

Azure Infrastructure as Code

Standardizing on supported cloud infrastructure blueprints is good for engineers, Agile teams, and businesses. Standards prevent organizational shortcomings of ad hoc scaffolding that has not been validated to support business needs. Businesses standardize development languages for custom applications, operating systems, remote access, network security, endpoint protection, and public clouds to support their business. Infrastructure as code (IaC) supports methods to standardize production-ready cloud networks, services, and security infrastructure deployment.

There are two very popular methods for deploying code to create an Azure network, VMs, and services.

- Azure Resource Manager (ARM) templates
- HashiCorp Terraform

As you learn more about developers using GitHub and leveraging the underlying Git service, GitHub has a great feature of version control to manage the life cycle of an application. To manage the infrastructure it needs to be deployed through code. By using code to build, test, change, and redeploy Infrastructure as Code (IaC) in Azure, you can create in-house customized solutions. With IaC, you can:

- Create standard secure virtual networks
- Test new VM deployments

- Update an infrastructure library for business-ready workloads
- Use automation and repeatable deployment models

Azure supports ARM templates natively through a JavaScript Object Notation (JSON) definition file so that it can be customized for your Azure subscription use. The JSON files support Azure resources, location sequencing, variables, and many deployment methods. ARM templates can be deployed using the portal, PowerShell, Azure CLI, and the REST API.

HashiCorp Terraform supports building and versioning IaC template libraries so that you can manage Azure services as well as AWS or GCP. Like ARM, HashiCorp's Terraform uses configuration files to generate plans for the "desired state" when it executes. It can create Azure VNets and VMs, enable DNS and Bastion Hosts, and create users and groups in Azure Active Directory—all by using code from a GitHub repository.

Azure Resource Manager templates complete work through the Azure API model, and Terraform uses providers to allow secure interaction with your Azure subscription. Refer to Chapter 11, where both ARM and Terraform are enabled to generate code that can be deployed in Azure.

ARM and HashiCorp Terraform are technology leaders. Using both deployment models solves a problem that you may not know your business encountered. Both deployment processes offer 24×7 support and world-class training to ramp up your team and can provide a deep pool of subject-matter experts to hire. Some businesses deploy Azure infrastructure using PowerShell or CLI scripts from an IaC library. Others use only ARM templates to deploy and manage Azure resources, and separate tools to manage on-premises and non-Azure workloads, like VMware, AWS, and Google Cloud Platform. Terraform allows your Azure team to develop a process to deploy IaC and use the same method to deploy to other clouds and on-premise.

Note Learn more about HashiCorp providers for Azure, AWS, GCP, and Alibaba cloud—and many other technology services—at `www.terraform.io/docs/providers/index.html`.

Let's also discuss building security into your IaC libraries. Microsoft offers a template to address this: Azure Blueprints. Use the Azure portal to deploy recommended security and policy models (see Figure 4-1).

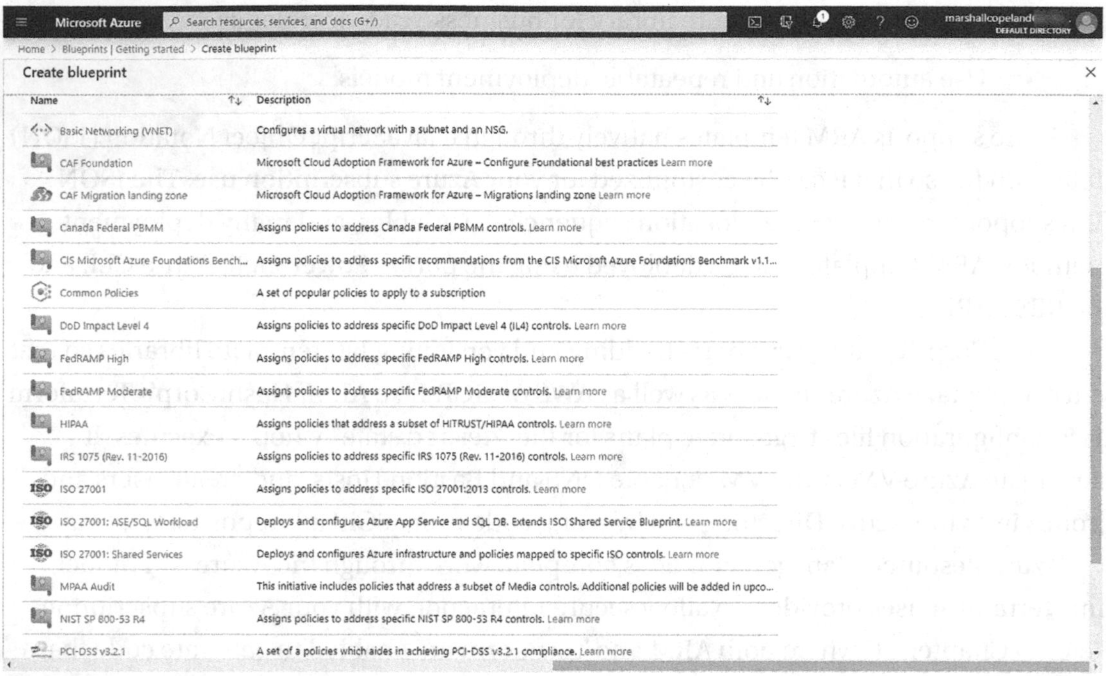

Figure 4-1. *Azure security blueprint examples in the Azure portal*

Azure App Service

Azure App Service enables many services under one umbrella, such as hosting web apps, and mobile back ends, and REST APIs, without the need to manage the infrastructure. The back-end services support high availability (HA) and scaling of services, but you must select the correct pricing tier.

Cloud services provide the ability to scale up and down based on the capacity of the service tier. The application must be architected with high availability as a requirement at the start of a development project because there are deployment methods that do not enable HA. There are two distinct compute platforms to select from before you can explore the features.

- Azure App Service on Linux
- Azure App Service (default)

Azure App Service on Linux was added after the Windows-based series. Hosting websites or web applications on Linux supports a different stack of services. For example, deploying programming language environment support in a Linux distro is slightly different than deploying a Windows-based app service. The following exercise offers greater insight into these differences.

EXERCISE: LIST LATEST APP SERVICE LANGUAGES

1. Log in to your Azure subscription portal (Free or Test subscription is fine). Use a role that supports starting the Azure CMD shell.
2. Start the Azure cloud shell in the upper right of the Azure portal, and select the Bash terminal, as seen in Figure 4-2.

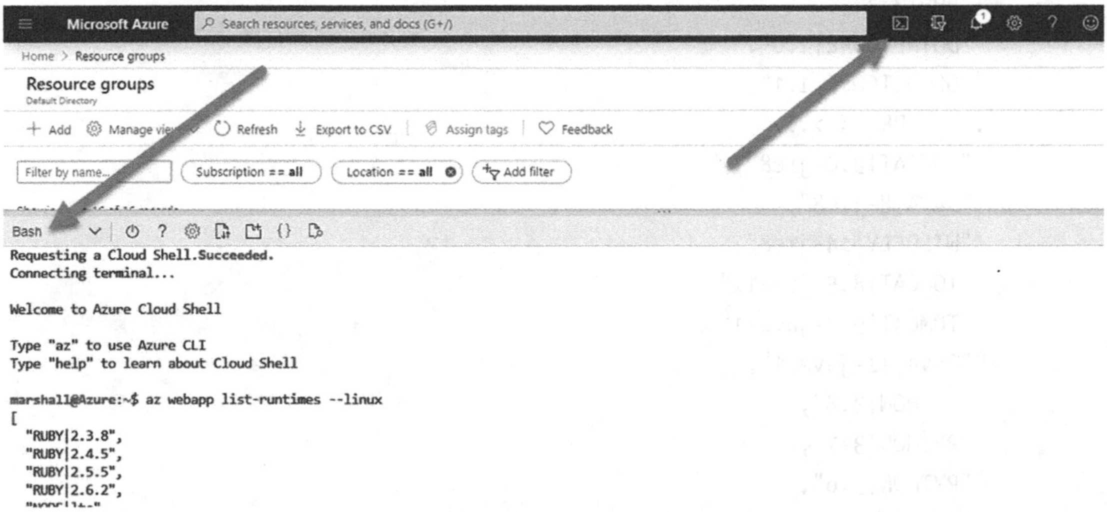

Figure 4-2. Use the cloud shell and select Bash as the environment (vs. PowerShell)

3. Type the following command:

```
az webapp list-runtimes --linux
```

4. Note that the list is long and includes the supported language versions available in your Azure App Service on Linux. (The following is a partial listing.)

```
 "RUBY|2.3.8",
 "RUBY|2.4.5",
 "RUBY|2.5.5",
 "RUBY|2.6.2",
 "NODE|lts",
 "NODE|12-lts",
 "NODE|10.12",
 "NODE|10.14",
... < BREAK > ...
 "PHP|5.6",
 "PHP|7.0",
 "PHP|7.2",
 "PHP|7.3",
 "DOTNETCORE|1.0",
 "DOTNETCORE|1.1",
... < BREAK >...
 "TOMCAT|9.0-jre8",
 "JAVA|8-jre8",
 "WILDFLY|14-jre8",
 "TOMCAT|8.5-java11",
 "TOMCAT|9.0-java11",
 "JAVA|11-java11",
 "PYTHON|3.8",
 "PYTHON|3.7",
 "PYTHON|3.6",
 "PYTHON|2.7"
```

5. Run the command once more without the - - `linux` extension. Type the following command:

```
Az webapp list-runtimes
```

6. Note that the list is different and starts with : aspnet | v4.7, …

In addition to the language support differences, there is a difference in deployment methods. Azure App Service on Linux supports FTP, a local install version of Git, GitHub, and Bitbucket.

There are many different App Service plans, and we'll review the highlights here; however, you should understand what is needed to support the architecture. An Azure App Service is a web service (Windows stack or Linux stack) running on a virtual machine (VM). You need to review current information on service plans, including Azure regions, VM instances, VM size, and pricing tiers.

Note The guidance provided on this topic is a snapshot from the time of writing. Services and tiers will change because demand drives cloud services.

If we look at the pricing tier, the categories include

- Shared compute tier: Free and Shared
- Dedicated compute tier: Basic, Standard, Premium, PremiumV2
- Isolated tier: Dedicated VMs on dedicated virtual networks

Each App Service tier supports either the Linux web stack and applications running on Linux VMs or the Windows web stack and applications running on Windows VMs. Each tier provides a subset of App Service features, and choosing the correct tier is critical to achieving application development requirements. The higher Azure Web Apps tiers offer more features. Go to `https://github.com/harris-soh-copeland-puca/azure-docs/blob/master/articles/app-service/overview-hosting-plans.md` for more information about the different Azure App Service plans.

If your application requires SSL certificates, custom domain names, or integration with Azure Traffic Manager (see Chapter 12), then review the App Service tier to find out which features are supported in which tier. The good news is that all the App Service tiers support scaling up and out.

Scaling up refers to more CPU, memory, and disk space for each VM in the tier. *Scaling out* refers to increasing the VM number with limits based on the pricing tier you selected. No change in code or redeployment of code is required to scale, and the updates take less than a minute.

Note More information on scaling app services or enabling features to support multicore CPUs with additional RAM is at `https://azure.microsoft.com/en-us/pricing/details/app-service/plans/`.

Summary

In this chapter, you learned about Azure development support for services and languages. This chapter is especially helpful for business executives and technology decision-makers to learn which Azure services support GitHub and Git. We overviewed two well-positioned deployment methods—ARM and HashiCorp Terraform. You gained insight into the Azure App Service and the need to understand features for scaling up and scaling out before you select a pricing tier.

CHAPTER 5

Ethical AI, Azure AI, and Machine Learning

This chapter serves as an introduction to the services in Microsoft Azure that support the most exciting part of the digital transformation wave that we are witnessing today.

Microsoft Azure, like all cloud providers, has its humble beginnings from IaaS, PaaS, and SaaS. In fact, these services continue to be important foundations and are still evolving, albeit with less fanfare compared to news about advancement in artificial intelligence (AI) and machine learning (ML). A field-programmable gate array (FPGA) is a good example of an infrastructure evolving to enable intelligence in cloud computing (see `https://github.com/harris-soh-copeland-puca/azure-docs/blob/master/articles/machine-learning/how-to-deploy-fpga-web-service.md`).

A large part of this second edition was rewritten with new content that was not present in the first edition, but that is not the only difference. Almost half the book has been dedicated to data, AI, machine learning, and advanced analytics. Two separate sections have been dedicated to these topics, respectively, and we have included more hands-on labs both in the book and added more to the book's GitHub (`https://github.com/harris-soh-copeland-puca`). If you are already familiar with the data, AI and machine learning services in Azure and want to dive into specific topics, feel free to skip this chapter and go directly to the later chapters that dive deeper into the technology.

If you are looking for a high-level overview of the Azure services that are available in support of this emerging trend, or you are looking for examples of how Azure is used and deployed by data scientists, modern data engineers, and data-driven decision-makers, then this chapter was written with you in mind. We start with the services that consume data and make our way down to where modern data services provide the information foundation that makes it all happen.

J. Soh et al., *Microsoft Azure*, https://doi.org/10.1007/978-1-4842-5958-0_5

Ethical AI

Before we get to the overview of the AI and machine learning capabilities in Microsoft Azure, it is important to take the time to discuss the topic of ethics as it pertains to the use of AI and the social issues related to AI.

Science Fiction and Reality: A Social Convergence

Hollywood science fiction has played its part in introducing intriguing effects of AI on society in movies like 2001's *AI: Artificial Intelligence* and 2002's *Minority Report*.

Both movies touch on extreme themes. In *AI: Artificial Intelligence*, audiences are left to ponder whether an artificial life form is worthy of the same protections as humans when an artificial child is built to possess emotions. In *Minority Report*, predictions made by AI are enforceable before the actual crime is committed.

As AI makes robots and digital assistants more human, the line between fiction and reality is indeed getting blurred. For example, contributing to Japan's issue of an aging population is the generation of *otakus*,[1] men who are in relationships with virtual girlfriends. A concept highly promoted in anime culture and gaming.

Machine learning, a subset of AI, uses algorithms to build mathematical models based on sample data for training and learning to make the most accurate predictions and decisions possible. How confident are we with machine-based decisions? Look around you at the Teslas, IoT devices, and smart homes. The US Navy and Boeing have a highly classified program (codenamed CLAWS) to develop AI-powered, Orca-class fully autonomous submarines that are outfitted with torpedoes, meaning these submarines can decide to kill indiscriminately. The obvious ethical question is, should a machine be able to kill without human intervention? The increase in concern regarding the need, or potential lack thereof, human intervention in AI decision making has led to the alternative, and growing popularity of not calling the acronym AI *artificial intelligence*, but rather *augmented intelligence*.

[1]In 2012, a 35-year-old otaku, who is a school administrator, married his virtual girlfriend named Hatsune Miku. `https://www.techspot.com/news/77385-japanese-man-marries-anime-hologram-hatsune-miku.html`

Note Another sign of the times is the explosion of fake news. Advancements in AI and machine learning are making it easier to create extremely convincing fake videos, known as *deepfake*. Experts fear that deepfake videos will create an even larger trust issue in journalism. These videos are also being employed in politics.

What Is Ethical AI?

Ethical AI is a study and governance surrounding the use of AI technologies in a way that does not violate human rights and endanger lives. We are not exactly at the point of having to address the rights of robots, so that part is still the domain of science fiction.

The impact of AI on life is so important. As we rapidly meet and surpass human parity in many areas, religious organizations have played a leading role in addressing this issue proactively. In February 2020, the Vatican in Rome released a guideline for ethical AI called "Rome Call for AI Ethics,"[2] to which Microsoft is one of the first to sign. Listen to Microsoft President Brad Smith's speech at `https://romecall.org`.

There are many discussions and representations of what ethical AI means, but the three principles in "Rome Call for AI Ethics" summarizes the core concepts: ethics, education, and rights.

Other organizations involved in the design and development of AI are also incorporating the important aspect of ethics. DeepMind is another example of an organization that is not only comprised of scientists, engineers, and researchers in the field of AI but also brings together philosophers and policy experts to form truly interdisciplinary teams to address the broad impact that AI has on society. It is indisputable that there is a need for accountability for the development and use of AI, perhaps more so than any emerging technology in recent history. With backing from large corporations like Google, organizations like DeepMind provides a forum to engage citizens, governments, and corporations to agree on fundamental concepts involving ethics. Find out more at `https://deepmind.com/about/ethics-and-society`.

[2]`https://github.com/harris-soh-copeland-puca/docs/blob/master/AI%20Rome%20Call%20x%20firma_DEF_DEF_.pdf`

> *AI-based technology must never be used to exploit people in any way, especially those who are most vulnerable. Instead, it must be used to help people develop their abilities (empowerment/enablement) and to support the planet.*
>
> —The Vatican

Microsoft AI Principles

Microsoft has a site dedicated to the company's AI principles at `https://microsoft.com/en/us/ai/responsible-ai` and is a leader in the charge to ensure ethics are deeply engrained in the development of AI technologies. The most important aspect of Microsoft's AI principles is that it applies to AI at scale since the technology is built into every service and shared across its entire portfolio. For example, threat patterns gleaned by AI in the Xbox service is shared across other services like Office 365, Azure, and Dynamics to help protect the entire cloud services portfolio. Even though Microsoft has an Office of Responsible AI tasked with putting the company's principles into practice, common ethical AI design principles are followed across all groups in the organization, from engineering to marketing.

> *An important hallmark of our approach to responsible AI is having [the] ecosystem to operationalize responsible AI across the company, rather than a single organization or individual leading this work.*
>
> —Microsoft

Microsoft's AI principles revolve around six key concepts.

- *Fairness*: AI systems must treat all people fairly and with no bias to age, culture, gender, or national origin.
- *Inclusiveness*: AI systems must engage and empower everyone, with no bias to age, culture, gender, or national origin.
- *Reliability and safety*: AI systems should perform reliably and safely.
- *Transparency*: AI systems should be understandable.
- *Privacy and security*: AI systems should be secure, protect, and respect privacy.
- *Accountability*: AI systems should have algorithmic accountability.

We dedicated a generous amount of time discussing ethical AI because it is a very important one as the technology evolves. For the rest of this chapter, we introduce the different AI technologies from Microsoft and look at some use cases. However, where applicable, we bring up specific ethical and legal considerations as it relates to the services.

Microsoft Cognitive Services

Microsoft Cognitive Services is a class of services that helps us build services that can interact with users more humanly. It is part of the AI family of capabilities. The goal of Azure Cognitive Services is to help developers create applications that can see, hear, speak, understand, and even begin to reason. The catalog of services within Azure Cognitive Services can be categorized into five main pillars: vision, speech, language, web search, and decision. Find out more at `https://github.com/harris-soh-copeland-puca/azure-docs/blob/master/articles/cognitive-services/Welcome.md`.

To make applications more human-like, we need to enable capabilities that go beyond how users traditionally interact with applications. That interaction was limited primarily to the lack of cognition. After all, it was only recently that computers could respond to spoken and understand spoken commands.

Measuring the advancement of computer cognitive abilities is based on test results against human performance. Where those results meet or surpass the capabilities of a human, then we would say we have reached human parity. So, how does a computer reach human parity for a capability? Humans make mistakes, such as incorrectly identifying something visually or did not hear certain words spoken in a sentence, so reaching human parity must take this into account. It does not mean the computer needs to be 100% accurate or have a 0% error rate. We provide examples of this comparison as we discuss each of the cognitive abilities.

Object Recognition

The advancement in AI at Microsoft culminated in an explosion of breakthroughs in the past two years. In the area of Computer Vision, Microsoft achieved human parity in 2016 by accurately identifying all the objects in a visual input with an accuracy of 96% compared to humans at 94%. Using a deep neural network called a *residual neural network* (ResNet) to train computers to recognize images, Microsoft went five times deeper than most other attempts to get the result (152 layers compared to 20 to 30 layers). Today, with the number of images available and the computing resources, computer vision is at 99% accuracy.

Through custom computer vision, we can train Microsoft's Vision cognitive services to identify images that fit the business need. The Custom Vision service uses a machine learning algorithm to apply your labels to images and hence provide customized image classifiers. To find out more about Custom Vision, visit `https://github.com/harris-soh-copeland-puca/azure-docs/blob/master/articles/cognitive-services/Custom-Vision-Service/home.md`.

Use Case Scenarios

Many use cases for object detection in Custom Vision apply in a public safety application. For example, images from the video feed of a security camera in a park setting can train a model to detect firearms. When a possible firearm is detected, which is not an object that should be in a park, law enforcement can be notified immediately.

In another example, a model can be trained to recognize wheelchairs. We can then provide medical facilities with the ability to quickly locate wheelchairs by accessing AI-driven cameras based on custom vision and object detection.

Face AI

Face AI is part of Microsoft Azure Cognitive Services and provides an API to

- Detect a face (face detection)
- Recognize a face (face verification)
- Detect emotion (perceived emotion recognition)

Face Detection vs. Face Recognition

Face detection is a specific form of object recognition in that the API is tuned to detect faces from a picture or video. It is important to differentiate face detection from face verification primarily because the latter falls under more stringent personally identifiable information (PII) protection.

Detecting a face does not equate to recognizing a face, but it is important to validate laws covering facial AI use are drafted to address this distinction. For example, in May 2019, San Francisco became the first US city to ban the use of facial recognition technology by police and city government agencies (see `www.npr.org/2019/05/14/723193785/san-francisco-considers-ban-on-governments-use-of-facial-recognition-technology`). In the same year, the American Civil Liberties Union (ACLU) sued multiple government organizations requesting the release and use of facial recognition (`www.cnn.com/2019/11/01/us/aclu-sues-federal-government-over-surveillance-from-facial-recognition-technology/index.html`).

Test drive the facial recognition at `https://azure.microsoft.com/en-us/services/cognitive-services/face`. Upload or provide a URL of two photos to compare whether they are the same person or different people. Figures 5-1, 5-2, and 5-3 show some of our test results.

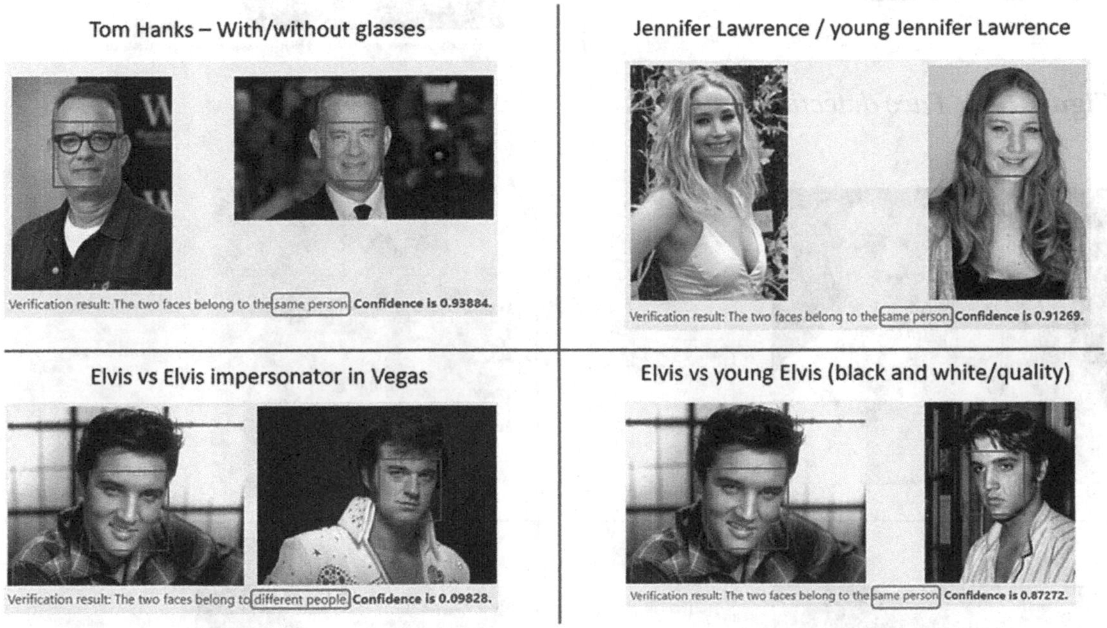

Figure 5-1. *Facial verification tests*

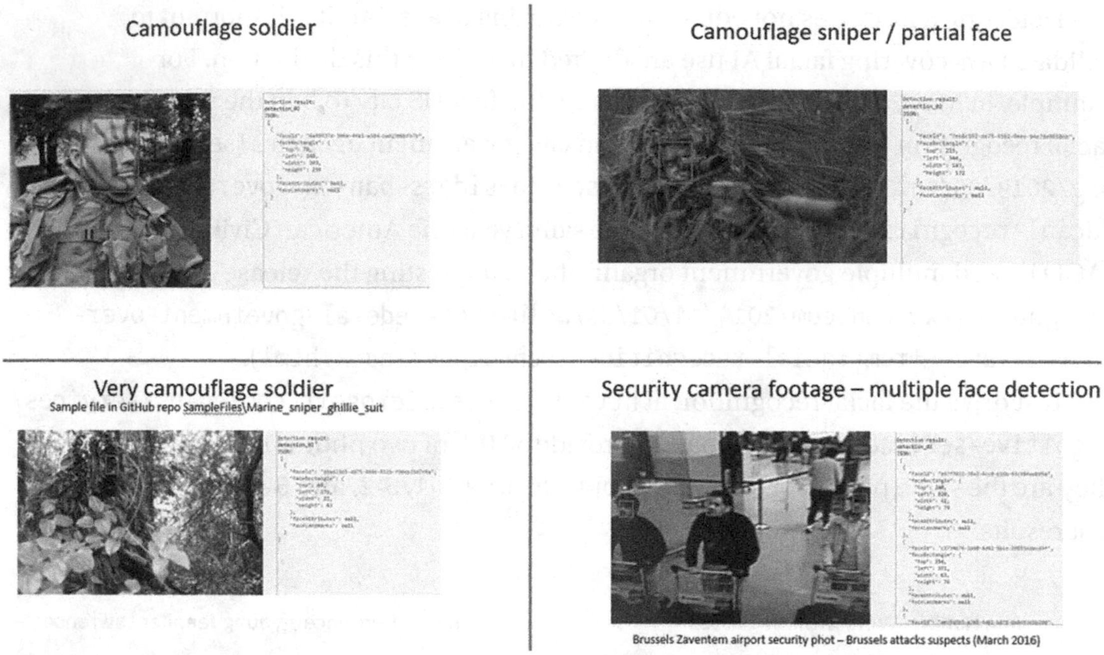

***Figure 5-2.** Face detection tests*

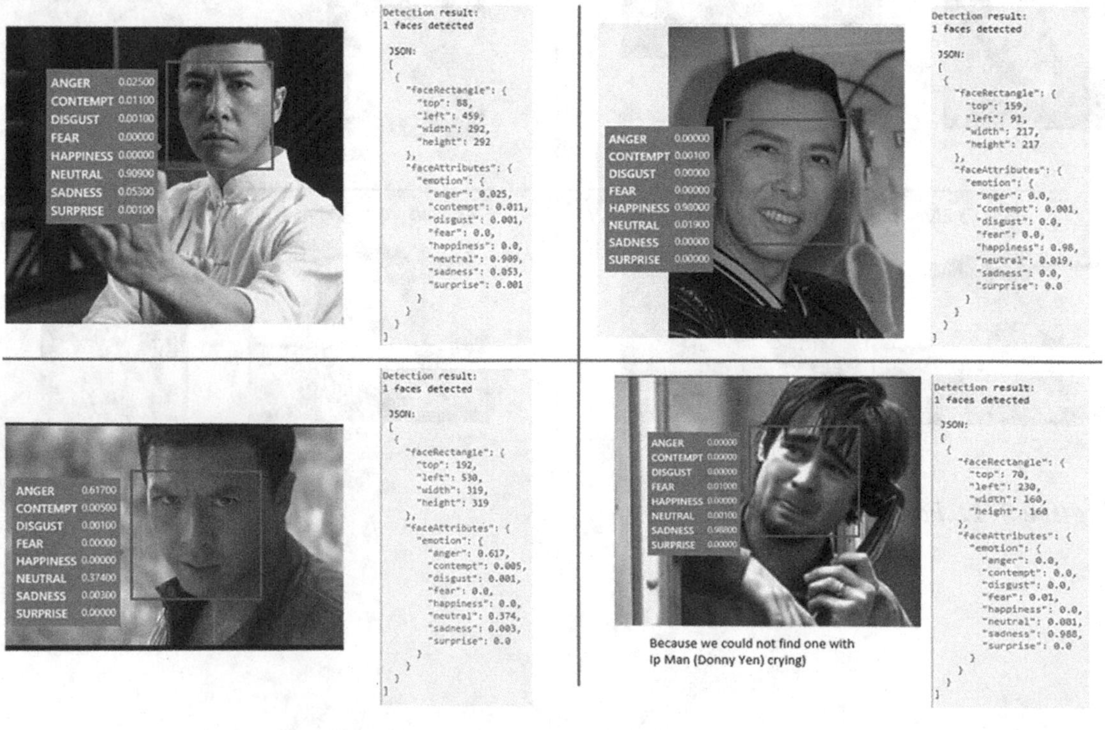

***Figure 5-3.** Tests for perceived emotion detection*

Use Case Scenarios

A use case introduced at a hackathon that we facilitated involved patient intake at hospitals. In this scenario, it is not uncommon to have patients who are unconscious and without ID. If these patients have been treated at the facility before, facial recognition will help emergency personnel identify the patient and their medical history to render treatment expeditiously.

Another use case can be one in a classroom setting. Perceived emotions from students can help teachers determine their emotional states, especially if the students are very young children who may not be comfortable voicing their feelings in the classroom.

Lastly, facial recognition and detection are widely used in public safety scenarios, as seen in the sample tests we conducted earlier.

Speech Services[3]

In 2017, Microsoft reached a 5.1%-word error rate. This means that for a transcription session, Microsoft's speech recognition can correctly transcribe 94.9% of the words spoken in an audio input. Compare this to the error rate of professional transcriptionists, which is 5.9%, as measured by the switchboard portion of the NIST 2000 test set where pairs of strangers discuss an assigned topic. At a 5.1%-word error rate, Microsoft's speech recognition reached[4] and surpassed human parity. Microsoft Speech service is the unification of speech to text, text to speech, speech translation, and speaker recognition.

Speech to Text

Speech to Text is a straightforward service. The two main scenarios for consuming this service is real-time transcription and post-transcription using a recorded audio file. At the time of writing, audio files must be .wav files. In our GitHub repo, we publish a project that accepts an incoming .wav file and translates it to text. This use case, dubbed CaseTalk, is based on a scenario where social workers visit rural communities that may not have good cellular and Internet connectivity.

[3]Microsoft Speech service has replaced Bing Speech API and Translator Speech.

[4]https://blogs.microsoft.com/ai/historic-achievement-microsoft-researchers-reach-human-parity-conversational-speech-recognition/

These social workers record their interviews with their wards on mobile devices or laptops and later transcribe the recordings. Since the social workers' time includes the commute to remote locations, the transcribed notes are not updated in a timely fashion. Such delays lead to long turnaround times to get aid to the community, and in some cases, entering potentially life-threatening situations. A simple speech-to-text interface was created to allow social and caseworkers to upload voice recordings and subsequently convert those to text via the speech-to-text API. This reduces the amount of work for caseworkers and reduces the time to get the appropriate assistance for community members.

Text to Speech

Advancement in text-to-speech technology allows computers to sound more human and in staccato and disjointed sounding sentences.

Microsoft has been investing in AI research for at least 25 years, with much of that research surrounding text to speech. For this cognitive skill, we thought it would be fun to demonstrate how computers sounded before. Some of us may remember the Apple II and Commodore 64 computers, and back then, there was a small text-to-speech program written in C called Software Automatic Mouth (SAM). So, we went looking for SAM and were pleasantly surprised to find a project by Sebastian Macke. He ported SAM so that it can be used in a web browser (see `https://simulationcorner.net/index.php?page=sam`).

Today, natural-sounding text-to-speech capabilities make following instructions provided by a computer a lot easier, increases the ability for call centers to push more functionality to automated attendants, and even appear on TV. See the world's first AI news anchor at `www.cnbc.com/2018/11/09/the-worlds-first-ai-news-anchor-has-gone-live-in-china.html`.

Speaker Recognition

Speaker recognition is the most recent addition to speech services, and at the time of writing, it is still in preview. It allows us to train using the voice of different speakers and subsequently identify the different speakers in a setting.

One use case scenario that this is applied to is speaker diarization in a courtroom, interview, or conference setting, where there are many known speakers and a need to identify who said what during the event. Speech diarization with speaker recognition can completely automate the role of a court transcriptionist. Speaker recognition allows post-processing of audio streams, which provides the ability to quickly search for things said by individuals.

Machine Reading Comprehension

In 2018, using the Stanford Question Answering Dataset (SQuAD), which is a reading comprehension dataset consisting of over 100,000 questions and answers based on Wikipedia articles, Microsoft reached an exact match (EM) score of 82.650%. The SQuAD dataset consists of 50,000 unanswerable questions, which were written to look like answerable ones. Scoring is based on a system's ability to answer questions when possible and to determine which are unanswerable questions and abstain from providing one. These scores are higher than the best human score, which is 82.304%, and therefore human parity was reached.

Machine Translation

A machine translation (MT) system is a data-driven system that combines rule-based and statistical methods into a hybrid system that is then capable of learning lexical and phrasal translations from the data derived from different languages.

In March 2018, Microsoft announced[5] an MT system that could perform as well as human translators in Chinese-to-English news translation. Incorporated in Microsoft Translator API, new models are available to convert Chinese, German, French, Hindi, Italian, Spanish, Japanese, Korean, and Russian to and from English. In some models, double-digit improvements have been made (e.g., 22% for Korean), as shown in Figure 5-4.

[5]Reference - `https://www.microsoft.com/en-us/research/publication/achieving-human-parity-on-automatic-chinese-to-english-news-translation/`

Translation quality improvements

Human evaluation results for news translation

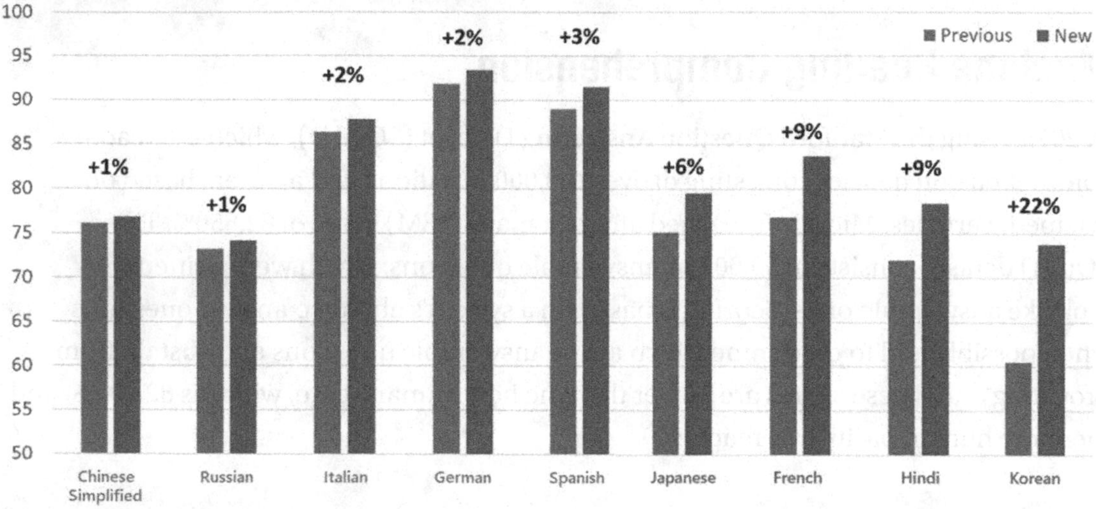

Source: Translator FY19 human parity evaluations, data collected in June 2019

Figure 5-4. *Human parity translation by language*

Use Case Scenarios

Imagine a scenario where there are more than two languages spoken in a single setting. Perhaps an international courtroom like the International Court of Justice, also known as the World Court. Cases involve multiple countries with 15 judges from different parts of the world. It is fathomable that more than one interpreter might simultaneously be needed because there may be more than one or two languages spoken during hearings.

Another use case scenario can be made for multinational organizations. With ecommerce, this is no longer the domain of large companies. Even small companies have global customers s and require translation—spoken and written—in many languages. A single AI service that provides multilanguage translations is more efficient, timely, and cost-effective than traditional means.

Text Analytics: Sentiment

Aside from transcription, translation, and understanding text, there is also sentiment. Sentiment describes the emotional aspect of a body of text, which would reflect the opinion and feelings of the author. Extracting sentiment out of text through AI provides more accurate responses, as Referenced in Figure 5-5. For example, if we have a stack of written reports to review, we may want the ability to prioritize by sentiment would ensure that the most negative reports are addressed first, assuming there are significant issues that warrant immediate action. The API provides advanced natural language processing over raw text and includes four main functions: sentiment analysis, key phrase extraction, language detection, and named entity recognition.

For more information on the Text Analytics API, please visit `https://github.com/harris-soh-copeland-puca/azure-docs/blob/master/articles/cognitive-services/text-analytics/overview.md`.

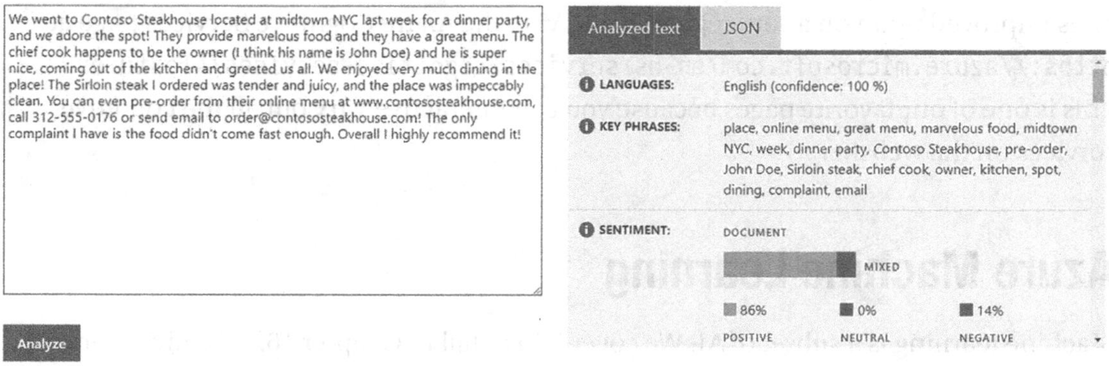

Figure 5-5. *Extracting sentiment from a body of text at `https://azure.microsoft.com/en-us/services/cognitive-services/text-analytics`*

Bots

All the cognitive services mentioned so far are used in digital assistants like Bots to communicate with users via a variety of channels like the web, Teams, SharePoint, and even voice (forthcoming). More than 300,000 developers are creating digital agents with Azure Bot Service.

Use Case Scenarios

In 2020, the world was in the midst of a novel coronavirus pandemic that shut down or overwhelmed many call centers. Bots were deployed at a record pace to help alleviate some of the load and efficiently get accurate information to citizens.

On a lighter note, there is a great case study by an esteemed colleague of ours, Eric Egland, an AI specialist, and his work with the State of California and the Eureka Bot. Eureka is the product of the Secretary of State's digital initiative to modernize and digitize the agency to make it easier to do business in California, and shortly after its launch in 2019, it has served more than 77,000 inquires. Most of these inquiries were offloaded from call centers. You can read the full story at `https://cloudblogs.microsoft.com/industry-blog/government/2019/08/15/eureka-chatbot-helps-california-stay-open-for-business/`.

There are many other AI and cognitive services such as video, search, anomaly detection, forms recognizer, and so forth. New capabilities are added, and existing ones improved upon on a very regular basis. Visit the Azure Cognitive Services page at `https://azure.microsoft.com/en-us/services/cognitive-services/#features`. This is one of our favorite pages because you can interactively try out all the cognitive services on the website.

Azure Machine Learning

Machine learning is a subset of AI. We cover it in detail in Chapter 16. The advancement in all the cognitive services mentioned in the previous section is based on Machine learning and the vast amount of available training data.

Machine learning trains models to not only recognize or detect, but also to predict outcomes and thus help drive decision making. Machine learning is fundamentally based on data science and statistical methods. The amount of data and statistical methods often requires a lot of memory and compute, which is an ideal fit for Azure.

In this section, we cover the options available in Azure that helps data scientists and researchers do their jobs. There are primarily two options: the initial implementation known as Azure Machine Learning Studio (classic) and the more recently released Azure Machine Learning. Table 5-1 summarizes the differences between the two offerings.

***Table 5-1.** Comparing Azure Machine Learning and Azure Machine Learning Studio (Classic)*

	Azure Machine Learning designer	Studio (classic)
	The designer is in preview, Azure Machine Learning is GA	Generally available (GA)
Drag-and-drop interface	Yes	Yes
Experiment	Scale with compute target	Scale (10GB training data limit)
Modules for interface	Many popular modules	Many
Training compute targets	AML Compute(GPU/CPU)	Proprietary compute target, CPU only
Inferencing compute targets	Azure Kubernetes Service for real-time inference AML Compute for batch inference	Proprietary web service format, not customizable
ML Pipeline	Pipeline authoring Published pipeline Pipeline endpoint Learn more about ML pipeline	Not supported
ML Ops	Configurable deployment, model and pipeline versioning	Basic model management and deployment
Model	Standard format, various depends on the training job	Proprietary, non portable format.
Automated model training	Not yet in the designer, but possible through the interface and SDKs.	No

Azure Machine Learning

Azure Machine Learning is a cloud-based environment for data scientists to train, deploy, automate, manage, and track ML models. It is often used in conjunction with cloud storage such as Azure Blob Storage and Azure Data Lake Store because of the potentially large amount of data being used in the ML process.

Azure Machine Learning supports all the tools and languages used by data scientists, such as R and Python. It also has tools such as Jupyter notebooks and supports open source add-ons such as PyTorch, TensorFlow, scikit-learn, and YOLO. It comes with a web interface called the Azure Machine Learning designer.

Azure Machine Learning supports classical ML, deep learning, as well as supervised and unsupervised learning. Azure Machine Learning also integrates with other Azure services, such as Azure DevOps, to help secure the data scientists' work through source control.

Machine Learning Studio (Classic)

Azure Machine Learning Studio (classic) is the initial implementation and ML offering in Azure. It is still available and should not be confused with Azure Machine Learning. See the differences in Table 5-1. Download the Azure Machine Learning Studio (classic) architecture to see all its capabilities at `https://download.microsoft.com/download/C/4/6/C4606116-522F-428A-BE04-B6D3213E9E52/ml_studio_overview_v1.1.pdf`.

Azure Databricks

Azure Databricks is the native implementation of Databricks in Azure and is provided as a PaaS offering. Azure Databricks provides all the tools and resources that data scientists and researchers need and is jointly managed by Databricks and Microsoft engineers.

Azure Databricks is provisioned as workspaces that contain the customizable compute clusters, the notebooks, datasets, and storage. Users can use Databricks File System (DFS) or mount external storage like Azure Blob Storage or Azure Data Lake Store to access data for projects. Azure Databricks notebooks allow users with different skillsets to collaborate because the notebooks support different languages like Python, R, Scala, and SQL. All notebooks can be source controlled using GitHub or Azure DevOps.

There are two types of compute clusters in Azure Databricks: default and high concurrency clusters. To optimize resources and reduce costs, the default compute clusters in Azure Databricks can automatically shut down due to inactivity. This threshold is set at 120 minutes, but this can be configured as needed. High concurrency clusters are configured to not terminate automatically. Visit `https://docs.microsoft.com/en-us/azure/databricks/clusters/configure` to find out more about cluster configuration.

Compute clusters can be customized with the desired libraries needed, such as PyTorch, scikit-learn, and TensorFlow, and so forth. Compute clusters can be pinned so that the customization is preserved even after the cluster is shut down due to inactivity.

Use Cases for Azure Databricks

Azure Databricks prepares raw data for downstream systems and analysis. Azure Databricks is a collaborative tool with a target audience of data scientists, data engineers, researchers, and business intelligence analysts.

Azure Databricks is usually front-ended by low latency ingestion solutions such as IoT hubs or event hubs and other types of storage serving nonstreaming data. Figure 5-6 depicts a typical architecture of an enterprise data pipeline architecture with data inputs from different sources (streaming and nonstreaming) with Azure Databricks as the data preparation environment before sending the prepared data to downstream datastores.

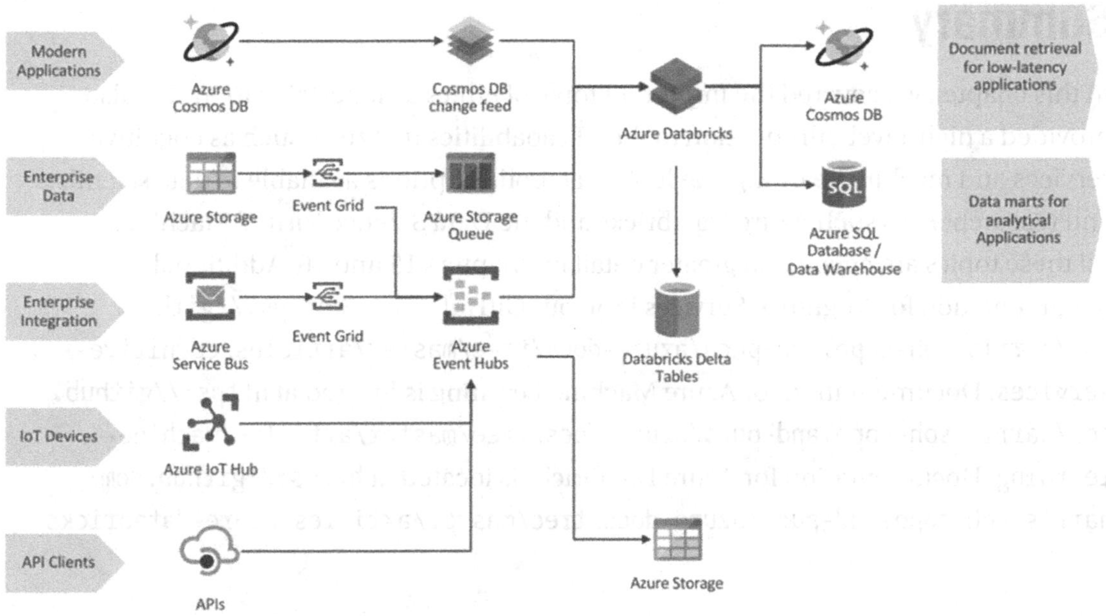

***Figure 5-6.** Data ingestion and manipulation pipeline involving Azure Databricks*

Azure Data Science Virtual Machines

In the most traditional approach, data scientists can always use regular virtual machines as their environment. This approach relies on the data scientist to completely customize a personally provisioned virtual machine with all the tools and libraries needed. Usually, it relies on the same virtual machine for compute and storage. It is not the most efficient and scalable model, but it is a common setup that is still widely used.

Microsoft Azure provides the data scientists that work in this setup with specialized virtual machine images in the gallery. It comes with preinstalled tools that are generally used in data science. This type of image is called a Data Science Virtual Machine (DSVM). Data scientists should choose this option over on-premises virtual machines or standard virtual machine images in Azure because of the specialized VM image and the ability to scale compute and storage resources for the VM as needed. Azure DSVMs are available with Linux or Windows operating systems. DSVMs can also be attached as compute to Azure Notebooks or in Azure Machine Learning Service to expand the compute power.

Summary

In this chapter, we covered the important topic of ethics as it pertains to AI. We also provided a high-level introduction to the AI capabilities in Azure, such as cognitive services and machine learning. We looked at tooling options available to data scientists and researchers as such Azure Databricks and the Data Science Virtual Machines. All these topics are covered in greater detail in Chapters 15 and 16. Additional documentation for Cognitive Services is on our GitHub repo at `https://github.com/harris-soh-copeland-puca/azure-docs/tree/master/articles/cognitive-services`. Documentation for Azure Machine Learning is located at `https://github.com/harris-soh-copeland-puca/azure-docs/tree/master/articles/machine-learning`. Documentation for Azure Databricks is located at `https://github.com/harris-soh-copeland-puca/azure-docs/tree/master/articles/azure-databricks`.

PART II

Planning and Adopting Azure

CHAPTER 6

Budgeting and Cloud Economics

How much value does the CIO's IT shop deliver? This is the most common debate on whether an organization can or should move to the cloud. *Cloud economics* is the evaluation of cloud costs compared to on-premises costs. Certain aspects of both are hard to determine but are usually quantifiable. For example, what does an administrator's time cost? We can determine that from their pay. What's the cost of the datacenter's square footage? Is the insurance or rent factored in? Can you recoup those costs if the datacenter is eliminated? Are your electric and water bills going to decrease because the workloads in the datacenter moved to the cloud? Is the virtual infrastructure you have provisioned utilized 24/7? Can you spin down the physical infrastructure when the virtual infrastructure is not using it? These are just a few of the questions that go into cloud economics.

In this chapter, we discuss a few more concepts that assist you in understanding your true *total cost of ownership* (TCO) in the cloud and on-premises.

Understanding Cloud Economics: CapEx vs. OpEx

Cloud economics is based on the philosophy that you only pay for what you use, and that you pay minimally, if at all, for what you aren't using. Since the 1980s, companies, and individuals had to budget for the computers they bought. These were often costly and bought in large numbers to satisfy a demand for a workload, whether it be people or an application on a server. Systems to run the application were architected, ordered, built on-premises, connected, tested, and eventually put into production. The timeline between the system purchase, and it is being put into production could take years in some cases.

J. Soh et al., *Microsoft Azure*, https://doi.org/10.1007/978-1-4842-5958-0_6

The initial purchase is called a *capital expenditure* (a.k.a. CapEx) because the IT systems are considered *fixed assets* and are expenses that a company capitalizes, which means they show it on their balance sheet as an investment. This would also mean they need to depreciate it, which is usually over a single-digit number of years; three to five years is common. This tight timeline would lead to a constant churn of architect, deploy, migrate, architect, deploy, migrate.

Now that you understand what CapEx is, a quick explanation of OpEx is needed. Operating expenses, or OpEx, are the costs a company incurs for running their day-to-day operations. Examples of OpEx include water, electricity, wages, and so forth. In short, OpEx represents how efficient a company is over time. Therefore, cloud computing fits into the OpEx model. There is no longer the lengthy timeline to architect a solution with what you know—hoping that you get it right and don't buy the wrong equipment, too much equipment, or not enough equipment. Cloud allows administrators to scale up or down, in or out, on a moment's notice, automatically if architected, with little to no impact on the workloads, and only billing for those resources used.

Some organizations still list cloud computing costs as CapEx, because of their budget and the evolving understanding of cloud services in their account and budget departments. CapEx at its very nature is the company's spend on physical assets. In most cases, around 99%, there are no physical assets acquired with cloud services. As organizations evolve, we'll see new ways in which they approach accounting and budgeting for cloud services.

Using Assessment Tools

Several assessment tools help administrators understand what they need to size a workload for the cloud. While it's safe to assume we know how to evaluate the size of a dataset, file share, or used drive, it's a little more involved to understand how much disk input/output (I/O) is in use, or how much network traffic comes from a given server or a given workload on that server. For example, if we have a "widget" workload running on a database server that generates *X* amount of network traffic, how much of that traffic is due to anti-malware software, OS updates, third-party products checking for updates or transmitting allowed data? If you host this widget workload in an Azure PaaS service such as Azure SQL Managed Instance, you are dropping that traffic from the workload running, since the OS and the associated management of it are handled by the cloud service provider.

There are many tools to scan an environment or system and generate a recommendation report on how the workload could be replatformed to Azure. These tools are frequently inaccurate due to their limited capture window. Ideally, a monitoring solution should evaluate a workload for just over 30 days to capture weekly or monthly cycles that may not exist in a smaller capture window. Solutions such as System Center can provide sizing and utilization data to the administrators on managed/monitored workloads. System Center may be too robust or not in use in each environment. Microsoft provides a free assessment solution, which is Azure Migrate.

Azure Migrate is a hub for all of your migration tools, including non-Microsoft tools. Azure Migrate allows customers to migrate servers, both physical and virtual, VMware and Hyper-V, databases, web apps, data, and other datacenter assets while providing end-to-end tracking through migration. Azure Migrate, which has its dashboard illustrated in Figure 6-1, allows administrators to create projects that track discovery and assessment data, and migration tasks. The tools that an administrator uses for discovery and assessment may be different from the tools used for migration, which allows a very flexible solution for migrations.

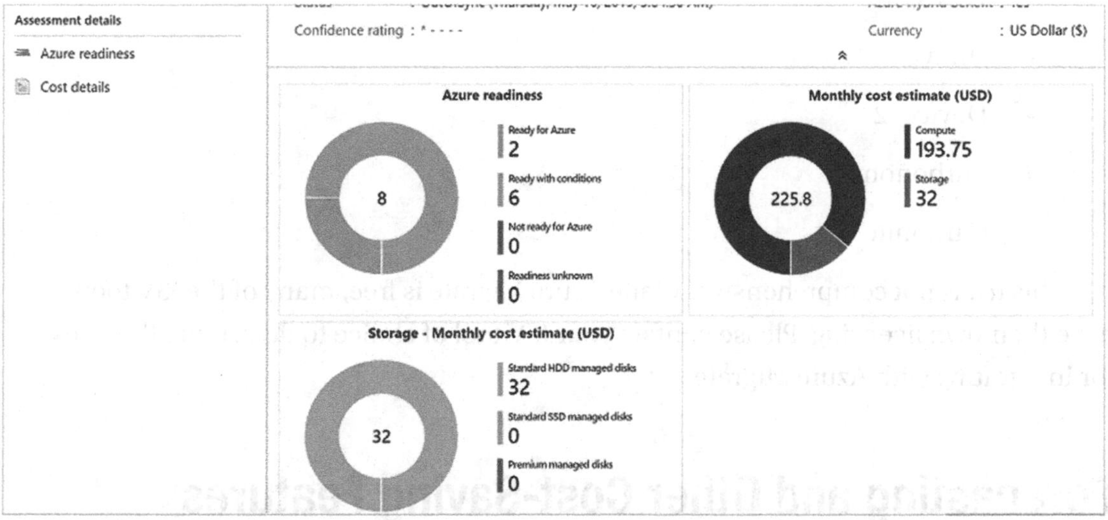

***Figure 6-1.** Azure Migrate server assessment report*

Azure Migrate includes Database Migration Assistant (DMA) and Database Migration Service (DMS), which assess and migrate on-premises SQL workloads to Azure IaaS VMs running SQL or Azure PaaS services, such as Azure SQL Database and Azure SQL Managed Instance. The DMA phase generates reports for customers identifying changes needed prior to migration. It is up to you to make these changes before using the DMS.

In September of 2019, Microsoft acquired Movere, a cloud migration partner. Movere's toolset includes their experience of more than 11 years discovering and assessing workloads. Within hours of deploying the Microsoft Movere solution, administrators and business owners are provided insights into their environment they usually haven't had before. Assessments with the Microsoft Movere solution can be initiated by contacting your Microsoft representative and engaging the Microsoft Solution Assessment team, formerly known as the Cloud Economics Program.

Microsoft has partnered with many ISV (independent software vendor) migration partners who have their offerings to plug into Azure Migrate. These ISV partners include

- Rackware
- Corent
- Cloudamize
- Lakeside
- UnifyCloud
- Device42
- Turbonomic
- Carbonite

This list is not comprehensive. While Azure Migrate is free, many of the ISV tools have their own licensing. Please contact your ISV tool of choice to determine their cost for integrating with Azure Migrate.

Forecasting and Other Cost-Saving Features

Microsoft Azure's Pricing Calculator for Azure (`https://azure.microsoft.com/en-us/pricing/calculator/`) is the best way to forecast your cloud consumption costs. You can run all of your "what if" or "how much would this cost" scenarios before ever spending any money in Azure.

Pricing Calculator reflects retail prices of Azure services given in their units. For example, a GB of Azure Storage costs approximately $0.02 per month, and an Azure Kubernetes Service (AKS) 8-core DS14 v2 node costs $1.48 per hour. Each service has its own metrics, in which the service is metered and billed. Some services are billed in batches such as notification hubs, where the first 10 million pushes are free, but each one million afterward is $10. As you can see, some units are measurements of storage or networking, and some are virtual hardware for an allotted time, an activity performed, and so forth.

If you have a Microsoft Volume License agreement, the Pricing Calculator can be adjusted to reflect your own discounted pricing. This can be done by signing in to the calculator using your credentials which has access to a Microsoft Customer agreement. Then configure your estimate. Scroll down to the bottom of the page and select Microsoft Customer agreement in the Licensing Program drop-down menu. Select the Billing Account and then Billing Profile and click Apply. The page refreshes to show you the pricing estimate with a Microsoft Customer agreement.

The Azure Pricing Calculator, shown in Figure 6-2, has an easy-to-use interface. The Products tab of the ribbon sorts the services by categories so you can easily find what you're looking for. As you click a tile, it is added to the calculator, where you can then configure the parameters of your workload. The calculator builds a running monthly run-rate of the services you have selected to estimate what the cost would be.

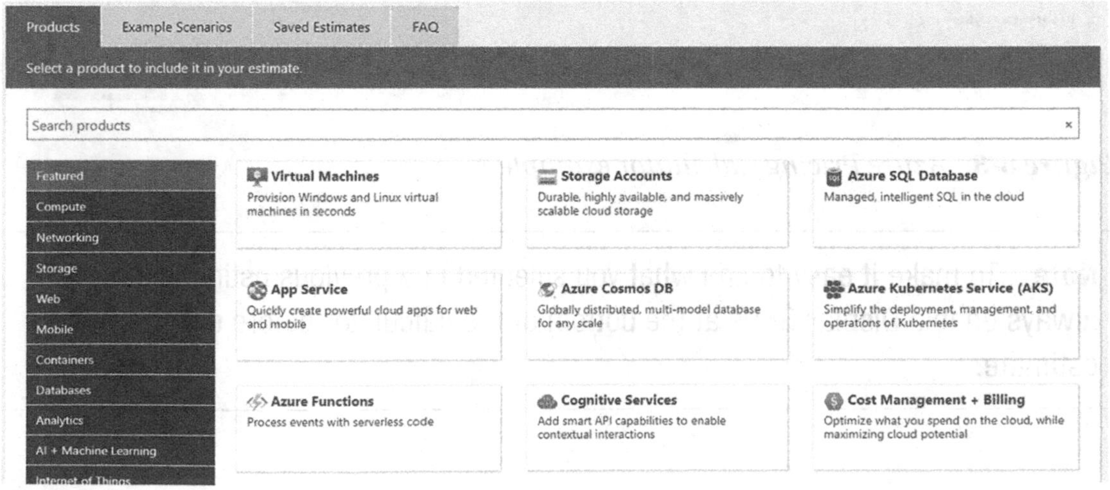

Figure 6-2. *Azure Pricing Calculator*

Each calculator model you build is exportable to Excel and can be saved online, assuming you logged into the website, and retrieved later and shared via links like OneDrive. This is handy for sharing estimation models of cloud workloads with customers, coworkers, and partners.

When building out models in the calculator, one of the most important things to do is make sure you have the right cloud or region selected. Prices do vary across clouds and regions. You would not want to estimate a workload running in Azure Government and have used the public Azure cloud as the region for estimation purposes. In Figure 6-3, the Azure services that make up this workload are added to the calculator to be estimated.

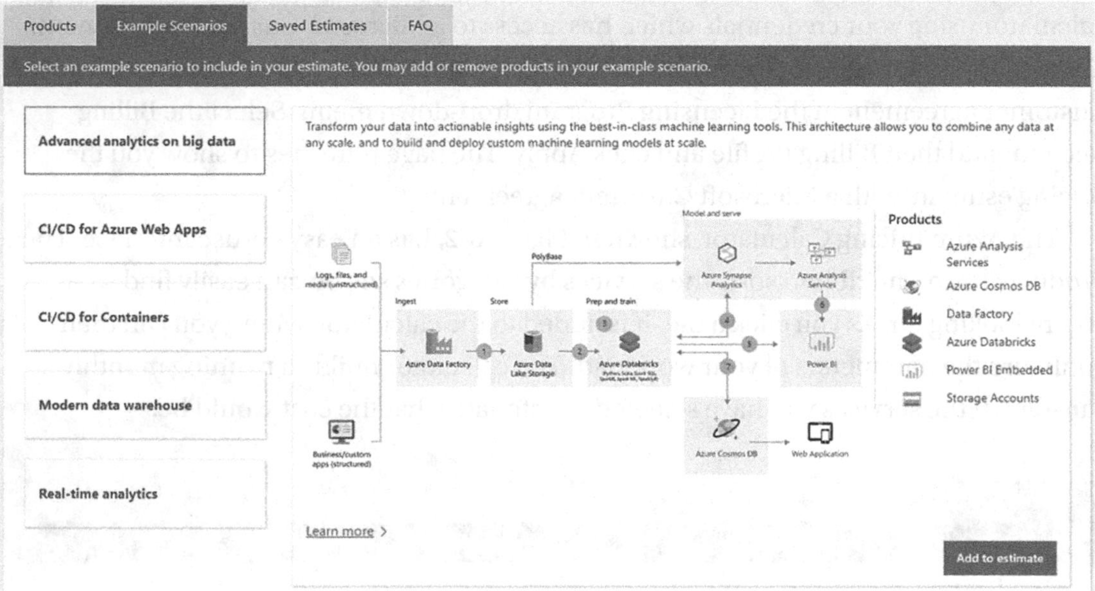

Figure 6-3. *Azure Pricing Calculator example*

Note To make it easy to find what you selected in a previous estimate, always enable Display SKUs at the bottom of the calculator before exporting the estimate.

Autoscaling

While autoscaling is a technical feature, it is important to mention it here due to how large of an impact it has on cloud costs.

Autoscaling is an Azure Monitor feature that allows various cloud services to increase or decrease the number of nodes presented as part of a farm or an array to serve a given workload. Figure 6-4 illustrates an easy example of autoscaling; at certain times, the website only needs two nodes to provide high availability, but at the busiest times, when it has thousands or millions of requests, it may need dozens to hundreds of nodes to satisfy the demand on the service.

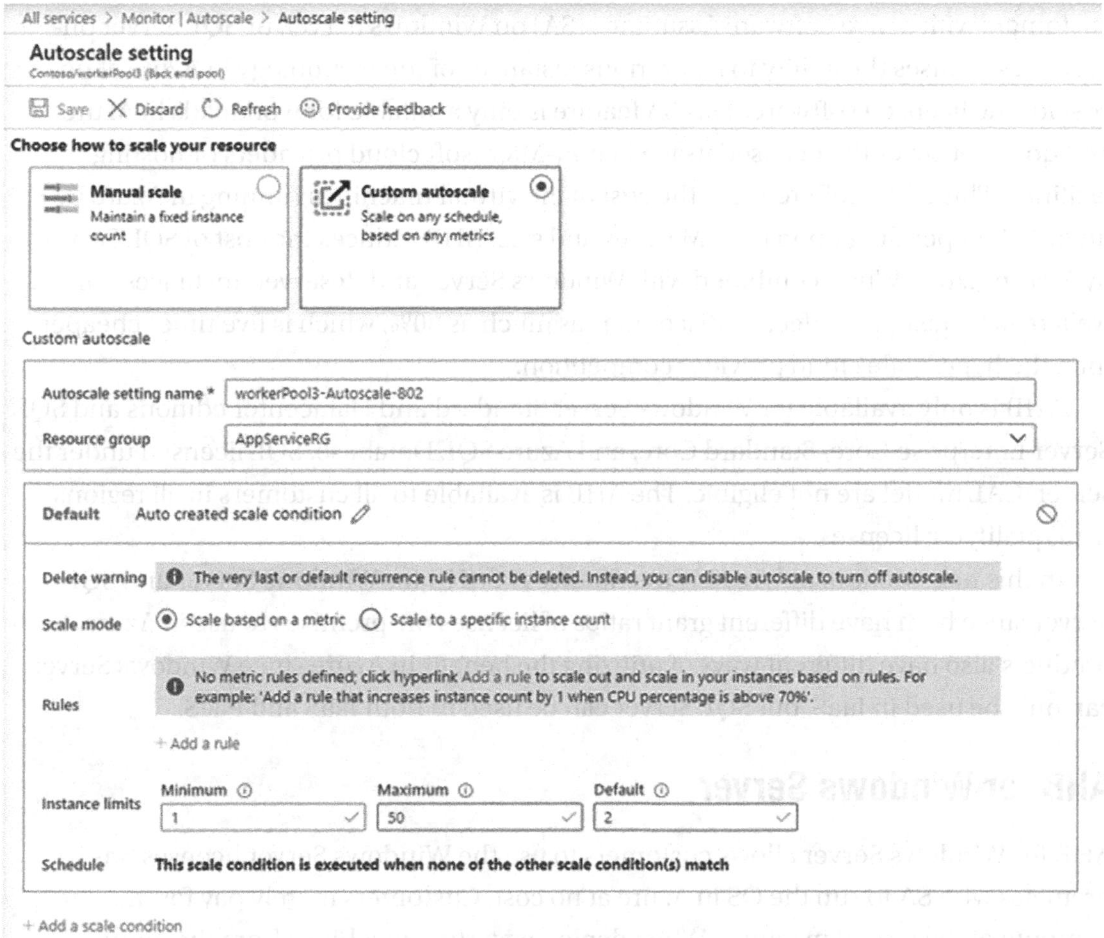

Figure 6-4. *Azure Monitor Autoscaling feature on a back-end WorkerPool*

Azure Autoscaling allows a dynamic adjustment of nodes based on any metric the administrator chooses to scale by. Autoscaling can also be invoked manually as part of a schedule if needed. For more information on how to configure autoscale rules, refer to `https://docs.microsoft.com/en-us/azure/azure-monitor/platform/autoscale-get-started`. Autoscaling allows you to scale down to as little as you want, including "off" to minimize what you spend on resources that aren't in use.

Azure Hybrid Benefit

Azure Hybrid Benefit (AHB) was formerly known as Azure Hybrid Use Benefit (AHUB). You'll see the AHB and AHUB acronyms still used today interchangeably. AHB provides customers with active Software Assurance (SA) on Windows Server, or SQL Server on-premises licenses the ability to run various instances of the technology in Azure at no cost for the licensed software. This SA feature is only available for workloads in Azure and does not cover the licensed usage in non-Microsoft cloud providers or hosting facilities. This SA benefit reduces the cost of the virtual machines running in Azure by up to 50% depending upon the VM series and size. AHB reduces the cost of SQL Server by 55% in Azure. When combined with Windows Server and Reserved Instances (which we'll review next), the effective discount is as much as 80%, which is five times cheaper than the hyperscale cloud provider competition.

AHB is only available for Windows Server Standard and Datacenter editions and SQL Server Enterprise Core, Standard Core, and Azure SQL Database. SQL licensed under the server/CAL model are not eligible. The AHB is available to all customers in all regions with qualifying licenses.

In this next section, let's review the nuances of AHB for Windows Server and SQL Server since both have different grant ratios of licenses on-premises to use in Azure. Both products also have different ways of utilizing the benefit in Azure since Windows Server can only be used in IaaS, but SQL Server can be used in both IaaS and PaaS.

AHB for Windows Server

AHB for Windows Server allows customers to use the Windows Server licenses on-premises with SA to run the OS in Azure at no cost. Customers merely pay for the compute of the virtual machine. When deploying virtual machines from the Azure

Gallery, the AHB offer can be utilized at deployment time from the very bottom of the Basics blade of the Create Virtual Machine wizard within the Azure portal virtual machines service, as shown in Figure 6-5.

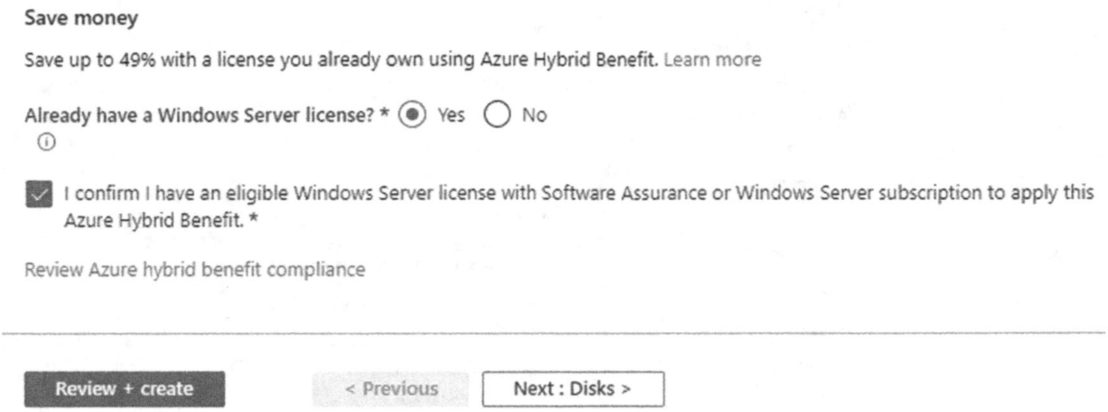
Save money
Save up to 49% with a license you already own using Azure Hybrid Benefit. Learn more
Already have a Windows Server license? * Yes No
I confirm I have an eligible Windows Server license with Software Assurance or Windows Server subscription to apply this Azure Hybrid Benefit. *
Review Azure hybrid benefit compliance
Review + create
< Previous
Next : Disks >

***Figure 6-5.** AHB virtual machine option when deploying from the Azure Gallery*

If administrators deploy virtual machines to Azure without enabling this feature, it can be enabled after the fact via the Azure portal also. As shown in Figure 6-6, by drilling down into a specific virtual machine and selecting Configuration from the virtual machine blade, administrators can enable AHB after the deployment also. This is a common oversight when deploying infrastructure as code (IaC). Also, when administrators deploy virtual machines to Azure from custom images, or through a migration tool such as Azure Migrate or Azure Site Recovery, the same steps should be taken to ensure compliance.

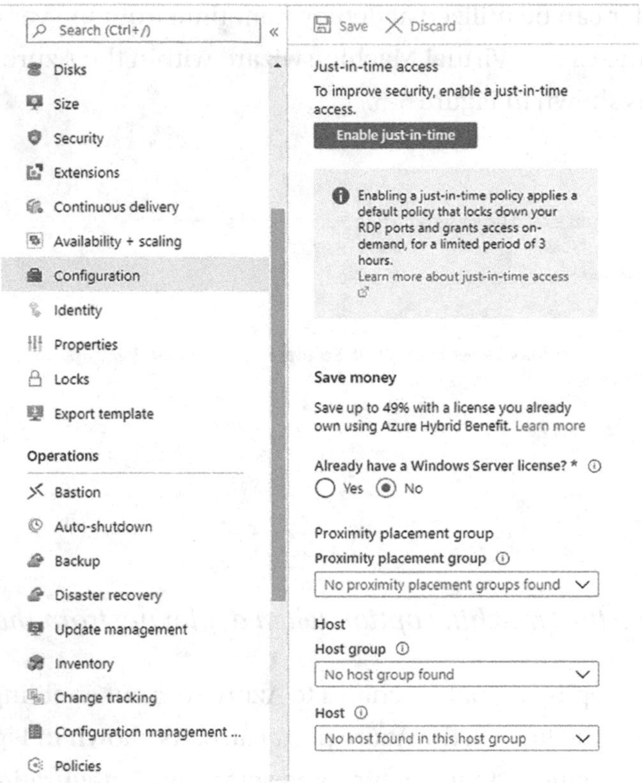

Figure 6-6. *Enabling AHB on existing virtual machines*

Converting virtual machines from Windows Server–licensed virtual machines to AHB can also be done via PowerShell or the Azure command-line interface (CLI). The one for PowerShell is as follows.

```
$vm = Get-AzVM -ResourceGroup "rg-name" -Name "vm-name"
$vm.LicenseType = "Windows_Server"
Update-AzVM -ResourceGroupName rg-name -VM $vm
```

The one for CLI is as follows.

```
az vm update --resource-group myResourceGroup --name myVM --set
licenseType=Windows_Server
```

Windows Server Standard and Datacenter editions have different grant ratios for AHB. Windows Server Datacenter with SA allows customers to run two Windows Server OSs in Azure simultaneously to the Windows Datacenter edition license used on-premises. Each of these two instances in Azure can utilize any virtual machine series with up to eight cores or one virtual machine up to 16 cores. Windows Server Standard edition can be used either on-premises, or in Azure, but not both simultaneously. Windows Server Standard edition also allows two instances in Azure that can utilize any virtual machine series with up to eight cores or one virtual machine up to 16 cores.

AHB for SQL Server

AHB for SQL Server is available to customers who have SQL Server licenses with SA. The AHB for SQL Server allows customers to use Azure SQL Database and Azure SQL Managed Instance, the PaaS services, or for SQL Server inside of virtual machines running on IaaS. When SQL Server images are deployed from Microsoft's Azure Gallery, the AHB benefits can be used for both. The Microsoft recommendation is to deploy SQL Server Azure Gallery images.

For Azure SQL Database, AHB entitles customers to one core of Azure SQL DB in the general-purpose service tier for each SQL Server Standard edition per-core license. SQL Server Enterprise Edition AHB entitles customers to one core of Azure SQL DB in the business-critical or hyperscale service tiers for each SQL Server Enterprise edition per-core on-premises license with SA. SQL Server Enterprise edition also entitles customers to use four cores in the general-purpose service tier per SQL Server Enterprise edition per-core on-premises license with SA, instead of the one in the business-critical or hyperscale tiers.

The general-purpose, business-critical, and hyperscale service tiers in Azure SQL Database are mapped out at `https://docs.microsoft.com/en-us/azure/sql-database/sql-database-service-tiers-general-purpose-business-critical`.

Reserved Instances

Azure Reserved Instances (RIs) are one of the commonly forgotten and overlooked values in the Azure platform from a cost and billing perspective. Azure Reserved Instances allow customers to commit to paying for a workload at a steeply reduced rate—as much as 72% off the regular pay-as-you-go model. Azure Reserved Instances can be bought in one- and three-year terms. Azure Reserved Instances can be paid upfront or monthly. The cost of up-front vs. monthly is the same and there's no fee for monthly payments. Azure Reserved Instances are only available for Microsoft Products/Services in Azure, not third-party solutions from the Azure Marketplace. Azure customers may exchange an Azure Reserved Instance, or reservation, for another reservation of the same type. Microsoft also supports refunding a reservation, up to

$50,000 in a 12-month rolling window, if you no longer need it. The maximum limit of the refund applies to all reservations in the scope of your agreement with Microsoft. For a detailed list of what can be covered by an Azure Reserved Instance, please refer to `https://docs.microsoft.com/en-us/azure/cost-management-billing/reservations/save-compute-costs-reservations`.

RIs can be scoped to an Azure subscription or a resource group. Discounted billing is applied to any resources in a subscription or resource group that meets the criteria of the RI. Administrators should think about resource groups as the more desirable target here. Experience has shown too often different resources are grouped in the same subscription. Applying RIs to a subscription can lead to the wrong resources getting the discounts if multiple are co-mingled. Administrators can scope RIs to a single resource group, a single subscription, or a shared subscription model, which means several subscriptions can be the target of a single RI.

You must monitor the utilization of RIs, which are "use it or lose it" discounts. If they are not utilized (for example, you applied them to DS series VMs, and an administrator scaled the VMs up to N series), you can exchange or refund RIs.

Microsoft estimates that there are 730 hours in one month. This is about 30.4 days. If you have workloads that run under approximately 300 hours per month, RIs may not be a cost-effective solution for your business' workload. It's safe to assume that any workload running 24/7 should be utilizing RIs to be as cost-effective as possible. Calculations should be done to see if RIs are cost-effective for each workload. The cost varies by the number of hours and by workload type.

An example of this is that a SharePoint farm is more cost-effective to run with a three-year RI than as two one-year RIs or pay-as-you-go, even knowing that it would be ending in about two years. For more information on RIs, please refer to `https://docs.microsoft.com/en-us/azure/cost-management-billing/reservations/save-compute-costs-reservations`.

Azure Cost Management + Billing

Azure Cost Management + Billing is an Azure service that has evolved from Microsoft's acquisition of Cloudyn in 2017. Azure Cost Management + Billing is an Azure service designed for managers, finance, administrators, and application owners. Azure Cost Management + Billing provides visibility and accountability for the services deployed and charges incurred for the various cloud resource usage. Azure Cost Management + Billing provides a level of financial governance as the Azure management group or subscription level. Azure Cost Management + Billing also supports the filtering of tags that apply to Azure resources.

Azure Cost Management + Billing supports every type of Azure offering. Figure 6-7 shows the consumption of a few services in a subscription, selected as the scope. The red dashed line represents a monthly budget, and the graph illustrates the expected trend against the budget. The meter graph illustrates the different resources being utilized and their costs. The Resource Type graph shows costs by that metric, illustrating how compute is the most expensive and networking is second-most expensive. Each of these graphs can easily be customized by the user to show the metrics they're interested in by using the drop- downs. Azure Cost Management + Billing dashboards can be saved and reused by others who have been granted access to them.

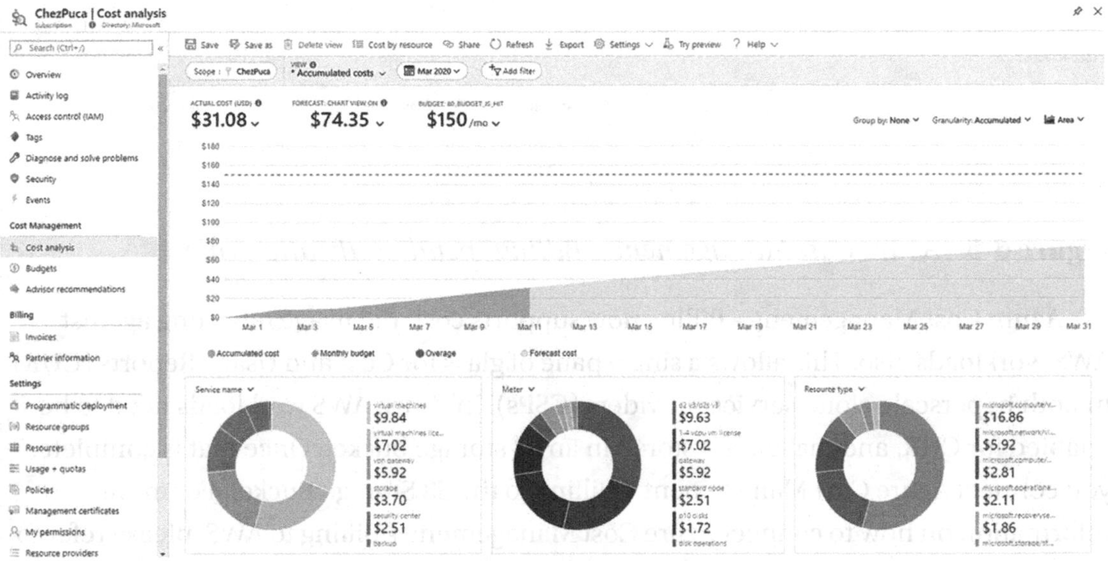

***Figure 6-7.** Azure Cost Management + Billing cost analysis*

Thresholds can be defined in the Azure Cost Management + Billing Budget blade. Administrators can specify single or recurring windows for which they want to monitor the costs. Any date range is available as a window, and rules can be created to give administrators advance notice of costs to prevent runaway expenses. Figure 6-8 shows a rule created to generate an email when 80% of my budget is hit. This rule and threshold are configured to reset monthly. Once exceeded, Azure Cost Management + Billing alert notifications are sent via email. While this shows only one generic address for the sake of the book, Azure Cost Management + Billing supports emailing numerous entries inside and outside of the organization.

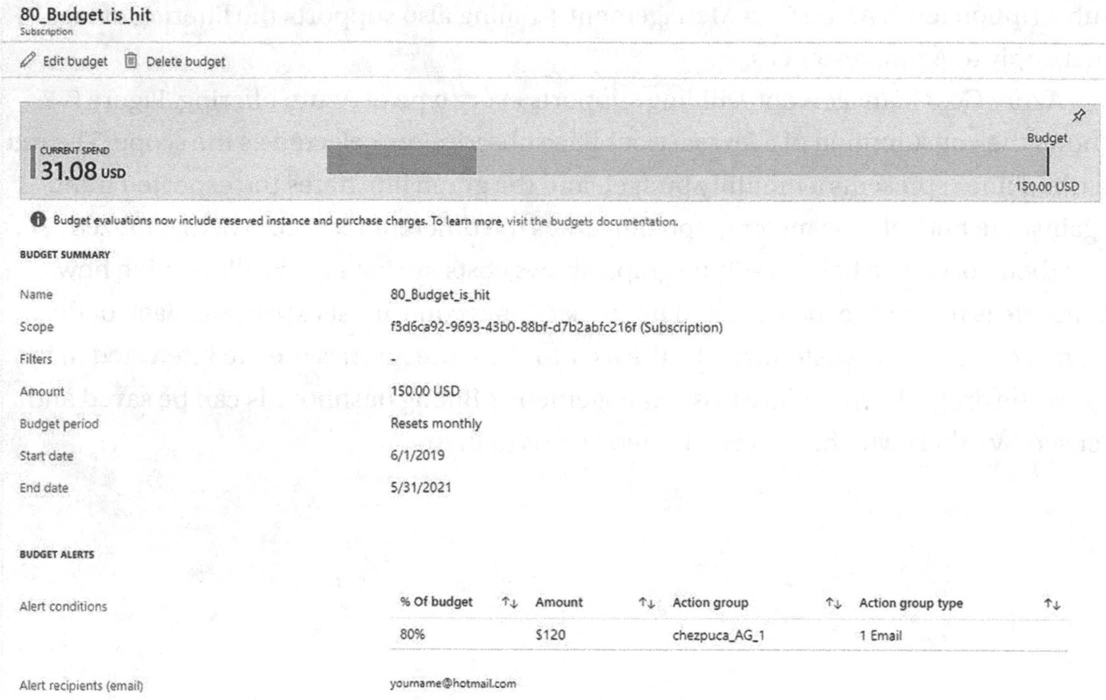

***Figure 6-8.** Azure Cost Management + Billing spend notification rule*

Azure Cost Management + Billing now supports cost and usage reporting against AWS workloads also. This allows a single pane of glass for Cost and Usage Reports (CUR) in both hyperscale cloud service providers (CSPs). In short, AWS workloads need to be enabled for CUR, and that data is stored in an S3 storage bucket. Once that is complete, you connect Azure Cost Management + Billing to the S3 Storage Bucket. For more information on how to connect Azure Cost Management + Billing to AWS, please refer to `https://docs.microsoft.com/en-us/azure/cost-management-billing/costs/aws-integration-set-up-configure#create-a-role-and-policy-in-aws`.

Summary

From assessment to calculator, and from the Software Assurance benefits of the on-premises licenses to Reserved Instances, Azure saves you money. Azure Cost Management + Billing lets you plan, monitor, and ultimately control your spending in not only Azure but AWS as well.

CHAPTER 7

Designing a Hybrid Datacenter

To understand what goes into a *hybrid datacenter*, you must first have a clear understanding of both public and private clouds. Both cloud types provide a variety of benefits over the traditional datacenter virtualization model. Cloud computing, in its most basic form, is the separation of the workload from the hardware (which virtualization does) and the operating systems and applications. This separation can exist on a single server at various levels—such as websites, SQL Server database instances, or the network layer—by using software-defined networking (SDN). Connecting to a cloud service provider (CSP) allows an organization to use the geographic distribution of cloud services to their advantage, without having to invest in real estate or the back-end processes associated with the acquisition, deployment, depreciation, updating, and retirement of the physical assets that make up the CSP infrastructure.

The term *hybrid datacenter* is the evolution of marketing terms. When the cloud was first discussed by various service providers, they were speaking of public clouds , where customers could go to consume their services over the Internet, or in some cases, over dedicated network connections. These public clouds were based on a shared, multicustomer, multitenant model. While these public clouds offered great economies of scale and low price points to customers, they were simply too constrained for certain workloads. Applications with multiple systems feeding into (or off of) them had too much complexity to move to public clouds. This created one of the varieties of private clouds, where the infrastructure was left on-premises.

Private clouds are frequently incorrectly referred to as such because of their virtual infrastructure. Private clouds are very similar to public clouds. IT clouds should provide the users high availability, disaster recovery, various levels of storage resiliency and performance, and workload elasticity where workloads can scale up and down or in and

J. Soh et al., *Microsoft Azure*, https://doi.org/10.1007/978-1-4842-5958-0_7

out. PaaS services may also be included, which allows multiple customers to use the same service without each requiring its own implementation. Yet, their data is logically segmented from each other to satisfy various security and regulatory compliance requirements.

Hyperconverged infrastructure (HCI) enabled hardware vendors to offer their customers software-defined compute, storage, and networking in a single platform. This is the first architecture from OEM vendors that truly allowed a private cloud as a turn-key solution. Prior to HCI, setting up a private cloud required very complex workflows to be manually coded, which allowed provisioning of storage, compute, and networking. HCI is ideal for customers whose workloads cannot move to the cloud, or the desire is to keep the workload local for performance reasons.

Air gapping is an example of regulatory compliance that drives HCI over a public cloud. The workload is not allowed to connect to another network, like the Internet or a LAN/WAN. Ultimately, connectivity, which we imply as bandwidth and latency, to the CSP is usually the bottleneck and key driver to keep a workload local to an organization. If the rate of change to the workload is too high, a given connection may not be able to keep up.

Globally, latency is the biggest connectivity challenge we face today from a networking perspective. The other key reason that a workload may need a private vs. a public cloud is when there are too many dependencies on other systems, where the overall effort to move a monolithic app and all of its dependent apps is too high or risky.

Networking Considerations

Networking is the foundation of cloud computing. In this section, we review the different methods of connecting to Microsoft Azure. While connecting to Azure over the Internet is a viable approach for certain workloads, the purpose of this chapter is to discuss networking in a hybrid model, so we'll review the methods to connect on-premises to Azure. Each of the connectivity methods described in this section is available in all regions in all Azure clouds.

Depending upon where in the world your connectivity requirements exist, you may have different product options and pricing from your telco partners. Network connectivity to Microsoft Azure usually has several components that make up the connection, and hence the pricing. In this book, we'll only be discussing the Microsoft part of the connectivity. Understanding your throughput requirements for both storage and networking is paramount to successfully architect a cloud solution.

Let's use a high-performance computing (HPC) workload as an example. If you have terabytes (TB) or petabytes (PB) of data that you need to move into the cloud to perform analytics against, and there's little time to do it, you may be better off performing the workload on-premises, or you may want to change the business process flow and have the data shipped to the cloud initially, instead of on-premises. An inverse example is if the data can be copied to the cloud from on-premises, the processing power of the cloud may be able to complete the workload so quickly that the timeframe consumed copying the data to the cloud may be negated.

Azure's connectivity options consist of VPN, including Point-to-Site (P2S), Site-to-Site (S2S), VNet-to-VNet, ExpressRoute through a cloud exchange co-location, ExpressRoute through a Point-to-Point Ethernet connection, or ExpressRoute through an Any-to-Any (IPVPN) connection. For a detailed breakdown of the various Microsoft Azure connectivity services, please refer to Chapter 9 of this book.

If you're interested in testing the latency to any Azure Datacenter, visit `www.azurespeed.com/Azure/Latency`. On this site, you can select whatever Azure region you desire, and test the latency in milliseconds (ms), as shown in Figure 7-1. It is important to note that you are testing from where you are running this web page, which means that any infrastructure you traverse is part of the test and adds to the latency. Your corporate office will likely test differently from a café or home. Figure 7-1 illustrates a test from an Xfinity home network to each of the USA Azure regions.

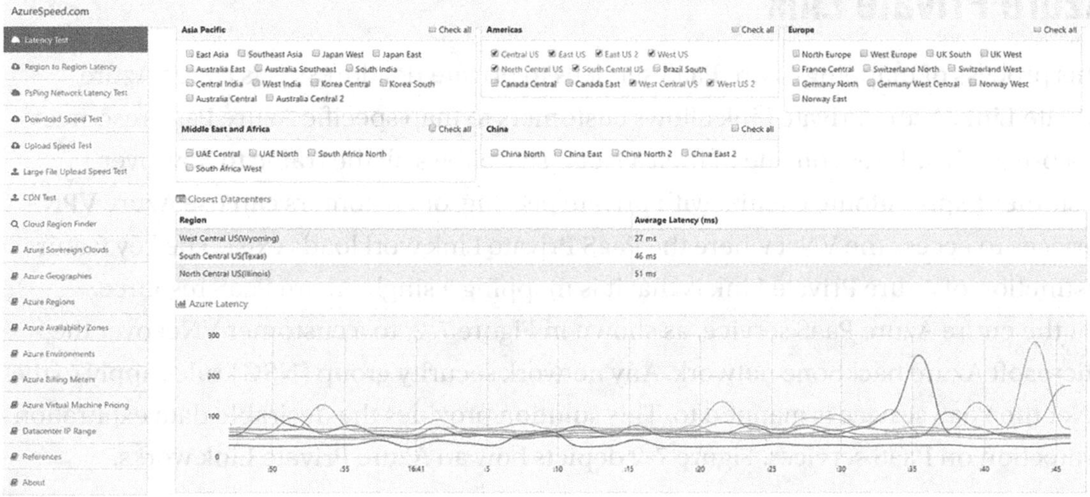

Figure 7-1. *Azure latency benchmarking*

In 2020, Azure's global network was the second-largest network in the world, with 58 regions across six continents and 140 countries. Azure has 130 points of presence (POP) across 80 metropolitan areas, and that does not include any of the POP city locations for Azure's content delivery network (CDN) from Akamai. Akamai is a Microsoft partner that has more 150,000 servers across the world, acting as the Internet's "edge." This partnership is a significant part of Azure's CDN.

PaaS Considerations

Azure PaaS services are exposed to the public via public IP addresses. These services can be accessed over the Internet or connected to over an ExpressRoute circuit. Due to the nature of the services using public IP addresses, many customers have concerns around security and privacy when traversing the Internet, regardless of the services using end to end encryption. ExpressRoute, which is a private, dedicated circuit, can have Microsoft peering enabled to connect to Azure PaaS services. Two new, completely different, services now exist within Azure that allows different methods of connecting to Azure PaaS services to private IP addresses; Azure Private Link and Azure service endpoints. These new connectivity methods provide a manner to connect to Azure PaaS services over private IPs, satisfying many of the security concerns.

Azure Private Link

This process of mapping Azure PaaS services to private IP addresses is called Azure Private Link. Azure Private Link allows customers to map specific Azure PaaS resources to a private IP address on one of their VNets. This allows all the traffic to flow over customer ExpressRoute circuits with private peering, or customers can use Azure VPN services to access the VNet where the PaaS Private Link workloads exist. The key feature distinction of Azure Private Link is that it is mapping a single Azure PaaS resource, not the entire Azure PaaS service, as shown in Figure 7-2, to a customer VNet over the Microsoft Azure backbone network. Any network security group (NSG) rules apply to the VNet the PaaS service is mapped to. This solution provides the desirable data exfiltration protection on PaaS services. Figure 7-2 depicts how an Azure Private Link works.

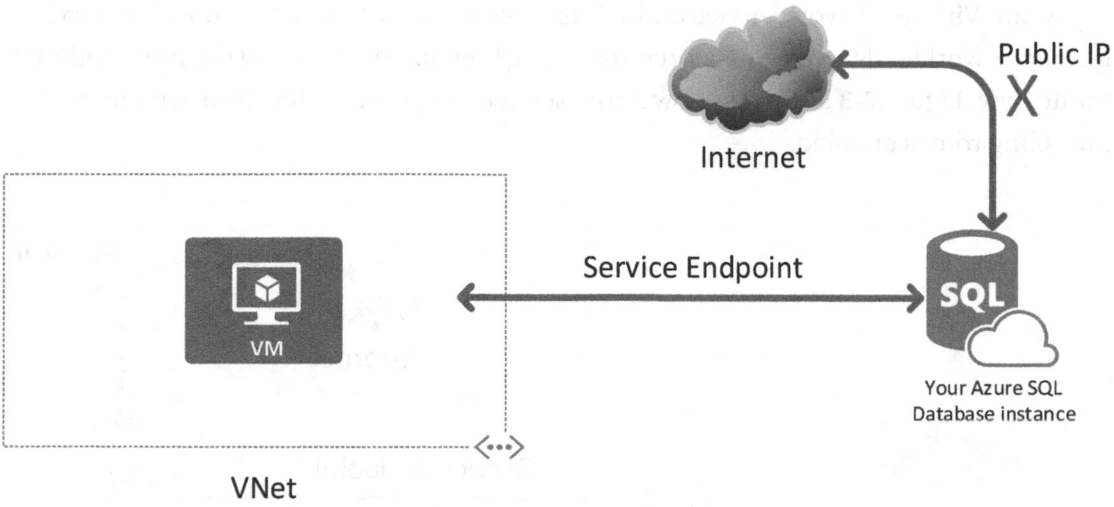

Figure 7-2. *Azure Private Link traffic flow*

A list of the PaaS services supporting Azure Private Link is at `https://docs.microsoft.com/en-us/azure/private-link/private-link-overview`.

Azure Virtual Network Service Endpoints

Azure Virtual Network service endpoints extend your VNet to the Azure PaaS services over the Microsoft Azure backbone network. This means that your VNet traffic does not go out over the Internet; it stays internal to Microsoft's network. This also means that the traffic to your PaaS service must go over the private connection, not the Internet. Traffic going out a VNet to an Azure PaaS service needs to go through a Network Virtual Appliance (NVA) or firewall to prevent data exfiltration. Azure Virtual Network service endpoints can only be used from IaaS workloads to PaaS workloads, not for on-premises to PaaS.

Force-tunneling lets organizations "force" all Internet traffic back to on-premises. This is a common architecture when there is a desire to log or monitor inbound or outbound Internet traffic. Force tunneling is common across many enterprises for this reason and required for most governments' networks. Since Internet-bound traffic must return to on-premise, workloads in Azure IaaS, such as VMs, need to traverse down to on-premise over VPN or ExpressRoute, then out the organization's Internet connection to get to the service. This is undesirable due to the long trip and latency associated with the large number of hops required to get from a VM in IaaS to a PaaS server, such as a SQL database.

Azure Virtual Network service endpoints allow you to get directly to the PaaS service from IaaS workloads, even when force-tunneling is enabled, providing the most optional traffic flow. Figure 7-3 illustrates how Azure service endpoints traffic flows with force-tunneling routes enabled.

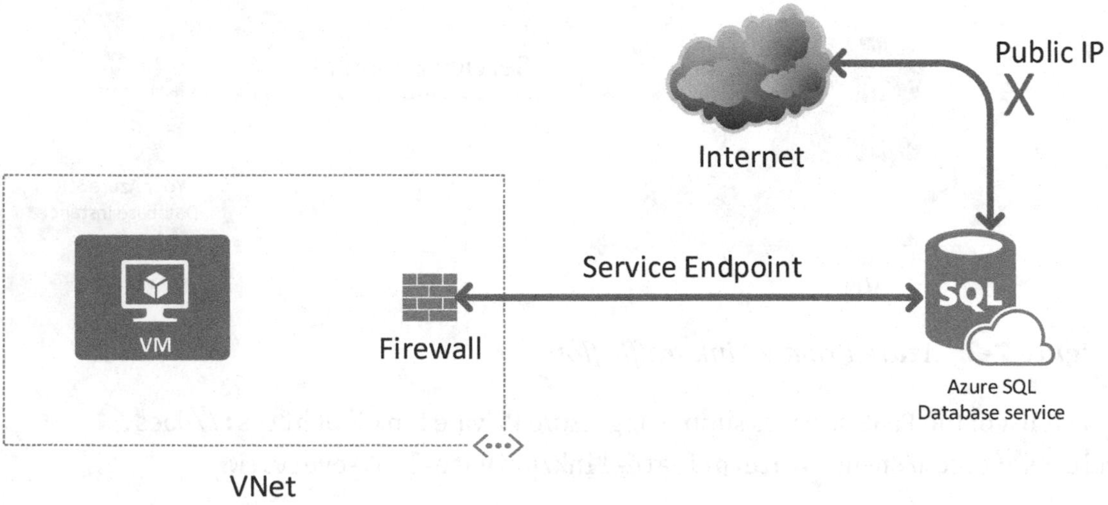

Figure 7-3. *Azure Virtual Network service endpoint traffic flow*

A list of the PaaS services supporting Azure Virtual Network service endpoints is at `https://docs.microsoft.com/en-us/azure/virtual-network/virtual-network-service-endpoints-overview`. For a detailed breakdown of the various Microsoft Azure connectivity services, please refer to Chapter 9 of this book.

Identity and Access Management

Identity is the foundation of all security. Microsoft Azure Active Directory is a highly secure cloud extension of Microsoft Active Directory and is Microsoft's *identity and access management as a service* (IDaaS) solution. Azure Active Directory (AAD) is Microsoft's hybrid identity utilizing conditional access (CA) and multifactor authentication (MFA) with a variety of MFA options, including smart cards, certificates, biometrics such as fingerprint and facial recognition with Windows Hello.

The Microsoft Azure Active Directory platform is an extension of on-premises user accounts, which authorizes (AuthZ) and authenticate (AuthN) users against a variety of Microsoft workloads (such as Office 365) and non-Microsoft workloads, including more than 2800 SaaS applications available in the Azure Active Directory Marketplace (`https://azuremarketplace.microsoft.com/en-us/marketplace/apps/category/azure-active-directory-apps`).

Azure Active Directory comes in several versions, including Free, Office 365, Premium 1 (P1), and Premium 2 (P2). Each of these versions builds upon the previous and total represent 49 distinct features. For a full list of these features and pricing, refer to `https://azure.microsoft.com/en-us/pricing/details/active-directory/`. Some of the more significant features include single sign-on (SSO), MFA, Self-Service Password Reset (SSPR), and Azure AD Join, mobile device management (MDM) autoenrollment, and privileged identity management (PIM).

Hybrid Identity is the creation of the cloud identity from some of the attributes of the on-premises identity. These attributes are synchronized via the Azure AD Connect sync process. Administrators can choose which attributes to synchronize via Azure AD Connect; for example, if some AD attributes contain PII, the administrators can choose not to sync those to AAD. There are approximately 200 attributes synchronized per use object for Office 365 Pro Plus, SharePoint Online, Exchange Online, Teams, Azure RMS, Intune, Dynamics, Windows 10, third-party apps, and a few other categories. For a detailed list, please refer to `https://docs.microsoft.com/en-us/azure/active-directory/hybrid/reference-connect-sync-attributes-synchronized#attributes-to-synchronize`. Figure 7-4 depicts how Microsoft Azure Cloud Services are layered on top of Azure Active Directory, which is usually synchronized for enterprise-size customers.

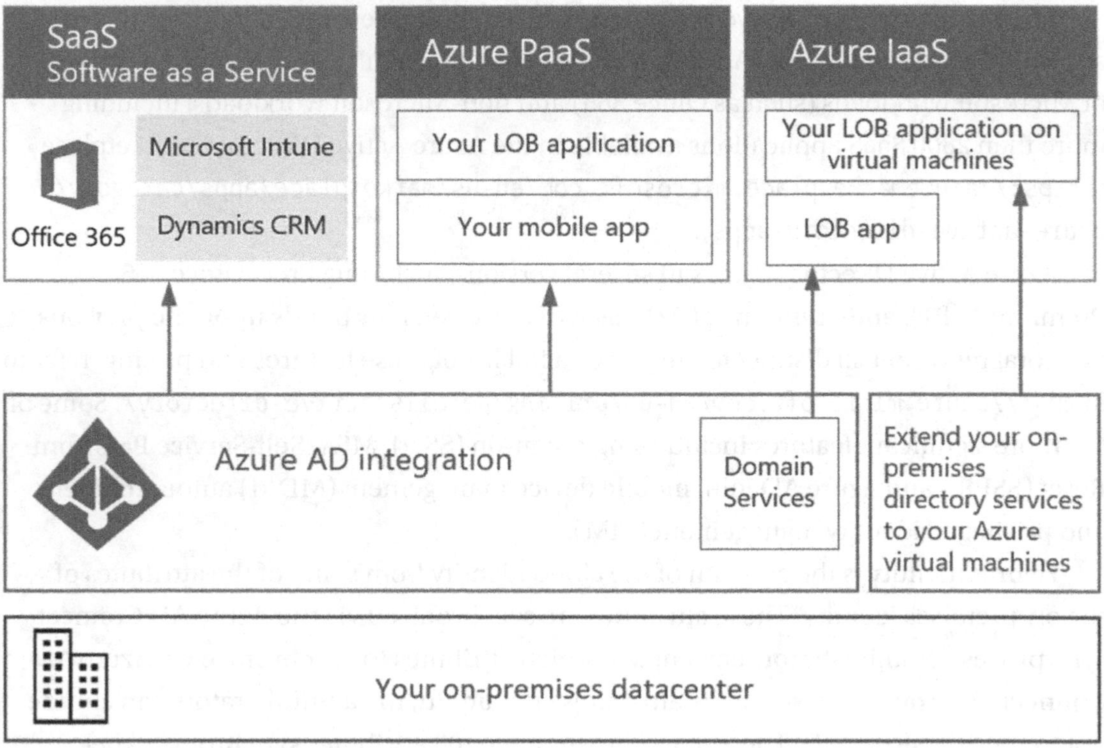

Figure 7-4. *Azure AD Hybrid ID cloud service in a hybrid datacenter*

Azure AD also includes Azure Domain Services (AAD DS), which allows administrators to join computers directly to the Azure AD domain, apply group policies (GPO), and use Kerberos/NTLM authentication without having to deploy domain controllers. Azure AD authenticates the systems and users with their corporate domain credentials.

Azure AD Domain Services is a highly available LDAP solution that works with cloud-only AAD and AAD that has been replicated from on-premises.

As shown in Figure 7-5, Azure AD includes a B2C offering that allows AAD Identity and Access Management (IAM) to customer-facing apps. Customers can use their existing corporate credentials, their preferred accounts in social media platforms (including Twitter, Facebook, Microsoft, Google, Amazon, LinkedIn, or local identities) to get single sign-on to the applications you have published. AAD B2C also supports third-party verification. Since the use of social media platform accounts can be enabled, a verification process is supported to validate the user is who they say they are. Figure 7-5 depicts the workflow for third-party verification.

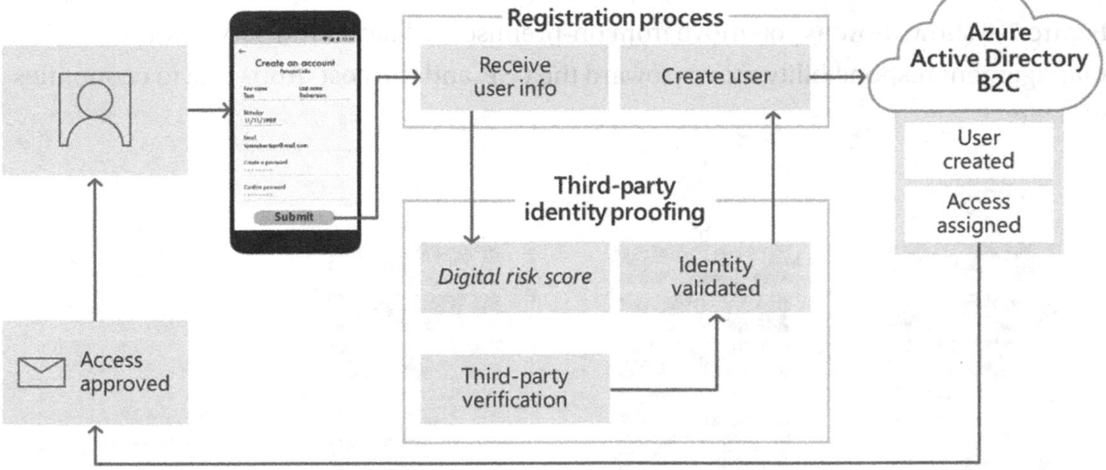

Figure 7-5. *Third-party verification of AAD B2C account*

For a thorough description of the Azure Active Directory B2C feature, please refer to `https://docs.microsoft.com/en-us/azure/active-directory-b2c/technical-overview`.

Security and Monitoring

Security is paramount for Microsoft Azure. Security in Azure is a partnership between you, the customer, and Microsoft, the CSP. Microsoft can only secure so much of the infrastructure. If you set up a web server that sends passwords in clear text, that's outside the realm of Microsoft's responsibilities. The responsibilities and controls for Azure services and application security vary depending upon which Azure cloud services you're consuming. Most organizations are completely responsible for their on-premises datacenter, or it may be shared with a managed service partner.

Figure 7-6 illustrates how as you move from IaaS to PaaS to SaaS, the amount of responsibility for the security and availability of the workload moves more toward the CSP. IaaS has Microsoft managing the Azure compute, networking, and storage "fabric." In contrast, the customer manages everything from the networking to the operating system environments (OSE) in the VMs up to the data layer. PaaS services allow Microsoft to manage more of the stack, including the operating systems and platforms hosting the services.

SaaS allows Microsoft to manage infrastructure, OS, applications, and data storage. Figure 7-6 shows how as you move from on-premises to SaaS cloud services, the management responsibility moves toward the CSP, and the cost drops due to economies of scale.

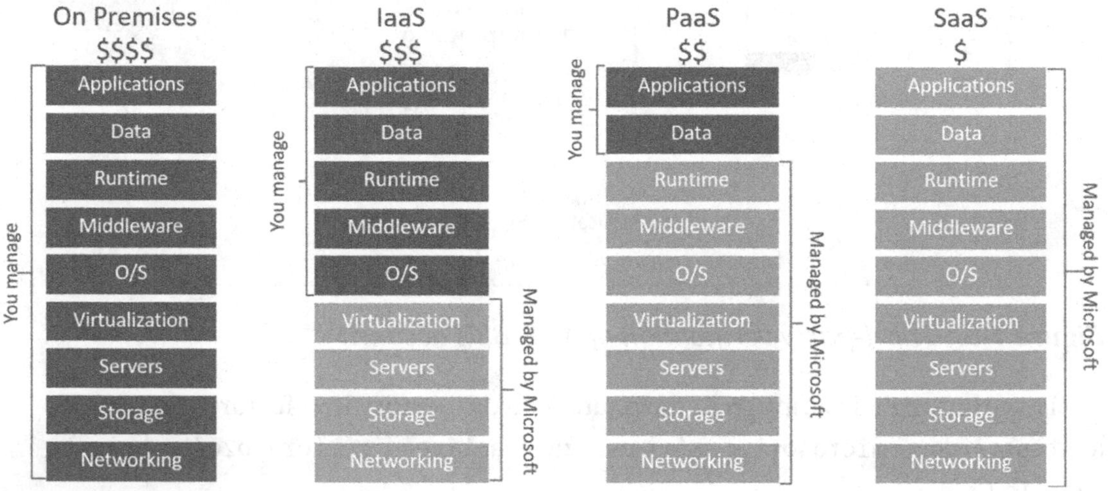

Figure 7-6. *Azure cloud service responsibility matrix*

At the time of publishing, Microsoft has approximately 800 NIST (National Institute of Standards and Technology) security controls across 262 Azure cloud services. Fifty of these services are IaaS, and 212 are PaaS services. Across these 262 Azure services, Microsoft maintains approximately 92 regulatory compliances, which include global, government, industry, and regional certifications. A full list of Microsoft regulatory compliance is at `https://docs.microsoft.com/en-us/microsoft-365/compliance/offering-home?view=o365-worldwide`.

The Microsoft Trust Center (`www.microsoft.com/en-us/trust-center`) should be your primary page for learning anything about Microsoft security, privacy, and compliance. This site is the home for where Microsoft details how we handle customer data, operations, and tools, including compliance offerings and audit reports of the Microsoft Azure clouds. If you're a US governmental entity and the Microsoft Azure SSP is required, please contact your Microsoft Account team.

Microsoft's commitment to security and privacy of customer data in the cloud is exemplified through industry-leading practices matured on some of the world's largest datacenters and cloud services. Hotmail has been a SaaS service for more than 20 years.

The following list outlines just some of the security principles implemented in each of Microsoft's cloud services.

- Customers own their data. It's yours; you can take it out of Azure whenever you want and have it permanently erased from all Azure servers/services.
- Customers control where their data resides, where it is copied to, and how it is secured
- Microsoft does not use customer data for anything. Microsoft does not even have access to customer data unless it is initiated via the Customer Lockbox for Microsoft Azure solution. For more information, refer to `https://docs.microsoft.com/en-us/azure/security/fundamentals/customer-lockbox-overview`.
- Privacy reviews are performed to verify requirements are being met.
- Microsoft directs data access requests from governments to the end customer whenever possible. Microsoft will go to court to challenge any invalid legal demands for data.
- Data is encrypted at rest by default at no charge. Customers can choose to encrypt again at the OS or service level, such as Transparent Data Encryption (TDE) in Microsoft SQL Server.
- Best-in-class data encryption is used for data in transit whenever the service allows. FTP is an example of a workload that can put a customer at risk. Transport Layer Security (TLS), the successor to SSL, is an example of communication encryption available between individual Azure deployments between Azure and on-premises workloads, and for Azure administrators and users.
- Azure Information Protection uses encryption, identity, and authorization policies to secure your data. You can see where your data went in the world, who viewed it, from where you can set expiration dates on your data, and you can revoke access to it if needed.

- Azure Key Vault allows customers to secure cryptography keys used by cloud services so that even Microsoft cannot access or see the keys.
- Earlier in this chapter, we briefly reviewed the ability of Azure AD to use conditional access policies, multifactor authentication, and managed access to third-party SaaS applications.
- Microsoft has been developing its Secure Development Lifecycle (SDL) since 2008. All Microsoft cloud services use SDL, which has evolved to include
    - Risk assessments
    - Attack surface analysis and reduction
    - Threat modeling
    - Incident response
    - Release review and certification
- The Microsoft Digital Crimes Unit (DCU) is part of the Microsoft Cyber Defense Operations Center (CDOC). The CDOC And DCU work with governments and law enforcement agencies globally to fight malware and go after "bad actors" on the web. Microsoft collects telemetry from the Windows OS, Azure AD, Office 365, and other cloud services. This data feeds the Microsoft Intelligent Security Graph, which is a data lake of billions of endpoints worldwide telling Microsoft where bad actors are operating from and letting Microsoft treat traffic from them accordingly.
- Microsoft operates under an Assume Breach methodology, in which teams are always trying to penetrate Microsoft's defenses, and other teams are always looking for them. When vulnerabilities are proactively found, they're escalated and remediated.
- Microsoft Azure supports multiple types of private connectivity to the customers' resources.

- Microsoft follows regulatory standards for overwriting storage before reuse or the physical destruction of decommissioned hardware. Faulty drives, both spinning and solid-state, and hardware are demagnetized and shredded.
- 24/7/365 physical security at datacenter locations.

For more information on Microsoft's security offering, please refer to `www.microsoft.com/en-us/security/business/explore/cybersecurity` and `www.microsoft.com/en-us/cybersecurity/content-hub`.

Summary

Microsoft has invested more than $1 billion annually in cybersecurity for over a decade. While most people may not think of Microsoft as a cybersecurity company, Microsoft has more than 3500 full-time employees working around the clock to secure their cloud services and technology down to the desktop and device. We hope that this chapter provided some insight into how these Azure services can be extensions of your on-premises IT infrastructure and enable hybrid cloud computing for your organization.

CHAPTER 8

Tools and Training to Up-Skill Existing IT Teams

This chapter focuses on competencies. You learn "how to learn" with an introduction to training options for teams and individuals as you prepare to support your business migration to the Microsoft Azure Cloud platform. We present a few cloud roles to consider and discuss how those roles relate to current IT on-premises teams. We then provide a matrix of the cloud training options for IT staff.

We overview the types of software tools needed to create a cloud engineer's laptop; security with portability is crucial to supporting flexibility. You learn about the types of tools needed to support a business in a hybrid cloud model. We discuss the pros and cons of the Windows operating system (OS) and macOS for specific tools. You should consider both versions now that all the foundational tools run on either—and to support the cloud developers who prefer Linux.

We highlight the framework that enables a continuous delivery process to build Azure infrastructure as code (IaC). We provide a high-level view of Azure Resource Manager (ARM) templates and HashiCorp Terraform. These tools are necessary in supporting an Azure infrastructure to build, plan, validate, test, destroy, and rebuild a new layer of code that can automate infrastructure deployment.

Available Training

You first need to ask and answer questions on how Azure cloud training can help your business. Who needs training? How much does it cost? How do you know if your staff is completing the exercises? Let's begin with the Azure cloud roles that are needed as applications, revenue-generating services are created and data is migrated to the cloud.

J. Soh et al., *Microsoft Azure*, https://doi.org/10.1007/978-1-4842-5958-0_8

Let's begin with the following. There are many other roles, but these three roles are foundational.

- Solutions architects
- DevOps engineers (developers)
- Administrators

The solutions architect's role in Azure is to understand how to create or develop a hybrid-cloud deployment network. Security is a crucial consideration in the design to enable the business and creativity of the DevOps engineer. Traditional security policies need to be reviewed and modified to support the cloud infrastructure mainly because security and IT tools for on-premises environments are often misaligned with the cloud infrastructure. Traditional vendors that build on-premises are consolidating to gain market sahre. As smaller startup businesses are acquired, their is a challenge to integration the smaller solutions to work seamlessly with the on-premises legacy applications. The integration can take years before the final products supports the public cloud.

Engineering teams have the historical role of development, building applications for the business, keeping them up-to-date, with Agile deployment methods. The role of DevOps combines the developer role with operations and introduces continuous integration and continuous delivery (CI/CD). Microsoft Azure supports many CI/CD methods to allow code updates and changes. The workflow for DevOps is also the focus of the cloud administrator to automate infrastructure deployment (see Chapter 11).

Continuous deployment of Azure services is more efficient after adopting many of the DevOps tools and engineering depth to deploy Azure infrastructure. Cloud administrators must do more than deployment using the Azure portal. They use the same tools; Visual Studio Code and PowerShell to deploy IaC from a Mac or Windows laptop. They use the same CI/CD processes to create, plan, test, deploy, revision software versions of Azure infrastructure deployment. They deploy the same code in test/dev and user acceptance testing (UAT) that is planned to be deployed in production.

There are many Azure cloud training options that provide on-demand and live training for beginning, intermediate, and advanced learners. Give your cloud operations team several hours a week to learn. Set expectations for deadlines, and it will pay off. If you purchase a team subscription for online access and do not support time to learn during the workweek, the knowledge gain will be slower and incremental. Set project hours to learn, but start to decrease many training hours as their skills increase.

It would not be fair to recommend one online training over another; however, there are features you need to consider when evaluating any training options for teams or evaluating for an individual consultant. One feature to recognize is professionalism, and that includes a clear, consistent level of audio, consistent speaker's ability to carry the topic to connect the dots and methods to answer your cloud support questions. Table 8-1 provides a starting place and then expand training features that are needed and the weight of importance.

Table 8-1. *Training Matrix for Online Training Considerations*

Azure Training Area	Cost	Weight- Importance
Unlimited access on demand	$	
Hands-On Lab	Included	
Live Training / in Person Option	$$	
Dedicated Training Option	$$	
Quizzes and Exam Simulator	Included	
Career Path Pre-Test (Metrics)	Included	
Management Portal (Metrics for Business)	$	
Sandbox Environment	$ or Included	
Activity Reporting (Metrics Individual)	Included	
Certification Focused Classes	Included	
Boot Camp (Options)	$$	

You should consider online platforms for cloud training options. One specific criteria to consider is it is incredibly cost-effective for beginning and intermediate cloud learning teams. However, based on your skill level and budget, traditional classroom training is always a great option. Trainers are often cloud deployment consultants who supplement the official curriculum with explanations of real-world challenges and how they were resolved.

Finally, if your company has a Microsoft EA contract there are training vouchers that normally expire at the end of the contract so plan to enable them earlier in the contract years. And if your company has a Premier Support agreement with specific hours allocated, those hours may be converted to create a hands-on workshop to focus on a very narrow and complex Azure deployment problem.

There are excellent online training programs available. The following are a few to consider.

- cloudacademy.com
- skillmeup.com
- opsgility.com
- pluralsight.com
- linuxacademy.com

When working across business divisions, there should be common ground to support up-skill training from a traditional on-premises datacenter to public cloud computing. Review the current roles in your business, how teams share and consider the need to remove the silos and technical separations.

If you are a manager of a team or executive directory, you need to adovcate for change in learning Azure public cloud. Every team member needs to agree with the business need to adopt the cloud. To build a successful team, IT operation roles change to cloud operation roles. Managers should ask hard questions like to support cloud adoption with questions like; is the right change for the business? The cost for training cloud operations support roles are similar to training cost for on-premise roles, and in some options a little less expensive.

Consider renaming positions, lateral movement, rather than deleting current roles and hiring for new roles. Consider hiring contractors to kick start the right engineering cloud projects. Roles are similar but not the same because all services are now virtual, no more rack and stack in Azure cloud.

Note Networking teams should learn about cloud-native DNS, firewalls, network security groups (NSG), and web application firewalls. The changes to third-party on-premises solutions like Palo Alto, Juniper, Fortinet, Barracuda, and Cisco enable features different from their virtual network appliances (VNA) counterparts.

Free is a great price to start training. Figure 8-1 may help you understand which systems are needed for a business in the cloud. As your business grows in the cloud, you made need artificial intelligence (AI) engineers and analysts, DevOps engineers that adapt to the cloud model, and agile deployment and security engineers. Azure cloud security, monitoring, alerting, and risk mitigations must be clearly understood to prevent data loss. Please don't view the results of the default search view, 1145 items because many of the training modules are less than an hour and some only a few minutes. Start at `https://docs.microsoft.com/en-us/learn/`.

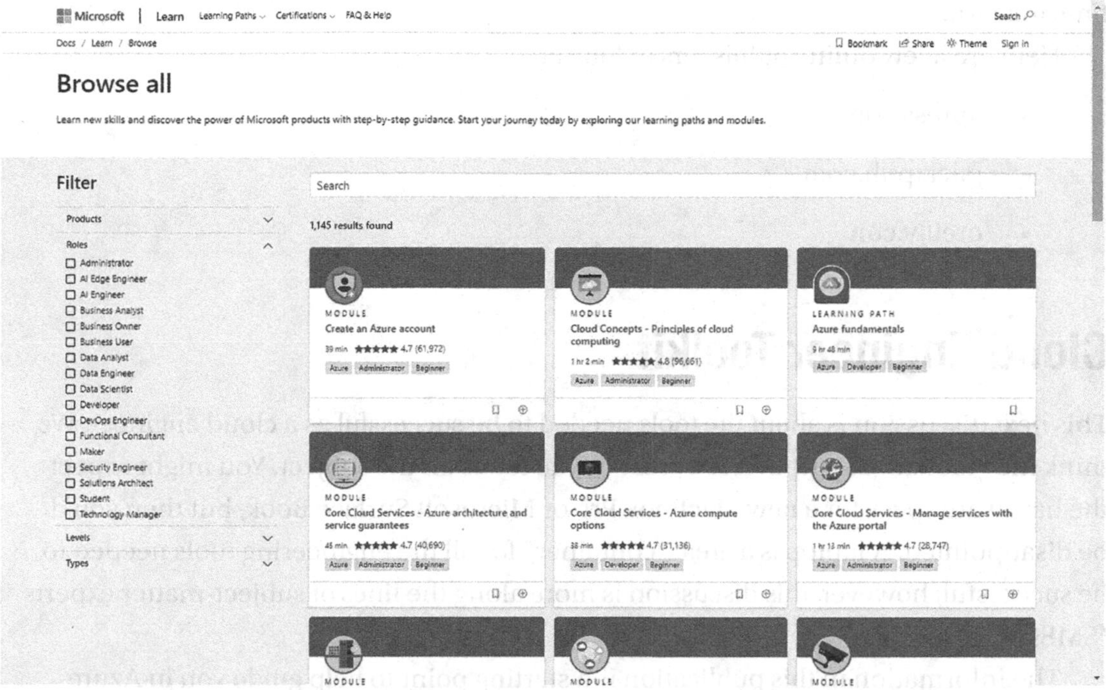

Figure 8-1. *Azure Learn website requires free registration*

Also, the business should consider cybersecurity training, a cloud security team is needed to gain insight into how best to protect your business from cyberattacks. Any Azure Public cloud opertions team should consider creating a security forensic lab in the cloud, as well as the forensic methods and common security language for cloud security. Ramp-up cybersecurity teams, red and blue teams on cloud penetration testing, digital forensics and updating cyberhunting skills, including hybrid design for a security incident and event management.

There are two cybersecurity industry leaders that offer live, team, online and classroom training. These two busniesses are:

- infosecinstitute.com
- sans.org

Book publishers also offer resources. Apress features ApressOpen, which offers free technology books. It also offers low yearly subscription options for online access to all its publications, like this one. Other publishers offer training classes with conferences posted on their subscription sites. There is no shortage of material, only a shortage of time to learn.

Here are a few online publishers to look at

- apress.com
- packtpub.com
- oreilly.com

Cloud Engineer Toolkit

This next discussion is about the tools needed to be successful as a cloud engineer. We think the "toolkit" description is a great way to focus on the subject. You might expect the hardware specs for a new MacBook Pro or Microsoft Surface Book, but then you'd be disappointed. A laptop is a great "container" for all the engineering tools needed to be successful; however, this discussion is more along the lines of subject-matter experts (SMEs).

The information in this publication is a starting point to help guide you in Azure Cloud Services that are interesting, growing, and have a growing demand in the market. The first step in assembling the cloud engineer toolkit is in the definition of an engineer as it relates to cloud and operations. Chapter 11 is all about infrastructure as code. You learn how to configure some of the tools to support Azure Resource Manager (ARM) templates and HashiCorp Terraform.

A successful cloud engineer includes a combination of other roles, including IT cloud operations, DevOps, and cybersecurity. You expect there to be IT cloud operations tools and development tools, but cybersecurity tools are part of the new cloud engineer role and should be included in the toolkit. You can install Azure cloud tools on macOS, Linux OS, or Windows OS.

Open your browser and download Visual Studio Code (VS Code) for your operating system from `https://code.visualstudio.com/download`, as shown in Figure 8-2. The first exercise installs VS Code on macOS.

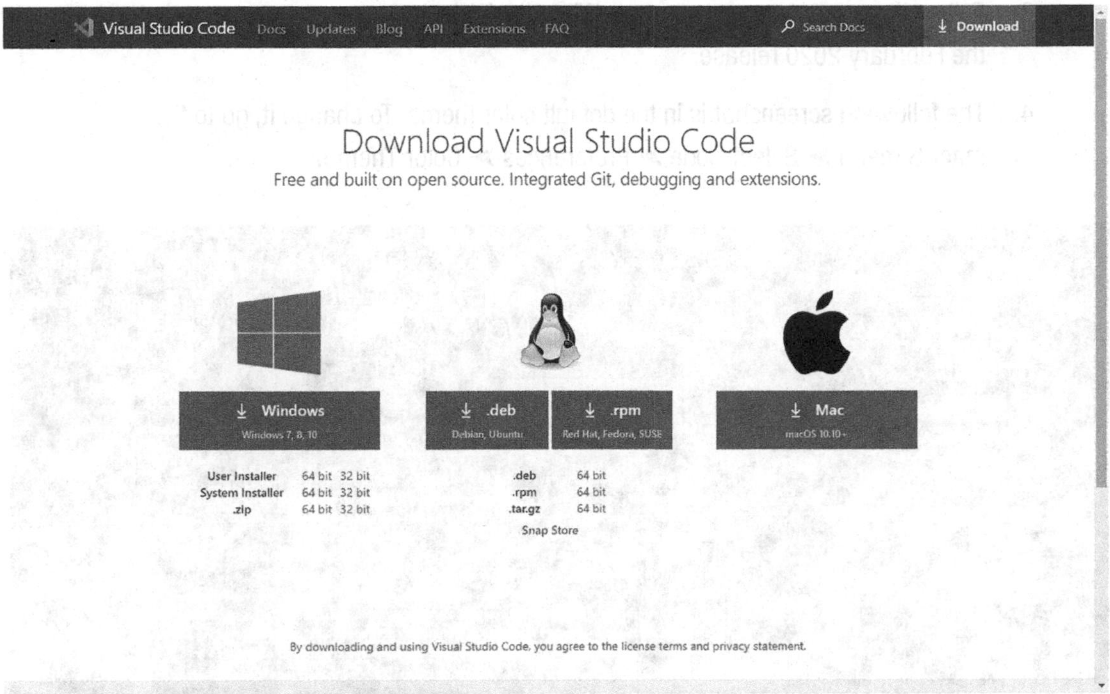

***Figure 8-2.** Visual Studio Code download for macOS, Linux, and Windows*

Now you can install Visual Studio Code for the Mac. It is quick and simple, with only a few steps to follow.

INSTALL VISUAL STUDIO CODE (MAC OS)

1. Install on a macOS laptop. Open your browser and go to `https://code.visualstudio.com/download`. Select the **macOS 10.10 +** button to download. Save the VSCode-darwin.zip file.
2. Click **Open** and allow the Visual Studio Code.app file to expand. Double-click to start the installation. macOS displays a warning: "Visual Studio Code.app is an app downloaded from the Internet. Are you sure you want to open it?" Click **Open** to continue.

3. Follow the prompts on your screen. When the Welcome screen opens, update to the February 2020 release.

4. The following screenshot is in the default color theme. To change it, go to the macOS menu ➤ Select Code ➤ Preferences ➤ Color Theme.

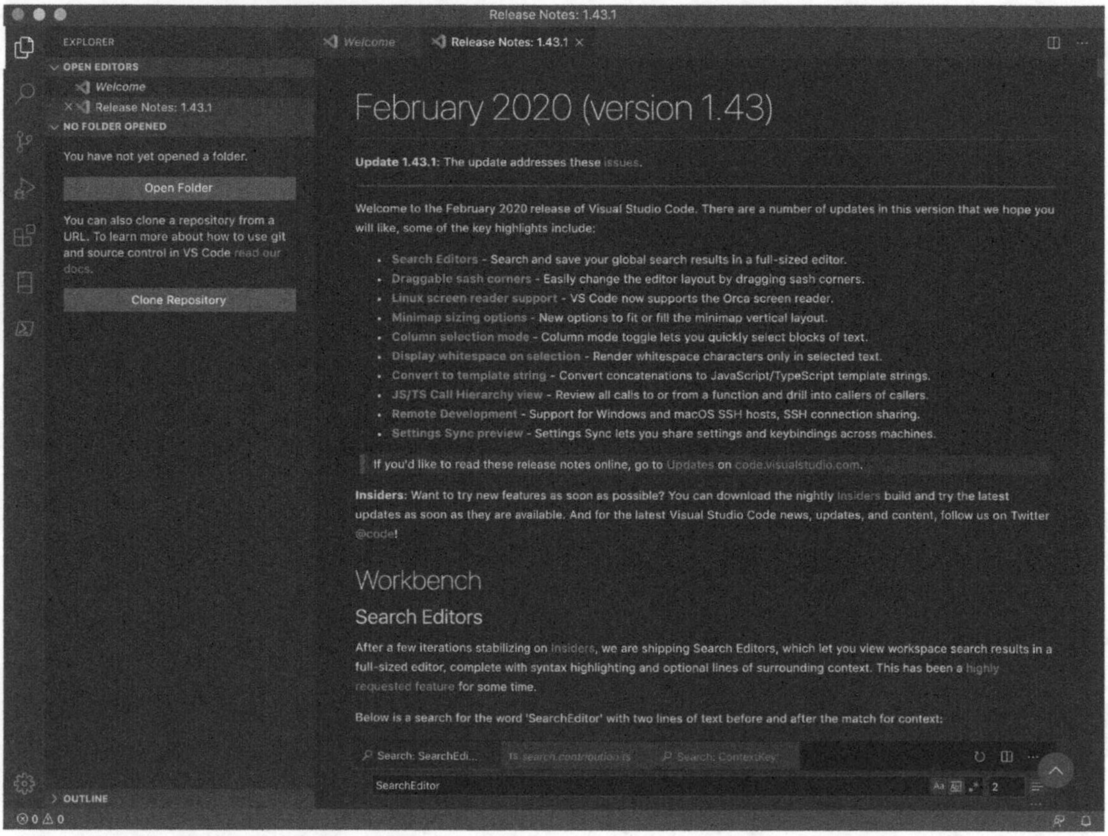

These exercises are short and easy to follow. You should create a similar set of installation guides for your business. Other cloud engineers would need the same toolkit installations.

INSTALL VISUAL STUDIO CODE (WINDOWS OS)

1. Install on Windows 10 laptop. Open your browser and go to `https://code.visualstudio.com/download`. Select the **Windows 7,8,10** button to download. Save the VSCodeUserSetup-x64-1.43.1.exe file (64-bit Windows 10 OS).

2. Click **Open** and allow the Visual Studio Code file to expand. Double-click to start the installation. Note the additional tasks, and leave the defaults. Click **Next** to continue.

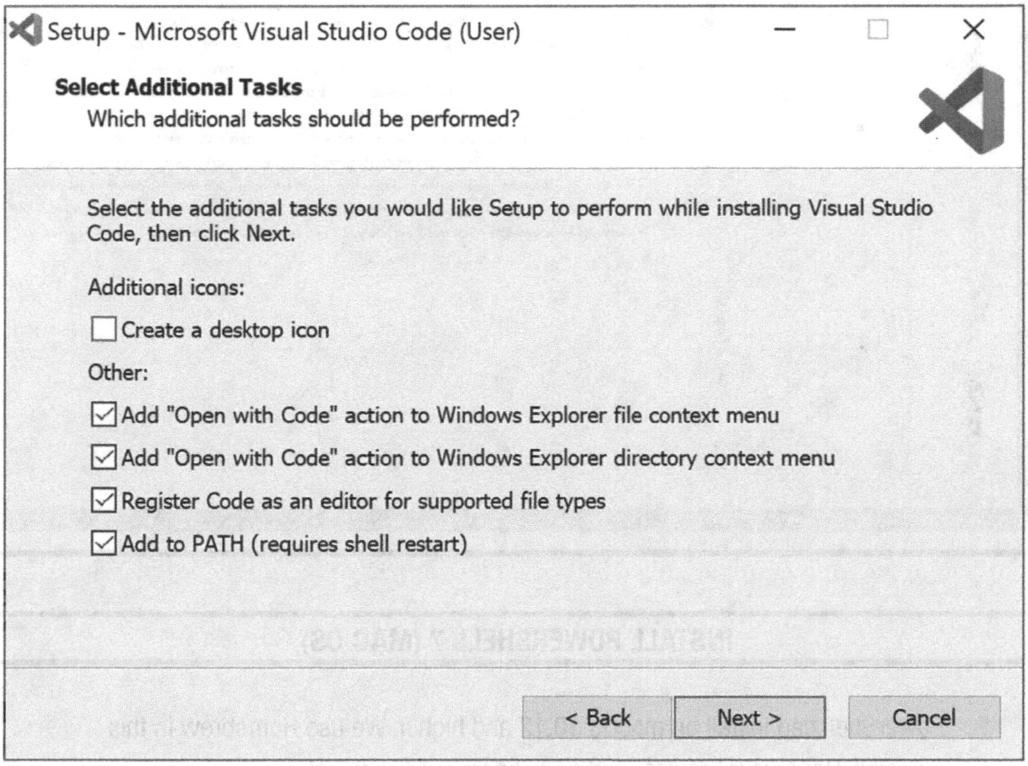

3. Review the screen settings and click **Install**. Note that the current updates are installed with the EXE file.

4. Update to the latest release to get updated and new features. To change the color, go to File ➤ Preferences ➤ Color Theme.

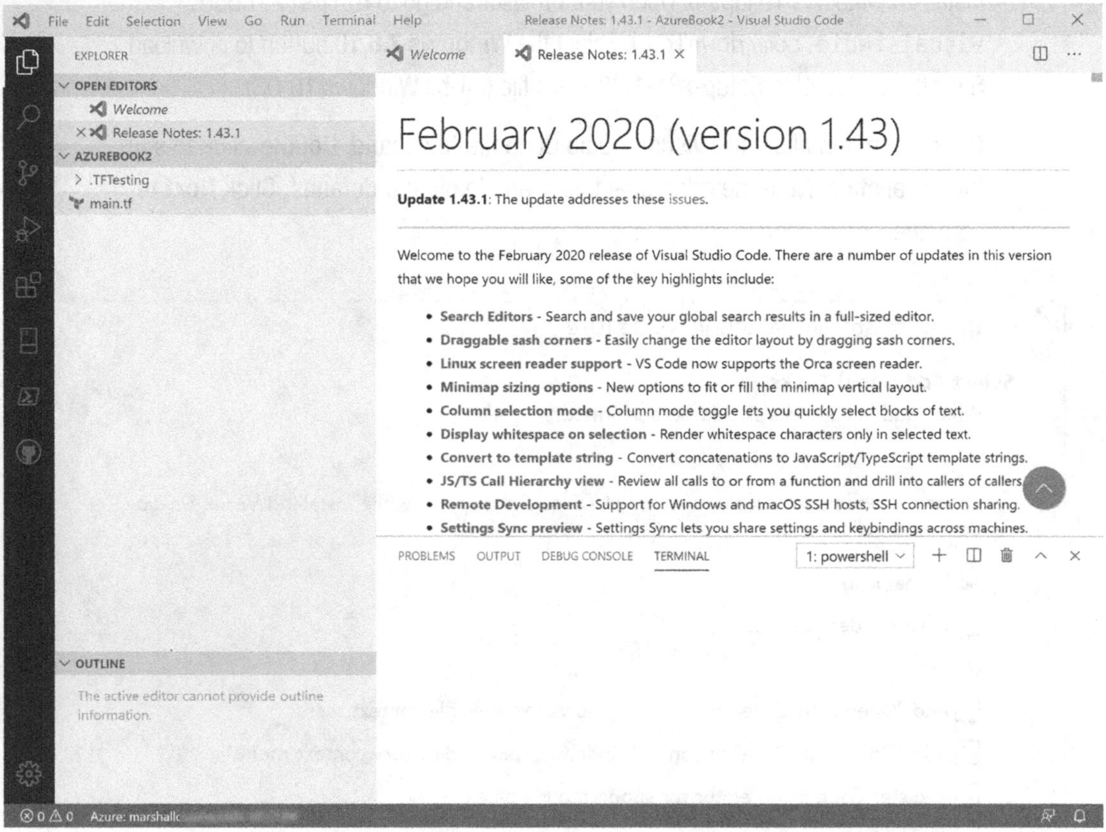

INSTALL POWERSHELL 7 (MAC OS)

1. PowerShell can install on macOS 10.12 and higher. We use Homebrew in this exercise. Open your browser and go to `https://brew.sh/`.

2. Open a Mac terminal window and copy and paste the following command: `/bin/bash -c "$(curl -fsSL https://raw.githubusercontent.com/Homebrew/install/master/install.sh)"`

3. Note that the installation script is a single line with no returns.

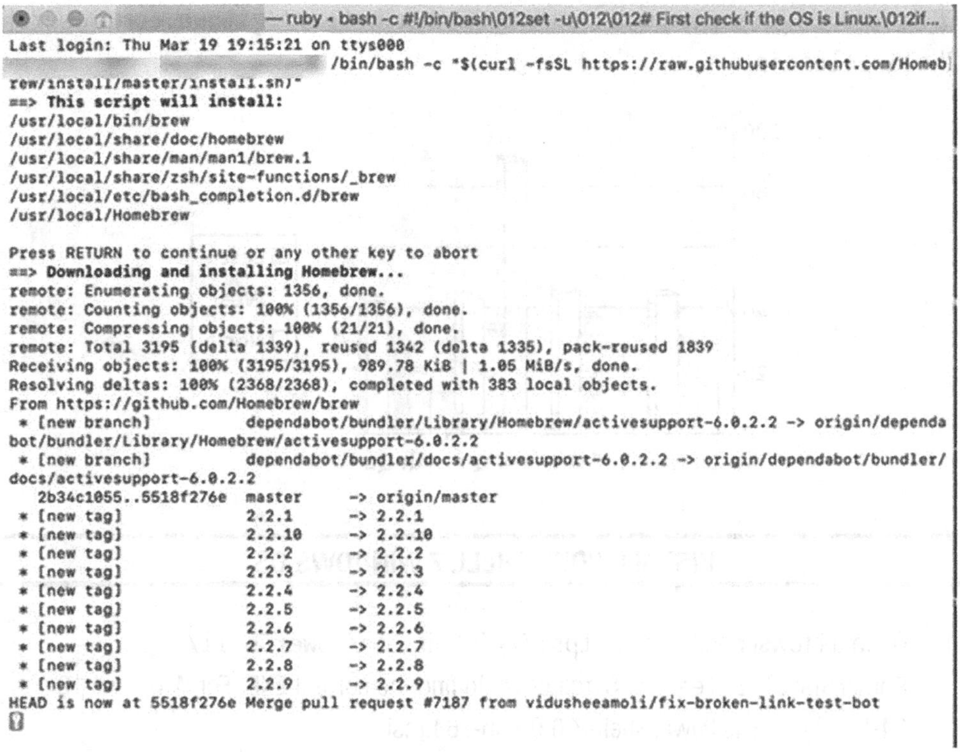
— ruby • bash -c #!/bin/bash\012set -u\012\012# First check if the OS is Linux.\012if...
Last login: Thu Mar 19 19:15:21 on ttys000
/bin/bash -c "$(curl -fsSL https://raw.githubusercontent.com/Homeb
rew/install/master/install.sh)"
==> This script will install:
/usr/local/bin/brew
/usr/local/share/doc/homebrew
/usr/local/share/man/man1/brew.1
/usr/local/share/zsh/site-functions/_brew
/usr/local/etc/bash_completion.d/brew
/usr/local/Homebrew
Press RETURN to continue or any other key to abort
==> Downloading and installing Homebrew...
remote: Enumerating objects: 1356, done.
remote: Counting objects: 100% (1356/1356), done.
remote: Compressing objects: 100% (21/21), done.
remote: Total 3195 (delta 1339), reused 1342 (delta 1335), pack-reused 1839
Receiving objects: 100% (3195/3195), 989.78 KiB | 1.05 MiB/s, done.
Resolving deltas: 100% (2368/2368), completed with 383 local objects.
From https://github.com/Homebrew/brew
* [new branch] dependabot/bundler/Library/Homebrew/activesupport-6.0.2.2 -> origin/dependa
bot/bundler/Library/Homebrew/activesupport-6.0.2.2
* [new branch] dependabot/bundler/docs/activesupport-6.0.2.2 -> origin/dependabot/bundler/
docs/activesupport-6.0.2.2
2b34c1055..5518f276e master -> origin/master
* [new tag] 2.2.1 -> 2.2.1
* [new tag] 2.2.10 -> 2.2.10
* [new tag] 2.2.2 -> 2.2.2
* [new tag] 2.2.3 -> 2.2.3
* [new tag] 2.2.4 -> 2.2.4
* [new tag] 2.2.5 -> 2.2.5
* [new tag] 2.2.6 -> 2.2.6
* [new tag] 2.2.7 -> 2.2.7
* [new tag] 2.2.8 -> 2.2.8
* [new tag] 2.2.9 -> 2.2.9
HEAD is now at 5518f276e Merge pull request #7187 from vidusheeamoli/fix-broken-link-test-bot

4. The installation guide warns that the script will install. Press **Return** to continue. You see the following text: `download/v7.0.0/powershell-7-0-0-o. Once the code is downloaded by brew you are prompted for your Mac password (to install on the HD)`. Homebrew is now installed.

5. Install PowerShell 7. From the Mac terminal, enter the following command: `brew cask install powershell`.

6. Test that PowerShell was installed. From the Mac terminal, enter the `pwsh` command.

7. In your Mac terminal window, you should see `PS /User/NAME/` as the prompt.

The next exercise provides you a process to install PowerShell for Windows OS. PowerShell is now an open source project, free to the community and distributed using the MIT license. To get started you can download at: `https://github.com/PowerShell/PowerShell/releases`.

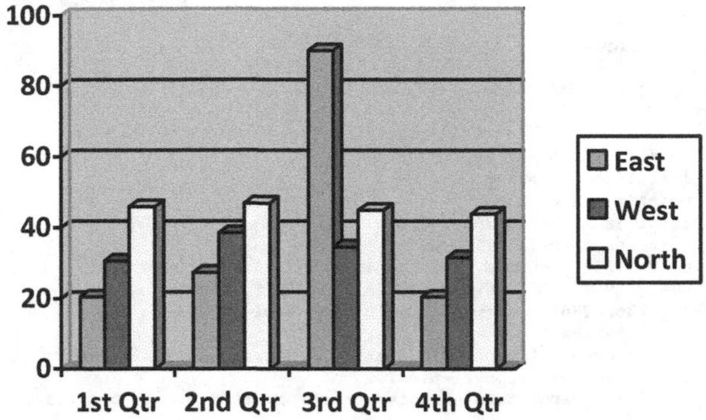

INSTALL POWESHELL 7 WINDOWS OS

1. Open a browser and go to `https://github.com/PowerShell/PowerShell/releases`. Scroll down to find the correct EXE. For Windows 10 64-bit, the EXE is PowerShell-7.0.0-win-x64.msi.
2. After the download is complete, open, and run the .MSI installer.

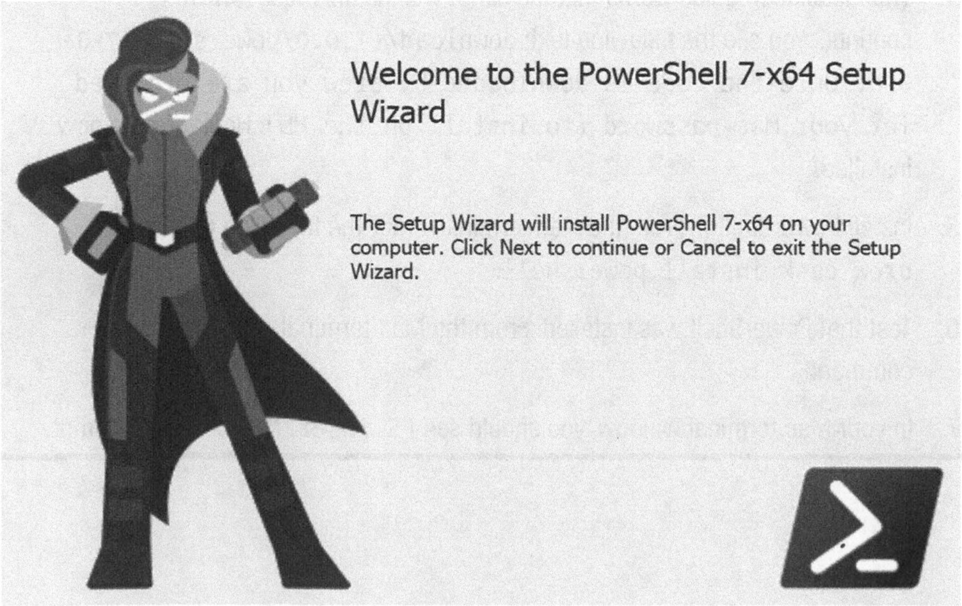

3. Continue using the install wizard. You should use the defaults to add PowerShell to the Windows path and support Event Logging. Click **Install** and when prompted, click **Complete** to start the PowerShell command-line window.

Azure Storage Explorer

Azure Storage Explorer is a cloud tool that can run locally. It is installed on your cloud engineering laptop to access Azure storage accounts. It allows you to visualize the storage files from the GUI (graphical user interface). You can download and install Azure Storage Explorer (see Figure 8-3) for macOS, Linux, and Windows from `https://azure.microsoft.com/en-us/features/storage-explorer/`.

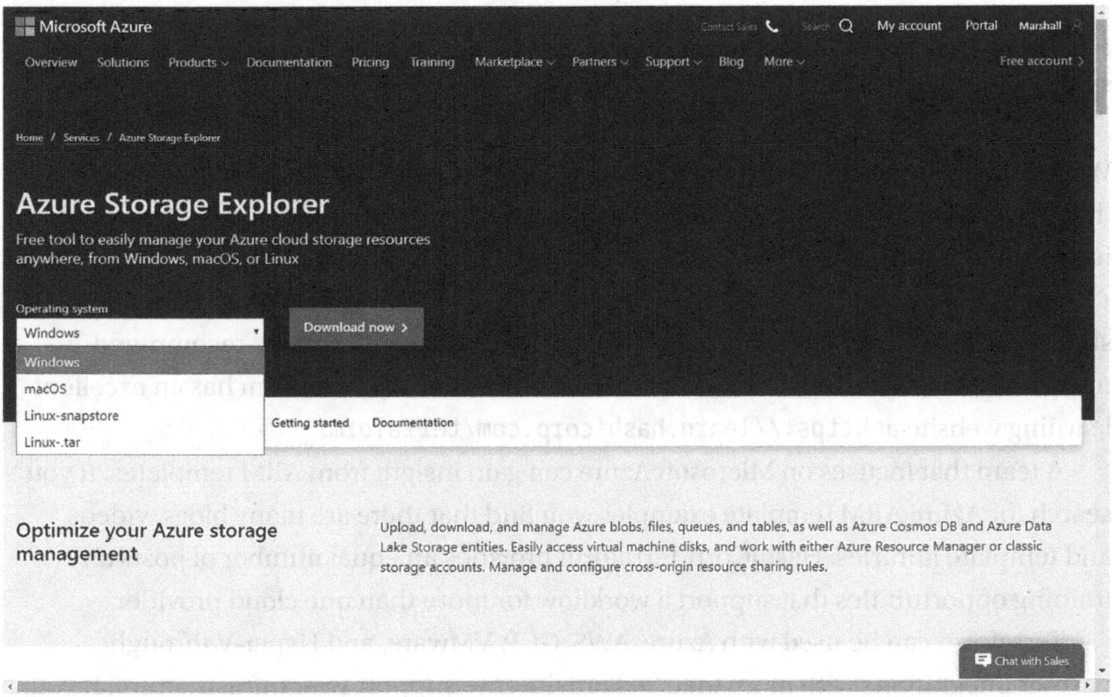

***Figure 8-3.** Azure Storage Explorer download page—select OS options shown*

Azure Storage Explorer is also available from your Azure portal. Simply open the portal and search for Storage Explorer, as shown in Figure 8-4.

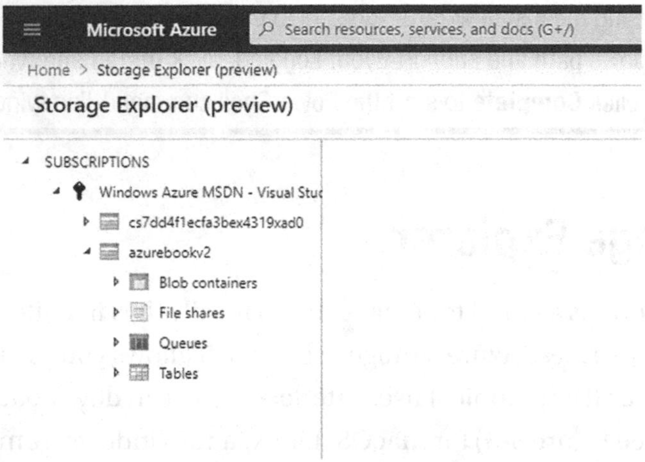

Figure 8-4. *Azure portal view of Azure Storage Explorer*

Azure Resource Manager (ARM) and HashiCorp Terraform

We start this discussion about the necessary tools to support IaC. We recommend that you read this overview and then go to the exercises in Chapter 11, which is about infrastructure as code.

You learned how to install Microsoft Visual Studio Code in this chapter, and Chapter 11 shows you how to configure both ARM and HashiCorp Terraform. We recommend using both, but if you do not have skills in either, HashiCorp Terraform has an excellent learning website at `https://learn.hashicorp.com/terraform`.

A team that focuses on Microsoft Azure can gain insight from ARM templates. If you search for Azure ARM template examples, you find that there are many blogs, videos, and template libraries. HashiCorp Terraform provides an equal number of posts and training opportunities that support a workflow for more than one cloud provider.

Terraform can be used with Azure, AWS, GCP, VMware, and Hyper-V through partner integrations with more than 200 providers to support your infrastructure. If your company needs a solution for a multicloud environment, creating a service delivery process that requires a change in cloud providers is an amazing concept.

One great feature for ARM template, from a file langue, JavaScript Object Notation (JSON) files, then deployment supports consistent infrastructure utilization, a known baseline from a library you create and maintain with version control. Templates can be maintained in a private repository, like Azure Blob storage or GitHub, and used in

Azure as a supported version. A *supported version* means that your team built the ARM template, tested it, and gave it a version control number, and can now deploy, delete, and redeploy with the same results.

HashiCorp Terraform modules use a file language called HashiCorp Configuration Language (HCL). The language syntax is structured like HTML, but it is human-readable to leverage IaC deployment to Azure or other clouds using nearly the same syntax. Let's look at two syntax examples (see Listings 8-1 and 8-2) to understand it better. The HCL "resource" is the declaration syntax public clouds.

Listing 8-1. HCL Using Azure Provider to Create a VNet

```
provider "azurerm" {
        version = "~>1.32.0"
}

resource "azurerm_virtual_network" "vnet" {
   name                = "azurebookv2"
   address_space       = ["10.0.0.0/24"]
   location            = "westus"
   }
```

Listing 8-2. HCL Using AWS Provider to Create a VNet

```
provider "aws"  {
    version = "~>2.0"
   regions = "us-west"
}

resource "aws_vpc" "azurebookv2" {
   cidr_block = "10.0.0.0/24"
}
```

In these examples, you declare the provider to use with HashiCorp Terraform. The HCL resources are different: AWS syntax vs. Azure syntax. HashiCorp uses HCL as a great middle-ground between readability and JSON files with all the necessary parentheses and curly brackets. With HashiCorp Terraform installed on the Azure portal, there are four main commands to run in the command-line interface (CLI) (see Chapter 11).

- `terraform init`: Initializes terraform configuration (in the VS Code directory)
- `terraform plan`: Shows what the deployment would look like but don't deploy
- `terraform apply`: Deploys the module into Azure
- `terraform destroy`: Deletes the Azure infrastructure

The "terraform plan" feature is nice to use on Azure; it provides information on what changes are going to be provisioned if you use "terraform apply". It is often used as a check or validation point to let you know how your Azure environment is going to change. It reviews the environment state and compares it to the Terraform module that you want to apply. The "plan" feature is native in HashiCorp Terraform but it is not a native feature in Microsoft PowerShell. Chapter 11 provides more information and examples that deploy code to get a better sense of its use and help you decide what is right for you and your team.

Version Control

Version control is necessary to maintain a known good infrastructure deployment template or module. GitHub is one of the online locations that provide a platform to support IaC versioning because it uses Git for control. Git filesystem is different than a traditional patch, where a file is replaced. Git records all the files and changes, tracking using in snapshots. Each commit to a project records the full "tree" state.

You can configure Terraform Professional to connect to GitHub using the OAuth workflow in Microsoft Azure Active Directory. The changes between GitHub and Terraform Pro are shared through the version control software (VCS) layer. Webhooks provides change notifications and triggers secure ingress and egress based on the managed permissions. HCL supports creating modules directly in GitHub. Listing 8-3 is an example code snippet.

Listing 8-3. Terraform Pro HCL Code Snippet for GitHub

```
Resource "github_repository" "harris-soh-copeland-puca" {
  Name          = "harris-soh-copeland-puca"
  Description  = "Azure Intelligent Cloud 2 Edition"
```

```
    private       = true
    template   {
    owner         = "github"
    repository    = "terraform-module-template"
    }
}
```

Version control is necessary for all of your code, including IaC templates or modules, but to start using GitHub, you need to install the service.

INSTALL GITHUB FOR WINDOWS

1. Open your browser and go to `https://desktop.github.com/`. Click the **Download for Windows (64bit)** executable. GitHubDesktopSetup.exe.

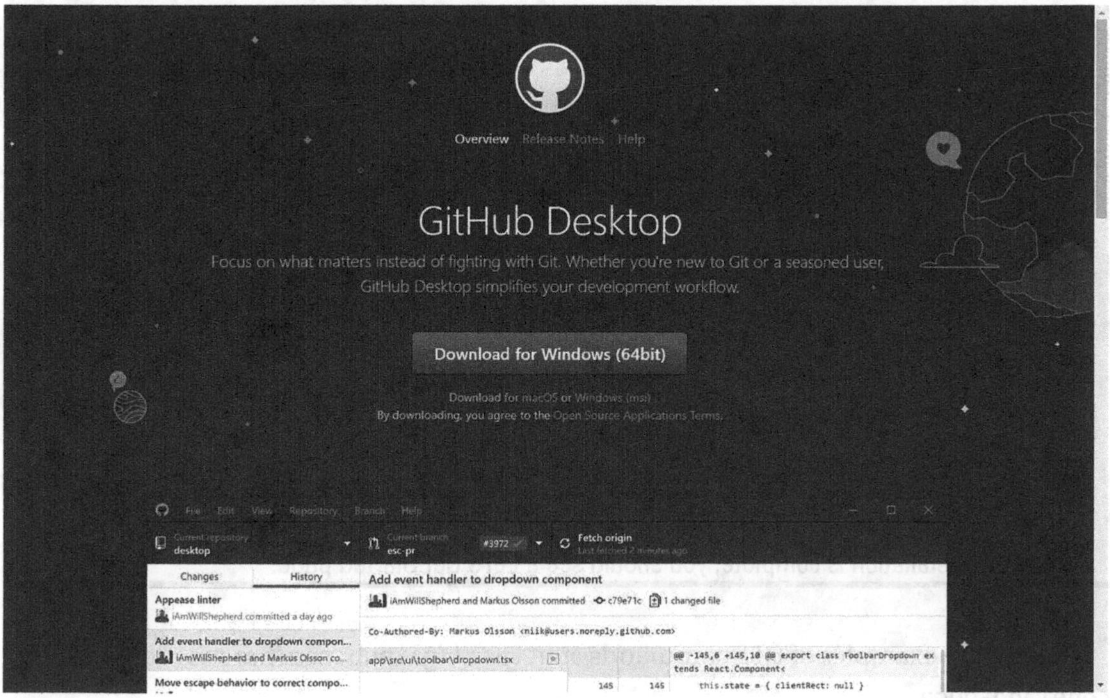

2. Click **Open** and then **Run**. You should follow the on screen prompts to complete the install. It is recommended to select the option to install Git Bash for Windows. This allows the use of Git command line commands and is more commonly used in DevOps teams.

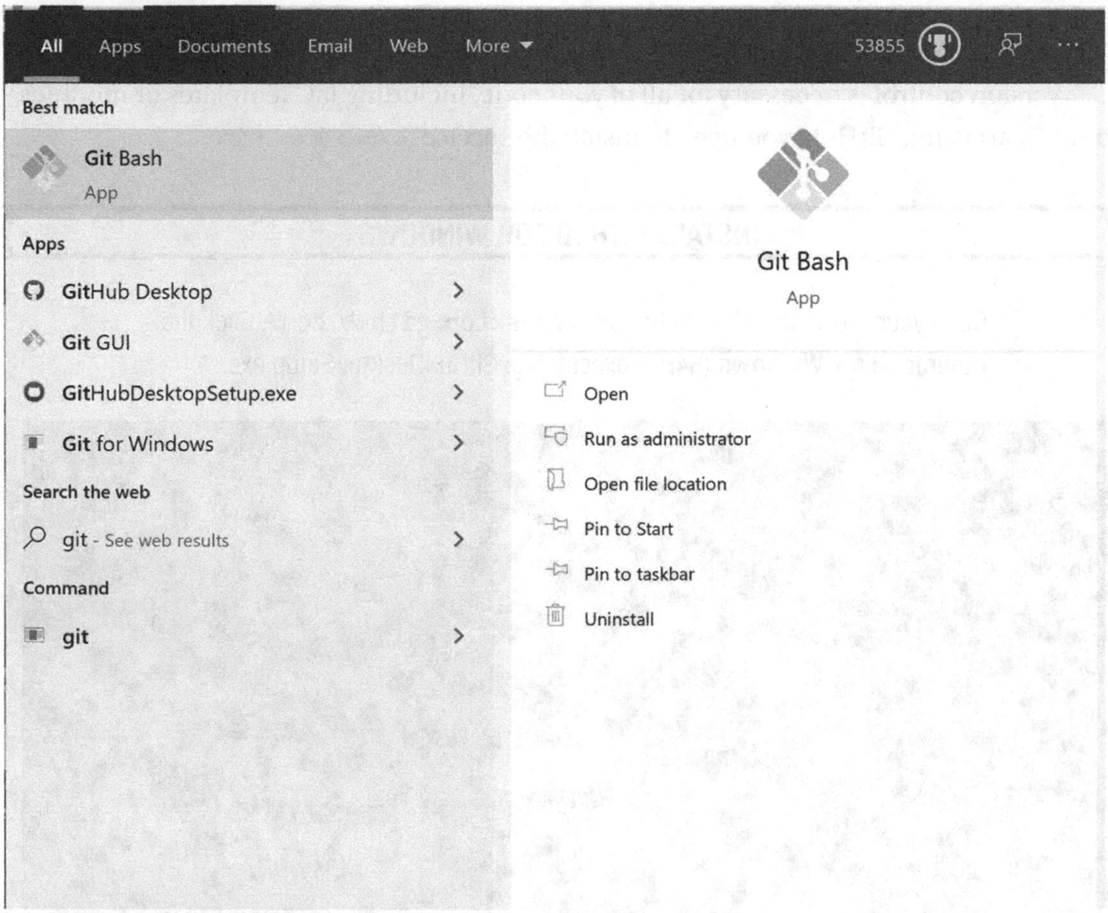

Once the installation is complete, you should see a Let's Get Started page.

There are examples of GIT commands at `https://github.com/harris-soh-copeland-puca`.

Summary

In this chapter, you were introduced to new cloud roles and learned how they relate to the traditional on-premises roles in IT operations. You now understand how the responsibilities of a traditional developer are used in a cloud engineer's role. You were introduced to many online training platforms that support these new cloud roles and reminded of the value of traditional classroom training. Customized training from Microsoft and Azure cloud "boot camps" by cloud providers were presented.

You then began installations to build your cloud engineering laptop with the tools needed to support cloud engineering roles. The operating system—Mac or Windows—is not a barrier. You learned that all the tools install in both OS options. You were introduced to ARM templates and Terraform modules, and you learned about supporting version control through GitHub.

You should start with the build on your laptop and then create a plan to use the tools from an Azure bastion host, which is discussed in an article on the GitHub repository (`https://github.com/harris-soh-copeland-puca`). You can read more about bastion-host region availability and support at `https://docs.microsoft.com/en-us/azure/bastion/bastion-faq`.

PART III

Using Azure for Infrastructure as a Service (IaaS)

CHAPTER 9

Implementing Azure Networking

Azure has multiple methods in which administrators can connect to their on-premises environment and extend their datacenter into the cloud. Different workloads, security considerations, and routing requirements of the various use cases may warrant a combination of a few different types of connections.

Azure hybrid networking includes

- Azure virtual network
- Azure Load Balancer
- Azure DNS
- Azure ExpressRoute
- Azure Traffic Manager
- Azure VPN gateway
- Azure Application Gateway

Connections directly over the Internet, VPN, and private ExpressRoute circuits are all options—and each has its unique nuances. We'll review this in this chapter. Figure 9-1 features four high-level Azure connectivity methods.

J. Soh et al., *Microsoft Azure*, https://doi.org/10.1007/978-1-4842-5958-0_9

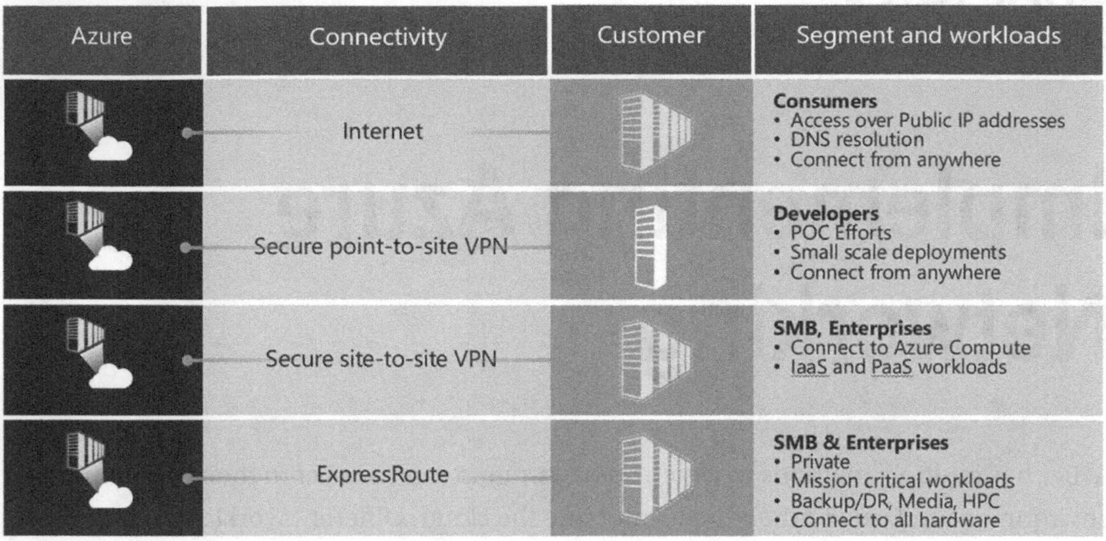
Azure
Connectivity
Customer
Segment and workloads
Internet
Consumers
• Access over Public IP addresses
• DNS resolution
• Connect from anywhere
Secure point-to-site VPN
Developers
• POC Efforts
• Small scale deployments
• Connect from anywhere
Secure site-to-site VPN
SMB, Enterprises
• Connect to Azure Compute
• IaaS and PaaS workloads
ExpressRoute
SMB & Enterprises
• Private
• Mission critical workloads
• Backup/DR, Media, HPC
• Connect to all hardware

Figure 9-1. *Azure hybrid networking connectivity types*

Internet Connectivity

Internet connectivity is the most basic method of connecting to Microsoft Azure. As shown in Figure 9-2, all the Azure PaaS services utilize public IP addresses, which means that the DNS for the workload and the connectivity to it is available to anyone on the Internet. This also means that all Azure PaaS services can be consumed over the Internet. Azure IaaS services need to be NAT'd (network address translation) from the private IP address the workload has on the Azure virtual network to a public IP address on Microsoft Azure's "Edge," or external network, connected to the Internet.

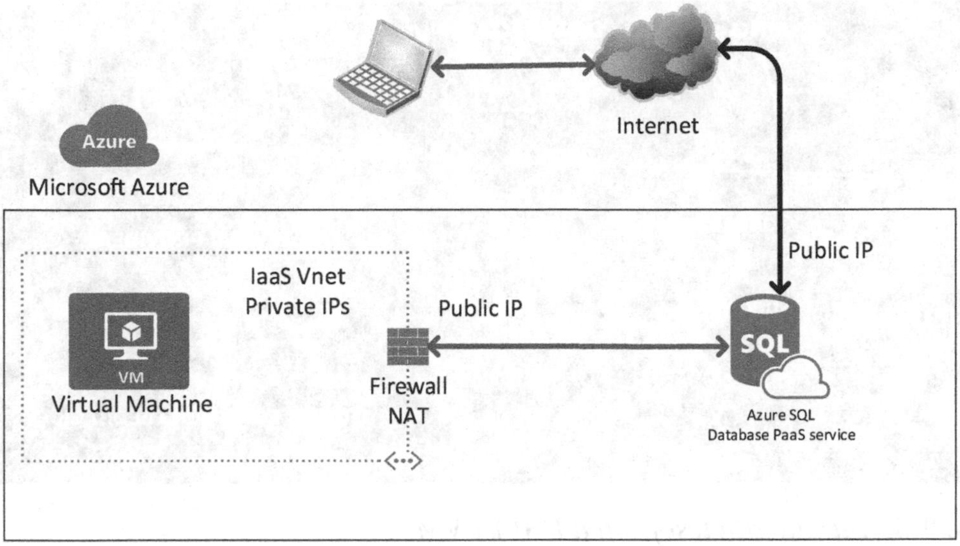

Figure 9-2. *Azure PaaS Internet connectivity from remote User and Azure VM*

Internet-based workloads in Azure work well for many use cases. When you don't need the workload to traverse a private or internal network, if the target user population of the workload is coming from the Internet, if the user population is a different organization, making the workload Internet-facing can have many advantages, including security. If you are making a workload external facing to "untrusted" systems and users, meaning they aren't managed by your organization, not coupling the Azure environment to your on-premises environment provides a security boundary. If a bad actor or malware were able to breach your workload, then the workload is all they would have access to, not on-premises.

Another advantage of Internet connectivity is the bandwidth available to the workload. This bandwidth is part of Microsoft's global network infrastructure, allowing high-speed, low-latency communication. Lower-end VMs typically see over 1Gbps down, over 500Mbps up, and extremely low latencies, as shown in Figure 9-3. This takes the burden off an on-premises Internet connection and reduces your on-premises exposure. When exposing workloads directly to the Internet, you get the full benefit of Microsoft's cybersecurity infrastructure, but you can still deploy your own security solutions if you want.

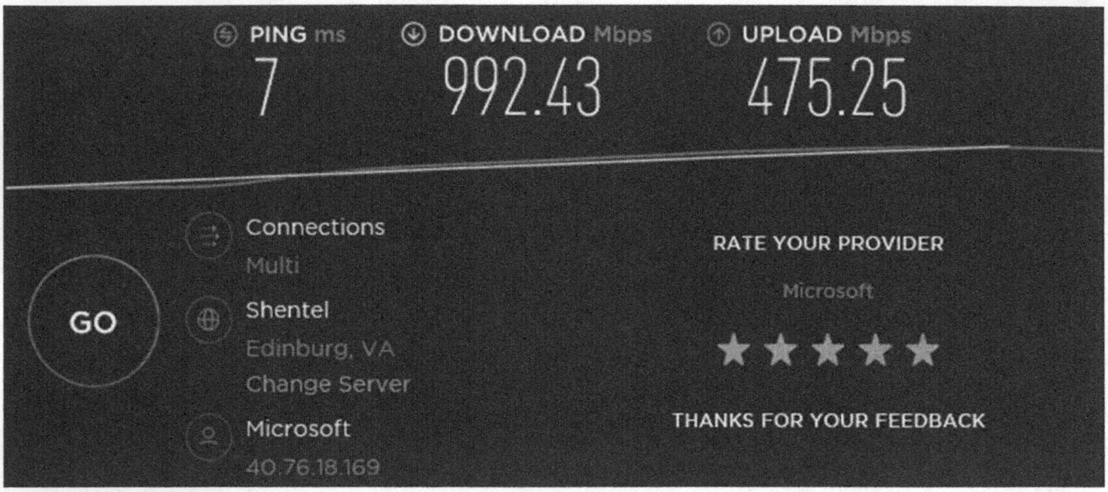

***Figure 9-3.** Bandwidth test from a DS1 v2 VM*

Azure VPN

VPN connectivity is frequently used when dedicated private circuits don't exist between locations that want to share IT services, such as Branch Offices or datacenters. VPN tunnels can either be initiated from the individual user's device from anywhere in the world, such as a coffee shop or house, known as Point-to-Site (P2S) VPN, or from an on-premises location to your on-premises datacenter. This is commonly referred to as a site-to-site (S2S) VPN tunnel, frequently used for "branch office" or low-cost office to office network connectivity. The key difference between P2S and S2S VPN tunnels is P2S VPN tunnels connect one resource to a remote datacenter or network, whereas S2S VPN tunnels connect many systems and users to a remote datacenter or network.

P2S and S2S VPN connections are designed to run over the Internet but can run on top of a private network connection. Both use the industry-standard protocols Internet Protocol Security (IPsec) and Internet Key Exchange (IKE). These protocols ensure the security of the connection. If the connection is broken or suspected of being tampered with, the connection drops as a security precaution. The connection then needs to be reestablished to continue communication to the remote endpoints or services. A P2S VPN connection usually requires the user to reinitiate the connection. You are likely familiar with this from having experienced this behavior on unreliable networks at hotels or cafés or having to use your smartphone as an Internet hotspot. S2S VPN connections usually have their tunnel reestablished automatically as soon as the first packets attempt to traverse the tunnel.

Azure VPN is provided by a service called a VPN gateway, which encrypts and sends all traffic to the on-premises location over the Internet, over Microsoft's ExpressRoute network connection, or between VNets in Azure (VNet-to-VNet). Azure virtual networks can only have one VPN gateway, just like a subnet can only have one default gateway address. Multiple networks can connect to a single Azure VPN gateway, thus allowing an administrator to create a virtual datacenter in the cloud and connect all their on-premises locations to it. This is the classic hub-and-spoke architecture, with the Azure virtual network as the hub. Figure 9-4 illustrates how different VPN connections can be used to join several different external resources to several cloud services.

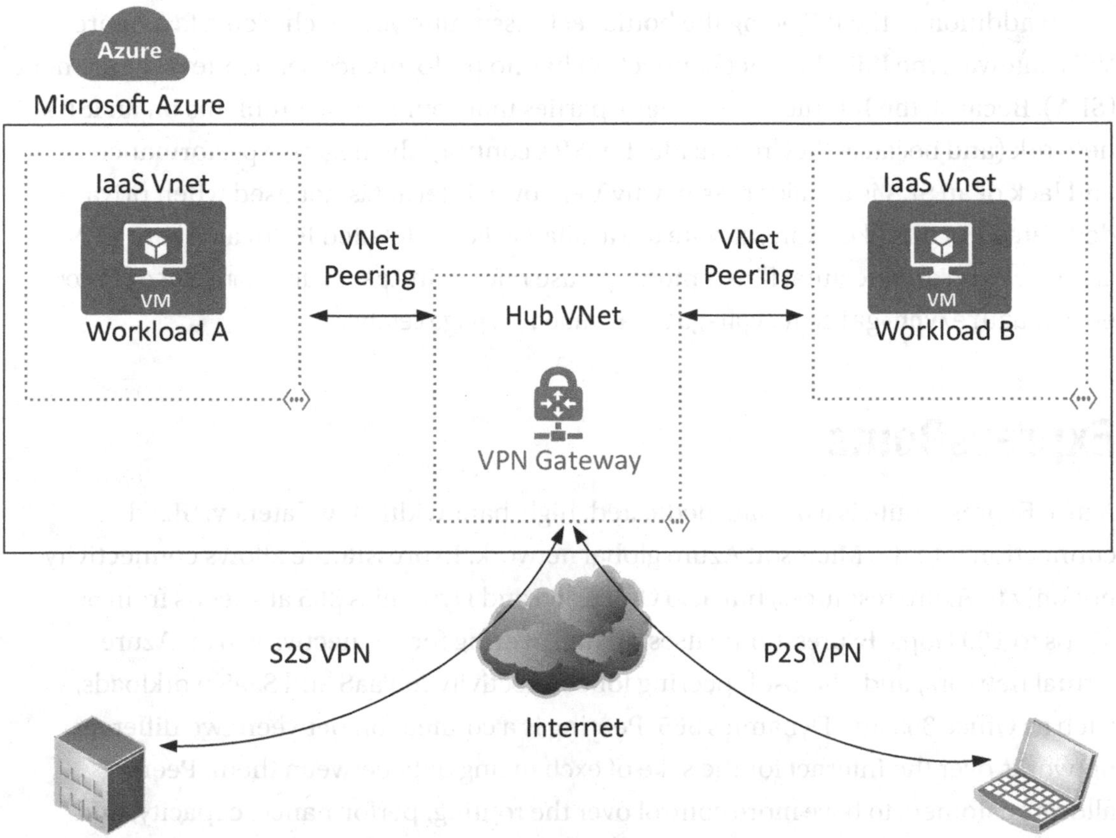

***Figure 9-4.** VPN hub and spoke topology*

A virtual network gateway is made up of VMs that are deployed to a specific subnet you create called the *gateway subnet*. The deployment of these VMs is the reason why standing up a VPN connection to Azure can take up to 45 minutes. The VMs provisioned when you create the virtual network gateway contain routing tables and run specific gateway services, which cannot be configured by administrators. Like all Azure services, if high availability is desired, administrators can deploy VPN gateways to Azure Availability Zones. This creates multiple gateways in an Azure region, which are physically and logically separated.

Azure VPN gateways come in several sizes, with varying performance metrics such as the number of concurrent connections, the connection speeds, and whether Zone Redundancy is an option for high availability. Azure VPN gateways range in speed from 100 Mbps to 10 Gbps. When Azure VPN gateways are used from on-premise to Azure, regardless of whether it is P2S or S2S, the Internet carrier is primarily responsible for the network latency and throughput; the ISP is usually the bottleneck.

In addition to the ISP being the bottleneck, assuming you've chosen a fast Azure VPN gateway, the ISP's Internet connection has no performance service-level agreement (SLA). Because the Internet has so many parties that could cause problems on an ISP's network (and because they're outside the ISP's control), the negative performance and lack of an SLA is a major reason why VPN-over-Internet is not used when private dedicated circuits like ExpressRoute are available. For a detailed list of all Azure VPN gateways and architectural illustrations, please refer to `https://docs.microsoft.com/en-us/azure/vpn-gateway/vpn-gateway-about-vpngateways`.

ExpressRoute

Azure ExpressRoute is a private, dedicated, high-bandwidth, low-latency, SLA'd connection into the Microsoft Azure global network. ExpressRoute allows connectivity not only to Azure resources, but also Office 365 and Dynamics 365 at speeds from 50 Mbps to 100 Gbps. ExpressRoute uses private peering for connectivity to an Azure virtual network, and Microsoft peering for connectivity to PaaS and SaaS workloads, such as Office 365 and Dynamics 365. Peering is a connection between two different networks over the Internet for the sake of exchanging data between them. Peering allows customers to have more control over the routing, performance, capacity, and redundancy. Therefore, the peering process is key to Azure services' connectivity when SLA high bandwidth or low latency is desired.

Microsoft updates the network addresses used for Azure PaaS workloads on a weekly interval, and SaaS services such as Office 365, on a monthly interval. Azure customers have one week of grace period to get these network addresses updated on their routing equipment. The use of the Border Gateway Protocol (BGP) allows the dynamic propagation of these routes as they change, further simplifying the administration needed for networking between the customer and the Microsoft Azure global network. BGP is used as the industry standard routing protocol whenever route changes need to be propagated quickly and frequently. This is common for cloud service providers due to their dynamic infrastructure. The following lists where Microsoft published these weekly network changes.

- Azure IP Ranges and Service Tags - Public Cloud
  - `www.microsoft.com/en-us/download/details.aspx?id=56519`
- Azure IP Ranges and Service Tags – US Government Cloud
  - `www.microsoft.com/en-us/download/details.aspx?id=57063`
- Office 365 URLs and IP address ranges
  - `https://docs.microsoft.com/en-us/office365/enterprise/urls-and-ip-address-ranges`
- Microsoft Dynamics CRM Online IP Address Ranges
  - `https://support.microsoft.com/en-us/help/2728473/microsoft-dynamics-crm-online-ip-address-ranges`

Each of the ExpressRoute routers can have ExpressRoute Private and Microsoft peering enabled for the various, IaaS, PaaS, and SaaS workloads, as shown in Figure 9-5. These IP ranges listed previously are added to the routers on the customer side of the connections illustrated in Figure 9-5. These routers are set up in an Active/Passive architecture. If they are utilized in Active/Active, the SLA is not supported.

In addition, ExpressRoute supports VPN failover for a redundant network connection. This allows customers to failover from ExpressRoute to a redundant VPN, with the understanding that the SLA on VPN is on the VPN gateway, not on the bandwidth.

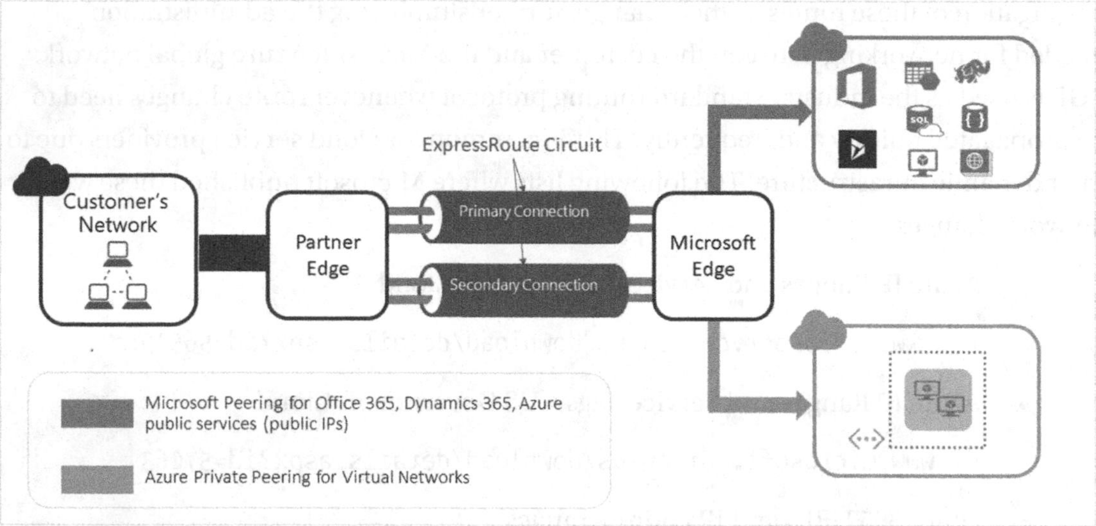

***Figure 9-5.** Peering types shown over the redundant ExpressRoute circuits*

In Figure 9-5, the ExpressRoute circuit connects the partner's Edge network to Microsoft's Edge network. This is an important point for clarification addressed earlier in the book. ExpressRoute connects one network to another; it does not connect a customer's enterprise network to an Azure "region." Route filters applied to the ExpressRoute connection determine what traffic can flow to and from Azure. Now that you understand the logical connections and routing domains to Microsoft Azure over ExpressRoute, we'll review how that works physically, in conjunction with the Internet and firewalls. Figure 9-6 depicts how logical connections work in parallel with the Internet.

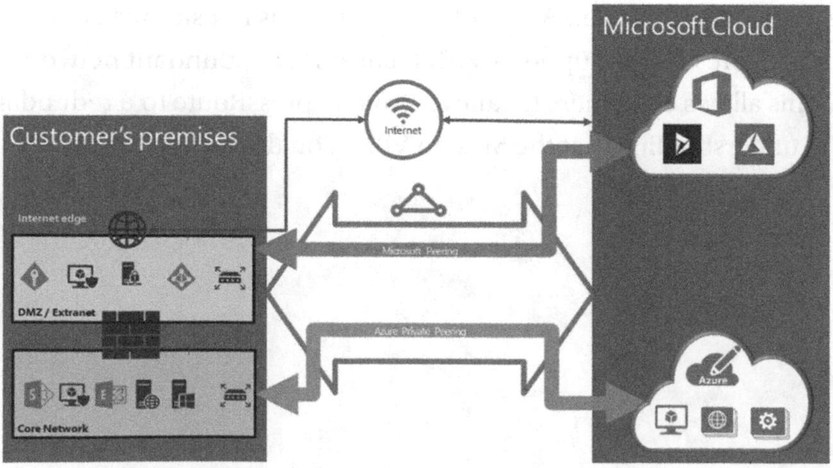

***Figure 9-6.** ExpressRoute peering topology*

In Figure 9-6, Microsoft peering from on-premises connects on the outside of the Internet-facing firewall, using a public IP address to peer with Microsoft's PaaS and SaaS services, which also use public IPs because they are Internet-facing. The private peering uses private IPs, as the name depicts, and comes from inside the environment to the IaaS VNet(s). Each of these peering types can be run in parallel, with multiple instances of each, or by themselves.

ExpressRoute locations are frequently referred to as peering locations, meet-me locations, or points-of-presence (PoP). These locations are managed by several Microsoft ExpressRoute partners, known as *connectivity providers*. AT&T, CenturyLink, Orange, and Tata Communications are a few of the connectivity providers.

At the time this chapter was written, there were 108 connectivity providers around the globe. Connectivity providers are usually ISPs, but many ISPs are not ExpressRoute connectivity providers. Each connectivity provider has specific locations that they make the Azure ExpressRoute service available, which is a subset of their actual public footprint. A detailed list of Azure ExpressRoute partners and peering locations is at `https://docs.microsoft.com/en-us/azure/expressroute/expressroute-locations-providers`. In Figure 9-7, Azure's public and enterprise ExpressRoute locations are different from the ones in the four Azure Government national clouds.

Figure 9-7. *Azure ExpressRoute meet-me locations for public and government clouds*

When you use an ISP not listed as a connectivity provider on the "Azure ExpressRoute partners and peering locations" page listed previously, customers can still connect to Azure through exchange providers. Exchange providers provide ExpressRoute at layer 2, or the data link layer, on the OSI model. We'll review Azure layer 2 ExpressRoute connections later in this chapter.

If ExpressRoute connectivity providers or exchanges aren't available in your geography, you may also connect to Azure through satellite operators. This should only be considered for Azure connectivity if lower latency options are not available. Satellite connectivity for ExpressRoute makes Azure one hop away but with a latency subject to the many hundreds of miles each way to communicate with the satellite. ExpressRoute over satellite may be the only option in locations like at sea or very remote locations of the globe.

ExpressRoute ports can be ordered in both a metered plan and an unlimited data plan. Both plans' costs include high-availability dual ports and are billed by the port speed monthly. ExpressRoute charges cited online and through billing reflect two ports on two routers. Both ExpressRoute data plans included unlimited ingress traffic, but only the unlimited data plan includes unlimited outbound traffic. The cost of egress traffic on the Metered Data plan varies by location. For example, North America is $0.025 per GB. A detailed breakout of ExpressRoute pricing is at `https://azure.microsoft.com/en-us/pricing/details/expressroute/`. ExpressRoute ports can be upgraded or downgraded at any time, but only upgrading the circuit can be done with no service interruption at this time.

Note Decreasing an ExpressRoute port speed requires deleting it and recreating a lower speed port. This causes service interruption.

Layer 2 ExpressRoute

Layer 2 ExpressRoute connections terminate a private circuit in a *cloud exchange*, where a cross-connect is established, usually between a customer's cage and the cloud exchange's cage for Microsoft Azure. Exchange providers (also referred to as *network service providers, fiber hotels, Internet exchange points*, or *peering points*) are where customers can bring in a circuit to their own infrastructure to exchange traffic with another network. The exchange providers' facilities are like colocations where circuits coming in from a customer, come into a cage for security reasons. The exchange provider runs cables from your cage to the cage where the Microsoft Azure global network is. This process of connecting through an exchange provider can drastically reduce connectivity and deployments times to approximately 30 days in some locations. Figure 9-8 depicts an Azure connection through an exchange provider.

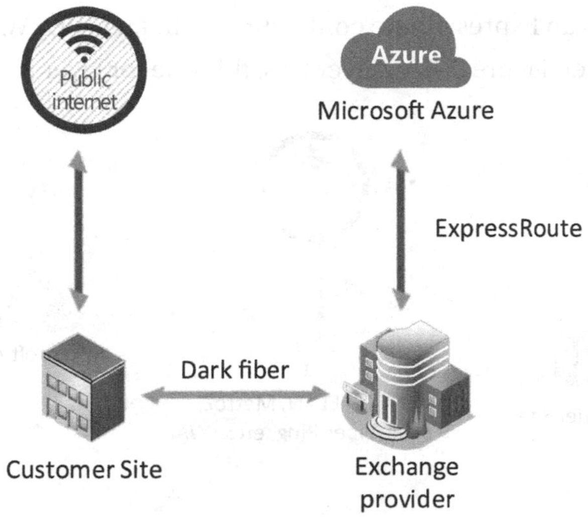

Figure 9-8. *Microsoft Azure ExpressRoute layer 2 connection*

The previous graphic illustrates the topology of the various pieces of a layer 2 ExpressRoute connection. Figure 9-8 does not depict the physical architecture for clarity reasons. For ExpressRoute connections to have an SLA, they must have two circuits with redundant routers on each end of the connection.

ExpressRoute has two connectivity models: layer 2 and layer 3. Layer 2 connectivity models are best used when a customer wants more granular control over the routing to and from the cloud or when they don't have a layer 3 network already in place. Layer 2 ExpressRoute connections require the customer to provide the networking equipment, and the expertise to configure that equipment.

Layer 3 ExpressRoute

Layer 3 ExpressRoute connections are usually part of a telco providers' Multiprotocol Label Switching (MPLS) network provided to the customer. The connections to Azure via ExpressRoute are merely ports on the mesh.

Think of an MPLS network as a spider web. Each connection on the spider web is a location on the WAN. If a single connection on the spider web is broken, that represents that location being offline, but no other location is affected. The other advantage of MPLS networks is the ability to create virtual direct connections across the WAN from one location to another, making them appear as a single hop, which you should notice by now, is what ExpressRoute does to Azure.

Figure 9-9 depicts an ExpressRoute connection from an MPLS WAN to Azure; note the differences between Figure 9-8 for layer 2 vs. this one for layer 3.

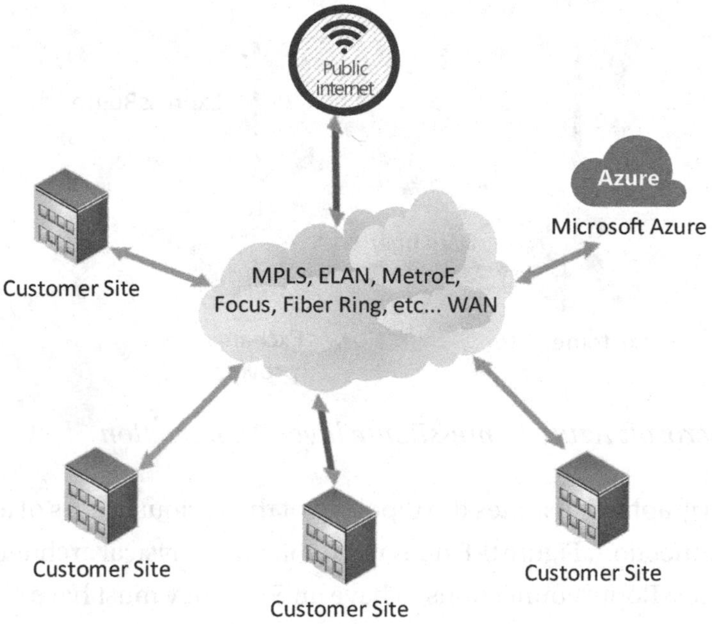

***Figure 9-9.** Microsoft Azure ExpressRoute layer 3 connection*

Layer 3 networks are usually managed by the telco, and the telco provides both the equipment and expertise for the configuration. Both the layer 2 and layer 3 ExpressRoute models require the use of two connections, between two routers on both the customer's and Microsoft's network edge, for a total of four identically configured routers, for Microsoft to guarantee the SLA. Point-to-point Ethernet connections are available to both layer 2 and layer 3 ExpressRoute customers, depending upon geography and the telco being used.

ExpressRoute Premium

ExpressRoute Premium is a collection of enhancements to the standard ExpressRoute service. ExpressRoute Premium is billed differently than the standard ExpressRoute. When using ExpressRoute for Office 365, the Premium SKU is required to support the increased routing requirement for all the Office 365 services. ExpressRoute Premium provides the following features.

- Increased routing table limit from 4000 routes to 10,000 routes for private peering
- Increased number of VNets and ExpressRoute Global Reach connections that can be enabled on an ExpressRoute circuit
- Connectivity to Office 365
- Global connectivity over the Microsoft core network

For more information on the thresholds of Azure services such as ExpressRoute, please refer to the "Azure subscription and service limits, quotas, and constraints" page at `https://docs.microsoft.com/en-us/azure/azure-resource-manager/management/azure-subscription-service-limits`. This is a page worth saving since the various service thresholds continually improve. For more documentation on ExpressRoute Premium, please refer to `https://docs.microsoft.com/en-us/azure/expressroute/expressroute-faqs#expressroute-premium`.

ExpressRoute Direct

ExpressRoute Direct is a special, turbo-charged version of ExpressRoute with ultra-fast port speeds. ExpressRoute Direct is only available from very select ExpressRoute locations, which is at `https://docs.microsoft.com/en-us/azure/expressroute/expressroute-locations`. The ports offered at these locations are dual 10 Gbps or 100 Gbps into the Microsoft global network. The ExpressRoute Locations page referenced here provides the most up to date list of which network Connectivity Provides support ExpressRoute Direct. ExpressRoute Direct may have the Premium add-on applied to it, and all other metrics are the same as standard ExpressRoute regarding egress and redundancy. The billing of ExpressRoute Direct is different than standard ExpressRoute ports since the billing starts 45 days after the port is requested, or once it is first used, whichever comes first. ExpressRoute Direct is provisioned through specific service providers at the defined locations, which enables fast onboarding. For a detailed list of the ExpressRoute Direct requirements and deployment workflow, please refer to `https://docs.microsoft.com/en-us/azure/expressroute/expressroute-erdirect-about`.

ExpressRoute Global Reach

ExpressRoute Global Reach is an Azure service that allows customers to network various on-premises locations across the Microsoft Azure global network. The various Microsoft networking partners provide the "last mile" to your locations. ExpressRoute Global Reach lets Azure be your WAN backbone. Figure 9-10 depicts how ExpressRoute Global Reach can connect your on-premises infrastructures. Without ExpressRoute Global Reach, customers connecting to Azure over ExpressRoute would only be able to connect to each other's Azure resources, not the on-premises resources.

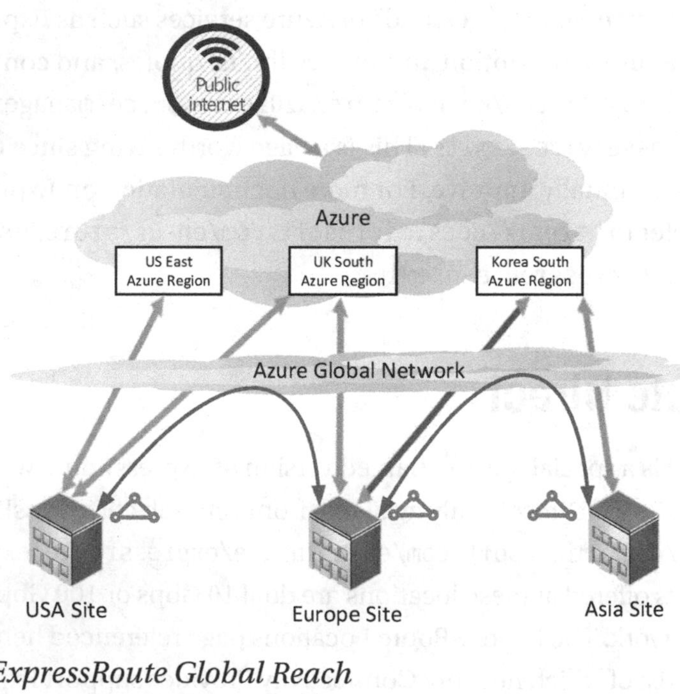

***Figure 9-10.** ExpressRoute Global Reach*

Note how in the previous figure, even the Internet is accessed via the connection to Microsoft Azure. This is not required for ExpressRoute Global Reach but was illustrated as an example of the networking possibilities when using Microsoft Azure. This Internet model could be applied to any of the ExpressRoute architectures if desired.

Implementing ExpressRoute

Creating an Azure ExpressRoute circuit in the Azure portal is quite easy, but remember that's only part of it. Follow these steps to create the ExpressRoute Circuit.

1. In the Azure portal, navigate to ExpressRoute Circuits and click **Add**.
2. Name the circuit.

Note Naming conventions should make it easy to understand which circuit to pick when selecting from several of them.

---

3. Choose the peering location.
4. Select the bandwidth that you plan to use. Remember that you can always upgrade with no service interruption, so start conservatively.
5. Select whether ExpressRoute Premium is required.
6. Select whether you want the unlimited egress traffic data plan.
7. Select the subscription.
8. Select the resource group.
9. Select the location in which you will be peering the Azure ExpressRoute circuit.
10. Click **Create**.

Figure 9-11 illustrates the form filled out to create the ExpressRoute circuit. Of course, like everything in Azure, this could have also been done as infrastructure as code.

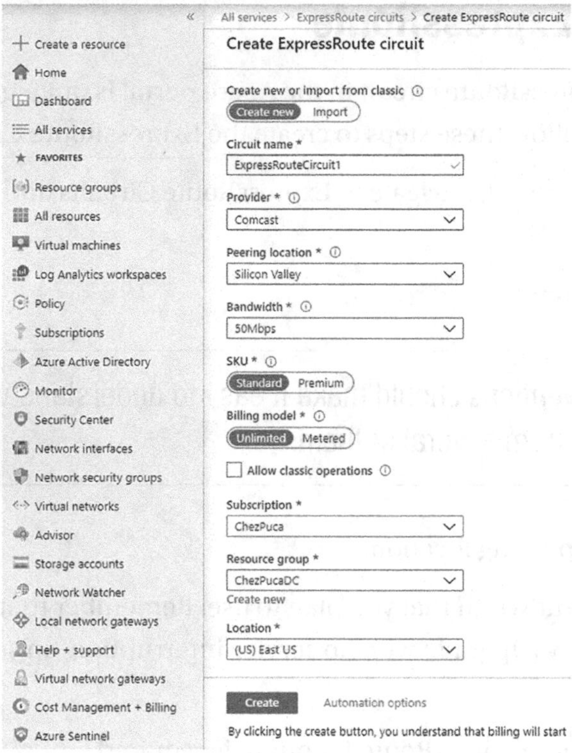

Figure 9-11. ExpressRoute circuit creation in the portal

Once the ExpressRoute circuit is created, the next step is to contact your network connectivity provider and provide them with the Service Key. There are a few key items you can view from the ExpressRoute circuit properties shown in Figure 9-12.

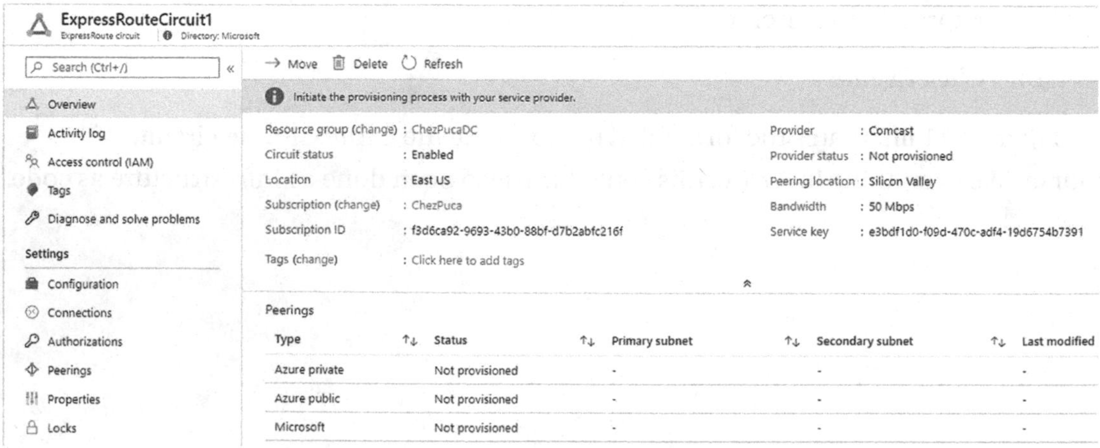

Figure 9-12. ExpressRoute circuit properties

The Subscription ID is needed for several things. This may be an individual subscription that your organization has set up for networking, to make it easy to track the charges or you may need to provide it to Microsoft for various support requests, such as enabling Microsoft peering for Office 365. The subscription can be scoped in Azure Cost Management and Billing. The service key is the GUID that must be provided to the connectivity provider to establish the connection. The connectivity provider may need other details such as VPN ID, VLAN ID, ASN, routing configuration if the provider manages, and so forth. In Figure 9-12, none of the peerings are provisioned. This is where administrators can check the status of their circuit as they work with their connectivity providers establishing the ExpressRoute connection. The ExpressRoute circuit status in the portal is the Microsoft side of the ExpressRoute connection.

Azure Virtual WAN

Azure Virtual WAN is a new Microsoft-managed cloud networking service that allows customers to connect multiple on-premises locations to Azure and network each of the on-premises locations together over the Microsoft Azure backbone in an automated and optimized fashion. Think of Virtual WAN as a competitor solution to an MPLS WAN, with the key differentiator being you still need the Telco for the last mile. Azure Virtual WAN allows Microsoft customers to use Microsoft as their WAN telco to the cloud and across their own WAN. Azure Virtual WAN implements a classic hub-and-spoke topology, where Azure is the hub, and each customer location is the end of a spoke.

Spokes can be

- On-premises locations
- Remote users
- VNets
- Internet

Azure Virtual WAN supports

- ExpressRoute
- S2S VPN
- P2S VPN
- VNet to VNet VPN

Azure Virtual WAN supports the following traffic flows.

- Branch to VNet
- Branch to branch
- Remote user to VNet
- Remote user to branch
- VNet to VNet
- Branch to hub to hub to branch
- Branch to hub to hub to VNet
- VNet to hub to hub to VNet

Azure Virtual WAN allows customers to choose their VPN endpoints are and which VPN *concentrator* in the Azure VNet is used. Azure Virtual WAN, illustrated in Figure 9-13, is like the MPLS network commonly used across enterprises today. Connections from on-premise don't connect to the VNet that the hub is associated with; they connect with the Hub itself. Virtual WAN endpoints must conform to the Azure VPN requirements of supporting IKEv2/IKEv1 IPsec. Azure Virtual WAN uses Azure Firewall to secure traffic. If customers want a third-party solution, they can use any of the Virtual WAN partner solutions for their software-defined WAN (SDWAN) provider. Azure Virtual WAN supports network virtual appliances (NVA), such as a Fortinet, in line from the Virtual WAN Hub, as a spoke that all traffic is routed through.

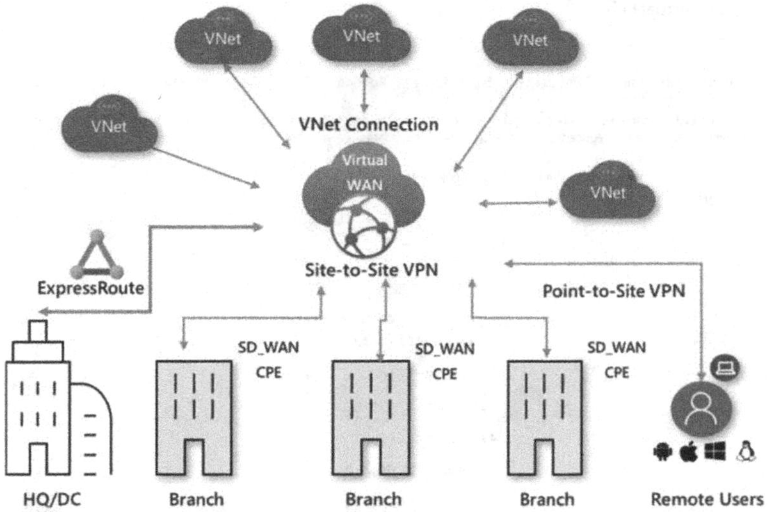

Figure 9-13. *Azure Virtual WAN spokes*

Azure Virtual WAN hub gateways are highly available and are defined by what Microsoft calls *scale units*. A virtual WAN gateway hub scale unit is a metric for how much throughput the gateway can handle. It is twice the number represented because, since it is highly available, there are two instances, and each has that throughput allocated to it. This means you should consider the size you choose as twice what you select. Figure 9-14 shows the Azure portal when defining the gateway scale unit.

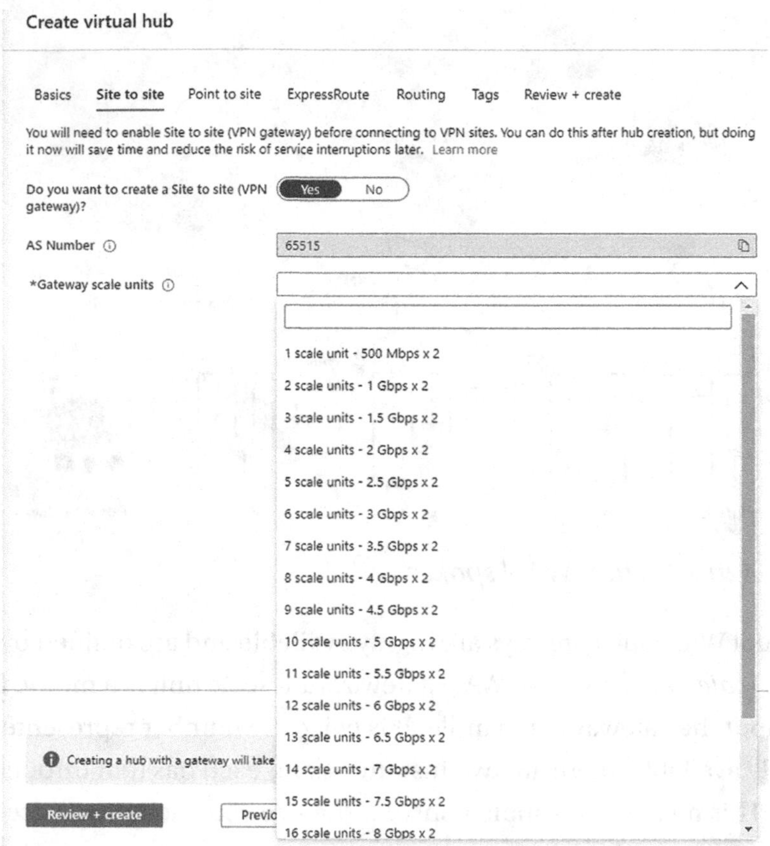

Figure 9-14. *Configuring Azure virtual WAN gateway*

Azure Virtual WAN P2S VPN connections can be performed via OpenVPN, which is an SSL VPN protocol and can be used from mobile devices such as Android, iOS 11.0+, Windows, Linux, and macOS 10.13+. Azure Virtual WAN P2S VPN connections can also be performed via IKEv2 connections.

For more information on Azure Virtual WAN, please refer to `https://docs.microsoft.com/en-us/azure/virtual-wan/virtual-wan-about`.

Implementing Network Security Groups

Network security groups (NSG) contain rules that allow or deny traffic to or from a resource within it. The resource NSGs can have the entire subnet or an individual VM as the resource it is controlling access to. A VM could end up having multiple NSG policies being applied to it at the subnet and VM level individually, making troubleshooting difficult sometimes. Diagnostic tools in Network Watcher (discussed next) make this easier to troubleshoot and administer.

The NSG is an SDN-based firewall solution that is configured, as shown in Figure 9-15. It is a very similar user experience as a firewall configuration. NSG policy is allowing inbound RDP traffic from any source to any source.

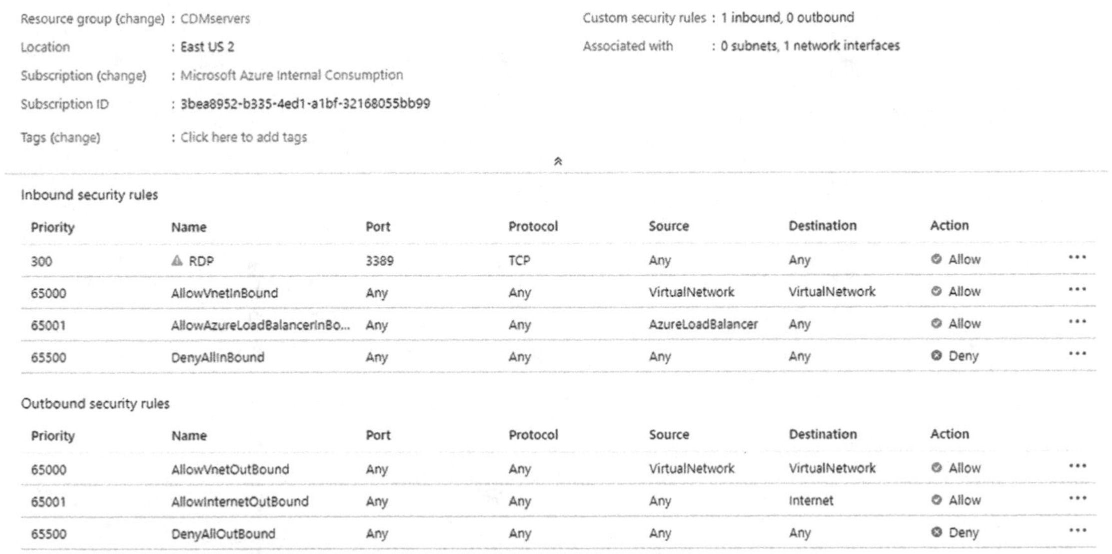
Resource group (change) : CDMservers
Location : East US 2
Subscription (change) : Microsoft Azure Internal Consumption
Subscription ID : 3bea8952-b335-4ed1-a1bf-32168055bb99
Tags (change) : Click here to add tags
Custom security rules : 1 inbound, 0 outbound
Associated with : 0 subnets, 1 network interfaces

Inbound security rules

Priority	Name	Port	Protocol	Source	Destination	Action
300	RDP	3389	TCP	Any	Any	Allow
65000	AllowVnetInBound	Any	Any	VirtualNetwork	VirtualNetwork	Allow
65001	AllowAzureLoadBalancerInBo...	Any	Any	AzureLoadBalancer	Any	Allow
65500	DenyAllInBound	Any	Any	Any	Any	Deny

Outbound security rules

Priority	Name	Port	Protocol	Source	Destination	Action
65000	AllowVnetOutBound	Any	Any	VirtualNetwork	VirtualNetwork	Allow
65001	AllowInternetOutBound	Any	Any	Any	Internet	Allow
65500	DenyAllOutBound	Any	Any	Any	Any	Deny

Figure 9-15. *NSG firewall rule configuration*

If you click NSG RDP Rule, a blade appears. It allows administrators to configure this specific NSG rule such that we can specify an IP address. Figure 9-16 illustrates how we can perform *port address translation* (PAT) on the inbound traffic to obscure the port we're exposing for RDP.

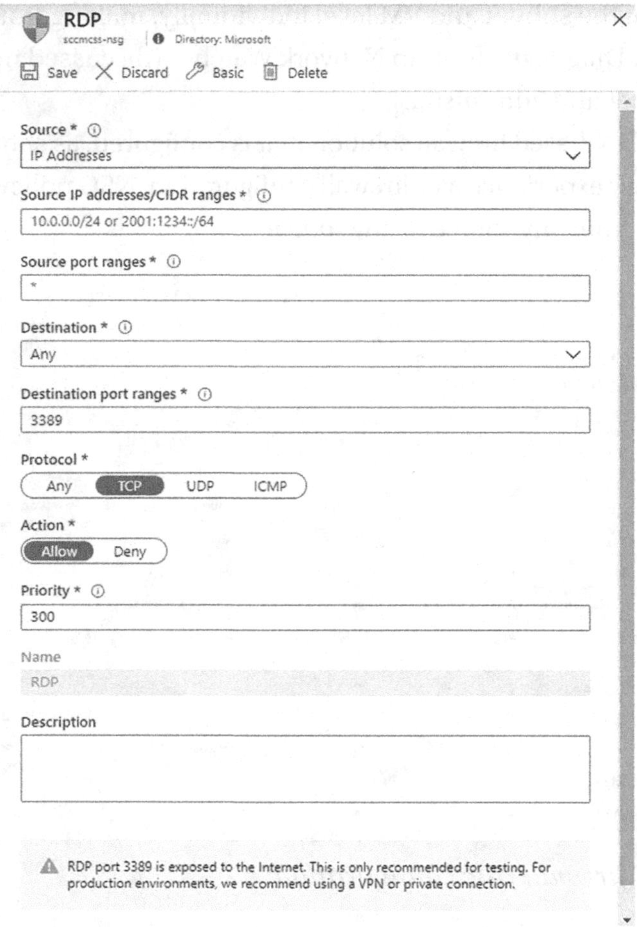

Figure 9-16. *NSG RDP rule modification*

Implementing Security and Monitoring for networks

Azure Network Watcher provides a series of tools to surface monitoring metrics on a variety of Azure IaaS networking resources such as virtual machines, virtual networks, application gateways, and load balancers. Azure Network Watcher will not work on Microsoft Azure PaaS resources. Azure Network Watcher is enabled automatically on the creation of a virtual network and allows administrators to diagnose problems on virtual machines, virtual networks, network security groups, and other resources by evaluating traffic flows, latencies, routing, traffic filtering, and other problems on these resources via diagnostic logging. These diagnostic logs are consumable in Azure Monitor and

Microsoft Power BI. For more information on Azure Application Gateway (AppGW) and network security groups, please refer to `https://docs.microsoft.com/en-us/azure/azure-monitor/insights/azure-networking-analytics`.

Network Watcher

Azure Network Watcher allows administrators to view resource-to-network relationships and network-to-network relationships; record the minimum, average, and maximum latencies over time; diagnose routing problems between VMs or virtual networks with *next hop* packet captures; test connectivity between network resources; troubleshoot and identify broken connections; and analyze network traffic logs from any network resource.

It allows administrators to enable diagnostic logging and IP flow, and verify packet capture and security group membership for Azure networking resources. This allows the manipulation of the resource's location, configuration, and sizing to evaluate those effects on performance. Since all the data from Azure Network Watcher is surfaced in Azure Monitor, alerts can be generated when specific counters or resources exceed a defined threshold. Figure 9-17 shows a simple RHES Linux VM running in Azure on a VNet protected by an NSG.

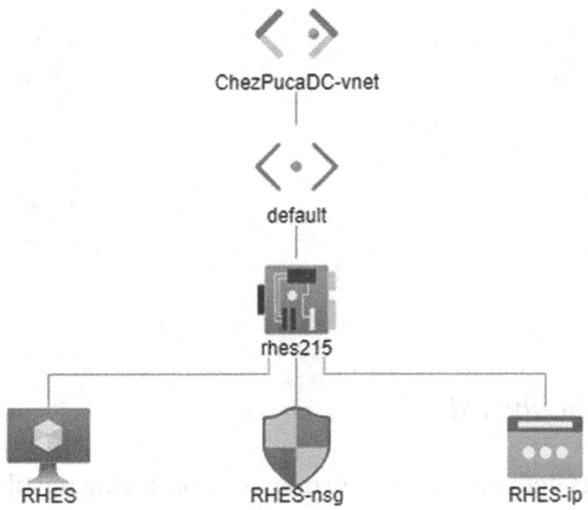

Figure 9-17. *Network Watcher topology view of a VM*

NSG flow logs allow administrators to view NetFlow, or ingress/egress, data per rule passing through the NSG. NSG flow logs can be enabled and configured per NSG, and each can have its data stored in its own Log Analytics workspace, or they can be combined. This is very useful in satisfying security requirements and regulatory compliance. NSG flow logs record five-tuple information about the flow (source/destination IP, source/destination port, and protocol) and if the traffic was allowed or denied. Administrators can choose to enable v2 of the NSG flow logs, which record bytes and packet data.

Network Performance Monitor

Network Performance Monitor (NPM) has been rolled into Network Watcher as a subcomponent. This allows administrators to have a single pane of glass, or single blade in the Azure portal, for all their network monitoring and administration. NPM is a hybrid monitoring solution that incorporates legacy stateful monitoring tactics with more dynamic approaches to monitoring endpoints and applications. Figure 9-18 illustrates the NPM dashboard.

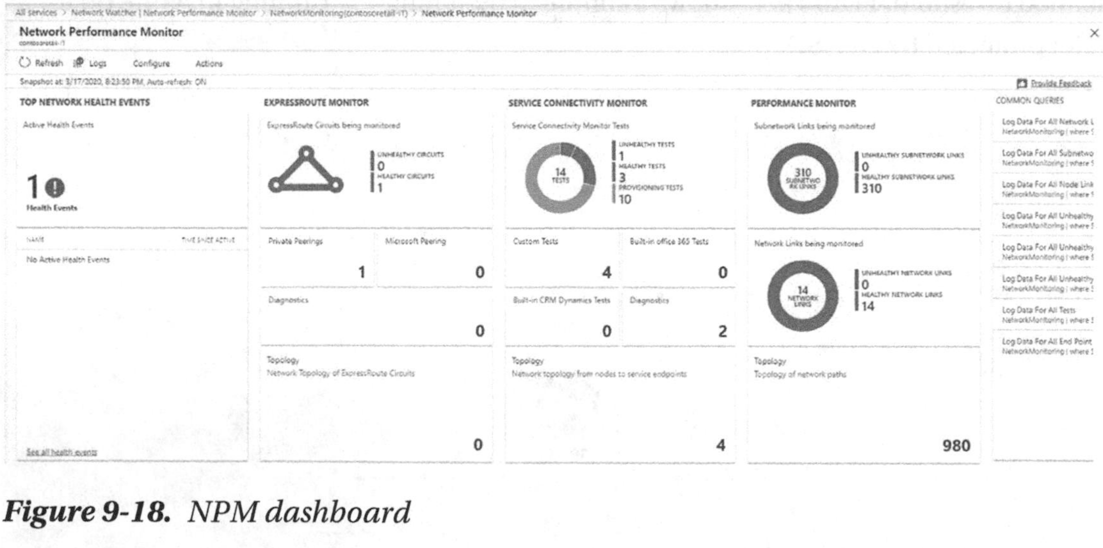

Figure 9-18. *NPM dashboard*

NPM, which has its network link performance-monitoring dashboard illustrated in Figure 9-19, can detect traffic blackholing, routing errors, and issues that conventional network monitoring methods aren't able to detect. NPM has three primary capabilities.

- *Performance Monitor*: Monitors across clouds and on-premises locations.

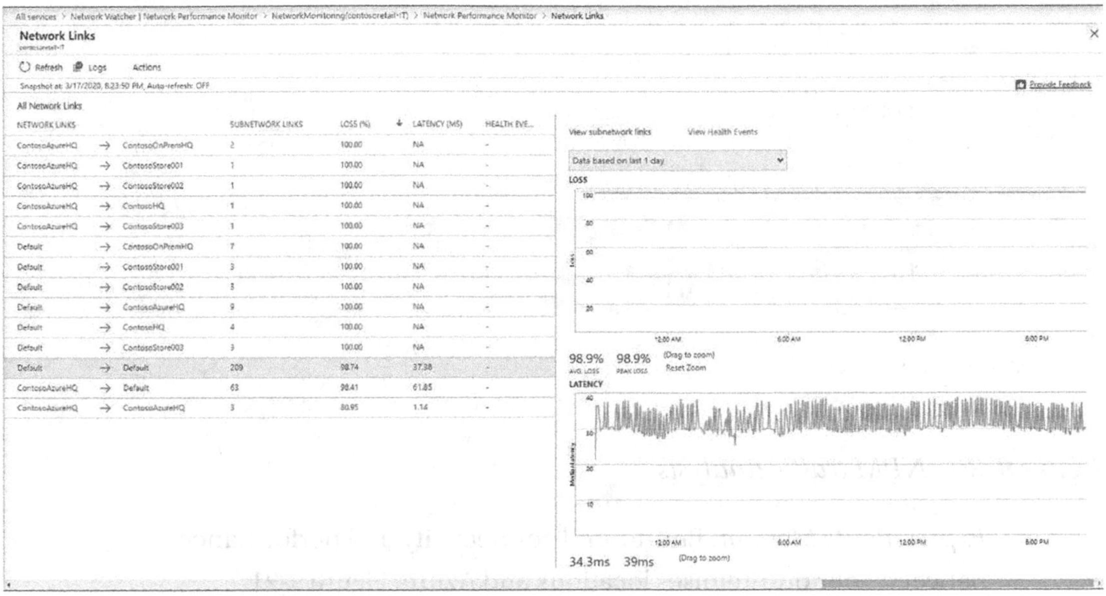

***Figure 9-19.** NPM latency and loss monitoring*

- *Service Connectivity Monitor*: Emulates a synthetic transaction from a user to a service, as illustrated in Figure 9-20. This is useful for identifying performance problems on applications as well as the end-user experience since you're testing from their endpoint, not within the same datacenter or network.

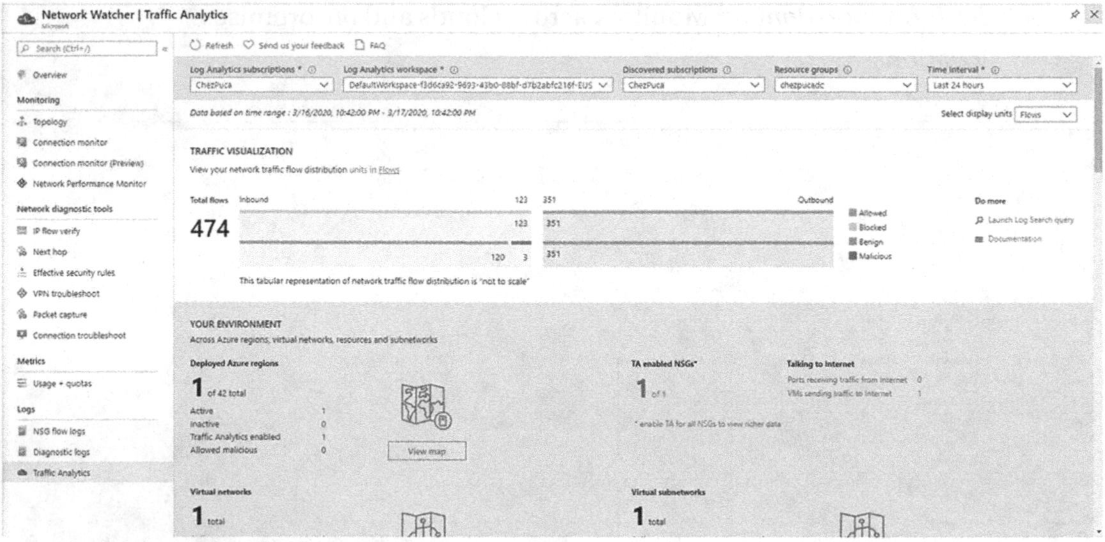

Figure 9-20. NPM traffic analysis

- *ExpressRoute Monitor*: End-to-end connectivity and performance between your on-premises locations and Azure. Figure 9-21 illustrates the global connectivity from the East US region.

NPM takes all the network monitoring capability built into Microsoft System Center Operations Manager and adds to it by leveraging cloud scale and analytics.

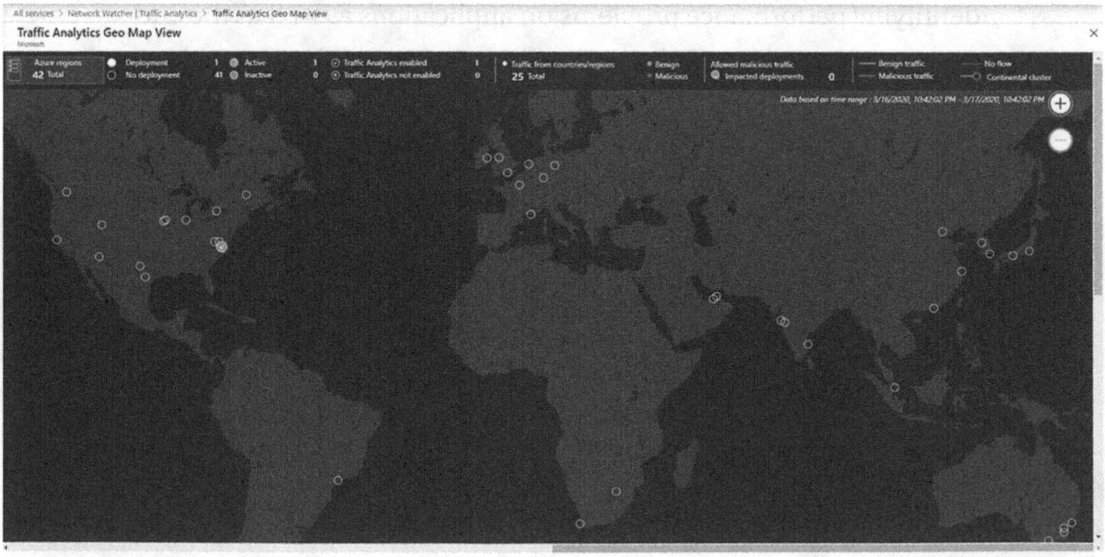

Figure 9-21. NPM traffic analysis map view

NPM performs its work via the same agent used for Azure Monitor, the Microsoft Management Agent (MMA). MMA can be downloaded from your Azure portal in the Log Analytics workspace blade.

Once configured, by following the instructions at `https://docs.microsoft.com/en-us/azure/azure-monitor/platform/agent-windows`, administrators can start monitoring their endpoints, services, applications, and network devices without the heavy infrastructure requirement typically found in most solutions today. Figure 9-22 illustrates how NPM can monitor the individual hops, latency between hops, and routes on a given workload.

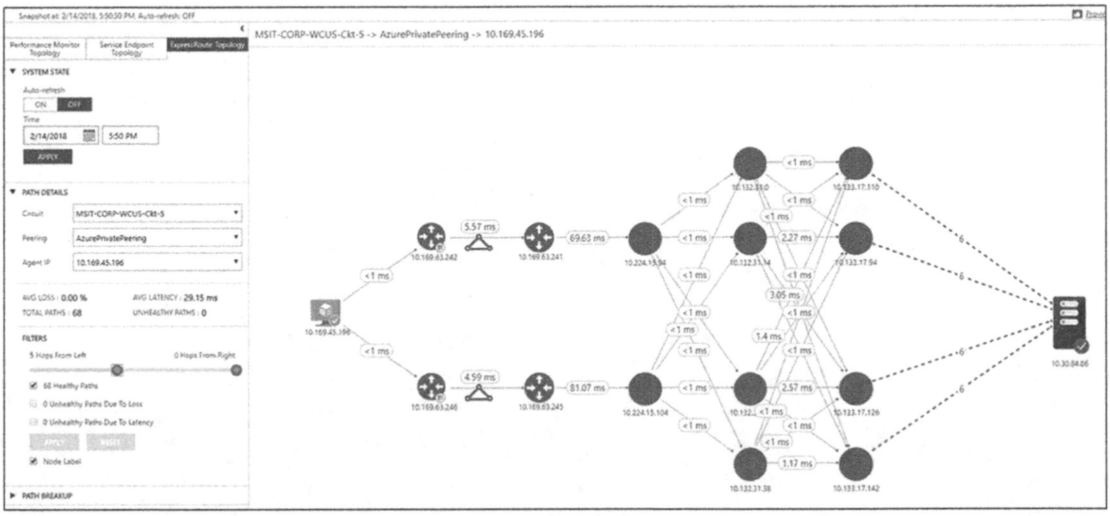

Figure 9-22. *NPM monitoring ExpressRoute layer 3 private peering*

Summary

We hope that you've seen that we can only scratch the surface of what's available in Microsoft Azure's networking portfolio. This should give you confidence that there is much more to the networking capabilities than we can cover in a single chapter. An entire book could be devoted to this topic. Microsoft has developed the second-largest network in the world, which shows in the solutions available to the customer—many of which are PaaS services that would have cost tens of thousands of dollars and countless hours to set up, maintain, and upgrade. To reiterate, all of this can be done as infrastructure as code and deployed via templates.

CHAPTER 10

Virtual Machines

Virtual machines (VMs) usually begin an organization's experience in the cloud because of a few key factors that make VMs the easiest cloud service to deploy. Most organizations have used virtualization on servers for more than a decade at this point, so there's a fair amount of familiarity with provisioning, operations, and management concepts.

VMs are a supported environment since the customer manages everything from the operating system up the stack. Tens of thousands of applications have been validated to run no differently on VMs. Microsoft and third-party vendors have had tools to migrate workloads from VMware, Citrix, Microsoft, and AWS virtualization solutions to Azure for many years.

Azure VMs run on a customized Hyper-V platform. The tools and processes are well used, understood, and trusted. Development and testing, applications running on VMs in the cloud, and extending your datacenter into the cloud are the top use cases for VMs in Azure.

In this chapter, we review some of the VM features released in Azure over the last few years. These new features include high availability, disaster recovery, scalability, monitoring, VM resources, and security. While this is not a complete list, we try to focus on the newer and more popular items that have received a lot of recognition from the global community.

Creating and Managing Virtual Machines

The life cycle of a VM in Azure is simple. Azure VMs can exist in several different states. These states determine whether the VM is available or not and if it is billed. This is important to understand because it directly impacts what you're billed for. Table 10-1 outlines the VM life cycle states and billing. It's worth repeating: we're talking about the billing of the compute, not the underlying storage, which is billed in blocks.

J. Soh et al., *Microsoft Azure*, https://doi.org/10.1007/978-1-4842-5958-0_10

Table 10-1. *VM Life Cycle State*

State	Description	Billing
Starting	Boot VM	Not billed
Running	Normal state of operational VMs	Billed
Stopping	Temporary state between "running" and "stopped"	Billed
Stopped	vHardware is still allocated to the VM and remains on the host	Disks are billed but compute is not
Deallocating	Temporary status	Not billed
Deallocated	VM has stopped, and vHardware is no longer allocated on host	Not billed

Costs for VMs vary by the series, size, Azure cloud, region, number of disks added to the VM, and if deployed from the Azure Shared Image Gallery (covered later in this chapter), and the amount and type of software preloaded in the VM.

Azure charges an hourly price for VMs based on processing power, memory, and storage capacity. For partial hours, Azure prorates to the minute.

Let's review reserved instances (RI). Azure Reserved Instances help you save money by committing to one- or three-year consumption plans on workloads such as Azure Compute. The commitment is targeted to specific subscriptions, resources groups, and VM series. Reserved instances are available on VMs and are specified as one- or three-year reservations. Azure reserved instances can save you up to 72% on the compute cost of Windows or Linux VMs due to the pre-committed nature of the reserved instance.

Let's agree to use 730 hours as the number of hours in a month; this equates to 30.42 days, which is the number we use for cost calculations due to the variety of 31-, 30-, and 28-day months. If you estimate the number of hours your workload runs, you find that usually 300 hours per month is the threshold. If you expect to run that many or more, Azure Reserved Instances is cheaper. You need to do this on a case-by-case VM series and size because Azure Reserved Instances are discounted differently depending on the series and number of cores.

It is safe to say that if you are running a workload all the time, or over half the month, it's a no-brainer that Azure Reserved Instances save you money. We have seen many examples where the three-year Azure reserved instance is cheaper than using a one-year and some pay-as-you-go due to the workload expected to retire in one or two years.

For more information on Azure reserved instances and how to apply them, please refer to `https://docs.microsoft.com/en-us/azure/cost-management-billing/reservations/save-compute-costs-reservations`.

Azure VMs have an industry-best monthly service-level agreement (SLA) of 99.9% for a single VM if you're deployed with premium storage. The SLA goes up to 99.95 when you have two or more VMs in an Azure Availability Set, which we cover later in this chapter. If you would like more specifics on any of Azure's services' SLAs, please refer to `https://azure.microsoft.com/en-us/support/legal/sla/`.

Operating Systems (Windows, Linux)

Microsoft Azure supports various Microsoft and Linux distributions. What Microsoft supports as an operating system environment (OSE) in Azure is different than what is supported on-premises, available in the Azure Shared Image Gallery, and the Marketplace. Each location has a unique list of systems that can be deployed, some of which in the marketplace are running hardened, proprietary OSEs, such as those made by firewall vendors for network virtual appliances (NVA).

Azure has many services, such as Azure Security Center and Log Analytics, that can run in a hybrid architecture, which means that they can run on VMs in Azure, as well as VMs and physical servers on-premises or in other cloud providers. This results in a very complicated support architecture. Microsoft supports only 64-bit OSEs in Azure. In early 2020, Microsoft supported the following Windows operating systems.

- Windows Server 2019
- Windows Server 2016
- Windows Server 2016 Core
- Windows Server 2012 R2 (64-bit)
- Windows Server 2012 (64-bit)
- Windows Server 2008 R2 (64-bit)
- Windows 10 (64-bit)

Microsoft maintains a subset of this list in the Azure Shared Image Gallery for customers to deploy images of these OSEs that have been patched and updated, from Microsoft directly, to minimize the gap of updates needed once the VM is deployed to make it current. The following OSEs are not available in the Azure Shared Image Gallery.

- Windows Server 2016 Core
- Windows Server 2012 (64-bit)
- Windows Server 2008 R2 (64-bit)

Note The (64-bit) instances listed are because that OS included a 32-Bit version.

Contrary to popular belief, Azure IaaS is not only for Microsoft-based OSEs. Microsoft has approximately 50% of the VMs in Azure running some version of a Linux distribution. Three years ago, that number was 40%. The following lists the Linux distributions available to Azure customers as of spring 2020.

- CentOS 6.3+, 7.0+, 8.0+
- CoreOS 494.4.0+
- Debian 7.9+, 8.2+, 9, 10
- Oracle Linux 6.4+, 7.0+
- Red Hat Enterprise Linux (RHEL) 6.7+, 7.1+, 8.0+
- SUSE Linux Enterprise (SLES)/SLES for SAP 11 SP4, 12 SP1+, 15
- openSUSE Leap 42.2+
- Ubuntu 12.04+

Microsoft requires Linux distribution manufacturers to update their images quarterly at a minimum. This is a more frequent cadence than what is seen from Linux distributors when comparing to the cadence of their version releases. Microsoft also works with these manufacturers to tune" their kernels for the Azure platform, incorporating new features and performance improvements. Azure-tuned Kernels include those from CentOS, Debian, SLES, and Ubuntu. For more information on the specifics of endorsed Linux distributions in Azure, please refer to `https://docs.microsoft.com/en-us/azure/virtual-machines/linux/endorsed-distros`.

Shared Image Gallery

The Shared Image Gallery is a service managed by Microsoft that replicates the images globally and exposes the gallery to customers at the tenant level, allowing RBAC to be utilized in the Shared Image Gallery across subscriptions. The Shared Image Gallery supports the versioning of images to facilitate change and release management across your cloud infrastructure. The Shared Image Gallery has a few resource types that assist in the management of your enterprise images in the cloud. The following list details these Resources and their purpose.

- *Managed image*: A basic image made from a Sysprep VM via the Windows Sysprep.exe tool or a generalized VM that allows repeated creation of VMs from a single image in storage. Figure 10-1 shows the Sysprep tool user interface. Linux systems use the Microsoft Azure Linux Agent waagent utility. The purpose of Managed Images is to quickly build VMs and preload apps and load configurations to minimize deployment times when the same installs and configurations are needed. For more information on how to use Sysprep to generate generalized installs, please refer to `https://docs.microsoft.com/en-us/windows-hardware/manufacture/desktop/sysprep--generalize--a-windows-installation`.

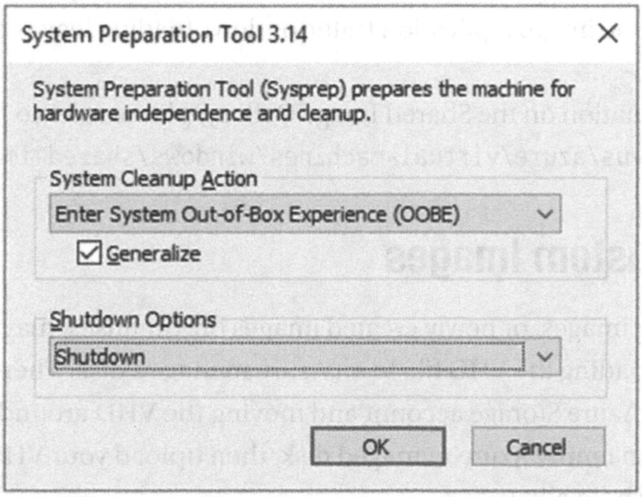

Figure 10-1. *Sysprep tool for master image preparation*

- *Snapshot*: A copy of a VHD that is in a deployed state. It is good for backing a point in time of a VM or a VHD that you may want to go back to for regression testing, rollback, cloning a disk, and so forth.

- *Image gallery*: A repository integrated into the Azure portal's virtual machines' service blade for managing and sharing images.

- *Image definition*: A description field where you can include information like the operating system, configurations, and release notes. The Image Definition field has three mandatory parameters for grouping and other management tasks: publisher, offer, and SKU. There are an additional nine optional parameters that may be used for easing resource tracking.
- *Image version*: Creates a VM when using a gallery. Multiple versions of an image are supported to make differencing the images as easy as possible.

Azure Shared Image Gallery includes high thresholds: 100 per subscription per region, 10,000 image versions per subscription per region, deployments up to 1000 VM instances in a single virtual machine scale set. It also leverages zone-redundant storage (ZRS) to mitigate entire zone failures in regions with Availability Zones, which we cover later in this chapter. Azure Shared Image Gallery may replicate from one Azure region to another automatically, making your images available locally to remote regions and workforces. The only billing associated with Shared Image Gallery is the storage and egress traffic when the image replication traffic or downloading leaves the Azure region it is located in.

For more information on the Shared Image Gallery, please refer to `https://docs.microsoft.com/en-us/azure/virtual-machines/windows/shared-image-galleries`.

Uploading Custom Images

Customer's existing images, or newly created images on-premises, may be uploaded to Azure easily by uploading the VHD file to an Azure managed disk. There is no longer a need to stage in an Azure Storage account and moving the VHD around afterward. Now you merely create an empty Azure managed disk, then upload your VHD to it, if it isn't over the 32 TB threshold allowed.

To upload your own custom on-premises images to Azure, follow these directions.

1. Download the latest version of AzCopy v10 from `https://docs.microsoft.com/en-us/azure/storage/common/storage-use-azcopy-v10#download-and-install-azcopy`.
2. Install the Azure CLI from `https://docs.microsoft.com/en-us/cli/azure/install-azure-cli?view=azure-cli-latest`.

3. Upload a VHD file. You can easily create one on Microsoft Hyper-V on any Windows OS from Windows 8 up. If you want a ready-made Windows 10 Enterprise VM with Visual Studio installed, download it from `https://developer.microsoft.com/en-us/windows/downloads/virtual-machines/`.

   The VHD needs to have a fixed-size disk; it cannot be a dynamically expanding virtual hard disk (see Figure 10-2).

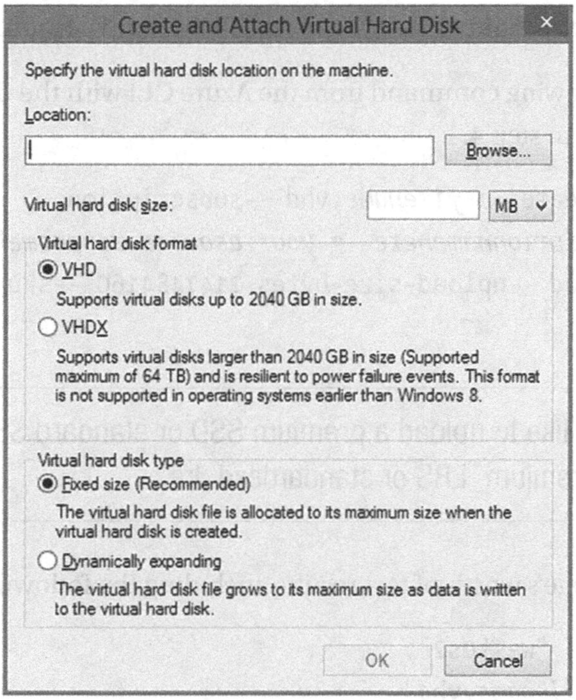

Figure 10-2. *Fixed-size disk type in Microsoft Hyper-V*

4. Determine the VHD file size in bytes.

Note Use the Size value from Windows Explorer, not the "Size on Disk" value.

---

5. Open a command prompt and type **az login**. This opens a browser to authenticate you to Azure from the CLI. You then see the list of subscriptions that you have access to.

```
You have logged in. Now let us find all the subscriptions to which
you have access...
[
  {
    "cloudName": "AzureCloud",
    "homeTenantId": "724243233.86f1.44af.91ah...."
```

6. Run the following command from the Azure CLI with the file size determined in step 4.

```
az disk create -n filename.vhd --subscription
yoursubscriptionnamehere -g yourresourcegroupnamehere -l westus2
--for-upload --upload-size-bytes 2147484160 --sku standard_lrs
--verbose
```

Note If you would like to upload a premium SSD or standard SSD, replace standard_lrs with premium_LRS or standardssd_lrs.

---

7. You see a page's worth of text results, including the following.

```
"location": "westus2",
"name": "filename.vhd"
"resourceGroup": "yourresourcegroupnamehere"
"sku": {
      "name": "Standard_LRS"
      "tier": "Standard"
},
Command ran in x seconds.
```

8. Look at the disk in the resource group blade in the portal. It is provisioned in a ReadyToUpload disk state, as shown in Figure 10-3.

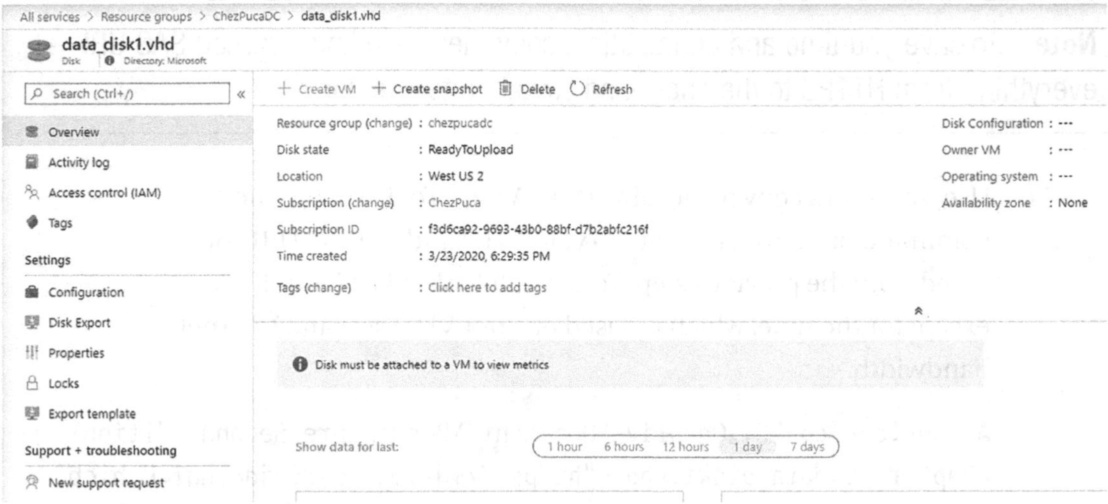

***Figure 10-3.** Disk in ReadyToUpload state*

9. To generate a shared access signature (SAS), which provides secure delegated access to resources in your storage account by securing it with the storage account key and the timeframe you specify at the end in seconds, follow the steps in Figure 10-3. Note how a 2 GB VHD is given 24 hours to upload.

   From the command line, run the following:

   ```
   az disk grant-access -n filename.vhd --subscription
   yoursubscriptionnamehere -g yourresourcegroupnamehere --access-
   level Write --duration-in-seconds 86400
   ```

10. It takes several seconds to show `-running...` You should see the confirmation shown in Figure 10-4.

```
C:\Users\anpuca>az disk grant-access -n data_disk1.vhd --subscription chezpuca -g chezpucadc --access-level Write --dura
tion-in-seconds 86400
{
  "accessSas": "https://md-impexp-qbgx5xsdnhq1.blob.core.windows.net/ff1j4r1r3p3f/abcd?sv=2017-04-17&sr=b&si=26cd10a8-de
1d-4913-85d8-584731db36fe&sig=TgO9aUwhDNEoIU%2FJEfErjKR0%2FLN6mUrpfCZfsAcO7lc%3D"
}

C:\Users\anpuca>
```

***Figure 10-4.** SAS generation success*

Note To save you time and aggravation, copy the preceding returned SAS URI—everything from HTTPS to the end—and save to a text editor.

11. Use AzCopy to copy the local VHD to Azure. To do so, run the command built from the path to your VHD and the SAS URI you saved from the previous step. Your result looks like Figure 10-5, except for the time, which is based on your VHD size and Internet bandwidth.

```
AzCopy.exe cp "C:\OneDrive\Documents\Book\Azure Second Edition\
Chapter 10\data_disk1.vhd" "https://md-impexp-df0jd4vhqf4k.blob.
core.windows.net/k5ph55c4qvbc/abcd?sv=2017-04-17&sr=b&si=7fb359dd-
c20d-47f4-b671-f6ed8eb2a5be&sig=Py3kYsySaDxhUyStp0yjG4S1q2QpdELW0r
%2FPqzRjcnY%3D" --blob-type PageBlob
```

Note AzCopy logs to C:\Users*%username%*\.azcopy, which is for troubleshooting.

```
C:\Users\anpuca>AzCopy.exe cp "C:\OneDrive\Documents\Book\Azure Second Edition\Chapter 10\
pexp-df0jd4vhqf4k.blob.core.windows.net/k5ph55c4qvbc/abcd?sv=2017-04-17&sr=b&si=7fb359dd-(
=Py3kYsySaDxhUyStp0yjG4S1q2QpdELW0r%2FPqzRjcnY%3D" --blob-type PageBlob
INFO: Scanning...

Job 46e13e00-6d5e-a74f-49bc-d67b3a7870cc has started
Log file is located at: C:\Users\anpuca\.azcopy\46e13e00-6d5e-a74f-49bc-d67b3a7870cc.log

0.0 %, 0 Done, 0 Failed, 1 Pending, 0 Skipped, 1 Total,


Job 46e13e00-6d5e-a74f-49bc-d67b3a7870cc summary
Elapsed Time (Minutes): 0.0333
Total Number Of Transfers: 1
Number of Transfers Completed: 1
Number of Transfers Failed: 0
Number of Transfers Skipped: 0
TotalBytesTransferred: 2147484160
Final Job Status: Completed
```

Figure 10-5. *SAS upload completed*

12. Revoke access to the VHD in Azure. This is necessary to change the status of the VHD from ReadyToUpload, as shown in step 8, to Unattached. Run the following command to revoke access:

```
az disk revoke-access -n filename.vhd --subscription
yoursubscriptionnamehere -g yourresourcegroupnamehere
```

13. By browsing the Azure portal to the disk, you see that its status has changed to Unattached, as shown in Figure 10-6. It is ready to attach to a VM or be used as your base image.

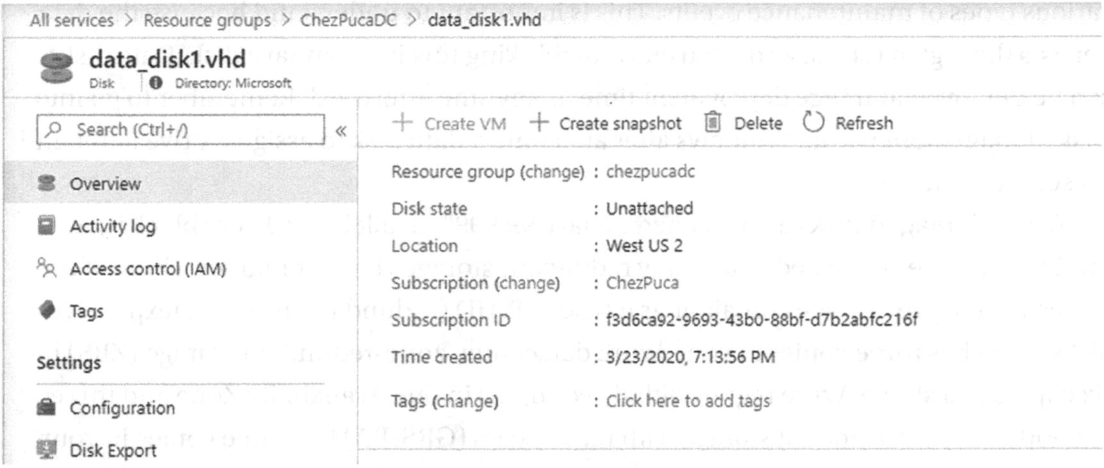

***Figure 10-6.** VHD successfully uploaded to Azure*

It is important to understand what was done with the shared access signature in this exercise. It temporarily (for a timeframe specified by the administrator) allowed access to an Azure resource group within a subscription and allowed the uploading of a file. Minimizing the timeframe and ensuring that access is revoked when the work is completed is imperative for security reasons. If anyone has access to the SAS, the token is in the string after the storage URI.

This is a simple exercise that allows you to upload any images you want to Azure very easily, including the "az login" step, in which there are only five steps to seed Azure with your virtual hard disks.

Virtual Machine Disks

Azure virtual machines (VM) use virtual hard disks (VHD) to store their OS and data. Disks are provisioned as specific, user-selected, sizes, and types. Azure disks are completely managed by Azure's fabric. The disks you create on top of this storage infrastructure include ultra disks, premium solid-state drives (SSD), standard SSDs, and standard hard disk drives (HDD). Each VM you deploy in Azure has an OS disk, as well as a temporary disk that is not a managed disk. It provides temporary storage for applications and is intended to be used like a swap file, but as an entire disk.

Data on temporary disks are destroyed under some events such as redeployment or various types of maintenance events. This is important to understand because the data persists through a reboot and lull users into thinking this is a standard disk. Data disks can be deployed at image deployment time or anytime afterward. Remember to go into Disk Management within Windows after attaching a data disk to assign a drive letter and present it to the OS.

Azure managed disks are designed to have 99.999% availability. Every block is, at minimum, triple replicated in a locally redundant storage (LRS) container. Think of the underlying Azure Storage container as a type of RAID (redundant array of inexpensive disks). LRS has three copies in your Azure datacenter, zone-redundant storage (ZRS) has six copies in a single Azure region with three copies in one Availability Zone and three in another. Geo-redundant storage with read access (GRS-RA) has three copies in your Azure region's datacenter and three copies in another Azure region's datacenter, with at least 600 miles between the datacenters for geographic zone fault tolerance. This storage architecture has led to Microsoft having an industry-leading 0% annualized failure rate.

Azure managed disks are integrated with Azure availability sets to ensure that all of your disks are not in the same storage scale unit (stamp) and to avoid another failure point. If a stamp failed due to hardware or software failure, your VMs would continue to run because the disks would be running in another stamp as part of the availability set.

Azure managed disks support role-based access control (RBAC) to assign permissions to a disk. RBAC permissions can be configured to prevent administrators from performing actions such as exporting the VHD. This is of importance to those who have severe lockdown procedures in place on virtual workloads. For example, this prevents someone from exporting a domain controller VHD to brute force its Security Account Manager (SAM) Active Directory (AD) offline without being detected.

Azure managed disks are automatically encrypted at the storage layer by Azure server-side encryption. This is done to ensure the data in Azure satisfies the various regulatory compliance requirements Microsoft is upheld to. Customers also can encrypt disks with their own customer-managed key instead of the Azure platform's. To protect your data and the OS or application level, Microsoft recommends you use Azure Disk Encryption, which is enabled in the Azure portal by going into the VM, selecting disks, clicking Encryption on the ribbon, and selecting your desired option, as shown in Figure 10-7. This encryption process is integrated with Azure Key Vault and allows you to manage your disk encryption keys.

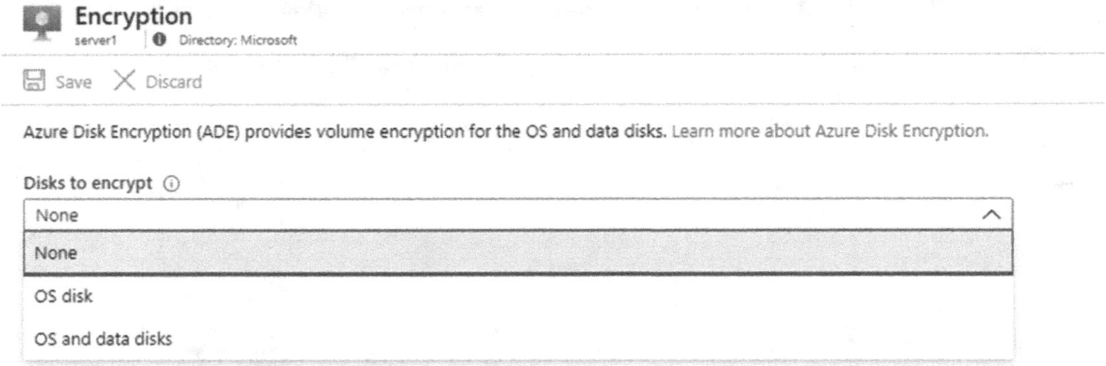

Figure 10-7. *Azure disk encryption on a VM*

Image Builder

Azure Image Builder is a new service that allows organizations to build baseline, gold, or master images for large groups of users or services with different requirements. They can also be easily customized to suit the specific needs of a user or service. Whatever the common denominator for your deployment, it can be built into a Master Image and patched at intervals to keep it current to streamline future deployments.

Azure Image Builder integrates with several configuration server solutions, including DSC, Chef, Puppet, Terraform, System Center Configuration Manager (SCCM), File Shares, and so forth. Once the images are created, they can be published to the Azure Shared Image Gallery for administrators to deploy in a streamlined process.

Monitoring the Health of Virtual Machines

Monitoring the health of VMs in Azure is accomplished in several ways. Microsoft provides basic telemetry data of a VM from the Azure portal on the Overview tab of the VM, as shown in Figure 10-8. These performance graphs illustrate CPU usage, network usage, total disk bytes, and disk IOPS. Mouse over any of the graphs, and you'll see the data for the point on which you are hovering.

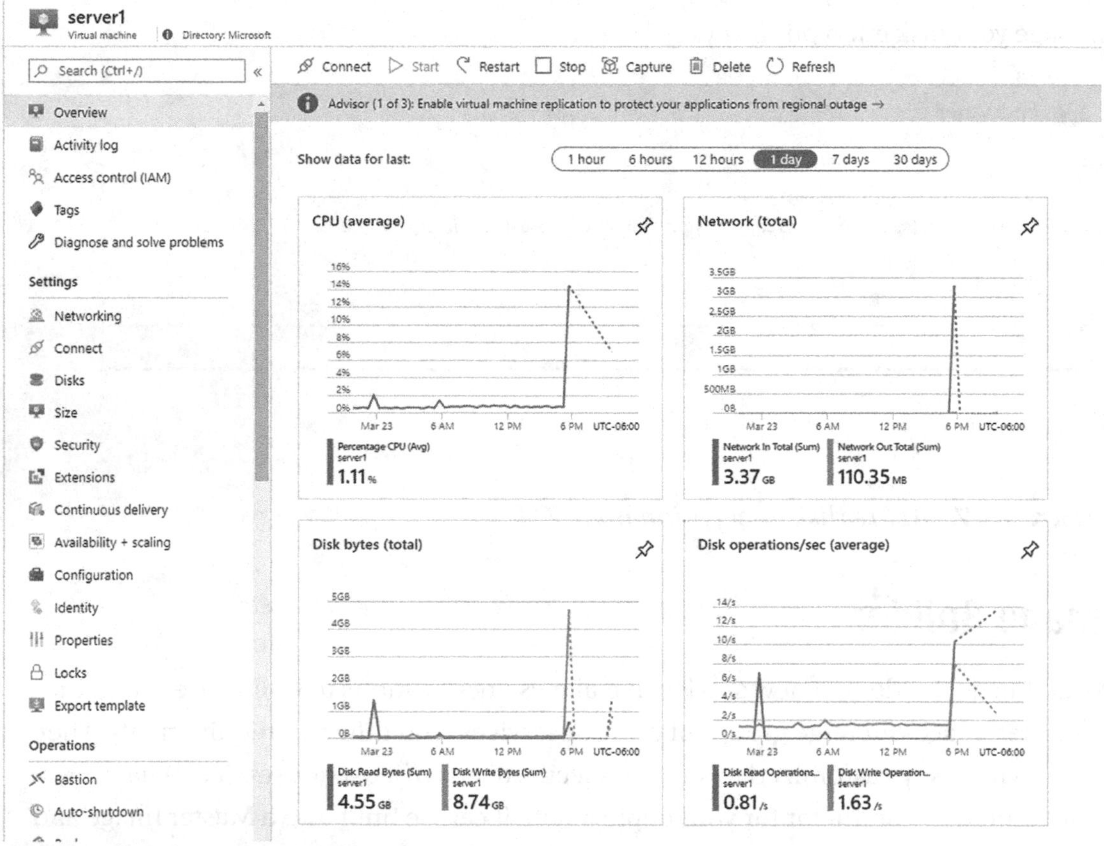

***Figure 10-8.** Azure portal VM monitoring*

Azure customers can enable Boot Diagnostics for an analysis of why a VM is not booting in Azure. It can be done at deployment time in the portal, via Azure Policy, Azure Scripting, or after deployment in the portal on the VM under the Boot Diagnostics section of the VM. Scroll down toward the bottom of the screen pictured in Figure 10-8. Boot Diagnostics, under the Support and Troubleshooting section of the virtual machine, writes the boot data into an Azure Storage account. You can use one Storage Account for multiple VMs. It is a best practice to keep that storage account local to the region the VMs are in and to have it named accordingly for the VMs that are writing to it.

It is highly recommended to enable the collection of guest OS diagnostics data. This can be done during the VM creation in the Azure portal, or any of the methods described earlier for enabling boot diagnostics. By adding this extension to Windows or Linux VMs, administrators get much more CPU, memory, and disk data. The key piece of monitoring here is access to how much RAM the guest VM is using. This is a requirement if the deployed service requires autoscaling, where the Azure autoscaling service would need to know what's in use within the VMs.

Alerts can be created for any of the performance and billing metrics Azure can monitor. These alerts are triggered by a performance counter exceeding or going below a threshold. Azure alerts are configured in the portal, by using templates, or from the Azure CLI. Azure alert rules include dynamic thresholds, where the monitoring alert rule adjusts itself dynamically for you by adapting to the changes of the counter.

Dynamic thresholds use machine learning (ML) to automatically detect metric patterns and adapt over time to their changes. This accomplishes suppressing alerts that may occur because of seasonality, such as daily, weekly, or month-end events that could naturally create spikes that are normal for that time. Ultimately, dynamic thresholds use the ML algorithm to filter out what is known as *noise* in the IT monitoring and management field.

Figure 10-9 shows how a dynamic threshold detected an anomaly in the CPU counter.

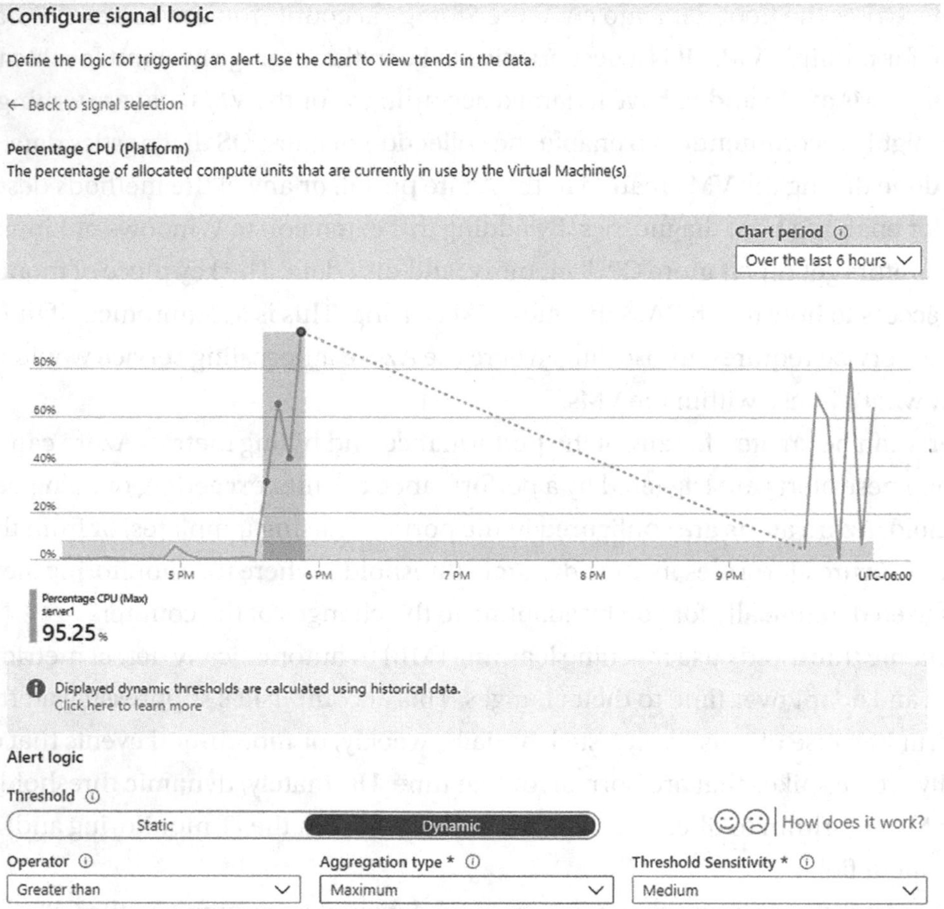

***Figure 10-9.** Azure dynamic threshold monitoring*

Azure Resource Health is another subcomponent of a VM that provides administrators insights into whether the Azure platform is experiencing issues that would be affecting the VM.

Azure Service Health is an Azure service that provides a view into the Azure portal. It identifies which service is having issues, what the issues are, their root cause once resolved, and the regions the issue is impacting. It provides time stamps and several other attributes relevant to the issue reported. Azure Service Health is a convenient and time-saving tool to use whenever you think you need to contact Microsoft about an issue you are experiencing.

To get the most robust and detailed visibility into a VM's performance, configuration, and operations, Azure Monitor and its Application Insights subcomponent should be deployed. Azure Monitor is an agent-based solution that uses the Microsoft

Management Agent to run within the Windows or Linux VM and send data to Azure Log Analytics workspaces. The data is then analyzed to determine if there are application configuration changes needed to satisfy best practices, performance issues, dependencies on other systems based on network connections, and so forth.

Application Insights, which is a feature of Azure Monitor, is the evolution of Microsoft's Application Performance Management (APM). Application Insights runs at the .NET or Java EE (pronounced J-2-E) application layer and detects performance anomalies to help administrators identify where the anomalies are coming from. The application monitored can be on-premises, in Azure, or any other cloud provider environment. Application Insights integrates with Visual Studio App Center and solves the age-old problem of application developers pointing their finger at the network, and system or network administrators pointing their finger at the application. Figure 10-10 shows the Azure Monitor providing basic health reporting in the dashboard of a virtual machine.

Application Insights monitors the following application metrics.

- *Request rates, response times, and failure rates*: Learn which pages are most popular, at what times of day, and where your users are. See which pages perform best. If your response times and failure rates are higher when there are more requests, then perhaps you have a resourcing problem.
- *Dependency rates, response times, and failure rates*: Learn whether external services are slowing you down.
- *Exceptions*: Analyze the aggregated statistics or pick specific instances and drill into the stack trace and related requests. Both server and browser exceptions are reported.
- *Page views and load performance*: Reported by your users' browsers.
- *AJAX calls* from web pages: Rates, response times, and failure rates.
- *User and session counts*.
- *Performance counters* from your Windows or Linux server machines, such as CPU, memory, and network usage.
- *Host diagnostics* from Docker or Azure.

- *Diagnostic trace logs* from your app so that you can correlate trace events with requests.
- *Custom events and metrics* that you write yourself in the client or server code, to track business events such as items sold or games won.

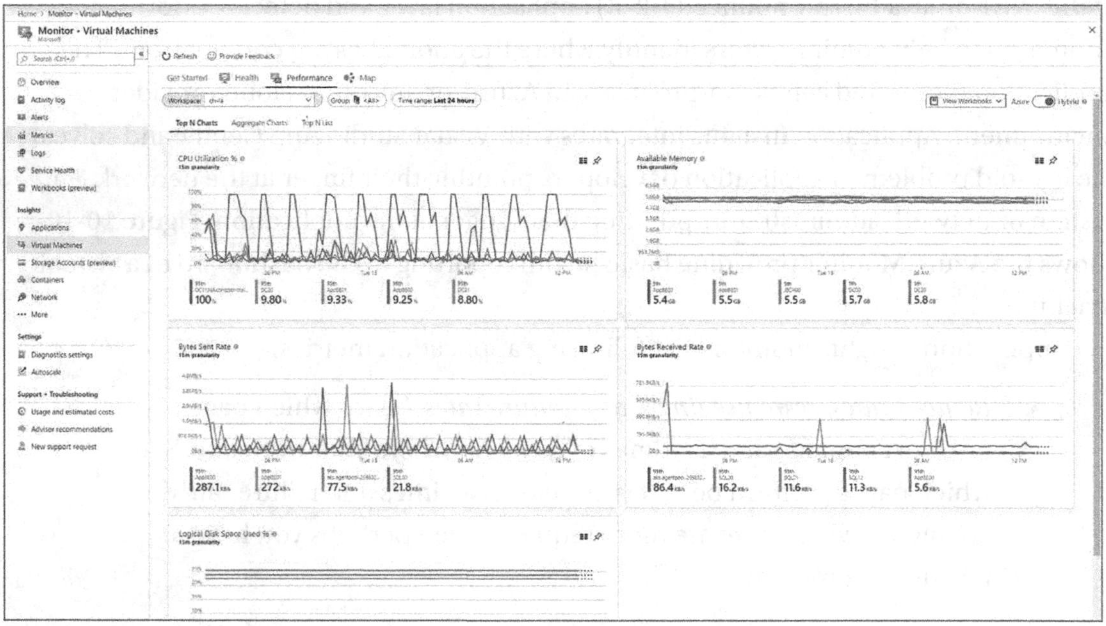

Figure 10-10. *Azure Monitor*

Figure 10-11 shows Azure Advisor recommendations on the security and configuration of a virtual machine. Azure Advisor provides tailored guidance on the resources monitored by Azure Monitor. The guidance provided by Azure Advisor is prioritized on the severity of the configuration detected and its risk exposure. Azure Advisor uses industry best practices to point out what's misconfigured or insecure and simultaneously provides actionable steps to remediate the vulnerability. In this case, we see how Azure Advisor can point out vulnerabilities both within the virtual machine and improvements available within the Azure fabric to improve the VM's availability.

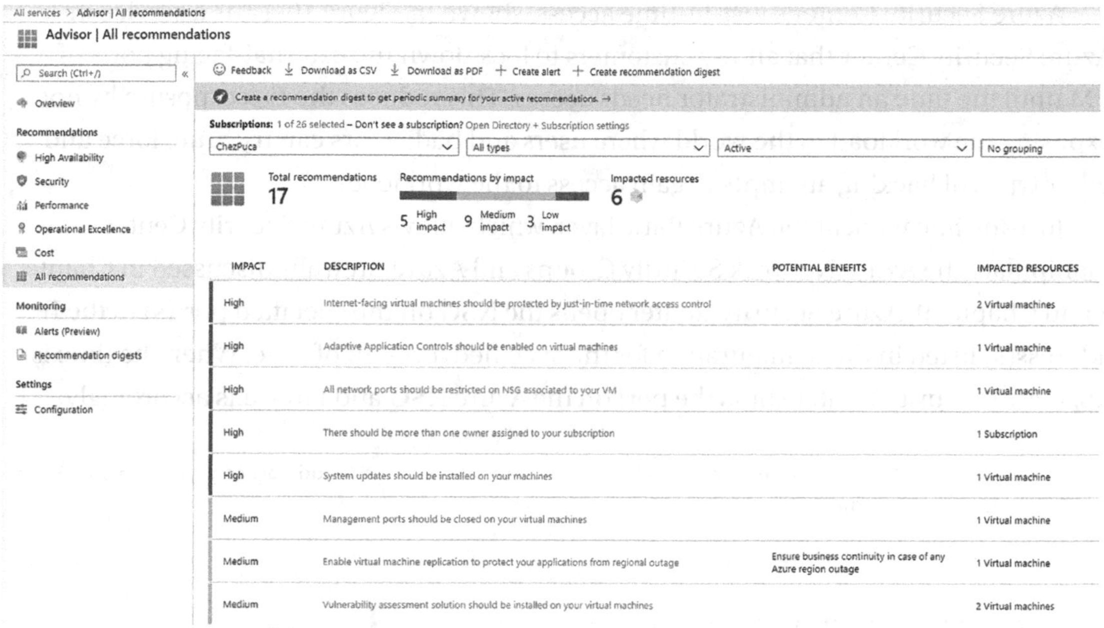

Figure 10-11. *Azure Advisor*

All the data is presented to the administrator in easy to view charts and graphs with weights applied to the various items discovered and reported to prioritize the most urgent at the top. The data collected and reported also surfaces in Azure Security Center, enabling you to focus on the tasks needed to properly secure your environment. In Azure Advisor, recommendations are made to give your workloads the best performing and most secure configuration.

Securing Virtual Machines

Azure secures VMs in several ways, including deployments based on Azure Blueprints, Azure Fabric, Disk Encryption, network encryption, and network shielding from various threats, including DDOS and known botnets.

Change tracking, security, and monitoring data in Azure Security Center identify risks with your configuration. Just-in-time (JIT) access in Security Center, prioritization of actions needed to harden your VMs in Azure Advisor, and more than 1300 policies enforce a security posture your organization needs for each specific workload.

Azure Security Center's just-in-time access, shown in Figure 10-12, is a service in Azure Security Center that allows customers to lock down the external-facing ports of VM until the time an administrator needs access. This reduces the risk exposure by not exposing the workload to the world where users and bad actors can try brute force and other types of hacking attempts to gain access to the workload.

Just-in-time work at the Azure Baric layer, which allows Azure Security Center to manipulate the Azure Network Security Groups and Azure firewalls discussed in Chapter 2 and Chapter 9. Azure Security Center opens the NSG on the specified port(s) to the IP address(s) listed in the configuration for the specified amount of time. When the time is up, Azure Security Center shuts the port on the Azure NSG and Firewalls accordingly.

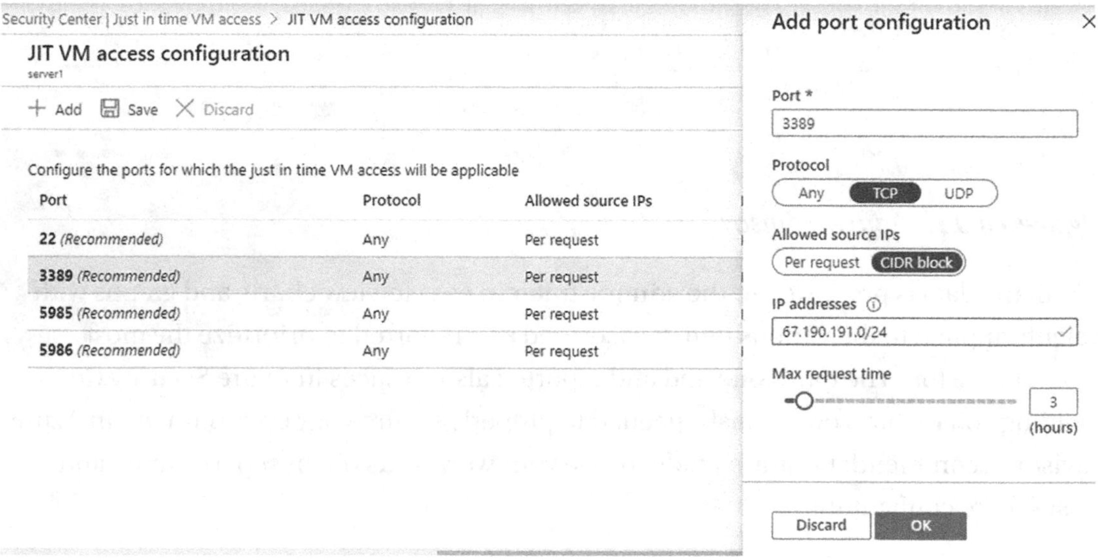

***Figure 10-12.** JIT VM access configuration*

Azure policies enforce the configurations to maintain consistency over time, personnel change, upgrades, and so forth. Azure Policy has similar behavior to Microsoft Group Policy Object (GPO). Still, it does not require the Windows system to be part of an Active Directory (AD) domain, and it works on Windows and Linux systems.

Azure Security Center (ASC) enables administrators to quickly assess how secure their various workloads are and prioritizes what they need to address based on a risk score determined by Microsoft's tickets and cybersecurity team weighing the importance of certain infrastructure deficiencies. The lessons learned by Microsoft Support and Security have directly influenced how Azure Security Center is designed and the data that manifests itself to each customer based on their global security posture experience.

The most common challenges addressed by Azure Security Center are

- Rapidly changing workloads
- Increasingly sophisticated
- Security skills are in short supply

Key benefits of Azure Security Center include

- Strengthens security posture
- Protects against threats
- Becomes secure faster

Azure Security Center is where administrators can go to check their Secure Score, which is a rank of where they are compared to where they should be from a security point of view based on the services deployed in the subscriptions viewed at the time. It is also where Azure policies, threat protection, regulatory compliance, recommendations, and several other security protections are surfaced in the Azure portal. Figure 10-13 shows the Azure Security Center dashboard.

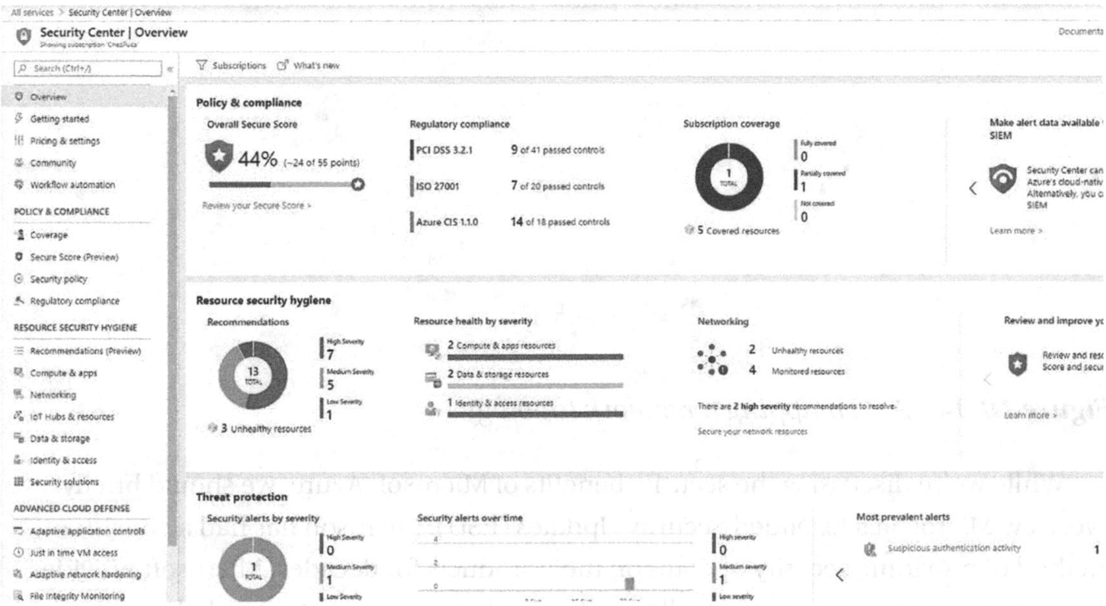

***Figure 10-13.** Azure Security Center dashboard*

Azure Security Center is covered in more detail in Chapter 2 as part of the native Azure services that help strengthen customers' security posture. Figure 10-14 shows how Azure Security Center can display the network topology as it provides continuous monitoring of the LAN and WAN and illustrates the relationship between resources talking on each. This is a demonstration of Azure Security Center monitoring over 400 resources across 100 virtual networks across approximately 25 subscriptions, some of which are on different Azure AD tenants also.

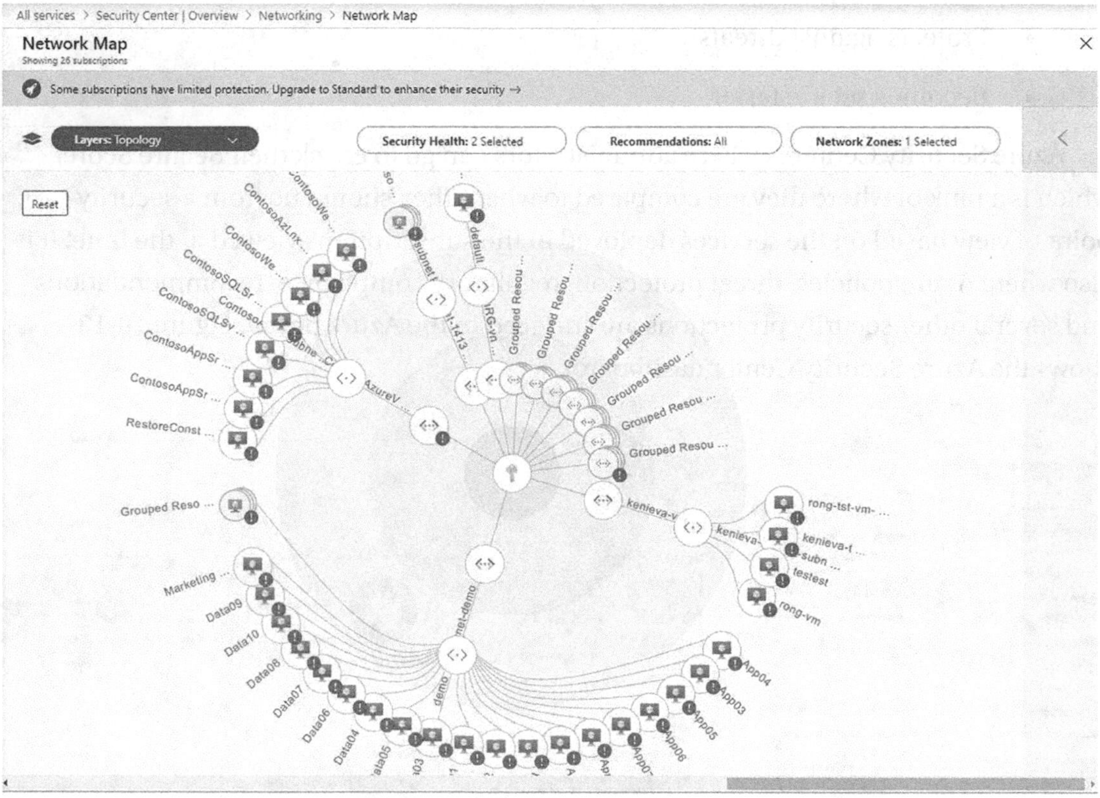

Figure 10-14. *ASC mapping a network topology*

While we're discussing the security benefits of Microsoft Azure, we should briefly overview Microsoft's Extended Security Updates (ESU). Microsoft has had a consistent method of providing security updates on their products for decades. Microsoft provides five years of mainstream support followed by another five years of extended support, which includes regular security updates. This provides a total of ten years of security-based support.

Once you have exceeded the ten-year threshold, you typically had only two options: get no security support or pay for extended security updates, which cost 75% of the cost of the licenses each year for up to three years. That's a total of 225% of the cost of the product over three years because it has not been upgraded for whatever reasons you may have. These frequently include a workload that is retiring or lack of vendor support for the newer OS or SQL platforms.

Many customers faced with Microsoft SQL Server 2008 and Windows Server 2008 hitting the end of their respective lives in July 2019 and January 2020. This process repeats for deployments of Windows Server 2012, which has an end of life in 2023.

You may be thinking, what does Microsoft Azure have to do with the boxed product end-of-life dates? There are a couple of benefits Azure provides with this issue. First, Azure SQL, the PaaS service, is continuously updated by Microsoft on the back end. This means customers never have to worry about end-of-life support issues with Azure SQL instances like Azure SQL Database or Azure SQL Managed Instance. Another benefit available only to Azure customers is the ability to move 2008 workloads, Windows, or SQL Server, to Azure, and get the extended support updates without having to pay the 75% cost of the license annually for the updates. This gives customers three more years to continue running the legacy database and operating systems while they determine an exit strategy.

For more information on the Microsoft Lifecycle Policy, please refer to `https://support.microsoft.com/en-us/lifecycle/selectindex`.

Troubleshooting

Some services have adjustable limits. When deploying virtual machines in Azure, there are several quotas administrators should be aware of. Your subscription has default quota limits in place that could impact the deployment of many VMs for your project. The limit on a per subscription basis is 20 VMs per region. This may seem, and is, quite small. This is to prevent administrators from mistaking deploying large deployments without realizing the financial implications of doing so. Limits can easily be raised by filing a no-charge Microsoft support ticket requesting an increase to the quota.

Quota increases do not apply to free trial subscriptions. Free subscriptions have several limitations placed on them, including quotas on monetary credits, and the number of and which resources are available. High-end compute series for VMs do not show up in free subscriptions. If you exceed your monetary credit in a free subscription, all the resources are shut down until the next billing cycle starts. For example, if you exceed your $50, $100, or $150 MSDN credit before 30 days have passed, the resources halt until the 30-day clock resets.

These are common causes for why administrators cannot start or resize virtual machines in Azure. For more information on Azure subscription and service limits, quotas, and constraints, please refer to `https://docs.microsoft.com/en-us/azure/azure-resource-manager/management/azure-subscription-service-limits`.

Other common issues with virtual machines include uploading a Windows VM as specialized, and it is generalized or uploading it as generalized, and it is specialized. Both generate timeout errors while the VM is stuck at the out-of-box experience (OOBE) screen. If uploading as generalized, the image must be Sysprepped. Collecting Azure VM Activity Logs can assist in troubleshooting VM deployments.

Improving VM Availability

In the following sections, we review the high availability and business continuity/disaster recovery solutions natively available in Azure. We review the primary services designed to provide these abilities to virtual machines in this chapter, not PaaS services. PaaS services have resiliency and zone-redundancy options built into them. There are also hundreds of solutions available in the Azure Marketplace from third-party vendors and OEMs. These solutions provide high availability and disaster recovery using software and licensing.

Availability Zones

Azure Availability Zones are separate from one another. The zones within an Azure region that have their own power, cooling, and networking. Availability zones protect workloads in an Azure region from datacenter failure, providing high availability within the Azure region. These Availability Zones provide an SLA on Azure VMs that utilize the zone redundancy an SLA of 99.99%.

Availability Zones support two categories of Azure Services.

- *Zonal devices*: Unique Azure services that can be pinned to an Availability Zone, such as a virtual machine or a managed disk.
- *Zone-redundant devices*: Azure services that are replicated across Availability Zones automatically as part of their services, such as zone-redundant storage or Azure SQL databases.

Note The numbering of Azure Availability Zones is not persistent in a zone. Availability Zone 3 in one subscription might be different from Availability Zone 3 in another subscription within the same Azure region. Do not rely on Availability Zone numbering across workloads to mean anything.

Because Azure Availability Zones provide a high-availability service within an Azure region, they support high-speed data transfers due to the distance being relatively small in comparison to cross-geography data transfers. This means Azure Availability Zones can support synchronous replication of the application and data across the zones for high availability. Administrators can then use services such as Azure Site Recovery (covered later in this chapter), for disaster recovery, by utilizing asynchronous replication across geography from Azure region to Azure region.

Availability Sets

Availability sets are a group of virtual machines deployed across a datacenters' multiple fault domains to mitigate hardware or large-scale outages at the rack or datacenter or datacenter where the virtual machines reside (see Figure 10-15). A fault domain is the hardware that the compute, storage, and networking run on. Availability sets make sure there is not only redundancy, but also a separation of the systems across hosts, racks, storage, networking equipment, and the power subsystem servicing all of these components. Availability sets allow Microsoft to provide and meet the SLA, even if hardware failure occurs. Virtual machines in an availability set are unique, with their own names and configurations, usually driven by the dependency of a commercial off-the-shelf (COTS) application.

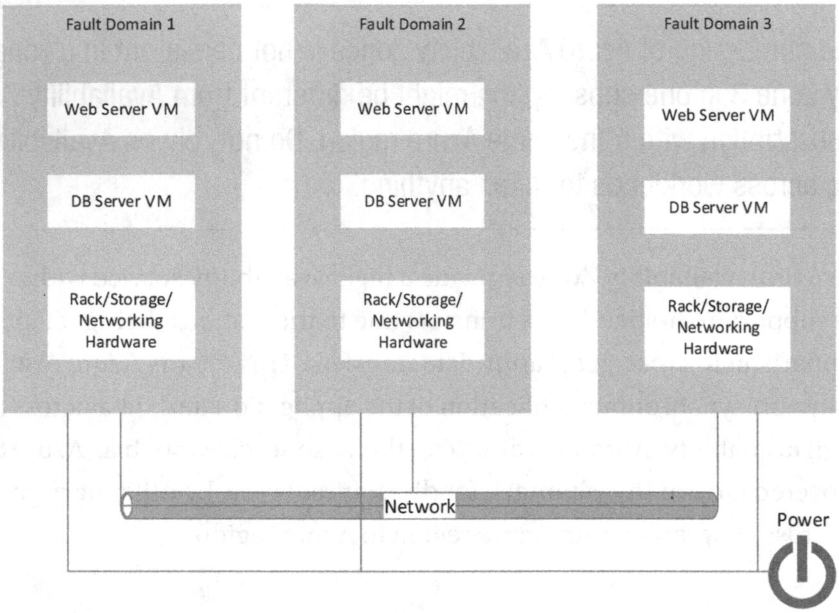

***Figure 10-15.** Azure availability set architecture*

Disaster Recovery

Disaster recovery (DR), also known as *business continuity/disaster recovery* (BCDR), is frequently confused with high availability (HA). The most basic definition of high availability is no disruption to the service for a long time. Most organizations' administrators define that as running a workload across maintenance windows without interruption. High availability is usually measured in uptime.

Disaster recovery—sometimes referred to as *continuous operations* or Continuity of Operations (COOP)—is the process of planning, defining, and instrumenting how an organization continues to provide essential services or mission-critical functions during an event that disrupts the normal business operations. The disruptions events planned for can vary from natural disasters to acts of terrorism or war, depending upon what the service is and its necessity after the disaster occurs. The key difference here is a small outage, which could be anywhere from minutes to days, could be considered acceptable. For this reason, disaster recovery services frequently employ asynchronous replication technologies to replicate data over long distances and away from the primary location, which would have been subjected to the disaster incident.

Microsoft Azure allows customers to replicate from one region to another region that is hundreds of miles or kilometers apart. Depending upon your geography, you'll find that 300 miles or greater are preferred for the Azure services predefined replication partners. This distance ensures the durability of customer data and workloads in the event of a regional disaster, such as an act of nature.

Due to the speed of light over fiber traveling at approximately 124,000 miles per second, synchronous replication is limited to approximately 100 statute miles as a rule of thumb, which gets about one millisecond of latency per 100 miles, or two seconds, if you're counting the round trip. Asynchronous replication technology becomes the preferred solution for long distances. Asynchronous replication is very tolerant of high-latency and can work over thousands of miles.

Azure Site Recovery

Cloud providers now have numerous disaster recovery as a service (DRaaS) solutions. Azure Site Recovery (ASR) is a disaster recovery solution that protects workloads by allowing Azure to be the target for failover in the event of a disaster for on-premises physical x64 systems, Microsoft Hyper-V virtual machines, VMware virtual machines, and Azure virtual machines, including on-premises Azure Stack virtual machines. Azure Site Recovery protects both Windows and Linux operating systems and workloads by replicating the blocks of data on the source systems to the disks on the targeted systems, which, if they are in Azure, are powered off virtual machines generating no cost.

Azure Site Recovery can failover workloads to Azure or another customer location. The failing over can be automated or approved as part of a workflow. Failing back to on-premises can also be performed once the disastrous event has been resolved. Figure 10-16 shows how ASR is enabled on a VM in an Azure region in two clicks and how the replication partner is predefined to leverage Microsoft Azure's global network backbone, which has been optimized for this type of traffic between Azure region pairs. The destination Azure region is configurable.

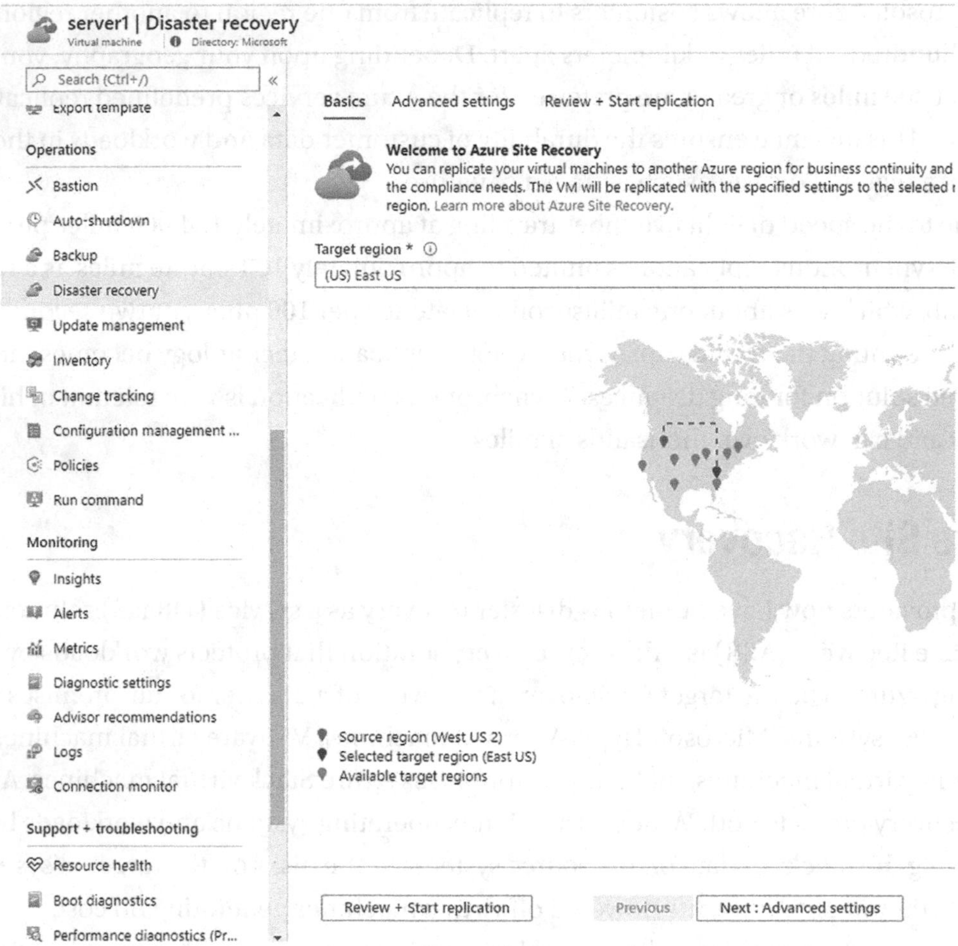

Figure 10-16. *Azure site recovery predefined replication*

Azure Site Recovery is frequently used as a migration tool, by failing over virtual machines to Azure and then leaving them running there. Azure Site Recovery also supports protecting Amazon Web Service (AWS) virtual machines and other cloud providers but lacks the ability to fail-back due to the lack of access to the source's infrastructure. Azure Site Recovery replicates data in an encrypted form and then stored the data on disks in Azure that are encrypted at rest as discussed in Chapters 2 and 7.

In relation to backups or disaster recovery, the terms *recovery point objective* (RPO) and *recovery time objective* (RTO) express the amount of data that is lost, and the timeframe expected to restore it. Azure Site Recovery provides continuous replication for Azure VMs, Azure Stack VMs, VMware VMs, and a replication frequency as low as 30 seconds for Hyper-V VMs.

You can further reduce RTO by integrating with Azure Traffic Manager to automate the DNS resolution of the workloads. We're not saying that this is the timeframe that you will get because that is dependent upon network latency, bandwidth, and the volume of change the protected workloads are experiencing. We're merely stating this is what the service provides and supports, and you what can expect when using the Microsoft backbone.

Azure Site Recovery is not a backup service. ASR does not restore to a point in time. It is continuously trying to mirror the source system to Azure. In doing so, a corrupted file on the source would be replicated to Azure as such. A changed file cannot be reverted to a previous version. These are tasks that Azure backup should be utilized for.

Azure Site Recovery supports the sequencing of multitier apps, which allows administrators to start one workload in an app before another workload that would be dependent on the predecessor. For example, you can start the database server before you start the web server that connects to the database server. Azure Site Recovery also allows administrators to test their DR plans by simulating failovers without impacting the production workloads.

Figure 10-17 illustrates how an n-tier app can be protected, provide automated failover, and client redirection to Azure.

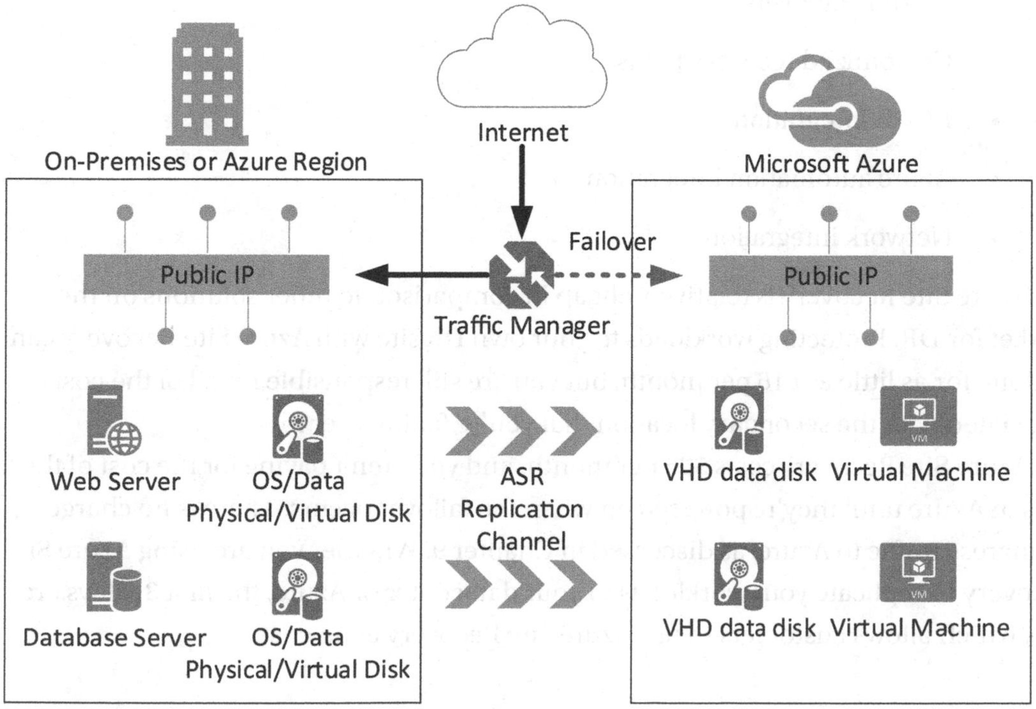

***Figure 10-17.** Azure site recovery protection*

An entire book could be written on Azure Site Recovery, the DR plans, architectures, and various possibilities from other cloud providers to using it as a migration tool. Several different Azure Site Recovery architectures could be deployed to address several workloads and requirements. For a quick guide on how to set up ASR for your workload, please refer to `https://docs.microsoft.com/en-us/azure/site-recovery/azure-to-azure-quickstart`. The following list outlines Azure Site Recovery's capabilities.

- Simple BCDR solution
- Azure VM replication
- On-premises VM replication
- Workload replication
- Data resilience
- RTO and RPO targets
- Keep apps consistent over failover
- Testing without disruption
- Flexible failovers
- Customized recovery plans
- BCDR integration
- Azure automation integration
- Network integration

Azure Site Recovery is relatively cheap in comparison to other solutions on the market for DR. Protecting workloads to your own DR site with Azure Site Recovery can be done for as little as $16 per month, but you are still responsible for all of the costs associated with the secondary location that you're failing over to.

Azure Site Recovery costs $25 per month, and you aren't paying for the cost of the VMs in Azure until they're powered on when the failover occurs. There is no charge for ingress traffic to Azure, as discussed in Chapter 9. Whether you are using Azure Site Recovery to replicate your workloads to your datacenter or Azure, the first 31 days are free, which allows customers to use Azure Site Recovery at no cost.

Scale Sets

Scale sets, also known as *virtual machine scale sets*, frequently confused with availability sets, are built from availability sets, but with identical virtual machines, making autoscaling and high availability, a much easier goal to achieve. Scale sets, illustrated in Figure 10-18, include the load balancing capability built-in the service; no third-party solution is required.

Scale sets have APIs that can be called to provide a virtual desktop infrastructure or VDI-like experience with deployments, imaging, updates, and so forth. For example, a scale set of 100 DS13v2 Ubuntu Linux virtual machines can be deployed in about five minutes, each having its own 4 TB data disk, which is only responsible for approximately 17 seconds of the overall deployment time!

These virtual machines each have 8 cores and 60 GB of RAM, providing 800 cores and 6 TB of memory to the service. This example illustrates the very rapid deployment and scaling capability provide by scale sets, while still incorporating all the resiliency of the availability sets, since they include no less than five fault domains.

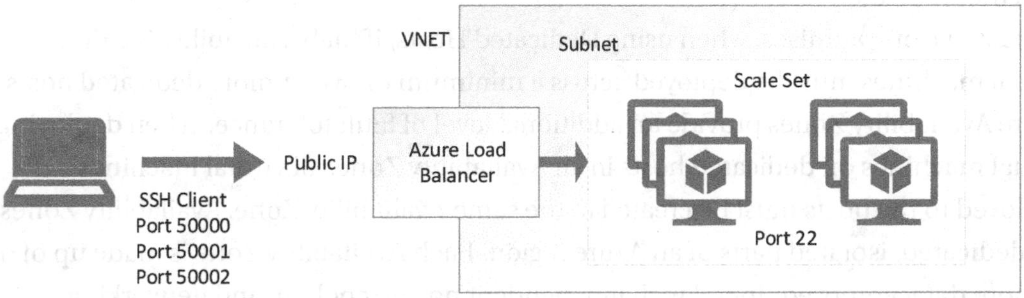

Figure 10-18. *Azure scale set architecture*

A sample template to deploy the scale set is at `https://github.com/Azure/azure-quickstart-templates/tree/master/201-vmss-public-ip-linux`.

Dedicated Hosts

Azure Dedicated Hosts were recently released as a new service enabling customers to use the same hardware customers' virtual machines are hosted on but without the sharing of resources across customers or subscriptions. Azure Dedicated Hosts' guests must all reside in the same Azure subscription. Customers may provision dedicated hosts within a region, Availability Zone, and fault domain, but they cannot use Scale Sets, and there are limited VM Series available. Check the Azure products available by region website at `https://azure.microsoft.com/en-us/global-infrastructure/services/` for a detailed list of which regions and VM series are available.

Dedicated Hosts support DSv3, ESv3, and FSv2. Dedicated Hosts allow Azure customers to isolate all of their VMs on the host from other customers' workloads while using the same shared network and storage. Maintenance windows may include updates to the Azure platform infrastructure to improve reliability, performance, security, and to launch new features. Dedicated Hosts provide customers the ability to opt-in or out of maintenance windows within an Azure region, for up to 35 days, to more finely control the maintenance impact to their workloads.

Customers are limited to 3000 vCPUs on dedicated hosts per Azure region. Like most Azure Quotas, this is a default setting and can be upgraded by filing a request through the Azure portal. This process usually takes a couple of days to be approved by the Azure provisioning team. When looking at Azure Quotas, it is important to evaluate all the quotas that may be in effect on a resource. For example, you may have a lower quota available for a specific virtual machine size within a certain region, which could be lower than the Dedicated Hosts quota.

Just like on-premises, when using Dedicated Hosts, if high availability is a desire, virtual machines must be deployed across a minimum of two or more dedicated hosts. Azure Availability Zones provide an additional level of fault tolerance. When deploying virtual machines on dedicated hosts in an Availability Zone, all virtual machines deployed to the hosts must be created in the same Availability Zone. Availability Zones are dedicated, isolated parts of an Azure region. Each Availability Zone is made up of one or more datacenters equipped with independent power, cooling, and networking.

When dedicated hosts are deployed, customers are billed per host. The number, size, and usage of the virtual machines on the host are no longer factored into billing. Customers only see a bill for the hosts; the virtual machines are on the billing, but with a price of $0. Storage, networking, and other services or licenses are billed as usual.

The Azure Dedicated Hosts service is different from most cloud services due to this billing model, where the customers are reserving the host entirely for themselves. This model is very similar to *colocation hosting*, but Microsoft owns the compute assets; customers are renting not only the space of the hardware footprint but the asset itself. A virtual machine's state has no impact on billing. A dedicated host with no virtual machines generates the same bill as one with dozens of virtual machines.

Proximity Placement Groups

Proximity placement groups are a new Azure resource that allows customers to group resources that have low latency requirements between each other, to minimize the impact of traversing an Azure region as much as possible. Proximity placement groups enable the co-locating VMs that need low latency to stay within the same datacenter within an Azure region. This is important because an Azure region may have dozens of datacenters, and the distance between servers in the same region could still be significant. Proximity placement groups are used with virtual machines, availability sets, or virtual machine scale sets. They provide the following features.

- Low latency between stand-alone VMs
- Low Latency between VMs in a single availability set or a virtual machine scale set
- Low latency between stand-alone VMs, VMs in multiple Availability Sets, or multiple scale sets (You can have multiple compute resources in a single placement group to bring together a multitiered application.)
- Low latency between multiple application tiers using different hardware types

When using virtual machines from different VM series, they're usually configured with different networking and storage capabilities. They have different hardware architectures, which indicates that they're likely in different racks. When moving existing virtual machines into a Proximity Placement Group for colocation purposes, Azure administrators should shut the virtual machine down to allow it to be moved across the Azure region infrastructure.

Note When seeking the lowest latency possible between workloads, place the virtual machines in a proximity placement group and the entire solution in a zone. When seeking the most resilient architecture, place your instances across multiple Availability Zones.

To create a proximity placement group (PPG) using the Azure CLI, try the following.

```
az group create --name myPPGGroup --location westus
az ppg create \
   -n myPPG \
   -g myPPGGroup \
   -l westus \
   -t standard
```

Next, place a virtual machine in the proximity placement group.

```
az vm create \
   -n myVM \
   -g myPPGGroup \
   --image UbuntuLTS \
   --ppg myPPG  \
   --generate-ssh-keys \
   --size Standard_D1_v2  \
   -l westus
```

Finally, measuring the performance of the virtual machine's latency is important to serve as a baseline to be referenced later. The act of measuring this is referred to as *benchmarking*. Many tools benchmark systems performance with their various virtual and physical hardware. Although Ping.exe measures access and latency, ideally, you want to simulate the workload as closely as possible to achieve the most accurate benchmark.

When using proximity placement groups, it is best to measure between two virtual machines vs. pinging Bing.com, where the results can naturally vary over time. Latency measurements are useful in the following scenarios.

- Establish a benchmark for network latency between the deployed VMs
- Compare the effects of changes in network latency after changes are made to the following.
    - Operating system or network stack software, including configuration changes
    - A VM deployment method, such as deploying to an Availability Zone or proximity placement group

- VM properties, such as Accelerated Networking or size changes
- A virtual network, routing, or filtering changes

ICMP is frequently blocked across network firewalls and routers. To measure latency, Microsoft provides two different tool options.

- For Windows-based systems: latte.exe (Windows)
  a. `https://gallery.technet.microsoft.com/Latte-The-Windows-tool-for-ac33093b`
- For Linux-based systems: SockPerf (Linux)
  b. `https://github.com/mellanox/sockperf`

Using these tools help ensure that only TCP or UDP payload delivery times are measured and not ICMP (Ping) or other packet types that aren't used by applications and don't affect their performance.

Spot Virtual Machines

Spot virtual machines allow customers to capitalize on running workloads on idle resources in Azure for a highly reduced price. Spot VMs are only available if Azure can provide the service. When Azure needs the capacity, Azure evicts Spot virtual machines. This means that the workloads run on Spot virtual machines must tolerate that type of service interruption.

Workloads like batch processing jobs and dev/test are good examples of Spot virtual machine uses cases. A Spot VM offers no high availability guarantees, and when Azure needs the capacity back, the Azure infrastructure evicts Spot VMs with 30 seconds notice. Production workloads that have any kind of SLA are not recommended.

Summary

While this chapter reviewed many of the features available to Azure virtual machines, it's hard not to feel like we barely scratched the surface of what's available. We hope this chapter provides some clarity around the various options available to make your workloads much more highly available and fault-tolerant.

CHAPTER 11

Infrastructure as Code (IaC)

When you read the term *infrastructure*, you may visualize hours spent in a fidget datacenter racking, stacking, cabling servers, and connecting network hardware. IT professionals recognize this work as part of their everyday job, some new to the datacenter, may not work in the cloud only and not in a professional on-premises datacenter. You learn to use tools to automate Microsoft Azure deployment of cloud services. The tools and processes to deploy software-defined datacenter components is commonly referred to as *infrastructure* as code (IaC).

In this chapter you learn how to use software to define data services and then create networks, servers, and applications. You learn how to use code to securely connect cloud services for user access. You learn to use enterprise ready tools to create a process for managing and provisioning cloud infrastructure as code using definition files.

Similar to an on-premises datacenter, new hardware with different motherboards and network interface cards and capabilities are brought online for new applications. Microsoft Azure development continues to enhance underlying hardware and refine hosting software so that you can redeploy IaC to support new services.

This chapter guides you in planning for and architecting business support for IaC. The topics include

- Overview of infrastructure as code
- An IaC example
- Azure Resource Manager (ARM) templates
- HashiCorp Terraform on Azure
- Deploying VNets with code (example)

J. Soh et al., *Microsoft Azure*, https://doi.org/10.1007/978-1-4842-5958-0_11

- Deploying VMs with code (example)
- IaC enhancement considerations
- Troubleshooting IaC

Overview of IaC in Microsoft Azure

There is a DevOps (development operations) relationship in deploying infrastructure as code to continuous integration and continuous delivery (CI/CD). The same types of tools used in engineering development are used to deploy IaC in Microsoft Azure and any major cloud. To be clear, the audience for this topic includes cloud architects and cloud administrators, who have the deep subject matter expertise to deploy cloud services using the Azure portal. Providing a codified workflow to create, re-create, and redeploy software-defined networks (SDN) and cloud infrastructure is a game-changer.

IaC workflow or processes support changing and updating existing SDN infrastructure safely and with predictability. For the discussions in this chapter, and as a cloud administrator or cloud engineer, you are expected to have previous experience in deploying Azure services like VNets, VMs, and security best practices using the Azure portal. Like engineering developers, IaC engineers adopted Agile development methods. They created a standard corporate integration with application code workflows like Azure DevOps, Git, GitLab, and other CI/CD pipeline tools like Jenkins.

In a datacenter (virtual or physical), over time, there is the problem of changing from the initial deployment, which is sometimes called *drift*. When physical servers are deployed and operating systems installed, the environment changes as maintenance is applied to systems. Cloud operations are always tasked to maintain stable production services, so Azure services must be immutable, and the deployment using IaC tools must guarantee repeatability. The word *immutable* is used in our IaC conversations to support the foundation of repeatability, reduce drift, and enable automation; all three are needed to support predictable and healthy Azure services deployment.

The next few topics provide an overview of SDN code and reusable modules to share and collaborate with other cloud engineers in your company or the community. There are many IaC tools; however, we focus on only two.

- Azure Resource Manager (ARM) templates
- HashiCorp Terraform

Azure Resource Manager is a service that creates software-defined networks and provisions idempotent configurations in an Azure subscription. ARM templates are defined in a JavaScript Object Notation (JSON) format to define the infrastructure and configure the application project. The ARM template uses a declarative syntax to deploy network infrastructure, storage, and virtual machines to Azure. The declarative JSON templates call the Azure REST API.

IaC allows cloud engineers to enable versioning control for security and stability and then provide that code to software developers. Development teams should leverage validated and tested production-ready SDN in their current Agile development cycle. The infrastructure is validated and tested to prevent deployment inconsistencies. Two examples of enabling IaC self-service model in an IT service management (ITSM) activity are

- Microsoft Azure Blueprints (and the rebranded next version)
- ServiceNow Azure Cloud Management Blueprint

The developers, operations, and business are disconnected. In this chapter, we want to identify IaC tools, including CI/CD pipelines, to support a transformation and a library of offerings to grow the business in a secure process.

Infrastructure as Code Example

We use an IaC example to reveal the toolset options for both Azure built-in and external tools as you progress through the steps to create and (optionally) deploy into your Microsoft Azure subscription. The exercise teaches the specific workflow processes needed to deploy software-defined networks and virtual machines using both Microsoft ARM and HashiCorp Terraform.

The exercise compares Microsoft ARM and HashiCorp Terraform processes and specifically guides you in creating virtual network and server components. This exercise is simple and not designed to provide a deep dive into Azure services automation steps. The guidance for building skills that enable you to master becoming highly efficient with either method of IaC library construction and automated deployment would require a dedicated book on both ARM and Terraform.

If you are new to developing code to deploy Azure services, this exercise is for you and business decision-makers. If you are skilled in IaC deployment to Azure, then this exercise may appear simplistic. The software template services were selected because they are critical to software-defined constructs that support real-world deployments, such as virtual machines, which has the most complex set of parameters, including Azure availability sets, network interface cards (NIC), and hard disk drives.

This exercise is used to introduces you to Azure virtual networks. The steps include the creation of VNets, with steps to configure a Network Security Group (NSG). The NSG is a software firewall that allows or denies IP traffic flow.

You can use the example in Figure 11-1 to create a new library with this IaC deployment reference model or add to your existing template repository.

Deployment of the Azure services used in this exercise for both ARM and HashiCorp Terraform includes

- IaC template basics
- IaC tool configuration
- Resources, parameters, variables

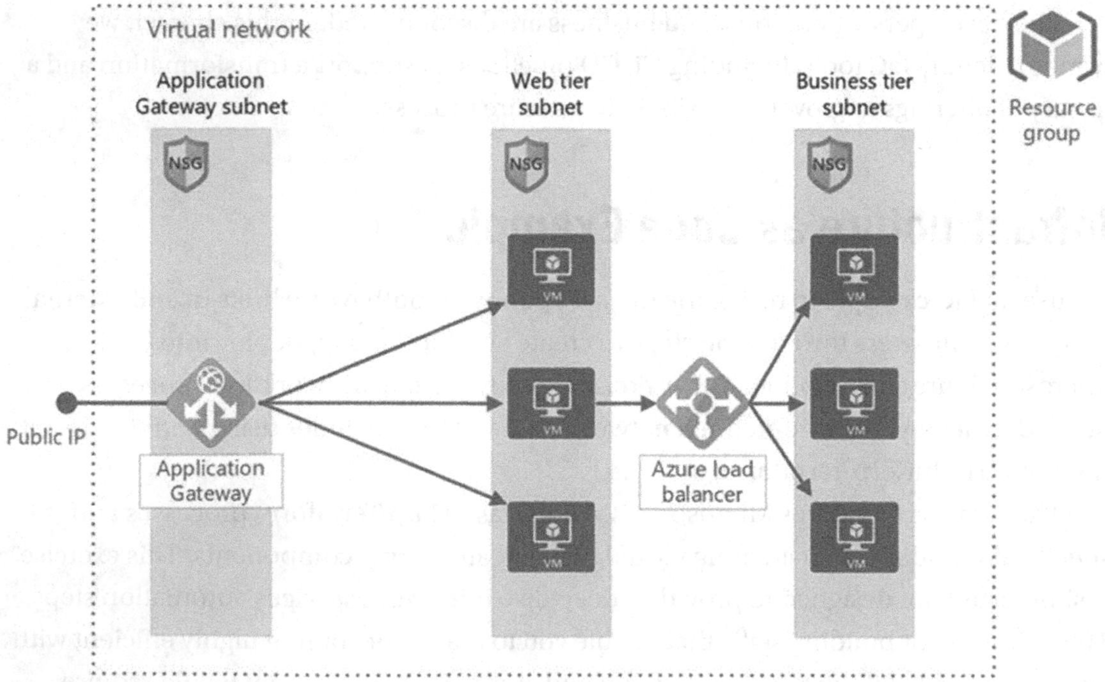

***Figure 11-1.** Infrastructure as code example*

Note All the code for the software-defined infrastructure—both Microsoft Azure ARM templates and HashiCorp Terraform—can be downloaded from `https://github.com/harris-soh-copeland-puca`.

ARM Templates

Infrastructure as code moved beyond PowerShell scripting with the introduction of Microsoft Azure Resource Manager (ARM) templates. ARM is an Azure management layer that enables resources in Azure to be created, updated, and deleted. Infrastructure as code resources in a template support software-defined networks, load balancers, virtual machines, and container runtimes like Kubernetes.

An often overlooked security feature is Azure role-based access control (RBAC), which is a direct feature of Azure resource management layer integration with Azure Active Directory (AAD). ARM templates work to create the virtual foundation, and additional tools are used to configure the applications for consistency and compliance.

Tools like Ansible, Chef, and Puppet are excellent applications for management across environments; they often support the cloud operations team after the network, server, and security infrastructure are created. ARM templates use JSON files that define configurations in Microsoft Azure in a declarative manner. Using templates in a software-defined format of JSON files ensures that the deployment is consistent and predictable.

There are many design areas supported by the JSON file format specifically for ARM; however, for this chapter, you need to be aware of only a few.

- Resource provider and version
- Resource location
- Parameters and variables

The application programming interface (API) layer of the Azure provider includes the methods, servers, services, applications, and users that interact with the resource. As API features are updated, the changes are reflected in version numbers from the resource provider. Each Azure region has resources supported for deployment that are used when deploying IaC.

An single example of a reusable library template would be the design of an ARM template. The ARM template should include the number of resources required such as a VM. You can create another ARM template that expands features, as an example, support for high availability. Azure Resource Manager supports the Azure API to create, update, and delete cloud resources. ARM templates should include version control. The version of resources then become a known resource supported by the Help Desk. The versioning numbers also support DevOps that includes continuous integration and continuous deployment (CI/CD).

JSON documents include many defined objects that are used in the software creation of Azure networks, virtual machines, and database services. Some of the types of object values include

- Numbers
- Strings
- Boolean
- JSON arrays
- JSON objects

You are not expected to become an ARM expert in this chapter; however, the level of detail is needed to help make informed decisions about investing in the creation of Azure ARM templates. Figure 11-2 provides a view of Azure QuickStart Templates. They are the same as GitHub ARM templates but, in an easy to search format.

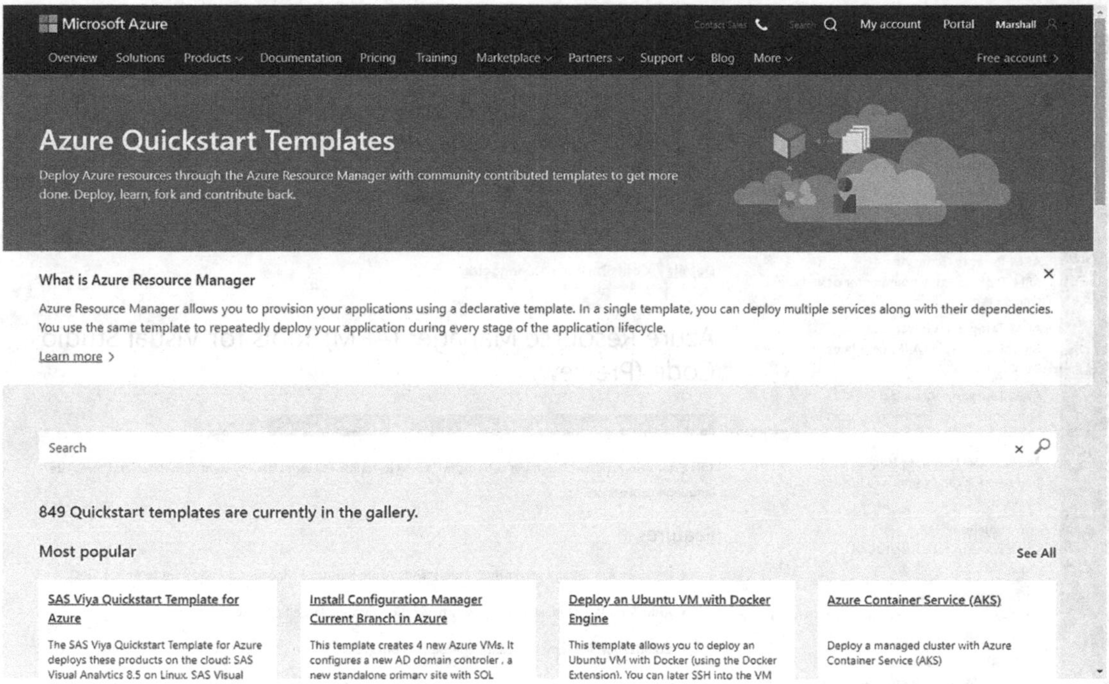

***Figure 11-2.** Azure quickstart templates in a searchable format*

Note Azure QuickStart templates are at `https://azure.microsoft.com/en-us/resources/templates/`.

Microsoft Visual Studio Code installation was covered in Chapter 8 when you were introduced to the tools and training necessary for an Azure cloud engineer. If needed, return to Chapter 8 to follow the installation instructions.

INSTALLING AZURE RESOURCE MANAGER (ARM) VISUAL STUDIO CODE EXTENSION

1. From your IaC laptop, open Visual Studio Code.
2. Select the Extensions option.

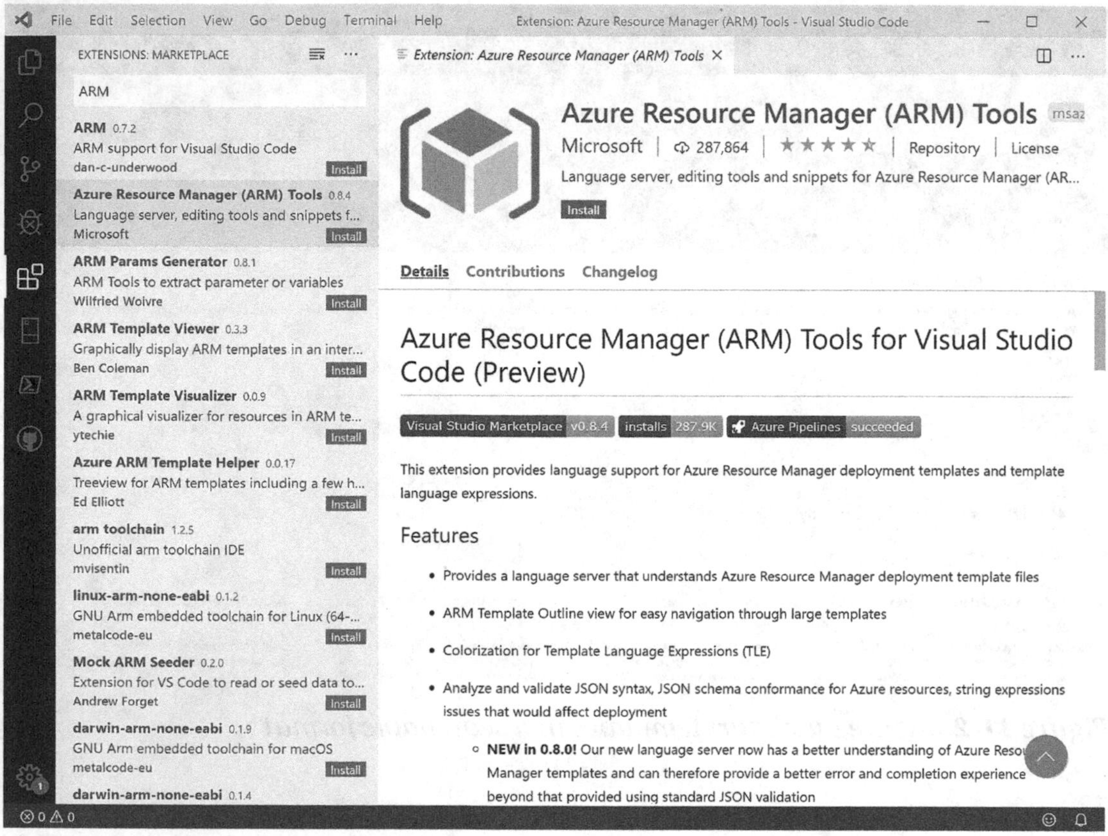

3. Search for the Azure ARM extension. Note the one created by Microsoft, and not another developer or corporation. Select the Install option.

4. Verify that the Terraform extension is installed by using the search bar. Type **@installed**.

5. The extension should appear in the list of installed extensions.

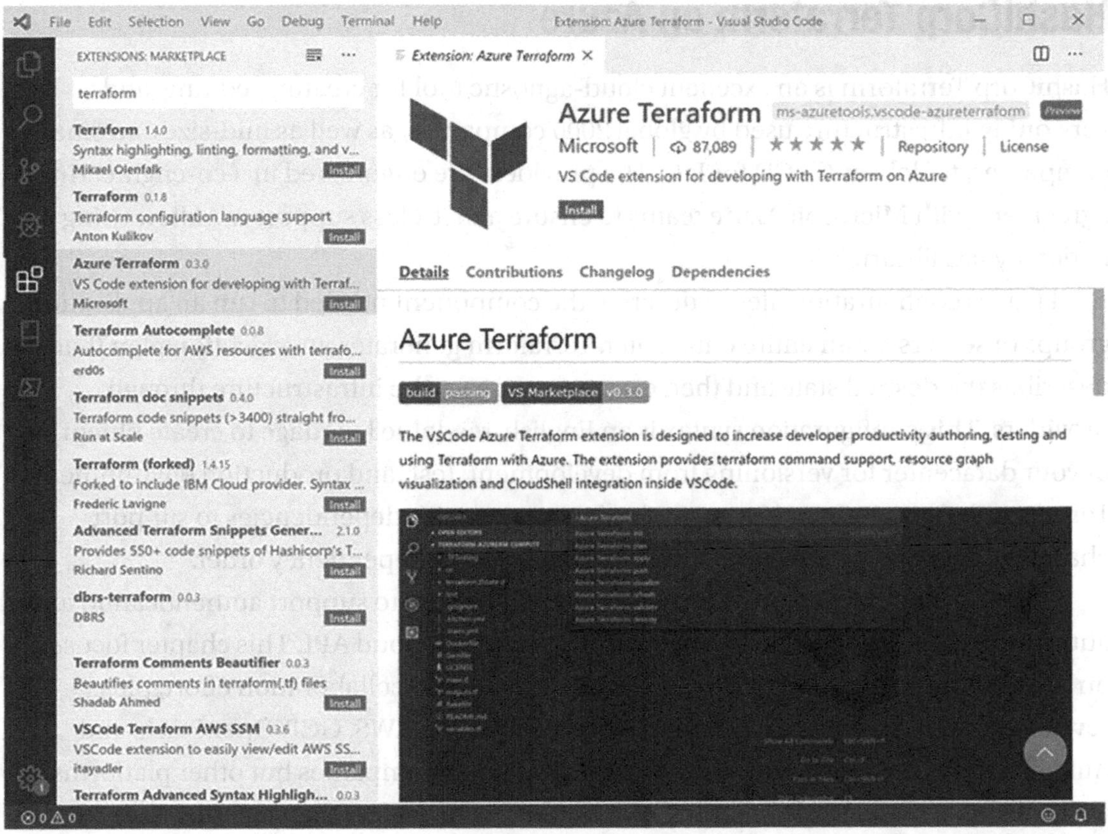

As Microsoft upgrades extensions and providers, the version numbers continue to increase.

Once the Terraform template is created, it is deployed from the Visual Studio Code PowerShell or Azure CLI terminals. Writing code to deploy Azure infrastructure and resources with VS Code is made powerful when you use variables for ARM templates. Variables are necessary in the VS Code structure, along with resources and output.

- $schema
- parameters
- variables
- resources
- outputs

With the installation of the extensions, you have a deeper understanding of the engineering effort between HashiCorp and Microsoft Azure.

HashiCorp Terraform on Azure

HashiCorp Terraform is an excellent cloud-agnostic tool for creating, editing, and versioning infrastructure used by global 2000 companies, as well as mid-size and smaller companies, to deliver CI/CD for IaC. The providers are engineered in a co-engineering agreement with Microsoft Azure teams to ensure a first-class support workflow using TF to deploy IaC libraries.

TF uses configuration files to describe the component needed to run an application, groups of servers, or an entire datacenter. Terraform generates an execution plan that describes the desired state and then executes to create the infrastructure through providers. This configuration syntax is an English-readable language to create blueprints of your datacenter for versioning from development, test, and production environments. Terraform has a core function to graph all resources with dependencies to support changes, additions, and reconfigurations in the correct dependency order.

Terraform leverages a provider, which is code written to support authentication and authorization, is responsible for interactions through a cloud API. This chapter focuses on the Microsoft Azure cloud provider, which has been a collaboration effort, please review Figure 11-3; however, all major clouds, including AWS, GCP, OpenStack, and Alibaba cloud. Terraform providers are not only cloud companies but other platforms as well. To gain a better understanding of the library of providers they include, Azure Stack, VMware, Chef, Cisco, Kubernetes, including directory services like Okta, Azure Active Directory, and databases platforms like MongoDB, MySQL, and network providers like Akamai, Cisco, Cloudflare, Palo Alto and more. Terraform allows the use of community versions of providers and validated providers. HashiCorp validated provider undergoes reviews and is often co-engineered between the two company engineering team.

Note There is an updated list of HashiCorp Terraform providers at `www.terraform.io/docs/providers/index.html`.

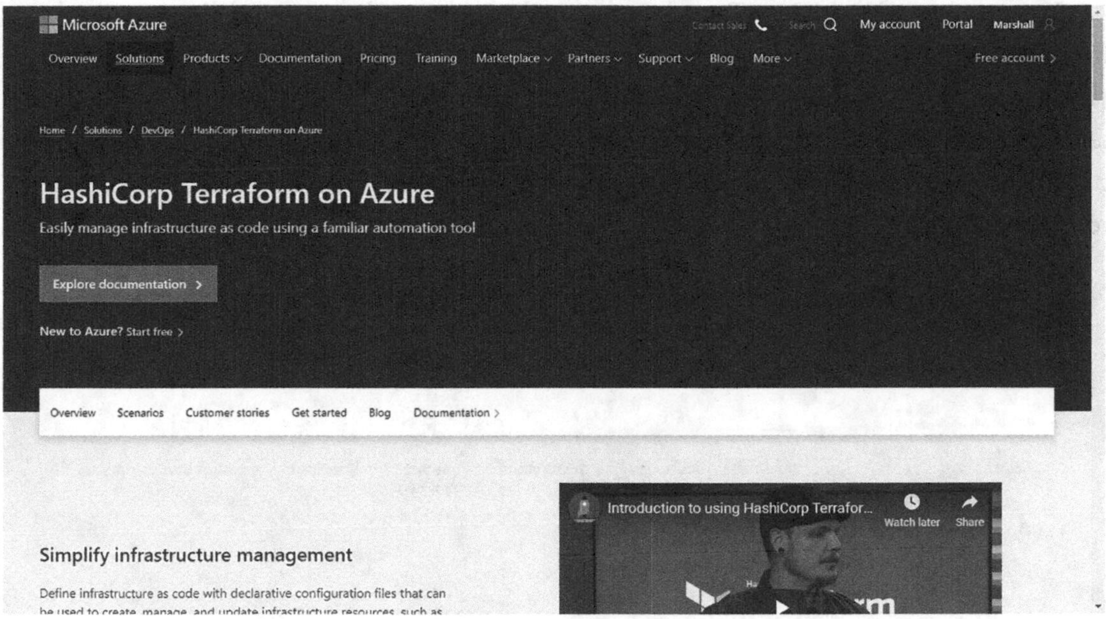

***Figure 11-3.** Screenshot of HashiCorp Terraform on Azure explore documents page*

You want to use HashiCorp Terraform and support the business using the IaC libraries through a standard framework and the Visual Studio Code integrated development environment (IDE). In Chapter 8, you learned the prerequisites and installation procedures for macOS, Linux, and Windows operating systems (OS).

Chapter 8 discussed

- Azure subscription
- Terraform Installation and configuration
- Visual Studio Code installation

Your IaC laptop must be configured properly to complete the exercises in this chapter if you deploy using HashiCorp Terraform or ARM. We realize your work may focus more on traditional operations, which requires more scripting with PowerShell or Azure CLI. Anyone who would like to become a subject matter expert (SME) will find that adopting developer tools and workflows are essential.

The HashiCorp Terraform community's open source (OSS) edition is a free download (as a single executable) to install on your local machine, as described in Chapter 8. (Note that this is the same version that is currently configured as the default in the Azure Cloud Shell.)

You can learn HashiCorp Terraform using the integrated command-line terminal from inside the Azure portal and watch the commands execute and validate by typing **terraform** in the command shell, as shown in Figure 11-4. The Azure cloud shell has the latest version of the Azure, and HashiCorp Terraform providers installed. The Terraform providers have been a joint engineering effort between Microsoft and HashiCorp, please reference Figure 11-5.

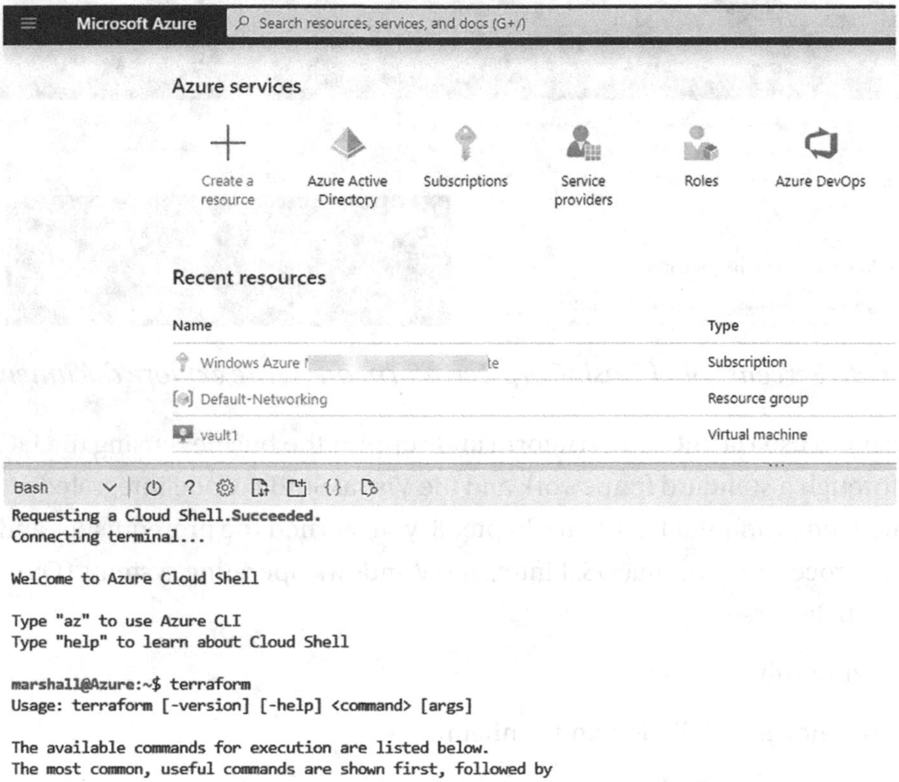

***Figure 11-4.** Validate the preinstalled Terraform using the Azure Cloud Shell*

To create an IaC laptop for this exercise, download and install Terraform locally. You should follow best practices and update the AzureRM provider to gain the latest functionality.

Note Validate the version of HashiCorp Terraform installed with the command extension: terraform –version.

INSTALLING HASHICORP TERRAFORM VISUAL STUDIO CODE EXTENSION

1. From your IaC laptop, open Visual Studio Code.
2. Choose the Extensions option.

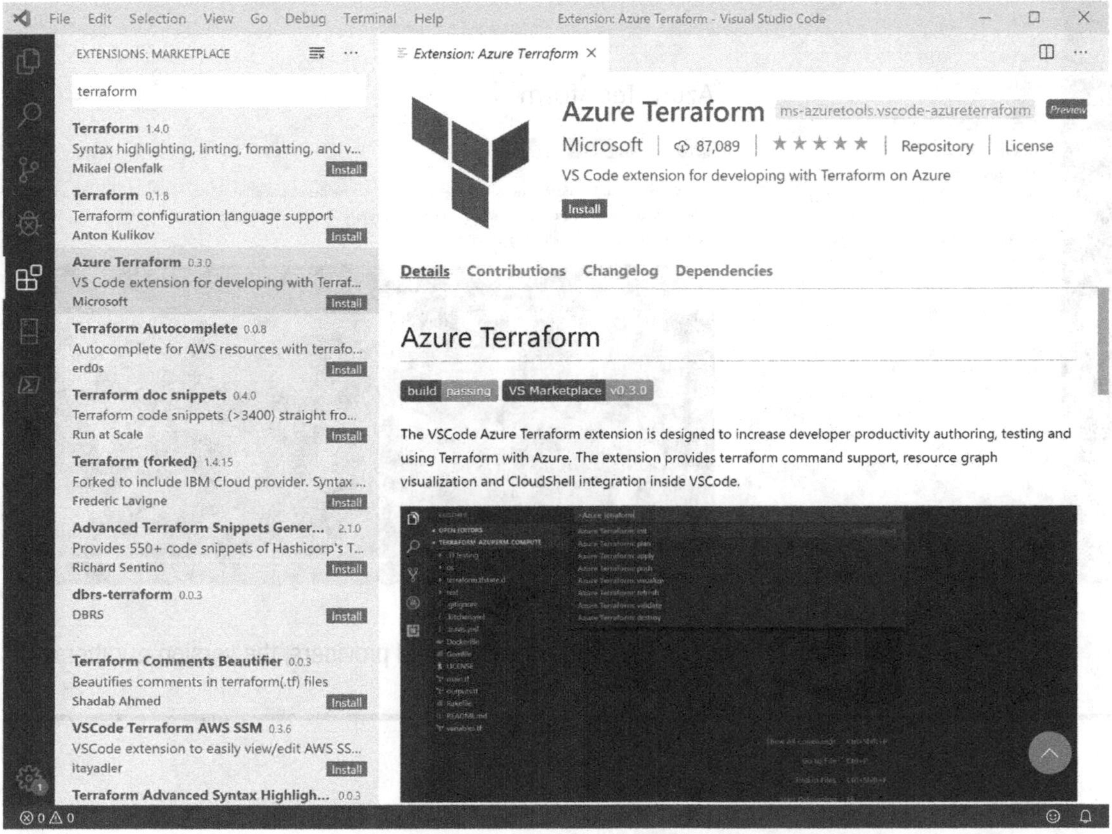

3. Use the Azure Terraform extension. Note the one created by Microsoft and not another developer or corporation. Select the Install option.
4. Verify that the Terraform extension is installed by using the search bar. Type **@installed**.
5. The extension should appear in the list of installed extensions.

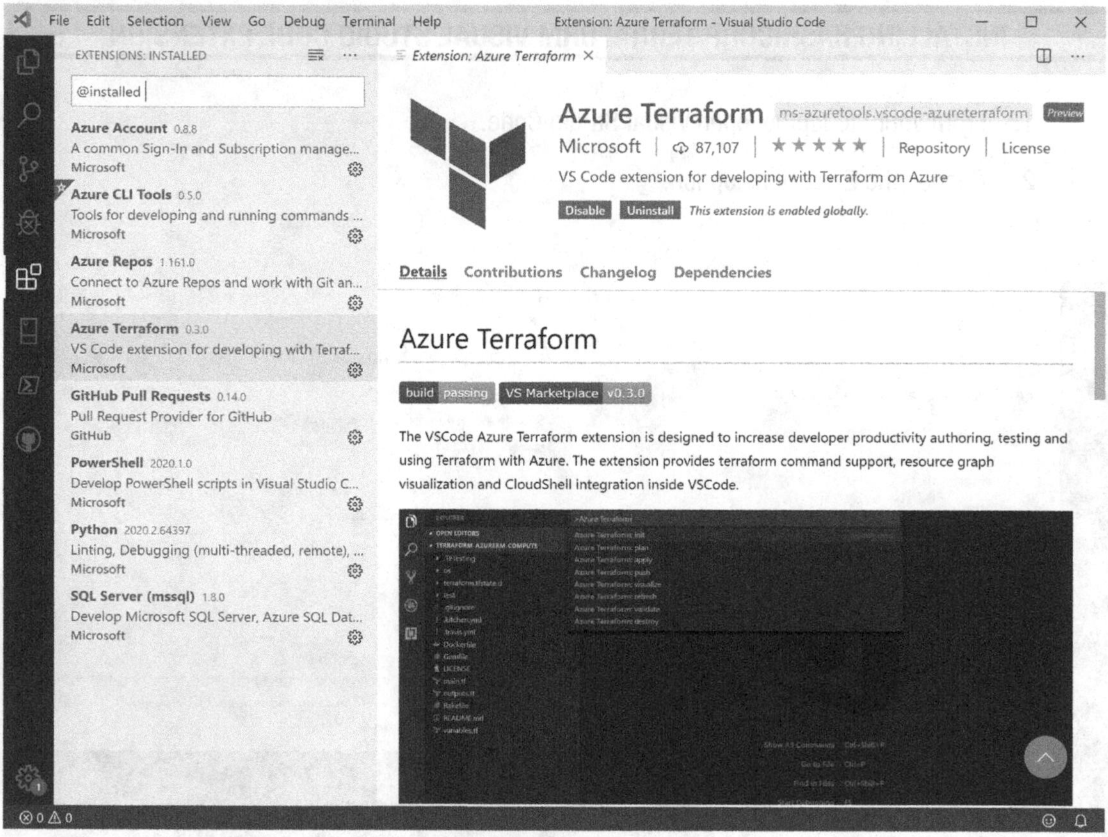

As a note, as Microsoft and HashiCorp upgrade extensions and providers, the version numbers continue to increase.

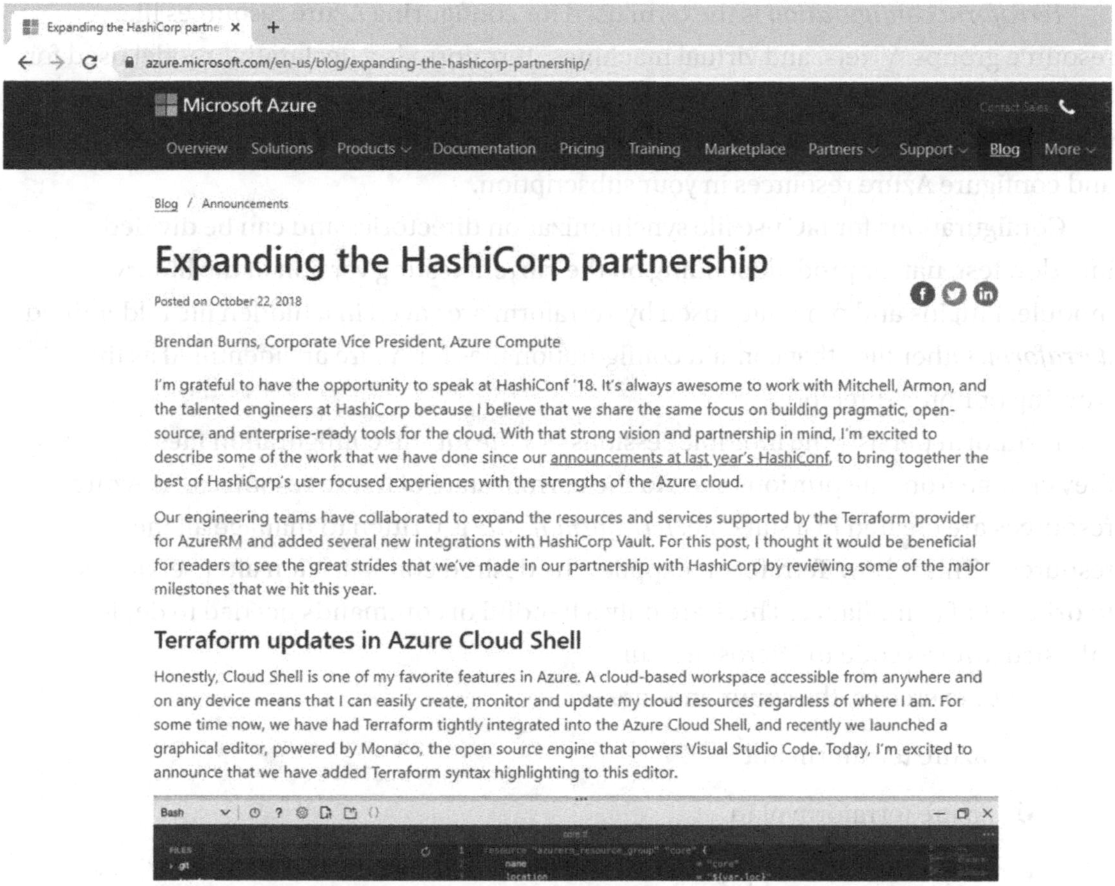

Figure 11-5. Microsoft and HashiCorp co-engineering blog post

Once the Terraform template is created, it is deployed from the Visual Studio terminal. Working with HashiCorp Terraform from the view of a DevOps engineer, you gain insight into the code structure now that the extensions are installed in Visual Studio Code (VS Code). Like ARM templates, Terraform uses a configuration file, and it is in one of two formats: HashiCorp Configuration Language (HCL) or JSON.

The HCL format uses less bracketing and is an easy-to-read file structure (easy for humans to read) but a machine-formal file structure. HashiCorp Terraform supports JSON as an alternative configuration file; however, with Terraform version 0.12 and later, the JSON files have a 1:1 mapping to HCL. The HCL configuration language format can be reviewed at `www.terraform.io/docs/configuration/syntax.html`.

Note Terraform 2.0 is the current version that continues support for ARM.

Terraform configuration is the term used for configuring Azure resources like resource groups, VNets, and virtual machines. Terraform is a declarative model used for building code modules and IaC libraries. This means that you write the code to create the desired state, and then Terraform communicates through Azure provide to create and configure Azure resources in your subscription.

Configurations for IaC use file synchronization directories and can be divided into dev, test, uat, or prod, depending on the current testing version of the library module. Plugins and other files used by Terraform are saved in a hidden file folder titled *.terraform*. Other files that contain configuration files for Azure are identified as the working or home directory.

Terraform persists the multiple sessions of *state* for the configuration files as they change from the previous state to the current state of Azure resources. As Azure resources are created in a state file, *terraform.tfstate* is written to manage all the resources. This is how Terraform reapplies the desired configuration after services start to drift out of compliance. There are only a handful of commands needed to deploy infrastructure as code to Microsoft Azure.

For our exercises, the commands are

- azure terraform init
- azure terraform plan
- azure terraform apply
- azure terraform destroy

Figure 11-6 shows the VS Code to interact with Terraform. It then invokes the Azure cloud shell to continue with the Terraform action.

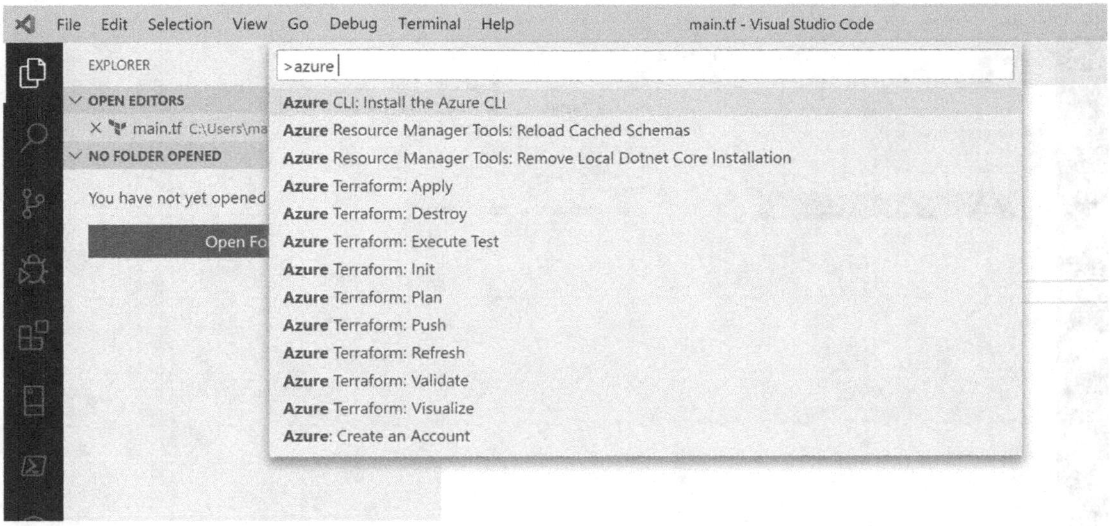

***Figure 11-6.** Visual Studio Code Azure Terraform commands*

Once the Terraform command is selected, the next action from VS Code is to open the Azure command shell to invoke the Terraform command in your Azure subsection, as shown in Figure 11-7.

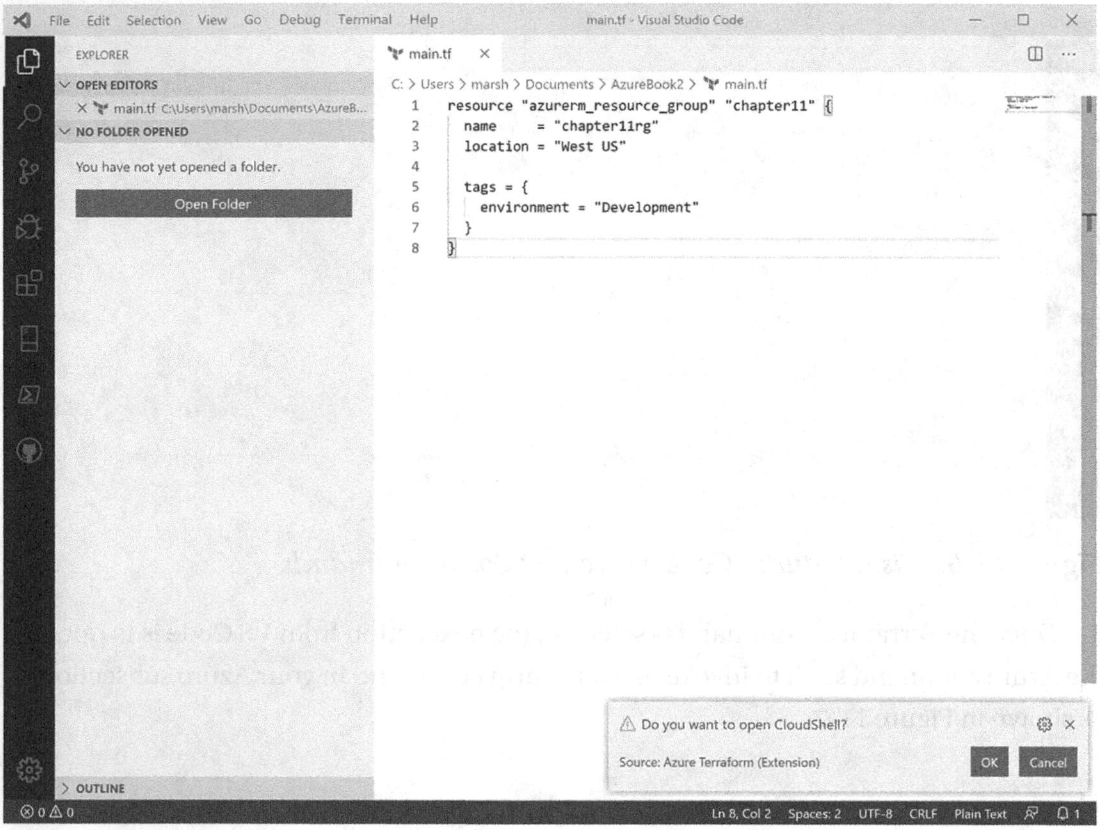

Figure 11-7. *VS Code prompt to open the Azure Cloud Shell to run the Terraform command*

Writing code to deploy Azure infrastructure and resources with VS Code is made more powerful when we use variables. The daily use of variables by developers is not specific to Terraform. A few of the directories that are used in VS Code for Terraform include

- main.tf
- outputs.tf
- variables.tf

You added the Terraform extensions to Visual Studio Code. You can optionally install NodeJS and GraphViz (not shown for exercises). These basic steps need to be added to a best practice installation guide to run HashiCorp Terraform on Microsoft Azure.

Deploy VNets with Code

This example begins with showing only a snippet of code for the creation of Azure virtual networks (VNets) showing two different configuration files. The ARM template for JSON is first, followed by the Azure TF HCL configuration file. The focus is to show the similarities between ARM templates deployed with VS Code PowerShell or CLI and HashiCorp Terraform HCL templates deployed from a VS Code terminal.

Note All the code for the software-defined infrastructure, both Microsoft Azure ARM templates and HashiCorp Terraform, can be downloaded from `https://github.com/harris-soh-copeland-puca`.

The first set of examples include the larger Azure network used for all the services needed in a Classless Inter-Domain Routing (CIDR) network. The /16 provides more than 65,000 subnets. The actual number is 65,536; however, Azure reserves five individual TCP/IP address for internal functions. The two subnets divided are /24, which provides 256 IP addresses in total. However, we need to take reservations into account as shown in Listing 11-1 for ARM and Listing 11-2 for Terraform.

Listing 11-1. ARM JSON Configure the Entire VNet and Two Subnets

```
{
    "$schema": "https://schema.management.azure.com/schemas/2015-01-01/
               deploymentTemplate.json#",
    "contentVersion": "1.0.0.0",
    "parameters": {
...
"variables": {
    "addressPrefix": "10.0.0.0/16",
    "subnetName": "webtier",
    "subnetPrefix": "10.0.1.0/24",
"subnetName": "businesstier",
    "subnetPrefix": "10.0.2.0/24",
...
```

```
"subnets": [
          {
            "name": "[variables('subnetName')]",
            "properties": {
              "addressPrefix": "[variables('subnetPrefix')]",
```

Listing 11-2. Terrform HCL Configure the Entire VNet and Two Subnets

```
resource "azurerm_virtual_network" "chapter11net" {
  name                = "${var.prefix}-network"
  resource_group_name = "${azurerm_resource_group.example.name}"
  location            = "${azurerm_resource_group.example.location}"
  address_space       = ["10.0.0.0/16"]
}
...
resource "azurerm_subnet" "webtier" {
  name                 = "webtier"
  virtual_network_name = "${azurerm_virtual_network.example.name}"
  resource_group_name  = "${azurerm_resource_group.example.name}"
  address_prefix       = "10.0.1.0/24"
}
...
resource "azurerm_subnet" "businesstier" {
  name                 = "businesstier"
  virtual_network_name = "${azurerm_virtual_network.example.name}"
  resource_group_name  = "${azurerm_resource_group.example.name}"
  address_prefix       = "10.0.2.0/24"
}
```

Deploy VMs with Code

This example begins by showing only a snippet of code for the creation of a virtual machine: Ubuntu Server. Listing 11-3 is the ARM template. Listing 11-4 creates the same Ubuntu Server version using Terraform.

Listing 11-3. ARM JSON Configure the Ubnutu Server

```
"ubuntuOSVersion": {
            "type": "string",
            "defaultValue": "16.04-LTS",
...
"storageProfile": {
                    "osDisk": {
                        "createOption": "fromImage",
                        "managedDisk": {
                            "storageAccountType":
"[variables('osDiskType')]"
...
"VariableForDiskSizeChapter11": {
      "type": "string",
      "metadata": {
        "description": "Size of each data disk in GB"
      ...
 "diskSizeGB": "[parameters(VariableForDiskSizeChapter11)]",
              "lun": 0,
              "createOption": "Empty"}
```

Listing 11-4. Terrform HCL Configure the Ubnutu Server

```
source_image_reference {
    publisher = "Canonical"
    offer     = "UbuntuServer"
    sku       = "16.04-LTS"
    version   = "latest"
  }

  os_disk {
    storage_account_type = "Standard_LRS"
    caching              = "ReadWrite"
  }
}
```

```
resource "azurerm_managed_disk" "data" {
  name                 = "data"
  location             = azurerm_resource_group.main.location
  create_option        = "Empty"
  disk_size_gb         = 20
  resource_group_name  = azurerm_resource_group.main.name
  storage_account_type = "Standard_LRS"
}

resource "azurerm_virtual_machine_data_disk_attachment" "data" {
  virtual_machine_id = azurerm_linux_virtual_machine.main.id
  managed_disk_id    = azurerm_managed_disk.data.id
  lun                = 0
  caching            = "None"
}
```

These views of creating a template library for both ARM and Terraform are very basic but a necessary place to start. As your skill increases with the use of both deployment methods, additional features are needed in the real-world deployment of Microsoft Azure infrastructure as code.

IaC Enhancement Considerations

The examples can be deployed as provided in this chapter but, with the understanding that other Azure services may be required to deploy or to be modify, dependent on your Azure subscription.

A list of the business requirements is needed before the IaC library examples can be deployed into production.

- Increase security by deploying Azure DDoS (distributed denial-of-services) protection
- Create a subnet and enable an Azure bastion host service
- Update the entire template to support high availability
- Deploy to another cloud provider

Note We purposefully show only a snippet of code for both ARM templates in JSON and HashiCorp Terraform and not a complete deployment solution.

You always want to improve security, and reduce risk. You can improve the overall Defense In Depth of Microsoft Azure while deploying IaC templates. However, if you want to enable an Azure DDoS plan for a specific region, first validate the service is available in the region that is exposed to the public IP address.

You also need to choose between the Basic and Standard plans. Basic is a free service. Standard has a usage cost and provides log streaming for SIEM (Security Integration Event Management) integration, real-time attack alerts and diagnostic logs, post-attack mitigation reports, layer 3 to layer 7 mitigation, and more. It can be enabled with IaC techniques with ARM, Listing 11-5. The HashiCorp Terraform code snippet, Listing 11-6 enables the Azure DDoS plan on an entire resource group using the network resource to enable the Azure protection plan.

The ARM and Terraform examples provide the same results using different language descriptors.

Listing 11-5. The JSON Format Needed to Add the DDoS service to Your ARM Template Code

```
{
  "name": "Chapter11-example",
  "type": "Microsoft.Network/ddosProtectionPlans",
  "apiVersion": "2018-08-01",
  "location": "Central US",
  "tags": {},
  "properties": {}
}
```

Listing 11-6. Terraform Code Snippet

```
{
resource "azurerm_resource_group" "chapter11" {
  name     = "chapter11-rg"
  location = "Central US"
}
```

```
resource "azurerm_network_ddos_protection_plan" "chapter11" {
  name                = "standard-protection-plan"
  location            = azurerm_resource_group.chapter11.location
  resource_group_name = azurerm_resource_group.chapter11.name
}
```

Note Learn more about Azure DDoS plans, features, and the types of attacks the service reduces at `https://docs.microsoft.com/en-us/azure/virtual-network/ddos-protection-overview`.

Create a TCP/IP subnet (with a public IP address) in Azure and include a bastion *host using ARM templates in JSON format, as shown in Listing 11-7.*

Listing 11-7. Bastion Host Using ARM Templates JSON Format

```
{
          "apiVersion": "2018-10-01",
          "type": "Microsoft.Network/bastionHosts",
          "name": "[parameters('bastion-host-name')]",
          "location": "[parameters('location')]",
}
```

HashiCorp Terraform code snippet, Listing 11-8, is used to enable Azure bastion host on an entire Azure virtual network with a public IP address using the network resource to enable the Azure bastion host. The term *bastion* is sometimes replaced with *jump-box*. The bastion host is a VM that has been "hardened" and less vulnerable to cybersecurity threats. You log on to the Azure bastion host from your laptop to perform administrative work on Azure resources, and not perform Azure administrative work directly from your laptop. You can read more about Azure bastion hosts at `https://docs.microsoft.com/en-us/azure/bastion/bastion-overview`.

Listing 11-8. Host Using Terraform Template

```
{
resource "azurerm_bastion_host" "chapter11" {
  name                = "chapter11bastion"
  location            = azurerm_resource_group.chapter11.location
  resource_group_name = azurerm_resource_group.chapter11.name
}
```

You can also create an Azure availability set. In our example, Listing 11-9 ARM, you set the number of Azure fault domains to 3 and the number of Azure update domains to 3. This code snip-it is used to show how to enable the VMs in the Azure subnet to be in Azure, Listing 11-10 Terraform.

Listing 11-9. ARM JSON Format

```
{
"type": "Microsoft.Compute/availabilitySets",
"name": "availabilityChapter11",
"apiVersion": "2018-10-01",
"location": "[parameters(Central US')]",
"properties": {
  "platformFaultDomainCount": 3,
  "platformUpdateDomainCount": "3"
 }
```

Create an availability set, and leave the default set to 3 and the number of Azure update domains at 3. This code enables the VMs in the Azure subnet to be in Azure.

Listing 11-10. HashiCorp Terraform Format

```
{
resource "azurerm_availability_set" "chapter11" {
  name                = "chapter11-aset"
  location            = azurerm_resource_group.chapter11.location
  resource_group_name = azurerm_resource_group.chapter11.name
  platform_fault_domain_count = 3
  platform_upgrade_domain_count = 3
}
```

An additional benefit, when you include Terraform to deploy infrastructure in Azure, is the same work flow when deploying to other cloud providers. You should include HashiCorp Terraform services for your next IaC platform for testing.

HashiCorp Terraform Cloud (free trial) is a service that does not run on-premises. If you need to have greater features not enabled in a cloud service, you should download HashiCorp Terraform Enterprise (free trial).

A short list of features supported by HashiCorp Terraform Cloud includes

- 24/7 phone support for mission-critical IaC
- Access control and security permissions with separation of roles
- Centralized logging for audit and compliance on any cloud provider
- Policy as code—HashiCorp Sentinel policy engine enforcement on any cloud provider

You can sign up for a free trial of the HashiCorp Terraform Cloud at `https://app.terraform.io/signup/account?utm_source=offerings&utm_campaign=tf_cloud_ga` (see Figure 11-8).

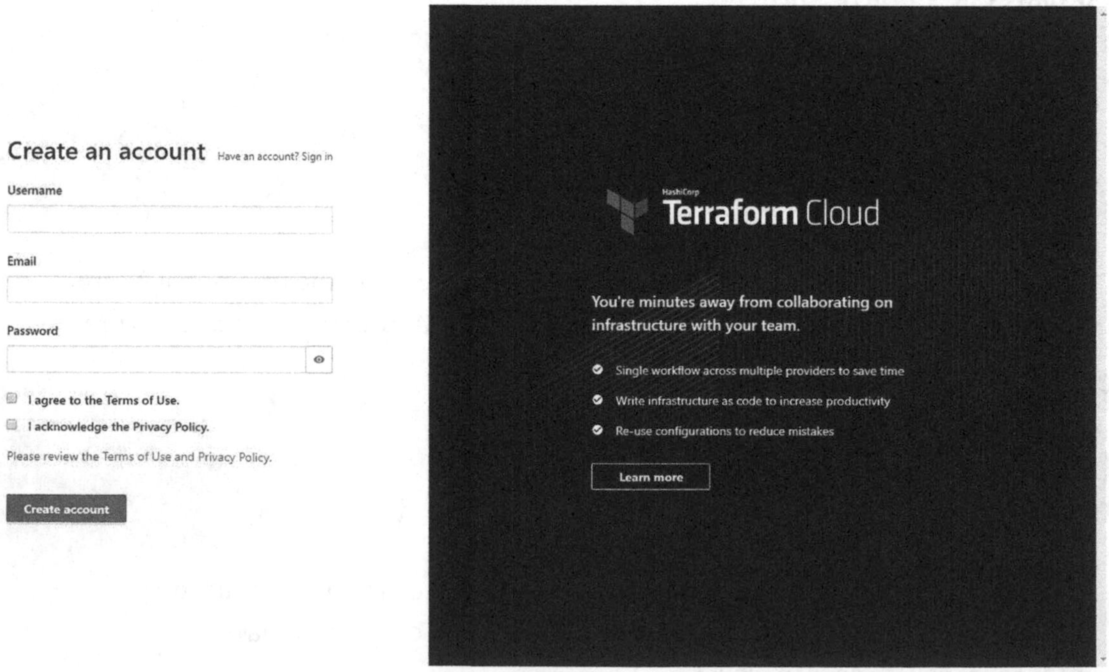

***Figure 11-8.** HashiCorp Terraform Cloud free signup page*

HashiCorp Terraform providers for Microsoft Azure have continued to improve over the last five years with more than 300 resources and 100 data sources added since version 1.0. HashiCorp TF AzureRM 2.0 brings three major improvements.

- Overhaul of the virtual machine and virtual machine scale set resources
- Introduction of custom timeouts
- Removal of deprecated resources

Troubleshooting IaC

You had a brief introduction to both ARM and Terraform to create your Azure infrastructure, and errors are part of the templating processes. Some of the common errors can be removed from ARM templates if you pay close attention to the bracketing required by JSON files.

JSON documents start and end with curly brackets, { }, and have a name/value pair, decorated by double quotes (" "). Some of the common errors are identified in the Microsoft Azure guide at `https://docs.microsoft.com/en-us/azure/azure-resource-manager/templates/common-deployment-errors`.

HashiCorp Terraform has the best architecture practices identified, which includes guidance on troubleshooting (see `www.terraform.io/docs/providers/oci/guides/troubleshooting.html`).

Subject-matter experts (SME) specialize in the pattern of building, testing, destroying, and rebuilding. The creation of a reusable Azure template library is an ongoing process and not a job role that allows the tools to be used once and then stored away.

Azure Blueprints

Azure Blueprints enable engineers and developers to build solutions using proven, hardened, templated, architectures that comply with organizational, industry, regulatory, and government requirements and policy. Blueprints enable rapid deployment to a secure and certifiable state of a cloud-hosted service in your organization, regardless of who the consumers of that service are. Blueprints allow architects to define roles, policies, templates, and resource groups. Blueprints enable bringing these components to a common architect to build, test, and deploy, commonly known as CI/CD, which means continuous integration and continuous delivery. Blueprints are what they are called—blueprints from which Azure services can be built.

Azure Blueprints are based on Azure ARM templates. Azure templates are declarative files for creating Azure resources in a reliable, repeatable, and auditable manner. Azure ARM templates let you deploy IaC. They are text files in which you define which Azure resources you want to deploy and how they are configured. ARM templates are test files in the JSON format. These JSON files can be edited in any text editor, and hence, can be versioned. The declarative approaches to infrastructure as code, policy as code, configuration as code, and role-based access as code provide a simple authoring experience that is integrated with Azure policy remediations, GitHub tasks, and provisioning with a variety of third-party solutions such as Terraform, Ansible, SNOW, and so forth. To learn more about defining resources in Azure ARM templates, please refer to `https://docs.microsoft.com/en-us/azure/templates/`.

The use of the native ARM templates allows Azure administrators to deploy resources as soon as they are available in the Azure cloud. There are no delays in compatibility and capability when ARM templates are the deployment plane. These deployments can be tracked easily in the Azure portal, providing visibility into the success or failure of the deployment. ARM templates perform checks before deployment to validate that they will succeed. These checks are known as what-if checks, which allow administrators to simulate what a change will do when deployed. It is a valuable featuresince there is no way to test in an existing environment, This feature validates preflight.

Multiple ARM template deployments can run concurrently, which is unavailable when using middleware to run IaC deployments. ARM templates can deploy Azure Blueprints across the Azure infrastructure for your organization.

ARM templates can be centrally stored and shared across the Azure ARM control plane in Azure TemplateSpecs, which is very similar to the Azure Shared Image Gallery discussed in Chapter 10. This allows the sharing of Azure templates, customized for your specific organization across Azure regions, subscriptions, and tenants. Azure TemplateSpecs can be deployed with the Azure portal, PowerShell, or CLI, or as nested deployments. Azure template artifacts and template linking will be available soon.

If you would like a tutorial on how to deploy an ARM template, please refer to `https://docs.microsoft.com/en-us/azure/azure-resource-manager/templates/template-tutorial-create-first-template?tabs=azure-powershell`. By leveraging

Azure ARM templates and Azure Blueprints, you can deploy cloud-hosted services in your organization to satisfy all of your security, regulatory, and organization requirements.

Summary

In this chapter, you learned about Microsoft Azure Resource Manager, an API management layer to create, edit, and delete Azure services. You were introduced to the IaC processes needed to build template libraries for blueprints to deploy Azure services consistently. You were introduced to two prominent methods for creating templates: ARM templates and HashiCorp Terraform. There was an example deployment designed to create the basic building blocks and then enhance the design with additional features. You were introduced to Azure Blueprints and the context of having a set of Azure IaC plans that may be deployed and updated with version control to create a consistent deployment process.

In Chapter 12, you continue to expand your Azure learning journey with Web Apps, monitoring, and integrating with Azure authentication methods. You learn about implementing connectivity between Azure Active Directory and other business connectivity for secure sharing of data.

PART IV

Adopting Platform as a Service (PaaS)

CHAPTER 12

Azure Web Apps

In Chapter 3, we covered all the platform as a service (PaaS) offerings. As you saw, there are many PaaS workloads in Azure, spanning different types of services. In future chapters, we explore data science and machine learning, specifically PaaS, network PaaS, and database PaaS. We repeat several times in this book that PaaS should be adopted whenever possible because of better service-level agreements, lower overhead in management, and ease in deployment.

In this chapter, we look at Azure Web Apps, one of the most common and extensively used PaaS and one of the earliest PaaS workloads in Azure.

What Are Web Apps?

The best way to describe Azure Web Apps is that it is hosted on an Internet Information Services (IIS) server or an Apache server. When you create a website or a web-based application like a .NET app, you need to publish it to an IIS server or an Apache server that is public facing. Once the website or application is published, users can see the site via URL.

The IIS or Apache server is responsible for running the published applications and responding to requests from users. There is often more than one application per IIS or Apache server, so the requests need to be routed to the right applications.

The IIS or Apache server also needs to handle user authentication for applications hosted on the server. When problems arise, the server administrators may need to troubleshoot or restart the IIS or Apache service. In IIS, server administrators may restart the application service pool to limit affecting all the other applications.

The management work involving IIS or Apache is moot if web apps are used.

J. Soh et al., *Microsoft Azure*, https://doi.org/10.1007/978-1-4842-5958-0_12

Hands-on: Deploying a Web App

In this hands-on exercise, we introduce the deployment of an Azure web app using the Azure portal. In future chapters, we look at similar exercises using automation tools like Azure Resource Manager (ARM) templates and infrastructure as code with HashiCorp's Terraform.

1. Sign in to your Azure portal to create two web apps in two different geographical regions.
2. In Azure Home view, go to **New ➤ Web App**, and click **Create**.
3. Create a new resource group for testing. Select the runtime stack (ASP.NET v4.7 because it has Azure analytics support) and the Central US region, as shown in Figure 12-1.

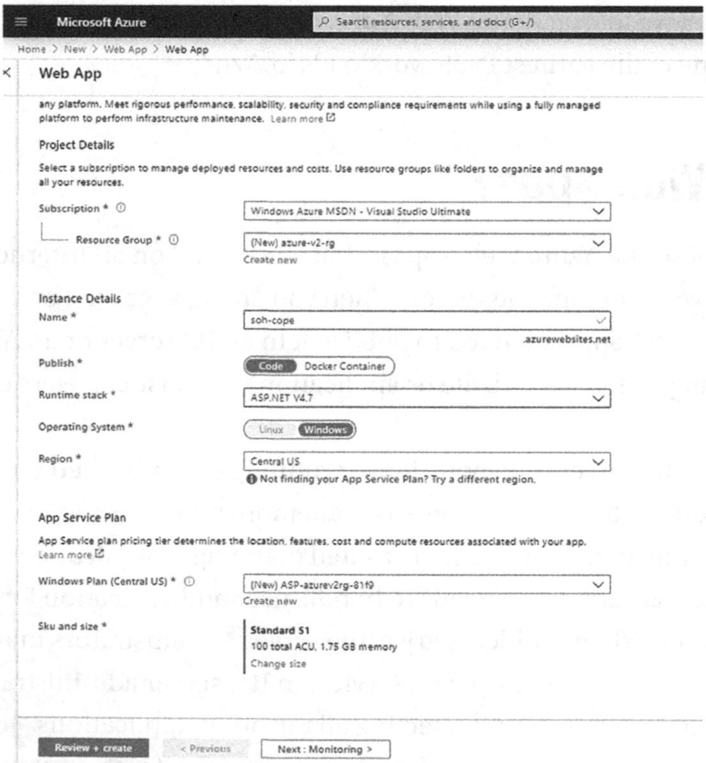

Figure 12-1. *Creating a web app*

4. Name this web app **soh-cope**.
5. Click **Next : Monitoring**.
6. Validate that Application Insight is enabled, select the default location, and click **Next : Tags**.
7. Tags are an easy method for identifying Azure services for different projects and billing purposes. Enter a name and a value and limit the resource to **Web App**. Click **Next : Review + create**.
8. Review the information on the Summary page, as shown in Figure 12-2, and then click **Create**.

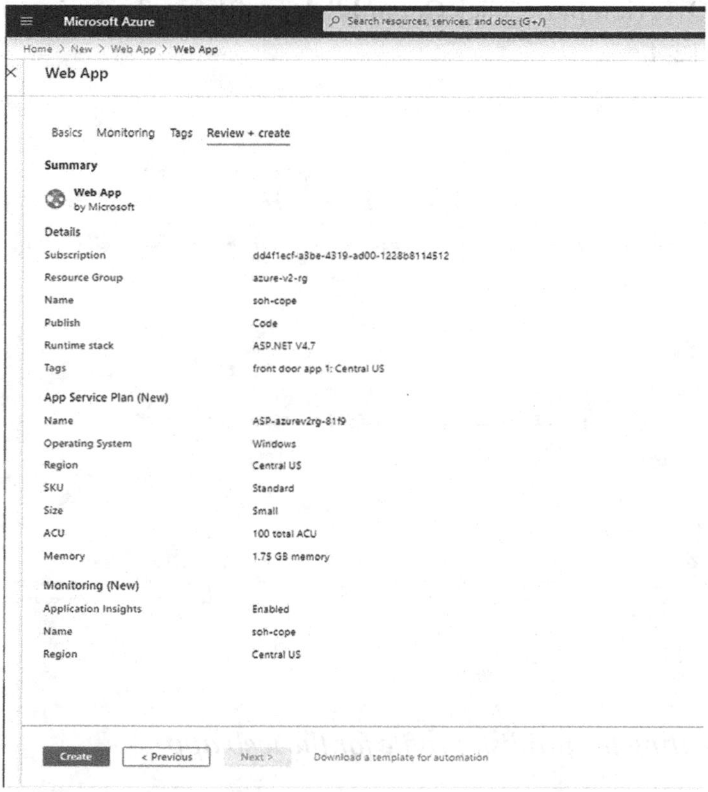

***Figure 12-2.** Pre-creation summary of web app*

9. Wait for the web app to be created. When done, you are notified and given the option to go to the resource, as shown in Figure 12-3. Click **Go to resource**.

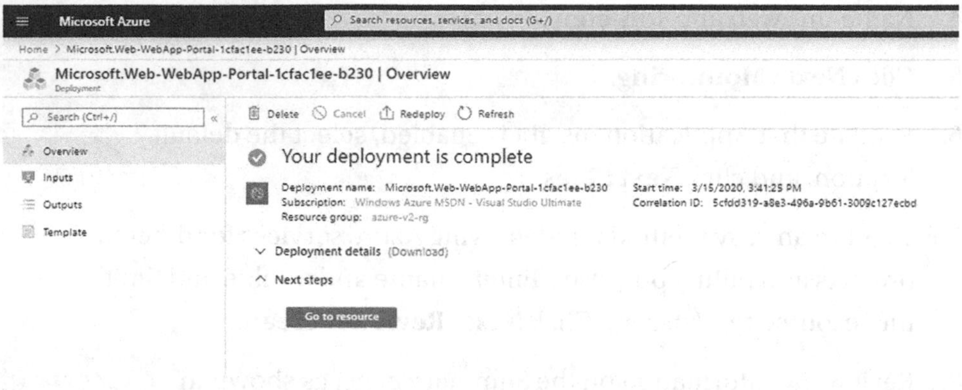

Figure 12-3. *Web app creation completed*

10. In the Overview pane, click **Get publish profile**, as shown in Figure 12-4.

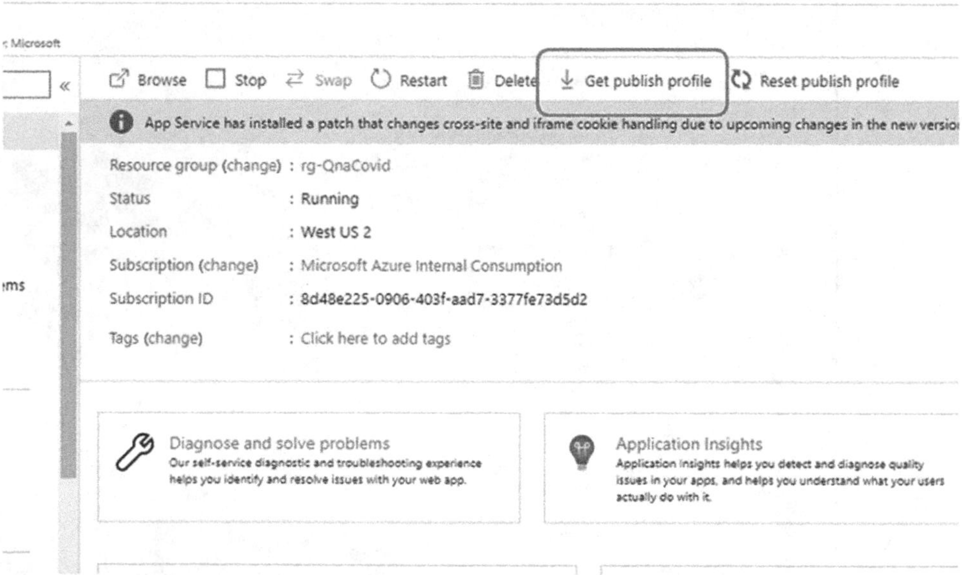

Figure 12-4. *Getting the publish profile for the web app*

11. Take note of the URL for this web app, as shown in Figure 12-5. The URL is <Web_App_Name>.azurewebsites.net. This is a routable and live website on the Internet, which is why the name of the web app has to be globally unique.

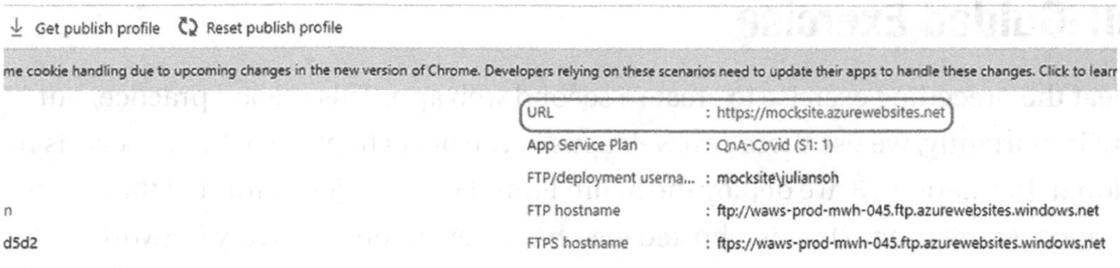

***Figure 12-5.** URL of web app*

12. Open another browser or browser tab and go to the web app's URL. You should see a page indicating that the site is properly configured and ready. Keep this tab open for now; you return to it after you publish your application to this web app.

You have successfully deployed a Windows-based web app, which is essentially a hosted IIS.

If you need a Linux-based web app (Apache), follow the same process, except choose a runtime stack that is available on Apache and select Linux as the operating system (see Figure 12-6).

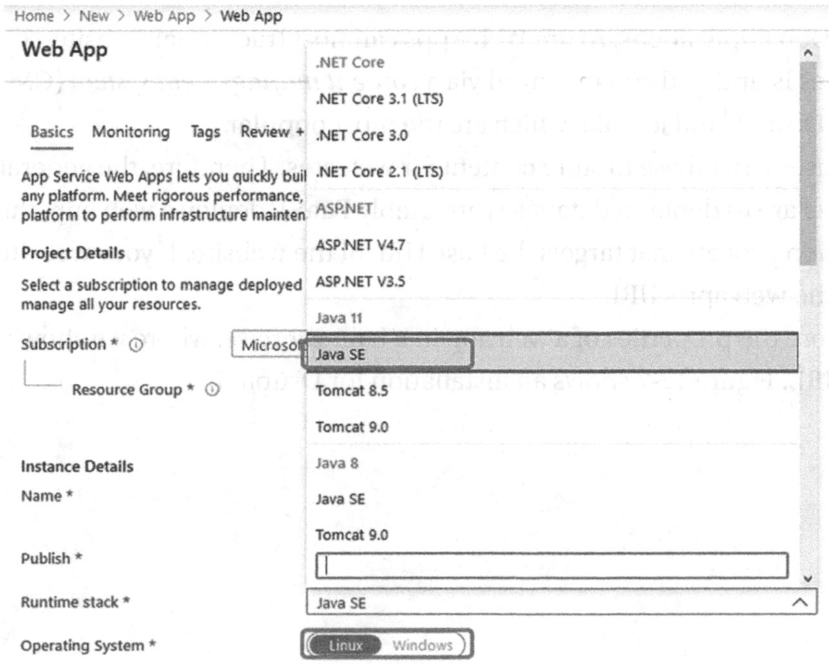

***Figure 12-6.** Selecting Linux because it supports the desired Java runtime stack*

Self-Guided Exercise

Repeat the preceding exercise to create a second web app. This is good practice, but more importantly, we use these two web apps in the next chapter, so this exercise is not optional. In Chapter 13, we deploy the Azure Front Door service in front of these two web apps. Azure Front Door is a hosted load balancer, content delivery network (CDN), and web application firewall (WAF) service. In fact, Azure Front Door is a network PaaS.

Use Table 12-1 to create the second web app in the **West Europe** region.

Table 12-1. *Information for Second Web App*

Configuration	Value
Web app name	soh-puca
Resource group	(New) azure-v3-rg
App service	ASP.NET v4.7

Content Management Systems on Web Apps

Aside from web applications, Azure Web Apps can host traditional websites. Content from websites is updated and managed via a *content management system* (CMS), such as WordPress, Drupal, and Joomla, which are the most popular.

A CMS uses a database to store content for websites. Therefore, the general requirements are to deploy a database (preferably PaaS), deploy a web app, then initiate the installation process that targets the base URL of the website. If your website is a web app, this is the web app's URL.

We explore the properties of a web app in a later exercise, where we show where to locate the URL. Figure 12-7 shows an installation for Drupal 7.

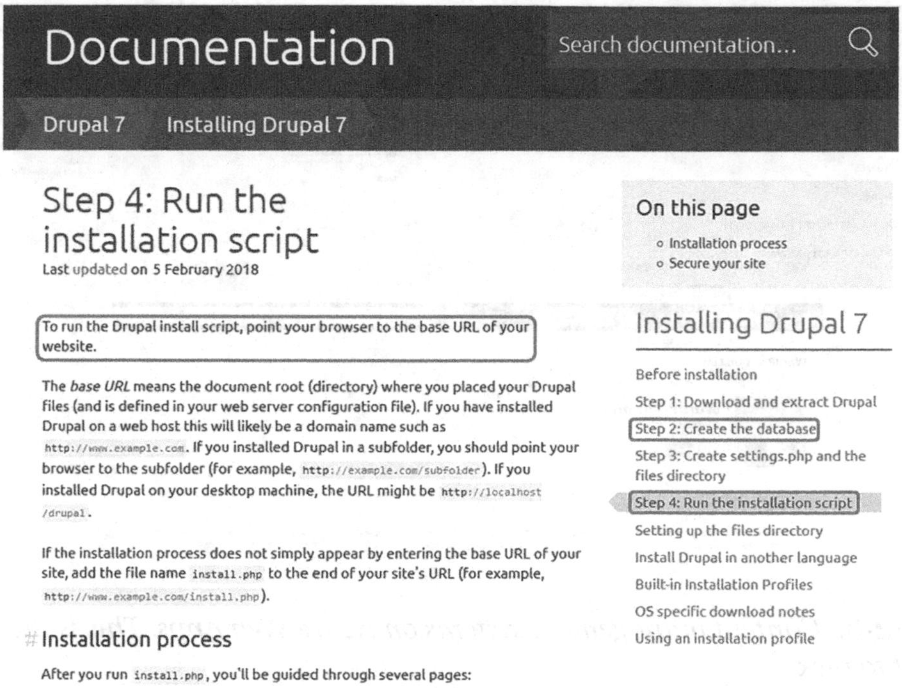

Figure 12-7. *Instructions for installing Drupal 7*

Alternatively, you can pick a deployment that includes the CMS already installed. On the Azure Marketplace, we found several CMSs that are ready to be deployed as a PaaS. The important thing is to make sure that the deployment is a web app, as shown in Figure 12-8, and not as a CMS on a virtual machine, as shown in Figure 12-9.

CMS solutions deployed over PaaS do not affect the way webmasters and content moderators update and maintain content. Only the platform has changed, and no operating system or underlying hardware needs to be maintained, so the overhead is reduced for system administrators.

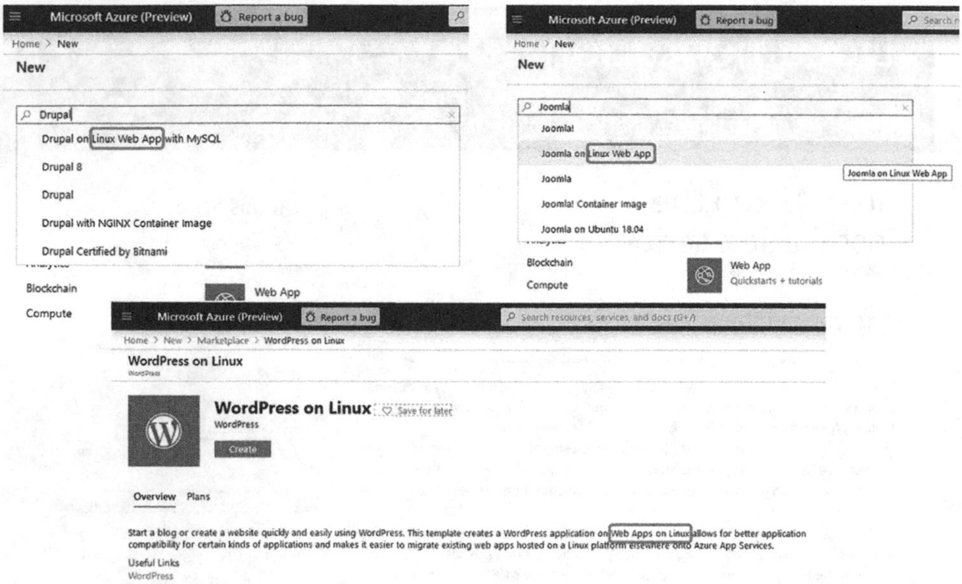

Figure 12-8. *Content management systems on Azure Web Apps. This is the option we want to pick*

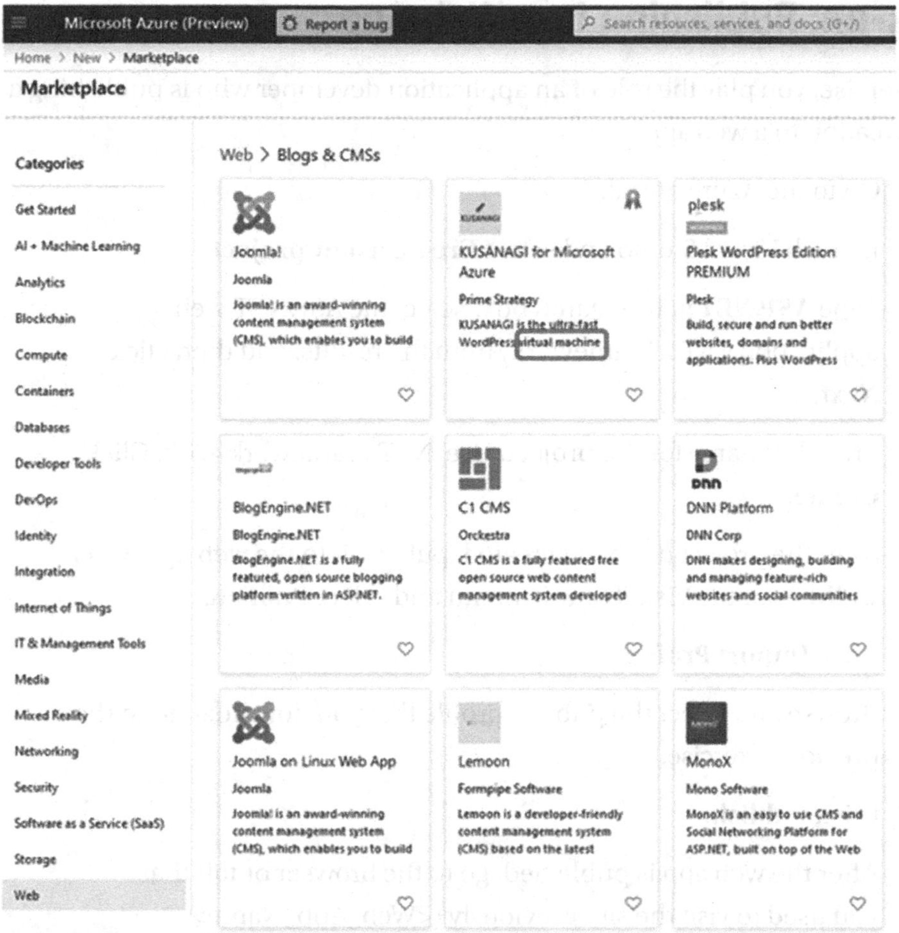

Figure 12-9. *Content management systems on a virtual machine. Not a web app/PaaS. This is the option we do not want to pick*

Using Azure Web Apps

Deploying an application to a web app, also known as *publishing*, remains the same for application developers and webmasters.

You can deploy applications directly from Visual Studio by publishing the application, or via FTP. If you are updating content in a CMS, you use the CMS's interface.

For the next hands-on exercise, we publish a .NET web application to a web app. In later chapters, we continue using this web app for other exercises as we make modifications to the .NET web application.

Hands-on: Publishing to a Web App

In this exercise, you play the role of an application developer who is publishing a .NET web application to a web app.

1. Go to the Azure portal.
2. Launch Visual Studio and select **Create a new project**.
3. Type **ASP.NET** in the search box. Select the ASP.NET web application (.NET Framework) from the results, and then click **Next**.
4. Provide a name for the project. Use .NET Framework 4.7.2. Click **Create**.
5. After the project has been created, publish it to the web app. Click **Build** from the Visual Studio menu and select **Publish**.
6. Click **Import Profile**.
7. Browse and select the publish profile that you downloaded in the previous exercise.
8. Click **Publish**.
9. After the web app is published, go to the browser or tab that you used to visit the site previously (<Web_App_Name>.azurewebsites.net) and click **Refresh**. You should see the ASP.NET application that you just published.

You can use the azurewebsites.net for your web application, but generally, you want to use a custom domain name. In this next exercise, we associate a custom domain to our website and look at other settings.

Hands-on: Adding a Custom Domain to a Web App

In almost all circumstances, you want your website to reflect the organization or entity. As such, a website that ends in azurewebsites.net is not desirable. In this exercise, you associate a custom domain name to replace azurewebsites.net as the suffix. To do this exercise, you need to have a custom domain name, and the app service plan for the web app must be a paid tier.

1. In the Azure portal and with your web app selected, under Settings, click **Custom Domains**.

2. In the Customs Domains pane, you see the IP address that has been assigned to this web app, and whether you want to enforce HTTPS traffic only. Take note of the IP address.

3. Go to your DNS service provider, or use Azure DNS, and create an A record for the custom domain name. Azure DNS was covered in Chapter 3, so if you are using Azure DNS, please refer to Chapter 3 if necessary. If you do not have a custom domain yet, you can purchase one through the portal by selecting Buy Domain at the bottom of the pane.

Note Alternatively, you can also use a CNAME record and point the custom domain to the <Web_App_name>.azurewebsites.net URL.

---

4. Click **Add custom domain**.

5. Enter the custom domain name and click **Validate**. The portal resolves the DNS for the custom domain name to confirm that it is pointing to the web app via an A or CNAME record.

6. If DNS is set up correctly, the type of record (A or CNAME) is automatically detected, and you are allowed to add the custom domain, as shown in Figure 12-10.

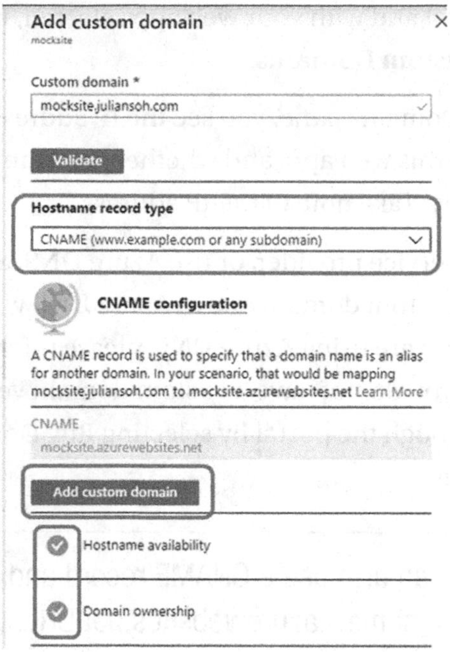

Figure 12-10. *Adding a custom domain*

7. Click **Add custom domain**.
8. Once the custom domain is added, it shows up as an assigned domain without an SSL, as shown in Figure 12-11.

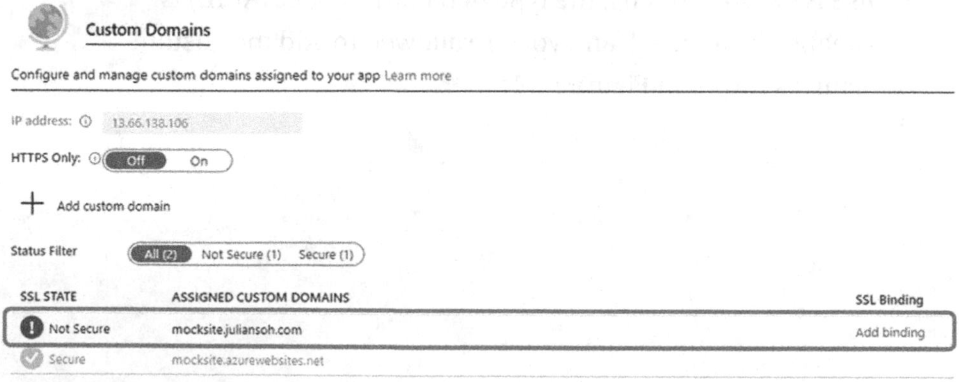

Figure 12-11. *Custom domain name added to the web app*

9. Open another browser tab and navigate to the custom domain name. It resolves to this web app.

Hands-on: Monitoring a Web App

You can monitor a web app to ensure that it is performing optimally. Performance monitoring is natively built into Azure Web Apps; it is called Application Insights.

1. Click **Performance** on the Azure portal, and then click **Turn on Application Insights**.
2. Select **Enable** to enable Application Insights. Select **Create a new resource** to capture performance statistics, as shown in Figure 12-12.

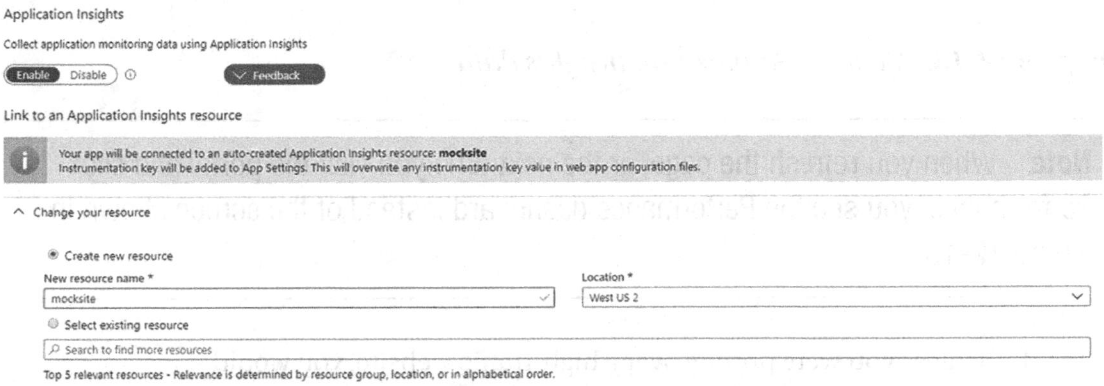

***Figure 12-12.** Turn on Application Insights and create a new resource to capture statistics*

3. When Application Insights is turned on, click **View Application Insights data**, as shown in Figure 12-13.

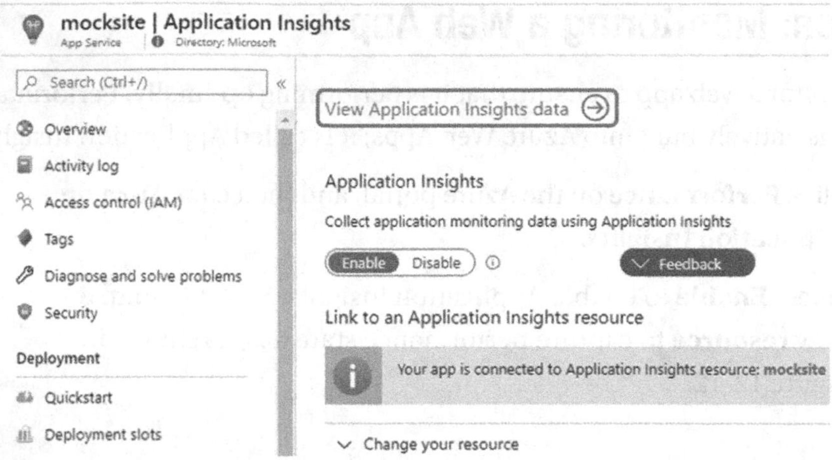

***Figure 12-13.** Viewing Application Insights data*

Note When you refresh the page, or the next time you visit the portal and click Performance, you see the Performance dashboard instead of the screen shown in Figure 12-13.

---

4. Unless you were porting over a high-traffic website, you would not see any statistics yet. Come back later or generate test traffic with a loading tool like open source k6 (see `https://github.com/loadimpact/k6`).

5. Once a load test is done, refresh the Applications Insights pane and look at the statistics, as shown in Figure 12-14.

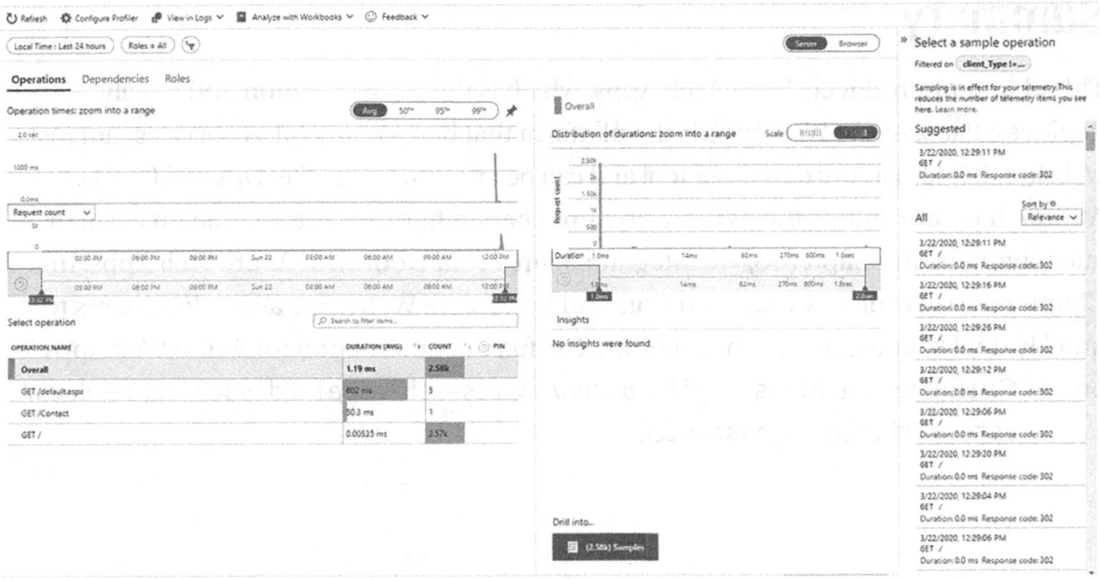

Figure 12-14. Application Insights statistics. Yours may look different based on layout and numbers

Hands-on: Self-Guided Exercises

Explore the other configuration options for Azure Web Apps and Applications Insights. Drill down to reports and add more metrics and filters. You can also create your own custom reports.

Look at the Authentication/Authorization pane and try out the different authentication methods if you need to secure your web app with login credentials.

Backup is another important topic that you can explore on your own. You can create periodic snapshots of your web apps and backups.

Note Securing your web app with TLS certificates is an important topic. We did not cover this topic in this chapter because it will be discussed in Azure Front Door in the next chapter. Communication between Azure Front Door and the web application pools containing web apps do not need to communicate over TLS.

Summary

This chapter introduced Azure Web Apps, which is the most common and widely deployed PaaS. Azure Web Apps is the platform that hosts many other services, not just websites. It is also a core developer tool and can be integrated with DevOps and CI/CD. Although we are ending the Azure Web Apps chapter here, we see it come up again in later chapters. In Chapter 13, we integrate Azure Front Door with Azure Web Apps. In Chapter 20, we explore CI/CD and slots and how Azure Web Apps allow developers to quickly deploy and manage applications. The full documentation for Azure Web Apps is on our GitHub repo at `https://github.com/harris-soh-copeland-puca/azure-docs/tree/master/articles/app-service`.

CHAPTER 13

Network Platform as a Service

Azure Virtual Network (VNet) should be the starting point before deploying any virtual machine, web app, or storage container. The virtual networks in your Azure subscription are the global and local networks used for connectivity in the cloud. Internally, VNet allows secure private connections for all of your business resources. Externally, it supports exposing public endpoints to the Internet for access by clients or cyberattacks.

This chapter provides information focusing on the Azure cloud-native networking services (i.e., platform as a service). You'll learn about the service, how it is used in the Azure platform, and why it is helpful to your business. In Chapter 2, you were provided an overview of Azure networking by creating a virtual network for all services and then dividing that network into subnets.

The address space used by the IP address is divided using Classless Inter-Domain Routing (CIDR). This range of IP subnets is represented by using a slash and a number (i.e., /16, /24, /128, and so on).

CIDR eases the work required by reducing the load on large network routers, which increases the size of the routing table. The aggregation of IP addresses through CIDR reduces the size of the routing tables; it is used inside Microsoft Azure for all VNets.

This chapter will not enable you to be a network architect, but you learn about the advantages of using Azure networking platform services, including how it helps route IP traffic and security.

Figure 13-1 visualizes the layers of service in the Azure network.

J. Soh et al., *Microsoft Azure*, https://doi.org/10.1007/978-1-4842-5958-0_13

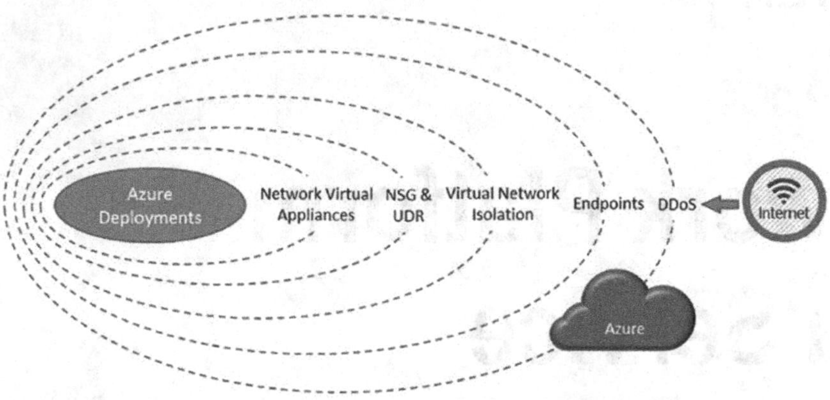

Figure 13-1. *Layers of Microsoft Azure network security visualization*

When you're working in the Azure portal, you can create a TCP/IP network. Figure 13-2 is a screenshot of the Azure portal during the final wizard journey page. The view displays creating a large virtual network, many subnets, and default network security services, including distributed denial of service (DDoS) protection and firewalls.

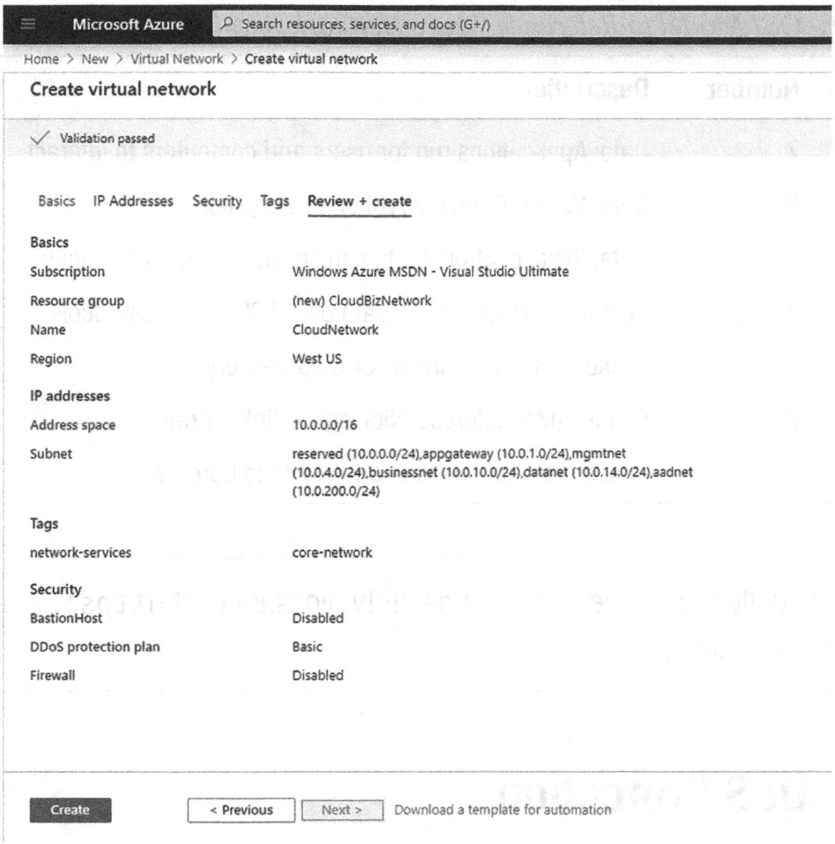

***Figure 13-2.** Azure portal view of virtual network platform services*

You should reference Figure 13-2 as you continue through this chapter and learn about the network services and security features, and how they support Microsoft Azure's network layer of defense. We don't want to go too deeply into a network layer and cybersecurity-focused discussion; however, a high-level reference of the Open Systems Interconnection (OSI) model is helpful.

Table 13-1 provides a conceptual view of the communication framework; you may reference this information as you read through this chapter.

Table 13-1. OSI Model to Reference Azure Network Services Support

Layer Name	Number	Description
Application	7	Data: Applications run for users and computers to interact
Presentation	6	Data: Usable Data, encryption / decryption
Session	5	Data: Sync, controls ports and sessions and connections
Transport	4	Segments: Host to host, data over TCP or UDP protocols
Network	3	Packets with IP address, for data delivery
Datalink	2	Frames (Mac address, Nic) logical link for data
Physical	1	Bits: stream for the Network Interface Card (NIC)

Note An excellent and free computer security glossary is at `https://csrc.nist.gov/Glossary`.

Azure DDoS Protection

Azure DDoS (distributed denial of service) protection is mitigation enabled with the "basic" service as part of the network platform (i.e., when you build a VNet). The service continuously monitors while providing defense against common network-level attacks. As a reminder, according to the National Institute of Standards and Technology (NIST), a DDoS attack is "a denial of service technique that uses numerous hosts to perform the attack." A simple definition is an overwhelming malicious attack to disrupt services and make them unavailable. This concept becomes clear as you consider the magnitude of globally coordinated DDoS attacks measured by the network bandwidth disruption, sometimes measured in terabits per second.

Before you can use the Azure network platform service DDoS, the purchase must be completed so that it appears as an option when you use the portal to create a VNet.

Figure 13-3 shows purchasing the service in the Azure portal. The DDoS protection service is a monthly recurring fee, but if you only use it for a portion of days or weeks, Azure offers a prorated bill for the hours and data used.

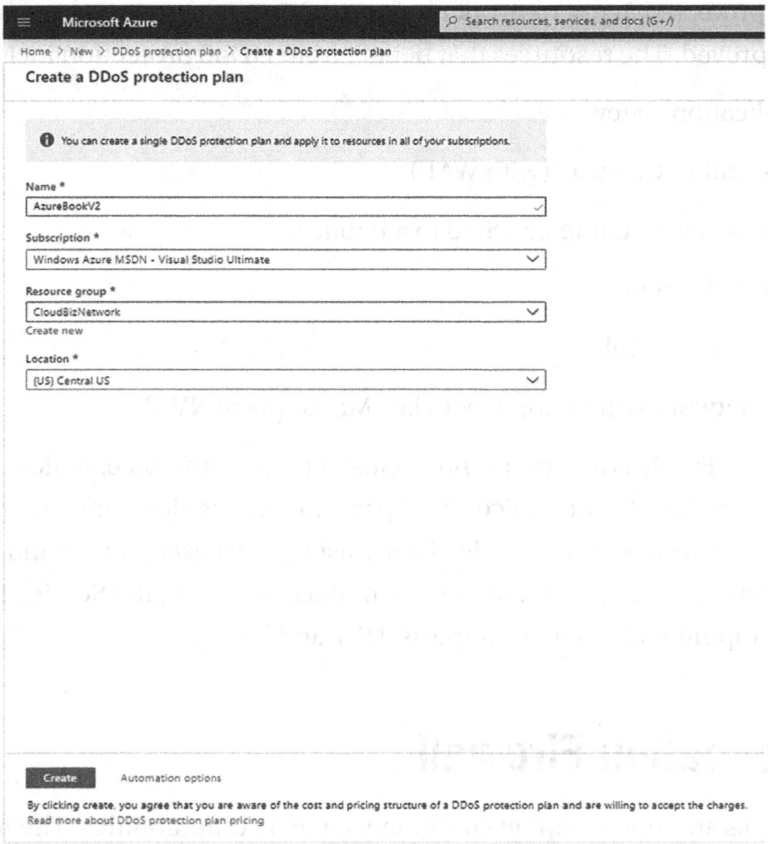

Figure 13-3. *Azure portal view to purchase the DDoS protection plan*

You are billed a service fee and a data processing fee for the protected resources in the Virtual Network plus. This cost is a service fee plus a calculated data processing on the egress bandwidth traffic (outgoing) from any VM (i.e., traffic from the VM to the Internet). IP traffic that travels across the ExpressRoute or virtual private network (VPN) gateway is not counted. As you continue to understand the services in Microsoft Azure that add to overall charges, consider the real-time analysis and storing application traffic for historical analysis storage are part of the data processing charges.

We all want to know how much a network cloud service costs. The worst answer is, “it depends.” The (retail) monthly charge at the time of writing is $2,944/month to protect 100 Azure resources. These resources (i.e., IaaS VM) can be across a single Azure tenant or multiple Azure subscriptions. Every resource over 100 costs another $30/month per VM.

The list of protected Azure network platforms continues to expand as services are added and improved. The resources that benefit from DDoS protection include

- Application Gateway
- Application Gateway (with WAF)
- IaaS virtual machine attached to a Public IP
- Load balancers
- Azure Service Fabric
- IaaS network virtual appliance (i.e., Marketplace NVA)

Azure Service Fabric is a platform node cluster that, as a service, scales and runs applications on the OS of your choice. DevOps teams can deploy applications in any programming language over the Service Fabric using guest executables and containers. You can optionally choose to implement communication using the Service Fabric SDK (software development kit), which supports .NET and Java.

Web Application Firewall

Malicious attacks attempt to exploit commonly known vulnerabilities. The Azure Web Application Firewall (WAF) follows defined rules based on the Open Web Application Security Project (OWASP) core rule sets 3.1, 3.0, or 2.2.9. The firewall allows the security administrator to create IP traffic rules that allow or deny IP traffic.

Creating a WAF can easily be completed following the Azure portal journey views, as shown in Figure 13-4.

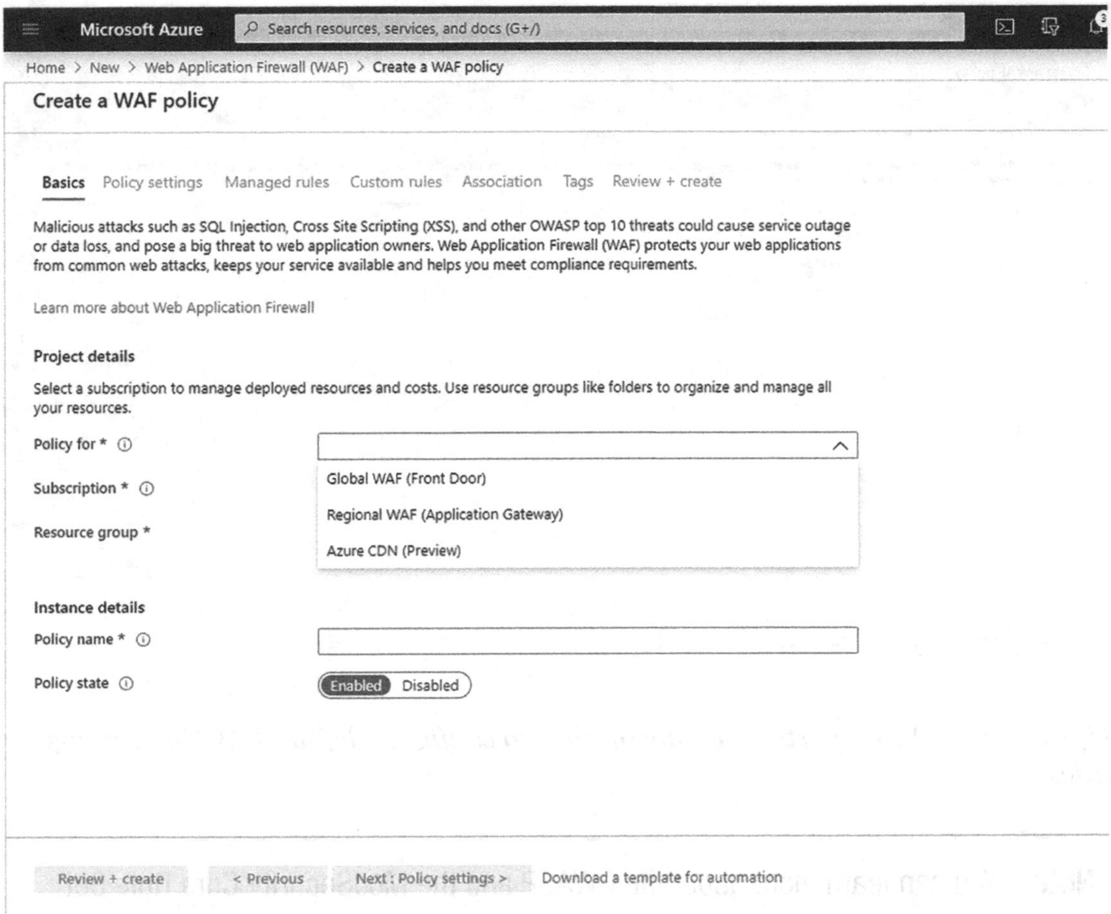

***Figure 13-4.** Azure portal view to create a web application firewall policy*

The WAF portal configuration enables the OWASP policies to be applied to different Azure services, including Azure Front Door and Azure Content Delivery Network (CDN), which are discussed in this chapter. After selecting the WAF policy and naming the default policies are enabled, as shown in Figure 13-5.

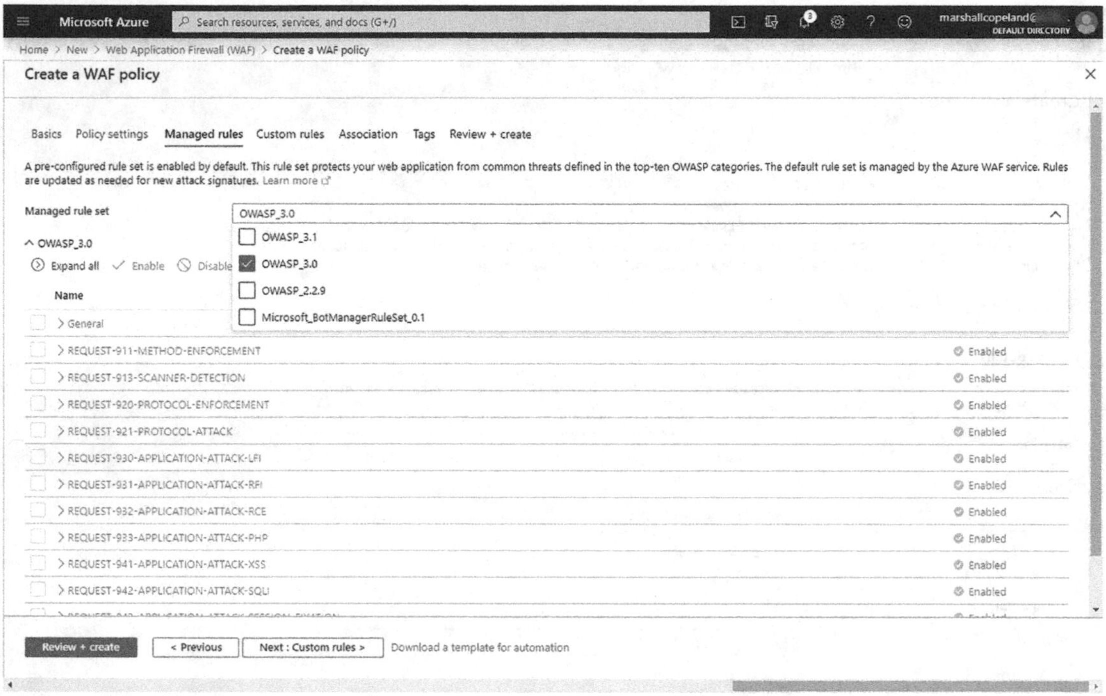

Figure 13-5. *Azure portal showing options to configure default OWASP managed rules*

Note You can learn more about the OWASP and the ModSecurity Core Rule Set used in Azure WAF at `https://owasp.org/www-project-modsecurity-core-rule-set/`.

The Azure Firewall supports creating custom rules but comes with built-in rules that reduce security risks based on the OWASP collection of top-10 application security risks. The firewall helps to educate developers and be more aware of web application security. The top-10 list from 2017 includes

- A1-Injection
- A2-Broken Authentication
- A3-Sensitive Data Exposure
- A4-XML External Entities (XXE)

- A5-Broken Access Control
- A6-Security Misconfiguration
- A7-Cross-Site Scripting (XSS)
- A8-Insecure Deserialization
- A9-Using Components with Known Vulnerabilities
- A10-Insufficient Logging and Monitoring

The program accepts contributions to its top 10 list.

Application Gateway

The cloud-native Azure Application Gateway provides Transport Layer Security (TLS) protocol termination (sometimes this is referred to using the older reference: Secure Socket Layer (SSL) offloading.) Azure Application Gateway manages web traffic based on HTTP request headers or URI paths, so this is marketed as a decision-based routing gateway. It routes traffic at the top of the OSI model at layer 7 (see Table 13-1). It is used primarily for web traffic with a built-in load balancer duplicate.

The traditional third-party (on-premises) application gateway, also called an application proxy, works at OSI Layer 4 - TCP and UDP. The support for an ephemeral IP address, port translation support protocols used for instant messaging, BitTorrent, and File Transfer Protocol (FTP). You should be aware of the application gateway total cost has a basic cost version (small, medium, large) and an integrated Azure firewall (small, medium, large) cost version, and both have versions have a data processing cost.

During the creation process, the front-end tab is an IP address that is typically set to public. You can create a new public IP address to separate it from the back-end tab. Add routing rules and configuration for your back-end servers, as shown in Figure 13-6. In this chapter's examples, we use the Microsoft IIS configuration templates in the GitHub repository.

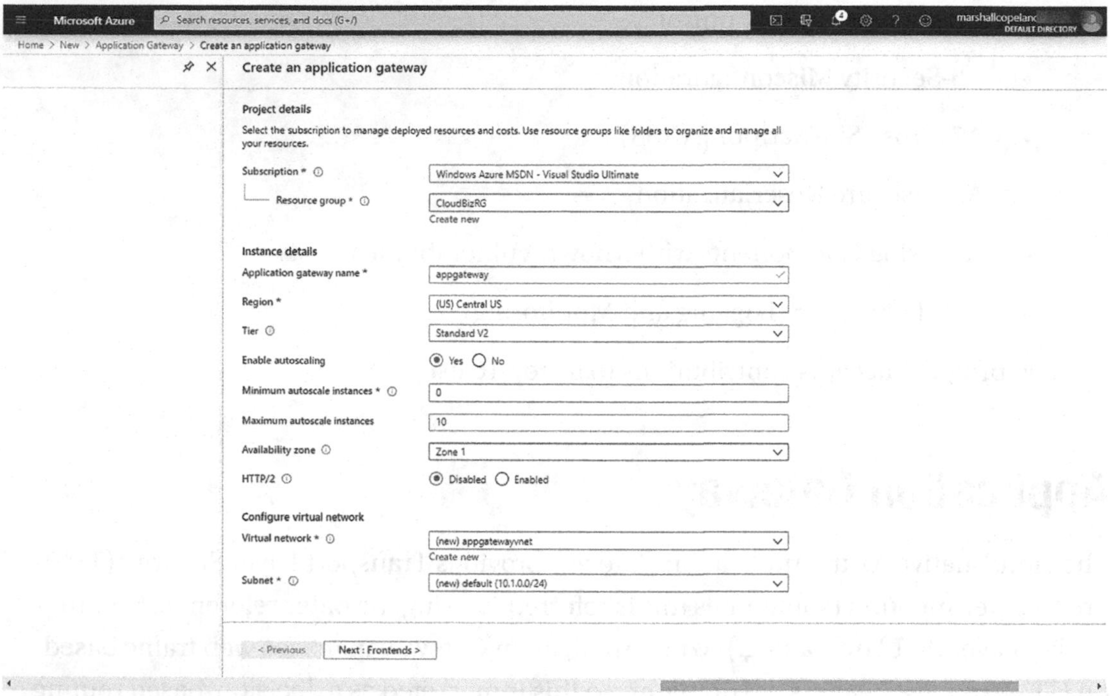

Figure 13-6. *Azure portal create an application gateway*

Load Balancers

Azure load balancers work at OSI layer 4 (refer to Table 13-1) to distribute incoming traffic across the different virtual machines. It is important to understand that at layer 4, the Transport Control Protocol (TCP) and Universal Data Protocol (UDP), allows hackers access to port scanning, they try to identify open network ports. Restricting access reduces the security risk using the configuration to narrowly allow traffic.

The load balancer requires the following.

- source IP address
- source port number
- destination IP address
- destination port number
- protocol type

Data that arrives at the load balancers front end (inbound) are distributed to the load on the back end (outbound). The Azure load balancers use health probes to determine the virtual machines in the Azure scale set to route traffic.

A public load balancer supports Internet traffic from a public IP address to a back-end pool of servers. The public IP is separated from the internal IP using network address translation (NAT). An internal load balancer uses private IP addresses only to route traffic inside a virtual network.

The health probes supported by the load balancer include

- HTTPS (HTTP probe with TLS wrapper)
- HTTP
- TCP

Creating a network to support a load balancer is discussed in Chapter 11; once the networks are configured, you can manually create the external or internal load balancer in the Azure portal, as shown in Figure 13-7.

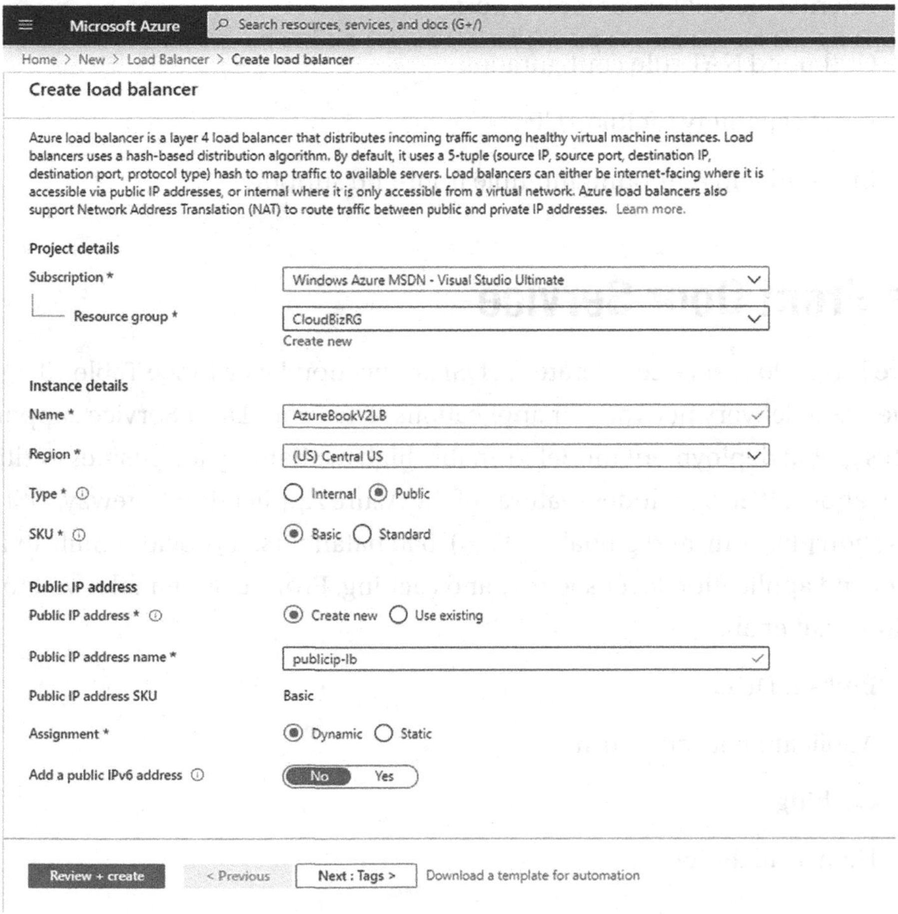

Figure 13-7. *Azure portal view to create the Azure load balancer*

Azure local balancers add a layer of security in the native cloud network platform that also reduces the risk of DDoS attacks when they are narrowly configured. Permitting IP-focused traffic and denying others reduces the security risk of server overload or traffic overload. There are two purchasing options or SKUs to choose, basic and standard.

Customization is very granular with the standard load balancer configuration. Also, Azure virtual machines scale sets and availability sets can only be connected to one load balancer, basic or standard, but not both. Once you select one of the SKU versions, it cannot be changed, only deleted and rebuilt.

Standard load balancers have many features, but the following are a few key features to help guide your decision.

- 1000 instances back-end pool size
- Internal load balancer for HA ports
- Outbound NAT rule configuration
- Reset capability for idle TCP
- Inbound and outbound multiple front-end support

Azure Front Door Service

The Azure Front Door service operates at OSI application layer 7 (see Table 13-1) and is classified as a delivery network for applications. The Front Door Service supports Microsoft's global deployment model to enable high availability for business-critical web applications. It also includes features of the Azure Application Gateway, OSI layer 7, acceleration platform, and global HTTP(s) load balancers. It provides built-in DDoS protection and application layer security and caching. Front Door enables you to build applications that enable

- Built-in DDoS
- Application layer security
- Caching
- High availability

Front Door services support web and mobile apps, cloud services, and virtual machines. Also, you can include on-premises services in your Front Door architecture for hybrid deployments or migration strategies to the Azure cloud. If you currently do not have a Front Door service, follow the exercise to create the servers for testing.

EXERCISE: CREATE FRONT DOOR SERVICE

Remember the two web apps that you created in Chapter 12? In this exercise, you deploy the Azure Front Door service and place these web apps behind it.

1. In the Home view of your Azure portal, select **Create a resource**. Enter **Front Door**, and select **Create**.
2. In the Basic Journey tab, enter a new resource group and location, and then click **Next : Configuration**. Your screen should look similar to the following screenshot.

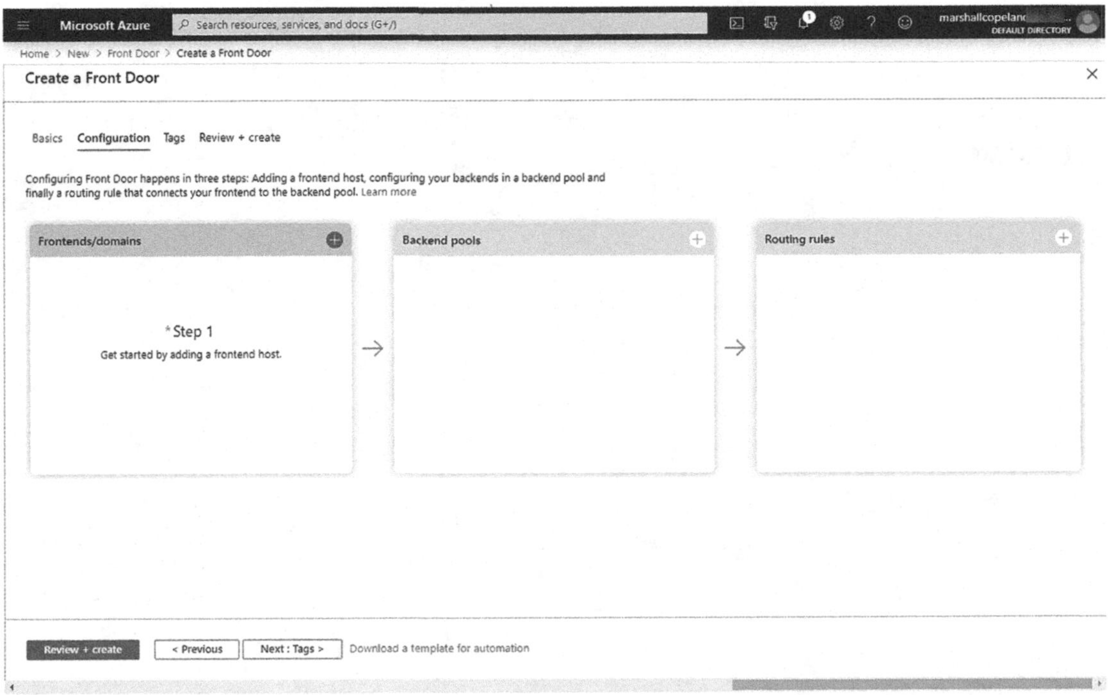

3. In the Step 1 square, click **+** to enter the front-end host name, similar to what's shown in the following screenshot. Notice that you have the option to enable session affinity (i.e., sticky connections; leave disabled for this exercise). Also, there is an option to enable WAF (leave it disabled for this exercise). Click **Add**.

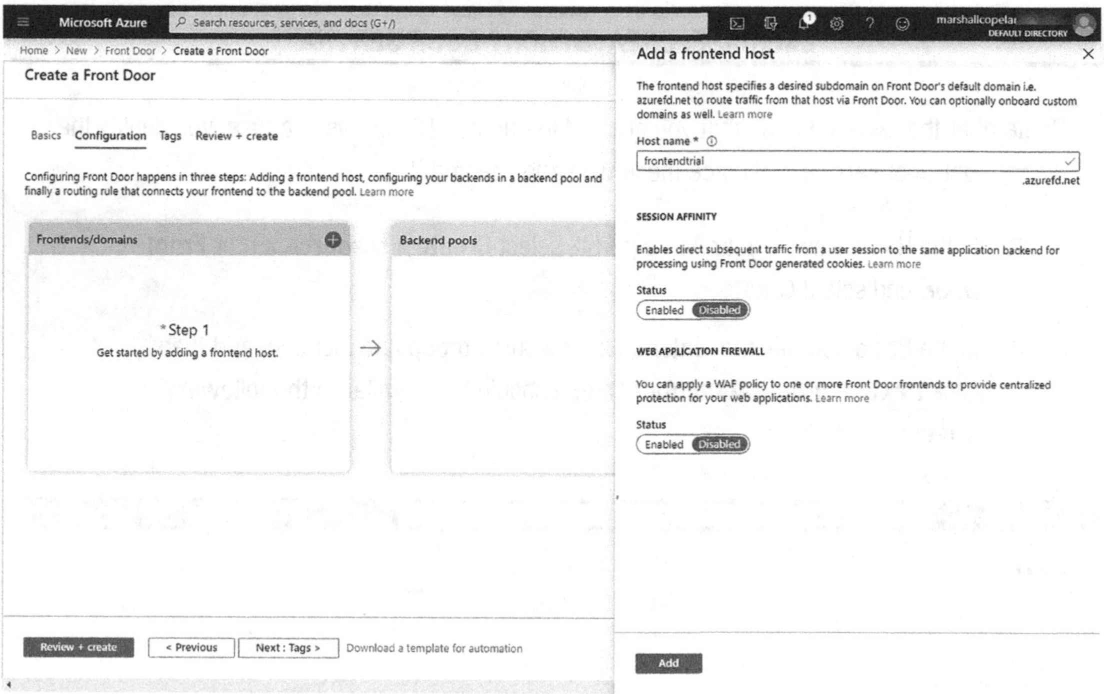

4. The next step is to add back-end pools. In the Step 2 square, click **+** in the top-right of the screen, and enter a unique name for the back-end pool, similar to what's shown in the following screenshot.

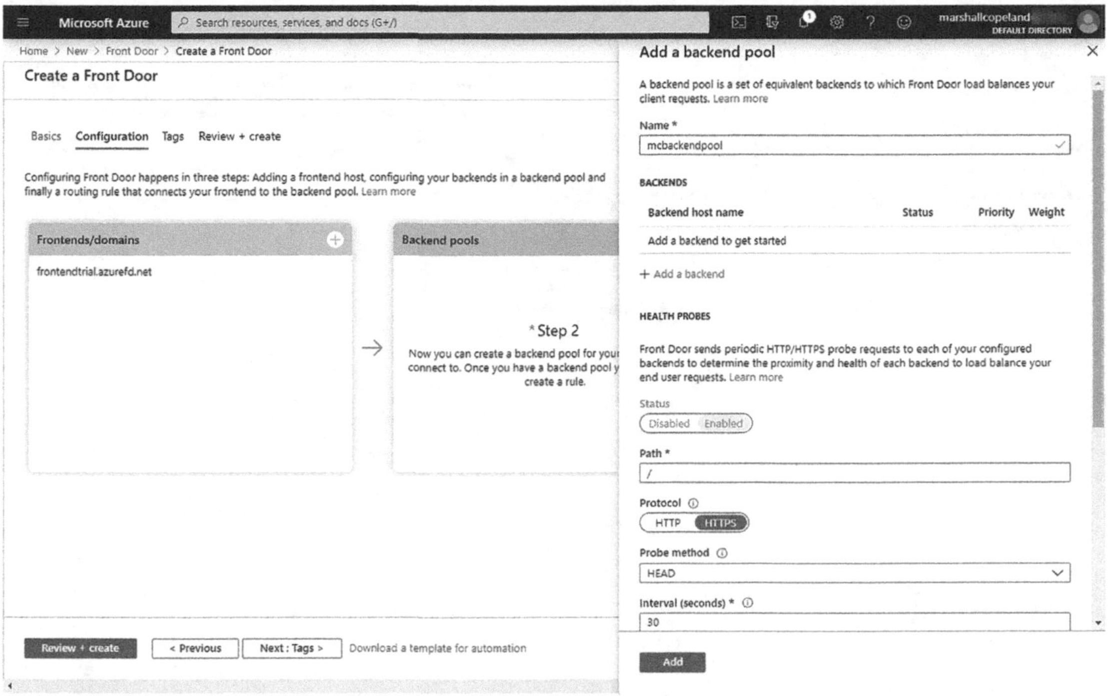

5. Click the **+**. Add a back-end label to add the first web apps from the earlier steps. The following screenshot should look similar to your screen.

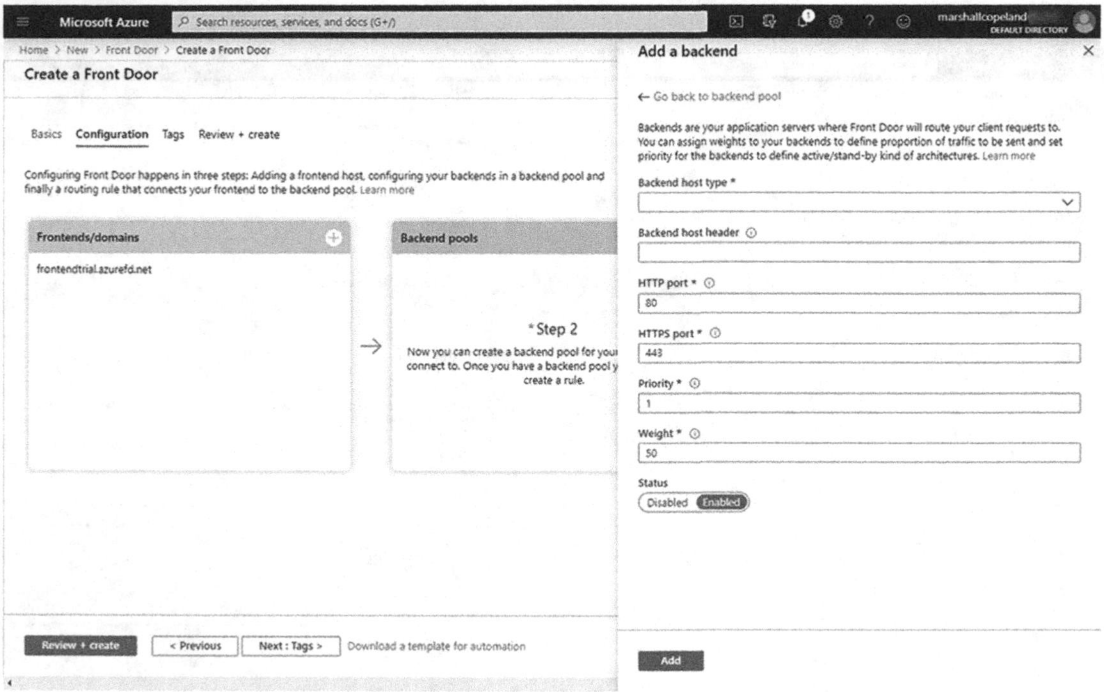

6. Select **App service** from the first drop-down menu. The back-end host name fills in automatically. Your screen should look similar to the following screenshot. Click **Add**.

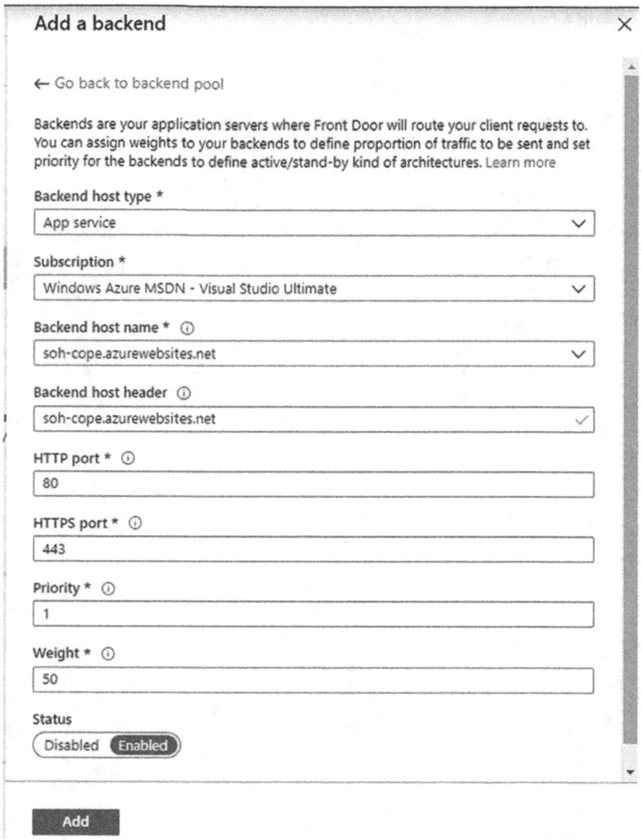

7. You need to add the second web app from West Europe. Click **+** and add a back end. Select **Backend host name** and then select the other web app. Your screen should look similar to the following screenshot. Select **Add**.

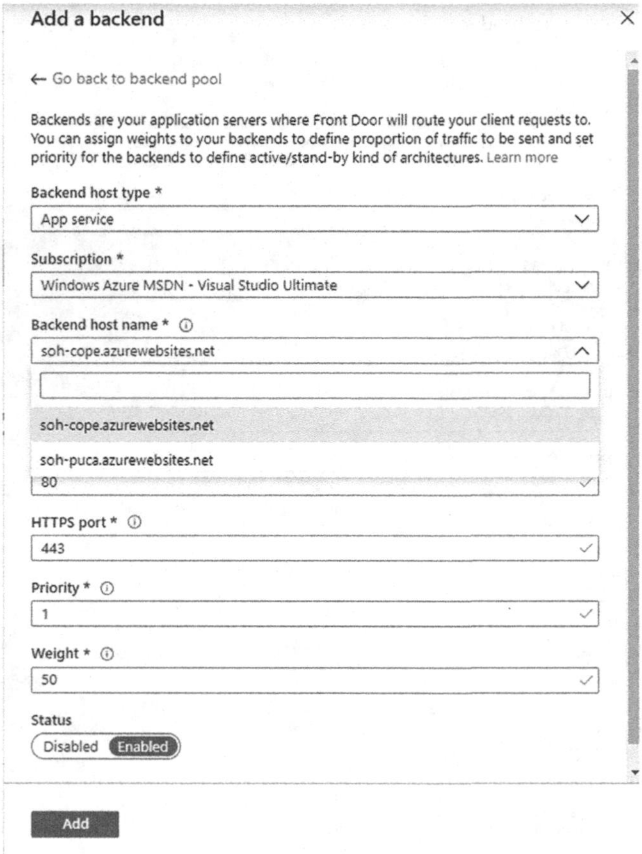

8. With both web apps configured (see Chapter 12) for the back-end pool, select **Add** to configure the routing rules. Select **Add**.

9. Enter a unique routing rule name. This connects the front-end request to forward to the back-end pool. Leave the other features at their default for this exercise. Click **Add**.

10. Your screen should show that the front end, back end, and routing rules are configured. Click **Next : Tags**.

11. Use the drop-down menu to select the Front Door app and location, and then click **Next : Review create**. Select **Create**.

12. The Azure portal changes to indicate your Front door deployment is underway. Wait for the completion, and select **Go to resource** to view the service.

13. The following screenshot should look similar to your Front Door screen.

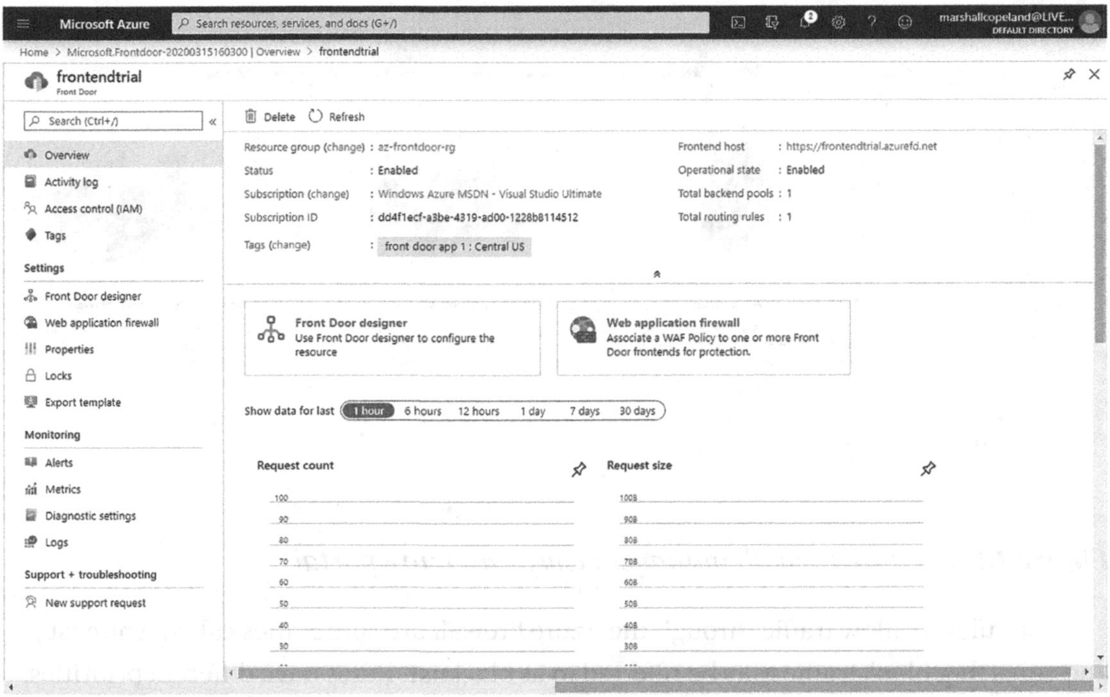

Azure Firewall

The Azure Firewall Manager portal view is shown in Figure 13-8 display a preview feature; however, the portal changes over time. As new features are added, the portal (real estate) is consolidated or reorganize with the underlying Azure Firewall APIs continued to be supported. The current API is at `https://docs.microsoft.com/en-us/rest/api/firewall/azurefirewalls`.

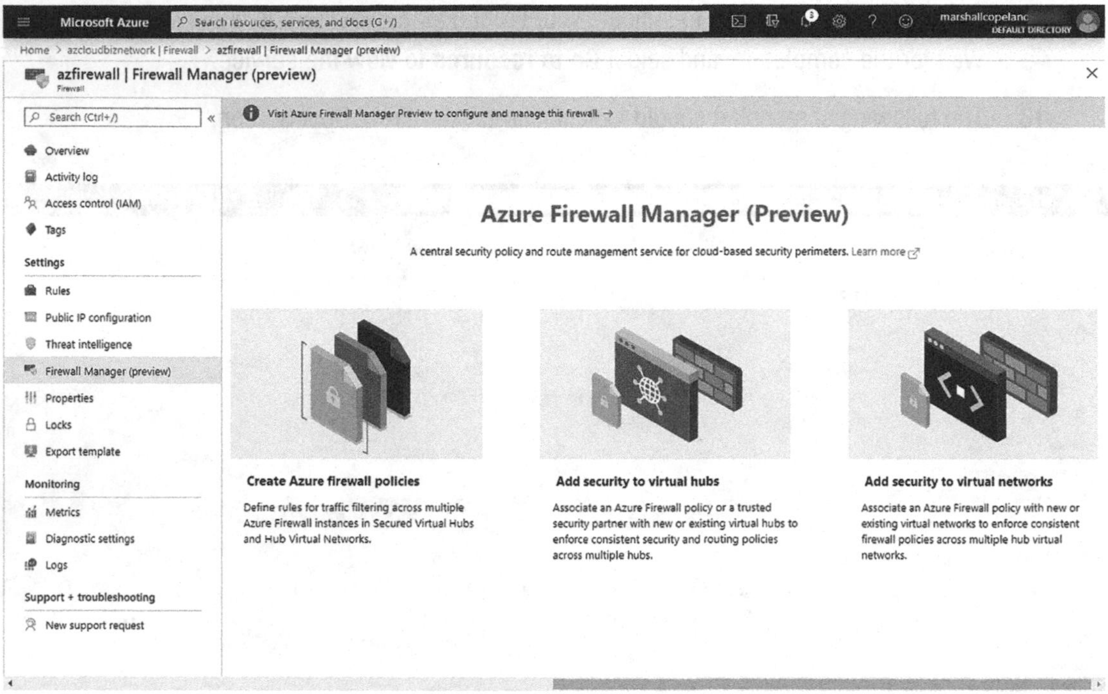

***Figure 13-8.** Azure firewall manager view from Azure portal*

The rules to allow traffic through the Azure firewall are sometimes called whitelist and rules that block traffic may be referred to as blacklist. Rules have different priorities, so the rule is tested, and if it matches, no future rules are tested. The rules are similar to a network security group (NSG) from Chapter 2 and Chapter 7. Rules contain a name, protocol, source type, source IP, destination type, destination address, and destination ports and must include a priority number (100–6500) and action (allow /deny).

Figure 13-9 shows the Azure portal to add a network rule collection.

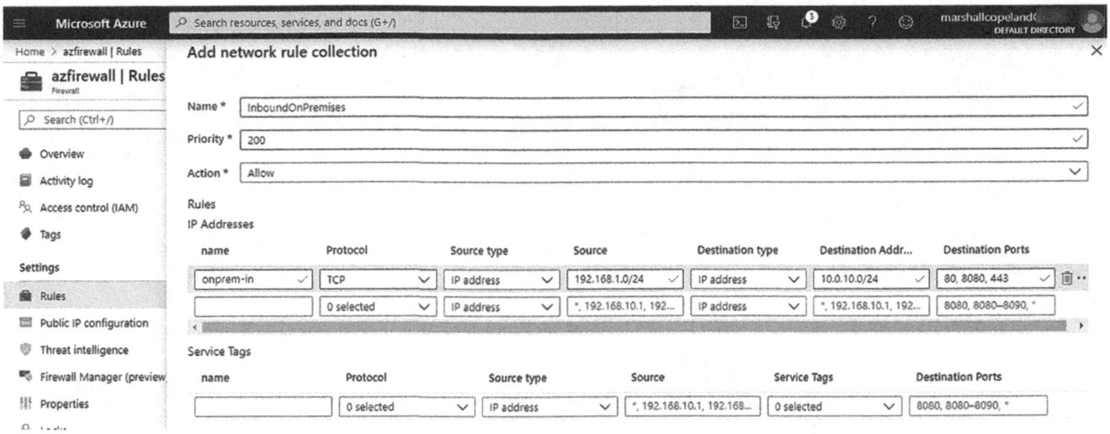

Figure 13-9. *Azure portal to add network rule collection with attributes*

Summary

In this chapter, you learned about the Azure network platform and its many services, including an out-of-the-box global network service that you can leverage. You learned about the DDoS protection built-in to Azure and additional options for granular control and analysis. Then, you learned about the security features in Azure Web Application Firewall and load balancers.

You learned about the use of application gateways to improve the customer experience. You went through an exercise to create Azure Front Door service, which included many Azure features like DDoS protection and web application firewalls. The final topic covered using Azure Firewall to create custom rules to allow or deny network traffic.

CHAPTER 14

Azure Storage

Over the years, the two foundational components that define Azure as a hyperscale cloud continue to be unmentioned pillars: compute and storage. Compute and storage are the foundational pillars for every private and public cloud. Infrastructure as a service is pretty much about compute and storage. We focused on compute in Chapter 2, and in this chapter, we dedicate time to cloud-based storage.

Cloud-based storage is not as ground-shaking and exciting as emerging technologies like artificial intelligence and machine learning, or the Internet of Things (IoT), or even Big Data, but these technologies all rely on storage to exist. In fact, they rely on a *lot* of storage.

The Difference Between Azure Storage and Azure Databases

Azure Storage, sometimes referred to as Azure datastores, is primarily designed for semi-structured or unstructured storage of content. It is separate from compute. That is what makes Azure storage inexpensive compared to Azure databases.

Azure databases are generally used for more structured data, and they are more compute dependent.

Cloud Storage and Storage Accounts

When we think of storage, the traditional hard drives, solid-state drives, thumb drives, and memory cards come to mind.

For enterprises, we think of storage area networks (SANs) and network-attached storage (NAS).

J. Soh et al., *Microsoft Azure*, https://doi.org/10.1007/978-1-4842-5958-0_14

Although cloud storage is physically backed by similar technologies, they may be offered as cloud services that are more in line with today's needs.

Storage in Azure is organized by objects called storage account s. A storage account is a logical container for the different types of cloud storage.

As seen in Figure 14-1, the types of storage that can share a storage account are

- Azure Blob storage
- Azure Files
- Azure Tables
- Azure Queues

Other types of storage may also be organized by storage accounts but would not be able to share the same storage account. For example, Azure Data Lake Store is another storage offering in Azure that is also housed in storage accounts but cannot share the same storage account with the other types of storage.

Figure 14-1. *Azure storage account Overview pane*

Azure Blob Storage

Azure Blob storage is the most economical and abundant storage that is available today. It derives its name of the term BLOB, which stands for Binary Large Objects, although it is usually represented in all lower case.

The definition of a blob is a large file, typically an image or any form of unstructured data. We talk about the different data types in Chapter 17, but for now, think of blobs as large files that are not suited to reside in databases. The hard drive on your personal computer can be considered blob storage because it houses different types and sizes of files that are organized in folders.

The following are the big differences between the storage on your personal computer and blob storage in Azure.

- Azure Blob storage is infinitely scalable and virtually limitless.
- Azure Blob storage is physically backed by at least three sets of infrastructure—from drives to power supplies. This is the default deployment and is known as locally redundant storage (LRS). LRS is the minimal deployment model (see Figure 14-1).
- Azure Blob storage can also be replicated to a remotely paired datacenter in Azure, which IS another three sets of infrastructure in that remote location. This is known as *geo-redundant storage* (GRS). Therefore, in a GRS configuration, data is being replicated across six sets of hardware spanning two geo-locations more than 500 miles apart,
- Azure Blob storage is the least expensive type of storage in Azure. To provide some context, at the time of writing, Azure Blob storage prices are \$0.03/GB/month[1] for the hot tier and as little as \$0.01/GB/month for the archive tier. This pricing is competitive among cloud providers, and Microsoft has demonstrated the willingness to continue making the price of storage competitive. Azure Blob storage should be considered enterprise-level storage so, it is economical to provide cloud storage in Azure than maintain on-premises hardware.

There are two types of Azure Blob storage.

- Block Blob storage is ideal for files up to 200GB in size. Block Blob storage is normally used for unstructured data of varying sizes, such as videos, photos, and other binary files.
- Page Blob storage is optimized to hold files that are used for random read and write operations. Therefore, they are often used to store the virtual hard disk (VHD) images of virtual machines in Azure.

[1]Azure workload prices may change, and different regions may have different prices. Prices mentioned in this book are to provide context and should not be assumed accurate.

To read, write, download, and upload files to Azure Blob storage, HTTPS PUT and GET methods are employed. To facilitate that, Azure provides public URL endpoints to access Azure Blob storage. However, Microsoft announced the Private Link service, which allows a public endpoint In Azure to be exposed with a privately owned IP address. Azure Private Link is discussed elsewhere in this book.

The URL to access blob storage in Azure is usually a .blob.core.windows.net suffix. Thus, accessing a blob stored in a container of a storage account looks something like this:

```
https://<StorageAccountName>.blob.core.windows.net/<ContainerName>/
<BlobName>
```

For more information about Azure Blob storage, we have forked Microsoft's extensive and evergreen documentation for Azure Blob storage to our GitHub repo at `https://github.com/harris-soh-copeland-puca/azure-docs/blob/master/articles/storage/blobs/storage-blobs-overview.md`.

Hands-on: Deploying Azure Blob Storage

In this exercise, you deploy an Azure storage account to deploy Azure Blob storage. You explore how to transfer files to and from Azure Blob storage and how to secure it.

As you start the deployment process, remember the relationship of the storage account to the blob containers and blobs, as seen in Figure 14-2.

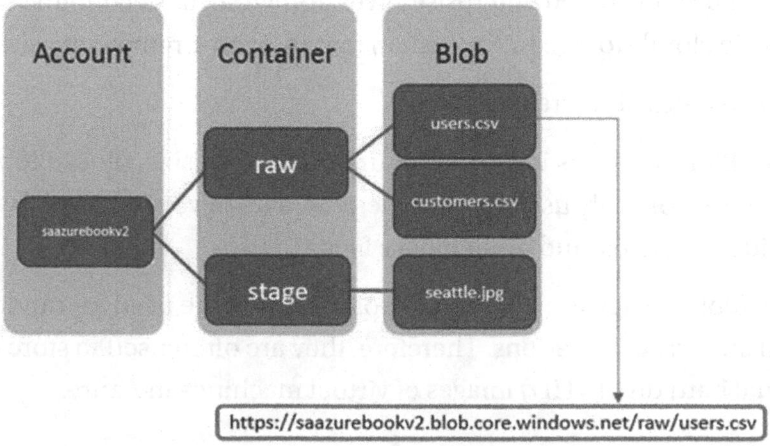

***Figure 14-2.** Structure and relationship of the storage account, blob containers, and blobs*

As with all the other hands-on exercises, we assume that you have an Azure subscription, or know to sign up for a free trial.

1. Go to your Azure portal at `https://portal.azure.com` and sign in.
2. Click **Create a resource**. Type **storage account** in the search box. Select **Storage account - blob, file, table, queue** when it appears in the search results.
3. Click **Create**.
4. Select the subscription to put the storage account in or create a new subscription for it.
5. Provide a name for the storage account. The name is used as part of the URL endpoint, so it must be globally unique. It must also be in lowercase and no special characters.
6. Select a location closest to you.
7. Select a performance level. Standard performance is backed by high-performance enterprise-level hard disk drives. Premium performance is backed by enterprise-level solid-state drives.
8. Leave the Account kind at StorageV2. StorageV2 accounts are recommended for almost all storage scenarios and incorporate all the functionality of StorageV1 and Blob storage. Both these storage types are still mainly provided for backward compatibility, for example, if there is a need to access the storage account using the classic model rather than the Azure Resource Manager (ARM) method. See `https://docs.microsoft.com/en-us/azure/storage/common/storage-account-overview#recommendations` for more details.
9. For this exercise, leave the access tier (default) as Hot unless you know for sure that this storage account is generally used for files that can tolerate some latency like near-line access. Blobs that are uploaded to this storage account are assigned this tier by default, and you can move the blob to the hot or archive tier after the upload.
10. Click **Next : Networking**.

11. Select **Public endpoint (all networks)**, and then click **Next : Advanced**.

12. Always keep the Secure transfer required option set to Enabled to enforce HTTPS communication.

13. Large file shares are disabled because you did not pick Premium as the storage type in step 7. Large file shares, if enabled, allow us to create file shares that are up to 100 TiB in size.

14. Leave **Blob soft delete** disabled. You can enable soft delete for additional protection against accidental deletes. The duration that deleted blobs are preserved if soft delete is enabled is based on the retention period, which you specify if you enabled this feature.

15. Leave the Data Lake Storage Gen2 Hierarchical namespace disabled because you are not deploying Azure Data Lake Services with this storage account. If you enabled Hierarchical namespace, it also means that you are specifying this storage account as an Azure Data Lake Store account, so you will not be able to deploy other storage types to this storage account.

16. Click **Review + create**.

17. Click **Create**.

18. After the storage account is deployed, click **Go to resource**.

You have just deployed an Azure storage account, but you have not deployed Azure Blob storage or any storage type.

In the following steps, you deploy Azure Blob storage by specifying the first container.

1. Go to the Overview pane of the Azure storage account created in the previous exercise if you are not already there.

2. Select **Containers** in the Overview pane, as seen in Figure 14-3.

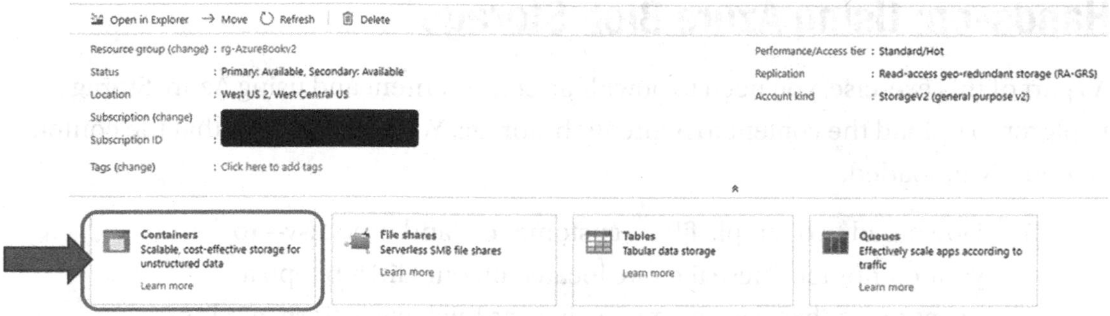

***Figure 14-3.** Containers (Blob) option in Azure storage account*

3. Click + **Container**, which is located at the top of the pane.
4. Type **raw** for the container name. This is because you are using this Azure Blob storage and container for exercises in later chapters (e.g., Chapter 19).
5. Leave the public access level as Private (no anonymous access).
6. Click **OK**.
7. Click + **Container** again and create another container named **stage**.
8. Your Azure storage account with Azure Blob storage should now look similar to what is shown in Figure 14-4.

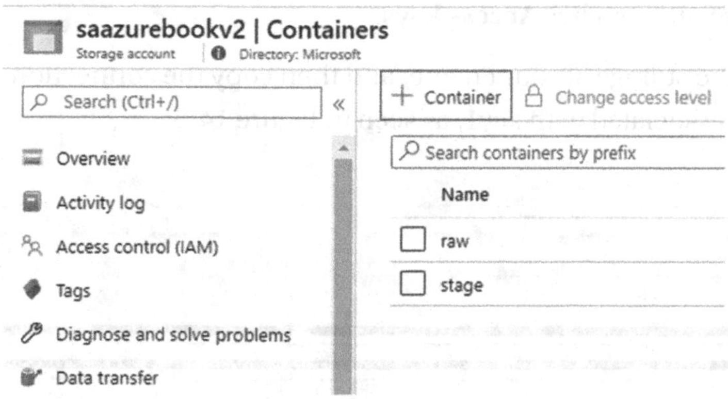

***Figure 14-4.** Azure Blob storage with two containers deployed*

You have now deployed Azure Blob storage; next, you need to store and retrieve files.

Hands-on: Using Azure Blob Storage

As part of this exercise, you need to download some content and using Azure Storage Explorer to upload the content to Azure Blob storage. You then confirm that the content is properly uploaded.

1. Download two sample files—customer.csv and users.csv—to your computer. These files are located on our GitHub repo at `https://github.com/harris-soh-copeland-puca/SampleFiles/blob/master/customer.csv` and `https://github.com/harris-soh-copeland-puca/SampleFiles/blob/master/users.csv` respectively. You will reuse these files for other exercises.

2. Download a picture file, seattle.jpg, from `https://github.com/harris-soh-copeland-puca/SampleFiles/blob/master/seattle.jpg`. You will use this file for exercises in later chapters.

3. Download Azure Storage Explorer from `https://azure.microsoft.com/is-is/features/storage-explorer/` and install it on your computer. This is the application that you will use to upload, download, delete, and browse containers and blobs in Azure Blob storage.

4. Go to the Azure portal and open the Azure storage account created in the previous exercise.

5. Under Settings, click **Access keys**.

6. Note the storage account name, and then copy the connection string associated with key1, as seen in Figure 14-5.

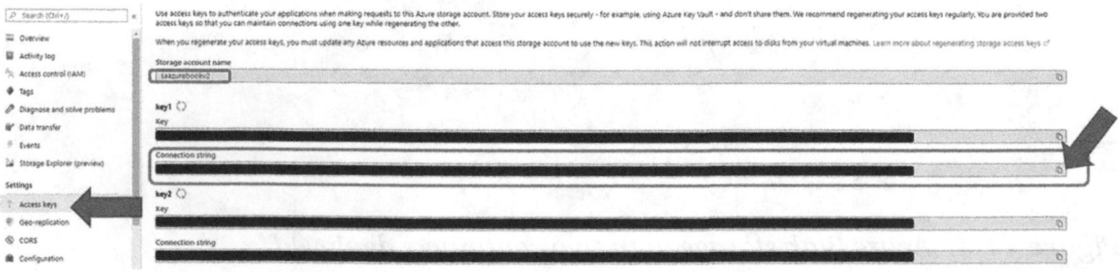

***Figure 14-5.** Storage account connection string*

7. Launch Azure Storage Explorer.
8. Click the **Connect** icon and select **Use a connection string**, as seen in Figure 14-6. Then click **Next**.

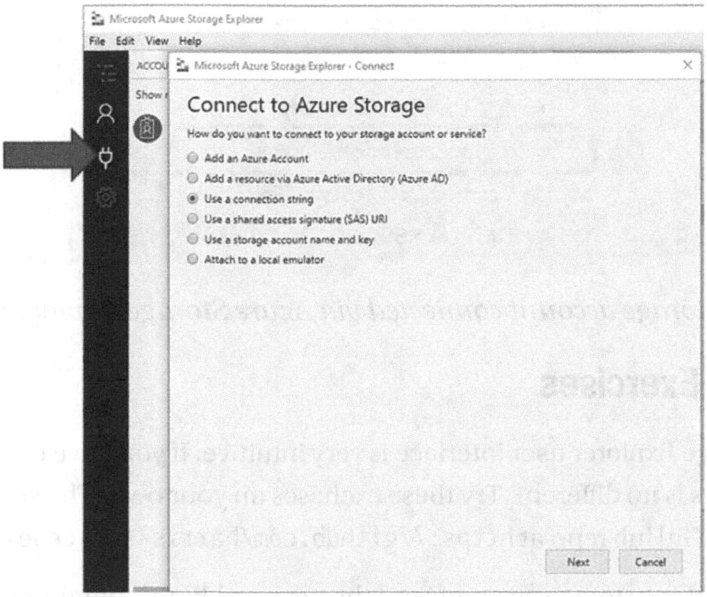

Figure 14-6. *Use a connection string to connect to Azure Blob storage.*

9. Paste the connection string that you copied in step 6 into the Connection string field. Notice that the display name is automatically populated with the Azure storage account name, as noted from step 6. Leave it like this, but you can change it if desired. This is the display name in Azure Storage Explorer. Click **Next**.
10. Click **Connect**.
11. Upon successful connection, you should see the storage account listed under Local & Attached ➤ Storage Accounts, as seen in Figure 14-7.

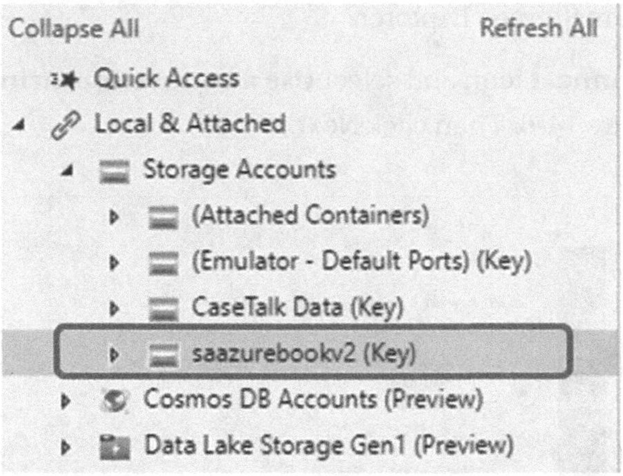

***Figure 14-7.** Storage account connected via Azure Storage Explorer*

Self-Guided Exercises

The Azure Storage Explorer user interface is very intuitive. If you have ever used an SFTP or FTP client, this is no different. Try these exercises on your own. The step-by-step guide is posted on our GitHub repo at `https://github.com/harris-soh-copeland-puca`.

1. Expand the storage account, and then expand Blob Containers. You should see the two containers created in the previous exercise.
2. Upload users.csv and customer.csv to the raw container. Upload seattle.jpg to the stage container.
3. Right-click **customer.csv** and change it to the archive tier.
4. Look for folder statistics and the activity history under Activities.
5. Try to access seattle.jpg from a browser. Change the container's public access level if you receive an error. Change it back after you are done experimenting. (Do not refresh the page. Reload it in a separate browser).
6. Try connecting to the storage account using a storage account name and a key instead of a connection string.
7. Try connecting to the storage account by adding an Azure subscription and not using a key.

8. Check out Storage Explorer from the Azure portal (in preview at the time of writing).

9. Create an empty folder.

Note Blobs in Azure Blob storage are stored in a flat system. The names of "folders" that blobs are stored in are part of the blob's file name. Therefore, if there are no files in a folder, the folder cannot exist. That is why when you try to create a folder, Azure Storage Explorer reminds you that folders are virtual in Azure Blob storage. The next section discusses hierarchical namespace (HNS) support in Azure Data Lake Store.

Next Steps: Azure Blob Storage

Microsoft's documentation on Azure Blob storage is on GitHub at `https://github.com/harris-soh-copeland-puca/azure-docs/tree/master/articles/storage/blobs`.

Azure Data Lake Store (ADLS)

Closely related to Azure Blob storage is the Azure Data Lake Store. Azure Data Lake Store is the only service that cannot share an Azure storage account with the other Azure storage options discussed in this chapter.

The Azure Data Lake Store covered in this book is the second generation of the service, often called Azure Data Lake Store gen2 or ADLS Gen2.

Azure Data Lake Store Gen 2 is built on Azure Blob with a few differentiating features, as follows.

- ADLS Gen 2 is better suited for certain scenarios involving analytics because it works better with text files than Azure Blob (applies to analytics involving text files and not video, of course).
- ADLS Gen 2 supports *hierarchical namespace* support, which is the ability to have a folder structure that is independent of the content. That means you can now have empty folders!
- ADLS Gen 2 costs more than Azure Blob storage and does not have an archive tier.

Provisioning an Azure Data Lake Store follows the same steps as deploying an Azure storage account with the exception that in the Advanced tab of the provisioning process, enable the hierarchical namespace option, as seen in Figure 14-8.

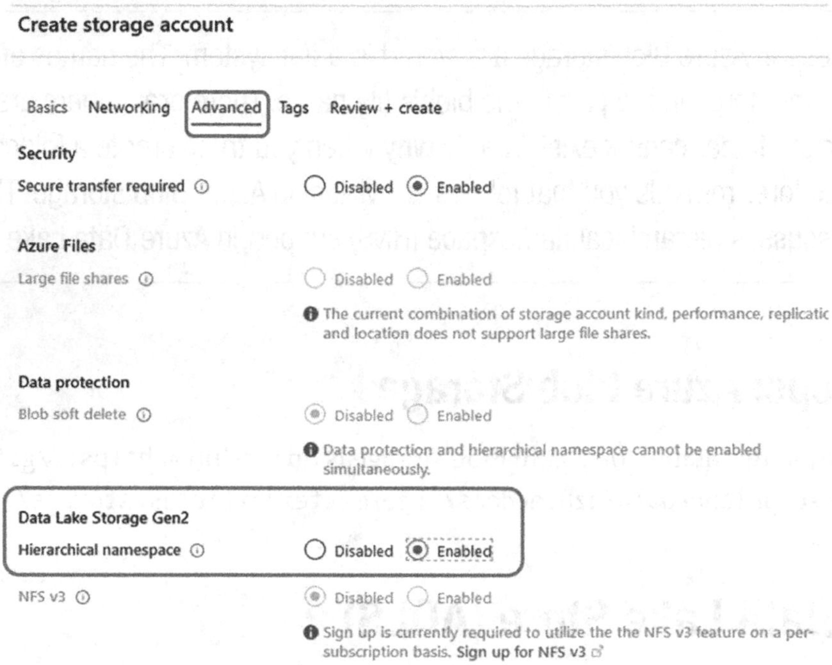

Figure 14-8. *Provisioning ADLS Gen2 by specifying HNS*

For more information regarding Azure Data Lake Store, please see the Microsoft documentation on this topic at our GitHub repo at `https://github.com/harris-soh-copeland-puca/azure-docs/tree/master/articles/data-lake-store`.

Azure Tables

Azure Tables is a nonrelational, key/value pair storage system. It does not require a schema and is a form of structured NoSQL datastore. Azure Tables are designed to be lightweight and optimized for simple and fast inserts and reads. Use case scenarios for Azure Tables include storing flexible datasets like user data for web applications, storage of lookup data or metadata, and so forth.

Note Azure Tables are *not* like the tables in a relational database. Therefore, you cannot do unions or joins between tables. The tables in Azure Tables are stand-alone.

What does *schema-less* mean? For example, if you have an online training website catered to members looking for a coach, the member table in a NoSQL datastore vs. the member table in a relational database would be different, as seen in Figure 14-9.

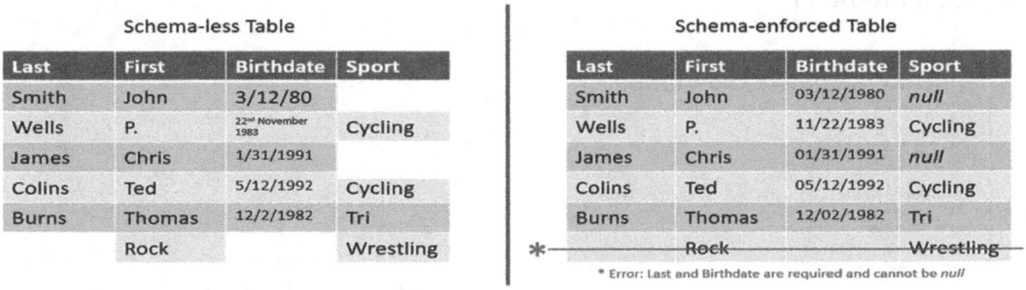
Schema-less Table
Last First Birthdate Sport
Smith John 3/12/80
Wells P. 22nd November 1983 Cycling
James Chris 1/31/1991
Colins Ted 5/12/1992 Cycling
Burns Thomas 12/2/1982 Tri
Rock Wrestling
Schema-enforced Table
Last First Birthdate Sport
Smith John 03/12/1980 null
Wells P. 11/22/1983 Cycling
James Chris 01/31/1991 null
Colins Ted 05/12/1992 Cycling
Burns Thomas 12/02/1982 Tri
* Rock Wrestling
* Error: Last and Birthdate are required and cannot be null

***Figure 14-9.** Difference between a schema-less table vs. a schema-enforced table*

Anatomy of Azure Tables

The architecture of Azure Tables is similar to Azure Blob because they both reside in an Azure storage account. Using the example of our online training website for members and coaches, this is graphically represented in Figure 14-10.

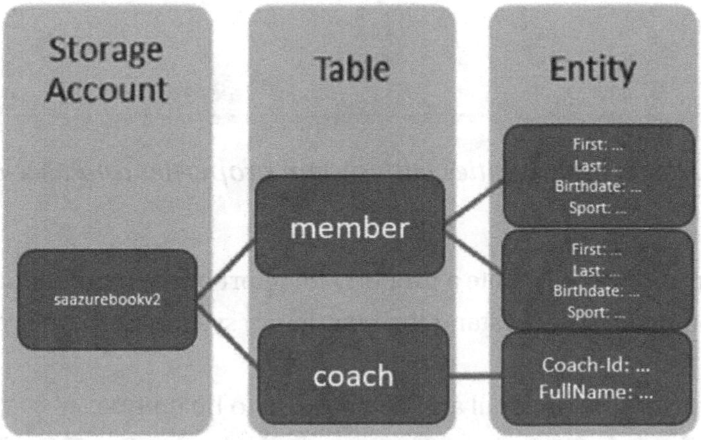

***Figure 14-10.** Structure of Azure Tables in Azure storage accounts*

Entities in Azure Tables can have any number of properties. A property of an entity in Azure Tables is akin to a field. Every Azure Table entity has three mandatory system properties.

- PartitionKey
- RowKey
- Timestamp

Using our online training website example, the member Azure Table has the entities shown in Figure 14-11.

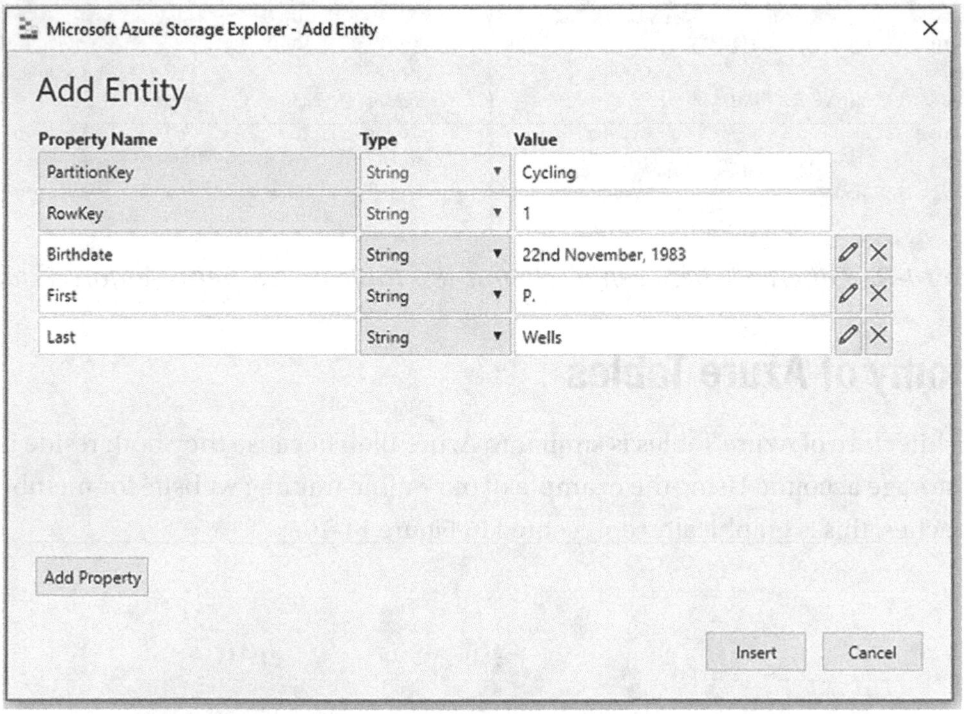

Figure 14-11. *Azure Table entities with system properties and user-defined properties*

But wait! Why did we not create a property for sport in the member table? To answer this question, you need to understand the mandatory system properties and how they are used.

PartitionKeys (PK) are optional and do not need to be unique.

RowKeys (RK) need to be unique. Therefore, only the first RowKey of all partitions can be blank.

Timestamps are automatically added to an entity upon its creation.

The primary key in an Azure Table is what uniquely identifies a row, and that primary key is a combination of the rows' PartitionKey and RowKey.

Azure Table primary key = PK + RK

All entities in an Azure Table are sorted by PartitionKey, followed by RowKey. Therefore, for efficient Azure Table operations, you should select a PartitionKey that best organizes the data. So, going back to our member table, the best PartitionKey would be Sport. RowKeys are then uniquely assigned to each member in the same PartitionKey. Figure 14-12 depicts the member table when taking the PartitionKey and RowKey into consideration.

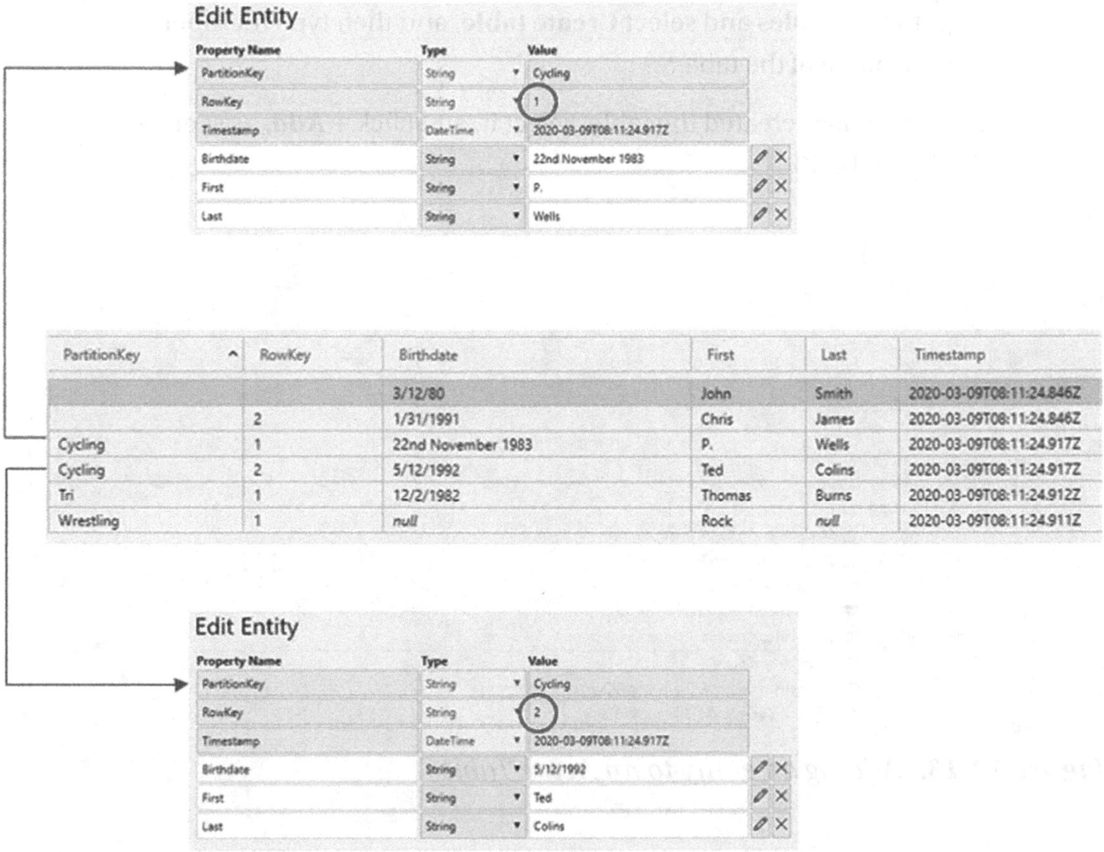

Figure 14-12. *Member table with Sport as the PartitionKey and unique RowKeys within the same partition*

Like Azure Blob storage, Azure Tables are accessed via an API endpoint using REST HTTPS; however, unlike Azure Blob storage, there is no option to allow anonymous access to Azure Tables.

Hands-on: Using Azure Tables

This exercise continues to use Azure Storage Explorer to manage tables and entities to visualize Azure Table operations.

1. Launch Azure Storage Explorer and navigate to the Azure storage account created in the previous exercise.
2. Expand Tables. You see several system tables that already exist.
3. Right-click **Tables** and select **Create table**, and then type member for the name of the table.
4. After you have created the table, select it, and click + **Add**, as seen in Figure 14-13.

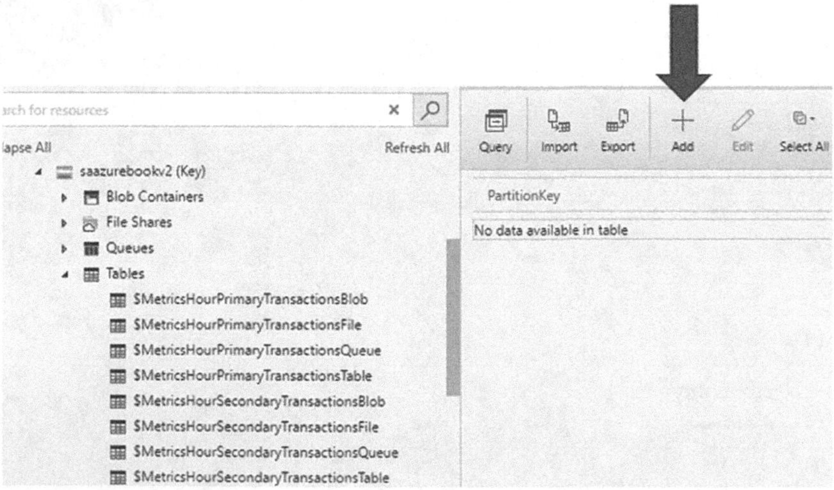

Figure 14-13. *Adding an entity to an Azure Table*

5. Add the first entity, as seen in Figure 14-11. Use the value of Sport for each member's PartitionKey and a unique RowKey. Click **Add Property** to add the first name, last name, and birthdate properties. You should only have to do this with the first entity. Subsequent entities remember those properties. If you delete a property for a new entity, it shows up as null.

Self-Guided Exercises

Try these exercises on your own. The step-by-step guide is posted on our GitHub repo at `https://github.com/harris-soh-copeland-puca`.

1. Explore how PartitionKeys and RowKeys are used by using Query in Azure Storage Explorer.
2. Try to create an entity with a non-unique RowKey in a partition.
3. Edit an existing entity.
4. Sort by columns in Azure Storage Explorer.
5. Export and import a table.

What format does it take?

Next Steps: Azure Tables

While you can use Azure Storage Explorer as a UI for Azure Tables, it is generally used as a rapid write and retrieve datastore. Data used by websites is a very common use case scenario. A Microsoft tutorial on Azure Tables using the .NET SDK is a good resource (see `https://docs.microsoft.com/en-us/azure/cosmos-db/tutorial-develop-table-dotnet`). When you first look at this tutorial, you might wonder why it refers to Cosmos DB instead of Azure Tables. The reason is that Cosmos DB is a multimodel database that uses the same Azure Table API. You do not need to follow the portion of the tutorial that tells you to deploy an Azure Cosmos DB. Start using the Azure Tables that you created in this chapter with the .NET SDK.

Note In Chapter 17, we explore Azure Cosmos DB, a schema-less datastore with Table APIs and similar characteristics. The main difference between Azure Cosmos DB and Azure Tables is that the latter is a subset of Cosmos DB. Azure Cosmos DB is a multimodel database (one of the APIs for Cosmos DB is the Azure Table API) with the option to replicate globally for performance reasons. In contrast, Azure Tables can only be geo-redundant to another region more than 500 miles away primarily for disaster recovery and business continuity. A Microsoft Azure Tips and Tricks article has a good summary of the differences (see `https://microsoft.github.io/AzureTipsAndTricks/blog/tip166.html`).

You can find Microsoft's documentation on Azure Tables at `https://github.com/harris-soh-copeland-puca/azure-docs/tree/master/articles/storage/tables`.

Azure Files

Azure Files offer shared storage for applications using the SMB 3.0 protocol. Azure Files only support SMB 3.0 because it is an Internet-secure protocol.

Traditionally, file shares are drives attached to servers and shared on the network, except in the case of Azure Files, there are no servers involved. As such, Azure Files is one of the simplest forms of serverless service to understand.

The easiest way to describe Azure Files is that it is a shared location that you can map a network drive letter to, and then use that drive letter in file explorer to access files.

The easiest use case for Azure Files is to connect them to virtual machines in Azure.

Hands-on: Using Azure Files

1. In Azure Storage Explorer, go to the Azure storage account created earlier in this chapter.
2. Right-click **File Shares** and select **Create File Share**.
3. Give the File Share a name. The File Share name is part of a URL, so it must be a valid DNS name. If the name is not acceptable, you see a red exclamation mark next to it.

4. After the File Share is created, select it, and upload a file.
5. Click the **Connect VM** option from the top menu in Azure Storage Explorer and copy the **net use** command provided in the popup prompt. Notice that the key is embedded in the command.
6. Remote to a VM in Azure and open a command prompt. Paste the command copied from step 5, and replace the drive letter in the command with the drive letter that you wish to use.

Next Steps: Azure Files

Azure Files offers an easy way to create File Shares that VMs in Azure can use. However, if you want to connect to File Shares via a drive letter from our on-premises computers, special network and security considerations need to take place, including opening port 445 in the firewall. Most ISPs block this port for security reasons because although SMB 3.0 is considered an Internet-secure protocol, older versions of SMB are not, but they use the same port 445.

For more information about connecting to Azure Files from on-premises networks and computers, see `https://docs.microsoft.com/en-us/azure/storage/files/storage-files-networking-overview`.

As with all the other topics, Microsoft's extensive documentation on Azure Files is at `https://github.com/harris-soh-copeland-puca/azure-docs/tree/master/articles/storage/files`.

Azure Queues

Azure Queues is another easy-to-understand serverless storage service that supports messaging. Message queues support asynchronous application-to-application communication, so like Azure Tables, Azure Queues are generally used by applications.

To facilitate a common communication protocol between applications and services, authenticated HTTPS is the access method to Azure Queues. A message added to Azure Queues is stored for a certain amount of time or until it has been processed by the receiving application and deleted.

The retention period of a message in a queue is specified by the application sending the message, and it can be in days, hours, minutes, or seconds.

Hands-on: Using Azure Queues

1. In Azure Storage Explorer, go to the Azure storage account created earlier in this chapter.
2. Right-click **Queues** and select **Create Queue**.
3. Provide a name for the queue and hit **Enter**.
4. After the queue has been created, click **Add Message**, as seen in Figure 14-14. Type **Message should stay for seven seconds** in the Message text and set the message option to 7 seconds. Then click **OK**.

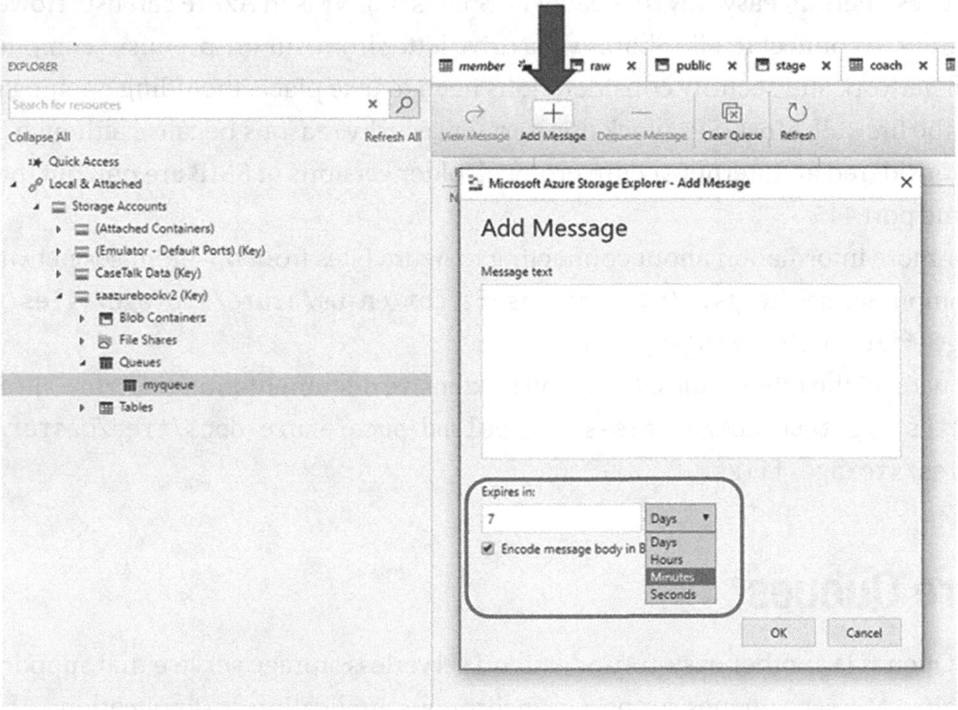

***Figure 14-14.** Creating and setting message options in Azure Queues*

Next Steps: Azure Queues

Getting into the development aspect using Azure Queues is beyond the scope of this chapter, but queues have served as a messaging method for a long time, so they are easily understood.

Microsoft's documentation on Azure Queues is at https://github.com/harris-soh-copeland-puca/azure-docs/tree/master/articles/storage/queues.

To quickly start using Azure Queues, read the documentation at https://docs.microsoft.com/en-us/azure/storage/queues/storage-dotnet-how-to-use-queues.

Summary

This chapter was written to provide you with a good primer on the different Azure storage options. As a reminder, the comprehensive documentation for all Microsoft Azure services is on our GitHub repo at https://github.com/harris-soh-copeland-puca/azure-docs.

PART V

Azure Data Services and Big Data

CHAPTER 15

Azure Cognitive (COG) Services

One of the most exciting areas in artificial intelligence is the area of cognitive sciences. Cognitive science is the study of how the brain functions—specifically, mental processing, awareness, and interaction. Cognitive science, as applied to technology, is about enabling software to interact with users at a more human level.

When we think of artificial intelligence in traditional science fiction, we envision robots that are modeled after humans. These robots can understand and carry a conversation, execute tasks with the same or better skill as humans, and can make decisions based on available information. These are all based on machines having cognitive abilities that are equivalent to those in the human brain.

We are at a point where artificial intelligence based on the cognitive abilities of machines is almost on par with humans in some areas. For example, advancement in camera and image processing technologies have made vision a cognitive ability that may be more effective at identifying and processing the immediate environment than the human eye can.

The ability to process information and understand different languages is another example where the cognitive ability of a machine may supersede the linguistic ability of many individuals.

Azure Cognitive Services

When we think of the brain's cognitive abilities, the ones that immediately come to mind are vision, speech, emotion, understanding, and decision making. Microsoft Research has invested significant resources in creating models that can recognize objects, understand language, and process facial characteristics to recognize age, gender, and emotion.

J. Soh et al., *Microsoft Azure*, https://doi.org/10.1007/978-1-4842-5958-0_15

These capabilities are then packaged into services that can easily be used by application developers, thereby making artificial intelligence available in a very turnkey way. Microsoft calls this the democratization of artificial intelligence.

Developers no longer need to be data scientists and have access to huge amounts of data to create models that can accurately identify people or certain objects. This work has been done, and such common models are made available for consumption.

Azure Cognitive Services has the following abilities.

- Vision
  a. Computer Vision: Analyzes content in images such as facial detection.
  b. Video Indexer: Analyzes and index content in videos.
  c. Form Recognizer: Extracts text and fields from tables and forms.
  d. Ink Recognizer: Recognizes handwriting and digital ink.
  e. Custom Vision: Trains the Vision cognitive services to identify content that is more customized to the business need. For example, a particular product or packaging, and not a common entity like "a person."
- Language
  a. Natural Language: Builds Language Understanding (LUIS) into applications, devices, and bots.
  b. QnA Maker: Leverages existing documents and FAQs as knowledge bases to create conversational capabilities.
  c. Text Analytics: Detects sentiment, key phrases, and named entities.
  d. Translation: Detect and translate languages.
- Speech
  a. Transcription: Transcribes audible speech into searchable text.
  b. Text to Speech: Converts text into lifelike and natural speech.

c. Speech Translation: Translates real-time speech into different languages.

d. Speaker Recognition: Identifies speakers based on trained audio.

- Decision Making

a. Anomaly Detection: Identifies anomalies, generally in time series data.

b. Content Moderation: Detects potential offensive or unwanted content.

c. Personalizer: Learns user behavior and provide a personalized recommendation that improves over time, thereby providing a very relevant and customized experience.

- Bing Search

a. Image Search: Finds images on Bing with full URL and metadata.

b. News Search: Uses keywords, search for news articles, including images, provider, and other metadata associated with the article.

c. Spellcheck and Proof: Uses Bing's spellcheck and proof-reading capabilities to analyze any given text.

d. Bing Search: Offers ad-free search results leverage Bing as the back-end search engine.

e. Video Search: Gets video-only search results with the related metadata.

f. Entity Search: Provides search results based on relevance, such as famous people, places, movies, TV shows, local businesses, and so forth.

All Azure COG services feature API endpoints that receive input from your application or device and return the relevant results in JSON format.

Explore the different COG services by visiting `https://azure.microsoft.com/en-us/services/cognitive-services/`. Each COG service has a landing page that features the ability to test the service and review the JSON result.

Quick Hands-on Introduction

Let's explore the COG services.

1. Go to `https://azure.microsoft.com/en-us/services/cognitive-services/`.
2. Scroll down and select **Language** under Azure Cognitive Services, and then select **Text Analytics**, as referenced in Figure 15-1.
3. Click the examples to use canned phrases, and observe the analyzed text, particularly the sentiment that was detected.

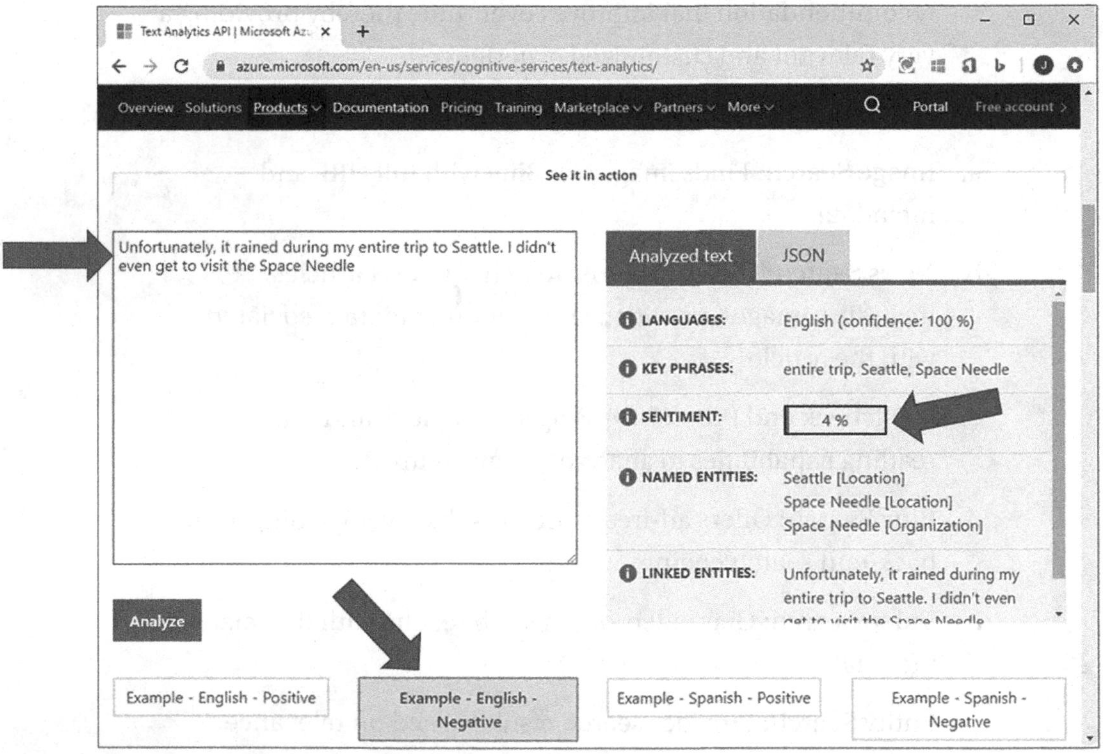

***Figure 15-1.** Negative sentiment of analyzed text*

4. Replace the text with your own text, and then click the **Analyze** button, and observe the detected sentiment. Is it what you expected?

5. Click the **JSON** tab, as referenced in Figure 15-2 to view the JSON results that were returned by the COG service.

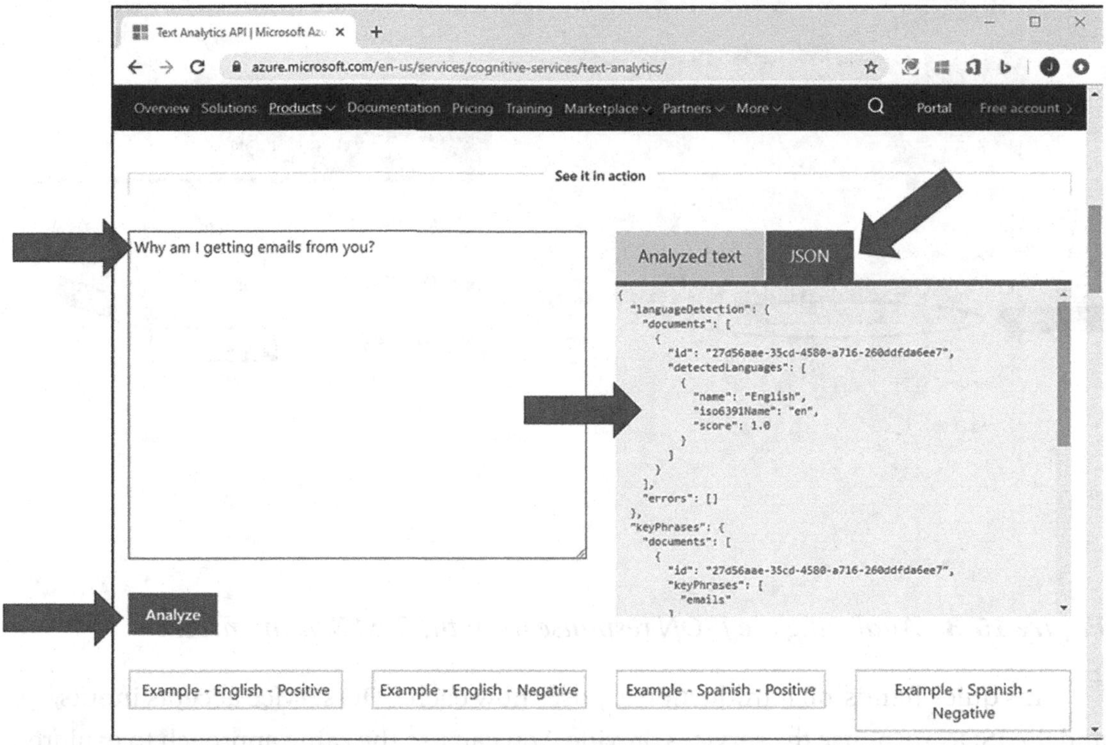

Figure 15-2. *JSON response from the COG service*

6. In the Sentiment array, there is an element titled **score**. This score determines the sentiment that was detected by the COG service. In our example, the graphic in the user interface showed 25%, as referenced in Figure 15-3 which is a roundup of the actual score of 0.24628770351409912.

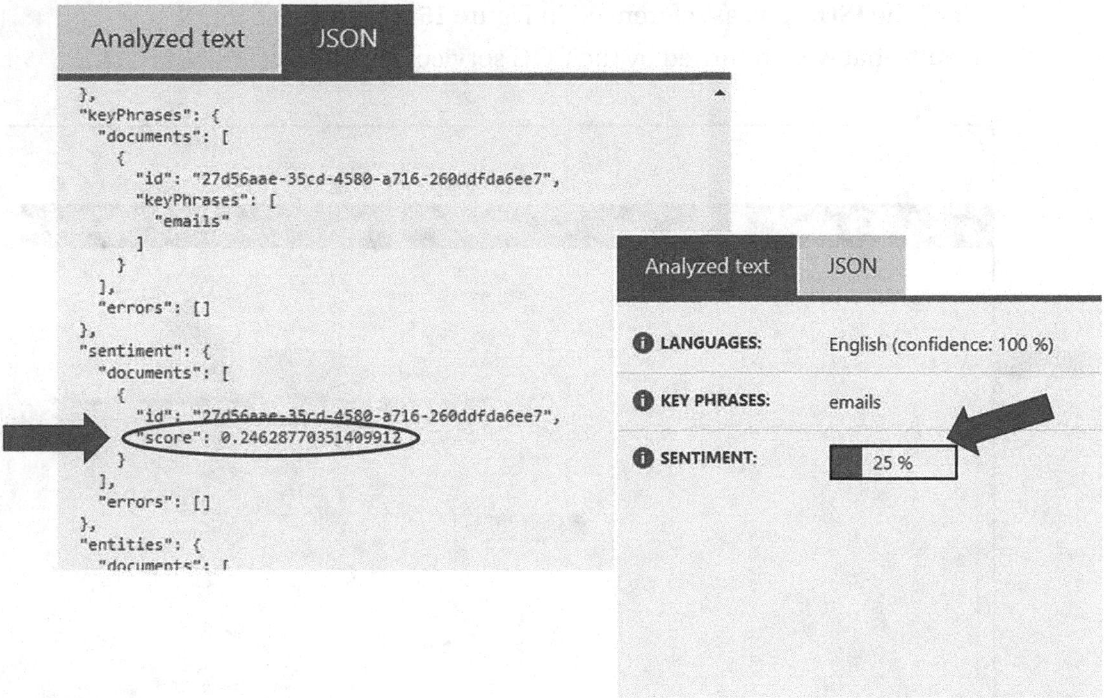

Figure 15-3. *Analyzing the JSON response from the Text Sentiment API*

This quick hands-on introduction exposes how each COG service accepts inputs, and the JSON response the services provide. You can use the same approach to explore the capabilities of all the Azure COG services.

With that in mind, let's apply this COG service in a practical scenario.

Hands-on Exercise

Scenario

Your organization currently has a website that accepts feedback via a webform. All feedback is free form and goes to a single email address. During peak times, the website may receive an extraordinarily high number of submissions.

You want to implement prioritization of feedback received so that they are directed to different individuals (email addresses) for proper handling. In particular, you want to make sure that you address any feedback that may be negative.

The solution you propose needs to be easily and quickly implemented and does not incur significant cost or management overhead on an ongoing basis.

Final Product

Let's create a C# web form that has a multiline field for users to provide feedback. Upon submission of the feedback, the text in the feedback field is sent to the Azure COG service, specifically calling the text sentiment analysis capability, and receive a sentiment score.

For this exercise, you simply display the score in a field on the same form. But in a real-world scenario, you can choose to route the feedback to the appropriate department based on the sentiment score. Figure 15-4 shows the solution in action.

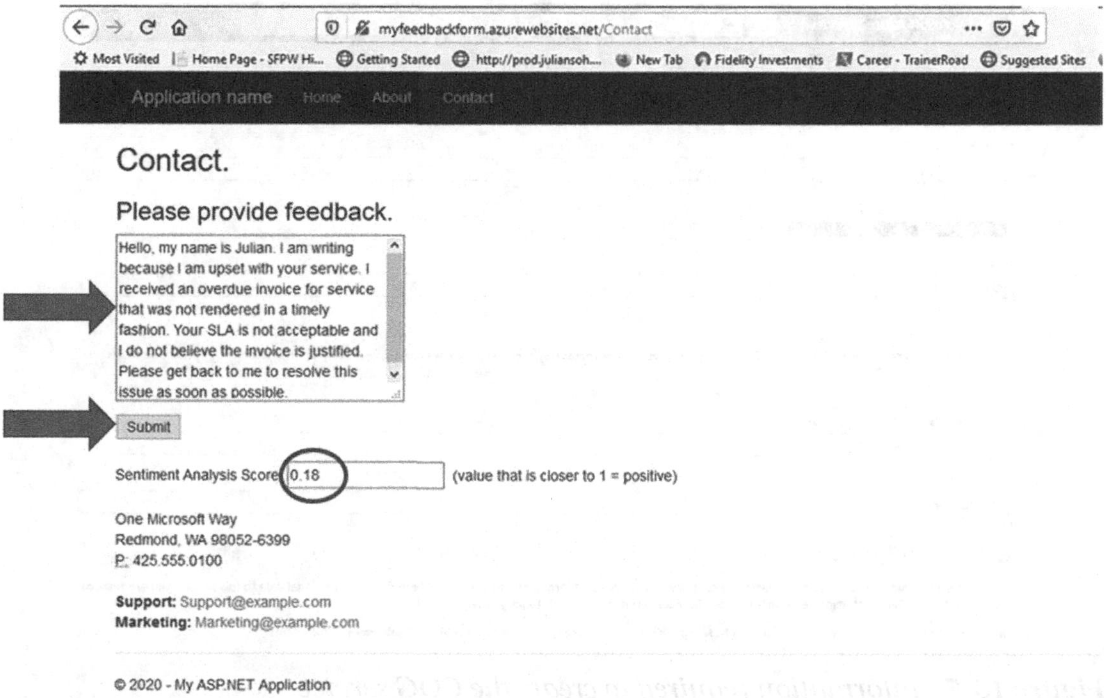

***Figure 15-4.** Feedback form with sentiment analysis capabilities*

Exercise

Make sure you have an Azure subscription or sign up for a free trial if you do not have one.

1. Sign in to the Azure portal and click **Create a resource**, as referenced in Figure 15-5.
2. Type **cognitive services** in the search box, and select **Cognitive Services** in the search results.
3. Click **Create.**
4. Fill in the required fields needed for the COG service for this exercise. Choose **S0** for the pricing tier, and then click **Create** when you are done.

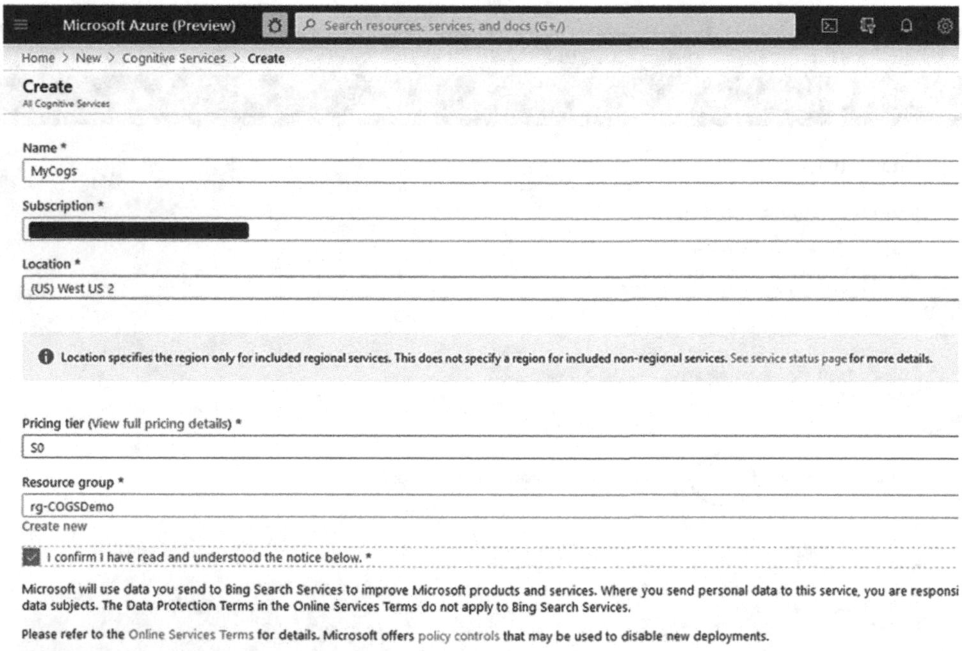

Figure 15-5. *Information required to create the COG service*

5. Once your COG service has been deployed, go to the resource, and retrieve your key and endpoint information, as referenced in Figure 15-6. These are in the Quick Start pane. Copy these values to Notepad or somewhere easily accessible. You will need to paste these values into your code later.

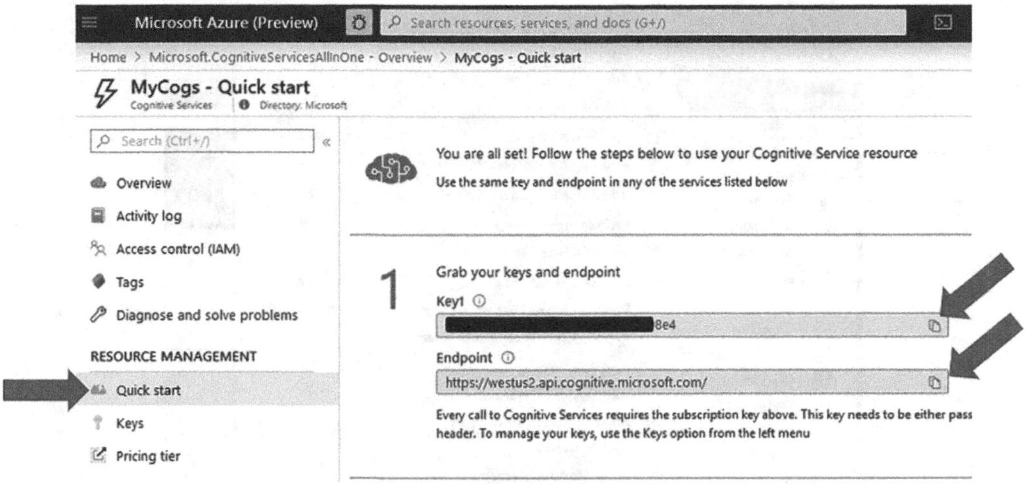

Figure 15-6. *Key and endpoint located in the Quick Start pane*

At this point, you can either continue following the steps in this exercise or clone the following GitHub repository for the complete solution at `https://harris-soh-copeland-puca.github.io`.

1. Open Visual Studio or your favorite integrated development environment (IDE). This exercise uses Visual Studio Community Edition 2019 as the IDE.

2. Create a new ASP.NET web application project (or open the project that you cloned from the GitHub repo).

3. Select Web Forms as the template for this project. By default, this template has a basic Web Application with three pages: Default.aspx, About.aspx, and Contact.aspx.Add the necessary packages. Under the Project menu, select **Manage NuGet Packages**, as referenced in Figure 15-7.

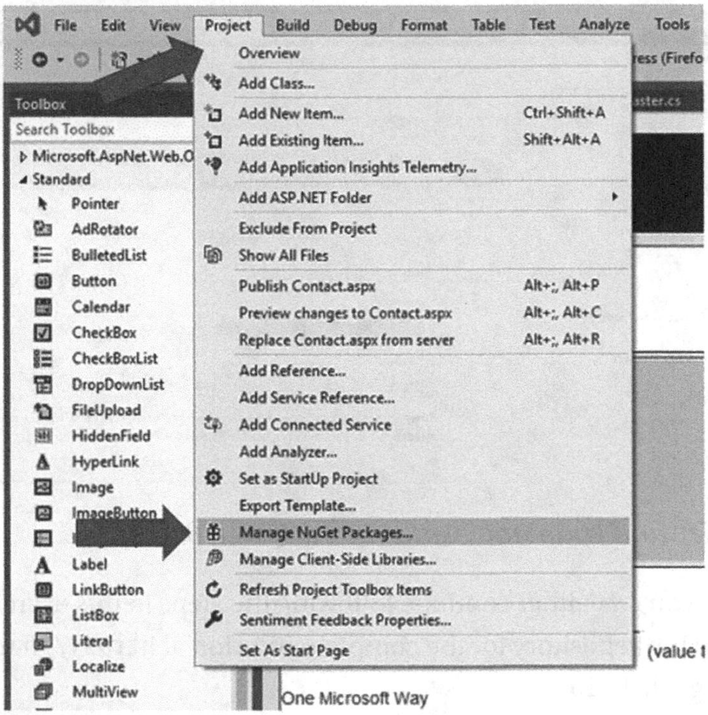

Figure 15-7. Add NuGet packages

4. Click the Browse menu option and type **Microsoft *Azure* cognitive services language** in the search box. Select Microsoft.Azure.CognitiveServices.Language.TextAnalytics in the results. Click **Install** to install the latest stable version of this package.

Let's modify the Contact.aspx page and add a feedback field, a submit button, and an analytics score field.

1. Open Contact.aspx and replace the code with the following.

```
<%@ Page Title="Contact" Language="C#" MasterPageFile="~/Site.
Master" AutoEventWireup="true" CodeBehind="Contact.aspx.cs"
Inherits="Sentiment_Feedback.Contact" %>

<asp:Content ID="BodyContent" ContentPlaceHolderID="MainContent"
runat="server">
    <h2><%: Title %>.</h2>
    <h3>Please provide feedback.</h3>
```

```
        <p>
            <asp:TextBox ID="txt_Feedback" runat="server" Height="162px"
            Width="464px" TextMode="MultiLine"></asp:TextBox>
        </p>
        <address>
            <asp:Button ID="Btn_Submit" runat="server" OnClick="Btn_
            Submit_Click" Text="Submit" />
        </address>
        <address>
            Sentiment Analysis Score: <asp:TextBox ID="txt_Score"
            runat="server"></asp:TextBox>
         (value that is closer to 1 = positive)</address>
        <address>
            One Microsoft Way<br />
            Redmond, WA 98052-6399<br />
            <abbr title="Phone">P:</abbr>
            425.555.0100
        </address>

        <address>
            <strong>Support:</strong>   <a href="mailto:Support@
            example.com">Support@example.com</a><br />
            <strong>Marketing:</strong> <a href="mailto:Marketing@
            example.com">Marketing@example.com</a>
        </address>
    </asp:Content>
```

2. Open Contact.aspx.cs and append the following to the top of the code.

```
using System.Net.Http;
using System.Net;
using System.Threading;
using System.Threading.Tasks;
using Microsoft.Azure.CognitiveServices.Language.TextAnalytics;
using Microsoft.Azure.CognitiveServices.Language.TextAnalytics.
Models;
using Microsoft.Rest;
```

3. Declare the following variables. Replace the values for the key and endpoint with the values that you copied from the portal when you first deployed the COG service.

```
private static readonly string key = "<replace-with-your-key>";
private static readonly string endpoint = "<replace-with-
endpoint>";
```

4. Create a new class named ApiKeyServiceClientCredentials.cs.

5. Add the following code to the ApiKeyServiceClientCredentials class.

```
using System.Net.Http;
using System.Threading;
using System.Threading.Tasks;
using Microsoft.Azure.CognitiveServices.Language.TextAnalytics;
using Microsoft.Azure.CognitiveServices.Language.TextAnalytics.
Models;
using Microsoft.Rest;
class ApiKeyServiceClientCredentials : ServiceClientCredentials
{
    private readonly string apiKey;

    public ApiKeyServiceClientCredentials(string apiKey)
    {
        this.apiKey = apiKey;
    }

    public override Task ProcessHttpRequestAsync(HttpRequestMessage
    request, CancellationToken cancellationToken)
    {
        if (request == null)
        {
            throw new ArgumentNullException("request");
        }
        request.Headers.Add("Ocp-Apim-Subscription-Key", this.
        apiKey);
```

```
            return base.ProcessHttpRequestAsync(request,
            cancellationToken);
        }
    }
```

6. Open Contact.aspx and double-click the button control that was added. This adds the code behind for that control. Then add the following code to the control.

```
var client = authenticateClient();
sentimentAnalysisExample(client);
```

7. Add the following method to the code to instantiate the TextAnalyticsClient object with your endpoint and an ApiKeyServiceClientCredentials object containing your key.

```
protected TextAnalyticsClient authenticateClient()
{
    ApiKeyServiceClientCredentials credentials = new ApiKeyService
    ClientCredentials(key);
    TextAnalyticsClient client = new TextAnalyticsClient(credentia
    ls)
    {
        Endpoint = endpoint
    };
    return client;
}
```

8. Add the following SentimentAnalysisExample() function, which takes the client that was created earlier and calls its Sentiment() function. The returned object contains the sentiment score, which you populate in the txt_score textbox.

```
        protected void sentimentAnalysisExample(ITextAnalyticsClient
        client)
        {
            System.Net.ServicePointManager.SecurityProtocol =
            SecurityProtocolType.Tls | SecurityProtocolType.Tls11
            | SecurityProtocolType.Tls12;
```

```
            var result = client.Sentiment(txt_Feedback.Text, "en");
            txt_score.Text = $"{result.Score:0.00}";
        }
```

9. Publish or run to debug this project. You should be able to enter some text in the feedback field, click Submit, and receive a sentiment score.

This exercise demonstrates how simple it is to consume COG services. It is a repeatable approach for almost all COG services. The democratization of AI allows developers to quickly incorporate these capabilities into their applications without the need to deal with complex models and algorithms. Just consume it!

Other Real-World Uses

There are many exciting applications for COG services. Some of the ones that we have come across from past projects include

- Text sentiment analysis on Twitter feeds
- Custom Vision to
    - identify blight, graffiti, and overgrown conditions from photographs submitted by property inspectors
    - identify unsafe workplace conditions (e.g., power cables not properly taped down or cluttered job site)
    - identify noxious weeds or invasive fish species
- License-plate recognition
- Language translation applications

Bots

Another exciting use case for COG services is the deployment of *bots* (also called *chatbots*) to websites. We are all very familiar with the standard Frequently Asked Questions (FAQ) pages that are a mainstay of almost every major corporate, retail, and commercial site. The problem with FAQs is that you need to search for the right terms.

The use of FAQs have grown exponentially, and as a result, we have observed that the well-meaning efforts of content managers to organize FAQs into proper categories or topics have caused fragmentation. So instead of making it easier for site visitors to get their questions answered, it has become more difficult because customers must navigate to the correct department, and then search the respective FAQs. Looking for an answer to a question at the wrong department's subsite may not provide you with the answer you seek.

Bots are an easily adopted AI solution that can help address this challenge. As simple as they are to deploy, which you will see shortly, bots provide a massive *return on investment* (ROI) in terms of customer satisfaction and the reduction in the number of calls flooding call centers.

QnA Maker

For this discussion, one of the capabilities leveraged in bots is a code-free back end called QnA Maker.

QnA Maker is a COG service that ingests FAQs and documents (PDF, Word, etc.) and then uses the content from these sources to answer questions and carry out conversations.

For example, if there is an FAQ that has these QnA pairs.

> Q: How much does a self-storage unit cost?
>
> A: It depends on the size of the unit.
>
> Q: How much does a small storage unit cost?
>
> A: $152/month
>
> Q: How much does an extra-large storage unit cost?
>
> A: $1,472/month
>
> Q: How much does a medium storage unit cost?
>
> A: $175/month

This FAQ can go on to list every type of storage unit and the associated cost, so the visitor has to read through the entire FAQ to look for the pricing, or it could point to a page with all the listed options, and the visitor must scroll through *that* list. Most likely, visitors would simply give up and pick up the phone to call, or worse, leave and go to a competitor.

Let's explore how to take this scenario and make it a much better user experience.

Hands-on Exercise Part 1: QnA Maker

First, let's mockup an FAQ page, or if you are ambitious enough, use an existing FAQ page from your site or someone else's site. All you need is the URL of the FAQ page!

1. Using the same project from the previous exercise, add an HTML page to the project. Add the following HTML to the <body> of the page.

```
<h2>Q: How much does a storage unit cost?</h2>
<div class="answer">A: IT depends on the size of the storage
unit.</div>
<h2>Q: How much does a small storage unit cost?</h2>
<div class="answer">A: $152/month</div>
<h2>Q: How much does an extra-large storage unit cost?</h2>
<div class="answer">A: $1,472/month</div>
<h2>Q: How much does a medium storage unit cost?</h2>
<div class="answer">A: $175/month</div>
```

2. Publish your project to a web app or a server that is accessible from the Internet. Refer to Chapter 12 if you need a refresher on spinning up a web app.

3. Open a browser and go to `https://QnAMaker.ai`.

4. By now, you should have an Azure subscription. If not, sign up for a free trial subscription.

5. Sign in using your Microsoft Azure credentials.

6. Click **Create a knowledge base**.

7. Follow the instructions for step 1, which is to create a QnA service in your Azure subscription. For this exercise, use the F0 for the pricing tier (three managed documents). If you need to add more URLs and or PDFs as sources, then select the **S0** (unlimited) pricing tier.

8. For the Azure Search pricing tier, use F (three indexes).

9. As per the instructions, after you have created a QnA service, you need to click the refresh button so that the drop-down menu options in step 2 are populated with the QnA service that you just created.

10. Provide all the required information in step 2, and name your KB in step 3. This also serves as the name of your bot. So, while you may intuitively want to name it something descriptive, we recommend that you use a short, friendly name. For this exercise, we have named our KB (bot) "Joe". Let's refer to him fondly by this name from here on out. This is by design because we want our bot to be personable, which is a subtle but important aspect, so keep that in mind when you start deploying bots.

11. In step 4, type the FAQ URL, but do not check the box for multiturn extraction. You can also define the personality of your bot by selecting one of the options under Chit-chat. For this exercise, we selected Friendly.

12. Click **Create your KB**.

Once QnA Maker has completed ingesting the FAQ, you can click the Edit menu to view the Question and Answer (QnA) pairs.

In our example, the four QnA pairs were correctly identified but notice that there is a total of 94 QnA pairs, as referenced in Figure 15-8. This is because additional QnA pairs were added to facilitate conversation, based on the *friendly* persona selected in step 12. You can see these conversational QnA pairs in the section titled "Source: qna_chitchat_Friendly.tsv".

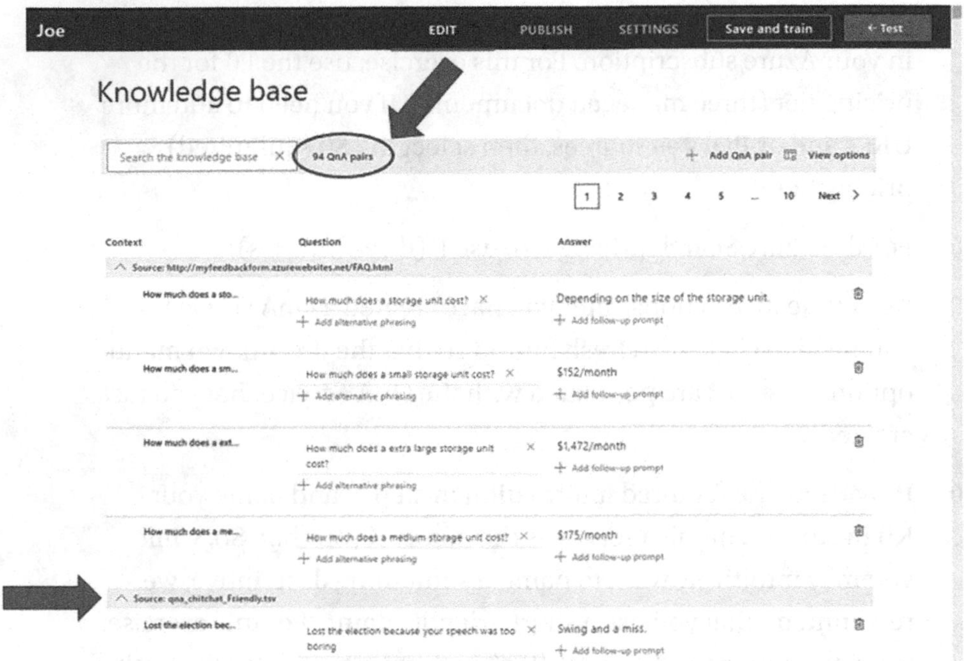

***Figure 15-8.** QnA Maker appending 90 Friendly conversational QnA pairs*

It is now time to test the interaction before attaching it to a bot. Click on the Test button at the top right corner of the page to start interacting with Joe. Figure 15-9 depicts this interaction. Notice that you do not need to phrase a question directly for Joe to provide the answer. This test is a good representation as to how Joe performs once the bot is deployed to the website.

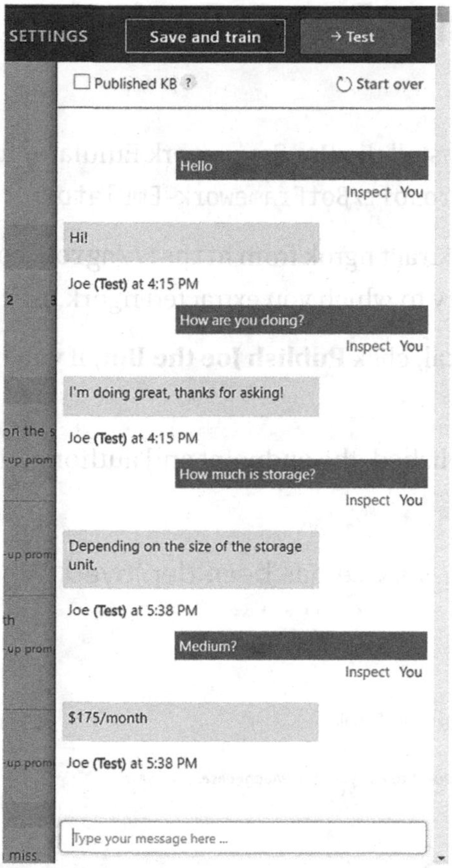

Figure 15-9. *Test interaction with Joe*

Note Click the Test button again to hide it.

If you need to fine-tune the responses, add more sources, or have Joe re-ingest new or changed content from existing URLs, go back to the Settings page. It is self-explanatory, so we will not go into detail here. Essentially, this exercise shows how you can implement a bot's back-end capabilities in a relatively short time. When you are satisfied with the content, click Publish.

Hands-on Exercise Part 2: Deploying Bots to a Website

1. Download and install the Bot Framework Emulator from `https://github.com/Microsoft/BotFramework-Emulator`.
2. Download and extract ngrok from `https://ngrok.com/download`. Note the directory to which you extracted ngork.exe to.
3. In the Azure portal, click **Publish Joe the Bot**, if you have not already done so.

Once Joe has been published, the endpoint and authorization information is made available.

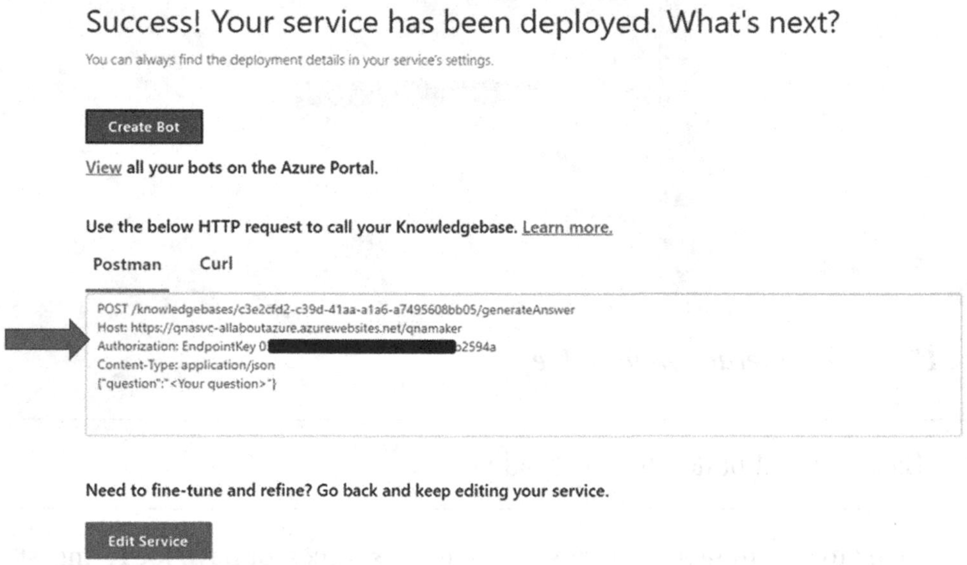

***Figure 15-10.** Information required to use Joe (bot)*

4. Click **Create Bot**, as referenced in Figure 15-10. This redirects you back to the Azure portal.
5. At the Web App Bot service creation pane,
    a. Provide a bot name (handle). It must be globally unique, so you may have to choose an instance name that is different from the bot's *display* name. In this case, we called our handle JoeTheBot, but the display name is still Joe.

b. Choose **S1** as the pricing tier but review the full pricing details if you want more information. (Bots are *not* expensive!)

c. Chose **C#** as the SDK language.

d. Note that the QnA Auth Key has already been generated and provided. Do not modify this.

e. Select an existing App Service plan or create a new one.

f. Leave Application Insights on and select a region closest to you.

6. Click **Create**.

7. After the bot has been created, go to the resource and test it by selecting **Test in Web Chat**, as referenced in Figure 15-11. Interact with the bot to confirm that it works.

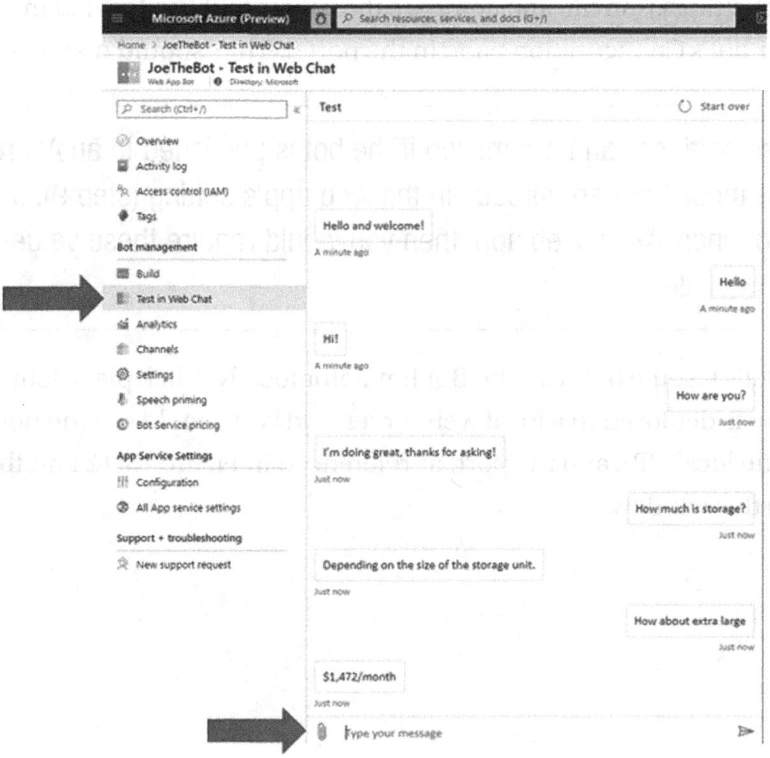

***Figure 15-11.** Testing the bot from the Azure portal*

8. Select **Configuration** under the App Service settings in the portal and copy the MicrosoftAppID and MicrosofAppPassword. You need these to configure the Bot Emulator for testing.

Note Click the icon that resembles an eye to unhide and copy the values.

---

9. In the Build pane, select **Download Bot source code.**
10. Select **Yes** to include settings. Wait for the zip package to be prepared, and then download it.
11. Unzip the package and open the QnABot.sln project with Visual Studio.
12. Since you chose to import settings, the authorization keys and endpoints for your project should have been configured. Open the AppSettings.json file and compare the values to those located in your bot's Configuration pane in the portal. They should match.

Note These settings can be removed if the bot is published to an Azure web app because these keys are already in the web app's setting (step 9). If you are publishing to a non-Azure web app, then you would require these values in the appsettings.json file.

For now, let's test the bot with the Bot Emulator locally. Click play/debug in Visual Studio. The bot is deployed to a local web server, and you should see the bot's web page. Take note of the local URL and the port, as referenced in Figure 15-12 and then minimize (do not close) this window.

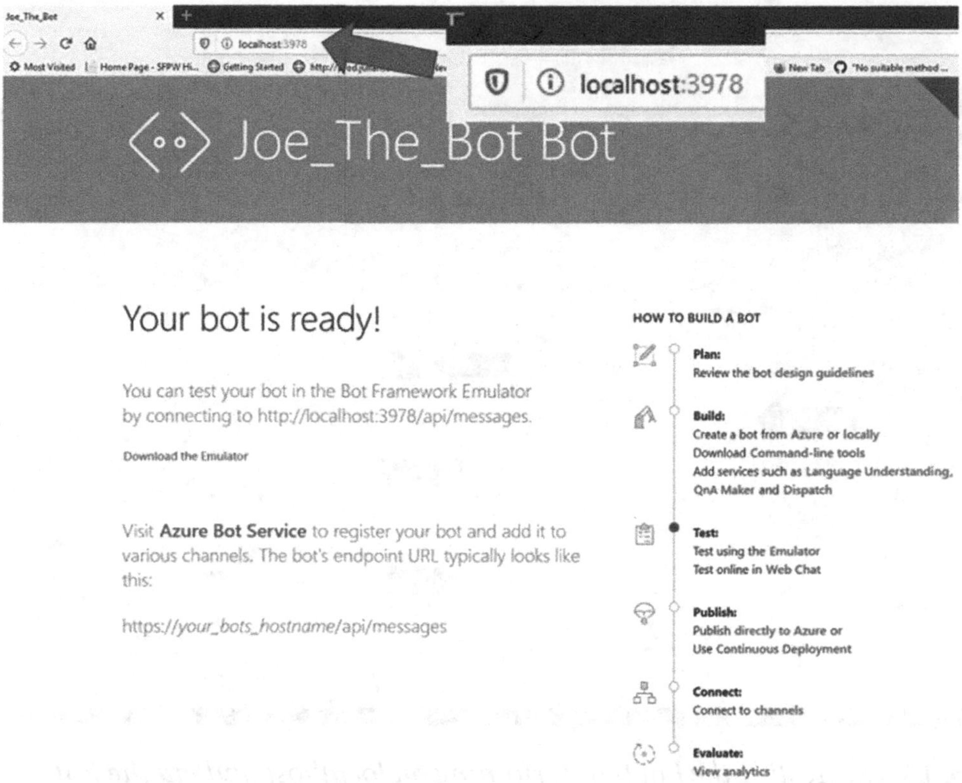

***Figure 15-12.** Bot published to LocalHost listening on port 3978*

1. Launch the Bot Framework Emulator. Click **File** and select **New Bot configuration**.
2. Enter a name for your bot.
   a. Enter the bot's URL from step 14, and append **/api/messages** to it.
   b. Enter the MicrosoftAppID from step 9.
   c. Enter the MicrosoftAppPassword from step 9.
   d. Click **Save and connect**.
3. Start interacting with the bot locally, as referenced in Figure 15-13. Note that if you close the bot web page, which you minimized in step 14, or if you stop debugging in Visual Studio, the bot stops responding to the Bot Framework Emulator.

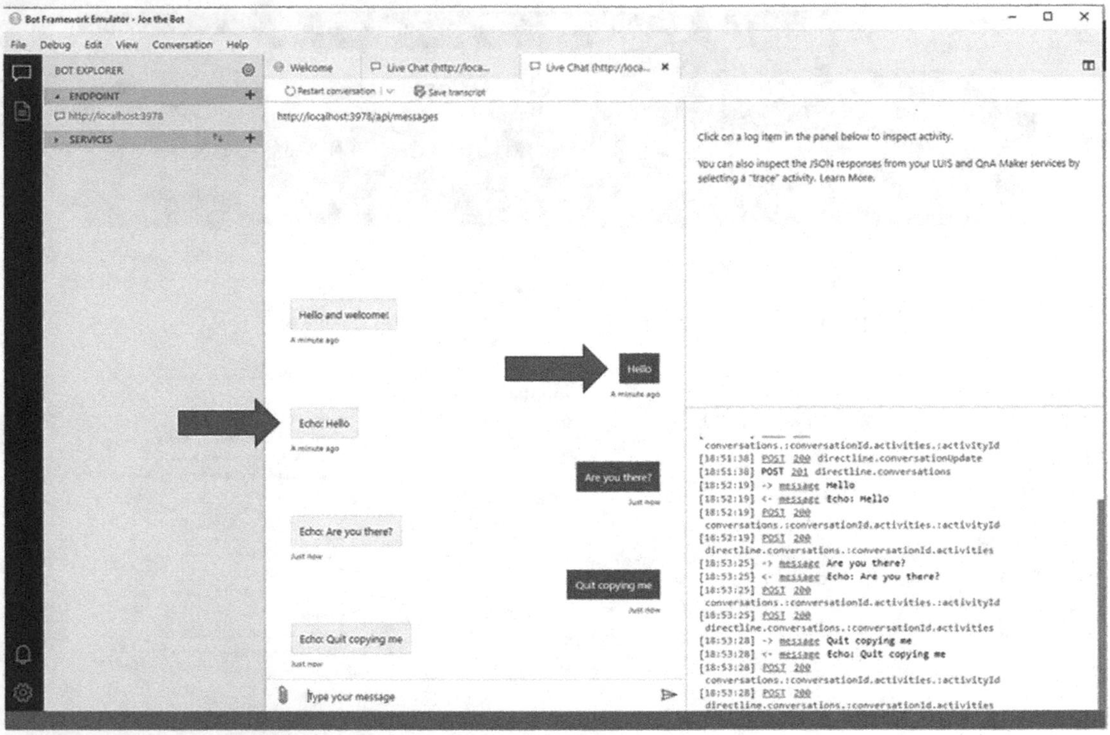

Figure 15-13. *Testing the bot that is running on localhost and via the Bot Framework Emulator*

4. Stop debugging in Visual Studio.

5. It is time to deploy the bot to a permanent location. To test the bot that is hosted remotely using the Bot Framework Emulator, you need to configure ngrok.

6. Click the gear icon located at the bottom-left corner of the Bot Framework Emulator. Browse or enter the path to ngrok.exe (from step 2), and select both checkboxes to bypass ngrok for local addresses, as referenced in Figure 15-14 and to run ngrok when the emulator starts.

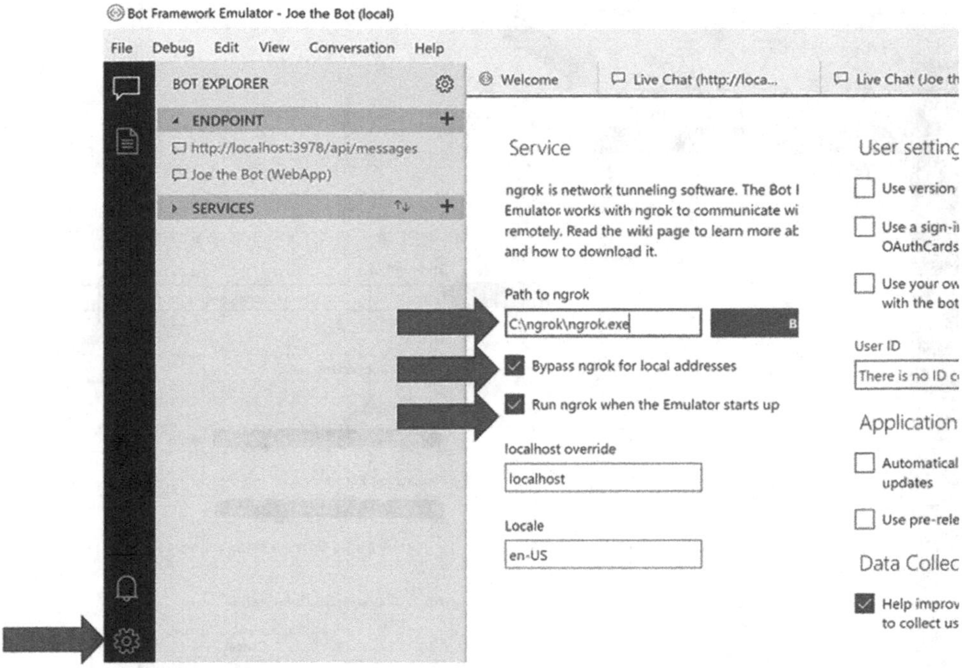

Figure 15-14. *Configuring ngrok*

7. In Visual Studio, publish your bot to a new web app. Refer to Chapter 12 if you need a refresher on how to deploy a web app.

8. Upon successful publication, you again see the bot page, but this time, notice that instead of a //localhost:3968 URL, it has a permanent URL (e.g., <your bot name>.azurewebsites.net). Take note of this URL. You can close this window this time, unlike in step 13, and it will not terminate the bot.

9. Let's test it one more time using the Bot Framework Emulator because the bot is now permanently hosted at the preceding URL. Click the + icon in the Endpoint menu to add an endpoint, and then enter the URL from the previous step with **/api/messages** appended to it, as referenced in Figure 15-15. Also, enter the MicrosoftApplicationID and MicrosoftApplicationPassword in the Application Id and Application Password fields. Click **Save**.

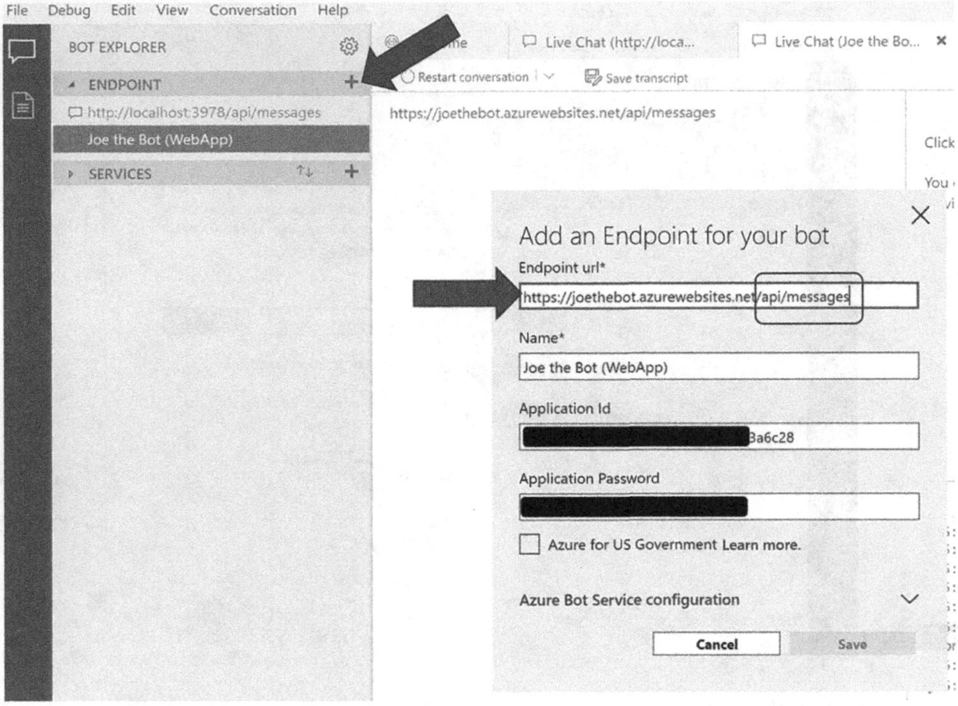

Figure 15-15. *Adding a remote endpoint for the bot*

10. As before, select the new remote endpoint and interact with your bot to confirm that it is responding as expected.

11. At this point, you can embed the bot on any webpage. For this exercise, let's build on the previous site (Sentiment Analysis) and make the bot available on that site as well.

12. In the Azure portal, click the **Channels** pane, as referenced in Figure 15-16. You should see Web Chat as an existing channel. Click **Edit**.

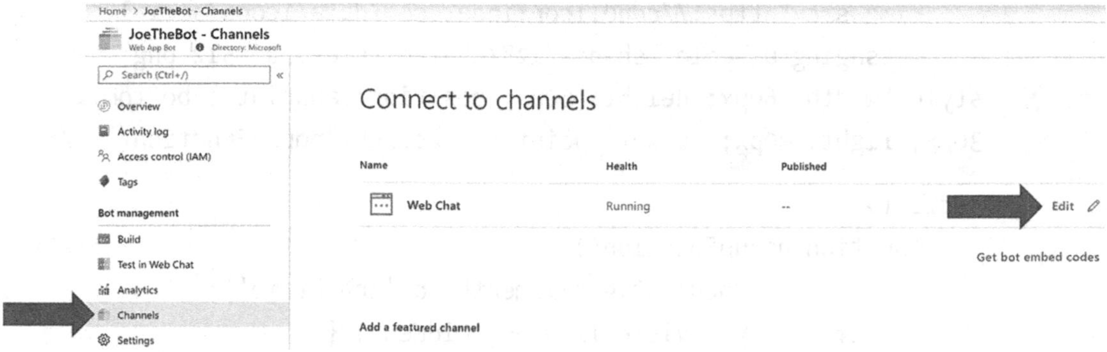

***Figure 15-16.** Editing the Web Chat channel*

13. Click **Show** to expose the first secret key and copy it to Notepad, as referenced in Figure 15-17.

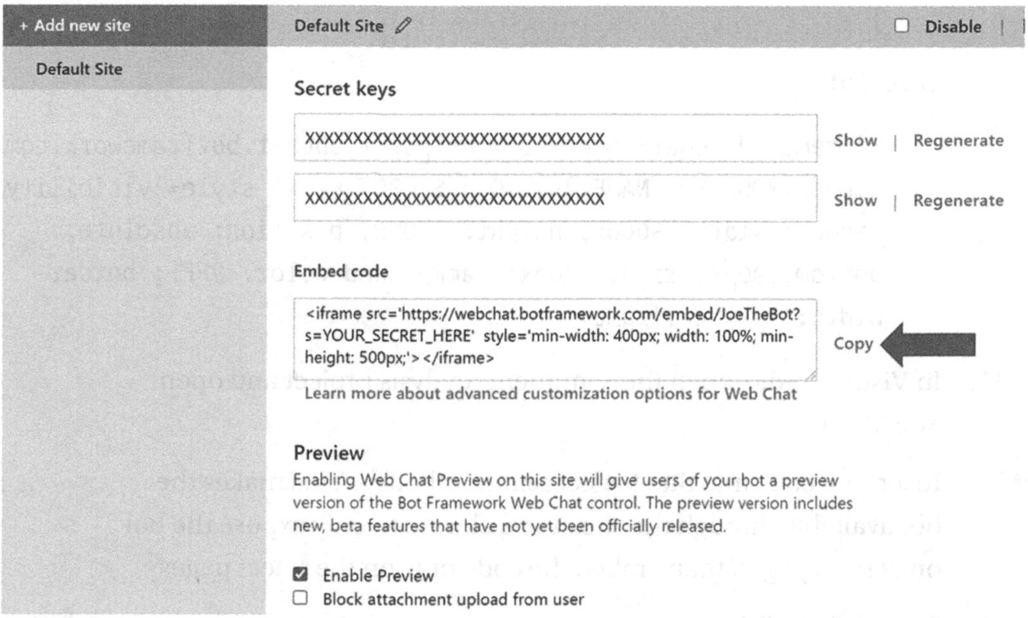

***Figure 15-17.** The embed code used in our web page*

14. Take note of the code in the **Embed code** field. You can choose to copy this code or use what we have provided here. Replace <YOUR_BOT_NAME> and <YOUR_SECRET_KEY> with the information you see in the Embed code in the portal and what you copied in the previous step.

```
    <img src="https://cdn0.iconfinder.com/data/icons/social-
    messaging-ui-color-shapes/128/chat-circle-blue-512.png"
style="width: 60px; height: 60px; position: absolute; bottom:
30px; right: 30px; cursor: pointer" onclick="popupFunction()" />

<script>
    function popupFunction() {
        var x = document.getElementById('chatFrame');
        if (x.style.visibility == 'hidden') {
            x.style.visibility = 'visible';
        }
        else {
            x.style.visibility = 'hidden';
        }
    }
</script>

    <iframe id="chatFrame" src='https://webchat.botframework.com/
    embed/<YOUR_BOT_NAME>?s=<YOUR_SECRET_KEY>' style='visibility:
    hidden; width: 500px; height: 600px; position: absolute;
    bottom: 90px; right: 20px; background-color: #FFF; border-
    width: 1px'></iframe>
```

15. In Visual Studio, open the Sentiment Analysis project and open Site Master.

16. Insert the code into Site Master before </body>. This makes the bot available through the site. If you choose to only expose the bot on certain pages, then embed the code only on the select pages.

17. Save and publish the project.

18. Go to the published website. You now see a chat icon in the lower-right corner of the site. Click it and start interacting with your bot.

Note In our GitHub repo, we have provided additional information on extending the capabilities of a bot, like performance monitoring and tracking the questions and responses provided by the bot. To learn how to set up telemetry data for your bot using Application Insights, please visit `https://harris-soh-copeland-puca.github.io`.

Summary

This chapter looked at two cognitive services in Azure: Sentiment Analysis and Bot. We built and deployed both capabilities into a website, so it now has the intelligence to determine the sentiment of a feedback form and enable visitors to interact with it in real time through a bot instead of having to search the FAQs.

From here, there are many opportunities to either implement other cognitive services capabilities or build on what we have accomplished so for. For example, a common next step for bots is to implement Language Understanding[1](LUIS) to help improve the bot's interaction with visitors or implement translation services to support other languages.

There are many ways to easily add AI capabilities to your applications by simply consuming the different COG services in very much the same way we have done so in this chapter.

[1]For more information about LUIS and how it is used in Bots, please visit `https://docs.microsoft.com/en-us/azure/cognitive-services/luis/what-is-luis`.

CHAPTER 16

Machine Learning and Deep Learning

The field of machine learning is an ever-changing and advancing landscape. For new and experienced machine learning (ML) practitioners alike, there is always more to learn. This learning and exploring can be done in Azure, marrying new advancements with a sophisticated platform and toolset. Machine learning is not new to Azure, however. Azure Machine Learning Studio has been prevalent since 2015, providing a platform for the development and deployment of ML models from within a drag-and-drop UI. Today, the offerings have advanced and become even more integrated across services in Azure (VMs, AKS, Databricks, Storage, etc.). They provide more ways for developers and data scientists to develop, deploy, and monitor custom ML models with SDKs or by using an integrated drag-and-drop interface that needs very little coding.

The first part of this chapter is a gentle introduction to ML and deep learning with examples in image analysis and alongside working with and thinking about data in the context of ML. Following this, the Data Science Virtual Machine, Jupyter notebooks, Azure ML, and Databricks are explored for data science tasks. Many code samples and walkthroughs are provided.

Introduction to Machine Learning and Deep Learning

At its core, ML is the process of mapping input to output without hardcoded rules. In other words, rather than using rules like "if, else, case, switch," ML uses systems that have seen and analyzed past data (or even streaming data) to make more "educated" guesses or predictions of future events.

J. Soh et al., *Microsoft Azure*, https://doi.org/10.1007/978-1-4842-5958-0_16

In classical programming, we write code (the rules or program) and provide data (input arguments and files) to receive an answer (return value). In contrast, in ML systems, labels or answers are provided along with the data to produce reusable "rules" or models, that in turn, may be used on new or "unseen" data to predict the labels or answers/return values.

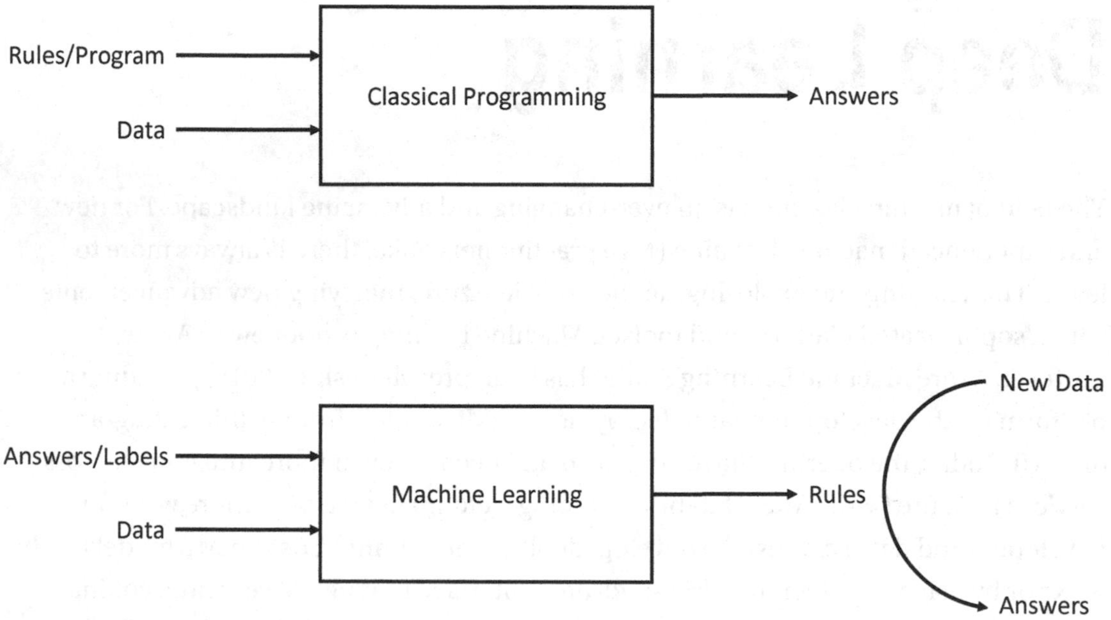

Figure 16-1. *Diagram depicting rule-based learning vs. a common type of machine learning system*

The production of an ML model is through a process called *training*. Usually included in training a model is an evaluation of that model on the part of the original dataset that had not been used in training—sometimes called the *held-out* or *test dataset*. After the production of a satisfactory trained model (according to an evaluation), it is used to gain insights on new data in a process called *inference* or *scoring*.

There are three general paradigms in ML, as shown in Figure 16-2, within which almost all ML algorithms fall. They are ways in which we can categorize different approaches to different types of problems and datasets. These paradigms apply to traditional ML as well as deep learning.

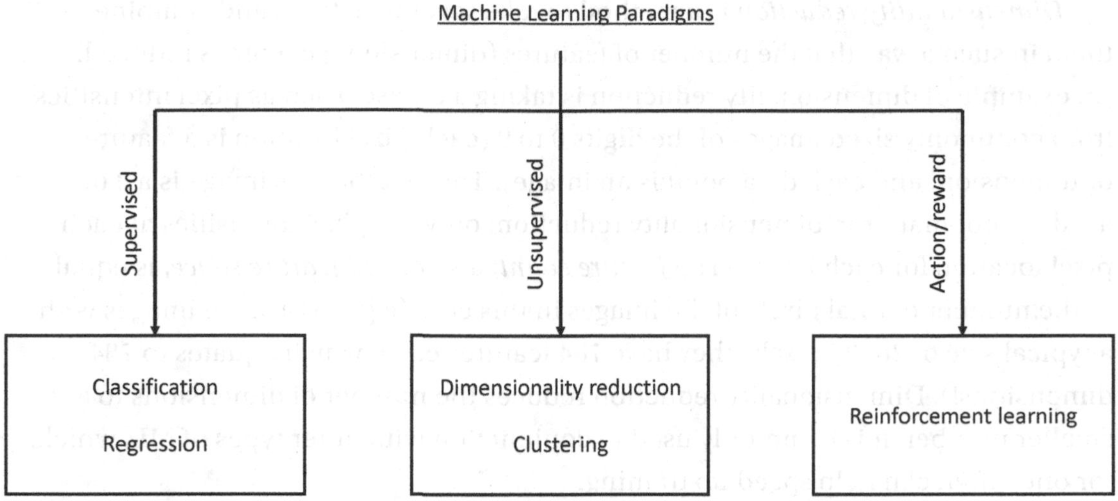

***Figure 16-2.** Machine learning paradigms. ML can be split according to the characteristics of the input data or signals into supervised, unsupervised or action/ reward- based*

In supervised learning, labels are provided at the beginning of training a model. Figure 16-1 depicts supervised learning, where data and the labels are provided to produce a model for tasks like classification or regression (see Figure 16-2). For instance, determining whether a patient has retinopathy, a dangerous eye condition, based on images of retinas from healthy patients and patients with this condition, is an example of a classification task. The labels for this task are binary: retinopathy or no retinopathy. Time-series analysis—where future events, like the demand for a product in a grocery store—is an example of a regression task. The demand for a product could be quantified as the number of items sold in a day. The future demand could then be predicted based on the demand from past days, or historical data. *Semi-supervised learning* is where a portion of the training data has labels, and the rest do not.

Unsupervised learning aims to understand the inner structure or organization in the input data and, thus, the input data does not need to be labeled. One common task is called *clustering*, where datapoints are formed into clusters that could answer questions such as how to group people who attend movies with input features such as age, gender, and income. Here, no label is trying to be predicted; rather, the goal is to find patterns and structure in the data. Based on how the data clusters, new characteristics may be inferred based on the age and income ranges, as well as, gender characteristics of the clusters.

Dimensionality reduction is a method to take several features and combine them in such a way that the number of features (dimensions) becomes reduced. An example of dimensionality reduction is taking a dataset such as pixel intensities from commonly sized images of the digits 0 to 9 (each pixel location is a feature or dimension, and each data point is an image). The fact that the image is a 3 or a 7 does not matter in dimensionality reduction; only the pixel intensities at each pixel location for each image. The *feature count*, also called *feature space*, is equal to the number of total pixels of the images in this case (e.g., for a set of images with a typical size of 28×28 pixels, they have 784 features each, which equates to 784 dimensions!). Dimensionality reduction reduces the number of dimensions to a smaller number. It is commonly used in conjunction with other types of ML, which, for one, often can help speed up training.

In reinforcement learning, a player (called an *agent*) learns how to optimally operate in an environment based on rewards and penalties assigned to it after taking actions in an iterative manner. For instance, imagine there is a maze that an agent is trying to get through to gain a big reward at the end, maybe a pile of gold or a large sum of points, but along the way, there are traps that take away points. The environment is the configuration or instance of this particular maze.

We begin with the agent at the entry-point to the maze—the initial state or location of the agent. Each turn by the agent through the maze counts as an action. At each turn, there is either a reward (award 1 point due to no traps or dead-ends encountered) or penalty (a trap or dead-end has been encountered—1 point removed). The summation of the points is the reward function in this case that the agent is trying to maximize. If the agent, through taking incremental actions (each turn or step), reaches the pile of gold, the agent has exited the maze successfully, and a new structure or set of conditions is created (new environment). The agent then begins again with some knowledge of how mazes work. After a certain number of rounds through different mazes, the agent has now learned strategies to make it through a maze to get the most points (it has maximized the reward function).

The examples in the next few sections focus on image analysis, as it is a good way to understand ML and important to many current scenarios. Text/natural-language, time-series, audio, speech, and other types of data are left for your exploration by using the resources provided on the book website at `https://harris-soh-copeland-puca.github.io/`.

Data Discussion

For use in an ML algorithm, data must be represented numerically, whether it's text, audio, image, or other types. For instance, image data, which is multidimensional by nature. Commonly, it has a red, green, and blue channel (and sometimes an alpha channel) if in RGB format. Each channel is a 2D array of numbers (where each number represents the intensity of a pixel). The channel 2D array (e.g., a red array) has the same width and height in pixels as the original image. The original image data (three 2D arrays) is the starting point for further image processing, such as padding, clipping, shrinking, and normalizing. Figure 16-3 shows how an RGB image is resized from its original dimensions down to 50×50 pixels.

***Figure 16-3.** An image is resized from 398×265 pixels to 50×50 pixels. Often in ML, an image must be resized before using in algorithms because the algorithms usually expect consistently sized inputs*

Figure 16-4 shows the separation of an image (a color RGB image - shown in black and white here) into the three channels, each of which are 2D arrays. It is a good example of data preprocessing for ML. The numbers equate to the pixel intensities in the range of 0–255. ML algorithms operate on all of these, and similar arrays of numbers, in different ways. Generally, they need an image as a multidimensional array of numbers, sometimes referred to as a *NumPy array* (because of the use of NumPy library) or a *tensor*(a common term in deep learning). Both terms, at their core, are simply arrays of numbers; however, they do sometimes come with a few other properties.

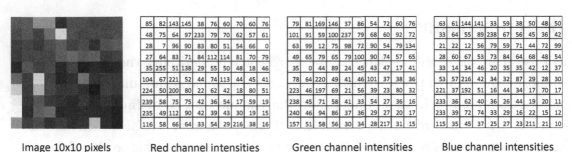

Image 10x10 pixels

85	82	143	145	38	76	60	70	60	76
48	75	64	97	233	79	70	62	57	61
28	7	96	90	83	80	51	54	66	0
27	64	83	71	84	112	114	81	70	79
35	255	51	138	29	55	50	48	18	46
104	67	221	52	44	74	113	44	45	41
224	50	200	80	22	62	42	18	80	51
239	58	75	75	42	36	54	17	59	19
235	49	112	90	42	39	43	30	19	15
116	58	66	64	33	54	29	216	38	16

Red channel intensities

79	81	169	146	37	86	54	72	60	76
101	91	59	100	237	79	68	60	92	72
63	99	12	75	98	72	90	54	79	134
49	65	79	65	79	100	90	74	57	65
35	0	44	89	24	45	43	47	17	41
78	64	220	49	41	46	101	37	38	36
223	46	197	69	21	56	39	23	80	32
238	45	71	58	41	33	54	27	36	16
240	46	94	86	37	36	29	27	20	17
157	51	58	56	30	34	28	217	31	15

Green channel intensities

63	61	144	141	33	59	38	50	48	50
33	64	55	89	238	67	56	45	36	42
21	22	12	56	79	59	71	44	72	99
28	60	67	53	73	84	64	68	48	54
33	14	34	46	20	35	35	42	12	37
53	57	216	42	34	32	87	29	28	30
221	37	192	51	16	44	34	17	70	17
233	36	62	40	36	26	44	19	20	11
233	39	72	74	33	29	16	22	15	12
115	35	45	37	25	27	23	211	21	10

Blue channel intensities

Figure 16-4. *An image separated into red, green, and blue channels. The pixel intensities are from 0–255*

Note ML algorithms that operate on other types of data such as text and speech that also need data to be represented by numerical values as arrays of numbers.

A preprocessing technique called *image augmentation* adds variation to the dataset by morphing a subset of the images (flipping, blurring, applying geometric transformations, lighting differences, etc.) to create a more generalized model that is used in diverse situations and usually with higher confidence. Data augmentation, more broadly, can increase the size of and add variation to a dataset. It is a very useful technique in the context of classical ML and deep learning for tasks of all kinds (image classification, sentiment analysis on text, acoustic event detection, etc.). Other types of preprocessing include extrapolation, tagging, aggregation, imputation, and probability techniques.

In supervised ML, it is extremely important to have a balanced dataset, that is, equal representation from all classes. This prevents class bias in the training process. Along those lines, the data should match the domain to get the question answered by creating the ML model. For example, to create a text-based system to answer questions from customers regarding how to file and monitor insurance claims for a particular firm, not all insurance-related documents across the Internet should be used to train the model, rather, only insurance claim questions and answers from that particular firm should be used. Also, one should always ensure to have the correct permissions to use the dataset to answer data science questions. As a final note, it is common to encounter biased datasets—ones that have inherent, built-in human prejudices. A dataset should be examined carefully, labels or feature characteristics should be checked (e.g., Do number ranges make sense? Are all classes represented equally and fairly?), and exploratory data analysis techniques should be used before using it in ML experiments.

Traditional ML

Traditional ML, also called classical ML, generally consists of simpler approaches than deep learning to solving similar data science problems (deep learning is addressed in a subsequent section). Traditional ML models often take less time to train, and the algorithms are generally easier to understand, thus, explain to others, however, at the cost of usually having to do much more manual preprocessing to address certain limitations in the algorithms.

Take, for instance, using classical ML to create an object detector. In this example, a window slides across an image incrementally, and at each increment, a classifier determines the types of objects in it. Object detection consists of two parts: localization (find the object; i.e., slide the window) and classification (name the object; i.e., run that portion of the image through a classification model).

Figure 16-5 shows the use of *histogram of oriented gradients* (HOG), which transforms an image into information-rich features (the preprocessing part). A support vector machine (SVM) is used for input with a large feature space to perform classification (the machine learning part). Here, HOG is used a *featurizer* on the raw input images before applying the classifier (the SVM). In traditional ML, it is common to have to carefully and extensively preprocess data manually, such as using HOG or other featurizers, in addition to using normalization methods, scaling, padding, and so forth. An example of the output of the HOG featurizer is shown in Figure 16-5.

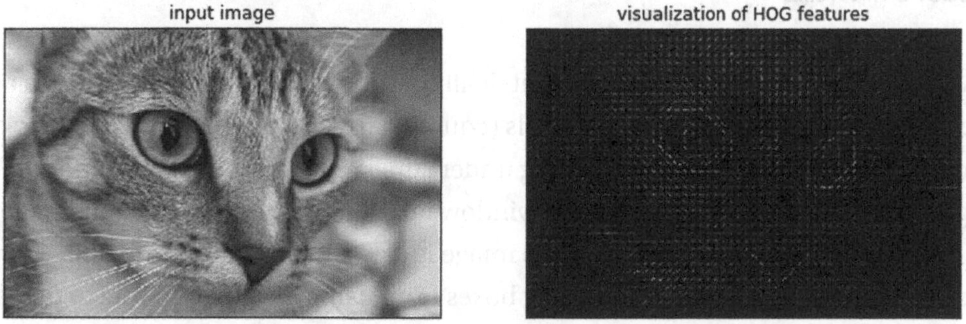

***Figure 16-5.** An input image (left) and the featurized image (right) created with the HOG method found in the scikit-image Python package*

An SVM classifier, also known as a *support vector classifier* (SVC), finds the best hyperplane that separates the dataset into the individual classes. As a simple example, imagine classifying flowers into three different species based on a petal length and sepal width, two features. The hyperplanes separating these classes may be visualized in Figure 16-6.

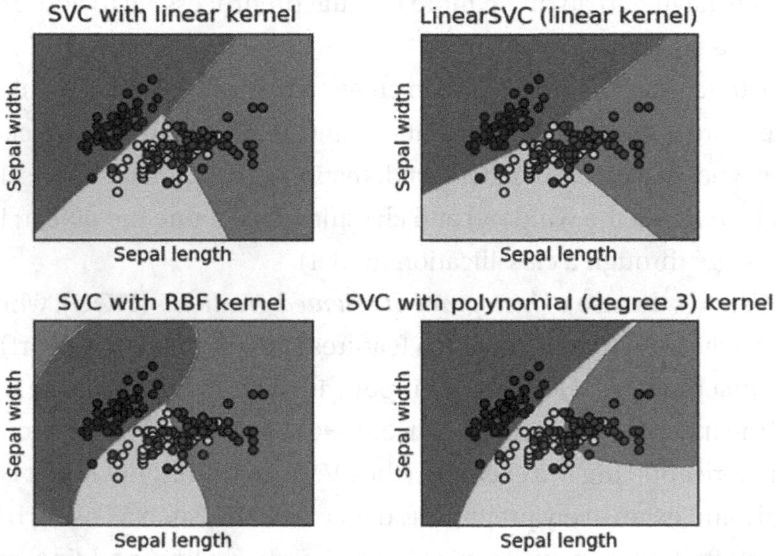

Figure 16-6. *Support vector classifiers (SVCs) showing the hyperplanes that separate three species of flowers. Source.* `https://scikit-learn.org/stable/modules/svm.html`

SVCs or SVMs are known to be good at dealing with larger feature spaces such as images with a height and width of 64 pixels (equating to 4096 features). SVM is one of the dominant classification algorithms falling under supervised learning techniques.

Again, in this example, a fixed-sized window incrementally slides over an image, and at each step, the window or portion of the image is classified as having the object or not. Figure 16-7 shows the resulting bounding boxes from using a trained model to detect an object in a new image that the model has never "seen" (for instance, detecting the head of a cat in a new image after training the algorithm on pictures of cat heads; the classes were "cat face" and "no cat face," where negative samples of non-cat images were used for "no cat face"). A histogram of oriented gradients was the featurizer to train the object detection model in Figure 16-7.

Figure 16-7. *Object detection with classical ML. Detecting cat faces*

For a Python Jupyter notebook code sample of Histogram of Oriented Gradients with an SVM for object detection, go to `https://github.com/harris-soh-copeland-puca/SampleCode/blob/master/Ch16/Ch16.Extra_Simple_Object_Detection_HOG.ipynb`. See documentation for more details on the HOG algorithm at `https://scikit-image.org/docs/dev/auto_examples/features_detection/plot_hog.html` and SVMs at `https://scikit-learn.org/stable/modules/svm.html`.

In the supervised learning case, as shown here, the ML model is trained by checking how far from the ground-truth (real) value the output is and comparing that to the model output (the prediction). This serves as feedback (through using a mathematical equation called a *loss function*) to the model that it is either getting better or worse at the task on which it is being trained. After some time, an ML model should perform better at the task as it converges on small loss values, an indication that the guesses are improving over iterations (called *epochs*) in the training process. Other types of ML models are trained similarly (iteratively and with feedback) such that a function gets minimized or maximized, which helps lead the training process to create a good model.

Neural Networks

There are three standard classes of neural network architectures, which are briefly touched upon here: feedforward, convolutional, and recurrent neural networks. Just as with traditional ML, a model is trained by looking at the output (e.g., a class label or bounding box) at each step of the training process and comparing it to a ground-truth value.

Feedforward neural networks have a simple structure compared to other types of neural networks. They are often used for more manageable tasks like the classification of large amounts of tabular data. Feedforward networks take input, process it through a single layer to multiple layers of nodes, which can get deep, formed into layers that interconnect like a multilayered cake. Each layer can have as many nodes as the ML practitioner wishes to add, but if too many nodes are added, there is a chance that the network overfits or becomes less widely applicable and understands only what it has been trained on. They can be *fully connected* or *dense*, in which all nodes are connected from one layer to the next. A typical example of a feedforward network is the multilayer perceptron.

Convolutional neural networks (CNNs) are made up of layers, like the feedforward neural networks, but they are a bit more complicated. These neural networks apply filters to images that are akin to scanning the image incrementally with a flashlight, but instead of an ordinary flashlight, however, this flashlight gets smarter as it scans an image and remembers parts of the image it has seen before, storing that information into a matrix of numbers. That matrix, in turn, is scanned again for more information in the next step or layer of the network. Often, different types of layers—pooling layers, for instance—are applied to help the CNN generalize better and speed up calculations. The first layers of CNNs are generally capable of picking up more coarse patterns; for images, this could equate to edges or circles. In subsequent layers, the network may learn more complex patterns such as ears or eyes and eventually in the final convolutional layers, entire faces. Usually, a CNN ends with a fully connected layer or two, which helps decide what class should be assigned to the input data. A typical example of a CNN is a ResNet-50 network, which is usually used for image classification and has 50 layers.

Recurrent neural networks (RNNs) are commonly trained for tasks around text analysis (sentiment analysis, named entity recognition, summarization, question, and answering, etc.). The structure is very different from a CNN. In RNNs, there is the concept of the cell. Inside this cell are different types of neural network layers. The cell takes inputs, the text data in numerical form (e.g., as a word embedding) and a hidden state (some take more information, but this is the simplest case). More complex RNNs can have more input and output types, but all-in-all the cell passes information from one instance of itself to another instance, which is what makes it recurrent. This process continues until the architecture is out of input data. RNNs have many variations, such as many to one, which is where an entire piece of text gives just one score, as is the case with sentiment analysis. Another form of an RNN is many-to-many, for which one example is machine translation, where one language is translated to another. A typical example of an RNN is the long-short term memory algorithm or LSTM.

There are other types of neural networks, such as deep reinforcement learning networks (trains models that can play the complex game of Go, for instance) and generative adversarial networks (trains models that can perform style transfer, for instance), which are left to you to explore further (resources are on the book's website).

To learn more about the differences between ML and deep learning, go to `https://docs.microsoft.com/en-us/azure/machine-learning/concept-deep-learning-vs-machine-learning`. Other helpful and in-depth resources on deep learning are on our website at `https://harris-soh-copeland-puca.github.io`.

Transfer Learning

Transfer learning is the process of taking a trained model (pre-trained) and fine-tuning it on new data with a different set, a subset, or entirely new class labels. The pre-trained or base model is trained on a high-quality, large dataset, such as ImageNet (1000 image classes) or the English Wikipedia corpus (over 3.6 billion words). In the fine-tuning phase of learning, less input data is needed as the model has general knowledge from the original, large dataset, upon which is was previously trained.

Transfer learning is commonly used across all types of ML tasks, from vision to language and speech. Additionally, transfer learning is used when there isn't enough data to train a network from scratch, or there's a pre-trained network that already exists for a similar task that has been trained on a very large dataset (see `https://builtin.com/data-science/transfer-learning` for more on this topic).

The Data Science Process

Just like creating and improving upon an application through cycles of development and productionizing, data science is an iterative process, as shown in Figure 16-8. The iterations of data science are a little different, however, from application development in the types of steps and resources needed. In fact, application development can very well include a data science process. This process is depicted in Figure 16-8.

The most important part of data science is asking the right question. The question usually comes from a business need or scientific study. A flawed question would be, how much money will I make next month? A better question is, by how many points will my Microsoft and Apple stocks increase over the next 28 days, and what will the mean predicted gain be at that time? Almost equally as important is to have relevant data to the question at hand.

After data acquisition, a good data science experiment begins with an exploratory data analysis step, which includes visualizing data such as the distribution of values or checking for outliers that could indicate mistakes in labels (which can happen on occasion) or calculations.

Usually, data is preprocessed in a certain way for the ML model to be trained, such as removing NaNs (for "not a number"), one type of data cleaning step. Data transformations are important, such as shaping an image from a 2D array to a long 1D array or making an RGB image grayscale. Another transformation type in the context of a time series experiment is log transforming the signal. It is said that data science is 80%–90% data processing and exploring, so becoming comfortable with data processing languages (e.g., SQL, Python, R) and ETL tools is very beneficial. Once the data is clean and transformed in a way that the algorithm can take as quality input, a model can be trained.

During the training process, different models may be tried, different algorithm parameters may be iterated over (hyperparameter tuning), and different ways of slicing and shuffling the dataset may be explored. Sometimes there is a need to go back to the cleaning and transformation data steps.

In the end, there is a better understanding of the problem space and datasets. The cycle continues as new data input changes the original dataset used to train the model; *data drift* may occur when the data becomes very different from the original dataset used to train a model and the model may not perform as well. A new model may need to be trained by going through the data science process periodically.

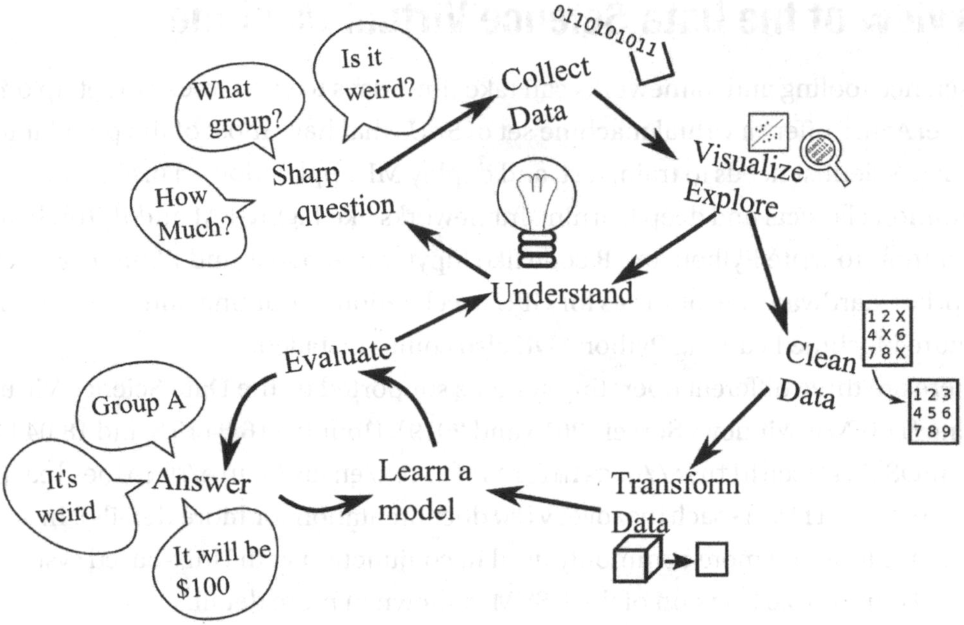

***Figure 16-8.** The data science process. Source:* `https://github.com/PythonWorkshop/intro-to-sklearn/blob/master/imgs/ml_process.png`

In summary, the data science process allows exploration and analysis of data and machine learning approaches in an iterative manner with improvements and better understanding along the way.

Prerequisites for Becoming a Successful Data Scientist

The following skills are very beneficial when becoming a data scientist, and all of them are practiced in this chapter.

- Git and GitHub for version control
- Python and/or R proficiency
- Jupyter notebook and a script editor (e.g., VS Code) experience
- Knowledge of how to preprocess data (image, text, time series, etc.)
- An understanding of classical ML and neural networks (completed!)

Overview of the Data Science Virtual Machine

Data science tooling and frameworks can take time, days to even weeks to set up on a machine. Azure offers a virtual machine set of SKUs that have most of the popular tools that a data scientist needs to train, test, and deploy ML applications. This includes all the common classical and deep learning frameworks like LightGBM and PyTorch, the popular tools to write Python and R code like Jupyter notebooks and RStudio, as well as, appropriate hardware and libraries for GPU acceleration of training and inference code. The Azure Machine Learning Python SDK also comes installed.

There are three different operating systems supported by the Data Science Virtual Machine (DSVM): Windows Server (2016 and 2019), Ubuntu (16.04 LTS and 18.04 LTS), and CentOS (7.4) (see `https://docs.microsoft.com/en-us/azure/machine-learning/data-science-virtual-machine/overview` documentation for more details). In general, data science tools are more commonly used in conjunction with Unix-based systems, so here, the Ubuntu 16.04 version of the DSVM is shown in more detail.

The DSVM for Linux with the Ubuntu OS makes it easy to get started with machine learning and deep learning on Azure. It contains popular tools for data science and development activities, including the following.

- Deep learning frameworks, such as PyTorch, CNTK, and TensorFlow
- The NVIDIA driver for GPU acceleration (when choosing N-series VM)
- TensorFlow Serving, MXNet Model Server, and TensorRT for test inferencing
- CRAN R
- Anaconda Python
- JupyterHub with sample notebooks
- Spark local with PySpark and SparkR Jupyter kernels
- Azure command-line interface
- Visual Studio Code, IntelliJ IDEA, PyCharm and Atom
- H2O, Deep Water, and Sparkling Water
- Julia

- Vowpal Wabbit for online learning
- XGBoost for gradient boosting
- SQL Server
- Intel Math Kernel Library

A Jupyter Notebook Overview

If your day-to-day work involves any data science, becoming familiar with Jupyter notebooks is an important skill. Jupyter notebooks are not necessarily a replacement for a full-fledged IDE or coding UI like Visual Studio, but they do have some advantages over such applications. Advantages include

- Quick and iterative prototyping
- Easy annotation that is presentation quality
- Shareable code and instructions for collaboration
- Notes and code combined in one place
- The ability to run anywhere the data science language (e.g., Python) and a browser are installed
- Integration into tools such as Visual Studio Code

Jupyter notebooks offer many different kernels for different languages and are predominantly used with data science languages like Python, R, F#, and Scala (a kernel is what interfaces with the programming language). Simply put, they provide a method of both annotating one's work (in the Markdown language or plain text) as well as writing code in blocks or small sections. The code blocks are run one at a time, which allows quick and easy prototyping and experimentation. Once a user is satisfied with the code, it may be exported to various formats, one of which is a script file (e.g., the Python .py file). The script file may then be run as one entire program at that point if so desired.

Figure 16-9 depicts a Jupyter notebook with free-form text annotation at the beginning (white background) followed by a Python code block (gray background). The example comes from a public source created by the Azure ML team.

Note Notebooks are used by the Azure ML team to demonstrate how to use its functionality with annotated examples. The Azure ML team maintains an official collection of Jupyter notebooks on GitHub at `https://github.com/Azure/MachineLearningNotebooks`.

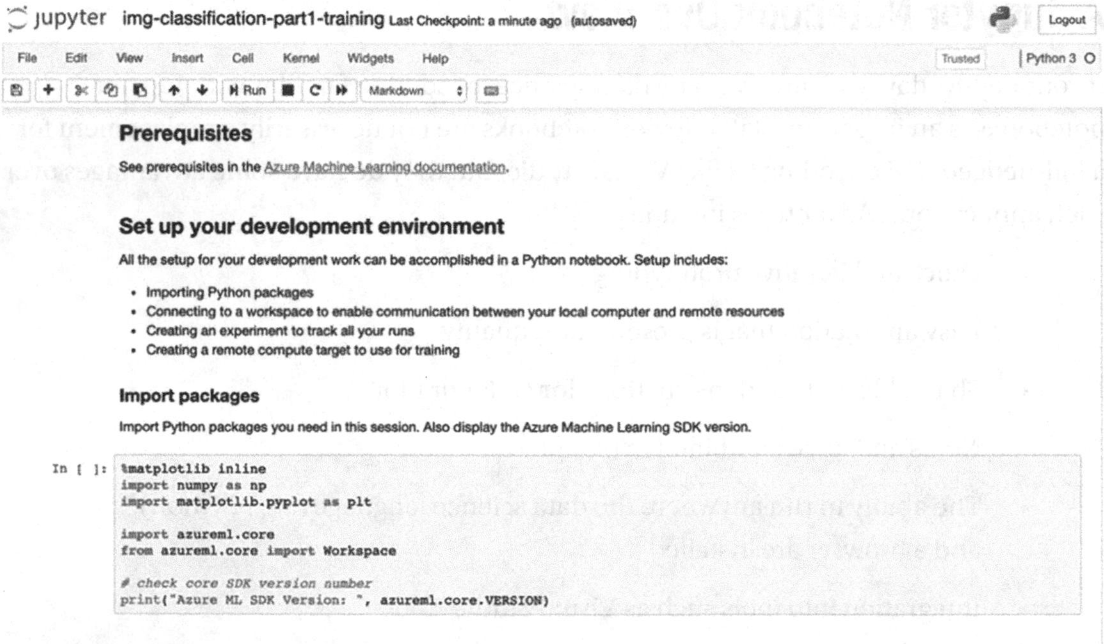

***Figure 16-9.** Example of a Jupyter notebook from the Azure ML official notebook collection on GitHub. Source: `https://github.com/Azure/MachineLearningNotebooks`*

Jupyter usage is explained in the next section, as well as how to write a simple Python program.

Hands-on with the Data Science Virtual Machine

Let's go through provisioning an Ubuntu Linux DSVM by using JupyterHub and the command terminal for some basic Python coding in a browser. The latest information on setting up the Linux DSVM is at `https://docs.microsoft.com/en-us/azure/machine-learning/data-science-virtual-machine/dsvm-ubuntu-intro`.

1. Go to the Azure portal and search for **Data Science Virtual Machine**. Select the Ubuntu version.

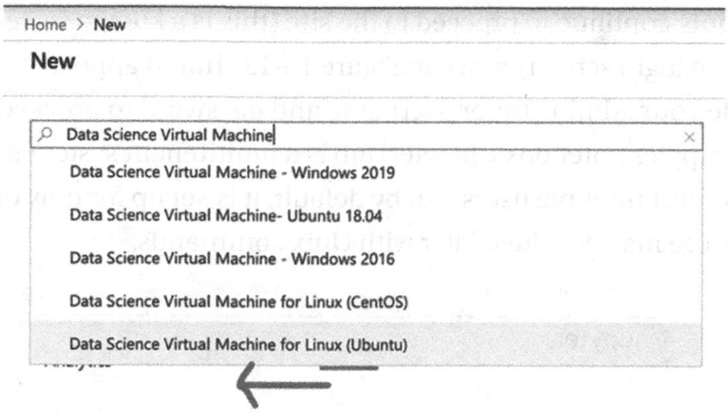

Figure 16-10. *Selecting the Ubuntu DSVM from the portal*

2. When provisioning, ensure you select **Password** as the Authentication type in the **Administrator account** section on the **Basics** tab (the first page after clicking **Create**). Also, it is **very important** that the **Username** for the account is all lower-case due to a limitiation with JupyterHub.

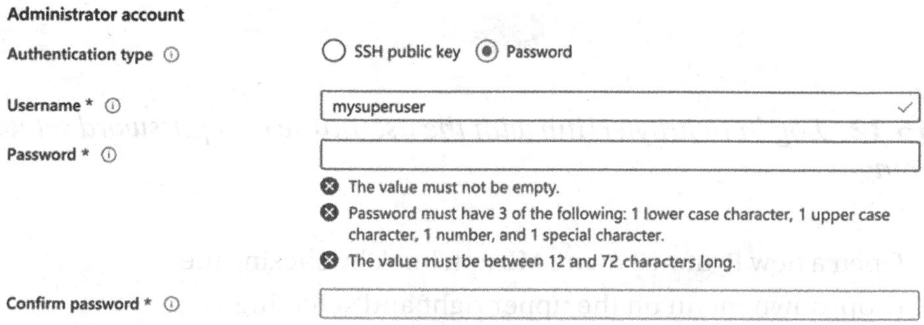

Figure 16-11. *When provisioning the DSVM, use the password method for authentication type*

3. Navigate to the public IP address listed on the Overview pane of the DSVM resource in the portal once provisioning has completed. Note down this IP address. Firefox and Chrome

browsers are best for use with JupyterHub. Enter the following URL and direct a browser window to it: https://THE_PUBLIC_IP_ADDRESS:8000. IMPORTANT: A certificate error may pop up; if so, simply continue to proceed to the site (this is a known issue). Next, the login screen shown in Figure 16-12 should appear. Provide your administrator username and password to proceed to the Jupyter notebooks. JupyterHub is a multitenant system that can support multiple users, but by default, it is set up for only one user. More may be added later with Unix commands.

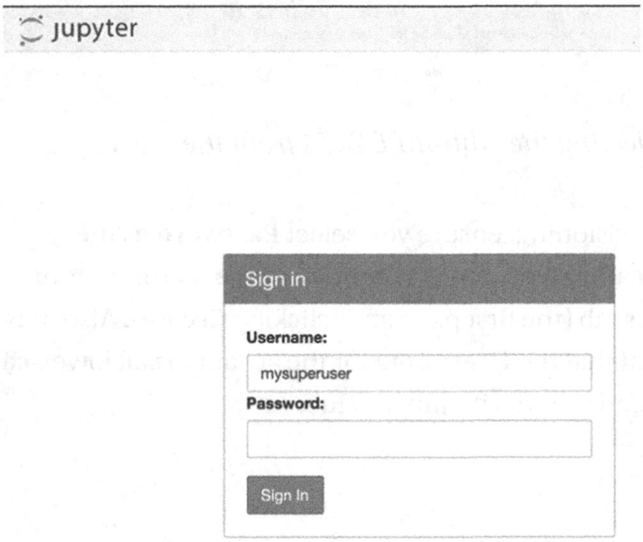

Figure 16-12. *Log in to JupyterHub with the username and password set when provisioning*

4. Open a new Python 3 Azure ML notebook by clicking the drop-down menu on the upper right and selecting **Python 3.6 – Azure ML** or the latest Python version with Azure ML.

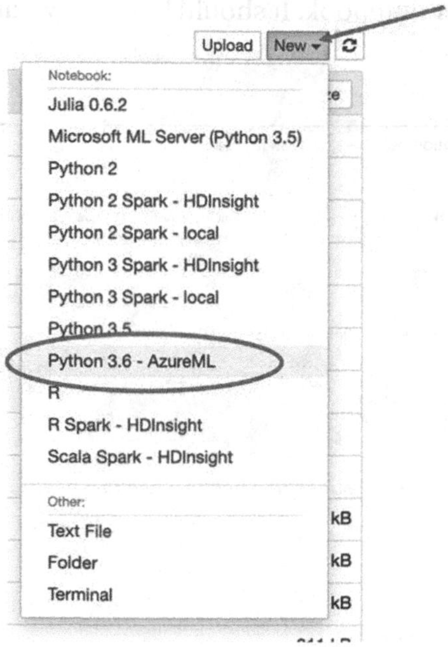

***Figure 16-13.** Selecting the right kernel in Jupyter on the DSVM*

5. Git clone the `https://github.com/harris-soh-copeland-puca/SampleCode` repo by type the following on the command line.

   ```
   git clone https://github.com/harris-soh-copeland-puca/
   SampleCode.git
   ```

6. Upload the Ch16/Ch16.01_Image_Manipulation.ipynb file to the DSVM through JupyterHub, confirm the upload, and then click the notebook file to open it.

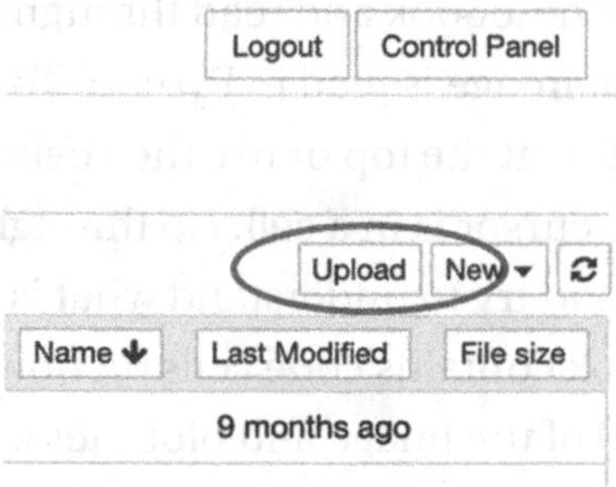

***Figure 16-14.** Upload button in JupyterHub*

An open a Jupyter notebook. It should look like what's shown in Figure 16-15.

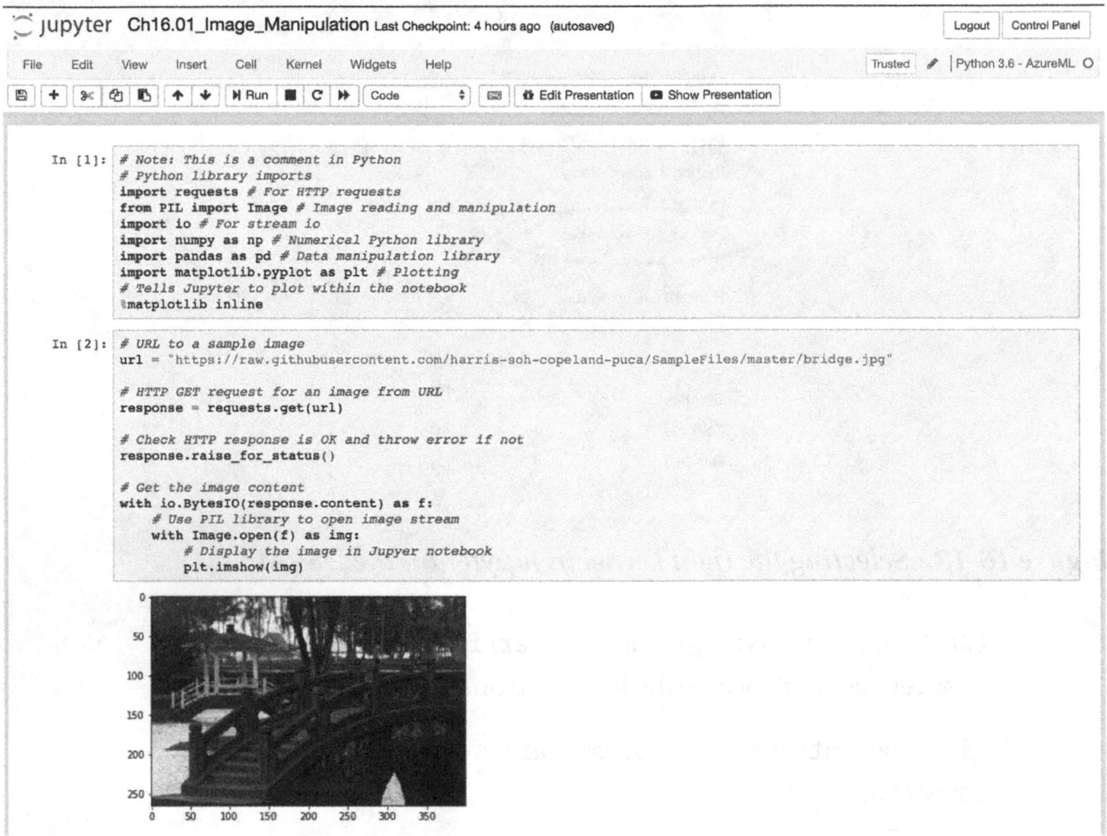

***Figure 16-15.** The Jupyter notebook including Python code on how to manipulate an image*

7. Follow along with the notebook and read through the comments to understand how an image is read in Python. To run a code-cell, use the Run button at the top or use the keyboard shortcut Shift+Enter when the cursor is in a cell. Go through each code cell of the notebook and try to understand what is going on. In addition, the notebook contains code cells on how to separate the color channels (RGB) of the image and plot them.

The Azure DSVM is not your only option, however, for working in the data science domain. For those getting started, the following article describes other options for setup: `https://rheartpython.github.io/navigating-ml/setup/`.

Overview of Azure Machine Learning

Azure ML is a cloud-based environment for training models, managing models, monitoring services, tracking experimentation, and deploying in an iterative or automated manner. The common workflow is shown in Figure 16-16.

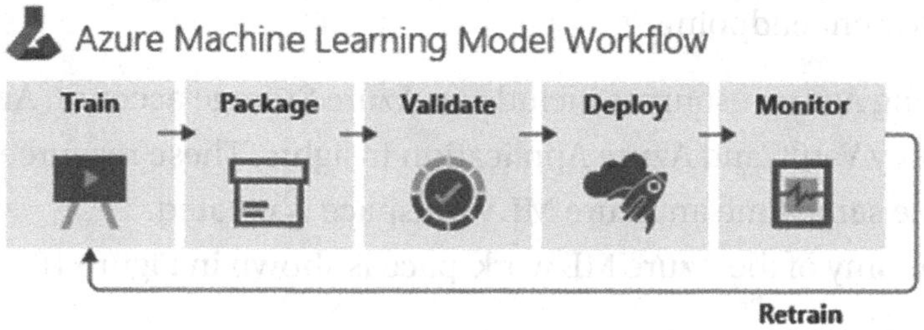

Figure 16-16. *Source: `https://docs.microsoft.com/en-us/azure/machine-learning/concept-azure-machine-learning-architecture`*

When training a model, think of Azure ML as your experimentation and deployment platform with integration into common frameworks like Scikit-Learn for classical ML or PyTorch and TensorFlow for deep learning. The ML practitioner has the choice to do their experimentation locally, on cloud VMs (like the DSVM) or Spark clusters like Databricks.

When the practitioner is satisfied with the model as measured by an appropriate metric (or "ruler" like accuracy), they may validate it on new, unseen data (part of our "data science process"). At this point, if the results are satisfactory, the practitioner or DevOps professional may deploy the model.

In Azure ML, there are a few different deployment paradigms. One is a cloud service and another an IoT edge device (e.g., an ARM32 IoT device like the Vision AI DevKit `https://azure.github.io/Vision-AI-DevKit-Pages/`). The cloud service can further be consumed by a Power BI dashboard.

Finally, a model may be monitored using Azure ML integrated with Azure Monitor for things like the health of the service. If it is an IoT Edge deployment, the device may be monitored with Azure IoT Hub from which messages and logs may then be analyzed.

An Azure ML workspace is a multitenant Azure resource, which is provisioned. Generally, it is shared by one team or organization of ML practitioners working on one or several projects. The workspace consists of the following pieces.

- User roles
- Compute targets
- Pipelines
- Datasets
- Registered models
- Deployment endpoints

The underlying Azure resources include an Azure Storage account, Azure Container Registry, Azure Key Vault, and Azure Application Insights. These resources are provisioned at the same time an Azure ML workspace is created.

The full taxonomy of the Azure ML workspace is shown in Figure 16-17.

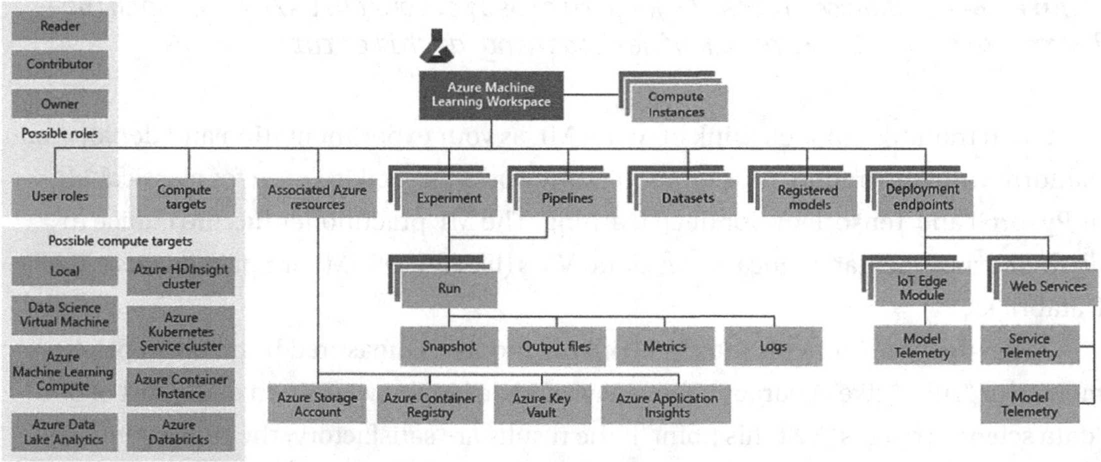

Figure 16-17. *Azure ML workspace taxonomy. Source:* `https://docs.microsoft.com/en-us/azure/machine-learning/concept-workspace`

Azure ML currently has SDKs in the R and Python programming languages. It can also be utilized with an interface called Designer, for a more of a drag-and-drop, no-code experience (however, in Designer, you can also write custom code as modules). In addition to the SDKs and Designer, Azure ML has a CLI extension to the main Azure CLI that integrates directly with the Azure ML workspace from the command line and a REST API.

Almost any Python or R training code may be converted to an Azure ML-friendly code, which allows the use of the Azure ML cloud compute to train models and services like Azure Kubernetes Service for deploying models. Not only does Azure ML have linked compute for training/deploying, but it also has mechanisms for taking a snapshot and versioning the code to train the model. Also, versioning the model itself is done by a process called *registering a model.* This is part of model management. Once registered, a model is associated with the Azure ML workspace for later retrieval simply by using the SDK.

Additionally, Azure ML provides automated ML (Auto ML) capabilities. Three types of tasks are automated: preprocessing (e.g., featurizing), choosing algorithms that are appropriate to use, and hyper-parameter tuning. Currently, regression, classification, and time-series forecasting are supported in Azure ML's Auto ML capabilities.

Hands-on with Azure Machine Learning: Training a Model

1. Provision an Azure ML workspace in the Azure portal, with the Azure ML SDK or CLI.

   In the portal, search for **machine learning**, select **Machine Learning,** and click **Create** when prompted. Fill out the information for provisioning, selecting **Basic** as the workspace edition (it can be changed later). Note, the Basic edition does not support Auto ML and a few other features. Create this resource.

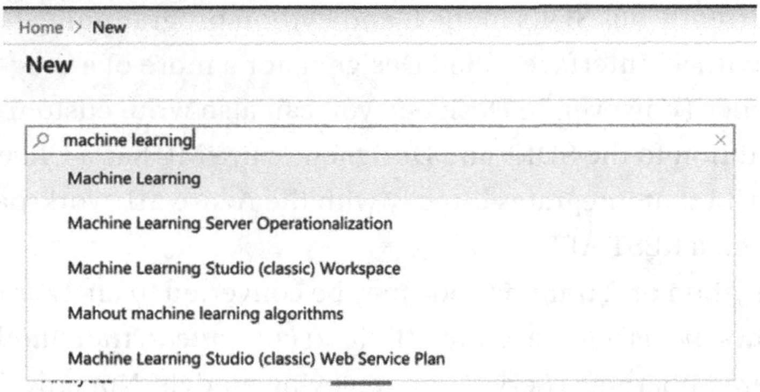

***Figure 16-18.** Provision an Azure ML workspace in Azure portal 1*

Once the workspace is provisioned, go to the resource, and download the config.json file directly from the Overview pane.

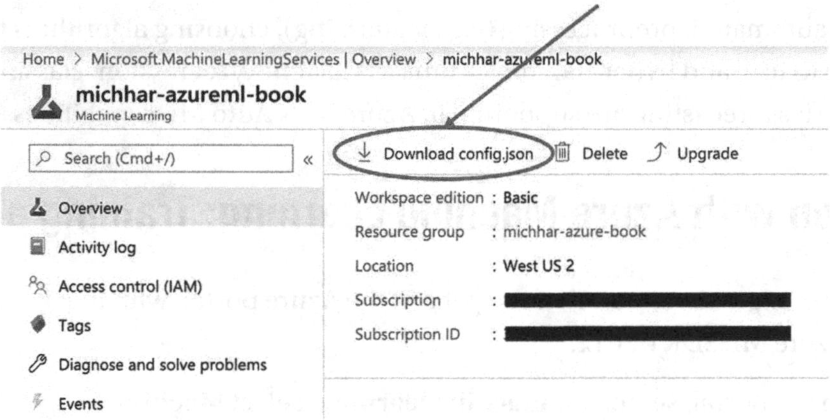

***Figure 16-19.** Download the config.json configuration file from the workspace in the Azure portal*

2. Start a Jupyter notebook system. Choices include

   a. JupyterHub on the DSVM

   b. Use Azure Notebooks (best if attached to a DSVM) at `https://notebooks.azure.com`

c. Locally, if Python 3 and Jupyter are installed. Start the Jupyter notebook locally with the following command on the command line.

```
jupyter notebook
```

Note The kernel may need to be set to the correct Python version and (on the DSVM, use Python 3.6 – Azure ML or the latest Python version with Azure ML).

---

3. In JupyterHub, open a terminal by selecting **New ➤ Terminal**.

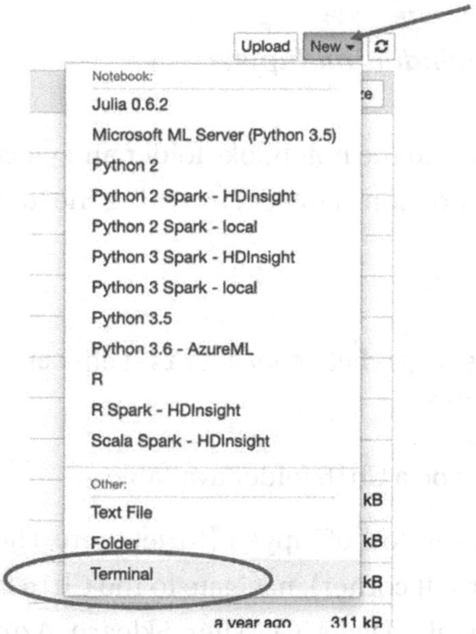

***Figure 16-20.** Open a terminal window in the browser from Jupyter*

This should provide an interface that looks as follows in Figure 16-21.

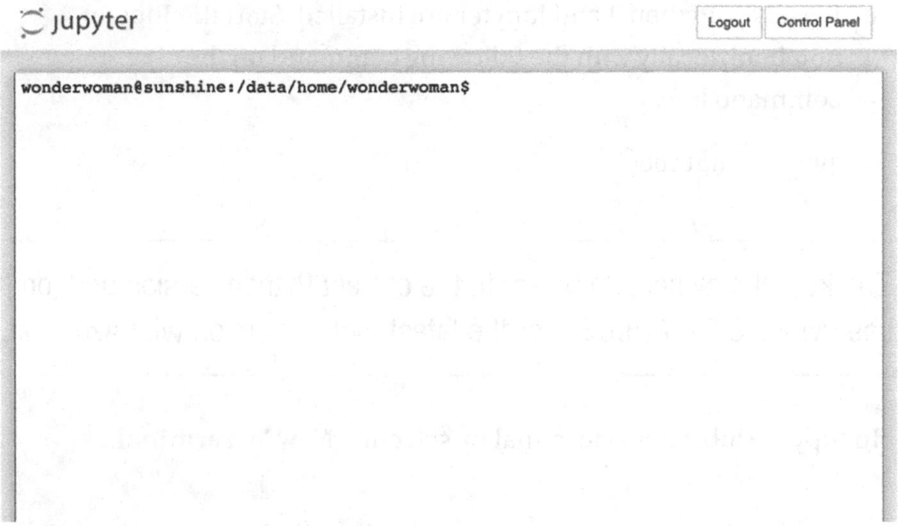

Figure 16-21. *Terminal window on Jupyter*

4. Change directory into the notebooks folder and git clone the following repo, if not done already, by typing the following into the terminal window.

```
cd notebooks
git clone https://github.com/harris-soh-copeland-puca/
SampleCode.git
```

There should now be a Ch16 folder available.

5. Back in the main window of Jupyter (to get there, click the Jupyter logo in the upper-left corner), navigate to the Ch16 folder, and open Ch16.02a_Train_Digits_Classifer_Sklearn_AzureML.ipynb. The **Python 3.6 - Azure ML** kernel, if on the DSVM, should be chosen if prompted. If a switch of kernels is needed, the Kernel option in the menu is the correct place to go, as shown in Figure 16-22.

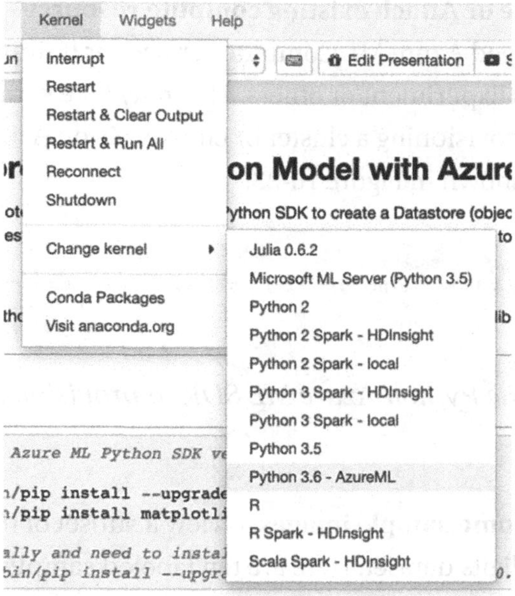

***Figure 16-22.** Picking the right Python Jupyter kernel for the notebook to use the right version of Python in the back end*

6. From the Ch16 folder, upload the config.json configuration file downloaded earlier so that the notebook has access.

7. Read through the introduction and then run the **Import packages** cell (a shortcut to run the code in a cell is to press Shift+Enter).

   The notebook trains a classical ML model (logistic regression) on the MNIST handwritten digits dataset that is now a part of Azure Open Datasets and accessible through the Python SDK. The original dataset is also accessible at `http://yann.lecun.com/exdb/mnist/`.

8. Run the **Connect to workspace** cell and log in to Azure through by following the interactive authentication instructions.

9. Run the **Create experiment** cell to create an Experiment for all the training runs for the scenario.

10. Run the **Create or Attach existing compute resources** cell to create a managed Azure ML Compute service for training ML models in this Experiment or others. This may take some time because it is provisioning a cluster of Linux VMs on Azure with the specification shown in Figure 16-23.

```
print("creating new compute target...")
provisioning_config = AmlCompute.provisioning_configuration(vm_size = vm_size,
                                                            min_nodes = compute_min_nodes,
                                                            max_nodes = compute_max_nodes)
```

Figure 16-23. *Using the Python Azure ML SDK to provision a compute cluster of VMs*

11. Run **Display some sample images** to view a subset of the MNIST handwritten digits dataset. Here are ten labeled sample images from this dataset.

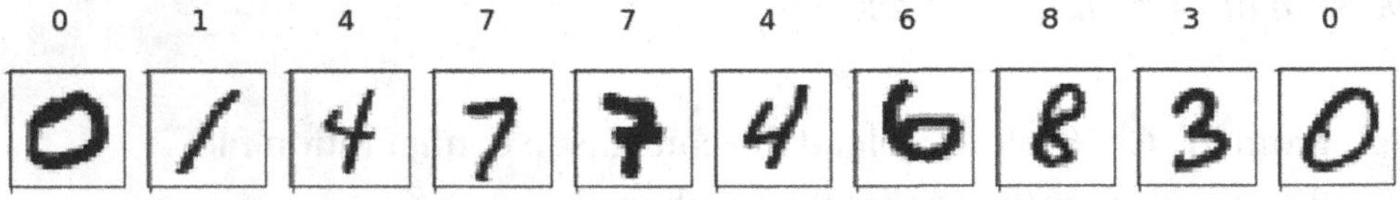

Figure 16-24. *Ten sample images from the MNIST handwritten digits dataset*

12. Run the **Create a directory** and **Create a training script**. Note, that the Jupyter cell magic %%writefile $script_folder/train.py appears at the beginning of the cell. This tells Jupyter to write a physical file to the path specified. Look in the folder with the Jupyter notebook to ensure the train.py was written to the sklearn-mnist subfolder. Notice the code that takes care of connecting the training process to Azure ML (Run context) as well as the code that trains a logistic regression classifier within this cell.

```
# get hold of the current run
run = Run.get_context()

print('Train a logistic regression model with regularization rate of', args.reg)
clf = LogisticRegression(C=1.0/args.reg, solver="liblinear", multi_class="auto", random_state=42)
clf.fit(X_train, y_train)
```

***Figure 16-25.** Set up the Run context to track training and then train the classifier*

The sklearn-mnist script folder is a crucial element of using Azure ML as the contents of this folder are uploaded to the Azure ML Compute (target compute context) to do the training. The compute takes a snapshot of this script folder. The snapshot currently has a size limit of 300 MB or 2000 files. Because of this, if needing to train on a large amount of data, one recommendation is that one uses a Datastore object (`https://docs.microsoft.com/en-us/azure/machine-learning/how-to-access-data`) that utilizes either the Blob Storage attached to the workspace or a separate Blob Storage. Another option is to have the training script download the data directly with code or use a Dataset object (`https://docs.microsoft.com/en-us/azure/machine-learning/how-to-train-with-datasets`) which helps keep track of that process. The Dataset object is shown in this notebook.

13. Run all the cells in the Create an estimator section to define the Python environment and create the Estimator, a wrapper object that understands the compute, training script, script folder, parameters for training script and Python environment.

14. Run the **Submit the job to the cluster** cell to begin training the model on the MNIST digits dataset. This creates a docker image, scales the cluster, runs the training job, and saves to an output folder with any created assets and sends this to the workspace upon completion.

15. Run the **Jupyter widget** cell to see the progress in detail of the job. The first time the job is submitted, it takes up to 10 minutes as it needs to create the docker image and scale the cluster to the right number of nodes. After running this cell, a link to the Azure portal

is provided. Click this link to see how it shows in the Azure portal for monitoring. If not using a Jupyter notebook, but rather scripts, it is helpful to know about this view.

16. Run **Get log results upon completion** to view the logs and prevent running other code until the run is complete.

17. Run **Display run results** to see the accuracy of the model on the test dataset.

18. The model is now available in the output folder as a Python pickle file. It is associated with the run in that workspace. Run the **Register model** cells to register the model and make it accessible programmatically (useful in future scripts that need to access/use this model). Note that the model now has a name and a version number.

Hands-on with Azure Machine Learning: Deploying a Model

This section is a continuation of the previous one. In this section, the model is deployed as an Azure Container Instance (ACI) service in the cloud as ACI is the quickest and simplest way to run a container in Azure, making it a good initial testing ground for Azure ML. Additionally, ACI doesn't require managing VMs or adopting higher-level services (see `https://docs.microsoft.com/en-us/azure/container-instances/container-instances-overview` for more information on ACI).

1. In the main window of Jupyter (to get there, click on the Jupyter logo in the upper left corner), navigate to the Ch16 folder, again, and open Ch16.02b_Deploy_Digits_Classifer_Sklearn_AzureML.ipynb. The Python 3.6 – Azure ML kernel, if on the DSVM, should be chosen if prompted.

2. Run the **Set up the environment** cells to import the packages and retrieve the registered model (physically downloads it with the SDK) that was trained in part 1.

3. Run the cells in the **Test model locally** section to download, load, and predict the test data locally before the service is created to ensure the code works as expected. If there are errors, try restarting the kernel and rerunning all cells up to this point. (Restart a kernel by going in the menu to Kernel➤ Restart & Clear Output.) After running, the **Example the confusion matrix** section, the plot shown in Figure 16-26 should be visible.

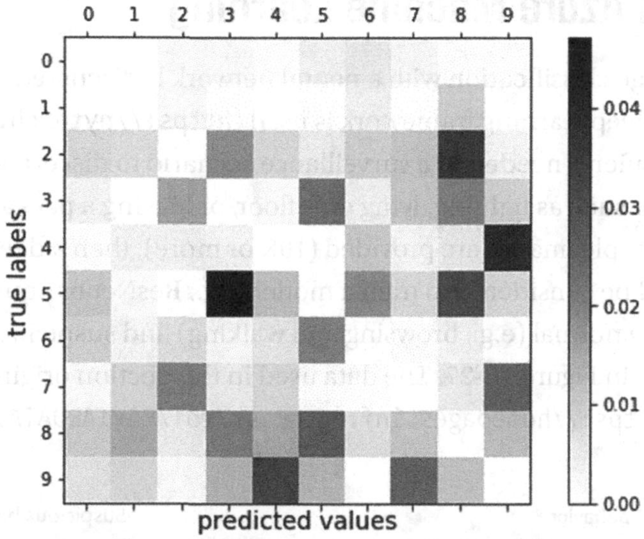

***Figure 16-26.** Confusion matrix for the handwritten-digits classifier. The darker the cell, the higher the error rate is. For instance, it is apparent that 5s and 3s are not discerned well, nor are 4s and 9s*

4. Run the cells in the **Deploy as a web service** section to create the scoring or prediction script (physical file) and the environment for scoring (a physical file). Create the deployment configuration for ACI, and deploy as a service in the cloud (which may take a few minutes as it's creating a docker image with the necessary files and packages, then pulling it down to the ACI). Take note of the scoring web service's HTTP endpoint for REST calls. At this point, any language that can make REST calls may be used with proper input data format and header.

5. Run the cells in the **Test deployed service** section to call the web service with the SDK and with a raw HTTP request.

6. Only the service (not workspace) can be deleted, as shown in the last code cell, to conserve Azure resources if it is no longer needed.

Use Case: Image Classification with a Deep Neural Network and Azure Machine Learning

In this section, image classification with a neural network is discussed. In the sample code, the PyTorch deep learning framework is used (`https://pytorch.org`).

Imagine a classifier is needed in a surveillance scenario to discern when there is suspicious behavior such as fighting, lying on a floor, or leaving a package in a public space. If enough sample images are provided (10K or more), then a deep neural network architecture should be considered to train a model (e.g., ResNet or SqueezeNet). Sample images representing normal (e.g., browsing and walking) and suspicious (e.g., fighting) behavior are shown in Figure 16-27. The data used in this section originates from the CAVIAR dataset (`https://homepages.inf.ed.ac.uk/rbf/CAVIARDATA1/`).

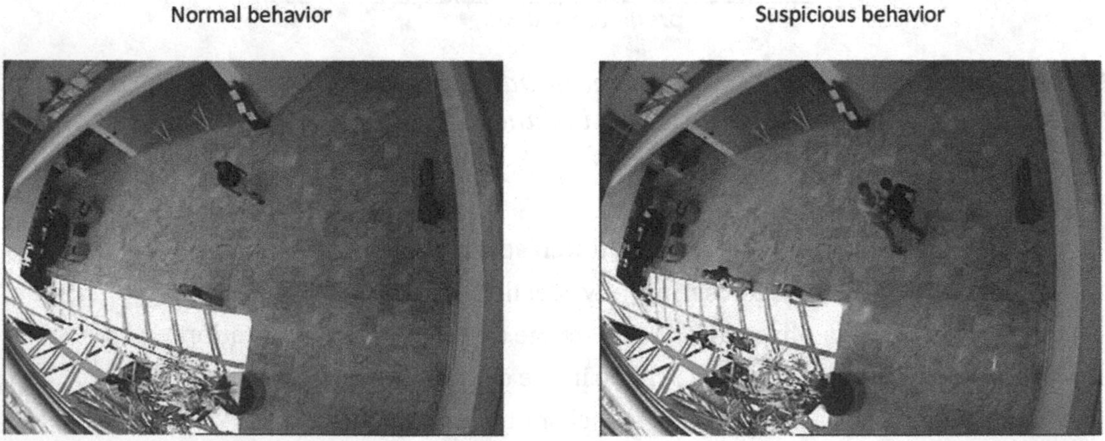

***Figure 16-27.** Normal and suspicious behavior images from the CAVIAR dataset*

Hands-on with Azure Machine Learning and PyTorch

In this hands-on section, a deep learning model for the classification of images into suspicious or normal behavior is created and evaluated using PyTorch and an AML Compute cluster with GPU-acceleration (NVIDIA GPU with CUDA/cuDNN preinstalled) using a Jupyter notebook coding environment.

1. Start a Jupyter notebook system. Some of the choices include
   - JupyterHub on the DSVM
   - Use Azure Notebooks (`https://notebooks.azure.com`; best if attached to a DSVM)
   - Locally, if Python 3 and Jupyter are installed. Start the Jupyter notebook locally with the following command on the command line.

     ```
     jupyter notebook
     ```

   Note that the kernel may need to be set to the correct Python version (on the DSVM, use Python 3.6 - Azure ML or the latest Python with Azure ML).
2. In JupyterHub, open a terminal by selecting **New ➤ Terminal**.
3. Change directory into the notebooks folder and clone, if not already done, the SampleCode repository by typing the following into the terminal window.

   ```
   cd notebooks
   git clone https://github.com/harris-soh-copeland-puca/
   SampleCode.git
   ```

   There should now be a Ch16 folder available.
4. Navigate to the Ch16 folder and open the Ch16.03_Train_Behavior_Classifier_PyTorch_AzureML.ipynb notebook. This notebook is based on a tutorial from the PyTorch public documentation for image classification. It uses transfer learning, which means we can use smaller datasets to train the model (`https://pytorch.org/tutorials/intermediate/quantized_transfer_learning_tutorial.html`). Ensure the config.json for the workspace is in the Ch16 folder, as well.

5. Run each cell in the notebook as was done in the "Hands-on with Azure Machine Learning: Training a Model" section.

6. In the Evaluation section, the accuracy is reported. Note, that even if it's low, the more data that is added to this training experiment, the better the accuracy. Also, changing the training parameters can help greatly in a process called *hyperparameter tuning*.

7. Check the workspace in the Azure portal for the Experiment, Run, and registered Model. A "Completed" status for the Run indicates success.

The next step is to create a scoring script and deploy it. An example is at `https://github.com/harris-soh-copeland-puca/Azure-AI-Camp/blob/master/day2/1.1.ImageClassificationAmlCompute/Deploy-PyTorch-AzureML-Compute.ipynb`.

IoT Devices and the Intelligent Edge

The Internet of Things, or IoT, refers to an Internet interconnected ecosystem of computing devices that are embedded into everyday objects, sending, and receiving different types of data continuously to and from other devices or the cloud. Examples of IoT devices are smartwatches, smart thermostats, network/Internet-connected cameras to monitor front doors, and temperature sensors that send data to alerting systems through the network. Devices may be controlled or monitored on cell phone, for instance, or an onsite computer system. They may be Internet-connected and monitored through a system like a Power BI dashboard in Azure. The device might not be connected to the Internet regularly, and some never connect to the Internet. Azure still helps IoT developers build entirely disconnected intelligent devices systems.

There are many Azure IoT projects available for the MXChip IoT DevKit (`https://aka.ms/iot-devkit`), a small, Arduino-based device, and other devices like it. The IoT DevKit, as a common example, can operate connected to wi-fi or in a completely disconnected scenario, incorporating cloud AI or running an ML model locally. Sample projects, integrated with Visual Studio Code, are provided with the Azure IoT Tools extension.

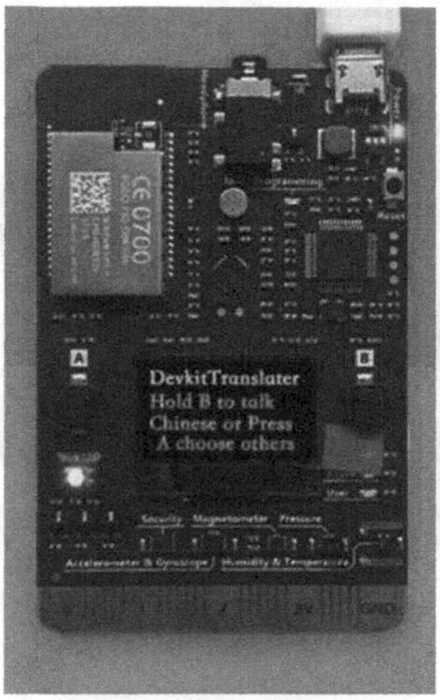

***Figure 16-28.** MXChip IoT DevKit that is wi-fi connected and running an Azure-based translator project found integrated with VSCode Azure IoT Tools extension. Source:* `https://microsoft.github.io/azure-iot-developer-kit/docs/projects/`

Not only is it easy to run cognitive services on constrained devices like the MXChip, but there are also advanced Azure services (e.g., Azure IoT Hub and Azure IoT Edge) that provide mechanisms to deploy ML models to devices. For instance, the NVIDIA Jetson Nano is a GPU-accelerated embedded device capable of running deep learning models efficiently. Azure IoT Edge may be set up on this type of Linux device to run AI models, coordinate their updates (as Azure IoT Edge modules), and monitor their output and health (in Azure IoT Hub). One example takes advantage of NVIDIA's DeepStream SDK (see `https://github.com/Azure-Samples/NVIDIA-Deepstream-Azure-IoT-Edge-on-a-NVIDIA-Jetson-Nano`).

Figure 16-29. *NVIDIA Jetson Nano, a Linux-based device in which Azure IoT Edge modules may be deployed. AI workloads are common to the Nano. Source:* `https://github.com/Azure-Samples/NVIDIA-Deepstream-Azure-IoT-Edge-on-a-NVIDIA-Jetson-Nano`

IoT Edge modules are docker containers with custom code, optionally supporting both Azure ML-built AI models or custom ML models trained elsewhere. They don't necessarily have to have any ML, but it is becoming a more popular option. They are capable of running on laptops and servers, as well as constrained Windows and Linux devices, like cell phones and ARM-based computing systems.

The intelligent Edge allows the creation and deployment of modules for AI such as object detection and optical character recognition (e.g., license plate recognition), audio analysis (e.g., a dog barking), speech to text and translation (e.g., helping medical professionals with charting), the Azure IoT Edge runtime, and tight integration with the Azure cloud through IoT Hub. More information and tutorials are on the IoT Edge documentation pages at `https://docs.microsoft.com/en-us/azure/iot-edge/`.

As a continuation of the projects in this chapter, deploy an Azure IoT module to an Azure Edge VM (VM in Azure specifically preinstalled with Azure IoT Edge runtime) by running this tutorial: `https://github.com/harris-soh-copeland-puca/Azure-AI-Camp/tree/master/day2/2.IoTEdgeModule`.

Overview of Spark and Databricks

When discussing Spark, it's helpful to know the difference between *scale-up* and *scale-out*. Scale-up and scale-out are ways to meet the increasing demand for computing resources from increasingly large workloads.

In its basic form, scale-up refers to adding more resources to a single machine or set of independent machines such as increasing memory or adding a more powerful processor.

With scale-out, there is a set of machines that share a common workload. Scale-out, in its basic form, is adding more machines to the pool that work on a single workload in unison. Parts of a workload and partitions of data are separated onto different worker nodes, which each perform calculations and, when finished with a task, return an answer to a cluster manager. This organization is shown in Figure 16-30.

This section is based on an excellent tutorial on Azure Databricks and Spark by B. Cafferky (`www.youtube.com/watch?v=ofYIsToVnTO`).

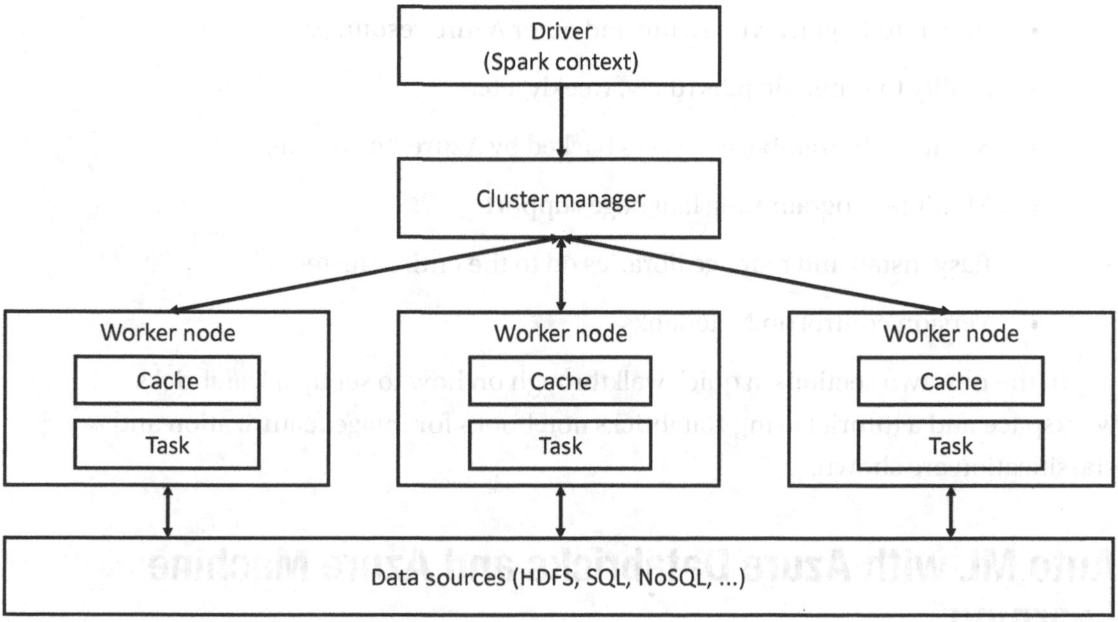

***Figure 16-30.** Apache Spark high-level architecture. Based on the information at* `www.youtube.com/watch?v=ofYIsToVnTO`

Spark is part of the wider Apache ecosystem or *zoo*, an open source collection of tools and libraries for scaling-out with distributed computing. An older approach to scale-out methodology was Hadoop Map Reduce. Spark is a newer take on this, and in some cases, hundreds of times faster than Map Reduce. Unlike Map Reduce, Spark aims to keep as much data in memory as possible to avoid I/O trips to and from the data source such as a Hadoop Distributed File System or SQL database.

Spark was invented by the founders of Databricks, which is one reason for the tight integration. Databricks has very tight integration, too, with Azure (VMs, data stores, ML, etc.), although it is relatively cloud-agnostic. Spark alone is not necessarily optimized for the cloud, nor simple to set up. However, running Spark on Databricks is far easier and comes with several advantages, including

- An easy-to-use UI and portal accessible through the Azure portal
- Notebooks as the developer tool (very similar to Jupyter notebooks)
- Easy Blob Storage integration
- Simple cluster creation and management
- Integrated tightly with Azure and other Azure resources
- Ability to schedule jobs (daily, weekly, etc.)
- Secure with role-based access backed by Azure Active Directory
- Multiple programming language support
- Easy install and manage libraries on to the entire cluster
- Version control on Notebooks

In the next two sections, a quick walkthrough on how to set up a Databricks workspace and a tutorial using Databricks notebooks for image featurization and classification are shown.

Auto ML with Azure Databricks and Azure Machine Learning

Auto ML, or automated machine learning, is a feature of Azure ML that aids in choosing the right ML model for the task (classification, regression, time series, etc.) by testing out many different algorithms and hyperparameters automatically within one run and measuring against a metric of choice. Models get ranked according to the metric, and the best one wins (see more at `https://docs.microsoft.com/en-us/azure/machine-learning/concept-automated-ml`).

MLFlow comes by default with Databricks to keep a data science project organized and standardized—from building models to deployment within Databricks. It is also compatible with Azure ML.

Hands-on with Azure Databricks and Auto ML

In this Hands-on section, an Azure Databricks workspace is created and used with the functionality of Azure ML called Auto ML.

1. Navigate to the Azure portal, click **Create a new resource**, and search for **databricks**, selecting **Azure Databricks**.

2. Click **Create** and fill out the template.

   a. Use a new resource group because many resources are created when provisioning Azure Databricks. Having them all in one clean resource group allows easier management.

   b. In the Pricing Tier, select **Premium** so that role-based access and security are enabled.

3. To get the code, it is easiest to download the Databricks notebooks in GitHub as a zip file (in fact, it contains the entire repository). Navigate to `https://github.com/harris-soh-copeland-puca/Azure-AI-Camp` and download as a zip file and unzip on the local computer.

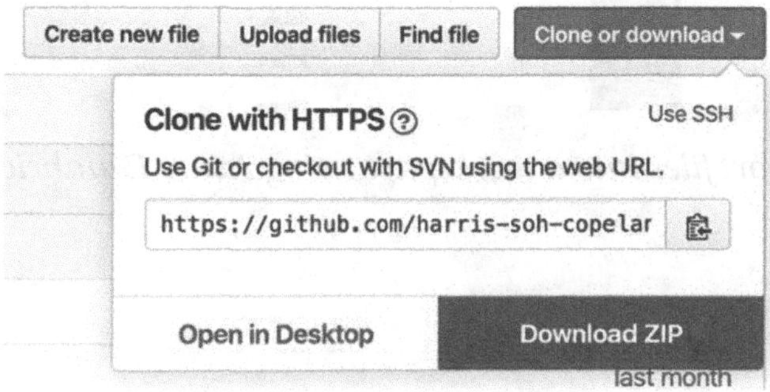

Figure 16-31. *Download a GitHub repository as a zip file*

4. In the Azure portal, navigate to the Azure Databricks service, and while in the Overview, click **Launch Workspace** to sign in to the Azure Databricks workspace using AAD credentials of the current Azure user.

5. In the Databricks menu on the left side, click **Workspace** and use the drop-down arrow to select **Import** and browse to the files under Azure-AI-Camp-master/day1/2.AutoMLDatabricks/ and select Model Training Classification III.dbc to import. This is a Databricks compressed file that can contain multiple files and folders. These may also be created from a Databricks workspace and exported. Note, many different types of files may be imported into Databricks, including plain Jupyter notebooks. Once imported, a single notebook should be visible under the Workspace menu item.

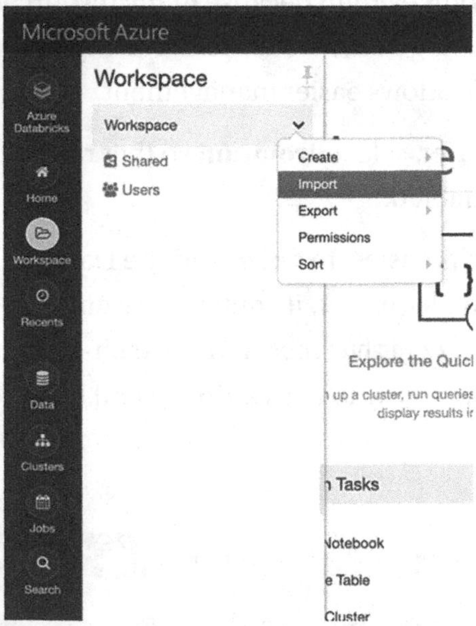

***Figure 16-32.** Import files into a workspace using Azure Databricks*

6. A cluster is needed to run the notebook. Navigate to Clusters in the menu, and click **Create Cluster**.

    a. Give the cluster a descriptive name as there might be other users in the workspace who use the cluster (concurrently or later).

    b. Keep the cluster mode on Standard, unless there are multiple users of this cluster concurrently and, in that case, it is a good idea to select High Concurrency.

    c. The pool can remain as None (this is for higher availability of nodes for the cluster).

    d. In Databricks Runtime Version, select **Runtime: 6.4 (Scala 2.11, Spark 2.4.5)** (non-GPU and non-ML version) or the default.

    e. In Autopilot Options, make sure that **Enable autoscaling** and **Terminate after** are selected. It is recommended to set **Terminate after** to 30 or 60 minutes to prevent getting charged for any unnecessary compute resource time.

    f. Ensure the Worker Type is set to default (of this writing, that is Standard_DS3_v2) with 2 Min Workers and 4 Max Workers. Note, a static fixed number of workers may also be specified.

    g. The Driver Type can remain at **Same as worker**.

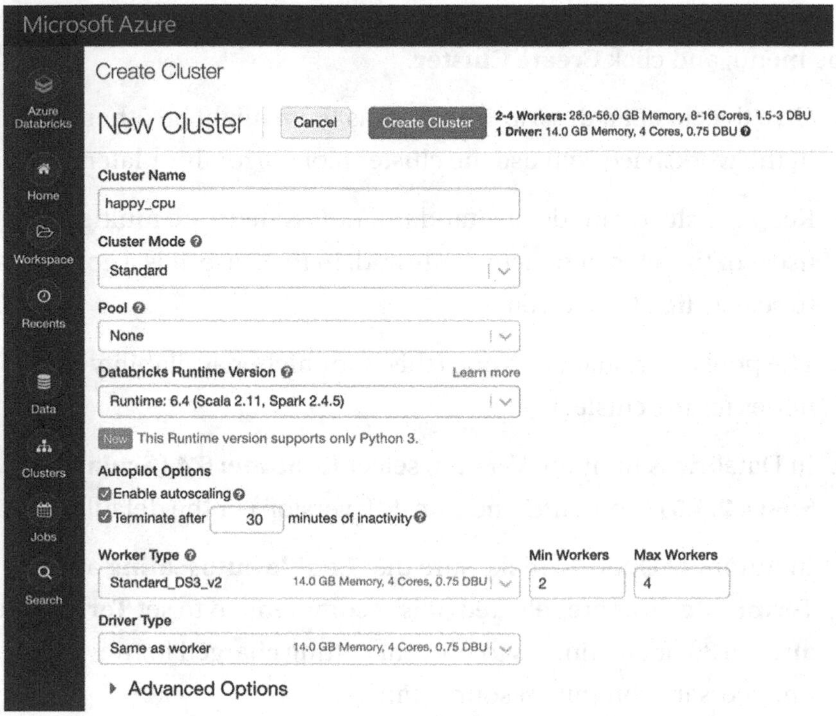

***Figure 16-33.** Creating a cluster in Azure Databricks*

h. Click **Create Cluster** to begin the provisioning process. This process could take several minutes, depending upon the size of the cluster specified. If the cluster stops, navigate back to the Clusters in the menu, pick the cluster, and click **Start** when ready to use.

7. Azure ML Python SDK needs to be installed on to the cluster. Navigate to Workspace in the menu and use the drop-down menu to select **Create** and then **Library**. For a Python package, select **PyPI** and type **azureml-sdk[automl]** (a version may be pinned with the use of == such as azureml-sdk[automl]==1.2.0 to ensure compatibility). Check the GitHub repo for the latest. Click **Create** to install the library to a cluster.

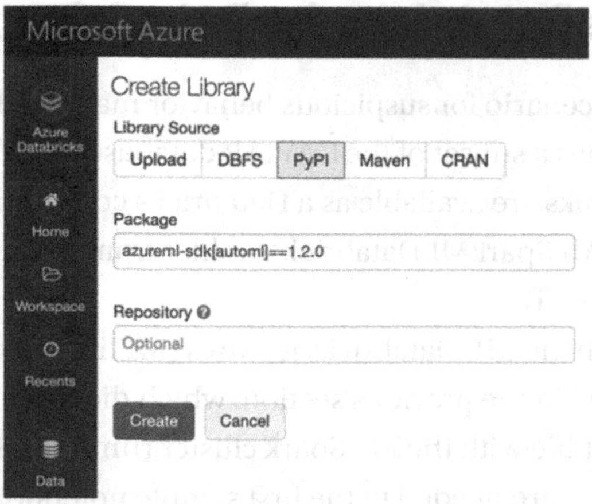

***Figure 16-34.** Installing the Azure ML Python SDK with Auto ML support on Databricks*

8. The next step is to ensure that the library is installed on the cluster. There should now be a Status on running clusters pane. Check the small checkbox next to the running cluster of choice (if it is not running, start the cluster). After checking the box, click **Install**.

9. Navigate back to the Model Training Classification III under Workspace and open it.

10. Fill in the cell that has placeholders for Azure subscription ID, resource group, Azure ML workspace name, and region of the Azure ML service started in an earlier section.

```
subscription_id = "<>" #you should be owner or contributor
resource_group = "<>" #you should be owner or contributor
workspace_name = "<>" #your workspace name
workspace_region = "<>" #your regionsubscription_id = "" #You should be owner or contributor
```

***Figure 16-35.** Filling in the details of the Azure ML workspace to connect with the notebook*

Interactive login to Azure is one of the next steps using a device login code.

This notebook should be very familiar if you worked through the previous Jupyter notebook hands-on sections because the controls are very similar, as are the process of using Azure ML to train and deploy. Use the instructions in the notebook as a guide to train and deploy the model to ACI for testing.

Use Case: Azure Databricks for Data Scientists

The surveillance video scenario for suspicious behavior may also be explored in Databricks. Databricks has a subset of the CAVIAR database preinstalled for tutorials and testing. Two notebooks are available as a Databricks compressed file in the Azure-AI-Camp/day1/3.AzureMLSparkMLDatabricks/ folder from the repository used in the previous section on Auto ML.

A second cluster with the ML Databricks features (MLlib) needs to be created alongside the one created in the previous section, which did not have Spark ML libraries. (Azure ML is not compatible with the ML Spark cluster runtimes; however, some features from this runtime are needed in the first sample notebook of this section). MLlib is a Spark ML library and has built-in algorithms and featurizers. The notebooks for this section take you through (1) data preprocessing (using MLlib to featurize an image dataset, created from videos) using the ML Databricks runtime and (2) training and using a logistic regression classifier to predict normal and suspicious behavior with Azure ML on a non-ML Databricks runtime.

Summary

This chapter laid a foundation of knowledge in machine learning, with examples in image data processing and analysis. The Data Science Virtual Machine, Jupyter notebooks, Azure ML, and Databricks for data science tasks were discussed. Images are not the only things that can be analyzed with machine learning, so you are encouraged to continue to learn and explore ways to use ML on Azure—whether on a local computer with the Azure ML SDKs, a DSVM or in an Azure Databricks workspace. Plentiful references and resources are on this book's website at `https://harris-soh-copeland-puca.github.io`. Machine learning can truly be a fascinating and lifelong study.

CHAPTER 17

Azure Data Services

Digital transformation is a term to describe how technology has changed our lives, how we interact with each other, and how organizations make business decisions. It is all possible because of the abundance of data available today. There is not only more types of data, but also the emergence of new types of data.

The volume of data has exploded exponentially in the last 30 years, especially since the early 2000s as more Internet-connected devices were adopted by organizations as well as consumers.

When the iPhone debuted in 2007, it ushered in the era of the smartphone. Entire countries that did not have the infrastructure of landlines leapfrogged developed countries in the adoption of cellular technologies. Applications have become untethered to computers and moved into the hands of mobile users creating social media content that is shared and reshared throughout the entire world. Social media unleashed different types of content such as video, conversation streams (streaming data), and photos.

Then came the Internet of Things (IoT) connecting devices to the Internet and sending data 24 hours a day, seven days a week. Smart homes and digital assistants monitor homes and make special orders via verbal commands or because an IoT refrigerator knows that something is running low and needs reordering. Organizations automate production lines and supply chains based on the conditions that IoT devices are tracking at every stage. You may have taken for granted the ability to track the delivery of the item you ordered from an Internet vendor as it traverses through a shipping company like FedEx or multinational carriers that seamlessly hand off a package from one shipper to another as it crosses international borders. This is all content and data that was not available before data was globally connected by public cloud.

To say that these examples are barely scratching the surface in terms of new content that never existed before is a huge understatement. There are so many use cases in any industry, vertical, consumer, and enterprise that generate rich content that now drives business decisions and touches our personal lives daily. The data abundance that has

J. Soh et al., *Microsoft Azure*, https://doi.org/10.1007/978-1-4842-5958-0_17

resulted in this age of digital transformation means that we need new tools, skills, and strategies to effectively harness the power of data-driven decision making. But before we can make sense of the data, we first need to efficiently store and manage data. For that, we need to better understand data as it exists today.

Data Trends

Data trends fall into four topical categories.

- Data types and volume
- Data analysis trends
- Data roles
- Data platform as a service (data PaaS)

Data Types and Volume

When we use the term *data* in the IT context, we automatically think of databases, SQL, tables, indexes, fields, and so forth. That is the traditional definition of data, also known as *structured data.*

However, not all data today fall into columns with fields and indexes. That is certainly not the case with videos or photos, aside from the metadata of such content. But you cannot afford not to classify them as data. For example, take the case of security video footage or videos captured by law enforcement body cameras. These are all content that is being used in *line of business* (LoB) applications and sometimes in court for legal proceedings. Therefore, they are truly the new data types that need to be handled differently. We call this content *unstructured data.*

Data also changes over time. Take a retailer, for example. Let's look at one type of product that a retailer might sell, like a backpack. This simple product can easily fit into a structured database with fields like size, color, weatherproof qualities, or not. Then came along a change in trend that introduced a single strap backpack. Should the retailer add a field for the number of straps or perhaps an indicator field for a single strap and apply it to the entire table? Recently there is also the trend for smart backpacks with charging capabilities for electronic devices. Then came along airport security (e.g., TSA-friendly) backpacks. The bottom line is that new features and trends are introduced to products every time. So instead of adding new fields to the entire table that affects the entire product class, it may be better to have those fields present only when applicable. This is called *semi-structured data*.

There is also another better way to define certain data relationships rather than a traditional key/value pair in columns. For example, it is easier to map out relationships of data points by representing them as vertices and edges. This is widely used in social media to map the relationships between people. The database that manages this kind of data is known as a *graph database*.

By now, you are probably no longer surprised you need more storage space than you purchased and continue to fall short all the time. Not too long ago, it was gigabytes, but today, we are commonly referring to consumer-based storage in the terabyte range. That is because video takes up a lot of space. Your chat history with shared and reshared content are space hogs. You need the backup of precious digital photos. The type of content and the social aspect of the content drives the amount of volume such content.

The introduction of different data types—semi-structured, unstructured, or graph requires different approaches in storing and handling such data. The footprint of such data contributes significantly to the volume of data that needs to be managed today.

Data Analysis Trends

You may have heard of *data-driven decision making*. Data scientists are one of the fastest-growing professions. Colleges are introducing data science curriculums and degrees. Online and distant learning opportunities for professionals who are already in the workforce see high enrollments in such programs.

At the same time, tools such as Databricks and technologies that support big data like Hadoop clusters are rapidly being deployed to support modern data analysis so organizations can take advantage of data-driven decision making. Why all this investment? Because data-driven decision making leads to better customer service, lower operational costs, and in many cases, improve and save lives. Knowing what, when, and why to carry out certain actions is always better than guessing. The simple rule of thumb is that more data improve the quality of decision making.

The problem is that more data also takes up more compute and memory, and the decision-making timing may be cyclical, but also have a rigid timeframe. In other words, it is pointless to spend more to deploy and maintain a big data analysis infrastructure if the activity is carried out once annually, but it is also pointless if the right decision is made too late.

Modern Data Roles

With new and modern data comes new and redefined roles. We briefly mentioned data scientists. These are the professionals who take the massive amount of data, often time from disparate data sources, and conduct data exploration, experiments, and analysis to find correlations between the data.

To make the data accessible so data scientists can do their jobs is the role of the modern data engineer. Data engineers should not be confused with database administrators, although we are seeing a natural transition of professionals from the database administrator roles to that of the data engineer. We have also seen data scientists serve as the data engineer as well, especially in smaller organizations.

In either case, the role of the data engineer is very defined. It is a role that makes the data available in a useable form for data scientists to do the analysis. Making data available involves moving, copying, cleaning, consolidating, merging, and updating data into a central and easily accessible location. It has its roots from the ETL (extract-transform-load) days.

Data engineers need to know which is the right repository for the type of data. For example, as discussed, unstructured data should not be stored in structured databases. So, the data engineer ensures the efficient and best storage medium for the different types of data.

Data engineers also need to ensure security for the data. In recent years, many privacy policies have had a worldwide impact, even though they may originate from certain jurisdictions. One good example is the General Data Protection Regulation (GDPR), which is a European Union (EU) law aimed at protecting EU citizens' privacy. Data security and access restrictions need to be in place to protect data belonging to EU citizens, but since we are in a global economy, EU citizens are no longer only in the European continent. Even small organizations are multinational if they do business on the Internet. Therefore, GDPR is a globally impacted regulation that everyone needs to adhere to. Using this single regulation as an example, all data engineers need to ensure GDPR data privacy, security, and notification requirements are in place. Throw in other regulations, such as *personally identifiable information* (PII), Health Insurance Portability and Accountability Act (HIPAA), Internal Revenue Service form 1075 (IRS 1075), and so forth. While there may be overlapping requirements, the data engineer needs to ensure that they are all adhered to.

What a data engineer should not need to do is to ensure the technology platform is always available and healthy. For example, the data engineer should not need to patch the SQL Database or Cosmos DB every month. The data engineer should not need to ensure the geo-redundant capability is working, just that it is in place if there is a requirement for geo-redundancy of the data in accordance with the organizations' business continuity and disaster recovery (BCDR) plan.

Data Platform as a Service

Data PaaS is the consumption of database services as a PaaS. This is a narrower definition of a PaaS to mean that it relates to data. It is sometimes incorrectly used interchangeably with data as a service (DaaS). We see DaaS as a definition of data available for consumption.

Data engineers deploying the right type of database to store data without having to manage the VM and the database engine and software is an example of PaaS.

Once data is cleaned, merged, consolidated, or the often used word is *wrangled* to the point where data scientists can analyze the data, or business users can browse to data repositories with their PowerBI tool and explore the data. Then this is considered data as a service. In Microsoft Azure, Azure SQL Database, and Cosmos DB are two examples of data PaaS. Azure Data Catalog is also an example of a data PaaS that is designed to deliver DaaS to the organization.

You have read from previous chapters the benefit of PaaS in other non-data specific terms, like Azure Cognitive Services and Azure Web Apps. The same benefits that PaaS delivers to these other areas are identical to the data realm: better redundancy, better resiliency, and better overall SLA. But remember our discussion regarding GDPR, PII, and all the numerous regulatory requirements?

Data PaaS offerings in Azure already legally adhere to these requirements. If there are required certifications in place, Microsoft already has the relevant documentation and certifications, so data engineers and organizations adopting the data PaaS can automatically ensure that the proper security requirements are in place.

The other data PaaS offers traditional on-premises databases. The common misconception for data PaaS is the network latency as it relates to data exchange since the data PaaS in the cloud is a remote location. Depending on the architecture and the use cases, this is often not the case.

If an application remains on-premises and pulls data in a traditional client-server approach, there is latency. This should be addressed with an application modernization effort, or, at the very least, combining the lessons learned in Chapter 12 from using web apps as PaaS integrated with data PaaS.

The other use case is in the field of data-driven decision making and the work of the data scientists. If the analytical tools are also PaaS, like Azure Databricks, and then there not be any latency issues. Of course, having to copy data on-premises to Azure take time from a transfer perspective, this is usually a batch process just by the nature of a data warehouse's role, which is an Online Analytical Processing (OLAP) role as opposed to Online Transaction Processing (OLTP). Furthermore, remember the discussion related to data volume, the ability to store large amounts of data, and then assign sufficient memory and compute to process the analysis against the data on a consumption basis rather than a capital expense yield significant savings.

Azure Data Services

Now that we have introduced the industry trends driving how data is used and the data engineer and data scientist roles in this modern era, we can focus on the actual data PaaS offerings in Azure.

The data PaaS in Azure is called Azure data services. It is a family of data specific solutions to address the replication, manipulation, and storage of the different types of data, at scale, and securely.

Like all PaaS, Azure data services have a financially backed service-level agreement that focuses on high availability. The published availability of Azure data services is summarized in Table 17-1.

Table 17-1. *Azure Data Services Availability SLA*

Uptime Level	Uptime Hours per Year	Downtime Hours per Year
99.9%	8,751.24	~8.76
99.99%	8,759.12	~0.88
99.999%	8,759.91	~0.09

Another key difference between on-premises databases versus Azure data services PaaS is that the cost of using Azure data services already factors in all licensing costs. In fact, software licensing is not even an applicable line item for Azure PaaS, such as Azure data services.

You can explore Azure data services at `https://azure.microsoft.com/en-us/services/#databases`, but this only shows the different databases. However, data services include technologies that are not databases in nature, such as IoT services that require IoT-specific data services (see `https://azure.microsoft.com/en-us/services/#iot`) and all the analytics tools, including Azure Data Factory and Azure Data Catalog (see `https://azure.microsoft.com/en-us/services/#analytics`). There are also elements of Azure data services that support hybrid integration of on-premises and Azure-based architectures, such as Azure SQL Database managed instance, which you can explore at `https://azure.microsoft.com/en-us/services/#hybrid`. Essentially, Azure data services have a significant footprint across multiple technologies because data is a very fundamental layer utilized by many different architectures and initiatives.

In this chapter, we focus on the core Azure data services as it applies to databases. Specifically, we look at

- Azure SQL Database
- Azure Synapse
- Azure Cosmos DB

Remember that there are other databases available in Azure as well, even proprietary non-Microsoft databases and open source databases, such as Azure Database for MySQL and Azure Postgres SQL.

Last, we also look at data storage technologies that support Azure data services particularly around extract-transform-load (ETL) and extract-load-transform (ELT) processes, such as Azure Blob and Azure Data Lake Services.

Azure SQL Database

Azure SQL Database should be the most familiar to audiences that have been using SQL Server. As the name implies, it is SQL Databases, not SQL servers, provisioned in Azure. Of course, the underlying technologies that support Azure SQL Database are SQL servers, but as a PaaS, you do not need to provision a VM, install the SQL Server engine, patch it, and test it before using it. You provision the SQL databases you need and start populating it with tables and data. It is the quickest and most time-saving way of getting access to a database.

There are three deployment models for Azure SQL Database.

- Azure SQL Database
- Azure SQL Database managed instance
- Azure SQL Database Elastic Pool

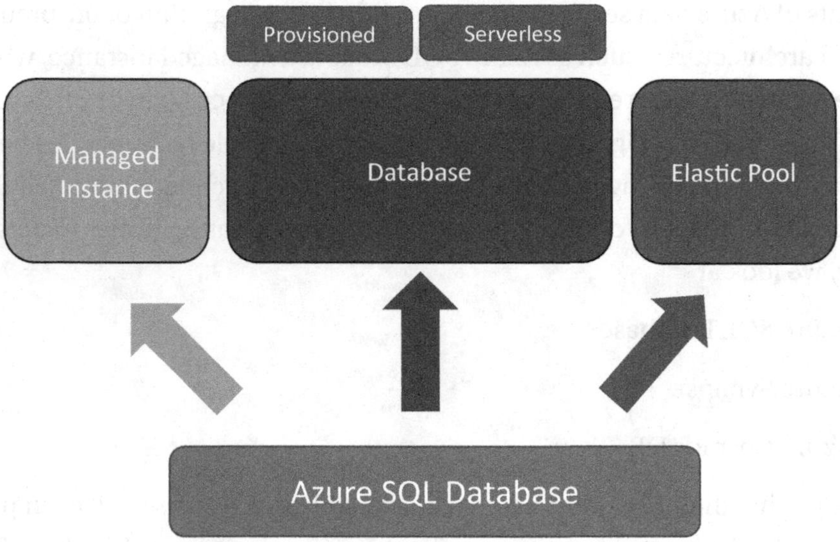

***Figure 17-1.** Three flavors of Azure SQL Database*

Azure SQL Database is the most common implementation and recommendation of consuming databases as a PaaS. Each deployment of Azure SQL Database is a deployment of a *single* scalable database.

Hands-on with Azure SQL Database

Azure SQL Database is best for modern cloud applications that need a scalable database that is fully managed, has built-in high availability, and promises the lowest administrative overhead.

Note One unique aspect of Azure SQL Database as a PaaS is that deploying Azure SQL Database as a PaaS would require pinning the database to a new or existing virtual SQL Server instance. This may sound confusing based on your knowledge of how PaaS work, but if you think about the way the SQL engine works, this makes sense. Traditionally, some capabilities are delivered at the server level (e.g., access security to ports used by SQL) and the other capabilities delivered at the database level. Therefore, to continue providing server-level capabilities for Azure SQL Database, a virtual instance of SQL server be created. Rest assured that you still not need to patch and manage this SQL Server. The hands-on section in this exercise clarifies any confusion concerning this topic.

1. As with all the other exercises throughout this book, we assume you already have an Azure subscription. Go to the Azure portal at `https://portal.azure.com`.
2. Click **Create a resource** and type **SQL Database** in the search box, and then select **SQL Database** in the results, as seen in Figure 17-2.

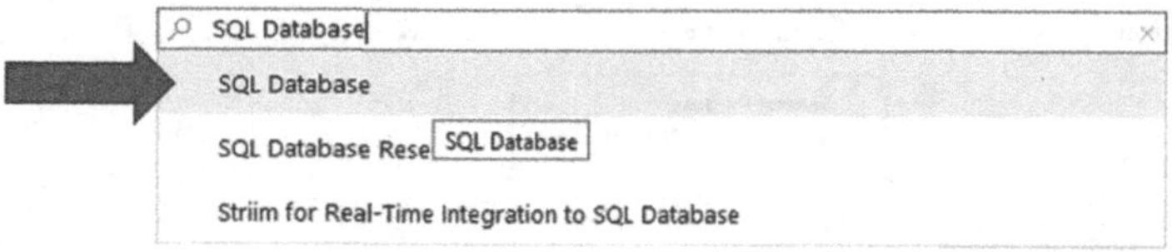

***Figure 17-2.** Selecting SQL Database from the results of the available service*

3. Click the **Create** button.
4. Select the subscription, an existing or new resource group, and a name, and then click **Create new** to create a new database server to host this database. In the future, when you create another Azure SQL Database, you can use this same database server. Unlike the traditional SQL server licensing model, there is no SQL core or CPU licensing associated with spinning up a server to support Azure SQL databases, but there are compute and storage charges incurred based on what you select. For example, the charges

for the server to support Azure SQL databases in Figure 17-3 is for a 2 vCore, 32GB server. Visit `https://docs.microsoft.com/en-us/azure/sql-database/sql-database-resource-limits-database-server` to learn more about the capacity limitations, but as an example, with this single database server deployment, you can reuse it for up to 5000 Azure SQL Databases.

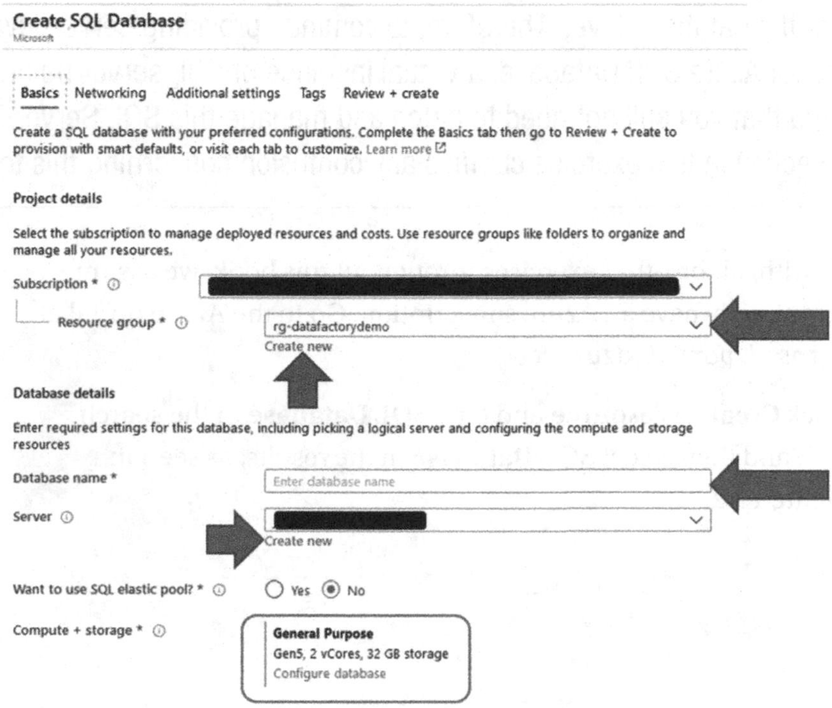

***Figure 17-3.** Deploying an Azure SQL Database instance*

5. In the New server pane, provide a name for the server and the admin login credentials. The admin credentials you enter here is the SQL dba credentials. Select the region to place this database server and click **OK**.

6. Select **No** for the SQL elastic pool for now. We discuss what elastic pool is later. Click **Configure database** in the Compute + storage section.

7. Take note of the different scale options: General Purpose, Hyperscale, and Business Critical. Look at the characteristics, such as the IOPS and latency for each option, as seen in Figure 17-4. Click each box to see other details. In an actual deployment, select the option that meets the performance requirements of your database. For now, once you have explored the different options, select **General Purpose**.

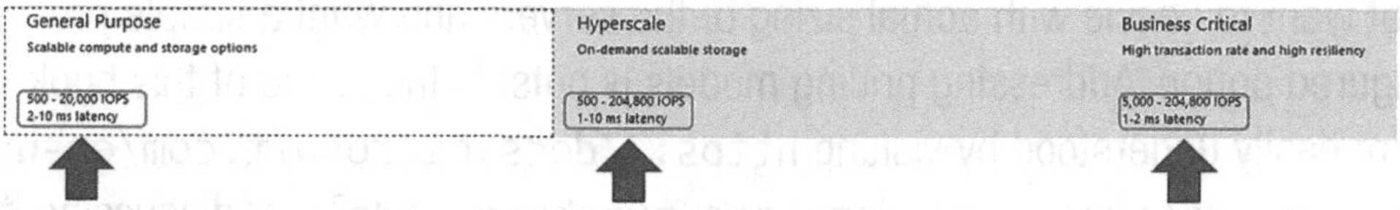

***Figure 17-4.** Different deployment options for Azure SQL Database based on the desired performance*

8. Next, you have the option to select Provisioned or Serverless for the Compute tier for your database. As their names imply, the Provisioned tier permanently allocate compute resources to the Azure SQL Databases that are allocated to this server. You are billed hourly so long as this server exists. The Serverless tier is based on dynamically scaled and assigned resources. During peak times, more resources may be assigned based on the sliders at the bottom of the page. During lower peak times, resources are deallocated to save money. When there is no activity in the databases, all resources are deallocated, and the database pauses until a request comes in. Therefore, there might be a slight delay if there is a period of database inactivity. If your application has unpredictable usage and can tolerate some latency, Serverless is the most cost-effective option.

9. For this exercise, select **Provisioned.**

10. Click **Change configuration** in the Hardware Configuration section. Take note of the different configuration types available. You see a compute optimized vs. memory optimized configuration option. Based on your application requirements, select a configuration that best meets your needs. For this exercise, accept the default Gen5 configuration and click **OK** at the bottom of the screen.

11. Use the sliders at the bottom of the screen to allocate the number of vCores and the space. You can always modify this later.

Note In this exercise, we are explicitly defining the vCores and Storage to allocate to this server. There is another option, which is called the *DTU billing option*. DTU stands for *database transaction units*. DTUs are a unit of measure that bundles compute, storage, and IOPS. It is an option for customers who do not want to hassle with actual sizing of the servers and want a simple pre-configured option. Addressing pricing models is outside the scope of this book but are easily understood by visiting `https://docs.microsoft.com/en-us/azure/sql-database/sql-database-purchase-models` or discussing it with your Microsoft representative. While on this topic, note that if you already own traditional licenses for SQL Server, you may obtain credit for the Azure SQL Databases you spin up in Azure.

---

12. Click **Apply**.
13. Click **Next : Networking**. You are not be adding a private endpoint for this exercise, but this topic was covered in Chapter 9; note that Azure SQL Database is a PaaS that you can allocate a private IP address as a hosted endpoint if needed.
14. Click **Next : Additional settings**. You are accepting the default options for this exercise and also skip creating tags. Click **Review + create**.
15. At this point, Azure deploy the database and a new database server instance to host that database. When the deployment is complete, go to the Azure database resource. In the Overview pane, you can see the server that it is hosted on, along with other important information like the status and location of the database. The database server name is represented as a fully qualified URL. Take note of this URL and click the server name, as referenced in Figure 17-5 which is also a link. This takes you to the database server resource.

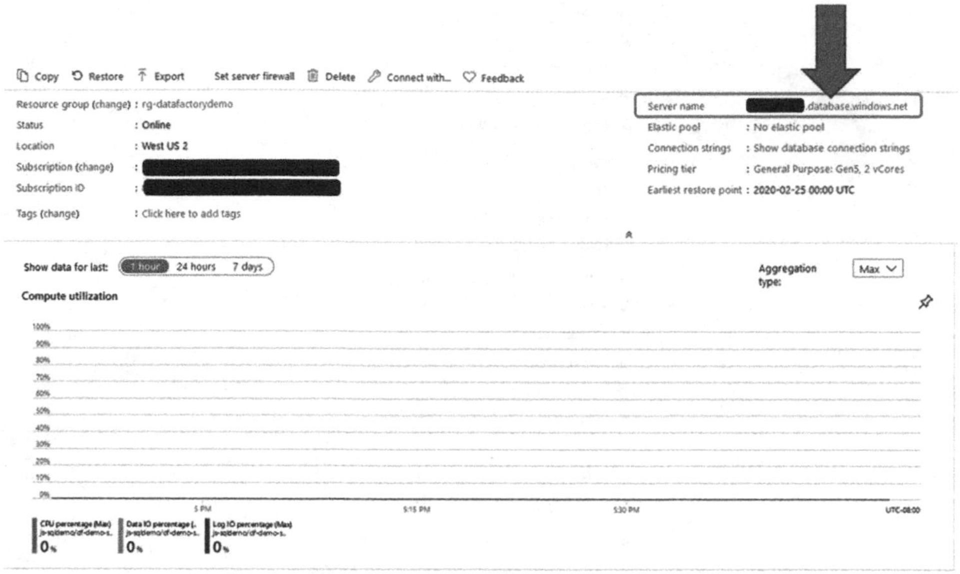

***Figure 17-5.** Overview pane of an Azure SQL Database resource*

16. Under the Security section of the menu on the left, click **Firewalls**, as referenced in Figure 17-6 and virtual networks.

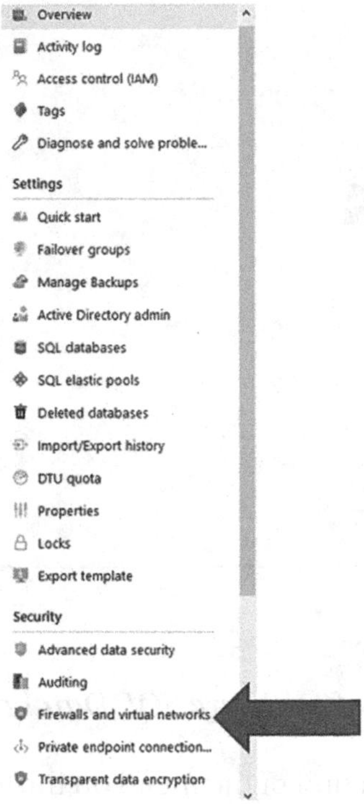

***Figure 17-6.** Configuring the firewall to allow access to this server and databases*

17. The Azure portal has detected the IP address of your computer, so if you click **Add client IP**, as referenced in Figure 17-7 it adds this address to the firewall to allow network-level access to the server. This is an important step if you wish to manage your Azure SQL Database using SQL Server Management Studio (SSMS). You can manually add ranges of IP addresses that you may want to allow access to connect to this database server. Actually, you may have to, especially if you are using network address translation that masks your IP address.

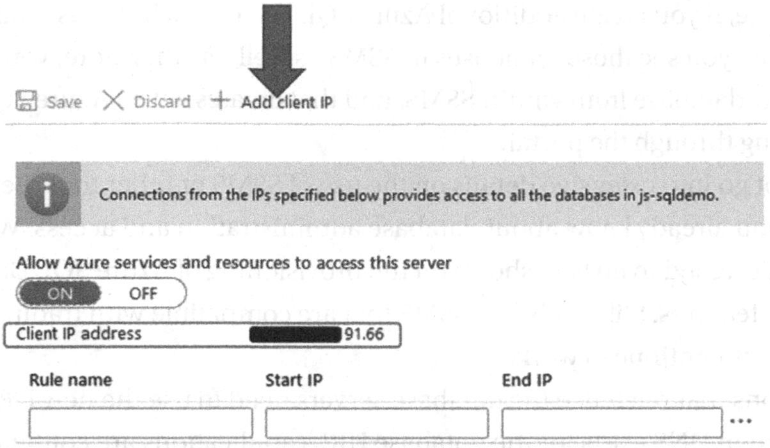

Figure 17-7. Adding a client IP address to Firewall ACL

18. Click **Save** and wait for the portal to update firewall rules.

At this point, you can access the Azure SQL Database that is hosted on this database server.

Assuming you are using SSMS as your client administrative tool, launch SSMS and connect to the server using the full URL of the server and the SQL dba login you created in step 5. Click **Connect**, as referenced in Figure 17-8. If your firewall is properly configured, as outlined in step 17, you are connected to the database server.

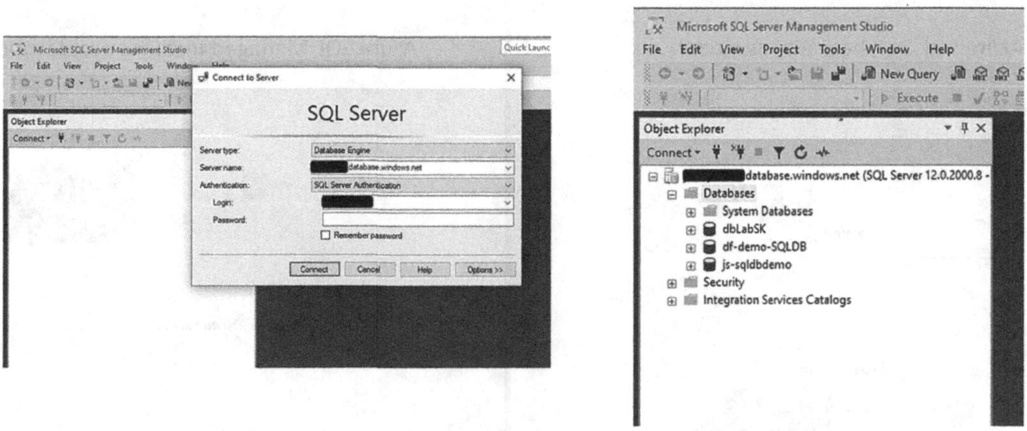

Figure 17-8. Connecting to the database server to manage an Azure SQL Database using SSMS

In the future, if you create additional Azure SQL Databases but reuse the same database server, you see those databases in SSMS as well. Furthermore, you can choose to create a new database from within SSMS, and that creates a new Azure SQL Database instead of going through the portal.

We did not go into extensive details on the use of SSMS or other tools because we assume that you already know about database administration and access. What this exercise was designed to do is to show you the provisioning of Azure SQL Database and the important features. Still, tools like SSMS that are compatible with traditional SQL server databases continue to work.

Applications that reference the database servers need to use the new URL, but if a CNAME record in DNS exists for the database URLs applications are configured to use, and the CNAME is repointed to the database server hosting Azure SQL Database, you likely would not need to make any changes to the applications themselves.

Azure SQL Managed Instance

Azure SQL Managed Instance is another deployment model of Azure SQL Database PaaS but with greater integration with a hybrid architecture.

Figure 17-9 depicts the difference in the access model between Azure SQL Database and Azure SQL Managed Instance, especially with the introduction of Azure Private Link for PaaS.

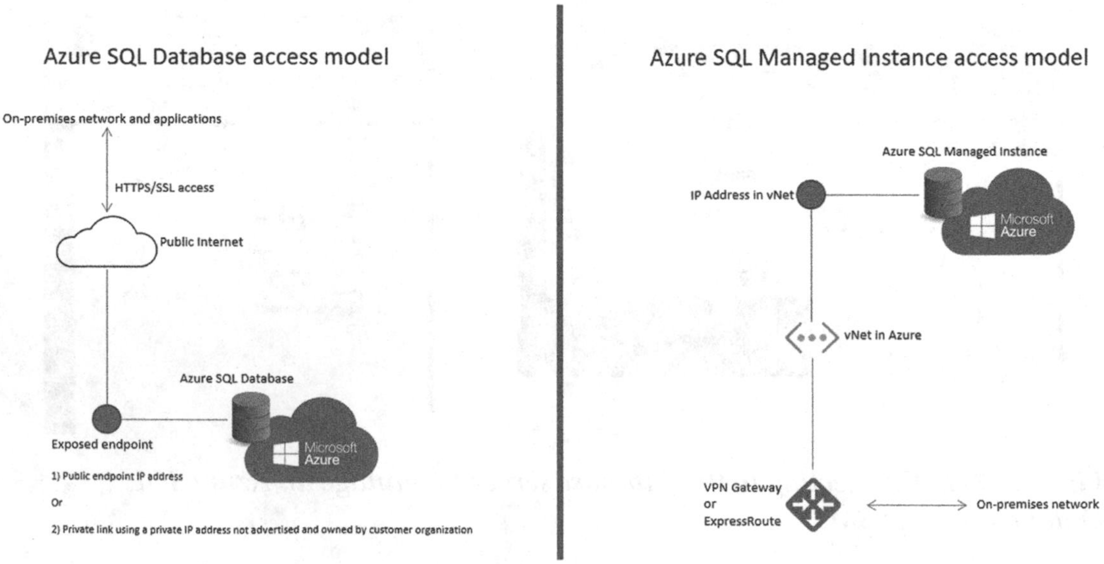

Figure 17-9. *Differences in access models*

Both Azure SQL offerings provide all the benefits of PaaS. For Azure SQL Databases, access to the database that has been provisioned on the virtual server instance is via a URL that is associated with a public endpoint (<host>.database.azure.net) as we saw in the previous exercise. With Private Link, that public endpoint can have a URL that is a private IP address owned by the customer organization, thereby further obscuring the endpoint for potential exploitation.

With Azure SQL Managed Instance, the database PaaS is tied to a virtual network (VNet), which is inherently private and isolated. This VNet is then connected to the on-premises network via a Site-to-Site VPN or ExpressRoute. We covered hybrid networking in Chapter 9.

Azure SQL Managed Instance is a new deployment option that provides native VNet integration for customers that have security requirements that mirror traditional on-premises SQL server deployments and are not exposed to the public Internet. It is also a model for applications that need to remain on-premises and access the database via a high-speed, dedicated link to Azure like ExpressRoute, where latency is minimized or eliminated.

Another important differentiator between Azure SQL Database and Azure SQL Managed Instance is that it has nearly a 100% compatibility with the latest SQL Server that is deployed on-premises. In fact, the capabilities in Azure SQL Managed Instance are greater than SQL Server on-premises. As such, Azure SQL Managed Instance makes it likely that customers can lift-and-shift on-premises databases that serve on-premises applications with minimal disruptions.

Deploying an Azure SQL Managed Instance is very similar to deploying Azure SQL Database, with the exception that you select an existing VNet or configure a new one to deploy Azure SQL Managed Instance to, and then provide an IP address that is in that VNet's virtual IP range.

Elastic Pools

The third Azure SQL Database deployment type is the use of Elastic Pools. Azure SQL Database elastic pool is a method of housing multiple Azure SQL Databases on a single Azure SQL Database server but letting Azure scale the capacity of the server based on a set price.

Elastic pools are most beneficial to software as a service (SaaS) application providers. In a SaaS delivery model, application providers may deploy multiple separate databases for each SaaS customer organization using a common application. Customer organizations may be different in size and have different peak usage. Traditionally, SaaS providers deploy infrastructure that can handle the peak utilization of all their customers to ensure that SLAs are met. This is often a costly strategy because there be times that the compute and IOPs remain idle. The solution is to house these customer databases on an elastic database server, so all the databases share the same resources on the server. It is up to the server to allocate and scale the right amount of resources to each database in real time based on current and historical consumption. This leads to predictable budgets for the SaaS provider without compromising the ability to meet published SLAs.

Hands-on with Elastic Pools

1. In the Azure portal, go to the Azure SQL Database that you deployed from the first exercise and click the name of the database server in the Overview pane, or you can directly go to the database server resource.
2. In the Overview pane, click **New elastic pool**, as referenced in Figure 17-10.

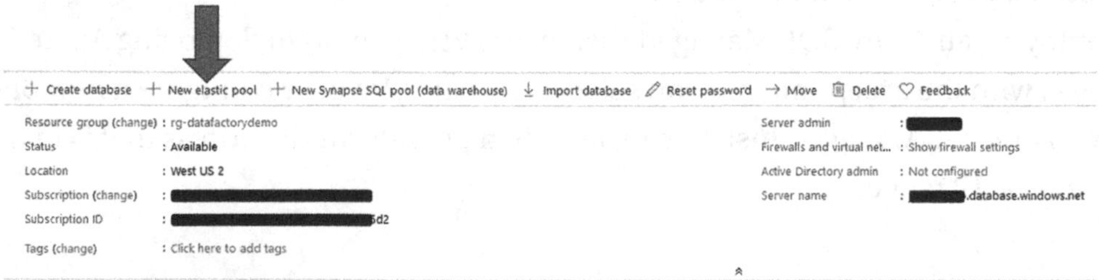

***Figure 17-10.** Adding a new elastic pool*

3. Provide a name for the elastic pool then click **Review + create**.
4. Note the estimated monthly cost for the Database server, and then click **Create**.
5. Once the elastic pool is deployed, click **Go to resource**.

6. Select **Configure**, and then click **Add databases**. Select the Azure SQL Database created in the first exercise to add to the elastic pool, and then click **Apply**, as seen in Figure 17-11.

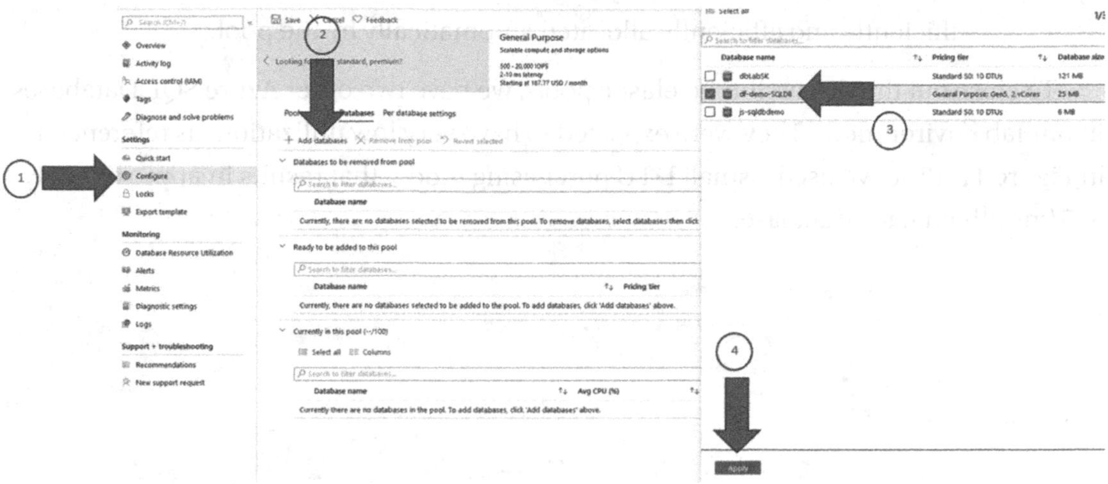

***Figure 17-11.** Adding an existing database to the elastic pool*

7. Click **Save** at the top of the pane.
8. After the changes have been implemented, click **Overview**. Click **Create database**.
9. Give the database a name and note that since you are creating this database from within the elastic pool pane, the options for the server are grayed out.
10. Click **Review + create**. Notice that the estimated cost for this database is stated as **Included in pool**, which means that the database server is scaled so that it remains within the budget as set when we defined the elastic pool's vCore and storage.
11. Click **Create**.
12. After the database has been created, return to the elastic pool resource, and click **Configure**.

13. At the bottom of the Configure pane, you see the average CPU, peak CPU, and storage that the two databases are using. Over time, you can tune the vCore and storage of the elastic pool so that the shared use of resources by all the databases in this pool are sufficiently and efficiently allocated automatically by the pool.

To close out the discussion on elastic pools, we have two other Azure SQL Databases in our lab environment. They were expected to have very low utilization, as referenced in Figure 17-12 so we used a small DTU purchasing model that results in approximately $15/month for each database.

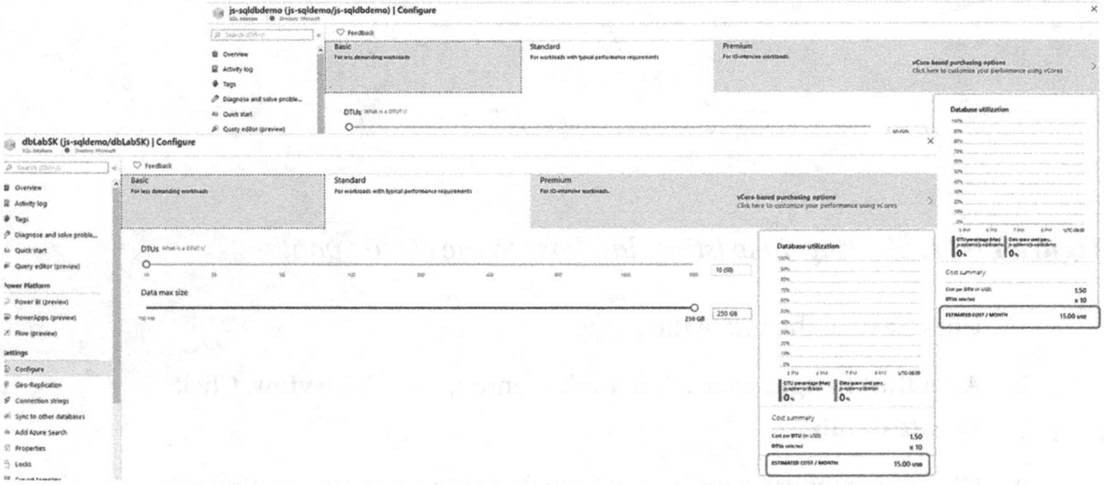

Figure 17-12. *Two databases purchased separately via the DTU purchasing models*

Repeating the steps 6 and 7 from the previous exercise, we added these two databases to the elastic pool because we know that there is enough capacity to accommodate these two databases. By doing so, we saved $30/month since both databases are now absorbed into the cost of the elastic pool.

Hands-on Tuning and Monitoring Azure SQL Databases

One of the benefits of using PaaS in Azure is the built-in performance tuning and monitoring capabilities. In this exercise, we explore these capabilities using the database we created earlier.

To observe the results of tuning, we first set up the test environment by downloading and installing HammerDB, which is a free load testing tool for databases.

Setting up the Test Environment

1. From the client machine that is conducting the test against Azure SQL Database, download HammerDB from `www.hammerdb.com/download.html` and install it. Take note of the directory in which you are installing HammerDB because you need to go to that directory to launch the application. The installation process may not create an icon on your desktop or Start menu. Make sure that this client machine's IP address is already added to the firewall for Azure SQL Database, which it would be if you are using the same machine against the same Azure SQL Database server in the first exercise.

2. After installation is complete, go to the installed directory and launch HammerDB by double-clicking and executing hammerdb.bat, as seen in Figure 17-13.

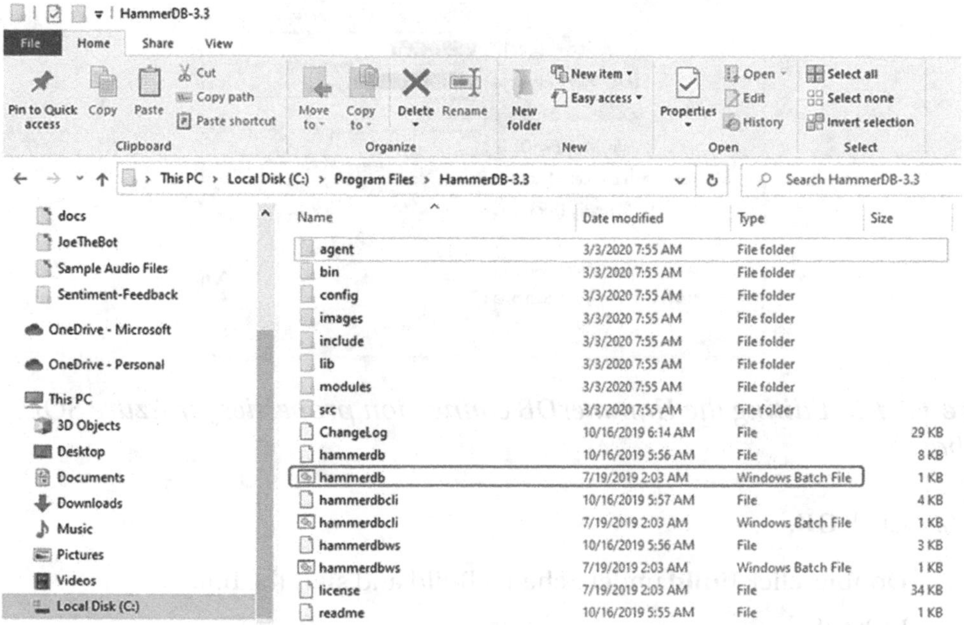

***Figure 17-13.** Locating and executing hammerdb.bat*

3. By default, HammerDB is configured for Oracle. Double-click **SQL Server** in the Benchmark panel and choose **TPC-C**, which stands for Transaction Processing Performance Council - Benchmark C.

4. Expand Schema Build and double-click **Options**.

5. Enter the information as you see in Figure 17-14. This creates a database named tpcc in Azure SQL Database and populates it with test schema and data. Pay close attention to edit the ODBC driver version, or the tool may be unable to connect to Azure SQL Database. Leave the number of Warehouses to 1, but guidelines suggest 10 to 100 warehouse per CPU. Leave Virtual Users to Build Schema at 1.

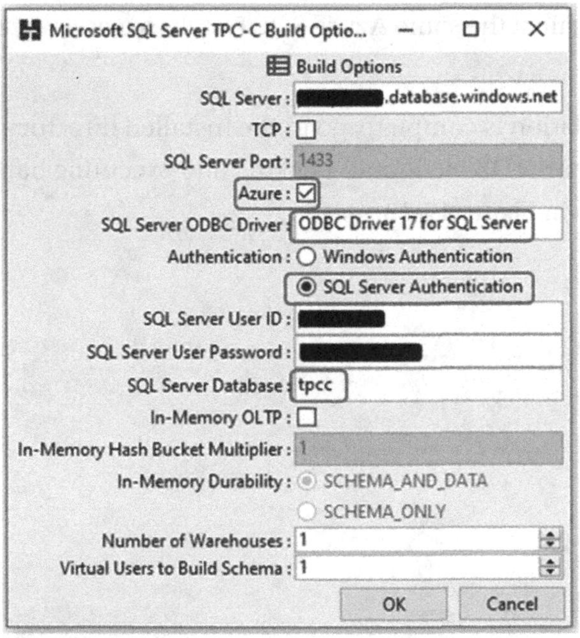

***Figure 17-14.** Editing the HammerDB connection properties for Azure SQL Database*

6. Click **OK**.

7. Double-click **Build** under Schema Build and start the build process.

8. After the build process is complete, the Azure SQL Database server has a new database named tpcc. You can verify that the database exists via SSMS or from the Azure portal, together with tables and sample data, as seen in Figure 17-15.

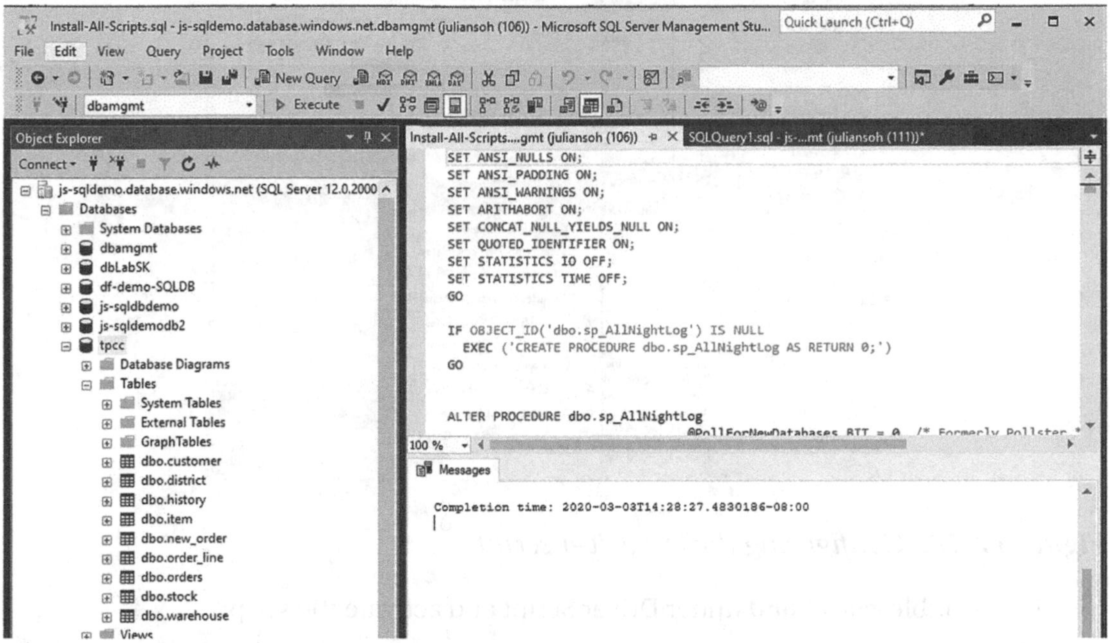

Figure 17-15. *New tpcc database with sample data*

9. Next, expand Driver Script in the Benchmark panel and double-click **Options**.

10. Configure the settings, as seen in Figure 17-16. Click **OK** when done.

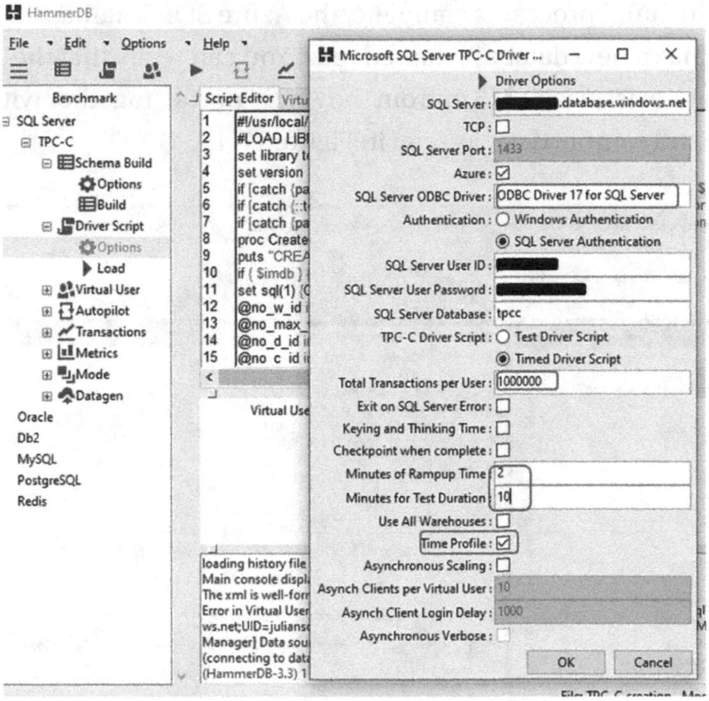

Figure 17-16. *Configuring the test driver script*

11. Double-click **Load** under Driver Script and activate the script.

12. Expand the Virtual Users section and double-click **Options**.

13. Create virtual users, as seen in Figure 17-17, and then click **OK**.

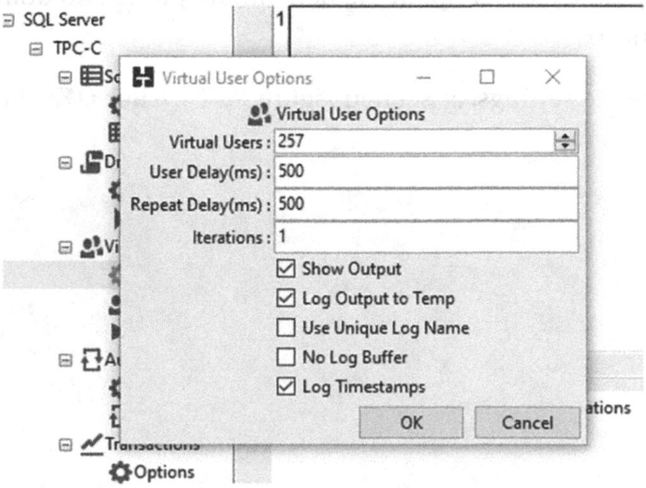

Figure 17-17. *Creating Virtual users that load test the tpcc Azure SQL Database*

14. Expand Autopilot and double-click **Options**. Configure Autopilot settings, as seen in Figure 17-18. We are going to ramp each stage of the test to get the results as we incrementally increase the load (number of users) according to the Active Virtual User Sequence. Then click **OK**.

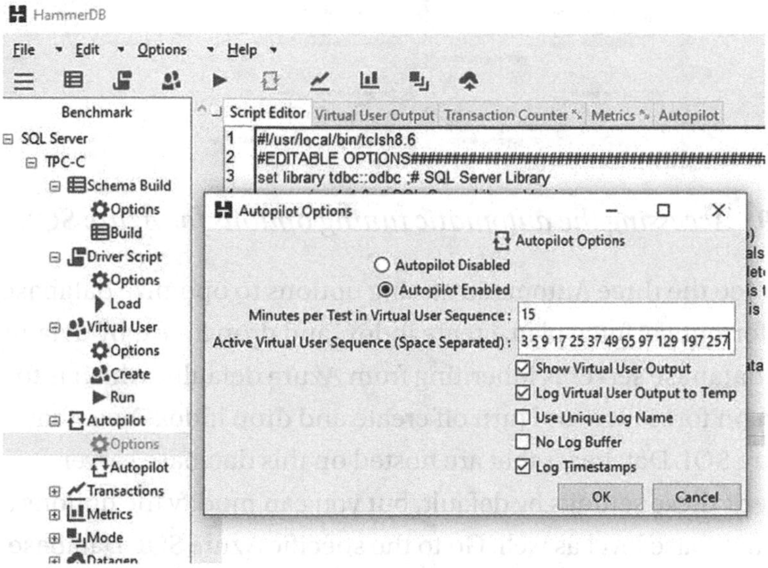

***Figure 17-18.** Configuring Autopilot to run the load test*

Leave HammerDB running for now because we are going to switch our attention to the Azure portal to look at performance statistics and turn on Automatic Tuning. We then come back to HammerDB to start the load testing.

Performance Monitoring and Automatic Tuning

First, we look at automatic tuning. Automatic tuning is a service that continuously monitors database usage and automatically tunes it for optimal performance. This is based on intelligent learning and AI capabilities within Azure.

1. In the Azure portal, go to the Azure SQL Database server that was created along with the Azure SQL Database from the first exercise.

2. In the Overview pane, select the Features tab, and then select **Automatic tuning**, as seen in Figure 17-19.

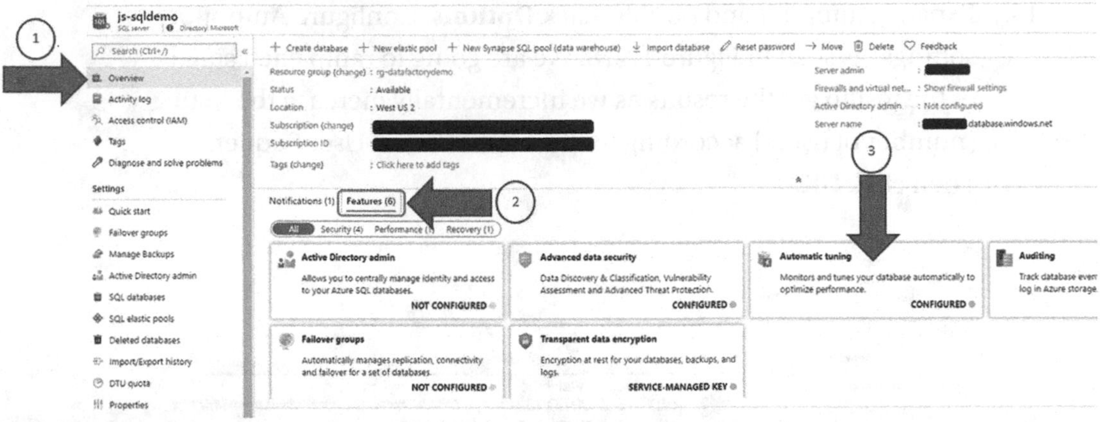

***Figure 17-19.** Accessing the automatic tuning options for Azure SQL Database*

3. You see the three Automatic Tuning options to optimize database performance: force plan, create index, and drop index. By default, the database server is inheriting from Azure defaults, which is to turn on force plan and turn off create and drop index. Note that Azure SQL Databases that are hosted on this database server inherit these settings by default, but you can modify the options at the database level as well. Go to the specific Azure SQL Database to stop inheriting these server settings and set its Automatic Tuning options.

4. Turn on Create Index.

5. Click **Overview**, and at the bottom of the pane, under SQL database, you should see the tpcc database that was created by HammerDB. Click **tpcc** to select it. The portal should take you to the tpcc Azure SQL Database resource.

6. Scroll down to Intelligent Performance and click **Automatic tuning**. Notice you have the same options as in step 3, but this is at the database level. Leave the settings as they are because you are going to use the server's settings from step 3.

7. Click **Performance recommendation**, as referenced in Figure 17-20. Azure tells you that the database is too new, and therefore there are no recommendations at this time.

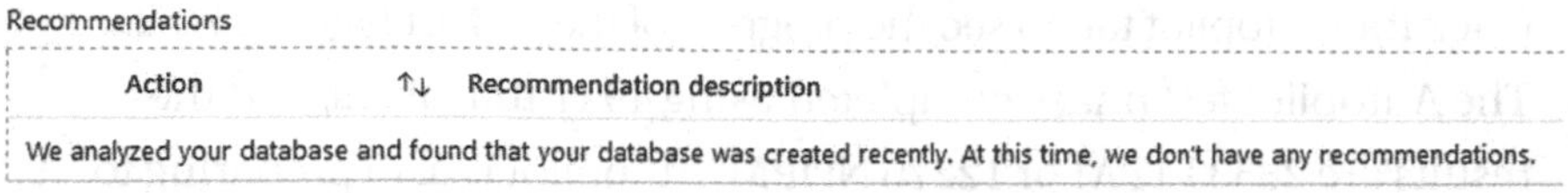

Figure 17-20. *Database performance recommendations*

Now that you have turned on Automatic tuning, you are ready to start load testing with HammerDB.

Load testing Azure SQL Database Server

1. Return to HammerDB and double-click **Autopilot** in the Benchmark panel. This starts the load testing process as virtual users are ramped up. You can stop the test at any time by clicking the Stop button, as seen in Figure 17-21, but the intent is for the script to run in its entirety.

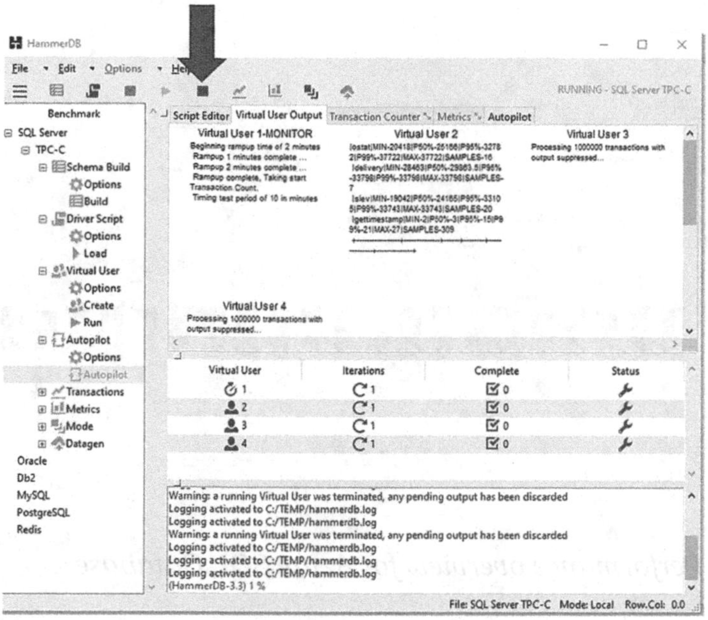

Figure 17-21. *Running the load test in Autopilot mode*

2. Click the Autopilot tab to see the progress of the test. In Figure 17-22. The Autopilot test phase completed using 49 virtual users, and the results are 28333 TPM or 12276 NOPM. Autopilot is also preparing to re-run the test with 65 virtual users. Notice that this is according to our settings from Figure 17-18 in step 14 when configuring HammerDB.

3. The setup for this test, as outlined in this exercise, takes up to an hour. When done, you can go scroll through the Autopilot window and gather all the TPM or NOPM data to determine performance at different user-level loads.

Analyzing Performance

1. Go back to the Azure portal and look at the Performance overview for the tpcc database. You should see tuning activity, top queries, and CPU consumption, as seen in Figure 17-22.

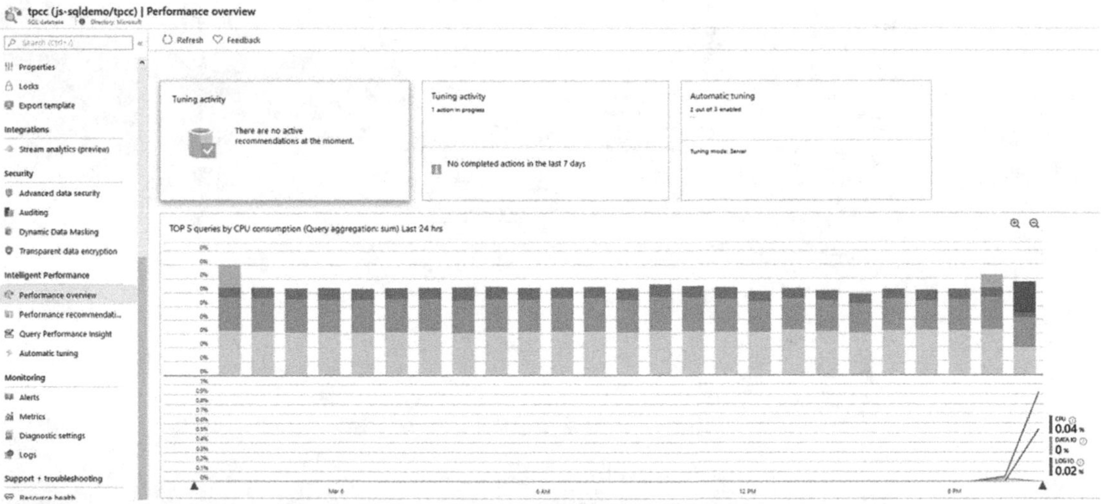

Figure 17-22. Performance overview for Azure SQL Database

Note You may have to run the HammerDB load test several times before Automatic Tuning has enough information to start implementing a tuning activity. Therefore, you may not see any Performance recommendations as well. If that is the case, re-run Autopilot in HammerDB to generate additional load history.

---

2. Click **Performance recommendation**. If there is enough information for Automatic Tuning to initiate an action, it is shown in this pane. Figure 17-23 shows a Create Index action resulting from Automatic tuning. The index is created, executed, and then validated. Refresh the page to see the different stages of the automatic tuning.

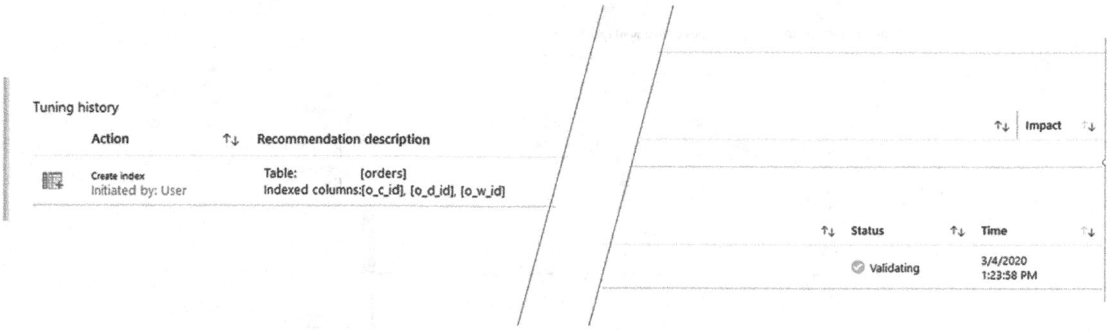

Figure 17-23. *Automatic Tuning in action (enlarged view)*

3. Explore all the performance details by clicking **Query Performance Insight**. You find interesting reports like longest-running queries and queries taking up the most resources. You can also create custom queries. You can click the reports and drill down to the details to get more granular information on the performance of the queries, as seen in Figure 17-24.

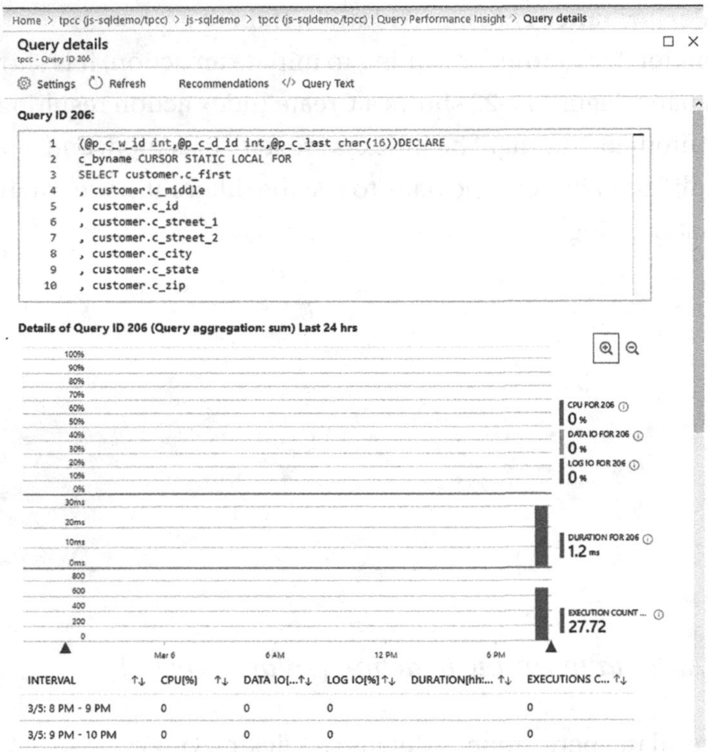

Figure 17-24. *Drilling down to look at the performance at the query level*

Next Steps: Self-Guided Assignment

Before we leave this exercise, create a table in the tpcc database that we are using in Chapter 19.

Launch SQL Server Management Studio (SSMS) and connect to the Azure SQL Database. Create this table in the tpcc database using the following SQL statement.

```
CREATE TABLE Users (
    PersonID int,
    LastName varchar(255),
    FirstName varchar(255),
    email varchar(255),
    ip varchar(255),
        gender varchar(10),
        comments varchar(max) null
);
```

This concludes our exploration of Azure SQL Database. For a detailed discussion and a much deeper dive on Azure SQL Database, a forked copy of Microsoft's extensive documentation on Azure SQL Database is on our GitHub repo at `https://github.com/harris-soh-copeland-puca/azure-docs/tree/master/articles/sql-database`.

Azure Cosmos DB

For the longest time, Microsoft was only associated with SQL Database. With Azure, Microsoft has not only embraced other database engines, including opensource, it has also recognized the need for modern databases that are better catered to handle semi-structured and unstructured data. Therefore, in 2017, Microsoft announced the release of Azure Cosmos DB.

Azure Cosmos DB is Microsoft's proprietary database service in the cloud that is

- Globally distributed
- Multimodel
- Schema agnostic (which is why it is a better fit for semi and non-structured data)
- Horizontally scalable
- Extremely low latency (millisecond response times) backed by high-performance Solid State Drives (SSD)
- Configurable database consistency levels

Cosmos DB can generally be classified as a NoSQL database at scale.

Use Cases for Azure Cosmos DB

Now that you know the key characteristics of Azure Cosmos DB, we can explore the use cases that make Azure Cosmos DB the preferred data source. The commonly shared requirements among the use cases are the need for low latency, data availability on a global footprint, and data that does not adhere to a strict schema.

Internet of Things (IoT)

IoT devices are usually deployed for real-time monitoring purposes and are found in sensors scattered in various locations. The kind of data generated by IoT devices is often referred to as *streaming data* and comes in high-frequency bursts. A low-latency database that supports real-time analytics is a key requirement for IoT deployments. An IoT solution generally uses a Cosmos DB that is front-ended by an Azure IoT hub or Azure event hub. The IoT hub or event hub can buffer incoming data streams at a rate of millions of events per second before funneling the data to Azure Cosmos DB for ad hoc querying.

Retail

Referring to our discussion at the beginning of this chapter, one of the data trends is the increase in semi-structured data types. The rise and expansion of eCommerce in the retail space is one area that is driving this data trend. Like the backpack product example, attributes of products that retailers carry change frequently over time. Being schema-agnostic makes Cosmos DB a great option for a product database.

If a retailer has a worldwide footprint, which is pretty much any retailer that sells on the Internet, and then a globally accessible database is desired for performance purposes. In this use case, the ability to configure a strong data consistency level that ensures site visitors always read the latest globally committed write may be important, so the latest inventory level or order is always being read.

Web and Social

Social media and websites are generally global services, so naturally, the globally distributed nature of Azure Cosmos DB makes it an ideal choice. Furthermore, data representing social interactions and relationships are better represented as a graph with nodes and vertices. Azure Cosmos DB, being a multimodel database, can be deployed with the Gremlin API so the data can be mapped as graphs.

Hands-on: Deploying Azure Cosmos DB

The comprehensive documentation for Azure Cosmos DB is at `https://docs.microsoft.com/en-us/azure/cosmos-db/`.

1. In the Azure portal and click **Create a resource.**
2. Type **Cosmos** in the search box and select **Azure Cosmos DB** in the search results, and then click **Create.**
3. Select the subscription that house the Cosmos DB, as referenced in Figure 17-25 and select an existing resource group or create a new one for this instance of Cosmos DB deployment.
4. Provide an account name, which must be globally unique. For this exercise, we named our Cosmos DB bot-conversations-cosmos.
5. Click the API drop-down menu and review the options. Select **Core (SQL).**

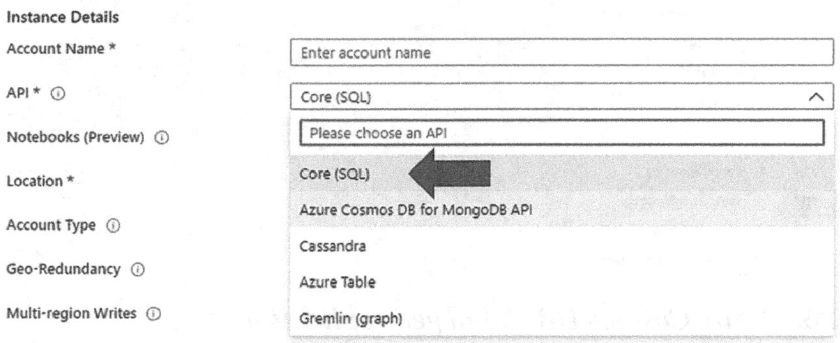

***Figure 17-25.** Deploying Azure Cosmos DB with MongoDB API*

6. Turn off the Notebooks option and select a location closest to you.
7. For account type, select **Non-Production**. This only customized the user interface in the portal by immediately enabling Geo-Redundancy and Multi-region Writes. It does not affect the SLA or the cost of the service instance, aside from the fact that Geo-Redundancy and Multi-region Writes are enabled.
8. Select the latest version.
9. Leave Availability Zones disabled, and then click **Review + create**.
10. Click **Create**.
11. Once the database is deployed, click **Go to resource**.

You have now deployed an instance of Azure Cosmos DB. Before populating it with data, let's explore some of the database features mentioned earlier.

1. Select the **Replicate data globally** menu option located under Settings. You should see a checkbox on a map indicating where your instance of Azure Cosmos DB was deployed, as seen in Figure 17-26. It should be in the location where you selected in the previous exercise.

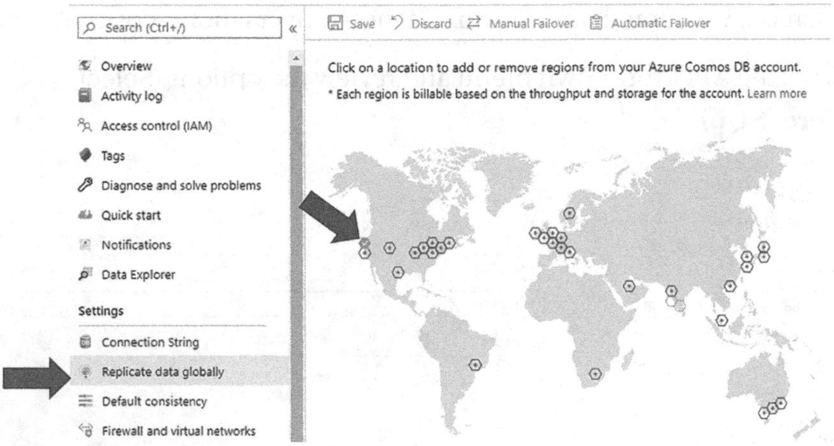

***Figure 17-26.** Azure Cosmos DB global geo-replication*

2. Other locations where you can replicate Azure Cosmos DB to are indicated by the pins on the map. Hover over a pin to identify the location.

3. Click a pin to select a location you wish to replicate Azure Cosmos DB in. For this exercise, we selected the Southeast Asia region.

4. Once you have selected a region to replicate the database in, by default, the new region is read-only. To enable read and write to the region, click **Enable for Multi-region writes**.

5. Click **Save**. Azure Cosmos DB starts replicating the database to the region that you have selected. In our exercise, the database is being replicated in Southeast Asia.

6. To disable geo-replication, click the newly replicated region, and then click **Save** again.

You have seen how easy it is to replicate to multiple locations throughout the world. Let's now use Azure

Cosmos DB to store data.

Hands-on: Using Azure Cosmos DB to Store Bot Conversation History

Remember Joe the Bot from Chapter 15? We are going to add more capabilities to Joe with the help of Cosmos DB. What we do in this exercise is to store conversation history. So, what are the benefits of storing bot conversation history?

Conversation history is a good source for analytics. For example, with conversation history, we can send that to Azure Cognitive Services for sentiment analysis to determine how satisfied customers are with their engagement with Joe. We can also mine conversation history to determine what were the top issues being asked. From a more traditional standpoint, conversation history may be a regulatory requirement or would be helpful in audits. There are many good reasons why conversation history should be stored.

Bot conversation history is stored in JSON format and is a built-in capability of the Bot Framework, known as the Bot Framework State Service. The conversations are stored as transactions into a memory object which we write to storage at the end of the session, in this case, Cosmos DB.

1. Launch Visual Studio and open the project for Joe the Bot from Chapter 15. If you rather pull the completed project from GitHub, go to `https://gitHub/harris-soh-copeland-puca/JoeTheBot` and clone the TrackConversation feature branch.

2. Add the Microsoft.Bot.Builder.Azure NuGet package.

3. In Solution Explorer, right-click the folder named Bots. Click **Add** and select **Class**.

4. Name the class **TrackConversations.cs** and add the following code to the TrackConversation class.

```
public class TrackConversation
{
    // Tracking what users have said to the bot
```

```
        public List<string> ConversationList { get; } = new
        List<string>();

        // The number of conversational turns that have occurred
        public int TurnNumber { get; set; } = 0;

        // Create concurrency control where this is used.
        public string ETag { get; set; } = "*";
    }
```

5. Open the QnABot.cs file and add the following headers to the top of the file.

```
using Microsoft.Bot.Builder.Azure;
using System.Linq;
```

6. In the QnABot class, add the following code containing values needed to connect to Cosmos DB as seen in Figure 17-27. You can get the Cosmos DB information from the Azure portal, as seen in Figure 17-28.

```
public class QnABot<T> : ActivityHandler where T : Microsoft.Bot.
Builder.Dialogs.Dialog
    {
        protected readonly BotState ConversationState;
        protected readonly Microsoft.Bot.Builder.Dialogs.Dialog
        Dialog;
        protected readonly BotState UserState;
        //Cosmos DB connection properties
        private const string CosmosServiceEndpoint = "<CosmosDB_
        URI>";
        private const string CosmosDBKey = "<CosmosDBKey>";
        private const string CosmosDBDatabaseName =
        "<CosmosDBName>";
        private const string CosmosDBCollectionName = "bot-
        storage";
```

```
// Create Cosmos DB  Storage.
private static readonly CosmosDbStorage query = new
CosmosDbStorage(new CosmosDbStorageOptions
{
    AuthKey = CosmosDBKey,
    CollectionId = CosmosDBCollectionName,
    CosmosDBEndpoint = new Uri(CosmosServiceEndpoint),
    DatabaseId = CosmosDBDatabaseName,
});
//End Cosmos DB connection properties
```

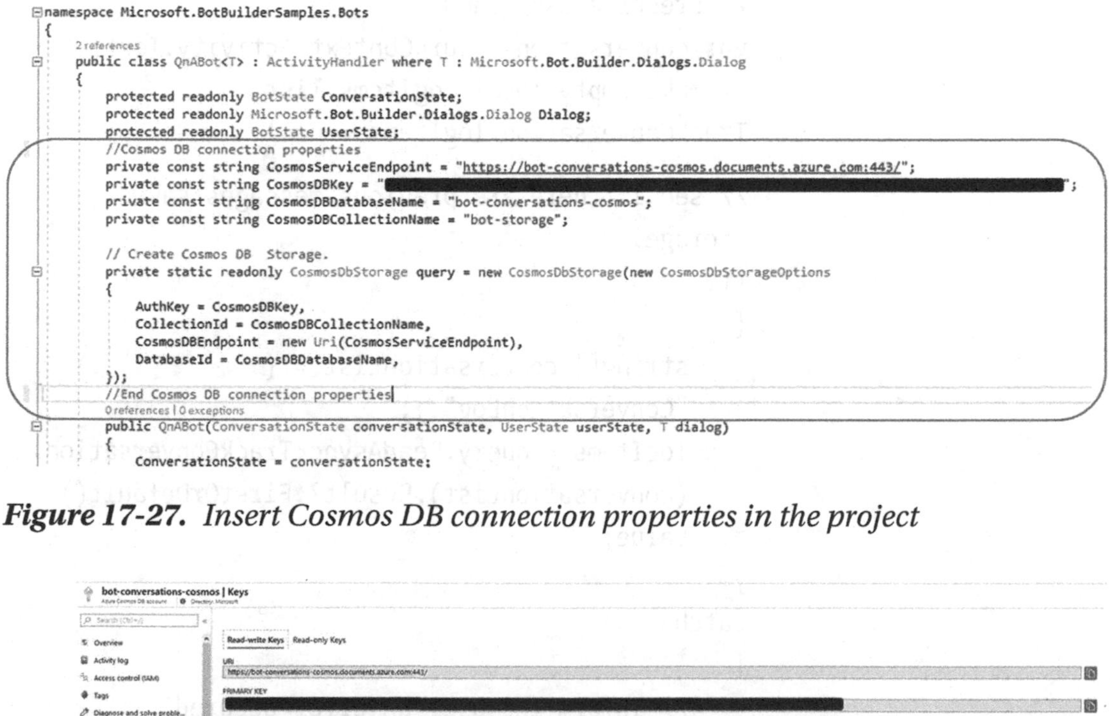
namespace Microsoft.BotBuilderSamples.Bots
{
2 references
public class QnABot<T> : ActivityHandler where T : Microsoft.Bot.Builder.Dialogs.Dialog
{
protected readonly BotState ConversationState;
protected readonly Microsoft.Bot.Builder.Dialogs.Dialog Dialog;
protected readonly BotState UserState;
//Cosmos DB connection properties
private const string CosmosServiceEndpoint = "https://bot-conversations-cosmos.documents.azure.com:443/";
private const string CosmosDBKey = "[redacted]";
private const string CosmosDBDatabaseName = "bot-conversations-cosmos";
private const string CosmosDBCollectionName = "bot-storage";
// Create Cosmos DB Storage.
private static readonly CosmosDbStorage query = new CosmosDbStorage(new CosmosDbStorageOptions
{
AuthKey = CosmosDBKey,
CollectionId = CosmosDBCollectionName,
CosmosDBEndpoint = new Uri(CosmosServiceEndpoint),
DatabaseId = CosmosDBDatabaseName,
});
//End Cosmos DB connection properties
0 references | 0 exceptions
public QnABot(ConversationState conversationState, UserState userState, T dialog)
{
ConversationState = conversationState;

Figure 17-27. *Insert Cosmos DB connection properties in the project*

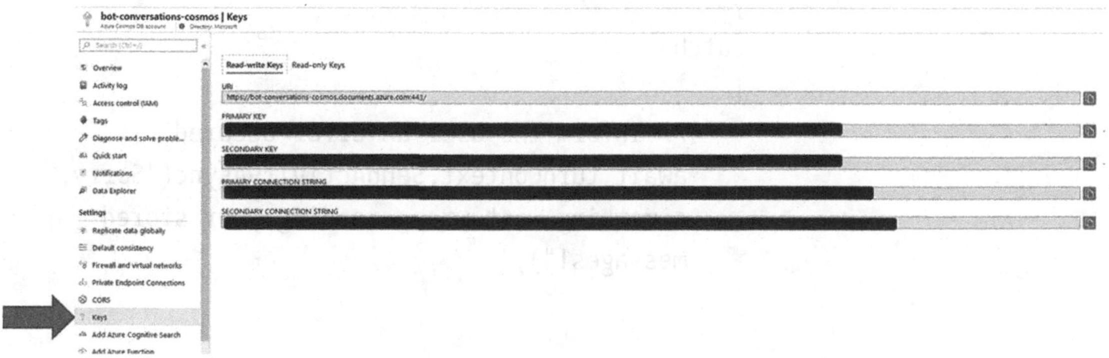
bot-conversations-cosmos | Keys
Overview
Activity log
Access control (IAM)
Tags
Diagnose and solve proble...
Quick start
Notifications
Data Explorer
Settings
Replicate data globally
Default consistency
Firewall and virtual networks
Private Endpoint Connections
CORS
Keys
Add Azure Cognitive Search
Read-write Keys
Read-only Keys
URI
https://bot-conversations-cosmos.documents.azure.com:443/
PRIMARY KEY
[redacted]
SECONDARY KEY
[redacted]
PRIMARY CONNECTION STRING
[redacted]
SECONDARY CONNECTION STRING
[redacted]

Figure 17-28. *Keys for Cosmos DB from the Azure portal*

7. In QnABot.cs, modify the OnMessageActivityAsync method so it looks like this.

```
protected override async Task OnMessageActivityAsync(ITur
nContext<IMessageActivity> turnContext, CancellationToken
cancellationToken)
        {    // Run the Dialog with the new message Activity.
            await Dialog.RunAsync(turnContext, ConversationState.
            CreateProperty<DialogState>(nameof(DialogState)),
            cancellationToken);

            {
                // preserve user input.
                var conversation = turnContext.Activity.Text;
                // make empty local logitems list.
                TrackConversation logItems = null;

                // see if there are previous messages saved in
                storage.
                try
                {
                    string[] conversationList = {
                    "ConversationLog" };
                    logItems = query.ReadAsync<TrackConversation>
                    (conversationList).Result?.FirstOrDefault().
                    Value;
                }
                catch
                {
                    // Inform the user an error occured.
                    await turnContext.SendActivityAsync("Sorry,
                    something went wrong reading your stored
                    messages!");
                }
```

```
// If no stored messages were found, create and
store a new entry.
if (logItems is null)
{
    // add the current utterance to a new object.
    logItems = new TrackConversation();
    logItems.ConversationList.Add(conversation);
    // set initial turn counter to 1.
    logItems.TurnNumber++;

    // Create Dictionary object to hold received
    user messages.
    var changes = new Dictionary<string, object>();
    {
        changes.Add("ConversationLog", logItems);
    }
    try
    {
        // Save the user message to your Storage.
        await query.WriteAsync(changes,
        cancellationToken);
    }
    catch
    {
        // Inform the user an error occured.
        await turnContext.SendActivityAsync("Sorry,
        something went wrong storing your message!");
    }
}
// Else, our Storage already contained saved user
messages, add new one to the list.
else
{
    // add new message to list of messages to
    display.
    logItems.ConversationList.Add(conversation);
```

```
                        // increment turn counter.
                        logItems.TurnNumber++;

                        // Create Dictionary object to hold new list
                        of messages.
                        var changes = new Dictionary<string,
                        object>();
                        {
                            changes.Add("ConversationLog", logItems);
                        };

                        try
                        {
                            // Save new list to your Storage.
                            await query.WriteAsync(changes,
                            cancellationToken);
                        }
                        catch
                        {
                            // Inform the user an error occured.
                            await turnContext.SendActivityAsync("Sorry,
                            something went wrong storing your
                            message!");
                        }
                    }
                }
            }
```

8. Debug the bot and test it with the Bot Emulator by carrying out a conversation, as you did in Chapter 15.
9. After a few lines of conversation, end your session and go to the Azure portal.
10. Go to the Cosmos DB resource and click **Data Explorer**.
11. Expand the database, followed by the container, and finally, Items.

12. Click **ConversationLogin** the Items. You should see the conversation that you carried out with Joe the Bot tracked, as seen in Figure 17-29.

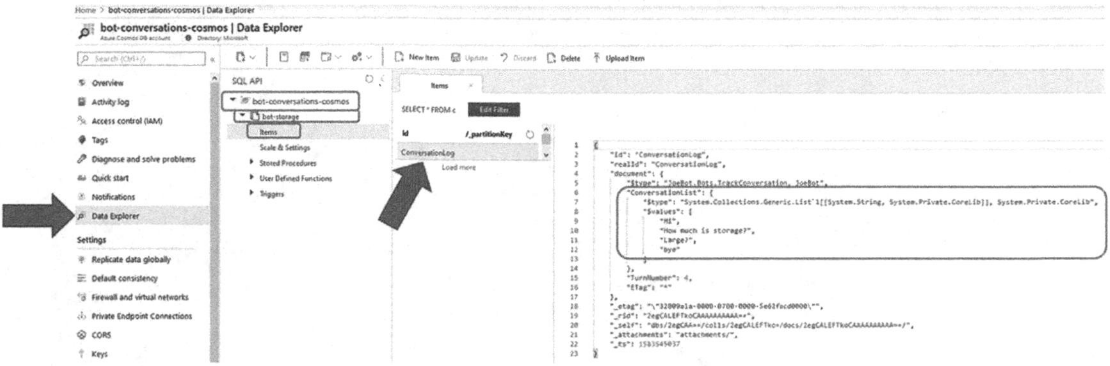

Figure 17-29. *Viewing the tracked conversation in Cosmos DB*

This concludes our discussion on and hands-on implementation of Azure Cosmos DB. Documentation on Azure Cosmos DB is on GitHub at `https://github.com/harris-soh-copeland-puca/azure-docs/tree/master/articles/cosmos-db`.

Summary

In this chapter, we only had time to cover Azure SQL Database and Azure Cosmos DB. We selected these two databases because they are the most prominent deployments in many of the projects we encounter today. However, keep in mind that Azure data services are very extensive and provide many other databases, including open source. We also omitted covering Azure Synapse in this chapter because it is not possible to do so in a limited amount of space. Data warehousing and analytics is a specialized topic that is better served by other resources, but in Chapter 16, we introduced advanced analytics using machine learning, deep learning, and Azure Databricks. In Chapter 19, you are introduced to data engineering, where we take a deeper look at data pipelines, data manipulation, and the concepts of a modern data warehouse, where we spend some more time discussing Azure Synapse.

Now that you know about the different data services in Azure, especially Azure SQL Database, in the next chapter, let's talk about strategies, tools, and best practices for migrating on-premises databases to Azure.

PART VI

Azure Services for Application Developers

CHAPTER 18

Migrating On-Premises Databases to Azure

In Chapter 17, we introduced database options and the benefits of consuming database services as a PaaS versus managing database servers.

This chapter covers the options that are available when migrating databases residing on database servers to Azure database PaaS. We mainly focus on migrating Microsoft SQL Servers to Azure SQL Databases, thereby eliminating the overhead of managing servers while realizing better service-level agreements.

We explore the migration tools, strategies, and options; going into detail about database migration is beyond the scope of this book. This is because database migrations usually impact applications, and a broader discovery to assess application dependencies should take place.

Bear in mind, however, that while the migration itself may be a complex activity, there are extremely very few scenarios where the needed capabilities can only be met if the databases remain on-premises. The benefits realized from having databases moved to Azure as a PaaS are worth the time taken to undertake such a migration.

Note While we can only cover the core migration tools like DMA and DMS in this chapter, Microsoft has a comprehensive Database Migration Guide that provides step-by-step guidance for many migration scenarios, including third-party source databases. The guide is at `https://datamigration.microsoft.com/`.

J. Soh et al., *Microsoft Azure*, https://doi.org/10.1007/978-1-4842-5958-0_18

Data Migration Assistant (DMA)

A good first strategy is to assess whether an on-premises database is a good candidate to migrate to Azure.

Microsoft provides a free tool called the Data Migration Assistant (DMA), which assesses the capabilities in a Microsoft SQL database to see if any issues need to be addressed before migrating the database to Azure SQL Database.

DMA tells you which features in use by the on-premises Microsoft SQL database will not be present in Azure SQL Database.

DMA is a good first step in the planning process to inventory and assess all the on-premises Microsoft SQL servers.

Not only is DMA an assessment tool, but it is also a migration tool that can copy the schema and the data from an on-premises database to Microsoft SQL Database; however, the Data Migration Assistant is designed as an assessment tool, and while it can serve as a data and schema migration tool, it is not designed to carry out an actual migration at scale. To execute migration at scale, please read the section on Database Migration Service later in this chapter.

We can also use DMA to migrate an on-premises SQL database to a Microsoft SQL Server on an Azure VM, but this scenario does not give you the benefits from using a PaaS, but we wanted to mention it anyway because there are scenarios where it is desirable to carry out this phased migration approach, for example, failing or aging hardware with databases that have migration blockers that may take time to remediate.

Hands-on: Setting up a Lab

In this exercise, you set up a lab environment that contains the following.

- A virtual machine with SQL Server 2016 SP1 or later installed
- A sample database that you can use DMA to analyze and migrate to Azure SQL Database

Let's start the exercise.

1. Create a VM or use an existing VM and install SQL Server 2016 SP1 or later.

2. Go to our GitHub repo and download the Wide World Importers sample OLTP database (WideWorldImporters-Full.bak) from `https://github.com/Microsoft/sql-server-samples/releases/tag/wide-world-importers-v1.0`
3. Copy WideWorldImporters-Full.bak to the program files\Microsoft SQL Server\MSSQL14.MSSQLSERVER\MSSQL\Backup directory.
4. Launch SQL Management Studio and connect to the Microsoft SQL Server.
5. Right-click **Databases** and select **Restore Database**.
6. Select **Device** as the source of the restore.
7. Click the Device ellipses and select **File** as the backup media type.
8. Click **Add** and select the WideWorldImporters-Full.bak file. Click OK.
9. Click **OK** again to start the restore.
10. When the restore is complete, check that there is now a WideWorldImporters database with sample tables.

Hands-on: Using the Data Migration Assistant for Assessment

In this exercise, you install the Data Migration Assistant and use it to assess the WideWorldImporters database.

1. Download and install the latest version of Microsoft Data Migration Assistant from `www.microsoft.com/en-us/download/details.aspx?id=53595`.
2. Launch the Data Migration Assistant. Then click + to start a new project.
3. Select **Assessment** as the project type and provide a name for the project. For this exercise, name the project **WideWorldImporters-Assessment**.

4. Select **Database Engine** as the assessment type, **SQL Server** as the source server type, and **Azure SQL Database** as the target server type, as shown in Figure 18-1.

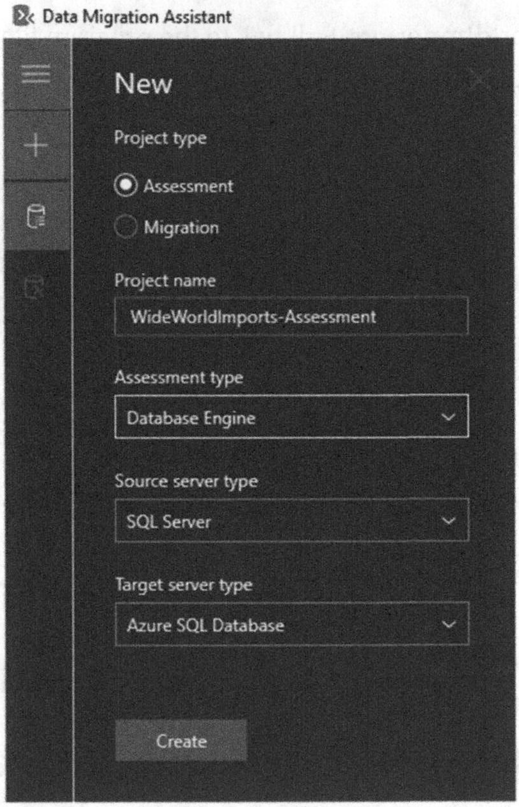

Figure 18-1. *Creating a new project in DMA*

5. Click **Create**.

6. You are presented with the different types of reports available, as referenced in Figure 18-2. Select both the **Check database compatibility** report and the **Check feature parity** report, and then click **Next**.

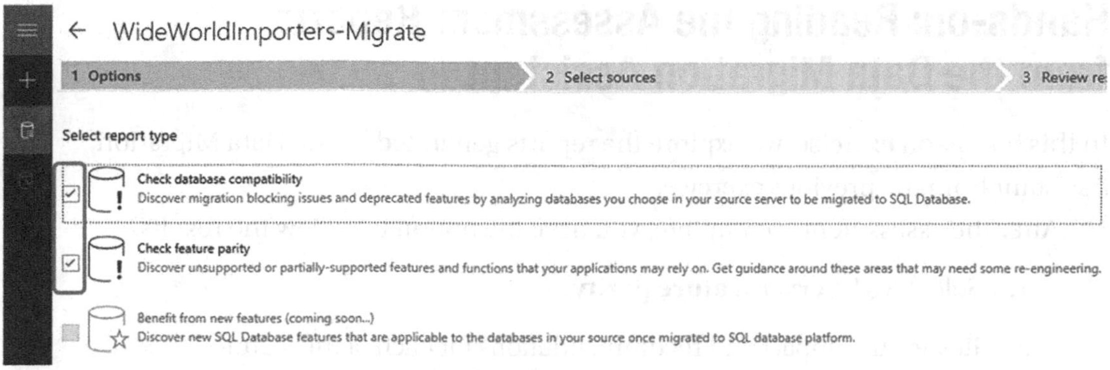

Figure 18-2. *Report types available in DMA*

7. Provide the connection information, as referenced in Figure 18-3 for the Microsoft SQL Server hosting the WideWorldImporters database, and then click **Connect**.

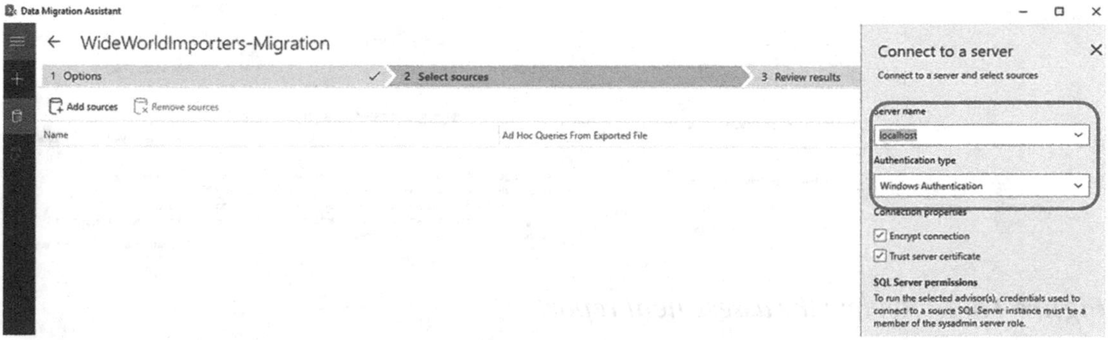

Figure 18-3. *Provide the connection information for the Microsoft SQL Database Server*

8. Select the WideWorldImporters database by checking the box next to it, and then click **Add**.

9. Click **Start Assessment**.

It may take a few minutes for the assessment to complete, but you have successfully initiated the assessment process. Next, we review the reports from the assessment.

Hands-on: Reading the Assessment Reports from the Data Migration Assistant

In this hands-on exercise, we explore the reports generated by the Data Migration Assistant from the previous exercise.

After the assessment is complete, you have the option to review the results.

1. Select **SQL Server feature parity**.
2. Review the impact and recommendations for each of the feature parity issues discovered as referenced in Figure 18-4. Pay close attention to the number of objects impacted because that is an indicator of the severity of the impacts.

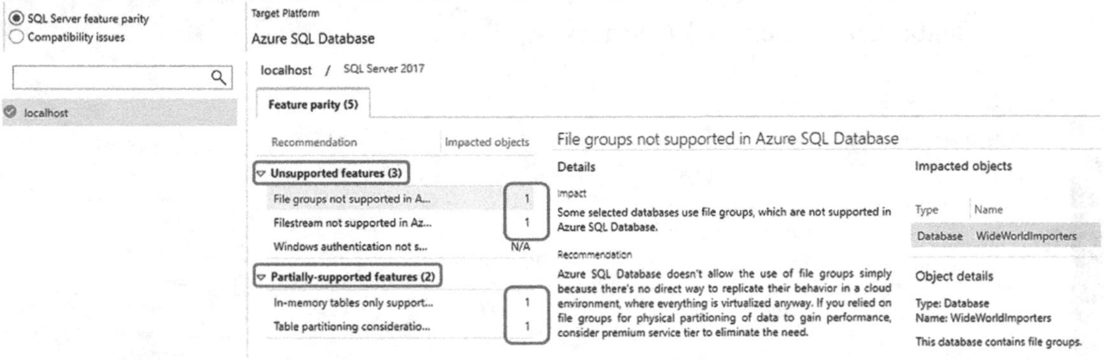

Figure 18-4. *Review the assessment report*

3. Repeat the same steps for the Compatibility issues report.

You might be wondering about the Upload to Azure Migrate option. We explore it next. Do not exit out of the Data Migration Assistant yet. Go to the next exercise.

Hands-on: Azure Migrate

Azure Migrate is a service that provides a central hub to manage all migration activities. It is not restricted to databases and includes servers, web applications, and virtual desktops. However, we are focusing on databases since that is what this chapter is all about. More information about Azure Migrate is at `https://azure.microsoft.com/en-us/services/azure-migrate/` and in our GitHub repo at `https://github.com/harris-soh-copeland-puca/azure-docs/tree/master/articles/migrate`.

1. Log in to the Azure portal and deploy Azure Migrate. We assume that you are familiar with deploying services in Azure, and so we will not go into detail on how to do so.

2. Once an Azure Migrate instance has been provisioned, go to the resource, and select **Databases**.

3. Add a tool and provide information about the project, as shown in Figure 18-5. Click **Next**.

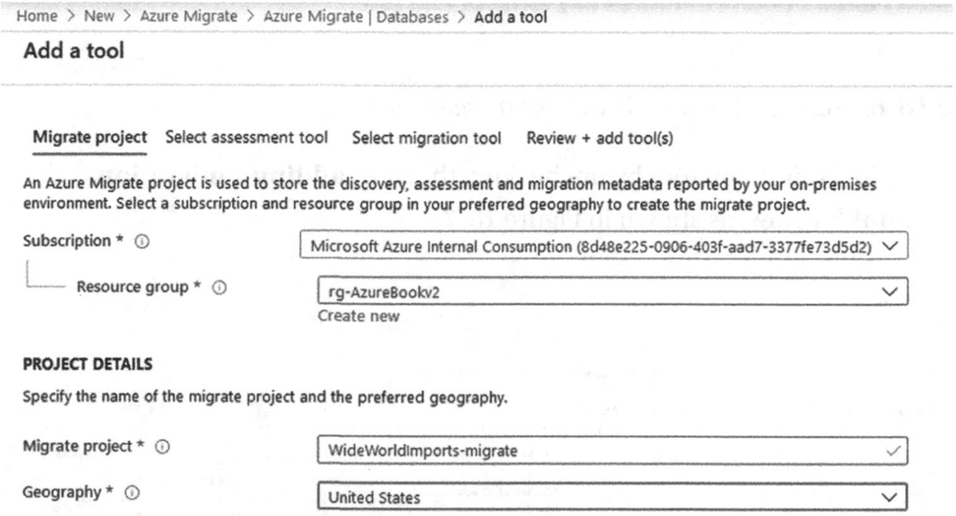

***Figure 18-5.** Set up the migration project*

4. Select **Azure Migrate: Database Assessment**, as shown in Figure 18-6, and then click **Next**.

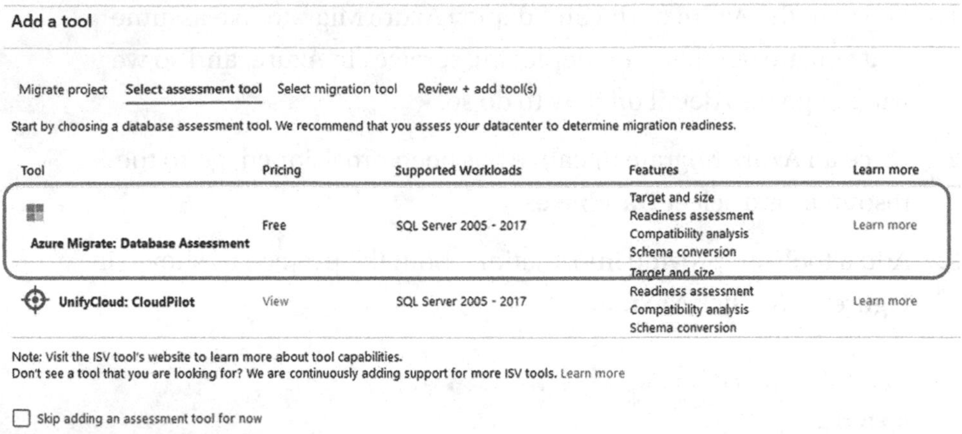

Figure 18-6. *Azure Migrate Database assessment*

5. Add a migration tool by unchecking the **Skip adding a migration tool for now**, as shown in Figure 18-7.

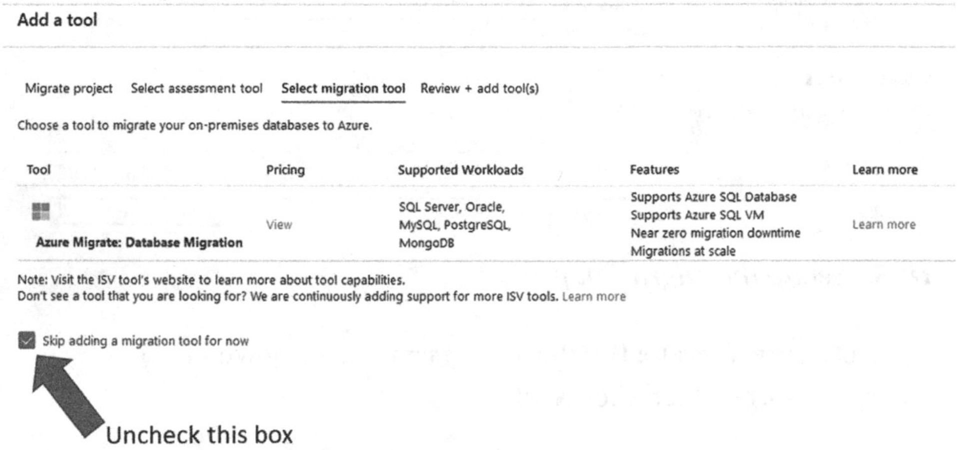

Figure 18-7. *Install a migration tool. Uncheck the box*

Once the tool is installed, you have Database Migration Service deployed in your Azure subscription.

We cover the Database Migration Service later in the chapter. For now, let's return to DMA and continue where we left off in the previous exercise.

Hands-on: Uploading an Assessment Report to Azure Migrate

1. In Data Migration Assistant, click **Upload to Azure Migrate**.
2. Select the subscription, and it should find the Azure Migrate Project created in the previous exercise.
3. Click **Upload**.
4. Go to Azure Migrate in the portal and select **databases**. Then click the refresh icon to see the report in Azure. As you carry out more assessments of other databases, uploading the reports to Azure Migrate gives you a centralized location for your reports.

Hands-on: Migrate Database Using Data Migration Assistant

In this exercise, you use DMA to migrate the schema and data from the WideWorldImporters database residing on a Microsoft SQL Server to Azure SQL Database.

1. Create a database. Using the Azure SQL Database server from Chapter 17, create an empty database and name it **WideWorldImporters**. Assign it to the elastic pool.
2. Start a new Data Migration Assistant project, but this time select **Migration** as the project type, as referenced in Figure 18-8, **SQL Server** as the source server type, **Azure SQL Database** as the target server type, and **Schema and data** as the migration scope.

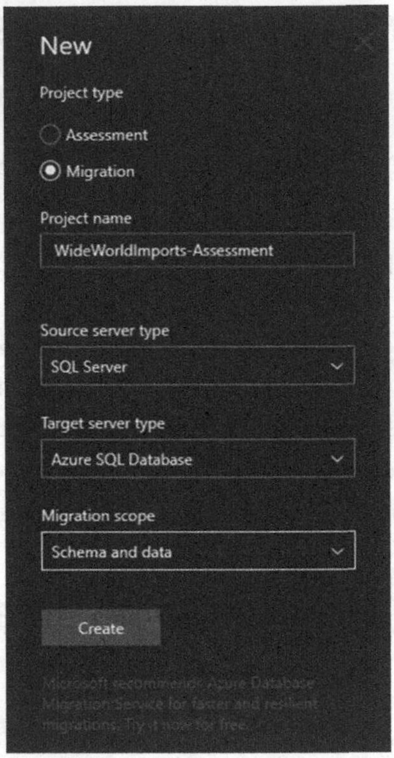

***Figure 18-8.** Setting up a migration project using DMA*

Note Notice the tip at the bottom that recommends using Database Migration Service because it is faster. That is indeed the case.

---

3. Click **Create**.

4. Provide a connection to the SQL server, and then click Connect.

5. Select **WideWorldImporters**, and then click **Next**.

6. For the target server, enter the connection information and credentials to connect to the Azure SQL Database server in your Azure subscription, as shown in Figure 18-9.

***Figure 18-9.** Credentials to the Azure SQL Database server*

7. Click **Connect**.
8. Select the empty WideWorldImporters database created earlier, and then click **Next**.
9. After the roles and schema have been generated, click **Generate SQL script**.
10. Click **Deploy schema**, as referenced in Figure 18-10. The progress of the deployment is shown in a pane to the right. Take note of any errors so that you can remediate them separately after migration.

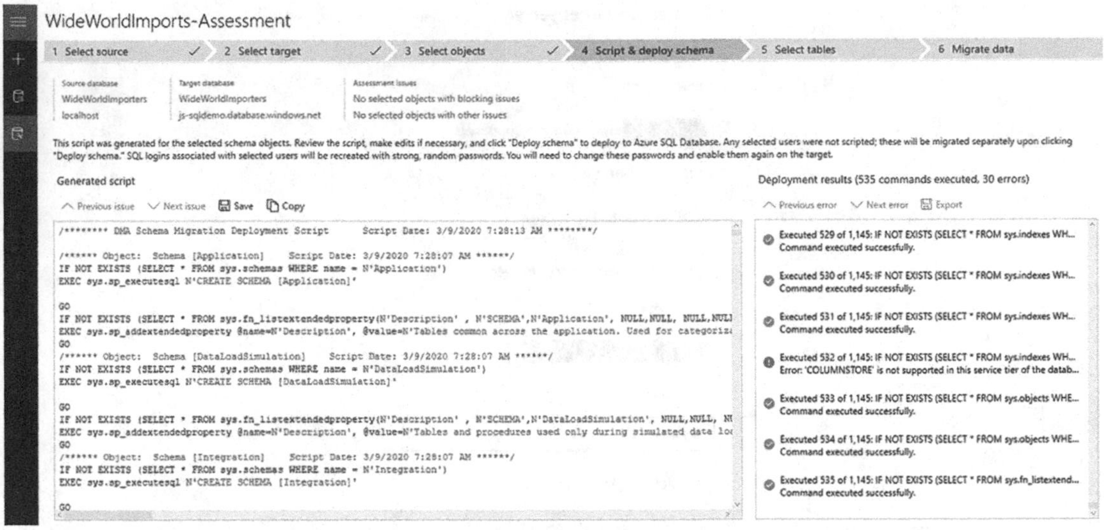

Figure 18-10. *Schema deployed to Azure SQL Database*

11. Click **Migrate data**.

12. Optional step. If you go to the Azure portal and look at the WideWorldImporters Azure SQL Database using the Query editor, as shown in Figure 18-11, you see all the tables. If you run a query, there will not be any rows because you have only created the schema at this point.

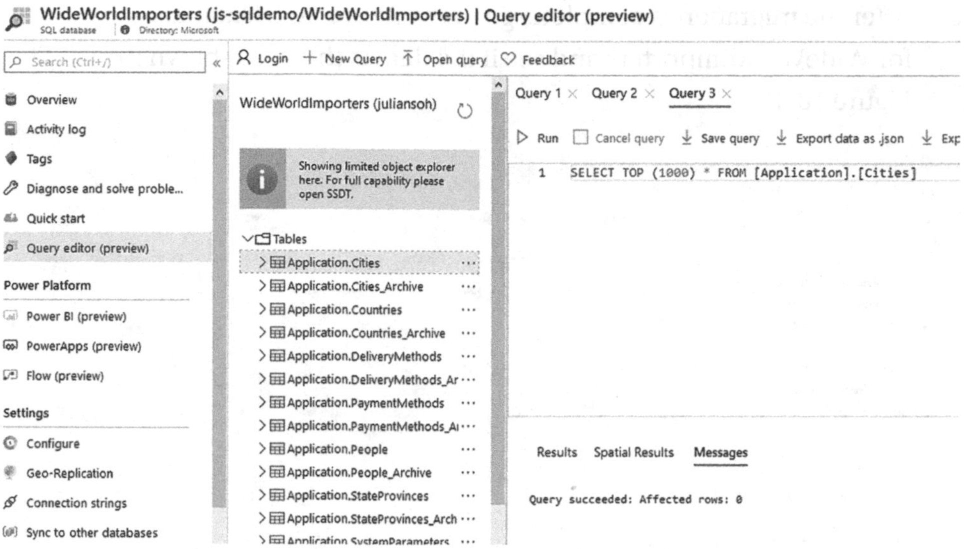

***Figure 18-11.** Viewing the WideWorldImports database in Azure SQL Database*

13. Click **Start data migration in Data Migration Assistant.**
14. Note the progress of the data migration as the database is migrating to Azure, as referenced in Figure 18-12.

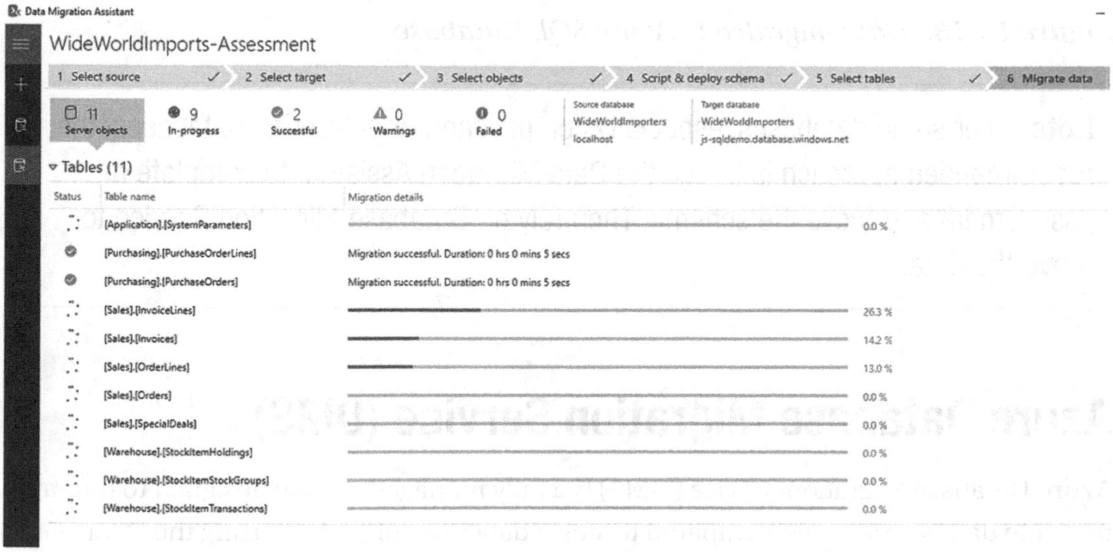

***Figure 18-12.** Data migrating to Azure SQL Database by DMA*

15. After the migration is complete, go to the Azure SQL Database for WideWorldImporters and see if the data is there, as shown in Figure 18-13.

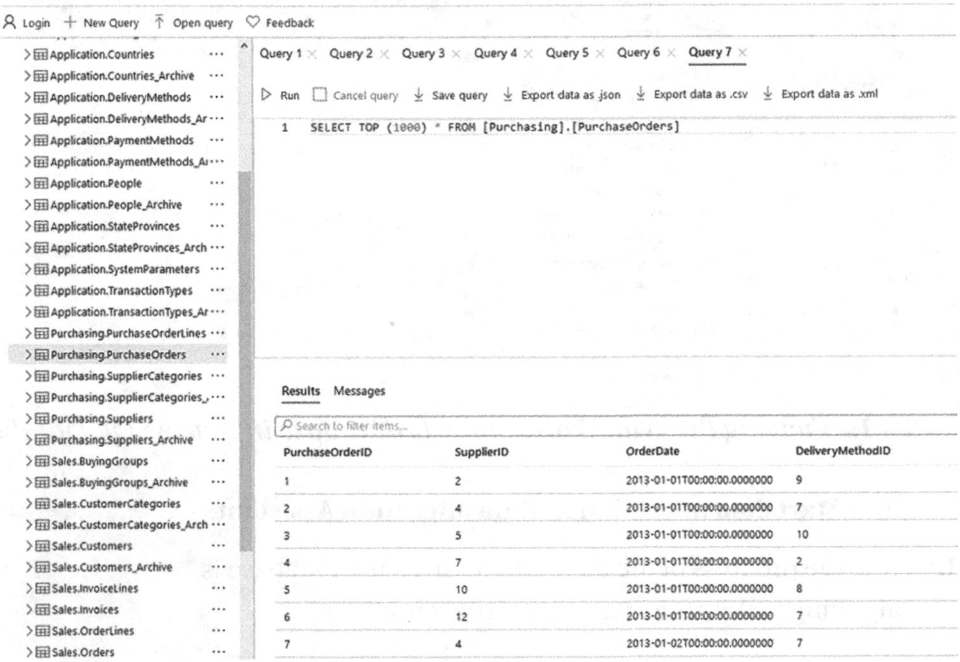

Figure 18-13. *Data migrated to Azure SQL Database*

Note For some databases, especially complex and or enterprise databases, the recommended approach is to use the Data Migration Assistant to complete an assessment and move the schema. Then rely on Database Migration Service to move the data.

Azure Database Migration Service (DMS)

Azure Database Migration Service (DMS) is a fully managed service designed to migrate multiple database sources, compared to single database migrations using the Data Migration Assistant.

Azure Database Migration Service can migrate from many database sources, unlike DMA.

The Azure Database Migration Service does rely on Data Migration Assistant to generate an assessment prior to performing the migration and schema migration. Because Azure Database Migration Service can synchronize data to facilitate a cutover at a specific time, it is the preferred choice for most enterprise scenarios.

Enterprises use Azure Database Migration Service to initiate the migration of a production database to the new service. Data is moved, and when the move is complete, the data continues to be synchronized in both environments until a cutover is initiated.

Hands-on: Deploying Azure Database Migration Service

Before you can deploy an instance of Azure Database Migration Service, you need to activate the service by registering the Microsoft.DataMigration resource provider.

1. Go to the Azure portal and type **subscriptions** in the search box at the top of the portal. Select **Subscriptions** in the search results.
2. For steps 3 to 7, refer to Figure 18-14 for reference.

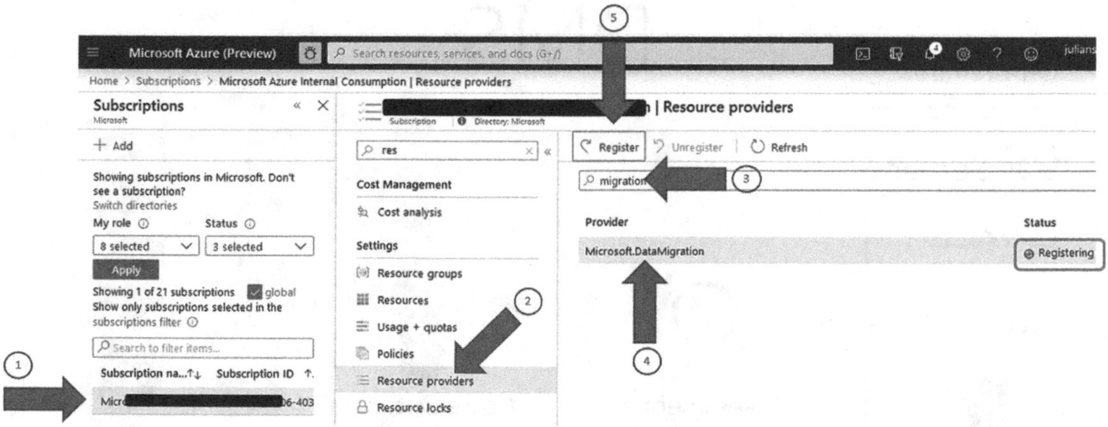

***Figure 18-14.** Registering the Microsoft.DataMigration resource provider*

3. Select the subscription in which you want to deploy the Azure Database Migration Service, and then select Resource providers.
4. Click Resource providers.
5. Type **migration** in the search box.
6. Select **Microsoft.DataMigration** in the Provider list.

7. Click **Register**, and wait until the status changes from Registering to Registered.

8. Once the Microsoft.DataMigration resource provider is registered, you can deploy Azure Migration Service by clicking **Create a resource on the Azure portal**. We assume that you are familiar with doing this by now, so we will not cover the steps on how to do it.

Hands-on: Using Azure Database Migration Service

After Azure Database Migration Service is deployed, you are ready to use the service to carry out the migration. Azure Database Migration Service uses the assessment from DMA to execute a migration.

Figure 18-15 shows the normal use of DMA as a precursor to using Azure Database Migration Service.

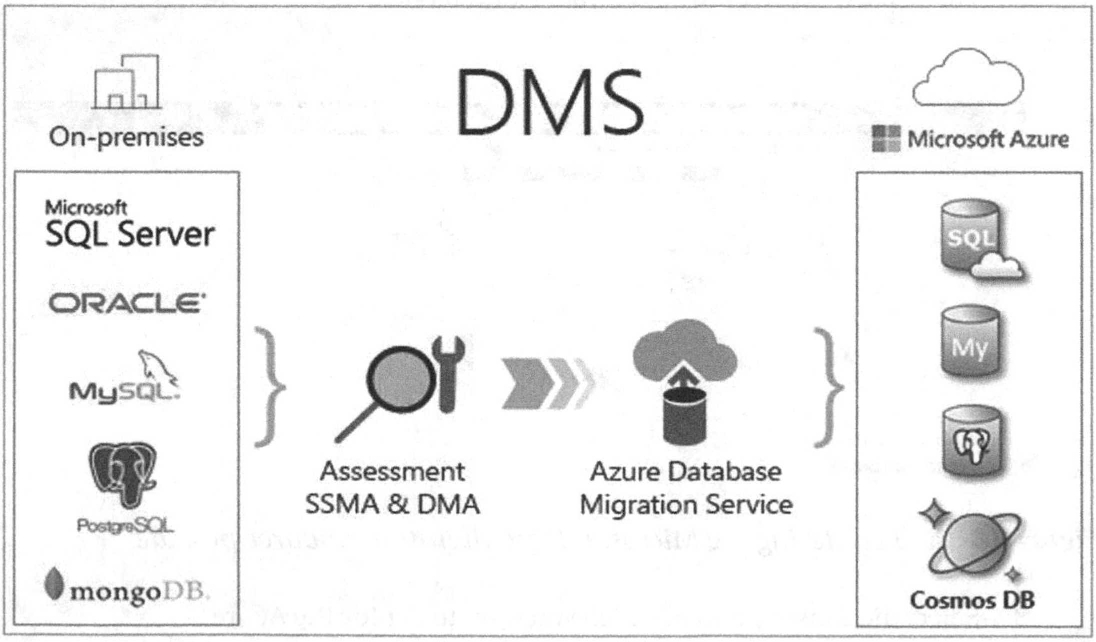

***Figure 18-15.** The use of DMA and Azure Database Migration Service*

For this exercise, you reuse the WideWorldImporters database assessment that you uploaded from the earlier exercise.

1. Go to the Azure Database Migration Service and click **+ New Migration Project**.
2. Enter WideWorldImporters-**migration** as the project name.
3. Click the **Source server type** drop-down menu and note the different database sources that Azure Database Migration Service uses, as shown in Figure 18-16. Select **SQL Server**.

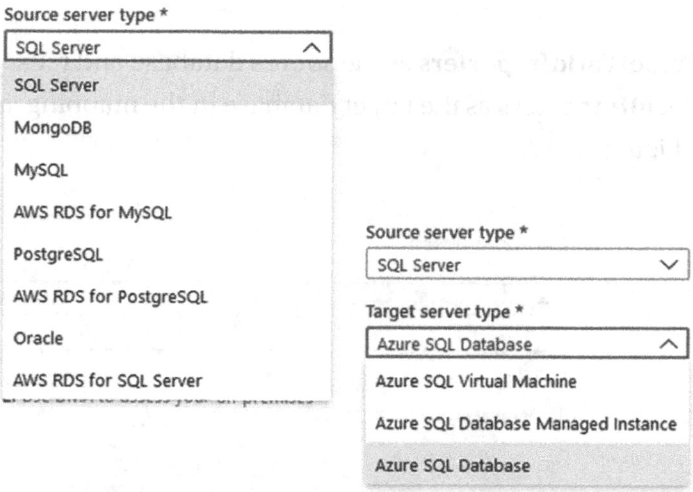

***Figure 18-16.** List of source and target database sources that DMS can use*

4. Click the **Target server type** drop-down menu and note the different database targets that Azure Database Migration Service can migrate to. Select **Azure SQL Database**.
5. Select **Offline data migration** for the type of activity. Azure Database Migration Service offers online or offline migration. With offline migrations, the database is stopped for the duration of the migration; application downtime begins at the time the migration starts. Online migrations carry out the migration while the database is not stopped until the final cutover. This limits the amount of downtime experienced by the applications.
6. Click **Save**.
7. Click **Create and run activity**.

8. Provide information for the following fields: Source SQL Server instance name, Authentication type, User Name, and Password.
9. Check the **Trust server certificate** box.
10. Click **Save.**
11. Provide connection and authentication information for the WideWorldImporters-dms Azure SQL Database server as the target.
12. Select **WideWorldImporters** as the source database and reuse **WideWorldImporters** as the target database in the mapping, as seen in Figure 18-17.

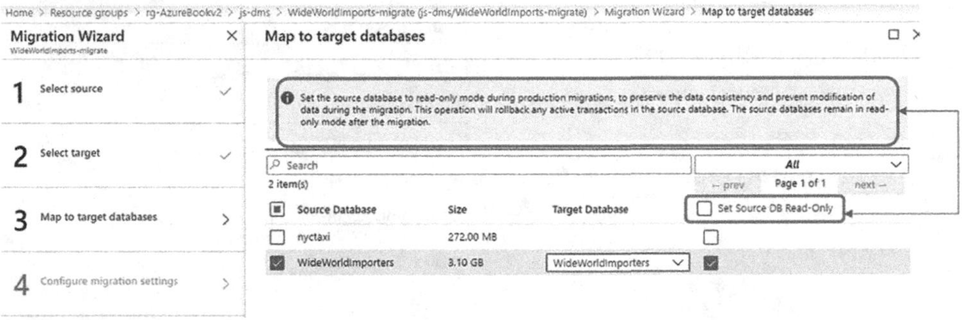

Figure 18-17. *Mapping the source and target databases in DMS*

13. Click **Save.**
14. Select the tables that you want to migrate. As warned, the target table is not empty. This is to be expected since you used DMA earlier to migrate data. The existing data in these tables are deleted before the migration, as seen in Figure 18-18.

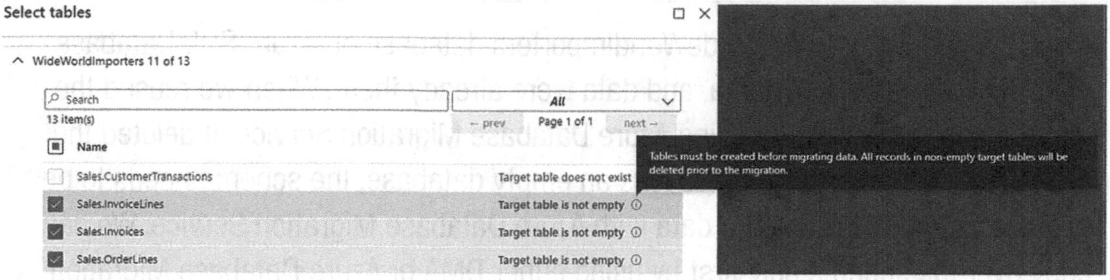

***Figure 18-18.** Warning that table is not empty, and data will be deleted*

15. Click **Save**.
16. Name the activity **WideWorldImporters-dms-migration.**
17. Click the **Validation** option and select **Validate my database(s)**, and then click **Save**.
18. Click **Run migration**.
19. The migration activity's progress is displayed in a new pane, as seen in Figure 18-19. Click **Refresh** to see the latest status.

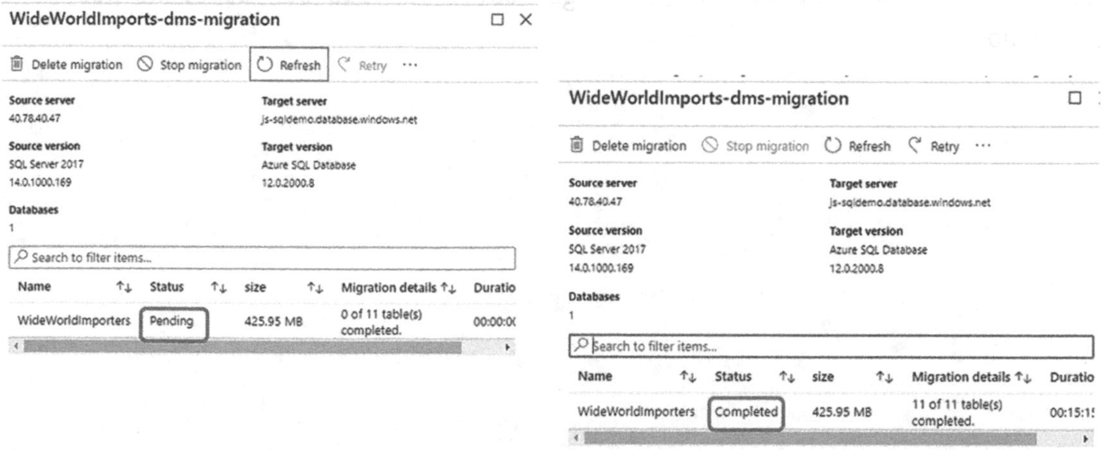

***Figure 18-19.** Status of DMS migration activity from pending to completed*

Note Since we used the WideWorldImporters database on Azure SQL Database with DMA, the tables, schema, and data were already there. When we reused the same database to migrate using Azure Database Migration Service, it deleted the data before the migration. If this was an empty database, the schema needs to be in place before migrating the data with Azure Database Migration Service. We can copy over the schema only first by using either DMA or Azure Database Migration Service.

Microsoft's comprehensive and continuously updated documentation for the Azure Database Migration Service is at `https://github.com/harris-soh-copeland-puca/azure-docs/tree/master/articles/dms`.

Summary

This chapter was written to provide you with a good primer on the different Azure Storage options. As a reminder, comprehensive documentation for all Microsoft Azure services is on our GitHub repo at `https://github.com/harris-soh-copeland-puca/azure-docs`.

CHAPTER 19

Data Engineering and the Modern Data Estate

In Chapter 17, we discussed data abundance and emerging data trends. Then in Chapter 18, we looked at database migration to Azure to better manage our data by providing more redundancy and protection. The reality is that data could exist on-premises, in the cloud, or both, and therefore there needs to be tools and processes to help manage the moving, copying, merging, and transforming of data.

Furthermore, when we talk about data in the cloud, we are not only talking about IaaS or PaaS. Data sources also reside in SaaS, such as in Office 365, Dynamics 365, SalesForce, SAP, and Oracle Service Cloud. Data in PaaS can reside in Amazon S3, Amazon Redshift, Google AdWords, or Azure SQL Database. So, data abundance is not only volume and type; it includes the vast diversity in storage and applications as well.

In this chapter, we explore the role of the data engineer and the tools and processes to manage this vast data estate. A data engineer prepares and cleans data so that it can be used in reports and analyses; this work is sometimes referred to as *data wrangling*. The quality of downstream workloads, including the success of advanced analytical capabilities like machine learning, depends on the quality of the available data, not just the quantity.

Terminology

There are a few new terms that describe the landscape of data engineering and the evolution of data transformation processes.

J. Soh et al., *Microsoft Azure*, https://doi.org/10.1007/978-1-4842-5958-0_19

Data Estate

Data estate is the term used to not only describe what type of data an organization owns and has access to but where that data resides. Traditionally, data is locked into individual databases and applications, which are often called *data silos* because it is very difficult to unlock that data. Today, data continues to exist in silos, but those silos expand from on-premises into different clouds. A successful digital transformation journey starts with knowing what kind of data you own, where it resides, and how to free it from silos so that it can unlock profound insights that can drive business transformation with AI and machine learning. So, the journey for digital transformation begins with knowing the state of your data estate.

Note There is a good tutorial about discovery and managing shadow IT in your network, which also addresses data silos. You can find this tutorial at `https://docs.microsoft.com/en-us/cloud-app-security/tutorial-shadow-it`.

Modern Data Warehouse: ELT vs. ETL

When we talk about data warehousing here, we are not talking about a product or a technology. We are talking about the strategies and processes that stages and transforms our data so that it is ready for data scientists and analysts to use.

Data in its most rudimentary form is known as *raw data*, and we put that raw data through stages of cleaning and enrichment, so that it becomes more meaningful. Traditionally, this is done via a process known as ETL (extract-transform-load). The idea behind ETL is to create a data pipeline that extracts data from some system, maps it to desired fields in another database, usually a data warehouse, and changes the format of the data to conform to the target field, and then load it into the database. Thus, going through the process exactly as implied by its name—ETL.

With the vast amount of data and the need to be dynamic, the modern approach is to reverse the order of the ETL to be agile. Therefore, instead of transforming the data and then loading it, the idea is to load the data as-is into some staging area and then transform it after the fact. This allows the data pipeline to operate efficiently in extracting or loading the data, since we are decoupling the transformation of the data from the process. If desired, which is often the case, a second separate pipeline can carry out the transformation, thereby streamlining the process. This process is known as ELT (extract-load-transform).

In many cases, ELT is driven by the speed of data; for example, take an IoT scenario. Bursting streaming data from IoT devices needs to be captured as soon as it comes in. There is no time to transform the data, and there may be different downstream systems that need all or a subset of this streaming data to make decisions, some of which need to be made in real time.

Modern Storage and Big Data

Storage for today's data needs to be reliable, fast, redundant, and capable of storing a lot of data (Big Data). Furthermore, it must be more economically viable than owning the infrastructure to deliver these capabilities. Moreover, storage for today's data needs must account for, and maximize the three Vs: volume, velocity, and variety.

Examples of storage options in Azure designed with these characteristics include Azure Blob, Azure Data Lake, Azure Queues, and Azure Tables. In this chapter, we focus primarily on Azure Blob storage and Azure Data Lake Services (ADLS).

Modern Data Platform Strategies

To optimize cost, one of the modern data platform strategies is to decouple storage from compute, which is a primary reason driving the modern data warehouse ELT approach. For example, if you load data into a SQL database, that database is supported by a database engine that relies on compute resources. By decoupling storage from compute, we can store raw and staging data in standalone storage like Azure Blob or Azure Data Lake Services.

Compute is used only when there is a need to analyze the data. PaaS services like Azure Databricks can access raw or staged data from Azure Blob or Azure Data Lake Services and spin up managed Spark clusters only when compute is needed. Upon being idle, the Spark clusters can be shut down without affecting the data storage. Likewise, data can be loaded into Azure Synapse, which is the new name for Azure Data Warehouse. Azure Synapse is a service that is built specifically for analysis. Therefore, it can load external data from Azure Blob using Polybase, and the database engine in Azure Synapse can also be paused. The strategy to decouple storage from compute can significantly reduce the cost of managing a data estate.

Separating storage from compute also gives organizations the ability to tier the data properly. Getting data to the end users at the right time can further affect costs by creating hot paths and cold paths. The data that is needed for real-time analysis goes to the hot path and therefore uses high-performance storage; whereas data that does not need to be analyzed in real time but still provides good insight (which is essential for machine learning and developing models) is served by a warm path.

In Chapter 14, we introduced Azure Blob and Azure Data Lake Services. We also looked at using Azure Storage Explorer to navigate and manage the data stored in Azure Blob and Azure Data Lake. In this chapter, we leverage the Azure Blob storage we created in Chapter 14 as part of our modern data warehouse pipeline process. The trend for future data solutions is to use Blob storage as the preferred source. Relational databases and sources are still common, but the trend for the three Vs continues to drive the adoption of Blob storage as the preferred source.

Azure Data Factory (ADF)

Azure Data Factory is a PaaS data orchestrator. The primary use case for Azure Data Factory is being the single tool to manage all data estate management activities, such as moving, copying, loading, transforming data. Azure Data Factory comes with many on-premises and cloud connectors to different types of data sources and applications to unlock the data within those sources. Like everything else, the best way to better understand Azure Data Factory is to get our hands dirty with some hands-on exercises. You start with an exercise to deploy Azure Data Factory and explore its interface and capabilities. Then there are more exercises based on a few use case scenarios.

We have also forked a copy of Microsoft's documentation for Azure Data Factory to our GitHub repo at `https://github.com/harris-soh-copeland-puca/azure-docs/tree/master/articles/data-factory`.

Hands-on: Installing Azure Data Factory

In this first exercise, you deploy an instance of Azure Data Factory and explore its user interface (UI) and some of Azure Data Factory's capabilities.

1. From the Azure portal, click **Create a resource**.
2. Type **Data Factory** in the search box, and then click **Data Factory** in the search results.

3. Click **Create**.

4. Give this instance of Azure Data Factory a globally unique name.

5. Keep V2 as the version to deploy.

6. Place this Azure Data Factory in an existing resource group or create a new one.

7. Pick a location closest to you.

8. Uncheck the checkbox to enable Git.

Note Git is a source and change control technology that can protect the artifacts in Azure Data Factory, such as pipelines, datasets, connections, and so forth. We highly recommend that you turn on Git even though we do not go through the steps here. We cover Git and source control in Chapter 21, and you can turn on Git after Azure Data Factory is deployed. At the time of writing, Azure Data Factory can only use GitHub or Azure DevOps but not other Git-based services.

---

9. Click **Create**.

10. After Azure Data Factory is created, click **Go to resource**.

For Azure Data Factory, the core user interface is the hosted authoring tool. There is no software to install, and you spend most of your time in the authoring tool.

Hands-on: Exploring Azure Data Factory

In this exercise, you explore the Azure Data Factory authoring workspace. This workspace is the core of Azure Data Factory and is the place where data engineers spend most of their time.

1. From the Overview pane of Azure Data Factory, locate and click **Author and monitor**. This launches the Azure Data Factory authoring workspace.

Note Instead of going to the Azure portal, selecting the Azure Data Factory instance, and then clicking Author and monitor, you can also go directly to the Azure Data Factory author workspace by going to `https://adf.azure.com`. If you have multiple subscriptions and or Azure Data Factory instances, you can select the correct subscription and Azure Data Factory instance.

2. From the left border, locate and click the pencil icon, which launches the authoring UI, as seen in Figure 19-1.

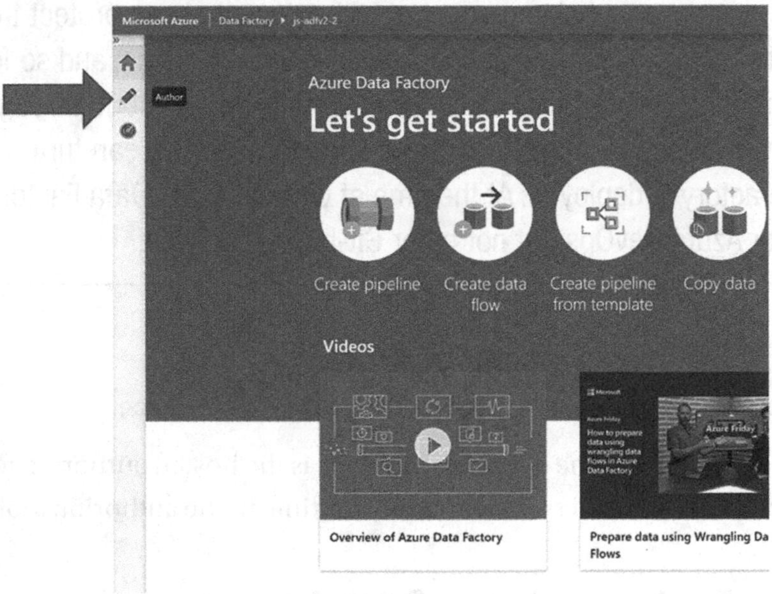

***Figure 19-1.** Authoring in Azure Data Factory*

3. When the authoring workspace is launched, locate the five different classes of Azure Data Factory resources—pipelines, datasets, data flows, connections, and triggers, as seen in Figure 19-2.

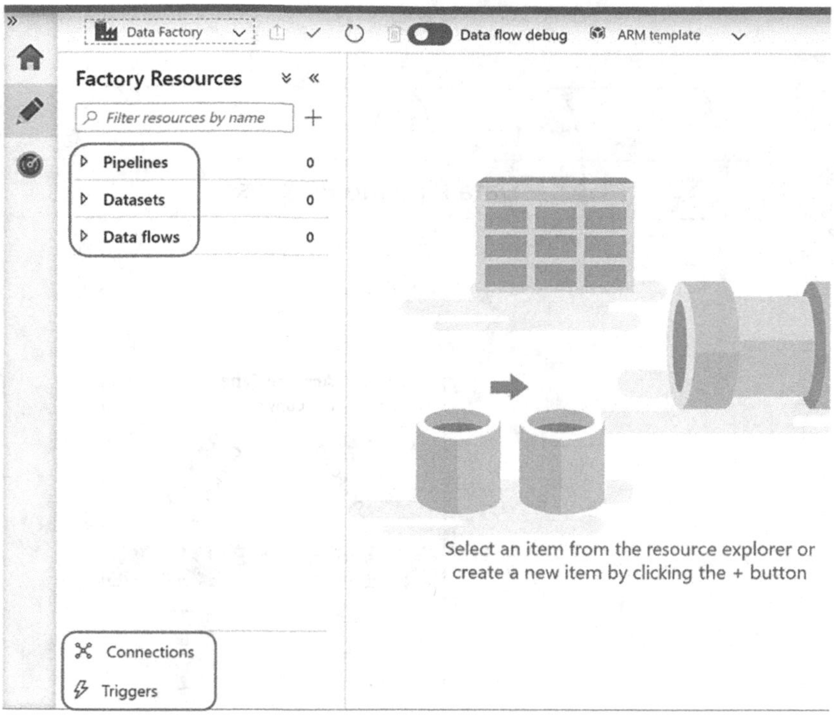

Figure 19-2. *Azure Data Factory resources*

Let's take a moment to explore these Azure Data Factory resources. These resources are the elements we use to build a data pipeline activity. Using these resources via the UI is a matter of dragging and dropping them onto the canvas to the right, or by clicking the + located next to the search box. Figure 19-3 depicts the relationship between the Azure Data Factory resources and how they are used as building blocks.

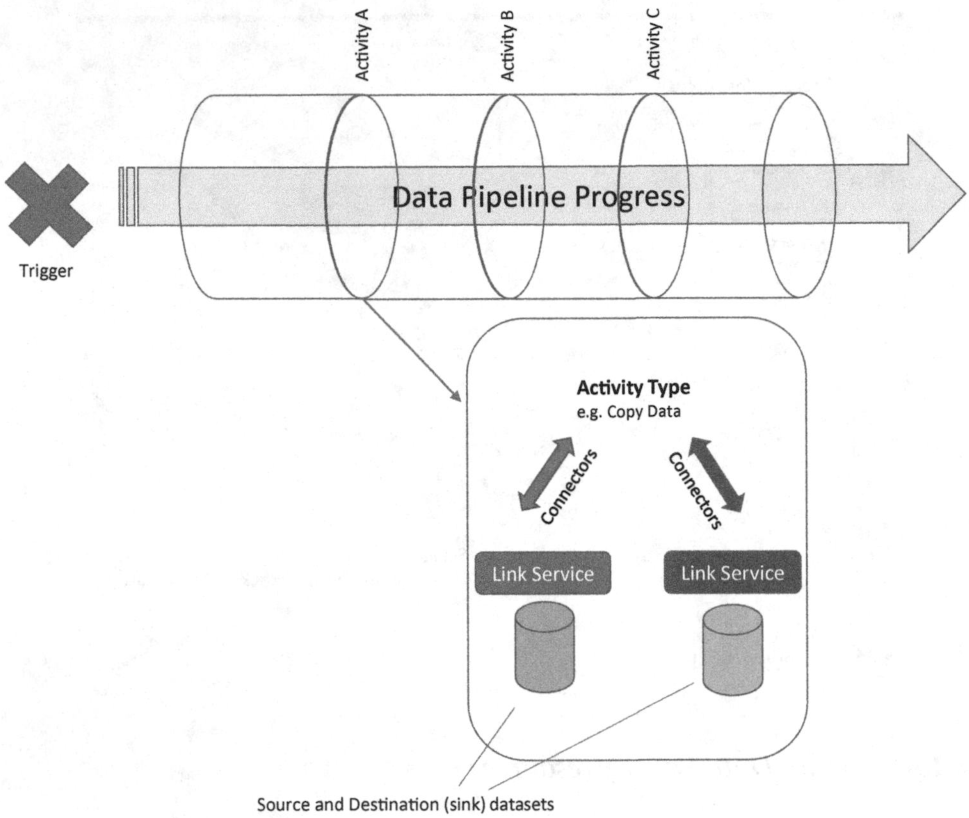

***Figure 19-3.** Architecture of Azure Data Factory resources*

Triggers

Triggers are quite self-explanatory. Triggers activate the data pipeline process. They are based on schedules, events, or timed intervals (tumbling window).

1. Click **Triggers** in the Azure Data Factory, and then click + **New**.
2. Observe the properties of the trigger object, as seen in Figure 19-4. Click **Cancel** for now because you are only exploring the trigger and not actually implementing it.

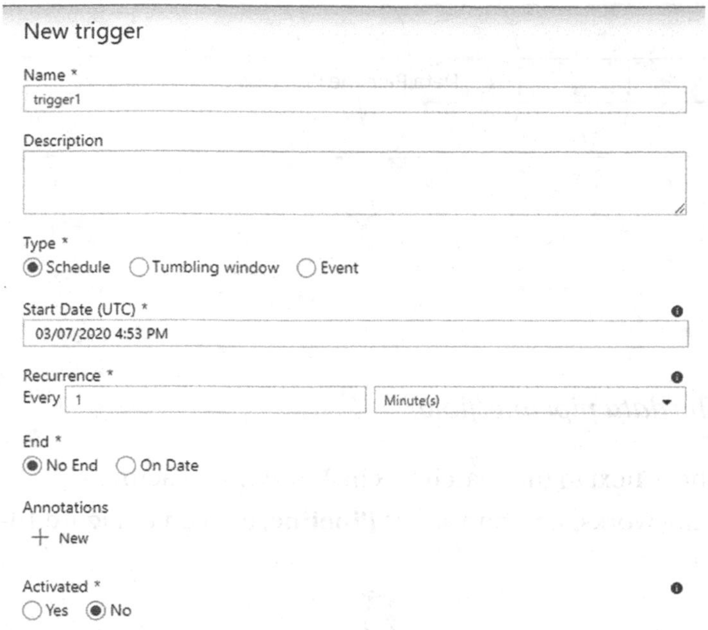

Figure 19-4. *Azure Data Factory trigger options*

Data Pipeline or Data Flow

The data pipeline or flow represents the orchestration work to be done by Azure Data Factory. It describes the sequence in which different activities need to take place to get the data into the right form and location. Figure 19-5 overlays the representation of the data pipeline onto how an actual pipeline may look like in Azure Data Factory. In the Figure, each of the boxes represents an actual Azure Data Factory activity that is carried out in sequence from left to right. Each activity has dependencies from the previous activity and may take parameters as inputs to control the workflow.

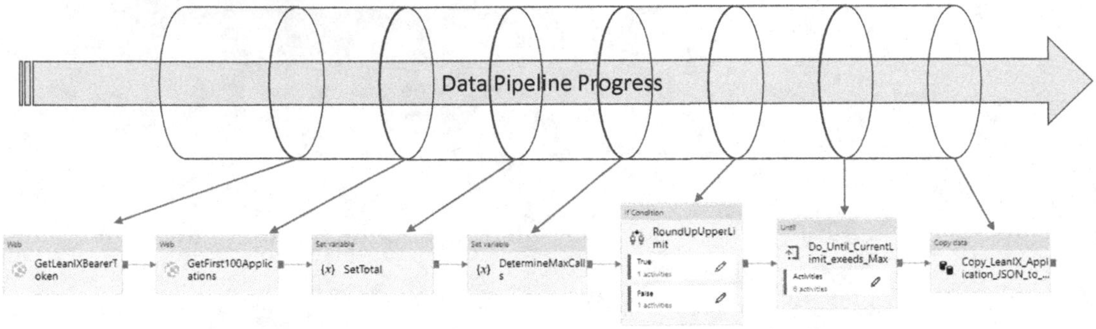

***Figure 19-5.** The data pipeline/flow*

1. Click the + next to the search box in Azure Data Factory's authoring workspace, and select **Pipeline**, as seen in Figure 19-6.

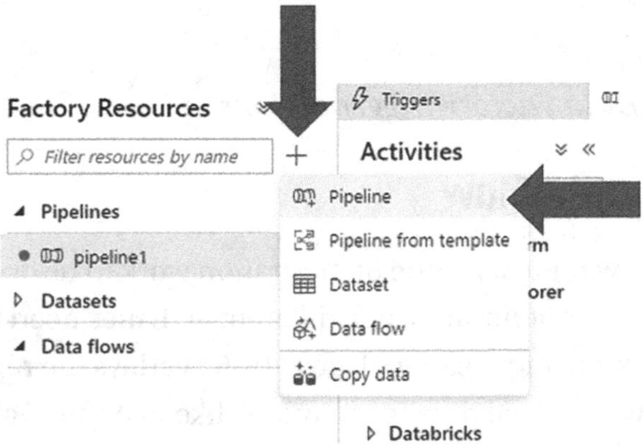

***Figure 19-6.** Creating a new pipeline in Azure Data Factory*

2. A new pipeline named pipeline1 is created and placed under Pipelines.
3. A new pane titled Activities appears. Explore the different types of activities that a data pipeline can hold. Locate each of the activities shown in Figure 19-5.
4. Expand **Move & transform** and drag and drop the **Copy data** activity to the canvas for pipeline1 on the right. Then change the name of this activity and see it change in the canvas as well, as seen in Figure 19-7. For this exercise, name this activity **Copy_from_Blob_to_Blob**.

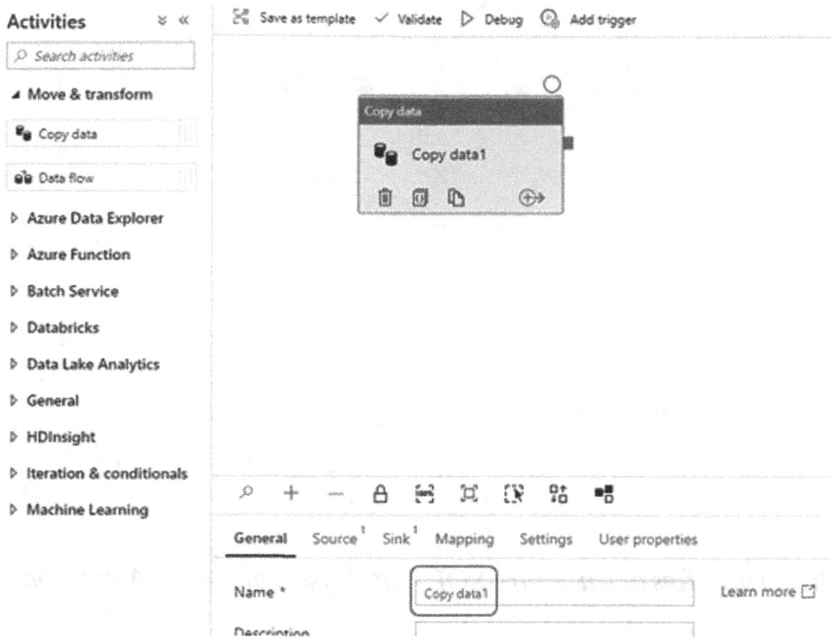

Figure 19-7. *Copy data activity in Azure Data Factory*

5. Click **Code** in the top-right corner of the canvas, and look at the JSON definition for this pipeline. Click **Cancel** when you are done.

Datasets

Datasets are the repositories where data is sourced or deposited. These repositories may be databases, such as SQL or Oracle. They can be from services like a REST API endpoint. Or, they can be from a SaaS API like SalesForce or Dynamics 365.

Figure 19-8 shows the properties of an Azure SQL Database dataset object in Azure Data Factory. Clicking the tabs for this dataset object shows the different properties that you must set up to establish connectivity to the data source, and ultimately the content. Each dataset object that is available in Azure Data Factory consists of unique and known properties that are specific to the data source type.

In this example, since the dataset is an Azure SQL Database, its property contains a field for the table that this dataset object should access. Compare this to the properties of a JSON dataset, which is essentially a file that resides in some location. The properties of such a dataset, as seen in Figure 19-9, does not contain a field to identify a table, but rather a file path and the encoding type.

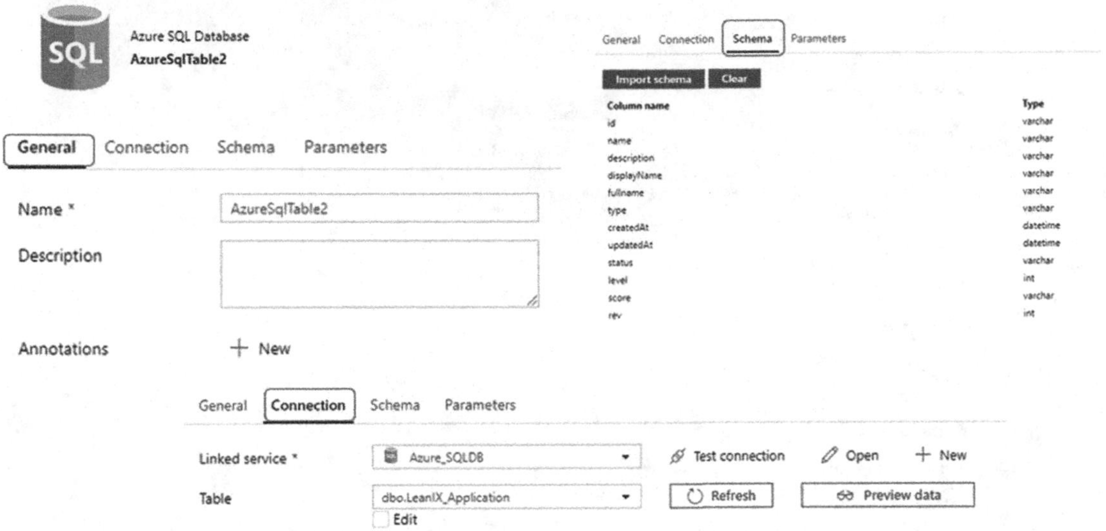

Figure 19-8. *Properties of an Azure SQL Database dataset in Azure Data Factory*

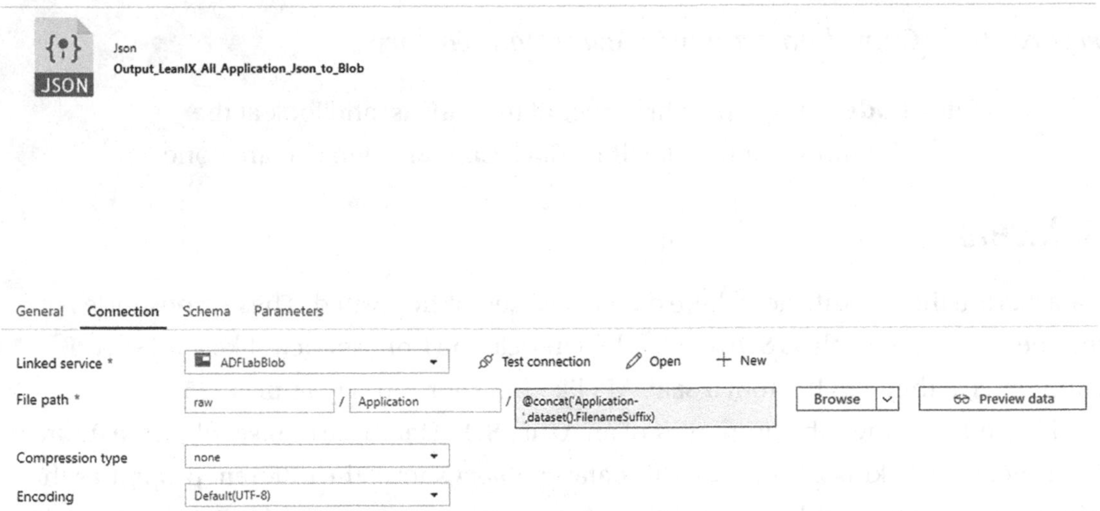

Figure 19-9. *Properties of a JSON file as a dataset*

1. Click the ellipses next to Datasets and select **New dataset**.
2. Browse through the different built-in datasets that Azure Data Factory can use. Click the Azure tab and select **Azure Blob Storage**.
3. Click **Continue**.

4. Select **DelimitedText** as the format, and then click **Continue.**
5. Give this dataset a name. For this exercise, use the name **CSV_on_Blob_raw**.
6. Click the drop-down menu to expand the Linked service options, and select + **New**.

For here, we are going to start defining the Linked service, which is a different Azure Data Factory resource that a dataset is dependent on. We continue this exercise in the next section.

Linked Services

Linked services are objects that define the connection to the location where a data source resides. The connection can be to a type of database engine, a file share, a REST endpoint, or even a SaaS. Generally, the core information required is to define the location and provide credentials for authentication. Once a connection is successfully established, and then it can be used as the transport layer to populate the datasets that are reliant on this connection. That is the role of a Linked service.

1. Picking up from the previous exercise, you should see the pane to establish a New linked service for Azure Blob storage.
2. Give this linked service a name. For this exercise, name it **Azure_Blob_LS.**
3. Leave AutoResolveIntegrationRuntime selected as the connect via integration runtime.
4. Leave Authentication method as the account key.
5. Next, remember the Azure Blob storage that you created in Chapter 14? You use that storage location in this exercise. So, open a new tab or a different browser instance and go to `https://portal.azure.com`.
6. Navigate to the Azure Blob storage resource built in Chapter 14 and retrieve the storage account name and one of the Access keys.
7. Go back to Azure Data Factory.

8. Select **Connection string**, and then select **Enter manually** as the option for the account selection method.

9. Copy and paste the storage account name and storage account key with the information that you retrieved in step 5.

Note When Azure Data Factory and Azure Blob storage are in the same Azure subscription, as is in this exercise, you could select From Azure subscription as the account selection method and browse for the Azure Blob storage instead of copying and pasting account names and keys. But, this exercise demonstrated that Azure Blob storage could reside in a different subscription, and the only way to access that location is via other authentication methods. In this case, we used an access key, but we could have used Azure Active Directory, Key Vault, or a temporary SAS key.

---

10. Click **Test connection** at the bottom of the pane and make sure the connection is successful. Next, click **Create**.

11. You have now created a Linked service and are back to finalizing the details of the dataset. Click **Browse** and select the **customer.csv** file located in the raw folder. This file is from an exercise in Chapter 14.

12. Click **OK**.

13. Check the **First row as header** box.

14. Click **OK** again to complete the creation of the dataset.

Datasets and Link Services

In the last two exercises, you created a dataset and its underlying linked service in a single sequence because of their dependencies. If you browse Azure Data Factory now, you see both objects exist in their respective locations in the editor. Because they are discrete objects, you can create a linked service object first and then use it in a dataset later. In fact, you can also reuse linked services. Now that we have a linked service to our Azure Blob storage in Azure Data Factory, we do not have to recreate another linked service. If we need a different dataset populated with another file from this same location, we just reuse this linked service.

Cloning

Any resource in Azure Data Factory can be cloned. In this exercise, we clone the CSV_on_Blob_raw dataset.

1. Click the ellipses next to the CSV_on_Blob_raw dataset and select **Clone**.
2. The dataset is cloned with the same name and _copy1 appended. So, you should see CSV_on_Blob_raw_copy1 as a new dataset.
3. Rename this dataset **CSV_on_Blob_stage**.
4. Click the Connection tab.
5. Remove the contents of the container, directory, and file name. Enter **stage** as the file path, as seen in Figure 19-10.

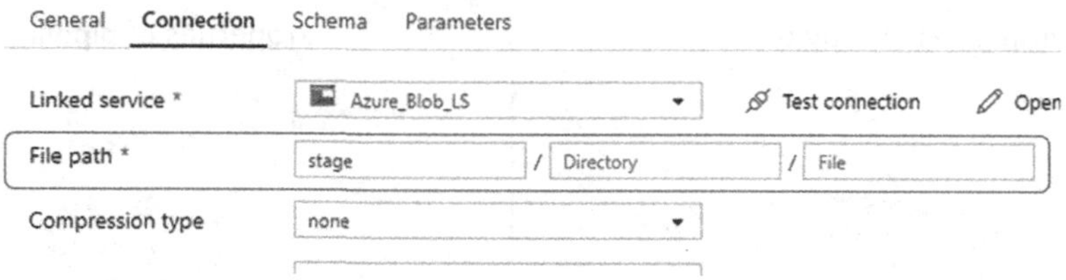

***Figure 19-10.** Editing file path for a dataset*

In this exercise, you explored the capability of cloning a resource like a dataset. In this modified dataset, we reused the linked service by not changing that field but pointed it to a different container in Azure Blob storage.

You can also clone resources that contain other resources. For example, when you clone an entire pipeline that contains activities, the entire pipeline is cloned. Just be aware that the individual activities contained in the cloned pipeline are *not* cloned. So, if you modify the properties of an activity in the cloned pipeline, it is the *same* activity referenced by the original pipeline.

Next Steps: Self-Guided Assignment

Before continuing, we leave it up to you to go through the preceding exercise once again to create another dataset for Azure SQL Database and its required linked service. Use the tpcc Azure SQL Database from Chapter 17. You need this second dataset with the customer table so that you can append the contents of the customer.csv file from Azure Blob storage to the table using a Copy Data pipeline in Azure Data Factory. Use Users_on_SQLDB as the name for the dataset, and Azure_SQLDB_LS as the name for the Azure SQL Database Link service.

Hands-on: Creating a Copy Data Pipeline

You are going to continue building pipeline1, which you created earlier in this chapter.

1. Select **pipeline1**.
2. On the editing canvas, click any part of the white space to unselect the Copy data activity. This ensures that the properties shown below the canvas belong to the pipeline, and not the activity. Compare the two screenshots in Figure 19-11.

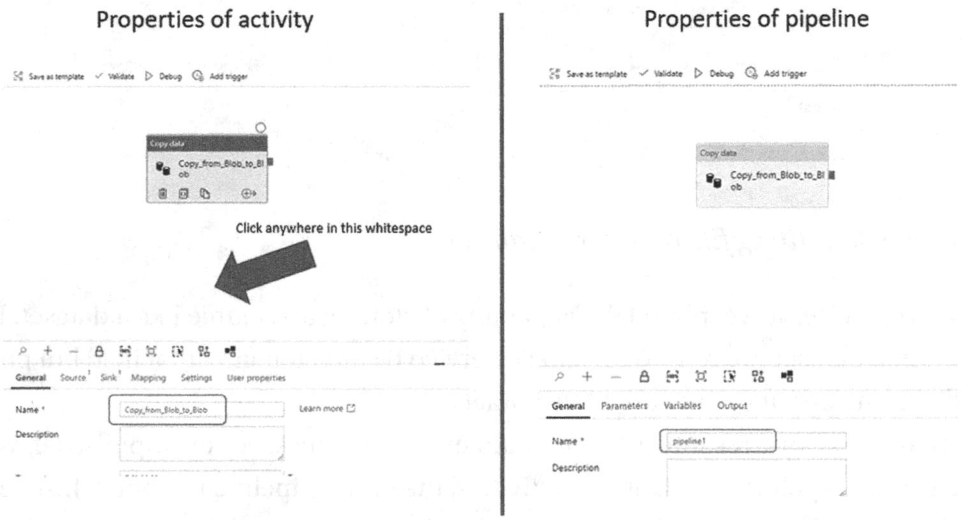

__Figure 19-11.__ Selecting the right properties to edit

3. Rename pipeline1 as **Copy_Blob_SQL.**
4. Select the **Copy_from_Blob_to_Blob** activity, and then click the Source tab in the properties below the canvas.
5. Click the **Source dataset** drop-down menu, and select **CSV_on_Blob_raw** as the dataset.

6. Click **Open** to open the dataset.
7. Select the **Connection** tab and check the **First row as header** box.
8. Select the Schema tab, and click **Import schema**.
9. Select **From connection/store** as the schema source. You should see the schema from the CSV file imported.
10. At the top of the canvas, select **Copy_Blob_SQL**.
11. Click the Sink tab in the properties pane beneath the canvas and select **CSV_on_Blob_stage** as the sink dataset.
12. Type **.csv** in the File extension box, as seen in Figure 19-12.

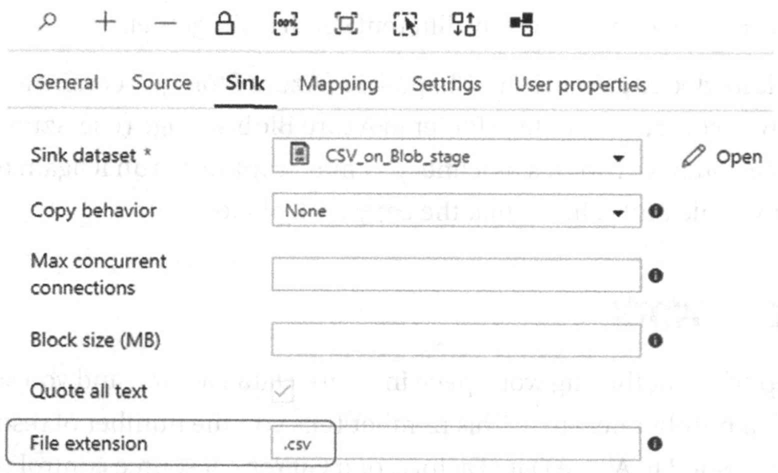

***Figure 19-12.** Specifying file extension*

13. Click **Open** to open the sink dataset properties and select the Connection tab. Make sure the **First row as header** box is checked.
14. At the top of the canvas, select the Copy_BloB_SQL tab to show the pipeline.
15. Click **Debug** to run this pipeline.
16. The properties pane beneath the canvas focuses on the Output tab. Click the icon that looks like a circled arrow to refresh and see the status of the pipeline, as seen in Figure 19-13.

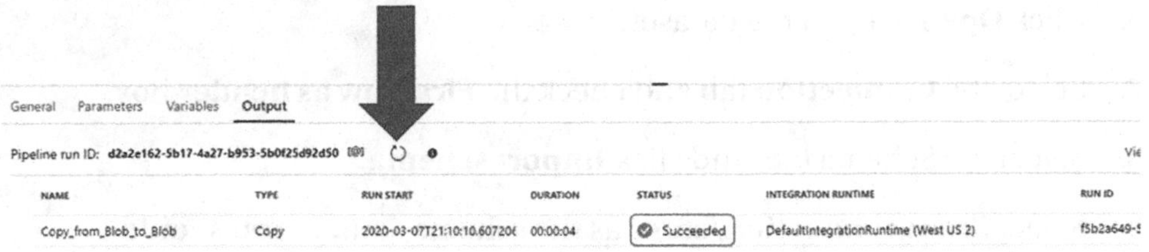

Figure 19-13. *Status of pipeline execution*

17. The pipeline should have executed successfully. At this point, this pipeline has a single copy activity that copied a CSV file from one container in Azure Blob storage to another container in the same Azure Blob storage. If you used a different linked service for the sink dataset, this file would have been moved to another Azure subscription or a completely different service altogether.

Using the knowledge gained from Chapter 14 (Azure Storage), confirm that customer.csv was copied to the stage folder in Azure Blob storage (use Azure Storage Explorer). Once you have run this pipeline, you may want to re-run it again to see the timestamp for the file and validate that the copy took place.

Saving Your Work

Look at the top of the authoring workspace in Azure Data Factory, and you see a Publish all button with a number next to it. This number tells you the number of resources that have not been pushed to Azure Data Factory, or a Git repo if source control was enabled.

Click Publish All. A separate pane appears; it lists the pending changes and new workloads that need to be published to Azure Data Factory, as shown in Figure 19-14.

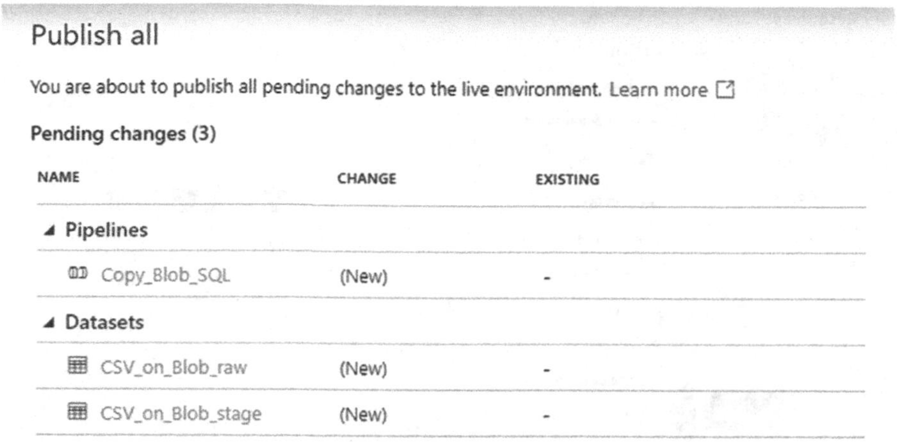

Figure 19-14. *Resources that need to be published to Azure Data Factory*

Click the Publish button, and the resources are pushed up to Azure Data Factory, GitHub, or Azure DevOps Repos, depending on your configuration.

Note Publishing in Azure Data Factory is akin to saving your work. It is important to note that all changes remain in the browser session until it is published. Therefore, if you close the browser session without publishing your work, all the changes are lost. During publishing, all changes are validated, and errors must be addressed before the work can be published. You can run a separate validation without publishing by clicking the Validate option located next to Debug.

Hands-on: Multiple Activities in a Pipeline

Usually, there are multiple activities in a pipeline. You can have one activity per pipeline, and then have one pipeline trigger another pipeline, as seen in Figure 19-15, but that is not the best method. The ability to execute another pipeline is useful when you are reusing existing pipelines to build a new process or for splitting up a pipeline that has too many activities and is therefore difficult to keep track of.

You may also want to time the execution of a set of activities against a second set of activities so that you can place them in two separate pipelines, and then trigger the execution of the second pipeline with the first pipeline if certain parameters are met.

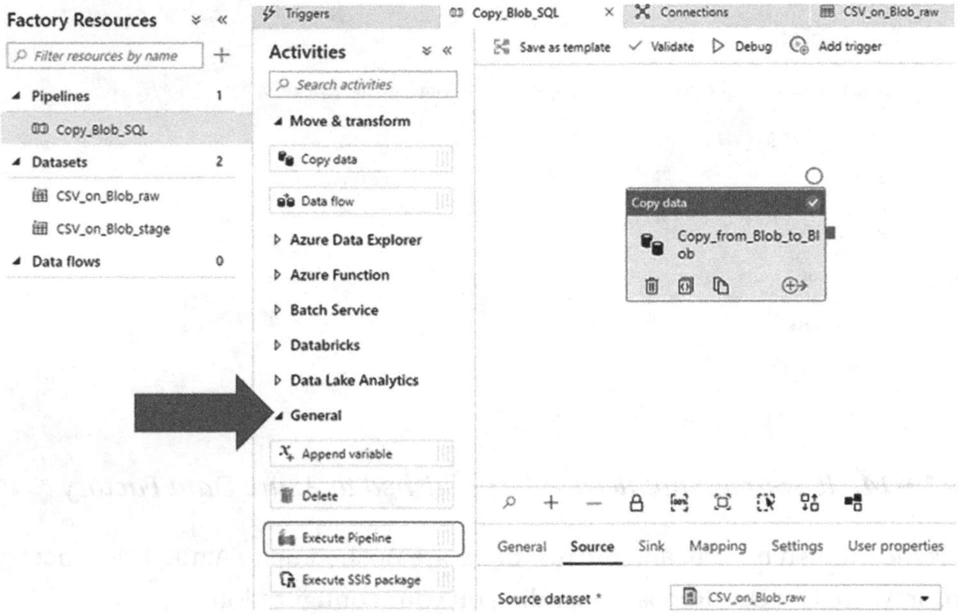

***Figure 19-15.** Executing another pipeline as one of the activities within a pipeline*

One easy strategy to adopt is to clone pipelines throughout the build stage so you can do unit testing as data is being copied and transformed from stage to stage.

In the preceding exercise, we now have a pipeline that copies data from one container to another (raw to stage) in Azure Blob storage, and we know it works. In this exercise, we continue building this pipeline by moving the data from the stage container to the Azure SQL Database dataset you created earlier as part of your self-guided assignment.

1. Click the **Copy_Blob_SQL** pipeline.
2. Expand **Move & transform**. Drag a new **Copy data** activity and place it to the right of Copy_from_Blob_to_Blob in the canvas, as seen in Figure 19-16.

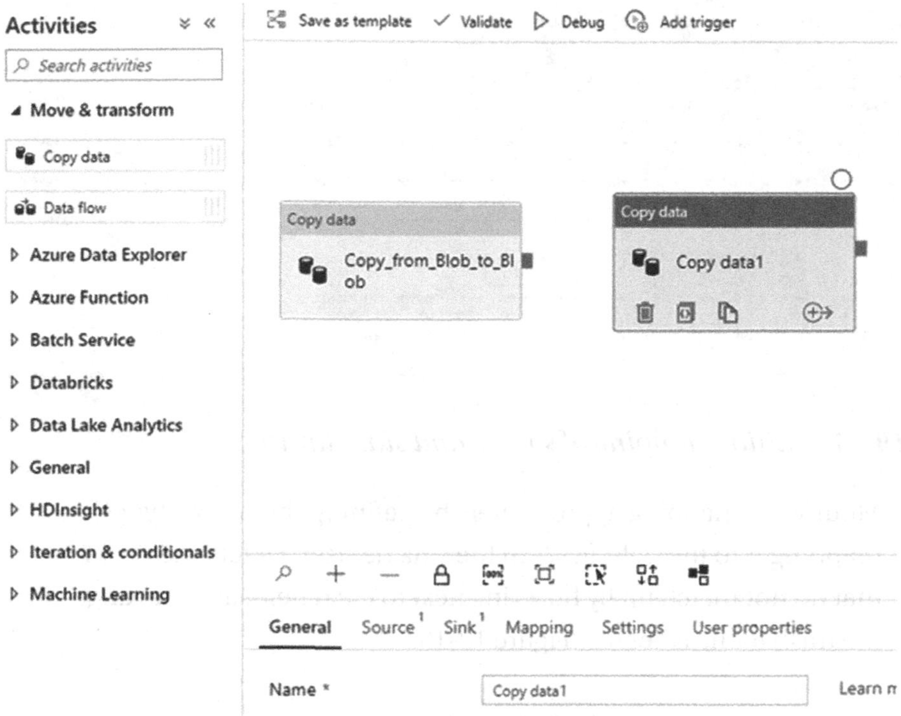

Figure 19-16. *New Copy data activity added to the pipeline*

3. Rename the new Copy data activity from Copy data1 to **Copy_from_Blob_to_SQL**.

4. Click the Source tab in the properties pane beneath the canvas and select **CSV_on_Blob_stage** as the source dataset.

5. Click **Preview data** to see the data in the CSV file. This confirms that Azure Data Factory can access the file and can successfully read its contents.

6. Select **Wildcard file path** as the option for file path type.

7. Click the Sink tab and select the **Users_on_SQLDB** dataset as the sink dataset.

8. Click the Mapping tab, and then click **Import schemas**.

9. Azure Data Factory attempts to map the fields between the source and sink datasets. Notice that it was not able to map several of the fields, as seen in Figure 19-17.

***Figure 19-17.** Initial mapping of source and sink datasets*

10. Modify the mapping appropriately by defining the source types, mapping it to the right fields in the sink dataset. Delete the fields that do not match up by hovering next to each field, and clicking the trash icon, as seen in Figure 19-18.

***Figure 19-18.** Mapping the source and sink datasets*

11. Next, click and hold down on the Success Output interface of the Copy_from_Blob_to_Blob activity. Connect a line to the input interface of the Copy_from_Blob_to_SQL activity, as seen in Figure 19-19.

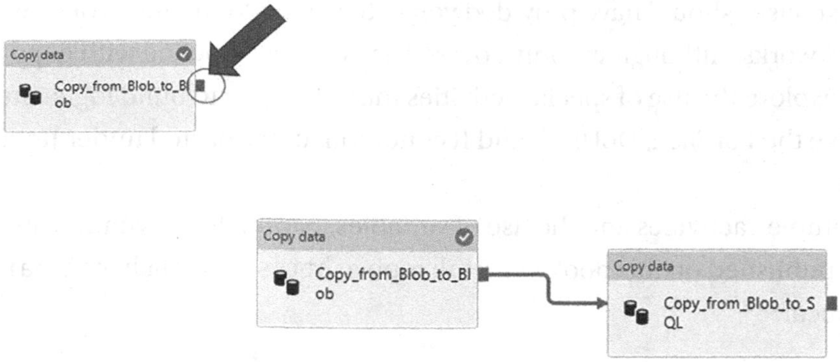

Figure 19-19. *Connecting two activities in a pipeline*

12. At the top of the canvas, click **Debug**.
13. The pipeline now runs in two stages. First, it runs the copy data activity to copy users.csv from the raw container in Azure Blob storage to the stage container in Azure Blob storage.
14. The pipeline then moves to the next copy data activity where it copies the fields in users.csv in the stage container in Azure Blob storage to the Users table in Azure SQL Database, using the mappings defined in step 10. The results of both successful stages are shown in the Output pane of the pipeline, as seen in Figure 19-20.

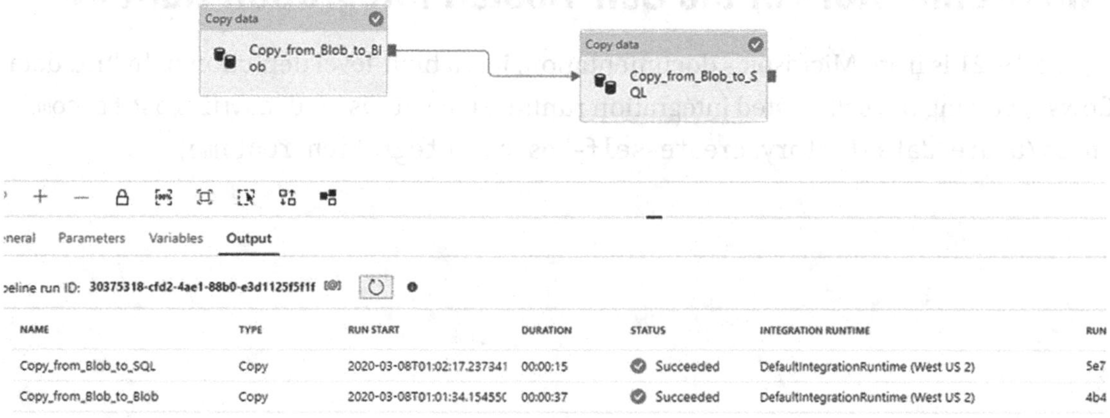

Figure 19-20. *Successful execution of a pipeline with multiple activities*

These exercises should have provided you with a good foundation for how Azure Data Factory works. Although we only covered a very basic pipeline with copy activities, you should explore the use of special activities that allow you to build logic into your pipelines, like the ForEach, DoUntil, and If condition loops located under Iteration & conditionals.

More complex activities and the use of variables, parameters, dynamically created content are published on this book's GitHub repo at `https://github.com/harris-soh-copeland-puca`.

Accessing On-Premises Data Sources

The existence of hybrid clouds is expected to continue. Therefore, there is a need for a scenario where Azure Data Factory must connect to on-premises data sources to copy or move data to the cloud or vice-versa.

This hybrid scenario is dependent on special software called the *self-hosted integration runtime* (IR). The self-hosted integration runtime is an Azure Data Factory agent that runs on a computer connected to an on-premises environment. It has access to the on-premises data sources and has outbound Internet connectivity to contact an Azure Data Factory instance. In that sense, the self-hosted integration runtime serves as a data gateway between the on-premises environment and Azure Data Factory.

The Architecture of the Self-Hosted Integration Runtime

Figure 19-21 is from Microsoft's documentation; it is a high-level depiction of hybrid data flows involving the self-hosted integration runtime (see `https://docs.microsoft.com/en-us/azure/data-factory/create-self-hosted-integration-runtime`).

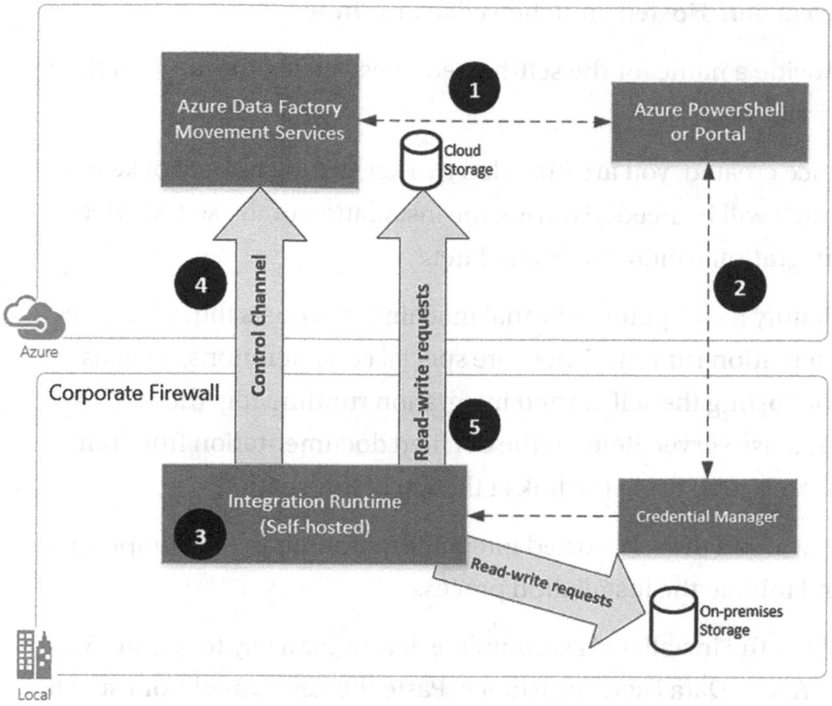

Figure 19-21. *High-level diagram of hybrid data flows using the self-hosted IR (Source:* `https://docs.microsoft.com/en-us/azure/data-factory/create-self-hosted-integration-runtime`*)*

Installing and Configuring the Self-Hosted Integration Runtime

Installing the self-hosted integration runtime is very extensively covered and very straightforward. You can find a forked copy of the latest instructions to install the self-hosted integration runtime at our GitHub repo at `https://github.com/harris-soh-copeland-puca/azure-docs/blob/master/articles/data-factory/create-self-hosted-integration-runtime.md`.

The installation and configuration of the self-hosted integration runtime include nine steps.

1. In the Azure portal, launch the authoring workspace in Azure Data Factory and click **Connections**.

2. Click the **Integration runtime** tab, and then click + **New**.

3. Select **Self-Hosted**, and then click **Continue**.

4. Provide a name for the self-hosted integration runtime, and then click **Create**.

5. Once created, you are provided two keys. Copy one set of keys, which will be needed during the installation of the self-service integration runtime software later.

6. Identify a computer or virtual machine that hosts the self-hosted integration runtime. There are special considerations, such as not hosting the self-hosted integration runtime together with a database server. Refer to the detailed documentation from our GitHub repo using the link at the top of this section.

7. Download the self-hosted integration runtime to the computer and initiate the installation process.

8. When the installation is complete, it asks for a key to register with an Azure Data Factory instance. Paste the key copied from step 6 and click **Register**.

Those are the steps for deploying a self-hosted integration runtime. When you look in Azure Data Factory, you should see the new self-hosted integration runtime, and its status should be Running, as seen in Figure 19-22.

***Figure 19-22.** Azure Data Factory showing the status of the self-hosted integration runtime*

Now, when you define datasets that are drawing from on-premises resources, you need to define a Linked service that utilized the self-hosted integration runtime instead of the default AutoResolveIntegrationRuntime.

AutoResolveIntegrationRuntime is an Azure-based integration runtime used to connect to any Azure or Cloud-based endpoint. Self-hosted integration runtimes access on-premises data sources or endpoints behind a firewall.

Summary

Azure Data Factory is a very powerful data orchestration tool without the footprint of multiple on-premises tools. It proves to be an extremely valuable tool in the data engineer's toolkit. Azure Data Factory is a cloud-based tool with an integrated code repository. Azure Data Factory has more than 90 connectors and a self-hosted integrated runtime; it can access data that resides anywhere.

There are many use case scenarios, connectors, and data flow examples that can be gleaned from the extensive documentation provided and updated by the Microsoft Azure Data Factory product group. A forked copy of the evergreen documentation for Azure Data Factory is at our GitHub repo at `https://github.com/harris-soh-copeland-puca/azure-docs/tree/master/articles/data-factory`.

Note Two data activities are important in the modern data world but are not covered in this chapter: data warehousing and data cataloging. This is because at the time of writing, Azure Data Warehouse was released as Azure Synapse Analysis, and Azure Data Catalog Gen 2 was in early preview. We provide updates to these two services at `https://harris-soh-copeland-puca.github.io`.

PART VII

Intelligent Cloud, Machine Learning, and Artificial Intelligence

CHAPTER 20

Developing and Deploying Azure-based Applications

Introduction

Azure is often referred to as one of only a few hypercloud offerings today. The term *hypercloud* indicates that it has a worldwide footprint, access to almost limitless resources (primarily compute, memory, and storage), and all of it on-demand and deployable within minutes.

This core characteristic of Azure brings new capabilities to developers because it allows applications to be more robust and resilient since resources can be allocated upward as needed, requests can be rerouted away from areas that are experiencing technical issues due to uncontrolled natural threats, and response times can be significantly improved since data and transactions are located closer to the end user's respective geographic location. There is also the ability to manage and deploy changes to versions of applications with minimal or no service interruptions.

These service-level agreements (SLAs) for applications have been around forever and are highly dependent on the underlying infrastructure. In this chapter, we cover built-in capabilities in Azure that helps improve SLAs that are impacted by application deployment efforts.

J. Soh et al., *Microsoft Azure*, https://doi.org/10.1007/978-1-4842-5958-0_20

Trends in Cloud-based Application Development

The characteristics and capabilities of a hypercloud like Azure changes the way developers think about designing and deploying applications, and thus drives certain trends we see today. Although there are many changes that affect developers and the way things are traditionally done, the major trends identified and discussed in this chapter are

- Platform as a service (PaaS)
- Azure Web Apps (as a PaaS)
- Containers (as a PaaS)
- Built-in monitoring, debugging, and performance insights

We selected these topics because they are prominent trends in cloud computing today. In the case of Azure, these are native capabilities that can easily be adopted and provide significant improvement in SLAs with minimal effort. You see how this is accomplished through the hands-on exercises in this chapter.

Platform as a Service (PaaS)

In Chapter 12, we introduced the topic of PaaS and made the case for its adoption. As a recap, we said that PaaS provided a layer of abstraction from the underlying infrastructure that forms the foundation of any application. No matter how advanced an application is, or how many different acronyms for new technologies and methods we hear today, the bottom line is that everything is supported by computers that are connected via network cables and powered from an outlet. Updating and replacing aging or faulty hardware, adding new hardware, and making sure the power is not disrupted by a vacuum cleaner, for example (yes, this has happened to one of the authors in an enterprise setting), are all considered "busy work" that does not contribute to value-added advancement but are very important nonetheless.

In this section on PaaS, we are going to explore additional SLA-contributing capabilities that developers who are deploying applications on Azure should take advantage of.

Slots on Azure Web Apps

Slots are a unique aspect of Azure Web Apps that is easily overlooked. It is easy to understand, adopt, and contributes to the quality assurance (QA) effort and reduces downtime when it comes time to cut over from one version of an application to another.

Problems like bugs may be caught during testing, but there are usability and user interface (UI) issues that surface only during user acceptance testing. Errors may also surface when an application is deployed from the dev/test environment to the production environment because of different settings like security or hardware. That is why most organizations try to maintain at least two identical infrastructures for the test and the production environments. This is a costly approach both in terms of capital expense and the labor needed to synchronize two environments. Slots in Azure Web Apps address these issues.

Hands-on with Slots on Azure Web Apps

Think of slots in Azure Web Apps as mirror environments of the web app. Every web app has one slot when it is first deployed. This slot is the default production slot that developers publish their web applications to. Subsequent slots can be configured as mirror environments and these can be slots for development, testing, QA, and pre-prod or staging purposes. The best part of slots in Azure Web Apps is that it does not cost extra to create slots in Azure Web Apps that are in the standard or premium App Service Plans, and since for production environments, the standard App Service Plan is the minimally recommended one, there is no reason not to use slots because it is a zero-dollar feature. Now that we have briefly made the financial case to utilize slots, this next exercise show how to get started with slots quickly.

1. In the Azure portal, go the web app for the Sentiment Analysis Feedback form you developed in Chapter 15.
2. In the Overview pane, note that the App Service Plan is Standard or Premium. If you followed the exercise verbatim, the App Service Plan for this project should already be Standard. The reason why we are pointing this out here is because slots are available only in the Standard plan or higher. Slots are not available in the Basic App Service Plan.

3. Select **Deployment slots**, as referenced in Figure 20-1 under the Deployment section from the menu on the left.

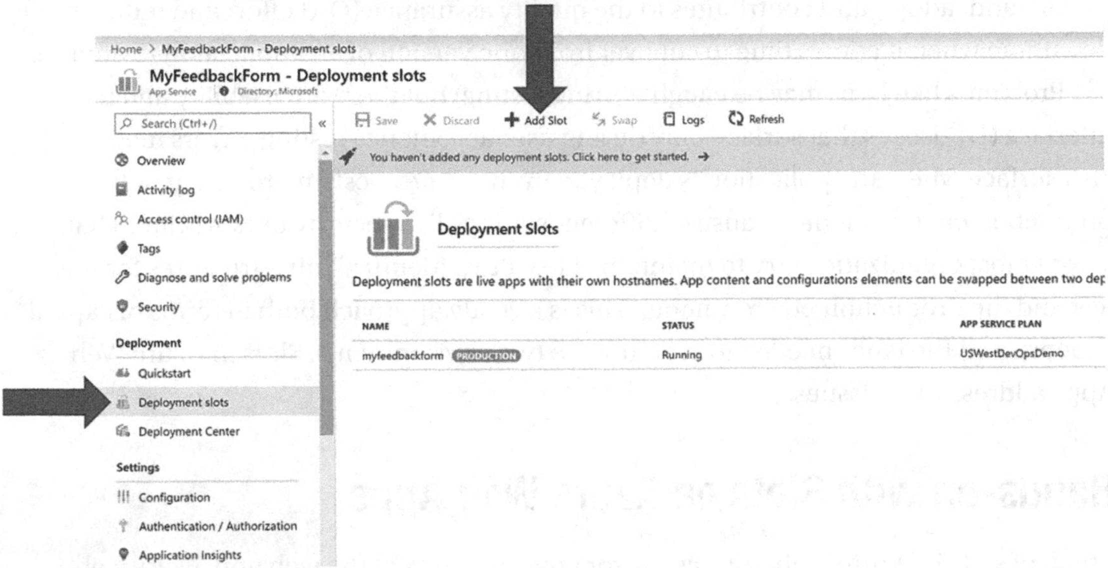

***Figure 20-1.** Add a deployment slot via the Azure portal*

4. Note that there is an active running slot, and 100% of the traffic is currently being routed to this slot. Click **Add Slot** from the top of the pane, as shown in Figure 20-1.

5. A new pane open. Type **Staging** as the name of this new slot, and for the Clone settings from dropdown box, select the default running slot. In our example, since our running slot is called myfeedbackform, this is the only other available option from which you can clone settings from.

6. Click **Add**.

7. It takes a time for the slot to be created, but once this is done, click **Close** to close the pane that appeared in step 5.

8. You see now two slots which are both running. The one you just created has the slot name appended to the default slot name separated with a dash (-). The newly created slot have 0% traffic routing to it.

9. Open another browser tab and go to the URL of the new slot (e.g., `https://myfeedbackform-staging.azurewebsite.net`). It should open to a generic landing page stating that the App Service is running, indicating the slot is live.

10. Go back to the portal and click the staging deployment slot, as shown in Figure 20-2. You be redirected to a new Web App page as if you are configuring a new and separate web app.

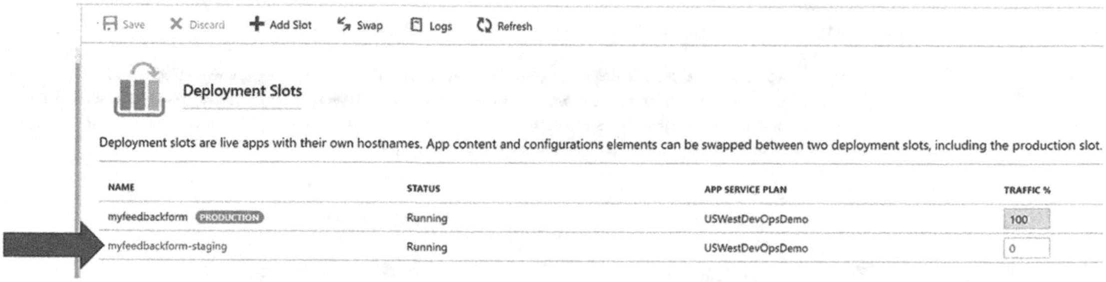

Figure 20-2. *Clicking the newly created staging web app*

11. Get the publishing profile of the staging web app by clicking the **Get Publish Profile** on the top of the pane.

12. Launch Visual Studio and open the Sentiment Analysis Feedback form project.

13. Make a modification to the project in order to simulate a new version to be released to staging for QA before moving the application to production. For example, for this exercise, you open the Default.aspx page and change lines 7 and 15 to describe this application. Figure 20-3 shows these changes.

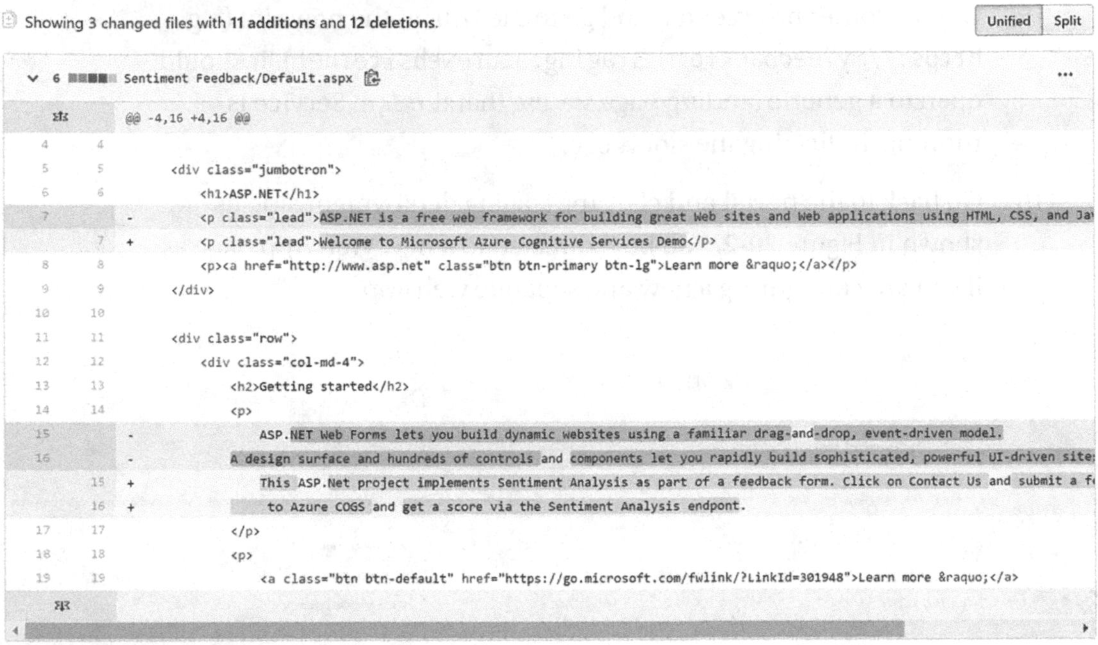

Figure 20-3. *Changes we made to Default.aspx to simulate staging a new release*

Note For something more visual, we also made a change to the code behind of Default.aspx to show the web app's process ID by using System.diagnostic. Display the process ID in a label control (named lbl_ProcessID). Our code for Default.aspx.c looks like this:

```
using System;
using System.Collections.Generic;
using System.Linq;
using System.Web;
using System.Web.UI;
using System.Web.UI.WebControls;
using System.Diagnostics;

namespace Sentiment_Feedback
{
    public partial clas _Default : Page
```

```
    {
        protected void Page_Load(object sender, EventArgs e)
        {
            int nProcessID = Process.GetCurrentProcess().Id;
            lbl_ProcessID.Text = nProcessID.ToString()
        }
    }
}
```

1. Publish this version of the Sentiment Analysis Feedback form using the publishing profile for the Staging slot. Remember you downloaded the publish profile for the Staging slot in step 11.
2. Once the application is published, you should be automatically directed to the URL of the application, or if needed, you can refresh the page or open a new browser tab and go to the URL for the staging web app. Any of these methods would show that the application is now published *on the same* web app as the production site but with different URLs.
3. Take note of the difference between the versions of the application that is in the production slot versus the staging slot by identifying the changes you have made in step 13. Better yet, if you did modify the application to display the process ID of the web app, take note of the process ID of the two versions. They should have different process IDs indicating that these are different applications running in different application pools.
4. At this point, you can continue testing all the application's capabilities in the staging slot by submitting a feedback and confirming that the application works.

What have you accomplished at this point? First, you created a separate slot from the same web app and we duplicated the settings from the production slot. That means you know there are no configuration settings that may be incompatible with this new version.

Secondarily, you can conduct user acceptance and QA testing without interrupting the production site.

Note While there is no additional cost in deploying to additional slots in an Azure web app, and even though one of the best use-case scenarios for slots is QA and user acceptance testing that usually occurs during staging, remember that all slots are supported by the same underlying resources defined by the App Service Plan. Thus, there are scenarios that may not be a good fit for slots. Stress testing is one such example. In a stress test, you are simulating traffic to an application to ensure that it works under peak loads. Unless you have configured autoscaling for the App Service Plan, stress testing a slot affects the version of the application in the production slot because the test cannibalizes the compute and memory resources shared between all slots.

Next, let's assume that the version of the application that we have deployed to the staging slot in the preceding exercise has passed user acceptance testing and QA. It is now time to deploy the new version of the application that is currently in the staging slot.

1. In the Azure portal, in the configuration pane for the web app, select **Deployment slots** in the menu on the left.

2. Then click the **Swap** menu option at the top of the pane, as shown in Figure 20-4.

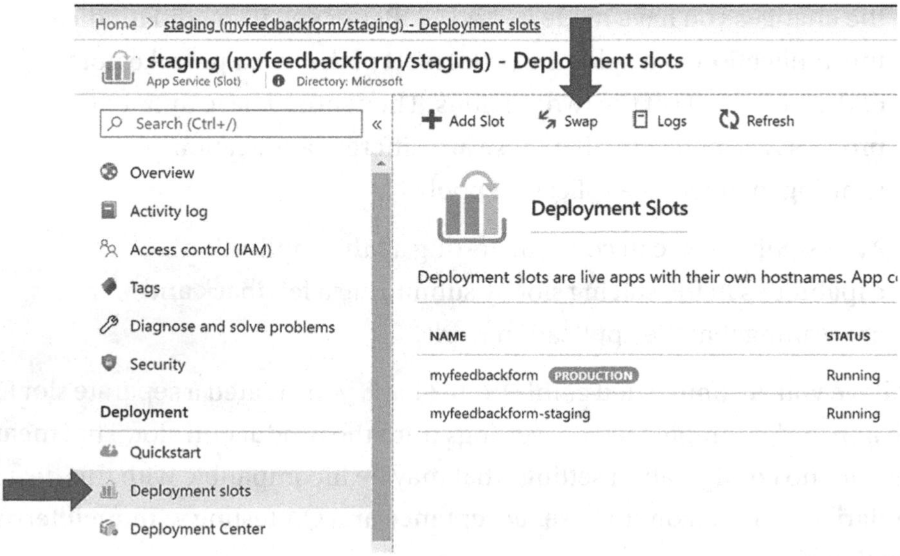

Figure 20-4. *Swapping slots*

3. By default, when the swap pane opens, it has the source of the swap set as the staging slot, and the target is the production slot. For now, ignore the **Perform swap with preview** checkbox and leave it unchecked.

4. Click **Swap** at the bottom of the pane.

5. When the swap is completed and successful, you be notified via a status bar at the bottom of the swap pane, as shown in Figure 20-5.

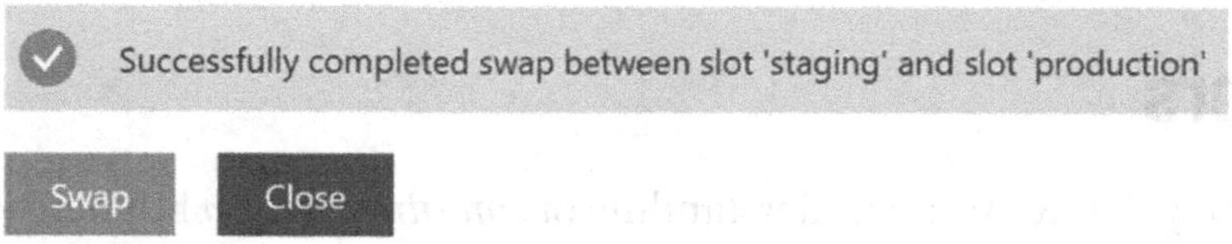

***Figure 20-5.** Successfully swapped slots*

6. Refresh the production site and you see that the application is now the version that was previously in the staging slot, and vice versa.

At this point, you have successfully deployed the latest version of the application by just swapping slots. URLs and settings were preserved, and there was no downtime when the swap occurred.

If you need to quickly roll back to the previous version of the application for whatever reason, all you have to do is reverse the swap by clicking swap and using the same source and target options. Remember that since the previous version is now in the staging slot, initiating a new swap is basically just reversing the first swap, but hopefully you do not have to do this because you had ample opportunity to carry out user acceptance testing and QA before the first swap!

Note There are several settings that do not get swapped but remain with the slot. For example, if you have a custom domain name for the production slot (very likely scenario and covered in Chapter 12), this custom domain does not get swapped and remains with the production slot. Therefore, when a user now visits the custom domain URL, it resolve to the new version of the application that is now occupying the production slot. If the custom domain name configuration had also been swapped and if for example the staging slot did not have a custom domain, and then the custom URL would point to the staging slot that now holds the previous version of the application, which defeats the purpose of the swap. Aside from custom domains, these settings are also not swapped and remain with the respective slots:

Publishing endpoints
Custom Domain Names
SSL certificates and bindings
Scale settings
WebJobs schedulers

Containers

We assume that you have some understanding of *containerization* but here is a quick primer.

Nothing has revolutionized the IT industry than the introduction of virtualization technology. Virtualization has helped us maximize limited hardware resources by significantly increasing the density of workloads that can be supported. For IT professionals, this usually takes the form of a hypervisor that creates multiple virtual machines (VMs) that share a physical infrastructure. As you saw in Chapter 2, hyperclouds such as Azure have maximized and automated the power of virtualization to provide IaaS for the masses.

For developers, virtualization occurs at the software layer, unlike IaaS, which occurs at the operating system (OS) layer, but both virtualization layers can be combined. Figure 20-6 shows the evolution of virtualization as well as the high-level differences and implementation options for IaaS virtualization and application virtualization using containers.

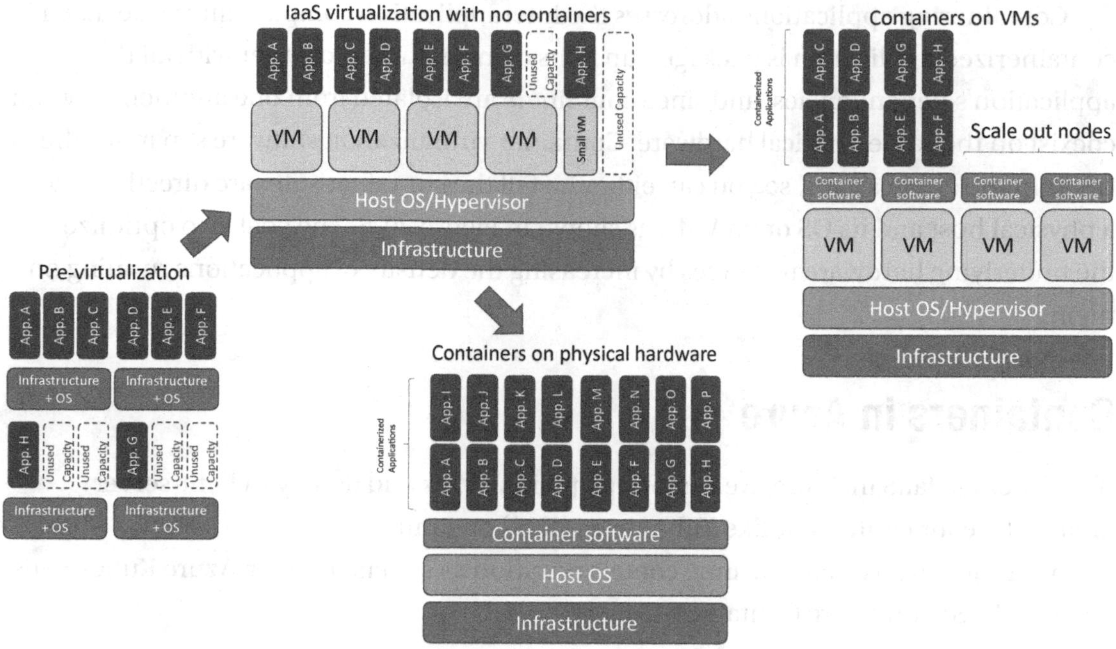

Figure 20-6. Evolution of virtualization

Prior to any form of virtualization technology, applications are tightly bound to the OS, which is in turn tightly bound to the physical hardware. Capacity and compatibility between applications determine the number of applications that can run on any given hardware. Therefore, there is a need for a large hardware footprint. For example, in Figure 20-6, during pre-virtualization, applications A/B/C are compatible with each other and thus can occupy the same physical infrastructure. Applications D/E/F are also compatible but need to occupy a new hardware infrastructure because there are not enough resources on the A/B/C's infrastructure. Applications H and G are not compatible with each other because there are conflicts in their respective software dependencies and thus must reside on their own separate infrastructure. This has the side effect of unused capacity that are still consuming resources such as power and cooling because the capacity is defined at the hardware layer.

With the introduction of IaaS virtualization, the OS can be virtualized into many VMs of different sizes. Applications that are compatible with each other can share a VM as long as there is enough capacity on the VM. Following along with the same example from before, applications G and H are still not compatible so we assign them their own VMs, choosing to have a larger VM for application G with spare capacity at the VM level for future applications, but scaling out a small VM for application H and leaving additional capacity on the physical infrastructure to spin up more VMs in future.

Containering applications addresses the interapplication compatibility issue. Each containerized application is packaged up in its own container together with all the application's dependencies, and since containers are isolated from one another, they can coexist on the same physical hardware. Container virtualization software separates the OS from the applications, so you can either install the container software directly onto a physical host and its OS or on VMs, as shown in Figure 20-6. The goal is to optimize the underlying hardware resources by increasing the density of applications running on them.

Containers in Azure

If we leverage IaaS in Azure, we can bring up Linux VMs and deploy a client-server architecture for containers, like Kubernetes (K8S) on Linux.

Alternatively, we can consume containerization as a PaaS by using Azure Kubernetes Service (AKS) and Azure Container Registry.

Note Azure Container Service (ACS) was retired on January 31, 2020. AKS was introduced in 2017 and has completely replaced ACS. See `https://azure.microsoft.com/en-us/updates/azure-container-service--retire-on-january-31-2020/`.

If your organization is already using on-premises containerization technology such as Red Hat's OpenShift, you can port your solution to Azure Red Hat OpenShift, which is an Azure PaaS jointly managed by Microsoft and Red Hat.

The bottom line is that you can take advantage of containerization without the overhead of managing an IaaS infrastructure for containers since the service is a PaaS offering in Azure.

Hands-on with Docker Images and the Azure Container Registry

In this exercise, we take our Sentiment Analysis feedback application and make it a container image.

1. Go to http://docker.com/products/docker-desktop. Download and install Docker Desktop. Windows 10 Pro or Enterprise edition is required if you are doing this on a Windows machine. A reboot after the installation may also be required

2. Launch Visual Studio and open the Sentiment Analysis Feedback project.

3. Right-click the project, select **Add**, as referenced in Figure 20-7, and then select **Docker Support**.

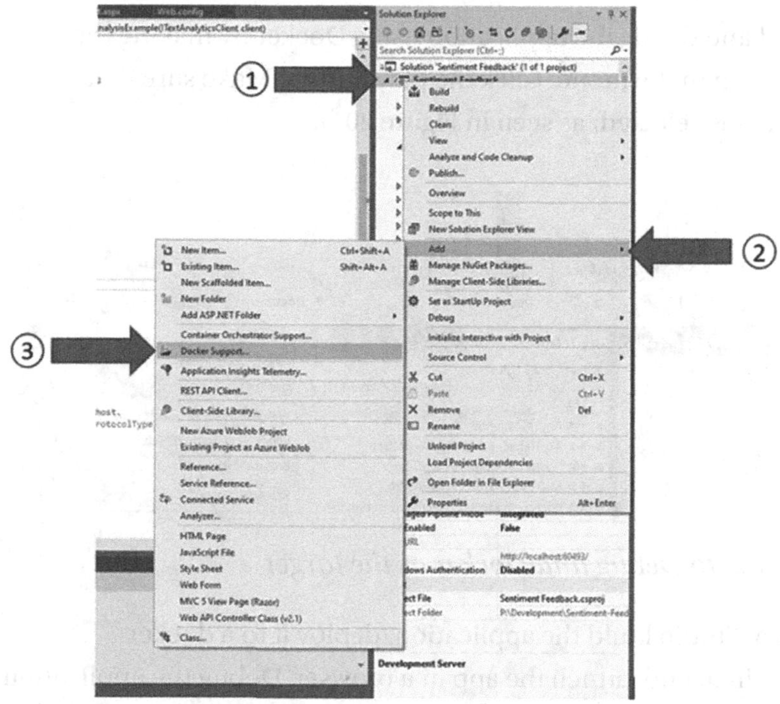

***Figure 20-7.** Adding Docker Support to an existing project*

4. Select **Windows** as the target OS when you see the Windows or Linux prompt.

5. This take some time as Visual Studio pulls the Docker images and dependencies during the build process. You can monitor the download and extraction process in the separately launched console window as seen in Figure 20-8 (this window may be minimized or hidden so you may not see it pop up).

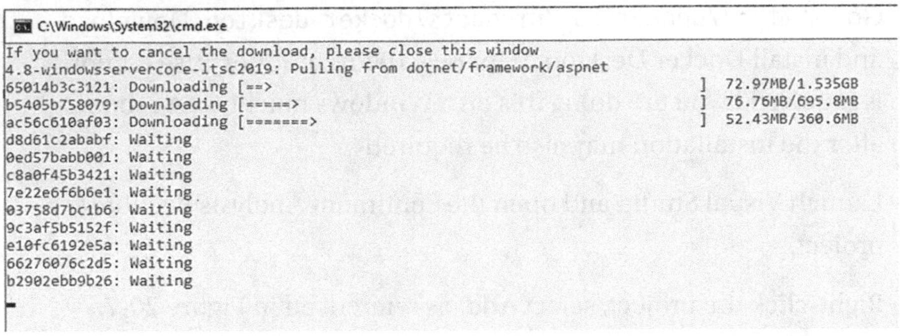

***Figure 20-8.** Docker downloading and extracting images*

6. Build and debug the application using Docker by making the selection in the menu. Click the play button. Make sure that Docker is selected, as seen in Figure 20-9.

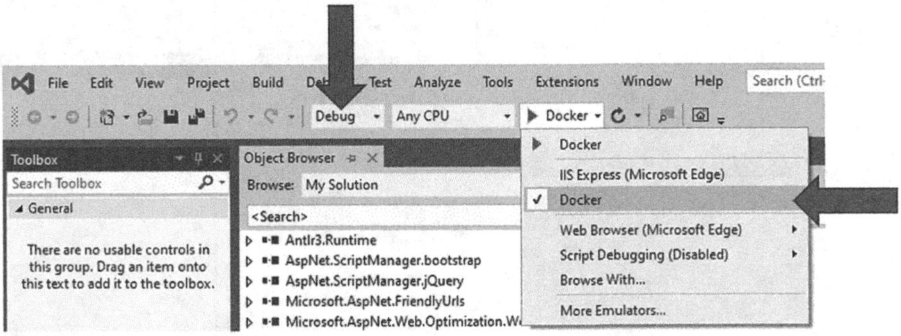

***Figure 20-9.** Set to Debug and Docker as the target*

7. Visual Studio build the application, deploy it to a docker container, and launch the app in a browser. Debug the application in the browser to make sure everything works.

8. In Visual Studio, press **Ctrl+Q** and type **Containers** in the search box. The Containers window opens, and you see the resources and dependencies that are in the container, as shown in Figure 20-10.

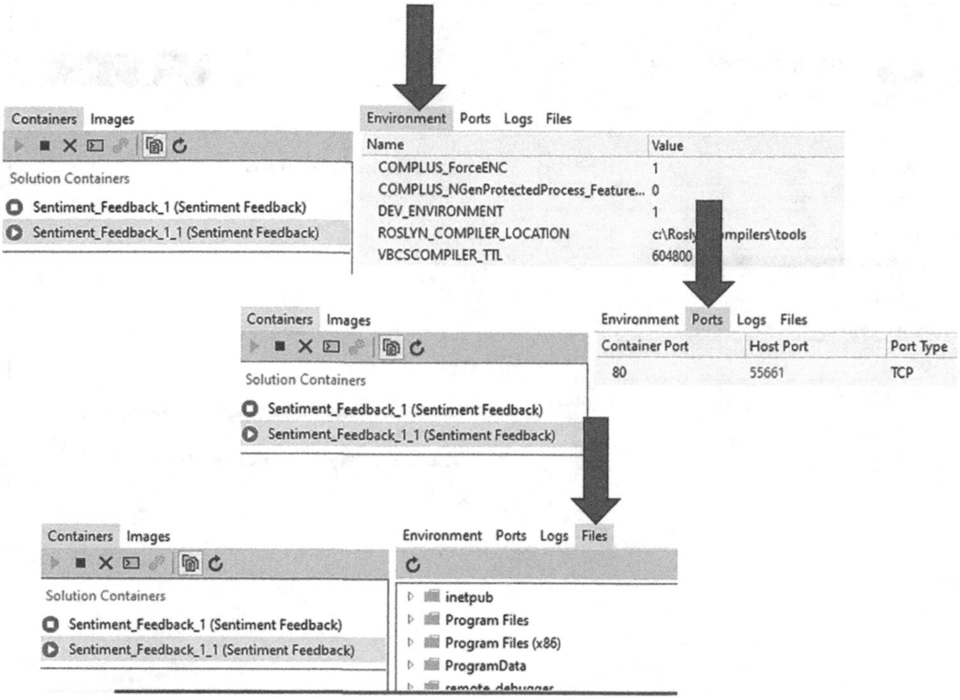

***Figure 20-10.** Browsing the envrionment, ports, and files in the container*

Stop the debugging once you have tested the application. Let's publish this application as a container image to Azure.

1. Right-click the project in Solution Explorer, and select **Publish**, and click **Start**.
2. Select **Container Registry** as the publish target, and then select **Create New Azure Container Registry**.
3. Click **Create Profile** as referenced in Figure 20-11.
4. Enter a globally unique DNS prefix, subscription, an existing or new resource group, SKU, and registry location. Then click **Create**.

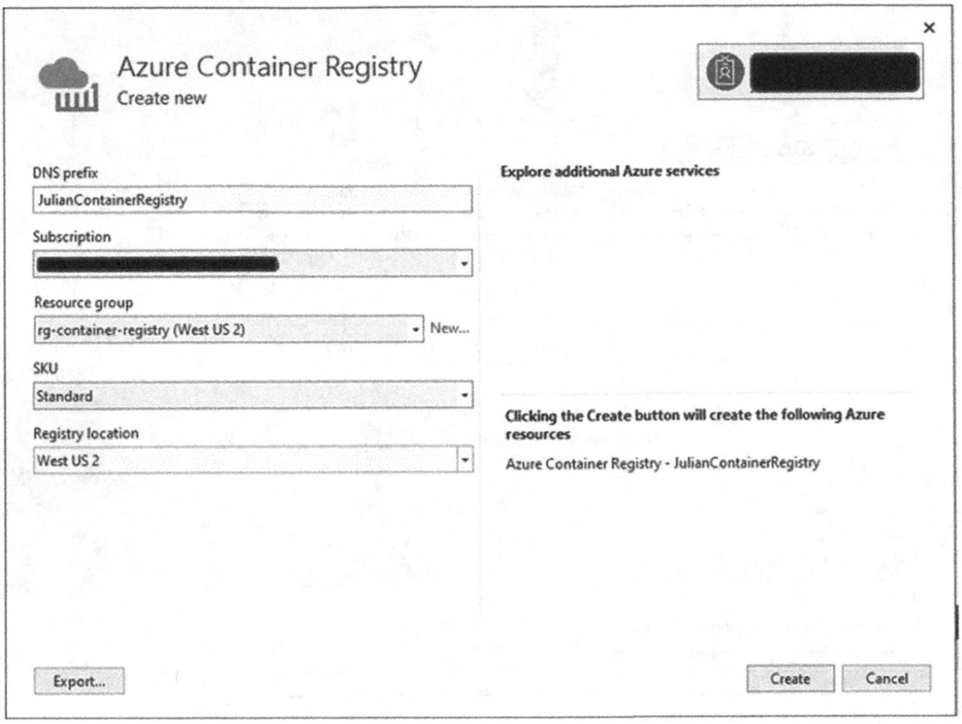

Figure 20-11. *Creating a new Container Registry in Azure*

5. In the next screen, click **Publish**. This deployment may take a while. Monitor the Output windows in Visual Studio and subsequent command windows that Docker Desktop launches during the deployment.

6. Docker pushes the application to Azure Container Registry.

Now that we have successfully published the Container image for our application, we can use that image on any host capable of running Docker images.

Hands-on with Azure Kubernetes Service (AKS)

AKS is a hosted PaaS that you can use to run your containerized applications. In the previous exercise, we added container support to our Sentiment Feedback application, tested it, and then pushed it to our private Azure Container Registry. In this exercise, we publish the container to AKS so the application goes live for the public.

For this exercise, you have the option to use the Azure CLI, but for the following steps, we use Cloud Shell from the portal.

1. In the Azure portal, click the Cloud Shell icon in the top menu, as shown in Figure 20-12.

Figure 20-12. Launching Cloud Shell from the portal

2. At the time of this writing, running Windows and Linux node pools in the same cluster is still a preview, so you must activate preview features. In the Cloud Shell, making sure that you are using Bash (not PowerShell) as the environment. Type the following.

```
az extension add --name aks-preview
```

Note Read the Windows Server container support and check when it move from Preview to General Availability at `https://azure.microsoft.com/en-us/blog/announcing-the-preview-of-windows-server-containers-support-in-azure-kubernetes-service/`

---

3. Check for available updates. Enter[1] the following.

```
az extension update --name aks-preview
```

4. Enable Windows Preview feature. Enter the following command to do so but be aware that enabling the Windows Preview feature may take a while.

[1]You may encounter an error if you just copy and paste the command into Cloud Shell. If so, type the command into Cloud Shell rather than using copy-paste.

```
az feature register --name WindowsPreview --namespace Microsoft.
ContainerService
```

5. Wait for the Windows Preview feature to be enabled. You can validate that the Windows Preview feature is enabled by continuing to enter the following command until you see the state change from Registering to Registered, as shown in Figure 20-13.

```
az feature list -o table --query "[?contains(name,'Microsoft.
ContainerService/WindowsPreview')].{Name:name,State:properties.state}"
```

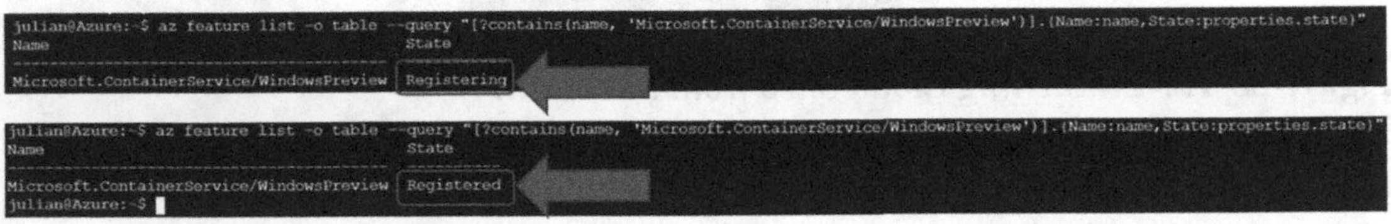

***Figure 20-13.** State of Windows Preview feature changing from Registering to Registered*

6. Once the Windows Preview feature is registered, enter the following command to refresh the registration.

```
az provider register --namespace Microsoft.ContainerService
```

7. You are now ready to create our AKS cluster that contain Linux and Windows nodes. If you are going to use an existing resource group, skip to the next step. Otherwise, if you want to put the AKS cluster in a new resource group, type the following.

```
az group create --name <Enter_Name_Of_Your_AKS_Cluster> --location
<Enter_the_region>
```

```
Eg. az group create --name rg-containers --location westus
```

8. Create the AKS cluster with Kubernetes version 1.13.5 and above. To check what versions are available by region, use the following command:

```
az aks get-versions --location <location> --output table
```

```
E.g. az aks get-versions --location westus --output table
```

```
julian@Azure:~$ az aks get-versions --location westus --output table
The behavior of this command has been altered by the following extension: aks-preview
KubernetesVersion    Upgrades
-------------------  ----------------------------------------
1.17.0(preview)      None available
1.16.4(preview)      1.17.0(preview)
1.16.1(preview)      1.16.4(preview), 1.17.0(preview)
1.15.7               1.16.1(preview), 1.16.4(preview)
1.15.5               1.15.7, 1.16.1(preview), 1.16.4(preview)
1.14.8               1.15.5, 1.15.7
1.14.7               1.14.8, 1.15.5, 1.15.7
1.13.12              1.14.7, 1.14.8
1.13.11              1.13.12, 1.14.7, 1.14.8
```

Figure 20-14. *Kubernetes versions in the West US region and identifying the latest non-preview version*

9. As seen in Figure 20-14, we identified the latest non-preview version of Kubernetes in the West US region is 1.15.7, which is greater than version 1.13.5, so we use this version for our cluster.

10. Create the AKS cluster

```
PASSWORD_WIN="<Select_a_Password>"

az aks create \
    --resource-group <Resource_Group_Name_From_Step_7> \
    --name <Name_Of_Cluster> \
    --node-count 1 \
    --kubernetes-version 1.15.7 \
    --generate-ssh-keys \
    --windows-admin-password $PASSWORD_WIN \
    --windows-admin-username azureuser \
    --enable-vmss \
    --enable-addons monitoring \
    --network-plugin azure
```

```
E.g.

PASSWORD_WIN="P@ssw0rd1234"
az aks create \
    --resource-group rg-containers \
    --name JulianK8S \
    --node-count 1 \
    --kubernetes-version 1.15.7 \
```

```
--generate-ssh-keys \
--windows-admin-password $PASSWORD_WIN \
--windows-admin-username azureuser \
--enable-vmss \
--enable-addons monitoring \
--network-plugin azure
```

Note If you already have an existing AKS cluster prior to enabling the Windows Preview feature, you are unable to apply the Windows Preview features to this cluster. You need to create a new cluster after the Windows Preview feature has been enabled.

---

11. Once the AKS cluster has been created, add a Windows node. You need to use the Windows node for our .NET Sentiment Feedback project.

```
az aks nodepool add \
    --resource-group <Resoucre_Group_Name_From_Step_7> \
    --cluster-name <Name_Of_Cluster> \
    --os-type Windows \
    --name npwin \
    --node-count 1 \
    --kubernetes-version 1.15.7

E.g.

az aks nodepool add \
    --resource-group rg-containers \
    --cluster-name JulianK8S \
    --os-type Windows \
    --name npwin \
    --node-count 1 \
    --kubernetes-version 1.15.7
```

12. Connect the AKS cluster to the Azure Container Registry from the previous hands-on exercise to which we pushed the Sentiment Feedback image to.

```
az aks update -n <Cluster_Name> -g <Resource_Group_Name_From_
Step_7> \
--attach-acr <acrName>
```

E.g.

```
az aks update -n JulianK8S -g rg-containers \
--attach-acr JulianContainerRegistry
```

13. Enter the following command to determine the details for the Windows node within the cluster so you can use it in the YAML file in the next step. This value ensure that the application is deployed to the correct node in the cluster. Locate the information in the output, as shown in Figure 20-15.

```
kubectl get nodes --show-labels
```

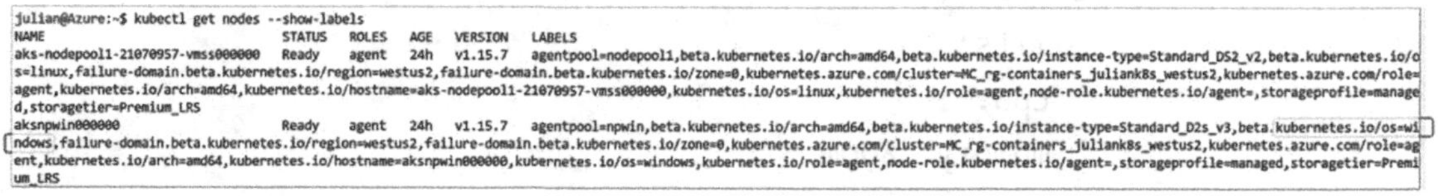

```
julian@Azure:~$ kubectl get nodes --show-labels
NAME                              STATUS   ROLES   AGE   VERSION   LABELS
aks-nodepool1-21070957-vmss000000   Ready    agent   24h   v1.15.7   agentpool=nodepool1,beta.kubernetes.io/arch=amd64,beta.kubernetes.io/instance-type=Standard_DS2_v2,beta.kubernetes.io/o
s=linux,failure-domain.beta.kubernetes.io/region=westus2,failure-domain.beta.kubernetes.io/zone=0,kubernetes.azure.com/cluster=MC_rg-containers_juliank8s_westus2,kubernetes.azure.com/role=
agent,kubernetes.io/arch=amd64,kubernetes.io/hostname=aks-nodepool1-21070957-vmss000000,kubernetes.io/os=linux,kubernetes.io/role=agent,node-role.kubernetes.io/agent=,storageprofile=manage
d,storagetier=Premium_LRS
aksnpwin000000                    Ready    agent   24h   v1.15.7   agentpool=npwin,beta.kubernetes.io/arch=amd64,beta.kubernetes.io/instance-type=Standard_D2s_v3,beta.kubernetes.io/os=wi
ndows,failure-domain.beta.kubernetes.io/region=westus2,failure-domain.beta.kubernetes.io/zone=0,kubernetes.azure.com/cluster=MC_rg-containers_juliank8s_westus2,kubernetes.azure.com/role=ag
ent,kubernetes.io/arch=amd64,kubernetes.io/hostname=aksnpwin000000,kubernetes.io/os=windows,kubernetes.io/role=agent,node-role.kubernetes.io/agent=,storageprofile=managed,storagetier=Premi
um_LRS
```

***Figure 20-15.** Locating the node information in the output*

14. Create the following YAML file using Visual Studio Code (`https://code.visualstudio.com/Download`) or your preferred lightweight IDE and save the file locally. You upload the file in the next step. Alternatively, you can also use the vi editor in Cloud Shell to create the YAML file instead of uploading it. Make sure that the YAML file references the correct Windows node that you determined in step 14, as shown in the following code and in Figure 20-16.

```
apiVersion: apps/v1
kind: Deployment
metadata:
  name: sentimentfeedback
```

```
  labels:
    app: sentimentfeedback
spec:
  replicas: 1
  template:
    metadata:
      name: sentimentfeedback
      labels:
        app: sentimentfeedback
    spec:
      nodeSelector:
        "beta.kubernetes.io/os": windows
      containers:
      - name: sentimentfeedback
        image: mcr.microsoft.com/dotnet/framework/samples:aspnetapp
        resources:
          limits:
            cpu: 1
            memory: 800m
          requests:
            cpu: .1
            memory: 300m
        ports:
          - containerPort: 80
  selector:
    matchLabels:
      app: sentimentfeedback
---
apiVersion: v1
kind: Service
metadata:
  name: sentimentfeedback
spec:
  type: LoadBalancer
  ports:
```

```
  - protocol: TCP
    port: 80
  selector:
    app: sentimentfeedback
```

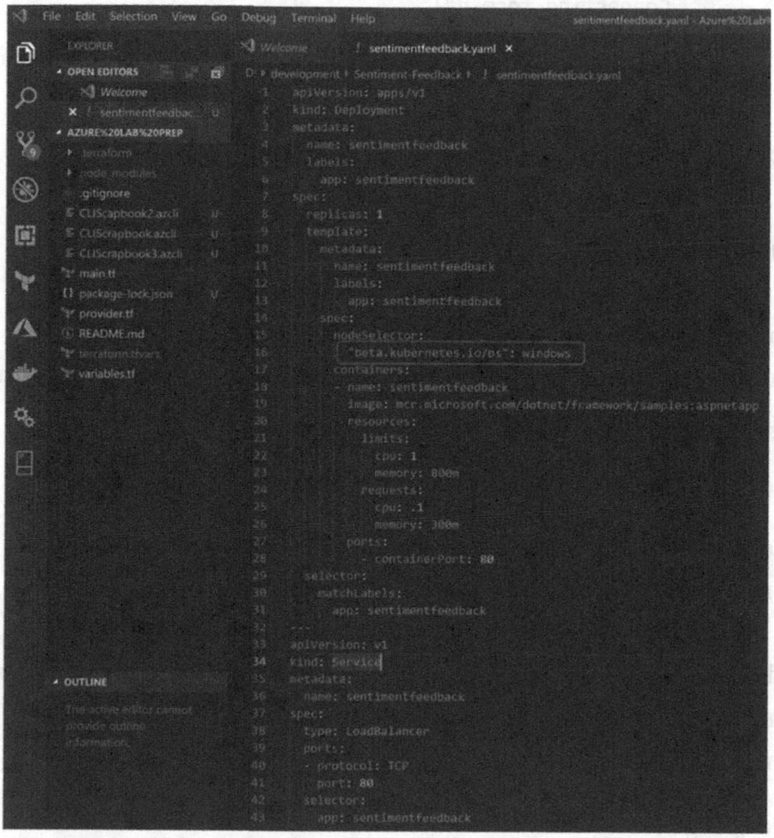

***Figure 20-16.** Visual Studio Code used to create the YAML file*

15. Upload the YAML file to the Cloud Shell by clicking the upload option in the Cloud Shell menu, as referenced in Figure 20-17.

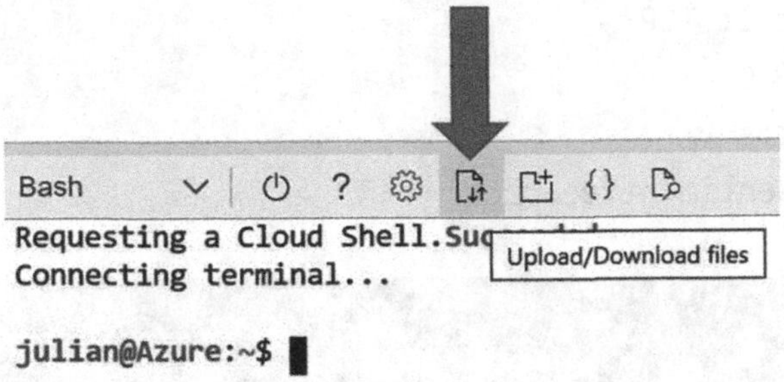

Figure 20-17. *Uploading files to the Cloud Shell environment*

16. You are now ready to deploy the Sentiment Feedback application by issuing the following command. It may take a while for the application to be deployed because it first needs to pull the container from ACR, and then the load balancer need to provision an external IP address for the application.

```
kubectl create -f ./sentimentfeedback.yaml
```

17. A deployment and a service be created for our application. To monitor the deployment, issue the following command. Initially, the External-IP shows Pending as the container is being pulled and as the load balancer acquires an IP address, but eventually an IP address is assigned, as referenced in Figure 20-18 and at that point, the application is accessible.

```
kubectl get service <servicename>
```

```
E.g.
```

```
kubectl get service sentimentfeedback
```

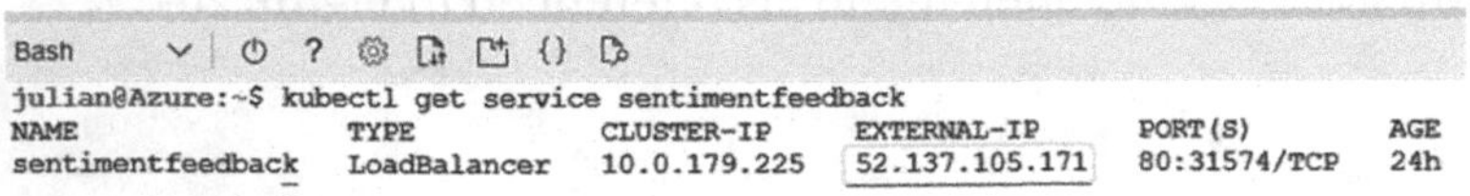
Bash
julian@Azure:~$ kubectl get service sentimentfeedback
NAME TYPE CLUSTER-IP EXTERNAL-IP PORT(S) AGE
sentimentfeedback LoadBalancer 10.0.179.225 52.137.105.171 80:31574/TCP 24h

Figure 20-18. *The assigned External-IP Address for the application*

18. To test the application, open a browser window and enter the external IP address in the address bar. You should see the Sentiment Feedback application that you developed in Chapter 15.

What we accomplished in the two hands-on labs was to take the Sentiment Feedback application that was developed in Chapter 15 and create a Docker image which we then pushed to Azure Container Registry.

We then deployed an AKS service with nodes that support Windows Containers and associated AKS to ACR so the Sentiment Feedback application image can be pulled and deployed to the Windows node in the AKS cluster.

This chapter has provided you the knowledge and hands-on experience to deploy containerized applications, but an in-depth exploration of all the capabilities of Kubernetes and Docker is outside the scope of this book. However, you have the fundamentals required to fully explore all the benefits of containerization with other resources dedicated to the topic.

Troubleshooting and Monitoring AKS

The last topic in this chapter is the built-in performance monitoring and insights associated with Azure-based applications. These capabilities can help troubleshoot issues and monitor performance.

You can manage, troubleshoot, and monitor AKS and ACS via the cloud shell using traditional methods like kubectl. For example, Kubernetes published a good cheat sheet of frequently used kubectl commands and actions at `https://kubernetes.io/docs/reference/kubectl/cheatsheet/` that can be used in the Cloud Shell.

Alternatively, the Azure portal also provides a graphical interface to AKS.

Hands-on Monitoring and Troubleshooting AKS

1. In the Azure portal, navigate to the AKS resource and click **Monitor Container**. Alternatively, you can click **Insights** in the menu along the left under Monitoring, as shown in Figure 20-19.

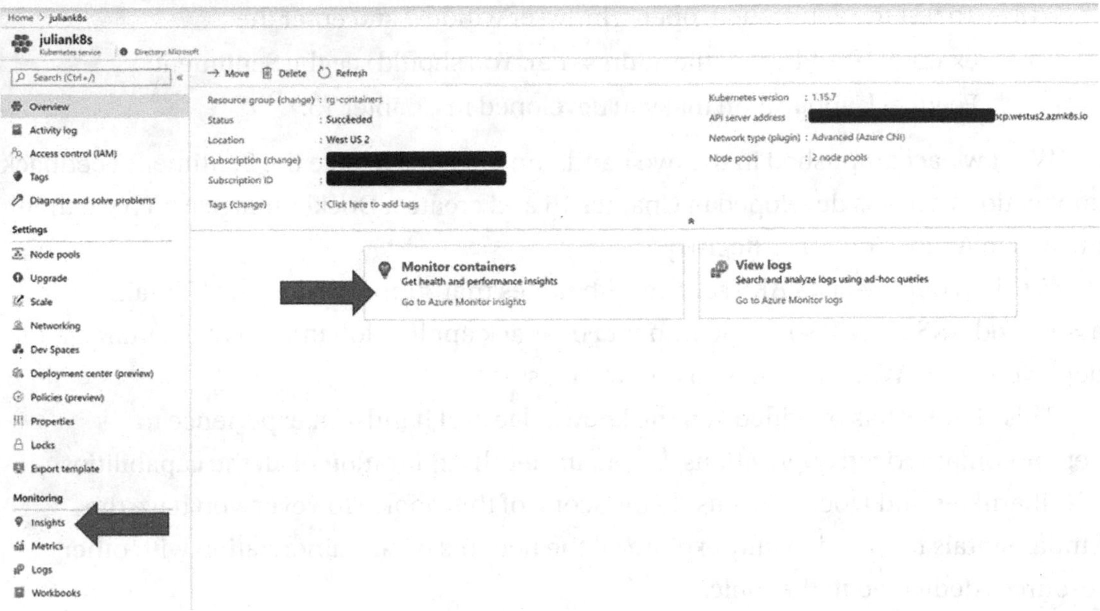

***Figure 20-19.** Monitoring and insights for the AKS resource in the Azure portal*

2. You see a dashboard with all the utilization information for the AKS cluster, such as node memory utilization, pod information, and so forth. You can also click **Time range**, as referenced in Figure 20-20 at the top of the dashboard to show only the statistics for a particular time frame.

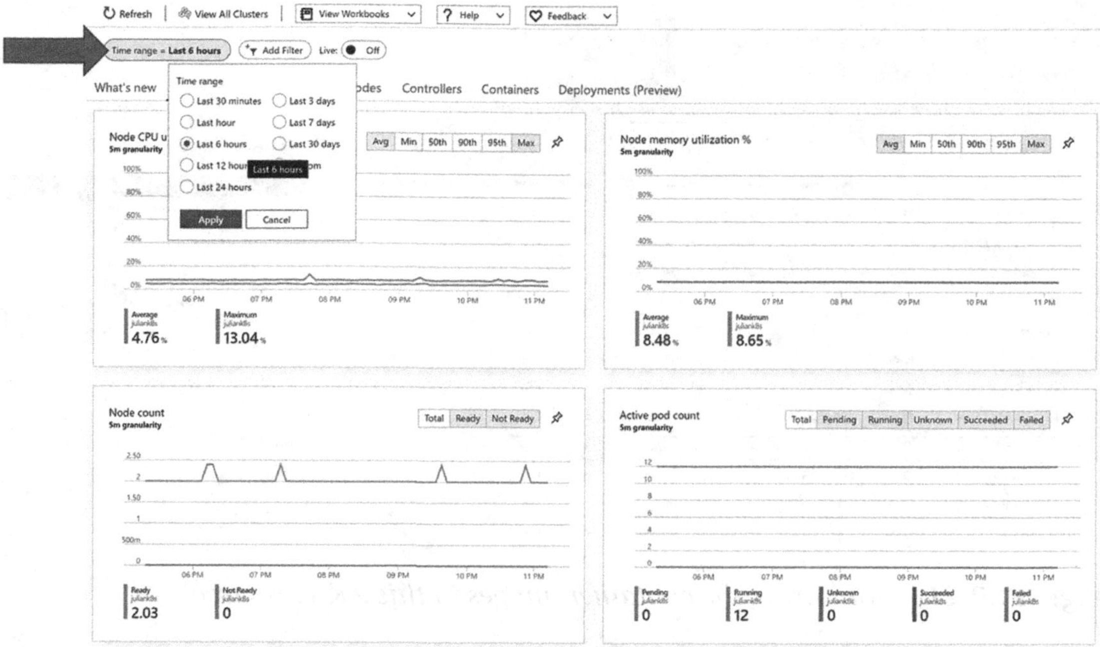

***Figure 20-20.** Setting the time range for the AKS dashboard*

3. Click **Deployments**, and you see the Sentiment Feedback application that you deployed in the previous exercise show up in the list of deployments. If you issued a command like `kubectl delete deployment sentimentfeedback` in the Cloud Shell and then click Refresh on this dashboard, the deployment disappears from the list.

4. Next, click the Containers

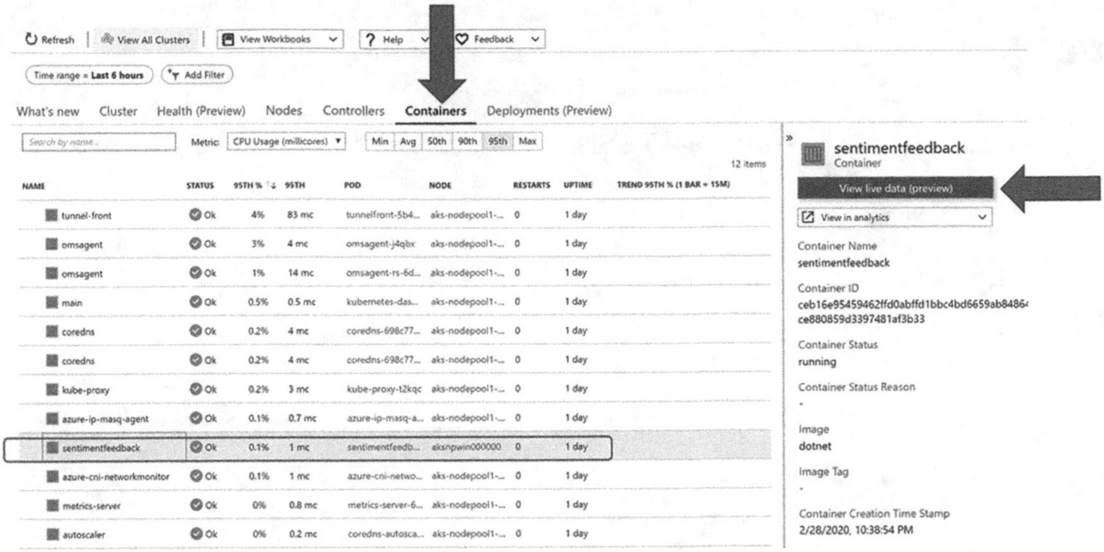

Figure 20-21. *Monitoring the container images in this AKS resource*

5. Click **View live data**. You can see events and logging information, if any. This not only applies to Containers, but also to Nodes and Controllers. Figure 20-22 shows a screenshot of the controllers' live data showing an error, therefore allowing you to troubleshoot the issue.

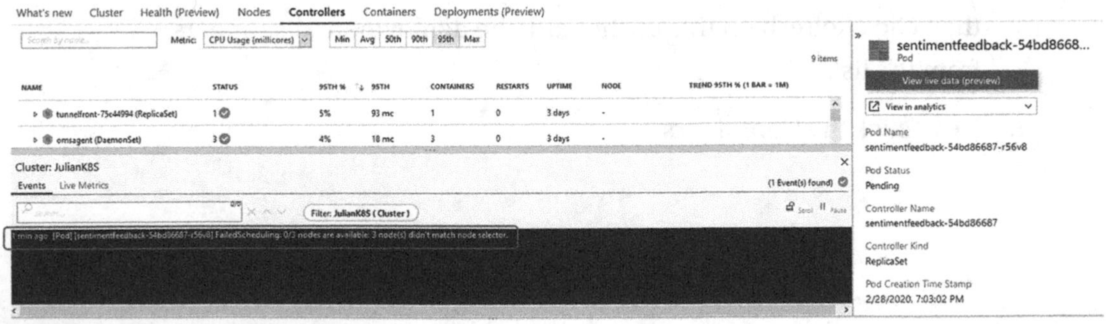

Figure 20-22. *Looking at the live data of an AKS resource*

Note As an example, the event message in Figure 20-22 is reporting node mismatch. This error told us that the application could not be deployed because it could not find the specified node in YAML or that the node AKS is trying to install this application to is incompatible. The final determination was basically the application was being pushed to the Linux node instead of the Windows node, and that allowed us to locate an omission in the YAML file.

Even though we only looked at some of the monitoring capabilities of AKS, almost all resources in Azure, especially PaaS like AKS and ACR, have Monitoring tools that you can access from the menu in the portal, as shown in Figure 20-23. Feel free to explore what is monitored in each resource and find out how to customize or drill down to the details.

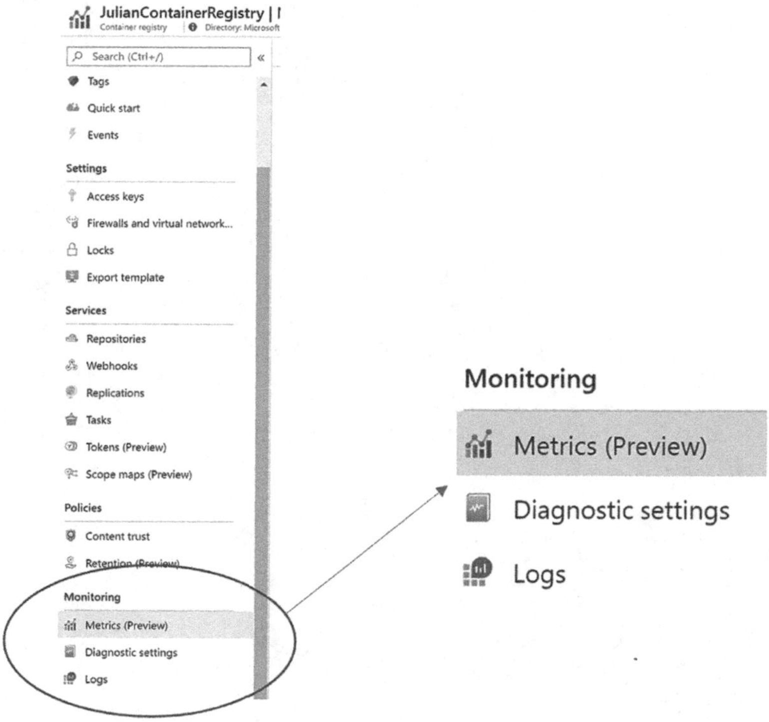

Figure 20-23. *Built-in monitoring for Azure resources, especially PaaS*

Summary

This chapter demonstrated two PaaS services that are prominent and popular among application developers: Azure Web Apps and containerization with Docker, ACR, and AKS. These are modern approaches to deploying and monitoring applications. Technologies such as Kubernetes are natively deployed in Azure and without significant configuration, you can use all the traditional commands in Cloud Shell to manage the service.

In the next chapter, you look at some automation features that take advantage of these new methods of application deployment and learn how approaches such as continuous integration and continuous deployment (CI/CD) are integrated into Azure.

CHAPTER 21

Continuous Integration/Continuous Delivery with Azure DevOps

One of the biggest benefits of Azure is the ability for organizations that adopt the public cloud to be exponentially agile. Services and solutions can be delivered in weeks and months instead of years. This accelerated life cycle for product and service delivery is based on agile concepts like *continuous integration and continuous delivery* (CI/CD).

In the previous chapter, we focused on how Azure changes the landscape for developers. In this chapter, we pick up where we left off and extend the discussion beyond the actual development of specific tasks and cover the development life cycle in Azure.

When we bring up DevOps when interacting with customers, we sometimes hear that the group we are meeting with are not developers. To successfully deploy modern cloud-based applications with maximum agility, all IT roles must work in concert. Therefore, the work among project managers, developers, data engineers, security personnel, infrastructure support, and all other IT professionals must collaborate to seamlessly deliver a successful solution. This entails complex coordination of activities that must be completed on time and per specifications.

This increased collaboration between the different IT groups is known as *DevOps*. DevOps itself is a compound term comprised of the words *developer* and *operations*, which most accurately highlights the interdependency between developers and IT professions.

J. Soh et al., *Microsoft Azure*, https://doi.org/10.1007/978-1-4842-5958-0_21

Azure DevOps is the implementation of the industry's practice of DevOps. The official definition of Azure DevOps is *"the union of people, process, and technology to continually provide value to customers."* So, although they share the same name, when we refer to "Azure DevOps," we mean the Microsoft service offering. When we simply say "DevOps," we are talking about DevOps as a discipline.

What Is Azure DevOps?

Azure DevOps is both a product and a practice. From a practice standpoint, Azure DevOps is designed to support the goal of breaking down the silos that we discussed earlier. It streamlines the software development/deployment life cycle (SDLC) by providing tools that facilitate planning, development, deployment, operations, and communication.

From a product standpoint, Azure DevOps is the new brand name for Microsoft Team Foundation Service (TFS) and is the overarching offering that comprises the following five tools.

- Azure Boards
- Azure Repos
- Azure Pipelines
- Azure Test Plans
- Azure Artifacts

Although we sometimes have to clarify whether we are talking about DevOps as a practice or DevOps as a set of tools, the thought behind blurring the line makes sense because it is beneficial to think of the tools and the practice as one and the same.

In this chapter, we focus on Azure Repos and Azure Pipelines as we demonstrate how to implement the basics of CI/CD. We are publishing information and exercises for Azure Boards, Azure Test Plans, and Azure Artifacts at the book's GitHub repository (`https://github.com/harris-soh-copeland-puca`).

Why Azure DevOps

As with any technology, we should take a moment to discuss why Azure DevOps is important from a business standpoint.

Predictability and Repeatability

In previous chapters, we looked at virtual machines and infrastructure as code, and how a cloud-first approach changes your IT operations. In Chapter 20, we also looked at how developers need to shift and transform when developing applications for the cloud. The number of services and capabilities come with an exponential increase in the number of variables in configuration at the application and infrastructure level. Furthermore, these two areas are interdependent, so a high level of coordination needs to occur between the two groups. Manual deployment of infrastructure and code is no longer a viable or scalable approach. With automation, we can ensure a consistent and predictable deployment every time.

Agile Deployment and Continuous Improvement

The term *agile* is used very frequently these days, and it no longer applies to only application development. The primary premise of the Agile practice is the rolling out, or retirement, of capabilities and changes in smaller increments in scope but more frequently. For application developers, this is now a fairly common practice.

For IT pros, the fast pace of deploying and retiring infrastructure is not a traditional practice; with significantly less hardware to provision and modern infrastructure (e.g., serverless apps and web apps), the same type of agility needs to be present at the infrastructure layer to optimize Agile across an IT organization.

Planning, Collaboration, and Workflow

If the IT pros and application developers in your organization tend to operate as silos, which is common in large and complex organizations, an area of improvement is the increased efficiency through better planning, collaboration, and some form of workflow that ensures timely deployment of resources. Through proper planning and the use of modern workflow tools, application developers are empowered to securely deploy their infrastructure during the development and testing phases. These infrastructure requirements can then be better communicated to IT pros when it comes time to formally provision infrastructure resources into production.

If these areas are part of your IT transformation journey, and they should be, and then services in Azure DevOps help you achieve those goals. How would they? This question is best answered as we explore each of the services in Azure DevOps. Once you have a better understanding of the roles that each service plays, we conclude this chapter with a discussion on the issues that you need to consider as part of designing and implementing Azure DevOps.

For now, it is important to note that while your organization may gain the most benefit by implementing Azure DevOps, there is no requirement to implement *all* five services, and there is no particular order of implementation. Although, we are presenting the services in the order that they are generally being implemented and keep in mind that there may be some dependencies between services when it comes to certain capabilities.

Provisioning Azure DevOps

For the hands-on exercises in this chapter, we deploy a new Azure DevOps environment and provision demo content into it.

1. Go to Azure DevOps at `https://devops.azure.com` and click **Start** for a free link to provision a new DevOps instance, or click the **Sign in** link if you already have Azure DevOps.
2. For this exercise, we generate a new demo project that already has content that we can use. Open a new browser tab and go to `https://azuredevopsdemogenerator.azurewebsites.net/` to generate the content.
3. Give the project a name. We recommend picking a name[1] that does not contain any spaces and is reasonable in length.
4. Use the drop-down box to select your organization, which should show the DevOps instance you signed in or created in step 1. We chose the default SmartHotel360 template, but you can click **Choose template** to see the different scenarios and pick the one that is most relevant to you.

---

[1]Refer to `https://docs.microsoft.com/en-us/azure/devops/organizations/settings/naming-restrictions?view=azure-devops` to learn about naming conventions and limitations. For example, you cannot use system reserved words like COM or PRN as part of a DevOps project name.

5. Leave the GitHub forking checkbox off because we are going to be using Azure Pipelines. However, since GitHub integrates well in Azure DevOps, you can choose to deploy another project with this checkbox checked so you can explore GitHub's integration with Azure DevOps.

6. Click **Create Project**.[2]

7. You should see the deployment progress of the demo project. Once the deployment is successful, you see a **Navigate to project** button.

8. Take a quick look at the project stats to get an idea of this project's artifacts, activities, and members.

9. Click the **Invite** link to add another user and enter the user's email address. If you are doing this exercise alone, use a different email account so that you can simulate a second user to collaborate with. Then click **Add user** and click **Add** on the next screen if you are not going to invite additional users. At some point, remember to accept the invite that was sent to the user's email address.

Azure Repos

We start exploring Azure DevOps with the Azure Repos service because we believe that this is a service that any organization should adopt.

Azure Repos securely stores an organization's IT assets, including source code, scripts, documentation, and any or all your IT artifacts. It includes the ability to control access and track changes to those assets over time, with the ability to keep historical information in the event you need to roll back changes. If you have heard or used GitHub before, which is also now a Microsoft company, Azure Repos is pretty much the same thing.

[2]If you get a warning that extensions are missing and needs to be installed, click Agree to acknowledge that the extensions are provided by third parties.

Note You can integrate GitHub with Azure DevOps; so if you already have assets stored in GitHub, you do not need to migrate them to Azure Repos. For example, when we cover CI/CD in Azure Pipelines, we highlight GitHub's integration with Azure DevOps.

Hands-on with Azure Repos

As with all the other exercises, the prerequisites for this hands-on exercise is to have an Azure subscription and to have provisioned the demo content from the earlier exercise. We assume that you understand fundamental Git concepts, such as commits, pulling, pushing, merging, and forking.

1. In the AzureHotel (Hotel 360) project, click **Repos** in the menu on the left.

   Repos is short for *repository*, so this is where all the artifacts related to this project reside. Artifacts are not only source code but can contain documentation, supporting files, and a markdown file called README.md. What you see here is a well-documented README.md that provides not only the description of this project but also instructions and screenshots. The general rule of thumb for README.md is to be as detailed as possible.

2. Locate and double-click **.Gitignore**. .Gitignore is a plain text file that is used for version control purposes. It tells Git which files it should ignore for committing and synchronization purposes. Generally, you can consider this a working file that Azure DevOps uses, and it is best you do not modify it manually.

3. Click the three ellipses in the top-right corner of the dashboard. You are presented with the options fork, download, or upload content to this repo.

Git clones the repo. The Clone button provides that functionality. Azure Repos' full source-control capabilities are also integrated into Visual Studio. Note that Azure Repos work with any Git compliant client.

Let's set up cloning through a popular Git client such as GitHub desktop.

1. First, you need the URL for this repo, so click **Repos** in the menu on the left, if you are not already there.
2. Copy and paste the URL into a temporary location, like WordPad. The URL should look something like `https://dev.azure.com/<username>/<RepoName>`.
3. Create a personal access token. Click the Account Profile icon on the top-right corner, and select **Personal access tokens**, refer to Figure 21-1, from the drop-down menu.

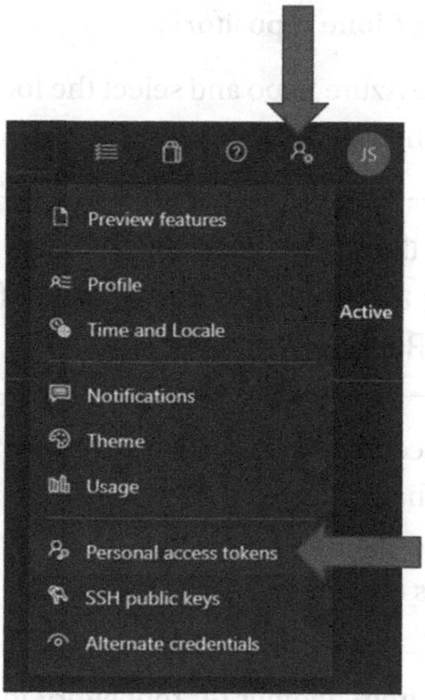

***Figure 21-1.** Creating personal access tokens in GitHub desktop*

4. Click the New Token option and provide a name. Note that this is equivalent to a username than a description.
5. Define an expiration date and review the granularity in access control you can achieve by looking at the options under Scopes ➤ Custom defined.
6. For this exercise, select **Full access**, and then click **Create**.

7. Copy and paste the generated token into WordPad as well. You need to use it in the GitHub desktop later. Note that you are unable to get this token again; you must regenerate a new token if you need to reauthenticate using this token.
8. Once you click **OK**, you see the new personal access token in the list of tokens. Select the token and note that you can revoke, edit, or regenerate a token.
9. Launch your preferred Git client, like GitHub desktop, which is used in this exercise.
10. Click **File** and select **Clone repository**.
11. Paste the URL of the Azure Repo and select the local directory to clone the repo to. Then click **Clone**.

Tip This does not enable the GitHub desktop to work with this Azure Repo. All the synchronization, push, pull, and branching operations in GitHub desktop are now fully integrated with Azure Repos in this particular repo.

This exercise walked you connecting a repo in Azure Repos to a Git client. What if you have an existing project that is located somewhere else, like GitHub or GitBucket? We can also import such projects into Azure Repos. Importing a repo includes all the project's artifacts as well as its revision history.

Note Importing a project from another Git repository to Azure Repos includes all artifacts, timelines, and its revision history at the time of the import. It does *not* continuously synchronize both repos, although there is a way to do so. This exercise does not cover synchronizing repos, but we do cover this topic in the book's GitHub repo.

Importing a Git Repo

1. Go to the Git containing the repo that you wish to clone into Azure Repos and retrieve the repo's URL.

2. Create a new Azure DevOps project, but without deploying any demo content this time.

3. Click **Repos** in the menu on the left and select **Import** under Import a repository as referenced in Figure 21-2.

4. Select **Git** as the repository type and paste the URL of the Git repo from step 1. Since our Git repo is a GitHub repo for this exercise, it is a GitHub.com URL.

5. Check the **Requires Authentication** box if the repo requires it (e.g., a private repo in GitHub), or leave it unchecked if it is a public repo.

6. If you checked the box indicating the source Git repo requires authentication, the option to provide a username and password/PAT appears; otherwise, click **Import**.

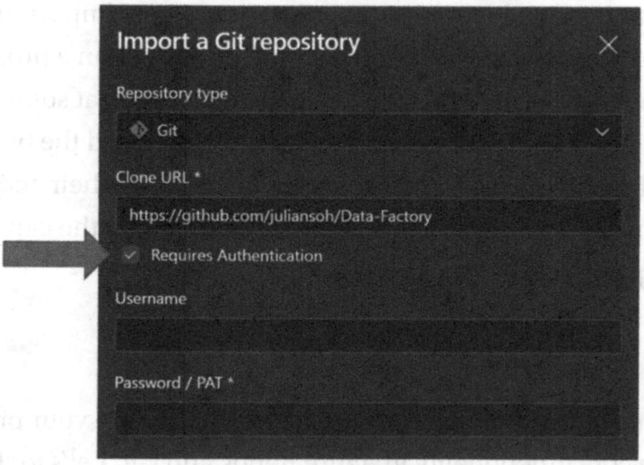

Figure 21-2. *Requires authentication checked, exposing Username and Password/PAT boxes*

7. Provide your Git username and password, and then click **Import**.

Note If you are using GitHub with multifactor authentication (MFA), providing a username and password is insufficient. Go to GitHub, click your user icon on the top right, and select Settings. Then select Developer settings and generate a new token. Use it in place of the password (keep using your GitHub username). If you are using some other Git repository with MFA, the approach should be similar.

8. Azure DevOps start importing all the items from the source Git into Azure Repos, including branches and the revision history.

Repository Operations

An exhaustive discussion about Git operations and concepts is beyond the scope of this book, but we want to address a few core principles that are important as you implement Azure Repos.

Azure Repo Goal

The goal of adopting Azure Repos and Azure DevOps as a whole is to streamline your development workflow through better collaboration. If you are in a development environment with many developers, this coordination is very important, so everyone does not step on each other's toes. If you are a lone developer on a project, you may want to test things and be able to roll back changes if needed. Then, at some point, you may want to share your project with users and other developers, and the best way of doing that is by inviting them to the repo and subsequently tracking their activities against the artifacts in the repo. With these goals in mind, let's explore the capabilities of Azure Repos that can help you achieve these goals.

Commits

Commits are actions that implement changes to the artifacts in your project's repo. In fact, commits are a core functionality in Azure Repos and Git. Let's look at commits through a hands-on experience.

1. In Azure DevOps, open the Hotel 365 demo project and click **Repos**.
2. For this exercise, you are going to select Visual Studio as your integrated development environment (IDE) to clone this repo to.
3. Azure DevOps launches Visual Studio, and an Azure DevOps dialog box opens, showing the URL of the repo to clone from, and the local path to clone to. Modify the local path if desired, and then click **clone**.
4. After the project is cloned to your local machine, locate README.md from Solution Explorer. Note that there is an icon of a lock next to the file name. This indicates that the file is under source control.
5. Open README.md and make a small change. For this exercise, we are going to add a comment to line 10. Notice that the lock icon next to the filename has now changed to a red check. The red check is an indicator that a change has been made to the file.
6. Click **File** in the Visual Studio menu and select **Save All**. Then right-click README.md and select **Compare with Unmodified**. Note that the changes you made in step 5 are highlighted.
7. Right-click README.md again and select **Commit**.
8. Provide a comment about the changes you made, and then click **Commit All**. This commits the changes that you just made to the local master branch on your local machine.
9. Note that at the top of the Team Explorer tab, which is where you should be, you are told to Sync your changes with the server if you want to implement the changes you made in step 5 with the Azure Repo for this project, as seen in Figure 21-3. Click **Sync**.

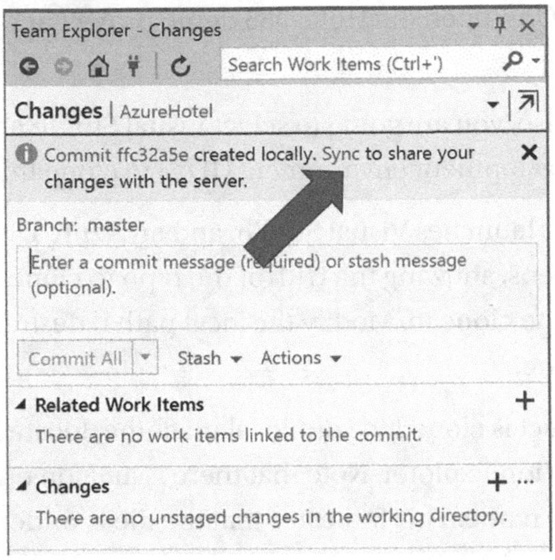

Figure 21-3. *Sync changes from the local repo to the remote repo*

Note If you do not see this message or a message to sync all changes in all files to Azure Repos, click the Home icon in Team Explorer and select Sync, as seen in Figure 21-4.

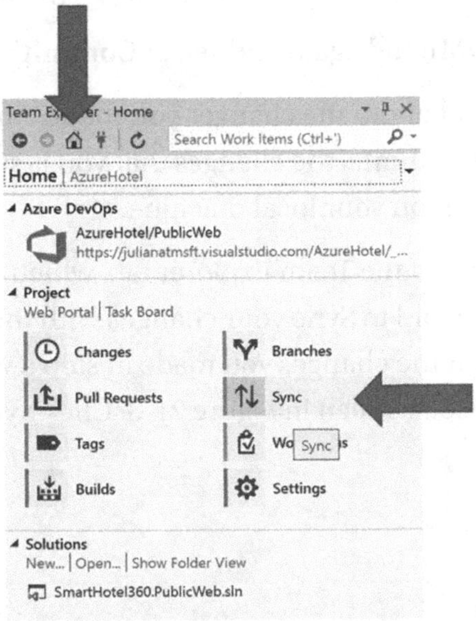

Figure 21-4. *Selecting Sync from the Home menu in Team Explorer*

10. The changes are pushed to Azure Repos. Go to Azure DevOps and refresh the repo page. You see the changes being reflected.

11. Click **Commits** in the Repos menu. You should see the commit that was initiated in step 9.

Branches

A branch is a version of a project. Every project has a Master branch, which represents the current version of all artifacts in a particular location. The locations are usually remote (on the Git server, in this case, Azure Repo) and local (on your PC).

When you initially clone a project, a copy of the master on remote is cloned to a master branch on your PC.

Let's explore the concept of branches.

1. In Azure DevOps, select **Repos**.

2. Note that there are four branches: dev, master, searchcities, and test as referenced in Figure 21-5. The default branch that is currently selected is master.

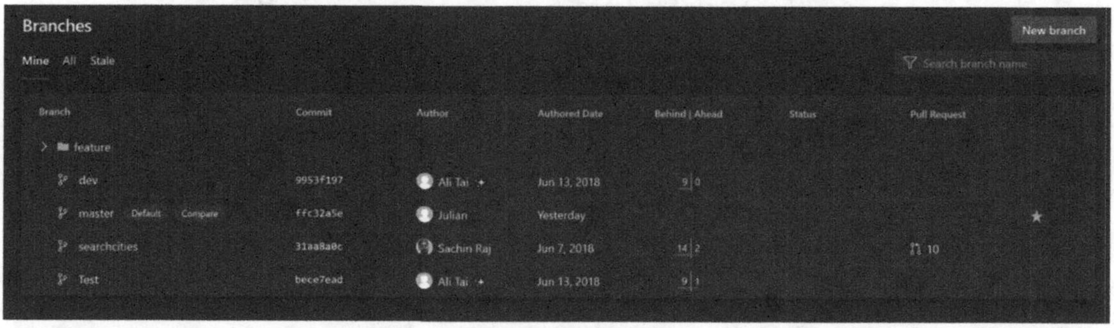

***Figure 21-5.** Branches shown in Azure Repos*

3. Look at the Behind | Ahead column. This column indicates the number of commits that have occurred in the respective branches and have not been reflected in master. For example, the searchcities branch is 14 commits behind and 2 commits ahead from master. Translated, this means that the artifacts in this branch have been modified twice since it was last synchronized with master on June 7, 2018 by Sachin Raj. Also, since June 7, 2018, master has received 14 commits, so that makes searchcities behind by 14 commits. So,

there are changes in the searchcities branch that are not reflected in master, and there are even more changes in master that are not reflected in searchcities.

4. Go to Visual Studio and click the Home icon in Team Explorer. Select **Branches**.

5. Expand remotes/origin, as seen in Figure 21-6. Notice that the branches are tracked in Azure Repos. Remotes/origin, as the name implies, is also the source (origin) from where you cloned this project. The master branch that is outside of the remotes/origin folder is the branch that exists on your PC, and that was where remote/origin was cloned to.

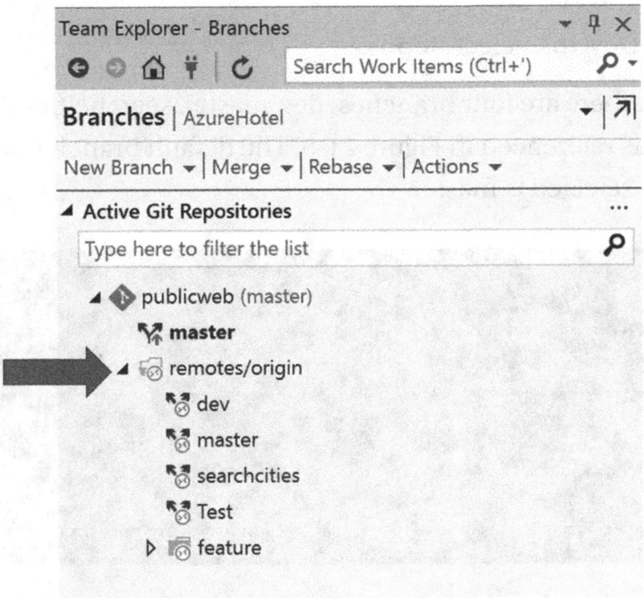

***Figure 21-6.** Remotes/origin as seen from within Visual Studio*

6. Double-click the **searchcities** branch in remotes/origin. This clones a copy of the searchcities branch to your local PC. Note the Output window to see which branch you have checked out, as seen in Figure 21-7.

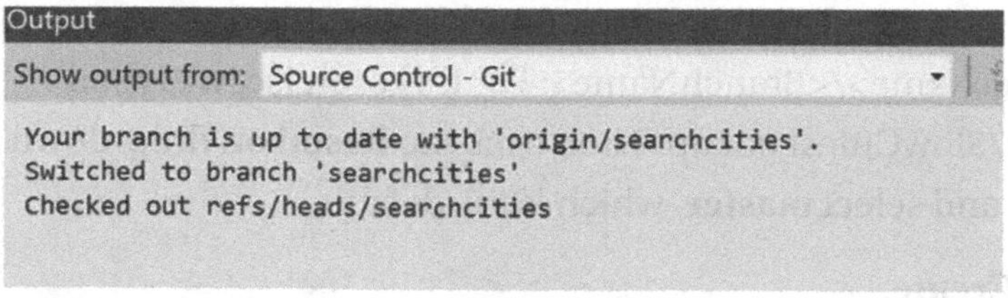

Figure 21-7. *Output showing branch being switched*

Note If you look at the contents of README.md in Visual Studio or via the command prompt, you notice that it changes accordingly depending on whether you have selected master or searchcities as the current branch in Visual Studio. This is because README.md differs between the two branches.

Now that we have a better understanding of branches, how would you use them?

One way may be to have different branches created for different contributors, perhaps naming each branch according to the contributor or developer. But this may still cause conflicts if two groups in different branches are working on the same concepts. Such conflicts would require intervention as to which changes to keep.

A better way uses *feature branches*, which are branches created to focus on specific features of a project. Look at the branches in the Hotel 360 repo. From the names of the branches, there seems to be a mix of how the branches are being utilized. The "dev" branch is presumably a work in progress, but its name does not specify what is being worked on. The branch named "Test" is probably a copy of the project that is being tested, but it is nine commits behind origin/master and one commit ahead, so the artifacts in the test branch are not the most current. Both these branches are named after activities, whereas the searchcities branch is named after a possible feature. One that perhaps incorporates the ability to search city names or zip code.

There is also a folder named features. Expanding the features folder reveals a branch named bot-widget. Now we are taking it a step further in terms of organizing our branches into folders.

Create branches in folders.

1. Click the **New branch** button at the top-right corner of Azure Repos.

2. When prompted for the name of the branch, type <FolderName>/<BranchName>. For this exercise, we typed bugfix/SlowCitiesLookup. Then click the **Based on** drop-down menu and select **master**, which is the default.

3. Click **Create**.

4. Your repo should look similar to Figure 21-8. Notice the new branch you created within the folder.

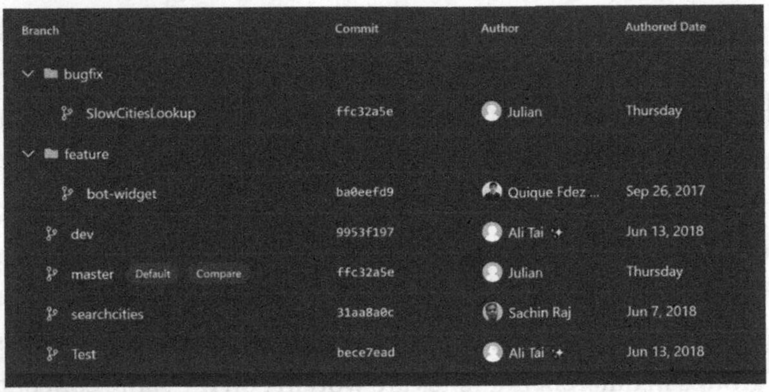

Figure 21-8. *New branch within a folder*

When creating and naming branches, follow a simple best practice of naming branches according to features and bug fixes and organizing them accordingly. Keep your strategy simple and select a descriptive naming convention. Figure 21-9 depicts how branches represent features or bug fixes that are being worked on. These branches are forked from master and are merged back once the work in the branches is completed and validated.

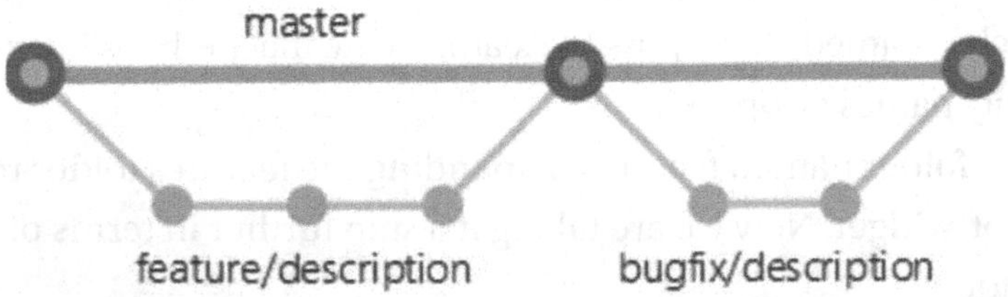

Figure 21-9. *Feature branches that are merged back to master*[3]

[3]Source: `https://docs.microsoft.com/en-us/azure/devops/repos/git/git-branching-guidance?view=azure-devops`

Another type of branching strategy that you can also adopt is the use of release branches. Unlike feature branches, where features and bug fixes are eventually merged into master, release branches are long-lived and do not typically merge back into master. Each Release Branch is a version of the application that would need to be supported until it is retired. Each release branch has its own feature branches specific to the release, as seen in Figure 21-10.

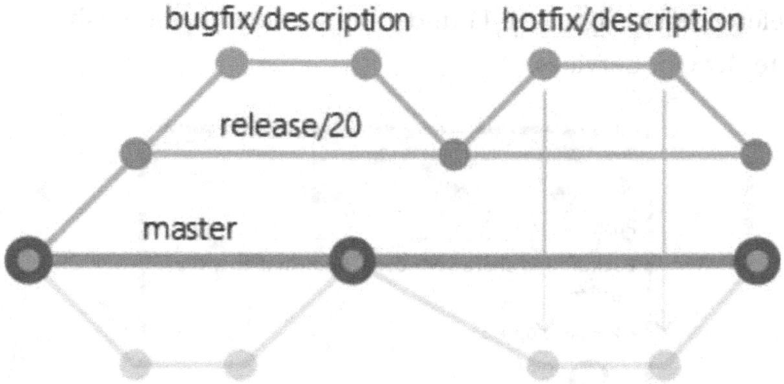

***Figure 21-10.** Release branches are long-lived and have feature branches*[4]

Note A more detailed discussion about adopting a good Git branching strategy is at `https://docs.microsoft.com/en-us/azure/devops/repos/git/git-branching-guidance?view=azure-devops`.

Hands-on with Azure Repos: Adding an Existing Project to Azure Repos

In Chapter 15, we built a web application that uses sentiment analysis. For this exercise, you add the project to Azure Repos to track the building of future features and releases.

[4]Source: `https://docs.microsoft.com/en-us/azure/devops/repos/git/git-branching-guidance?view=azure-devops`

1. From Visual Studio, open the Speech Sentiment project from Chapter 15.
2. Click the File menu and select **Add to Source Control**.
3. Click the Home icon in Team Explorer and click **Sync**.
4. Since you just added this project to Source Control, you are prompted for a destination to publish to. Click **Publish Git Repo**, as referenced in Figure 21-11 under the section labeled Push to Azure DevOps Services.

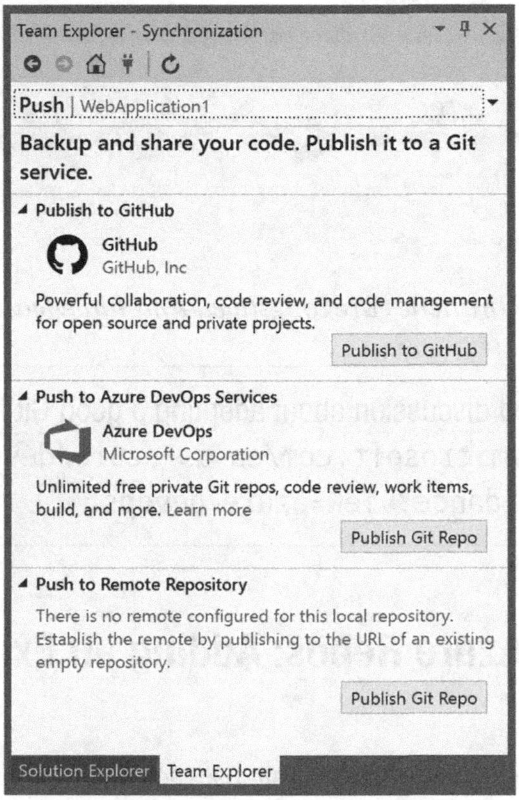

***Figure 21-11.** Push to GitHub, Azure DevOps, or any other Git repo*

5. Select or add your Azure DevOps login, and then pick the organization associated with the login, provide a name for the project, and click **Publish Repository** as referenced in Figure 21-12. For this exercise, name this project SentimentAnalysis.

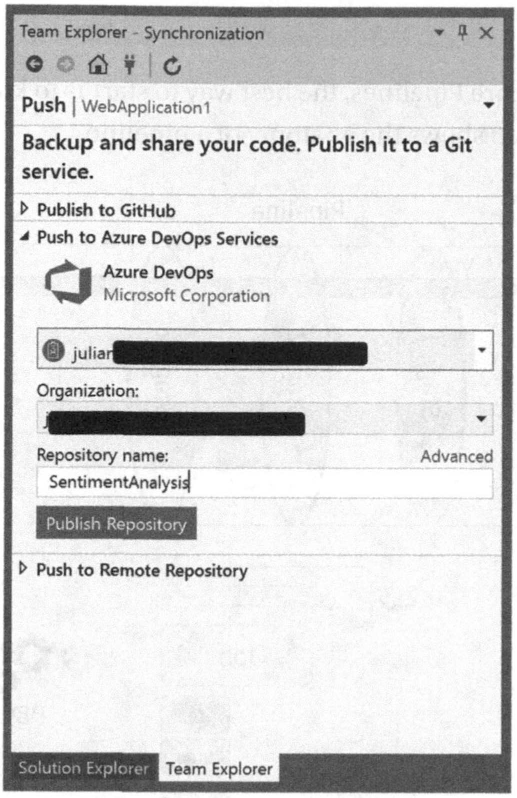

Figure 21-12. *Creating and pushing to the Azure Repo*

6. Once the push is complete, go to Azure DevOps and browse your projects. You should see SentimentAnalysis project in the list.

There are many more features in Azure Repos that we do not have time to cover in this book, such as Repo policies and tags, but what was covered should help you get started with Azure Repos and explore the other features on your own.

Azure Pipelines

Azure pipelines are tasks that involve building, testing, and deploying your project. It is commonly known as the enablement of continuous integration/continuous delivery (CI/CD).

Azure Pipelines work with Azure Repos and any Git service, such as GitHub and BitBucket.

Key Concepts

To better understand Azure Pipelines, the best way to start is to know the building blocks of a pipeline. Figure 21-13 shows the anatomy of a pipeline.

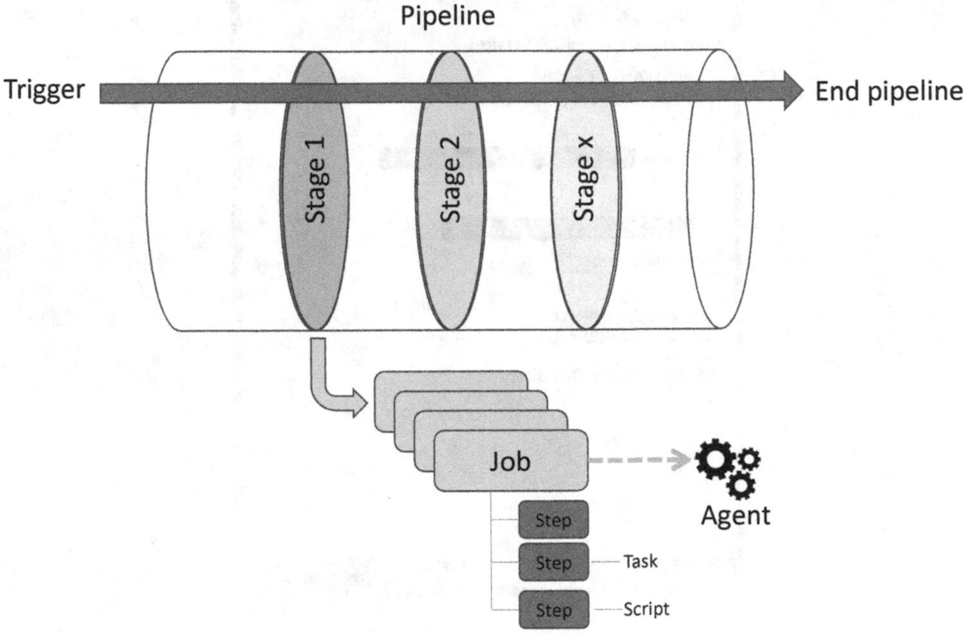

Figure 21-13. *Anatomy of a pipeline*

- A pipeline is comprised of one or more stages. When a pipeline is triggered manually or automatically, it executes each stage that is within the pipeline.
- A stage in a pipeline is a container for one or more jobs.
- A job has one or more steps, and a step can either be a task or a script. A task is the smallest building block in a pipeline.
- For a job to execute its tasks or scripts, an agent needs to be assigned. The agent is responsible for executing the tasks and scripts.

Hands-on with Azure Pipelines: CI/CD

1. From Azure DevOps, open the SentimentAnalysis project from the previous exercise and click **Pipelines**.
2. Select **Builds** and click **New pipeline**.
3. Azure Pipelines provide you with two options to create a new pipeline. You can have it generate a YAML file defining the pipeline, or you can choose a classic editor. For this exercise, we used the classic editor, so click the **Use the classic editor** link at the bottom of the screen.
4. Select the SentimentAnalysis repo as the source, and then click **Continue**.
5. Click **Azure Web App for ASP.NET** to select this template, and then click **Apply**.

Note This template builds the application and then deploys it to an Azure web app. Therefore, it is a complete CI/CD template because changes are incorporated when the master is changed (CI) and then deployed to a targeted Azure web app (CD). You could have created a CI-only pipeline if you had selected the ASP.NET template. You could also have created a CD-only pipeline. The reason why you want to do this instead of using a single CI/CD pipeline is to stage deployment separately from new updates (e.g., deploy a new version every quarter or at the end of every week).

---

6. Based on the template selected in step 5, the editor defines the tasks needed for this build job. It also highlights tasks that require attention or more information, as seen in Figure 21-14.

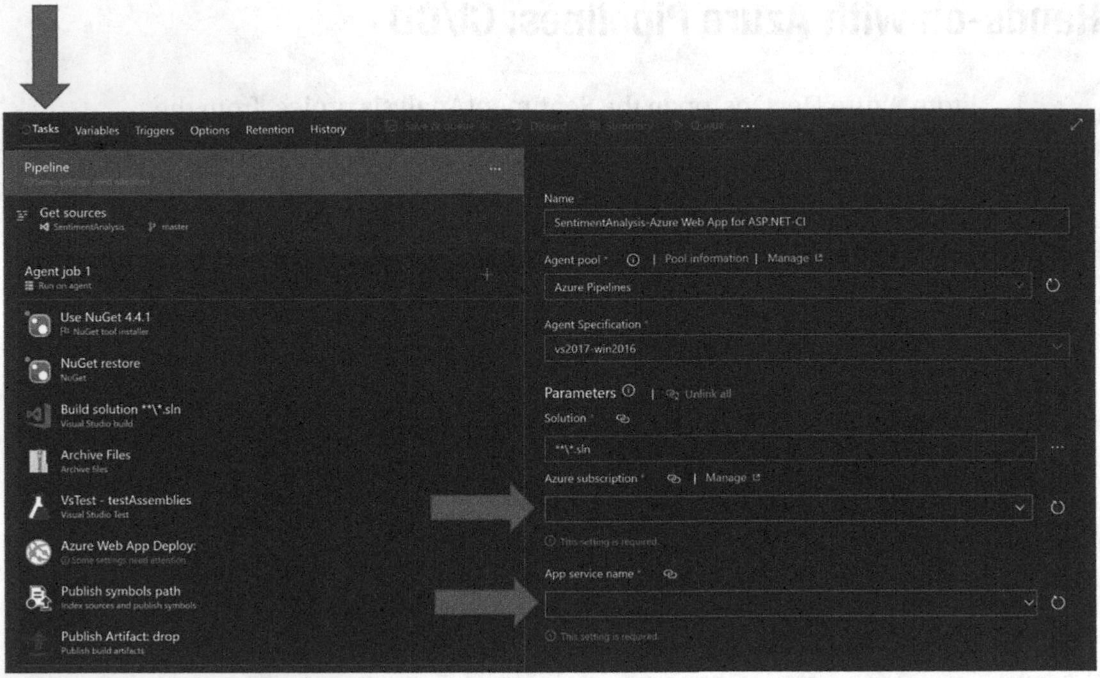

Figure 21-14. Tasks in the build stage of the pipeline

7. To see the details of a task, click it, as seen in Figure 21-15. The circle at the end is checked, which indicates that the task is selected. The pane on the left displays the parameters and details related to that task. Tasks are carried out from top to bottom. To reorder the sequence of tasks, hover over the dotted bar of a task, and the cursor changes to one with up/down arrows. Click, hold down, and drag the task to rearrange the order.

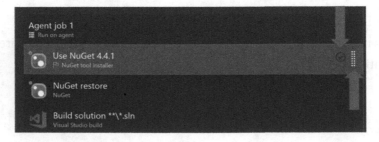

Figure 21-15. Select or move a task

8. Select the **Azure Web App Deploy** task. It requires information about the subscription and web app you wish to deploy this application to. We use the web app that was created in Chapter 12. Select the subscription and the web app from the drop-down menu. Set the app type as a web app on Windows.

9. Select **Triggers** at the top of the screen.

10. Ensure that the **Enable continuous integration** box is checked. By default, it should be. Be aware that you can add a schedule that restricts CI to a particular day and time, but we do not do it for this exercise.

11. Click **Save & queue** and select **Save & queue** from the drop-down options.

12. Provide a Save comment for this pipeline. Then click Save and run.

13. An agent is provided, and the job runs for the first time. The status of each task is shown. You can see which tasks completed or failed and which are still pending, as seen in Figure 21-16.

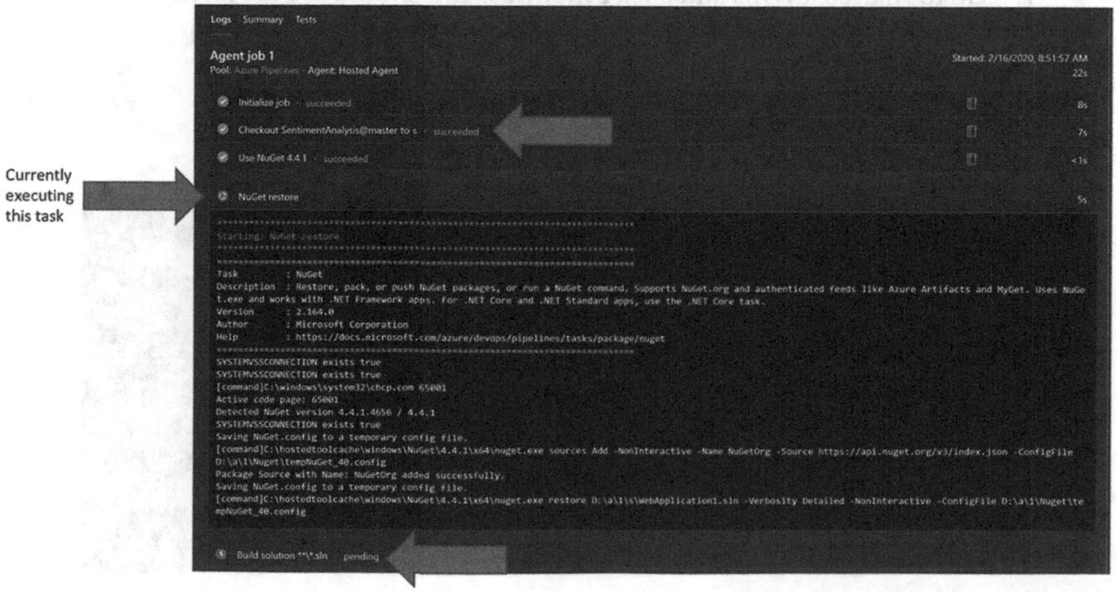

Figure 21-16. *Verbose log for a running job*

In the previous exercise, you created a build pipeline that was triggered whenever there is a change in master. In the next exercise, you test to make sure the trigger kicks off the entire CI/CD effort.

1. In Visual Studio, make a small change to the SentimentAnalysis project. For this exercise, all we did was change the Default.aspx page so that there is a minor change in the text on this page.
2. Click **File** and select **Save All**.
3. Within Visual Studio, in Team Explorer, click the Home icon and select **Changes**.
4. Enter a description for this commit or use the following commit message: "A minor change to the header for Default.aspx page to Chapter 21 CI Demo 2." Then click **Commit All**.
5. After the commit, sync the changes with the server as suggested at the top of Team Explorer.
6. In Outgoing Commits, you should see the commit that you named in step 4. Click **Push** to send the changes up to Azure Repo.
7. Go to Azure DevOps and click **Pipelines**. You should see the latest commit being built. The description of the commit you provided in step 4 describes the build, as referenced in Figure 21-17. Note the build number as well.

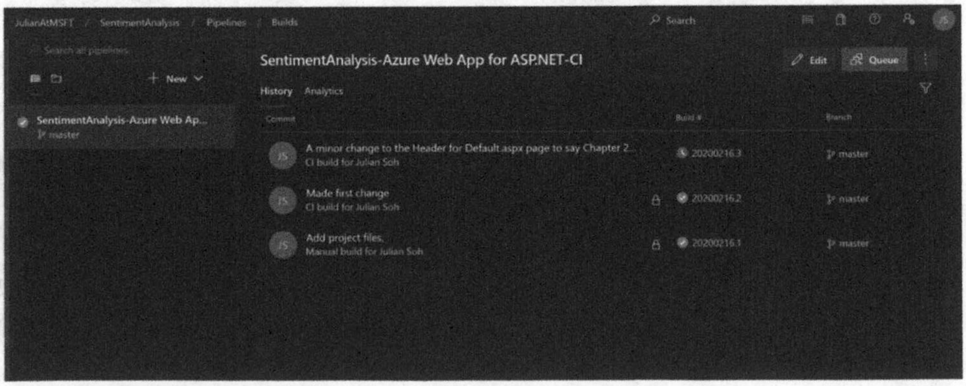

***Figure 21-17.** Pipeline automatically triggered by a change in the master*

8. Open a browser and view the website. It should now reflect the changes you made in step 1 without you having to publish the project like you had to in Chapter 12.

9. Go back to Visual Studio and in Team Explorer, click the Home icon, and select **Builds**.

10. You should see the build history, as referenced in Figure 21-18 for this project based on the build number. The build number that you noted in step 7 should be the latest.

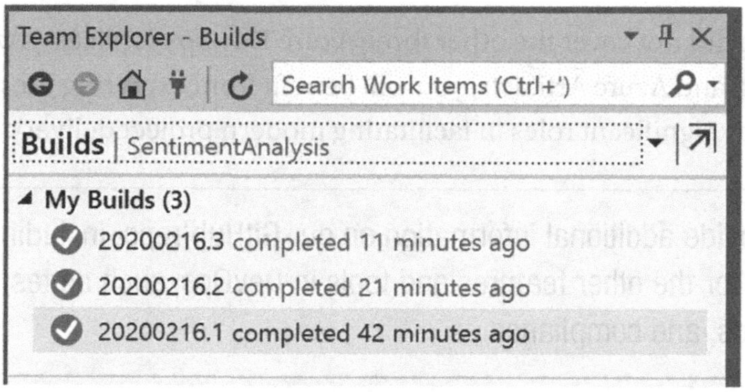

***Figure 21-18.** Build history as seen in Visual Studio Team Explorer*

There is a lot more that can be accomplished through Azure Pipelines. You can build complex automation, configure notifications, connect to other Git services like GitHub instead of Azure Repos, and managing libraries and releases. Covering the breadth of its capabilities is beyond the scope of this book, but you can expand your knowledge through Microsoft's extensive online documentation or other sources. This chapter and the exercises covered here have provided you with the necessary foundation and hands-on experience to fully understand and explore Azure Pipelines and CI/CD.

The next step we recommend that you do is set up the governance for CI/CD. We saw how to add Team Members to an Azure DevOps project, so governance that identifies roles such as reviewers and administrators ensure that nothing gets inadvertently pushed to the production environment.

A good resource to explore is Azure DevOps Projects, which sets up everything you need for developing, deploying, and monitoring your application. Learn more about it at our GitHub repo at `https://github.com/harris-soh-copeland-puca/azure-docs/blob/master/articles/devops-project/overview.md`.

Summary

In closing, Azure Repos and Azure Pipelines are the two services that facilitate CI/CD. With proper governance in place, the product or service delivery life cycle can be significantly optimized.

Although we did not cover the other three Azure DevOps services—Azure Boards, Azure Test Plans, and Azure Artifacts, you will benefit from exploring these services because they play significant roles in facilitating modern project delivery.

Note We provide additional information on our GitHub repo, including examples and exercises for the other features and tools in DevOps, such as test plans, artifacts, boards, and compliance.

Azure Boards provide visual tracking of user stories and tasks. It allows you to implement the Agile methodology that your organization adopts. It has a Kanban board to help visualize the stages of various user stories and their associated tasks. The tasks can be cross-referenced to specific builds in Azure Pipelines, so status updates in Azure Boards are in sync and reflect actual progress. In fact, the writing of this book was managed as a project using boards in Azure DevOps. Figure 21-19 is a screenshot of the board in our project.

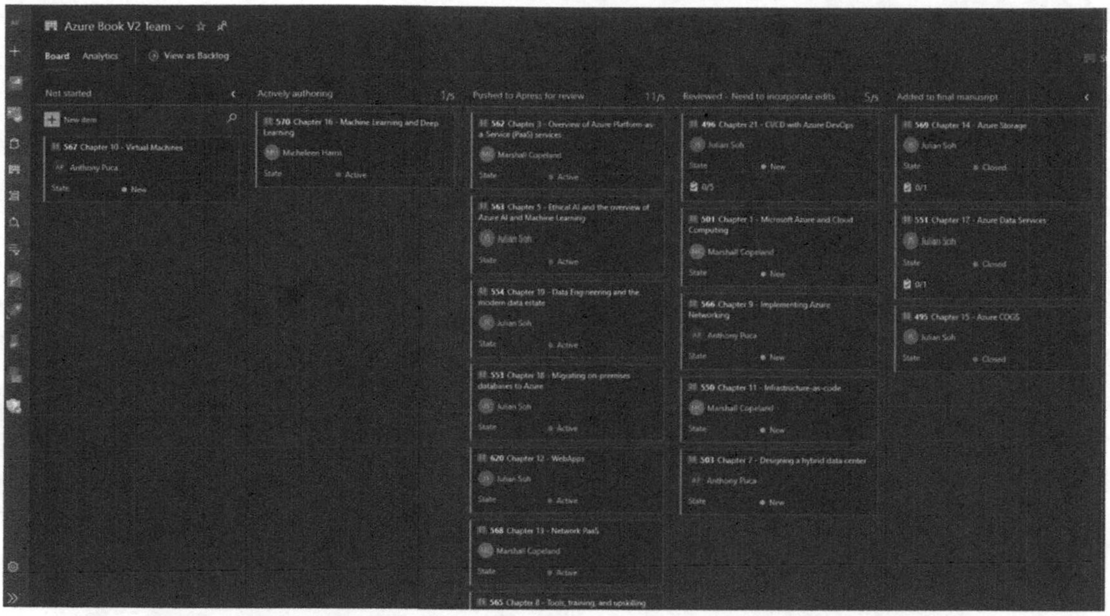

***Figure 21-19.** Managing the production of this book using Azure Boards*

Azure Test Plans provide the quality assurance needed at the sprint or milestone stages of a project. Azure Test Plans allow manual or automated testing or both. Proper and timely testing ensures not only a quicker to market product, but also ensures that quality is not compromised as a result of the shortened timelines in the development life cycle.

A developer is probably aware of packages and package management and deployment services like NuGet to roll out and share code. It is a foundation for any modern development platform. In fact, we used a NuGet package for our COGS hands-on exercise in Chapter 15. Azure Artifacts provides the ability to create and distribute packages to and from feeds like NuGet and npm. It introduces the concept of connecting multiple feeds, private and public, and allowing you to organize and control access to your packages. Reusing code through packages is another key strategy in modern application development that shortens the development life cycle. Packages that have been tested ensure that quality is consistent throughout the projects that incorporate such packages.

Azure DevOps is a fully integrated suite of tools that help streamline the development life cycle, and it is not just for developers. The integrated services bring together project managers, stakeholders, and IT professionals from the planning phase through delivery and beyond.

Index

A

J. Soh et al., *Microsoft Azure*, https://doi.org/10.1007/978-1-4842-5958-0

D

E

F

G

H

I

J

K

L

M

N

O

P

Q

R

S

W, X, Y

Z